Paul,

With appreciation and gratitude from all your colleagues for your valuable contribution over the years to the work of the Joint Nature Conservation Committee

December 2001

JOINT NATURE CONSERVATION COMMITTEE

Coasts and seas of the United Kingdom

Region 12   Wales: Margam to Little Orme

edited by
J.H. Barne, C.F. Robson, S.S. Kaznowska & J.P. Doody

Joint Nature Conservation Committee
Monkstone House, City Road
Peterborough PE1 1JY
UK

This report has been produced by the Coastal Directories Project of the JNCC
on behalf of the project Steering Group

JNCC Coastal Directories Project Team

Project directors Dr J.P. Doody, Dr N.C. Davidson
Project management and co-ordination J.H. Barne, C.F. Robson
Editing and publication S.S. Kaznowska, F.J. Wright
Information systems M. Jones
Administration & editorial assistance C.A. Smith, J.A. Mitchell, R. Keddie, E. Leck, S. Palasiuk

The project receives guidance from a Steering Group which has more than 200 members. More detailed information and advice comes from the members of the Core Steering Group, which is composed as follows:

Dr. J.M. Baxter *Scottish Natural Heritage*
R.J. Bleakley *Department of the Environment, Northern Ireland*
R. Bradley *The Association of Sea Fisheries Committees of England and Wales*
Dr. K. Hiscock *Joint Nature Conservation Committee*
Prof. G.A.D. King *National Coasts and Estuaries Advisory Group*
Prof. S.J. Lockwood *MAFF Directorate of Fisheries Research*
Dr J.P. Doody *Joint Nature Conservation Committee*
C.R. Macduff-Duncan *Esso UK (on behalf of the UK Offshore Operators Association)*
Dr. D.J. Murison *Scottish Office Agriculture & Fisheries Department*
M.L. Pickles *National Rivers Authority*
Dr. H.J. Prosser *Welsh Office*
Dr. J.S. Pullen *WWF UK (Worldwide Fund for Nature)*
Dr. G.P. Radley *English Nature*
Dr. P.C. Reid *Plymouth Marine Laboratory*
M.J. Roberts *Water Resources and Marine, Department of the Environment*
S.L. Soffe *Countryside Council for Wales*
M.L. Tasker *Joint Nature Conservation Committee*
R.G. Woolmore *Countryside Commission*

Recommended citation for this volume:
Barne, J.H., Robson, C.F., Kaznowska, S.S., & Doody, J.P., *eds*. 1995. *Coasts and seas of the United Kingdom. Region 12 Wales: Margam to Little Orme*. Peterborough, Joint Nature Conservation Committee.

Recommended citation for a chapter in this volume (example):
Davidson, N.C. 1995. Chapter 4.1 Estuaries. *In*: Barne, J.H., Robson, C.F., Kaznowska, S.S., & Doody, J.P., *eds*. 1995. *Coasts and seas of the United Kingdom. Region 12 Wales: Margam to Little Orme*. Peterborough, Joint Nature Conservation Committee.

Region 1: ISBN 1 873701 75 6
Region 2: ISBN 1 873701 76 4
Region 3: ISBN 1 873701 77 2
Region 4: ISBN 1 873701 78 0
Region 5: ISBN 1 873701 79 9
Region 6: ISBN 1 873701 80 2
Region 7: ISBN 1 873701 81 0
Region 8: ISBN 1 873701 82 9
Region 9: ISBN 1 873701 83 7
Region 10: ISBN 1 873701 84 5
Region 11: ISBN 1 873701 85 3
Region 12: ISBN 1 873701 86 1
Region 13: ISBN 1 873701 87 x
Region 14: ISBN 1 873701 88 8
Region 15: ISBN 1 873701 89 6
Region 16: ISBN 1 873701 90 x
Region 17: ISBN 1 873701 92 6
Set of 17 regions: ISBN 1 873701 91 8

Contents

Foreword

Information is vital for sound policy formulation. Decision makers at national and local level need to know more than just the scale, location and importance of natural resources that are of value to humans. They have to understand how human activities affect the value of those resources and how to conduct those activities in an environmentally sustainable way. This is true for virtually every activity that impinges on the natural environment. In the coastal zone the complexity of the relationships between the physical and biological systems adds another dimension to the problems of formulating management policy.

I am pleased, therefore, to be introducing the *Coasts and seas of the United Kingdom* series. The Coastal Directories project, of which this series of seventeen regional reports, covering the whole of the UK coast, is an important product, has brought together an encyclopaedic range of information on our coastal resources and the human activities that are associated with them. Amongst the topics covered are the basic geology of the coasts around the United Kingdom and measures taken for coast defence and sea protection, the distribution and importance of the wildlife and habitats of our coasts and seas, including fish and fisheries, and the climate and sea level changes to which they all are subject.

In addition to the value of the information itself, the way the project has been run and the data collected has made an important contribution to the quality of the product. A wide range of individuals and organisations concerned with the conservation and use of the coastal margin have collaborated in collating the information, their variety reflecting the extent of the interplay between the coastal environment and human activities. These organisations included the Ministry of Agriculture, Fisheries and Food, the Scottish Office Agriculture and Fisheries Department, the National Rivers Authority, the Countryside Commission, the Scottish Office, the Welsh Office, the Department of the Environment, the Sea Fisheries Committees, English Nature, Scottish Natural Heritage and the Countryside Council for Wales, together with local authorities, voluntary conservation organisations and private companies (notably those in the oil industry, through the UK Offshore Operators Association). I am also pleased to be able to acknowledge the contribution made by the staff of the Joint Nature Conservation Committee. As the work has evolved since the first meetings of the Steering Group in 1990, the value of involving such a broad span of interests has been highlighted by the extent to which it has allowed new approaches and information sources to be identified.

The regional reports will be of value to all who live and work in the maritime areas of the UK, where informed management is the key to the sustainable use of resources. The reports should become indispensible reference sources for organisations shouldering new or expanded responsibilities for the management of marine Special Areas of Conservation under the EC Habitats Directive. In addition, the reports will make an important contribution to the implementation of the UK Biodiversity Action Plan.

Selborne

The Earl of Selborne
Chairman, Joint Nature Conservation Committee

How to use this book

These notes provide some general guidance about finding and interpreting the information in this book.

Structure

The book is divided into ten chapters, each split into sections containing summary data on the topics shown in the Contents list. Chapter 2 provides a general physical background to the region. Sections in Chapters 3, 4 and 5 have been compiled to the following standard format:

- **Introduction**: presents the important features of the topic as it relates to the region and sets the region in a national context.
- **Important locations and species**: gives more detail on the region's features in relation to the topic.
- **Human activities**: describes management and other activities that can have an effect on the resource in the region.
- **Information sources used**: describes the sources of information, including surveys, on which the section is based, and notes any limitations on their use or interpretation.
- **Further sources of information**: lists references cited, recommended further reading, and names, addresses and telephone numbers of contacts able to give more detailed information.
- **Acknowledgements**

Sections in the remaining chapters all have the last three subsections and follow the other elements as closely as practicable, given their subject nature.

At the end of the book there is a list of the addresses and telephone numbers of organisations most frequently cited as contacts, as well as a core reading list of books that cover the region or the subject matter particularly well. Finally there is a full list of authors' names and addresses.

Definitions and contexts

The word 'region' (as in 'Region 12') is used throughout this book to refer to the coastal and nearshore zone, broadly defined, between the two points given in the title of this book. The area covered varies between chapter sections, depending on the form in which data is available. Coverage is usually either coastal 10 km squares, sites within one kilometre of Mean High Water Mark, or an offshore area that may extend out to the median line between the UK and neighbouring states. Inland areas of the counties concerned are not included unless specifically stated.

'Britain' here means Great Britain, i.e. including only England, Scotland and Wales. 'United Kingdom' also includes Northern Ireland.

The term 'North Sea Coast', as used here, means the coast of Britain covered by *The directory of the North Sea coastal margin* (Doody, Johnston & Smith 1993): that is, from Cape Wrath (longitude 5°W) along the east and south coasts of Britain to Falmouth (again longitude 5°W), and including Orkney and Shetland.

The 'West Coast', as used here, normally includes the coast and seas from Falmouth to Cape Wrath along the west coast of Britain. Only where explicitly stated have data for the Isle of Man and/or Northern Ireland been included in West Coast descriptions.

Sites within each chapter section are described in clockwise order around the coast, incorporating islands within the sequence. Maps and tables are numbered sequentially within their chapter section; for example in section 5.4, Map 5.4.1 is the first map referred to and Table 5.4.2 is the second table.

Throughout the book, the information given is a summary of the best available knowledge. The sites mentioned as important, the numbers and distributions of species, archaeological features discovered and information on all the other elements of the natural and man-made environment are as known at December 1994, unless otherwise stated. The fact that no information is presented about a topic in relation to a locality should not be taken to mean that there are no features of interest there, and fuller details should be sought from the further sources of information listed at the end of each section. Note, however, that under the Environmental Information Regulations (1992; Statutory Instrument No. 3240) you may be asked to pay for information provided by organisations.

Acknowledgements

This regional report is one of a series of products from the Coastal Directories Project of the JNCC. The compilation and publication of the series has been made possible by generous contributions from the members of the Coastal Directories Funding Consortium listed below:

Arco British Ltd [1]
Avon County Council
Ceredigion District Council
Cheshire County Council
Chevron UK Ltd [1]
Cleveland County Council
Clwyd County Council
Clyde River Purification Board
Colwyn Borough Council
Copeland Borough Council
Countryside Commission
Countryside Council For Wales
Cumbria County Council
Cunninghame District Council
Department of the Environment
Department of the Environment for Northern Ireland
Devon County Council
Dorset County Council
Dumfries and Galloway Regional Council
Dyfed County Council
English Nature
Fife Regional Council
Forest of Dean District Council
Gwynedd County Council
Hamilton Oil Company Ltd [1]
Highland River Purification Board
Isle of Man Government, Department of Industry
Isle of Man Government, Department of Local Government and the Environment

Isle of Man Government, Department of Transport
Kyle and Carrick District Council
Lancashire County Council
Lincolnshire County Council
Marathon Oil UK Ltd [1]
Ministry of Agriculture, Fisheries and Food Directorate of Fisheries Research
National Rivers Authority
Neath Borough Council
Norfolk County Council
North Cornwall District Council
Nuclear Electric plc
Preseli Pembrokeshire District Council
Scottish Natural Heritage
Scottish Office Agriculture and Fisheries Department
Scottish Salmon Growers Association Ltd
Sefton Borough Council
Solway River Purification Board
Somerset County Council
South Pembrokeshire District Council
Standing Conference on Regional Policy In South Wales [2]
Stroud District Council
Tayside Regional Council
Torridge District Council
UK Offshore Operators Association [3]
Vale of Glamorgan Borough Council
Water Services Association
Welsh Office
World Wide Fund For Nature (UK)

Notes

[1] Funding from these companies was given to the Cardigan Bay Forum to fund the supply of information to the project.

[2] Members of the Standing Conference on Regional Policy in South Wales are: Blaenau Gwent Borough Council, Cardiff City Council, Dinefwr Borough Council, Gwent County Council, Llanelli Borough Council, Lliw Valley Borough Council, Mid Glamorgan County Council, Monmouth Borough Council, Port Talbot City Council, South Glamorgan County Council, Swansea City Council, Taff Ely Borough Council, West Glamorgan County Council.

[3] The UK Offshore Operators Association is the representative organisation for the British offshore oil and gas industry. Its 34 members are the companies licensed by HM Government to explore for and produce oil and gas in UK waters.

We thank publishers and authors indicated in the figure captions for permission to reproduce illustrations. Crown Copyright material is reproduced with the permission of the Controller of HMSO.

This collaborative project involves many other branches of JNCC in addition to the project team listed on page 2. These are: Marine Conservation Branch (Keith Hiscock, Tim Hill, Bill Sanderson, Colin McLeod), Vertebrate Ecology and Conservation Branch (Deirdre Craddock, David Stroud, Steve Gibson), Species Conservation Branch (Nick Hodgetts, Deborah Procter, Martin Wigginton), and Seabirds and Cetaceans Branch (Mark Tasker, Paul Walsh, Andy Webb). We thank them all for their help and support.

The project has also received widespread support from the country conservation agencies: Countryside Council for Wales, English Nature, Scottish Natural Heritage and the Department of the Environment (Northern Ireland). We are grateful to the many regional and headquarters staff listed below as well as the representatives on the Core Steering Group.

The editors would like to thank the members of the Cardigan Bay Forum and the many people who have provided information or editorial assistance for the report or given their time to comment on drafts. Where appropriate, individual acknowledgements are given also at the end of each section.

Nigel Ajax Lewis, Glamorgan Wildlife Trust; Miran Aprahamian, NRA; Roger Bamber, Fawley Aquatic Research Laboratories Ltd.; Mr R.F. Beale, West Glamorgan County Council; Trevor Beebee, University of Sussex, Brighton; Tricia Bradley, RSPB; Blaise Bullimore, CCW; Alastair Burn, EN; Andrew Burr, Department of Transport; Tony Cadwalladr, CCW; Frances Cattanach, North Wales Wildlife Trust; Clive Chatters, Hampshire Wildlife Trust; Tim Cleeves, RSPB; Phil Coates, SWSFC; Bill Cook, NW & NWSFC; Keith Corbett, Herpetological Conservation Trust; Martyn Cox, The Crown Estate; Peter Cranswick, The Wildfowl & Wetlands Trust; Joan Edwards, The Wildlife Trusts; Brian Elliott, Dyfed Wildlife Trust; Matthew Ellis, CCW; Stephen Evans, CCW; Ben Ferrari, National Monuments Records Centre; Ian Francis, RSPB; Chris Fuller, CCW; Mike Gash, CCW; Tony Gent, EN; David George, Natural History Museum; Lucy Gilkes, CCW; Tony Green, Cardigan Bay Forum; Wells Grogan, Marathon Oil; Paul Harding, Institute of Terrestrial Ecology; John Hartley, AMOCO (UK); David Hewett, North Wales Wildlife Trust; Richard Howell, NRA; Eira Hughes, CCW; Antony Jensen, University of Southampton; Rod Jones, CCW; Graham King, National Coasts and Estuaries Advisory Group; J.W. Lambert, NRA; Owain Lewis, Neath Borough Council; Barry Long, CCW; Colin Macduff-Duncan, ESSO; Steve May, Field Studies Council Research Centre & Dyfed County Council; Thomas McOwat, Dyfed Bat Group; Clive Morgan, Cardigan Bay Forum; A J Murray, The Crown Estate; Elwyn Owen, Wales Tourist Board; Steve Parr, CCW; Frank Parrish, The Crown Estate; Mike Pawson, MAFF; Lindsay Pickles, NRA; Iowerth Rees, CCW; Ivor Rees, University of Wales Bangor; Jane Rees, North Wales Wildlife Trust; Chris Reid, Plymouth Marine Laboratory; Peter Rhind, CCW; Mandy Richards, CCW; Mike Roberts, Department of the Environment; Mark Robins, RSPB; Chris Rollie, RSPB; David Rye, Milford Port Health Authority; Pat Sargeant, EN; Alister Scott, Cardigan Bay Forum; John Sharpe, RSPB; Duncan Shaw, Irish Sea Forum; Pauline Simpson, Institute of Oceanographic Sciences; Rebecca Sinton, RSPB; Peter Slater, Standing Conference on Regional Policy in South Wales; Sarah Soffe, CCW; Mr P M Stainer, NRA; Phil Stone, Cardigan Bay Forum; Chris Stroud, Whale and Dolphin Conservation Society; Stephanie Tyler, RSPB; C. Vivian, MAFF; Sarah Welton, Marine Conservation Society; D.C. Williams, West Glamorgan County Council; Ray Woolmore, Countryside Commission.

Chapter 1 Introduction

1.1 The Coastal Directories project

Dr J.P. Doody

The Coastal Directories project sets out to collect and collate summary information that will provide an overview of coastal and marine resources and human activities at national and regional levels. It also provides an index to more detailed references and other sources of information.

Information on the coastal resource and its use is vital to the development of policy for environmental management. Because of the inter-related nature of the many components of the coastal zone, including both habitats and species, coastal management requires a knowledge of the interactions between human activities and the physical functioning of the zone and its biological components. In addition, it is essential to adopt a wide-ranging approach to collecting and collating this information.

For these reports, the definition of the coastal margin encompasses all the main marine, coastal and maritime zones, from offshore waters to terrestrial maritime habitats. By their nature the limits of the coastal, shoreline and marine zones are indistinct, as tidal movement, storms and the effects of sea level rise influence their relative positions. A wide definition of maritime habitats has been adopted here: tidal areas (mudflats, sand flats, saltmarshes and transitions to brackish marsh, swamps and salt-influenced grasslands) are included; rocky shores, shingle beaches, cliffs subject to salt spray, and terrestrial features including sand dunes and shingle structures that are maintained by marine processes are also covered. In addition, we have considered areas where combinations of these habitats occur. Examples include estuaries where lagoons or land claimed from the sea, such as coastal grazing marsh, form part of the functioning system. Also covered are habitats used by coastal species for at least part of their life cycle.

In the marine and nearshore environment we have not set any artificial limits to the areas to be discussed, except those imposed by the availability of information or the limits of national jurisdiction. A minimum distance of 35 km offshore has been agreed as a notional limit to the coastal zone for the Coastal Directories project, but in effect the median line between Britain and neighbouring states may be said to form the boundary in many instances. The offshore limits of geomorphological processes, affecting both the coast and the subtidal waters, and the seaward boundaries of nearshore benthic plant and animal communities, are important factors.

Because of the potentially wide influence of human use, the area from which we have derived data is occasionally wider than the strictly coastal zone. Fisheries, infrastructure development and sources of pollution are among the activities for which it is difficult to define a precise limit. The historical context, derived from archaeological evidence, must also be taken into account. However, when all these interactions are revealed they will help to inform the process of planning and delivering coastal management so that it allows for sustainable use and the maintenance of biological diversity.

1.1.1 Origins and aims of the work

Recognising the significant gaps that existed in scientific understanding of the North Sea, the Second International Conference on Protection of the North Sea established the North Sea Task Force in 1987. Under the guidance of the International Council for the Exploration of the Sea (ICES) and the Oslo and Paris Commissions, it organised a co-ordinated programme of research and monitoring with a primary aim of producing an assessment of the North Sea (the *Quality Status Report* (QSR)) by 1993.

The Coastal Directories project began following a suggestion in 1989 by the UK at the second meeting of the North Sea Task Force to include consideration of coastal habitats and species of conservation importance in the North Sea QSR. The work initially involved the collection and collation of information along the coastal margin of the North Sea, from Cape Wrath around the North Sea and the English Channel to the Fal Estuary. Funded as a joint project between the Department of the Environment and the Nature Conservancy Council (NCC), the information was compiled during 1990 and 1991 and a draft *Directory of the North Sea coastal margin* was circulated for comment in August 1991.

The principal original aim was to produce "a comprehensive description of the North Sea coastal margin, its habitats, species and human activities, as an example to other North Sea states" (North Sea Task Force 1993). It was hoped that this would help to ensure that habitats and species were considered in the QSR. The programme fulfilled this original aim, and the QSR published in 1993 included descriptions of both habitats and species in several of the sub-regional reports, together with an assessment of the human impacts on the ecosystems.

The *Directory of the North Sea coastal margin* was published in December 1993 (Doody *et al.* 1993). It was presented to Ministers at the Intermediate Ministerial Meeting on the North Sea held in Denmark in the same month.

The North Sea Task Force was wound up in December 1993 following completion of the QSR. Continuing work was subsumed into a new Assessment and Monitoring Committee (ASMO) under the 1992 Convention for the Protection of the Marine Environment of the North East Atlantic (the OSPAR Convention). The new OSPAR Convention requires that assessments similar to the *North Sea Quality Status Report* be produced for all the constituent parts of the north-east Atlantic and for that area as a whole (which we have called for simplicity 'the West Coast') by the year 2000. The Irish Sea will be one of the first areas subject to assessment. The extension of the Coastal Directories project to the West Coast of Great Britain (thereby covering all the coast not included in the *Directory of the North Sea coastal margin*, and also including the Isle of Man and Northern Ireland) and the production of regional reports such as this one contribute to that assessment.

1.1.2 Methods - the North Sea and West Coast Directories

Throughout the work on the directories a simple approach to compiling the information has been adopted. This has involved identifying existing sources of compiled information at national, regional and local levels. The *Directory of the North Sea coastal margin* was largely produced by staff within the Nature Conservancy Council (NCC); following reorganisation of the NCC in 1991, responsibility for the work has rested with the Joint Nature Conservation Committee (JNCC). Table 1.1.1 shows how the Coastal Directories project is managed.

At the outset it was agreed that the work should involve a wide variety of individuals and organisations concerned with the conservation and use of the coastal margin, to reflect the complex nature of the habitats and species and the wide-ranging influence of human activities. Initially, a small group of individuals and organisations (including the Ministry of Agriculture, Fisheries and Food (MAFF), the National Rivers Authority (NRA), the Countryside Commission (CC), the Scottish Office (SO), the Welsh Office (WO), the Department of the Environment (DoE) and the conservation agencies for England, Scotland and Wales (English Nature, Scottish Natural Heritage, Countryside Council for Wales)) was invited to help steer the project and to identify and provide information. As the work evolved from the first meetings in 1990, the value of this approach was highlighted by the extent to which new approaches and information sources were identified.

Unlike for the preceding work on the North Sea coastal margin, which was funded principally through the DoE and the NCC/JNCC, a decision was made to seek funding for the continuation of the work on the West Coast from a consortium of private organisations and public bodies, including coastal local authorities. Early in 1993, JNCC appointed a co-ordinator for this work, part of whose responsibility was to obtain funding for the project. In the event a large number of organisations agreed to participate and showed a keen interest in the development of the work. Members of the Funding Consortium are listed in the Acknowlegements section of the book.

This interest was reflected in the extent of external funding that the project received (including an injection of funds from the UK Offshore Operators Association, see below), and in the commitment shown by the steering groups, which meet regularly. Of particular importance is the annual Main Steering Group seminar: so far it has reviewed the *Role of the Directories in the development of coastal zone management* (January 1994), and considered the *Use of electronic storage and retrieval mechanisms for data publication* (February 1995).

1.1.3 The Coastal Directories' contribution to coastal management

As the work on the *Directory of the North Sea coastal margin* proceeded, the emphasis of the approach changed. In the UK during the period 1990 - 1993 there was a considerable upsurge of interest in the principles of coastal management. The House of Commons Environment Committee examined the issues during November 1991 and in January/February 1992 and published their report on *Coastal zone protection and planning* in March 1992 (House of Commons Environment Committee 1992).

That report, together with other initiatives at UK and European levels, continues to encourage a more integrated approach to management issues. The dialogue between the project consortium members has confirmed the importance of the Coastal Directories in providing basic resource information to support these new approaches. Increasingly, therefore, the Directories are seen as providing essential information to inform the development of coastal zone management policy at national levels.

The Directories provide information that complements the sectoral approach (control of different activities by separate regulations) currently being promoted by a range of Government reports. These include PPG 20: *Coastal planning* (Department of the Environment/Welsh Office 1992), and the two consultation documents that followed up the House of Commons Environment Committee report: *Development below low water mark* (Department of the Environment/Welsh Office 1993) and *Managing the coast* (Department of the Environment/Welsh Office 1993). MAFF too is promoting the setting up of 'coastal cell groups', to encourage sustainable shoreline management.

1.1.4 Regional reports

The coastal management developments fostered interest in the Coastal Directories project, and also increased demand for information at a regional level. It was decided, therefore, to produce a series of regional reports to cover the whole

Table 1.1.1 The structure of the management arrangements

Group	Role	Undertaken by
JNCC Coastal Conservation Branch (CCB)	Day to day management	Head of CCB
Management Board	Liaison & executive decisions	Country agencies/JNCC Coastal Conservation Branch
Core Steering Group	Steer work, provide information and support	See page following title page
Main Steering Group	Review progress, consider new developments, provide advice	All Steering Group members, conferring annually at Steering Group Meeting

coast of Britain, in addition to the two overview volumes (*The Directory of the North Sea coastal margin*, published in 1993, and the *West Coast Directory*). Discussions among consortium members indicated that early completion of the regional volumes should be the priority. Seventeen regions were identified for which reports are being prepared. These provide a more detailed level of information than the overview volumes, to help set each region in a national context and facilitate the preparation of regional plans.

It was also recognised that the summary data in the regional reports is valuable in preparing and assessing applications for oil and gas licensing around the coastal margin. An injection of funds from the United Kingdom Offshore Operators Association (UKOOA) made possible the early production of reports for most of the potential licensing areas in the 16th Offshore Oil and Gas Licensing Round.

The areas covered by the complete series of regional reports are shown in Map 1.1.1: Regions 1 - 10 cover the area of the *Directory of the North Sea coastal margin*; Regions 11 - 17 deal with the area of the *West Coast Directory*.

1.1.5 Outputs

The reports are published as conventional paper reports; in addition a first version using UKDMAP (the electronic atlas developed by the British Oceanographic Data Centre, Birkenhead) was published in 1994 (Barne et.al, 1994). Other forms of electronic publication are being evaluated. The position on publication as at March 1995 is shown in Table 1.1.2.

1.1.6 Further sources of information

A. References cited

Barne, J., Davidson, N.C., Hill, T.O., & Jones, M. 1994. *Coastal and Marine UKDMAP datasets: a user manual.* Peterborough, Joint Nature Conservation Committee.

DoE/Welsh Office. 1992. *Planning policy guidance - coastal planning.* PPG 20. London, HMSO.

DoE/Welsh Office. 1993. *Development below Low Water Mark - a review of regulation in England and Wales.* London, HMSO.

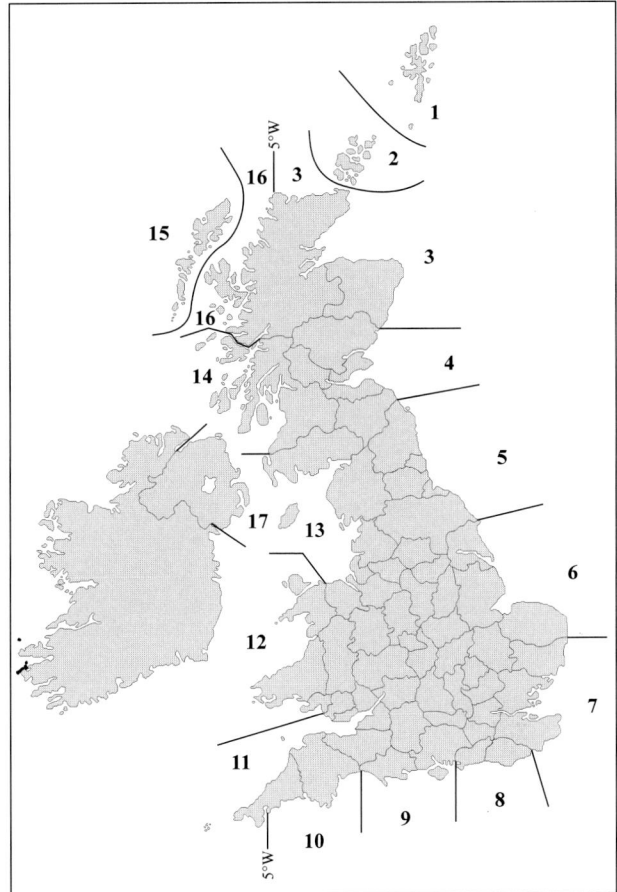

Map 1.1.1 Regions in the series. Region names are given in Table 1.1.2.

DoE/Welsh Office. 1993. *Managing the coast: a review of coastal management plans in England and Wales and the powers supporting them.* London, HMSO.

Doody, J.P., Johnson, C., & Smith, B. 1993. *Directory of the North Sea coastal margin.* Peterborough, Joint Nature Conservation Committee.

House of Commons Environment Committee. 1992. *Coastal zone protection and planning.* Second Report. 2 volumes. London, HMSO.

North Sea Task Force. 1993. *North Sea quality status report.* London, Oslo and Paris Commissions.

Table 1.1.2 Provisional titles and publication dates of the Coastal Directories reports	
Directory of the North Sea Coastal Margin	Published 1993
Regional Report 1. Shetland	Publication due 1997
Regional Report 2. Orkney	Publication due 1997
Regional Report 3. North-east Scotland (Cape Wrath to St Cyrus)	Publication due 1995
Regional Report 4. South-east Scotland (Montrose to Eyemouth)	Publication due 1995
Regional Report 5. North-east England (Berwick-on-Tweed to Filey Bay)	Publication due 1995
Regional Report 6. Eastern England (Flamborough Head to Great Yarmouth)	Publication due 1995
Regional Report 7. South-east England (Lowestoft to Dungeness)	Publication due 1996
Regional Report 8. Sussex (Rye Bay to Chichester Harbour)	Publication due 1996
Regional Report 9. Southern England (Hayling Island to Lyme Regis)	Publication due 1995
Regional Report 10. South-west England (Seaton to Falmouth Bay)	Publication due 1996
Regional Report 11. The Western Approaches (Falmouth Bay to Kenfig)	Publication due 1996
Regional Report 12. Wales (Margam to Little Orme)	Published 1995
Regional Report 13. Northern Irish Sea (Colwyn Bay to Stranraer)	Publication due 1995
Regional Report 14. South-west Scotland (Ballantrae to Mull)	Publication due 1996
Regional Report 15. The Outer Hebrides	Publication due 1996
Regional Report 16. North-west Scotland (Loch Linnhe to Cape Wrath)	Publication due 1996
Regional Report 17. Northern Ireland	Publication due 1996
West Coast Directory	Publication due 1996
Coastal and marine UKDMAP datasets: Version 1	Published 1994

B. Further reading

Bird, E.C.F. 1984. *Coasts - an introduction to coastal geomorphology.*
    3rd ed. Oxford, Basil Blackwell.

C. Contact names and addresses

Type of information	Contact address and telephone no.
Information about the Directories project and UKDMAP version	*Project Co-ordinator, Coastal Conservation Branch, JNCC, Peterborough, tel: 01733 62626
Sales outlet for the regional volumes, the Directories and other JNCC publications	Natural History Book Service Ltd, 2-3 Wills Road, Totnes, Devon TQ9 5XN, tel: 01803 865280

* Starred contact addresses are given in full in the Appendix

Whitesands Bay, St David's Head, Dyfed. Rocky cliffs and sweeping sandy bays are characteristic and important features of this region and are popular with holidaymakers for their beauty and tranquility. Photo: JNCC Geological Conservation Review.

1.2 Regional summary

Dr J.P. Doody

1.2.1 Introduction and scope

This chapter gives a brief introduction to the character of the region and the extent of its human use and development, summarising the information presented in the following nine chapters. Region 12 covers the major part of the coastline of Wales, including the whole of its west coast. The area is influenced by south-westerly and westerly Atlantic winds, has a varied geology and has an open, predominantly agricultural hinterland. Major industrial development is concentrated in the south, particularly around Swansea Bay. Much of the coast is unspoiled and includes thirteen sections designated as Heritage Coasts. Two National Parks also include substantial coastal sections and the area is a popular tourist destination. Map 1.2.1 shows the main locations in the region that are mentioned in the text.

1.2.2 General description of the coastline

The coast is 1,322 km long when measured at high water mark as shown on the 1:50,000 Ordnance Survey maps, which is 84% of the total coastline of Wales and 7% of that of Great Britain. From south to north the rocks from which the coast is constructed are progressively older. In the south, rocks of the Carboniferous period (300 million years) include the sediments (shales and limestone) of the Coal Measures. The bulk of the area north of Pembrokeshire is composed of rocks of Lower Palaeozoic age (570 - 400 million years), though even older rocks occur on Anglesey and the Llyn Peninsula. The nature of the underlying rock, together with the more recent influence of glacial action, including the deposits of material left as the ice retreated, provide the basis for the present-day landscape. Offshore there are thick deposits of sedimentary rocks, which are younger than those on the land but pre-date the glacial period.

In the south several large estuaries and associated sand dunes and saltmarshes surround Swansea and Carmarthen Bays. These are separated by the Gower Peninsula, a popular tourist destination. Swansea Bay includes the only substantial area of infrastructure development to have caused major loss of coastal habitats. Here the sand dunes and estuaries of the area around Swansea, Neath and Port Talbot have largely been destroyed by various urban, industrial and port developments, including one of Europe's largest steel works. By contrast, the estuaries of Carmarthen Bay are largely intact and include complete sequences of habitats that have been lost, by enclosure, from many other sites in Great Britain.

The Pembrokeshire Coast National Park includes the limestone cliffs, with their rich grasslands, around St. Govan's Head and the exposed westerly-facing headlands and adjacent cliffs of St. Anne's and St. David's Head, where important cliff and cliff-top heathland vegetation occurs. Together with the offshore islands and their internationally important breeding bird colonies and the marine interest in the waters around Skomer and the adjacent Marloes Peninsula, the whole area is of exceptional conservation interest. Milford Haven is also of special interest: the site of a major oil terminal, it still retains much of its natural beauty and wildlife importance.

The southern part of Cardigan Bay, the Ceredigion coast, is remote, with cliffs and small sandy bays. North of Aberystwyth the coastline has a generally more low-lying topography. Here the coastal fringe includes a sequence of estuaries (Dyfi, Mawddach and Glaslyn) and enclosing sand dunes of considerable interest for their structure, history and vegetation. Cardigan Bay is an important marine area and has some of the least polluted coastal waters in Wales.

The northern rocky coast, with its cliffs and offshore islands, supports cliff-face and cliff-top plant communities of considerable importance, ranging from the limestones of Great Orme's Head to the geologically older, heath covered slopes of Holy Island coast and the cliffs of the Llyn Peninsula. On the south-west corner of Anglesey there are several sand dune systems, of which Newborough Warren is the largest, with more than 1,000 ha of wind-blown sand.

Offshore of Region 12, marine life is also very rich. Both sub-littoral and littoral habitats exhibit a wide range of variation. Milford Haven (a drowned river valley), the waters around Skomer Island and Ynys Enlli (Bardsey Island) and the Menai Strait are all nationally important marine areas.

1.2.3 Coastal habitats and species

The coast of Region 12 includes a mixture of all the main coastal habitat types, with nationally important examples of sea cliffs, sand dunes and saltmarshes. The sea cliffs and cliff tops, particularly those associated with the offshore islands, also support important sea bird colonies. The estuaries are numerous and ecologically varied, though not large in a national context. There are no nationally important examples of shingle structures and only one lagoon with nationally important brackish-water invertebrates.

Sand dunes

The region includes a high proportion of the total area of sand dune in Great Britain (14%). The prevalence of onshore westerly winds has encouraged the growth of a number of large systems. These include two of the ten largest areas of wind-blown sand in Great Britain, on Anglesey (Newborough Warren) and the Pembrey Burrows in the south (1,257 and 1,559 ha respectively). Both of these sites have been extensively planted with pines intended to prevent sand movement. This has reduced the area of open habitat, with losses of 56% and 45% for Pembrey and Newborough respectively, based on measurements taken from OS 1:50,000 scale maps. As with other sites in Britain and the Netherlands this is thought to have contributed to a lowering of the water table within the dunes, which may have affected the development of the important and characteristic dune slack vegetation.

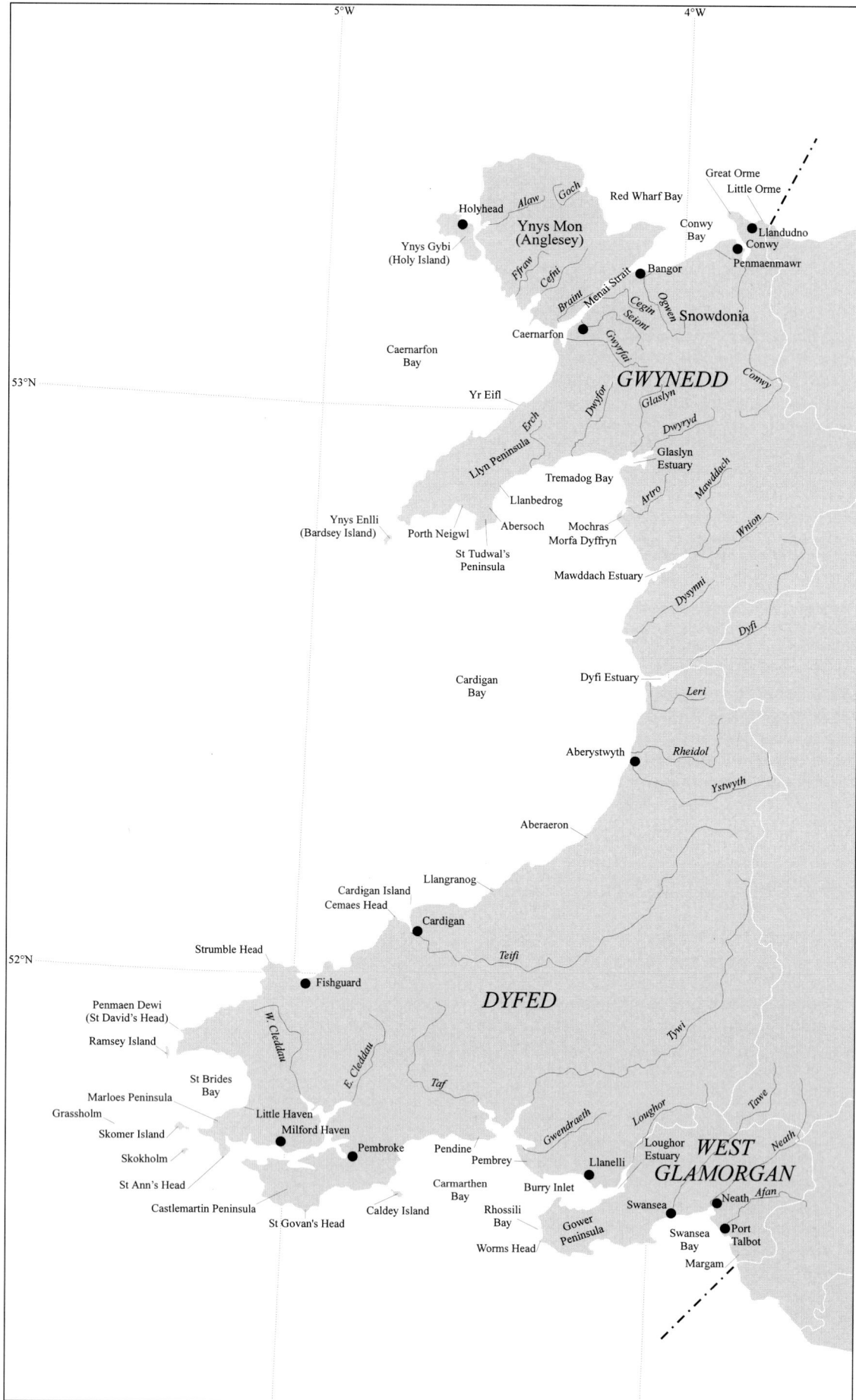

Map 1.2.1 Rivers, major towns and other coastal locations. The dashed lines show the coastal limits of Region 12.

The vegetation of the dunes is predominantly composed of species-rich calcareous communities, which are dependent on periodic low-level grazing for their survival. They include a number of fungi that are restricted to sand dunes and a rare liverwort that is confined to dune slacks in this area. The richness of the sand-dune vegetation is matched by its invertebrate fauna, which includes both species characteristic of open sandy habitats and rarer species including those of wet slacks. In some areas a reduction in grazing levels has led to an increase in the growth of coarse grasses and scrub development at the expense of the species-rich grassland.

Recreational activity has locally increased the extent of sand movement at several sites, including the National Nature Reserves of Morfa Harlech and Morfa Dyffryn.

Saltmarshes

Both large and small saltmarshes occur within the region. They are mostly grazed and support a relatively rich vegetation. The absence of major enclosure for agriculture is an important element in sustaining a complete zonation (all the stages of development of saltmarsh, from the water's edge to the limit of tidal influence) at several estuarine sites. Thus the saltmarshes of the Loughor Estuary (notably Llanridian Marsh) have the true marsh-mallow in their upper levels - a species absent from many other sites where saltmarsh enclosure has taken place. Within the region, where saltmarshes are enclosed by a sand spit, transitions to sand-dune vegetation may include elements of the Mediterranean flora, including sharp rush *Juncus acutus*, which helps provide a geographical link between the communities of the colder north and those of the warmer south. Significant areas of upper saltmarsh are dominated by sea rush *Juncus maritimus*, another species that is common and characteristic of the Mediterranean flora.

Although these areas have been relatively free from destruction by enclosure, compared with those in the south-east of England, many estuaries do show loss of habitat. This loss includes the development of grazing marsh on former saltmarsh, though even the larger areas in the region, such as Malltraeth Marsh on Anglesey (1,365 ha) and the grazing marshes associated with Carmarthen Bay and the Dyfi Estuary, are still relatively small when compared with the extensive grazing marshes of other regions.

Cord grass *Spartina anglica* is a major factor in saltmarsh development around the region. Extensive areas occur in almost all the estuaries, and at some sites, such as the Dyfi estuary, there is a correlation between a loss of wintering waders such as dunlin and the spread of cord grass (Davis & Moss 1984). At the Malltraeth estuary, which is part of the National Nature Reserve at Newborough, a programme of control underway for several years has prevented encroachment onto the tidal flats.

Estuaries

The region includes 23 estuaries identified in the Estuaries Review (Davidson *et al.* 1991). They are ecologically varied, though not among the largest in Britain. The Loughor Estuary and Milford Haven are the largest estuaries (each in excess of 5,000 ha) and represent 60% of the resource in the region. However, they are small by comparison with the major estuaries such as the Wash (65,000 ha) and Morecambe Bay (45,000 ha), the two biggest estuaries in Great Britain. The Welsh mudwort *Limosella australis* is of particular note, as it is a typically North American species, found at a number of estuarine sites in the region, though nowhere else in Europe.

Sea cliffs

The cliffs and cliff tops of the Gower and Castlemartin peninsulas are rich in plant species, with a wealth of lime-loving plants including several rare species. Similarly, Great Orme's Head in the north is also important for a number of rare plants that inhabit the limestone cliffs and cliffs tops. These are, botanically, among the most species-rich cliff sites in Britain and compare well with those of the Dorset coast and the Isle of Wight.

On the headlands of Strumble Head and St. David's in the south-west and Holy Island in the north-west there are good examples of maritime and para-maritime vegetation on sea cliffs. These cliffs are composed of older, more resistant rocks and support communities that include examples of acid-loving vegetation. On the more exposed cliffs, a sequence of salt-spray influenced vegetation with typical maritime plants such as golden samphire and sea thrift grade into maritime heath, with a close-cropped and sometimes extensive vegetation composed of heather, bell heather and western gorse. In the late summer these slopes provide a spectacle of purple and yellow flowers covering the cliff tops. Another feature in these exposed cliffs, particularly in Pembrokeshire, is the presence of a closely wind-pruned shrub community of privet and blackthorn, which is often so dense as to be completely impenetrable. The oceanic climate is also important for the presence of a number of lichen populations, which require the damp conditions of the cliff-top grassland and coastal woodlands to survive.

The cliffs in the region are not only important for their rich and varied vegetation but also have some significant seabird populations. Some of the very few remaining colonies of the chough in Britain occur on the cliffs of Gwynedd and Dyfed.

Islands

One of the features of the coast is the presence of a number of islands important for nature conservation. Notable amongst these are Ynys Enlli in the north, and Ramsey, Grassholm, Skomer and Skokholm in the south. Each of these has its own suite of breeding bird species, which attract thousands of visitors each year. Access by boat from the mainland is limited, but regular trips take place, landing on the islands or sailing round them. Skomer Island is one of the most visited offshore island sites anywhere in Britain. The written history of nearby Skokholm Island, by R.M. Lockley, charts the farming history and wildlife interest in a series of classic books (Lockley 1943a, 1943b, 1946 and 1969).

1.2.4 The marine environment

The importance of the region's marine habitats is reflected in the number of sites identified as potential Marine Nature Reserves. The waters around Skomer Island are now the UK's second (and Wales's first) designated statutory Marine

Nature Reserve, and the Menai Strait and Ynys Enlli, along with part of the Llyn Peninsula, have both been identified for potential future designation. The particular value of the marine communities lies in the great diversity of their flora and fauna, associated with the turbulent and clear waters, which are relatively free from pollution when compared with other parts of southern Britain.

Benthic (sea-bed) communities

The waters off the Pembrokeshire coast have a high density of sites of marine biological importance. A wide range of shore types occur here, ranging from exposed bedrock on headlands to sheltered sandy bays. The exposed limestone cliffs west of St. Govan's Head have some of the finest examples of rocky shore communities in Wales. Sublittoral habitats around Skomer Island exhibit an outstanding range in a very small area. The whole of the Milford Haven/Daucleddau estuary system is one of the best examples of a ria system (drowned river valley) in Britain, with a wide range of benthic habitats and communities.

In Cardigan Bay, the sub-littoral, shallow boulder reefs ('sarnau') provide outcropping hard substrates which are subject to strong wave action and tidal currents and are especially rich in species.

In the north the Menai Strait includes rich tide-swept communities tolerant of extreme current strengths. Again the range of communities throughout the area is large, developing on rocky shores and in sandy bays and muddy inlets.

Fish

This region contains all eight of the British species protected under national, European and international legislation. However, only the lamprey, lampern and the two shad species are considered threatened in a national context. These four species are recorded throughout the region and are particularly associated with the estuaries and coastal waters around Gwynedd and south Wales. The south Wales estuaries feed into the Bristol Channel, where a population of shad occurs that is of considerable importance, being the only one in the UK known to be viable.

Marine mammals

The grey seal is present throughout the region (common seals rarely visit and do not breed in the region). Breeding is concentrated around the Pembrokeshire coast, with a small population around Ynys Enlli. The colonies represent approximately 5% of the national population of grey seals. The diversity of regularly-recorded cetacean species is not particularly rich in the region, although a total of fourteen different species have been recorded offshore. However, Cardigan Bay is noteworthy for having the only recognised resident community of bottlenose dolphins in England and Wales.

Archaeology

Offshore from Region 12 there is an extensive former coastal plain, which was populated by Mesolithic and Neolithic peoples when sea-level was much lower (by up to 40 m) than today. Submerged forests offshore provide evidence

for a former wooded landscape, and other prehistoric land surfaces are now buried beneath the extensive dunes of the west coast.

More recent history is derived from onshore sites, which testify to Roman occupation, though surprisingly little survives from the next 700 years. In modern times the presence of coal provided the impetus for the development of ports on the south coast, mirroring the Bronze Age importance of the north Wales coast, which was also rich in relatively accessible mineral resources.

Birds

Cliff-nesting choughs are present on Anglesey and in Pembrokeshire, representing about 26% of the British population. The peregrine falcon also breeds on the more inaccessible cliffs. The seabird colonies on the islands of Skomer, Skokholm and Grassholm are the most important in the region. Wintering waterfowl occur in nationally important numbers at three sites, Burry Inlet and Carmarthen Bay in the south and Lafan Sands in the north. The rocky nature of much of the rest of the coast restricts the size of available sites and the numbers of waterfowl using them.

1.2.5 Site protection

The value of the area for nature conservation is reflected in the large number of official site protection measures that have been applied to a large proportion of the coast. The total number of sites and the area of the main designations are given in Table 1.2.1. In addition to these there are three Areas of Outstanding Natural Beauty, two National Parks and thirteen Heritage Coasts, including a Marine Heritage Coast pilot project in Ceredigion.

Table 1.2.1 Summary of main site protection measures

Site type	Total area in this region (ha)	No. of sites in region	% of area of GB coastal sites
Sites of Special Scientific Interest	38,229	176	5.5
National Nature Reserves	6,793	12	8.0
Marine Nature Reserve	1,500	1	51.9
Ramsar sites	9,418	3	4.0
Special Protection Areas	10,753	7	4.3
Local Nature Reserves	3,045	8	22.8
National Trust sites	6,840	88	10.9
Wildlife Trusts sites	1,128	38	4.8
RSPB Reserves	1,603	8	4.3

The extent and importance of the interest is reflected in the approach to coastal management being adopted by Arfordir. This group is a partnership of practitioners in Wales promoting integrated coastal management and 'best practice' environmental management for the whole of the Welsh coast.

1.2.6 Human activities and infrastructure development

Early occupation of the region dates back to prehistoric times, when scattered settlements existed along the coastal fringe. Sea routes were of major importance and there is considerable evidence of the importance of the area from Roman times. The ports of Swansea (coal and steel), Fishguard, Holyhead and Milford Haven (oil) are the only significant port and port-related developments in the region, though there are a number of smaller, older ports.

Carmarthen and Swansea Bays, with their gently shelving sub-tidal areas, are important for shellfisheries. Cockles are abundant and gathered commercially in the Loughor Estuary and Traeth Lafan; other species are more widely dispersed and are not considered to be important for major fisheries. The *Spartina* marshes on the west coast are known to be valuable as nursery areas for sea bass.

The majority of the coastal hinterland is in agricultural use. Although some areas of coastal land within estuaries have been enclosed, this represents much less of an incursion than has occurred in many estuaries in other regions. By contrast, the ploughing of the grassland and heathlands of the cliff tops has affected a number of areas and a relatively higher proportion of cliff-top than estuarine land. In some places the cliff-top margin has been left as a narrow strip with little or no surviving interest. At the same time the decline of rough grazing on the cliff tops and slopes has caused further loss of species-rich grassland and heath, as bracken and scrub have spread.

There is a concentration of tourist use and associated facilities in some parts of the region, which can put pressure locally on coastal habitats such as sand dunes. Where problems have arisen, such as on the National Nature Reserves at Ynyslas and Whiteford, management of people by providing access and walkways and the rehabilitation of

the habitat has protected the conservation interest. Generally the level of use of the area for tourism has been in keeping with the nature of the environment.

The oil industry represents a major development, located principally in Milford Haven. Offshore exploratory drilling has recently (1992) taken place some 10 km north of the tip of the Llyn Peninsula and exploration is likely to increase. Industrial development in the area of Swansea Bay and to a lesser extent around Llanelli represents an incursion into the natural coastal habitats of the area, with major losses of sand dunes and estuarine saltmarsh and tidal flats. Amenity barrages, such as the half-tide barrier on the Loughor Estuary and the recently constructed barrage on the Tawe Estuary, continue the process of land claim and could potentially affect other estuaries in Wales.

1.2.7 Local Government boundaries and re-organisation

The proposed new Unitary Authorities are shown on Map 1.2.2. All are wholly within the region except Aberconwy and Colwyn, parts of which are in Region 13.

1.2.8 Further sources of information

A. References cited

Davidson, N.C., Laffoley, D.d'A., Doody, J.P., Way, L.S., Gordon, J., Key, R., Drake, C.M., Pienkowski, M.W., Mitchell, R.M., & Duff, K.L. 1991. *Nature conservation and estuaries in Great Britain.* Peterborough, Nature Conservancy Council.

Davis, P., & Moss, D. 1984. *Spartina* and waders - The Dyfi Estuary. *In:* Spartina anglica *in Great Britain,* ed. by J.P. Doody. Huntingdon, Nature Conservancy Council. (Focus on nature conservation, No. 5.)

Lockley, R.M. 1943a. *Island farm.* London, H.F. & G. Witherby.

Lockley, R.M. 1943b. *Dream island days.* London, H.F. & G. Witherby.

Lockley, R.M. 1946. *The island farm.* London, H.F. & G. Witherby.

Lockley, R.M. 1969. *The island.* Andre Deutsch.

B. Further reading

Steers, J.A. 1964. *The coastline of England and Wales.* 2nd ed., 112 - 183 (Geology and geomorphology). Cambridge, Cambridge University Press.

Robinson, A., & Millward, R. 1983. *The Shell book of the British coast,* 185 - 229 (General setting and history). Newton Abbot, David and Charles.

Gillham, M.E. 1977. *The natural history of the Gower, South Wales.* Cowbridge and Bridgend, South Wales, D. Brown & Sons.

Balchin, W.G.V., *et al.* 1971. *Swansea and its region.* Swansea, British Association for the Advancement of Science.

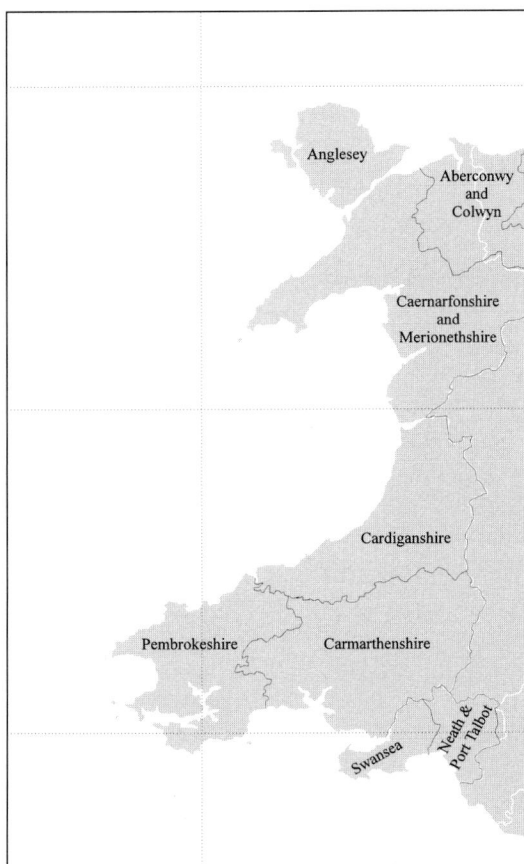

Map 1.2.2 Unitary authorities proposed under local government reorganisation

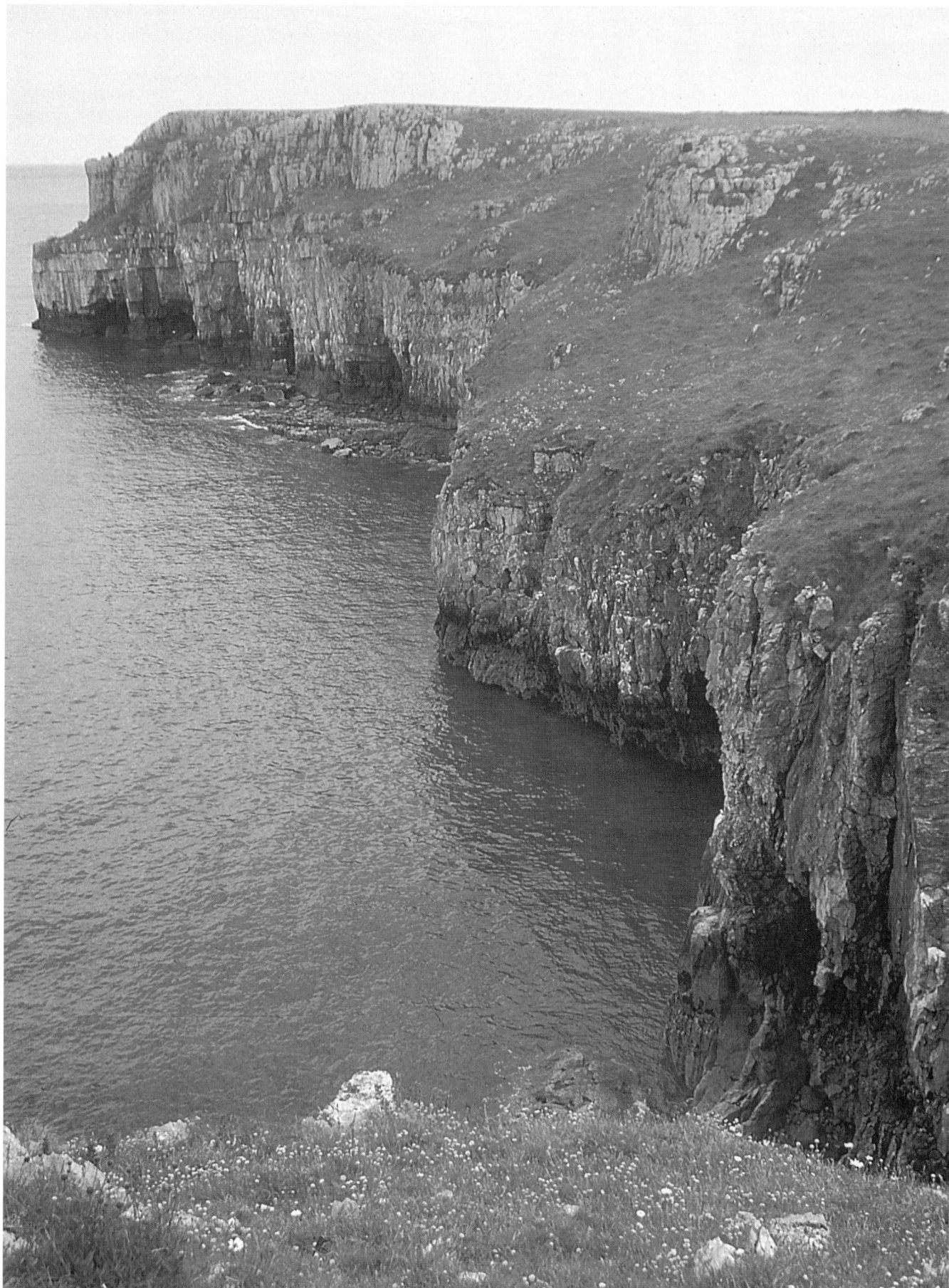

Stackpole Head, Dyfed (Site of Special Scientific Interest). These limestone cliffs are nationally important for both their geological interest and their plants and animals. Photo: J.P. Doody, JNCC.

Chapter 2 Geology and physical environment

2.1 Coastal geology

Dr C.D.R. Evans

2.1.1 Introduction

This section describes the geological structure, stratigraphy (history of the rock units) and glacial history of the region and relates them to the coastal landforms.

The Palaeozoic and Precambrian rocks of the region hold a special place in the history of geological science in that names of many stratigraphic units, now used world-wide, were derived from them (Table 2.1.1). A broad range of these rock units and their associated structures are well exposed along these coasts.

2.1.2 Stratigraphy

Map 2.1.1 shows the onshore coastal geology of the region. Locations mentioned in the text are shown on Map 1.2.1.

Swansea Bay – St. Bride's Bay

Swansea Bay, lying on the southern flank of the south Wales syncline, is surrounded by poorly exposed, locally carbonaceous shales of the Coal Measures. The bulk of the Gower Peninsula comprises shelly, coral-rich Carboniferous Limestone but an inlier of Old Red Sandstone conglomerates outcrops at Rhossili Bay. The bays along the south coast result from erosion of softer shales, which form synclinal cores in the Millstone Grit. Numerous faults and folds traverse the rocks of southern Gower. Glacial deposits, raised beaches and cliffs are found along this southern coast, though mantling glacial deposits are absent inland.

The coast of Carmarthen Bay north-west of Gower is formed largely of sand dunes backed by alluvial flats. Red Marls of Old Red Sandstone age reach the coast at the confluence of the Rivers Tywi and Taf.

Southern Pembrokeshire is composed of a wide variety of rocks ranging in age from Precambrian to Carboniferous,

Table 2.1.1 Geological column

Era	Period	Epoch	Age of start (million yrs)	Stratigraphic units mentioned in the text	Significant geological events
Cenozoic	Quaternary	Holocene	0.01		Rapid sea-level rise
		Pleistocene	1.6		Glaciations (Devensian, Wolstonian, Anglian)
	Tertiary (Neogene)	Pliocene	5.1		
		Miocene	25		
	Tertiary (Palaeogene)	Oligocene	38		Subsidence of sedimentary basin in Tremadog Bay
		Eocene	55		
		Palaeocene	65		
Mesozoic	Cretaceous		144		
	Jurassic		213		Subsidence of sedimentary basins in Cardigan Bay and St George's Channel
	Triassic		248		
Palaeozoic (Upper)	Permian		286		
	Carboniferous	Stephanian			Armorican earth movements
		Westphalian		Coal Measures	
		Namurian		Millstone Grit	
		Dinantian	360	Carboniferous Limestone	
	Devonian		408	Old Red Sandstone	Caledonian earth movements
Palaeozoic (Lower)	Silurian		438		
	Ordovician		505		
	Cambrian		590		
	Precambrian			Holyhead Quartzite	

Note: Stippling = ages of rocks with important or extensive exposures along the coast of the region. Hatching = underlie Quaternary deposits at Mochras (see Map 2.2.4).

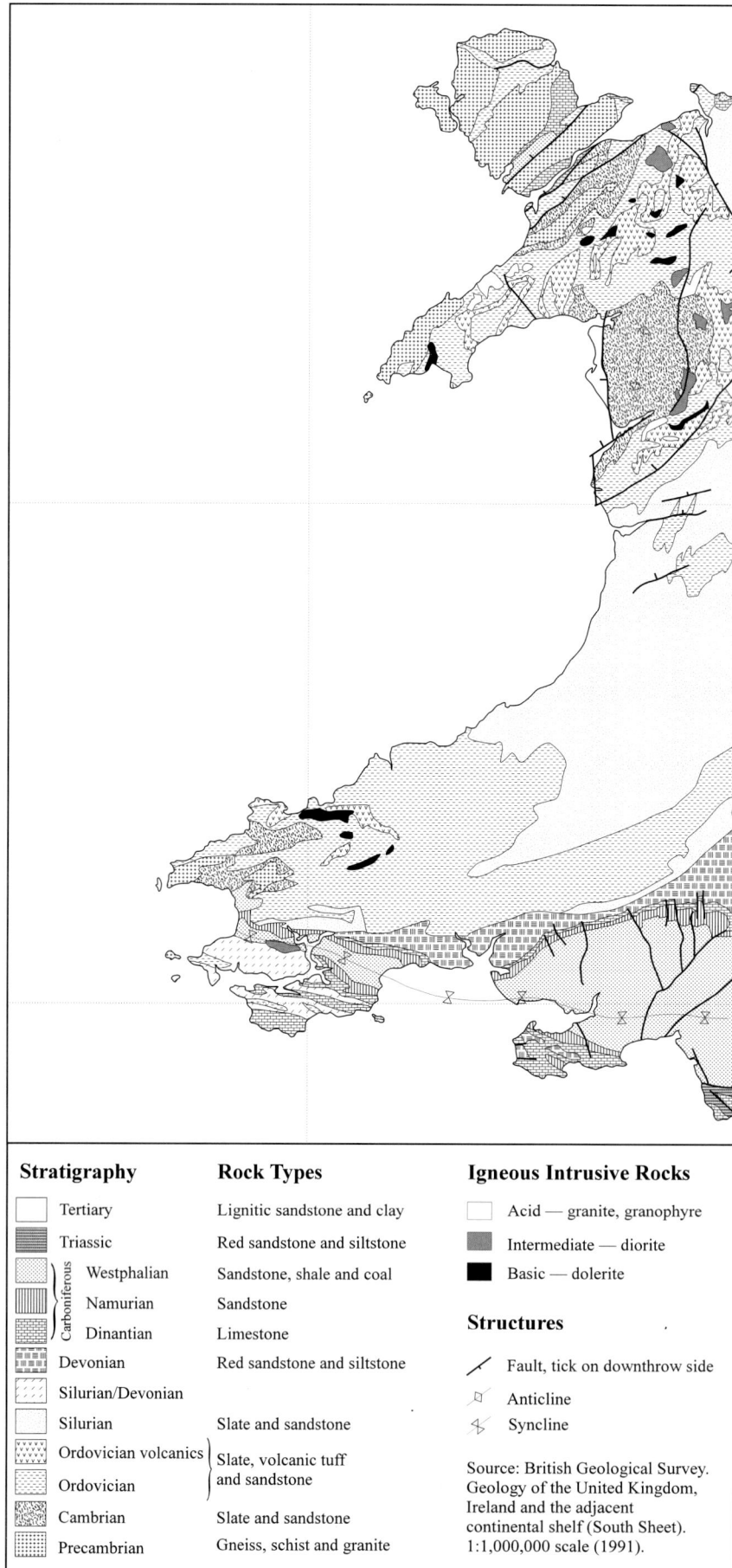

Stratigraphy

		Rock Types
☐	Tertiary	Lignitic sandstone and clay
▦	Triassic	Red sandstone and siltstone
▨	Westphalian	Sandstone, shale and coal
▥	Namurian	Sandstone
▦	Dinantian	Limestone
▦	Devonian	Red sandstone and siltstone
▨	Silurian/Devonian	
☐	Silurian	Slate and sandstone
▨	Ordovician volcanics	Slate, volcanic tuff and sandstone
▨	Ordovician	
▨	Cambrian	Slate and sandstone
▦	Precambrian	Gneiss, schist and granite

(Westphalian, Namurian, Dinantian grouped as **Carboniferous**)

Igneous Intrusive Rocks

☐ Acid — granite, granophyre

▨ Intermediate — diorite

■ Basic — dolerite

Structures

╱ Fault, tick on downthrow side

⋈ Anticline

⋈ Syncline

Source: British Geological Survey.
Geology of the United Kingdom,
Ireland and the adjacent
continental shelf (South Sheet).
1:1,000,000 scale (1991).

Map 2.1.1 Onshore coastal geology

which are formed into a series of complex, tight and locally overturned folds. The area south of Milford Haven is similar to the Gower peninsula, with continuous high cliffed sections delimiting the onshore plateau surface. To the north, inliers of Ordovician volcanic, sedimentary and intrusive rocks form Skomer island, the mainland to the east and an elongate zone which reaches the coast south of Little Haven. The coast along the southern part of St Bride's Bay is formed of folded and faulted Coal Measures with numerous coal seams.

Cardigan Bay

From the northern shores of St Bride's Bay to Fishguard, the extensive raised plateau surface is terminated at the coast by steep cliffs. The intrusive rocks within the Precambrian to Ordovician sequence form isolated hills that rise above the plateau surface and form steep, high sea cliffs, while erosion of the softer slates has resulted in narrow bays, and the thicker, more resistant volcanic rocks form promontories such as Strumble Head.

The coast sweeping north-eastwards from about Fishguard to the Dyfi estuary is formed of well-bedded Ordovician and Silurian slates and sandstones in major and minor folds, and is locally faulted. From north of Cardigan to Llangranog the rocks are mostly slates. The cliffs along this section of coast are higher than to the south and reach a maximum height of nearly 200 m at Cemaes Head. Some of the small, steep-sided valleys along the coast between Cardigan and Fishguard are glacial overflow channels, and the steep cliffs backing the coast around Aberaeron are blanketed by glacial till.

Northwards from the Dyfi to the Glaslyn estuary the coast is formed of extensive sand dunes and alluvium, backed by steep cliffs of Cambrian grits and shales. The dunes and alluvium extend furthest into Cardigan Bay at Mochras, which is underlain by nearly 2,000 m of Tertiary and Jurassic sediments. These rocks are typical of those forming the sedimentary basin in Cardigan Bay. The steep bedrock cliffs along this section of coast mark major faults, which form the boundary to this basin.

Llyn Peninsula – Great Orme's Head

The eastern Llyn peninsula is formed mainly of Ordovician sedimentary, volcanic and intrusive rocks. The intrusions form peaks along the northern part of the peninsula which slope steeply into the sea at Yr Eifl. The acid igneous intrusion at Llanbedrog forms a prominent upstanding coastal feature that contrasts with the bays at Porth Neigwl and Abersoch, which are carved into softer Ordovician slates. Much of the western part of the peninsula is formed of highly resistant Precambrian rocks similar to those found on Anglesey. They include a wide range of metamorphic and igneous rock types.

The northern coasts of the Llyn, Arfon and southern Anglesey are traversed by major NE-SW faults. The Menai Strait in part follows the path of some of these faults, which mark the boundary between the high ground of Snowdonia to the south-east and the lower plateau that forms much of Anglesey to the north-west.

Anglesey is formed of a range of Precambrian and Palaeozoic rocks, with a general NE-SW structural trend. The east and west coasts of the island are aligned at right angles to this structural trend, and this results in a varied coastal morphology. The relief of the island is generally low, except where more resistant units, such as the Holyhead Quartzite near South Stack, form high ground. Carboniferous Limestone occupies Red Wharf Bay, parts of the Menai Strait shores and the easternmost extremity of the island, and extends eastwards under Conwy Bay to reappear at the Great Orme. The fault system along the Menai Strait dies out to the east but is replaced by the more southerly Aber-Dinlle fault, which extends eastwards, occupying the low ground to the south of the Great Orme. The coast at Conwy Bay is formed generally of low ground, but where intrusive rocks are close to the fault, as at Penmaenmawr, spectacular cliffs fall steeply into the sea. South of the bay the ground rises steeply into the foothills of eastern Snowdonia. The Great Orme, north of Llandudno, is a spectacular upstanding mass of Carboniferous Limestone, which continues as a faulted outcrop eastwards towards Colwyn Bay and into Clwyd.

2.1.3   Structure

North of St Bride's Bay the form of the coast is controlled by NE-SW structures associated with the Devonian Caledonian earth movements. The coasts of southern Cardigan Bay and the Llyn peninsula, along with the Menai Strait and the valleys of the Mawddach and Dyfi, lie parallel to structures of this age. The region is flanked offshore by basins containing thick sequences of Mesozoic sedimentary rocks that are younger than the onshore rocks.

Across the southern part of the region, westwards to St Bride's Bay, the geological structures are aligned approximately E-W, and are associated with the Upper Carboniferous Armorican earth movements (see Table 2.1.1). The main structure here is the south Wales syncline, which encloses the south Wales coalfield in Glamorgan and extends westwards into south Pembrokeshire.

2.1.4   Glacial history

The ice-sheet that originated from the Welsh landmass during the last glaciation reached its maximum southern extension along the southern coast of the area. However, the contemporaneous ice-sheet filling the Irish Sea extended as a broad tongue well to the south, into the Celtic Sea. The interaction of the two ice-sheets along the northern and western coasts of Wales led to the deposition of especially complex glacial deposits. Evidence from offshore boreholes and isolated coastal sections suggests that more extensive, earlier (Anglian and Wolstonian) ice-sheets once covered the region.

2.1.5   Further sources of information

A.   Maps

British Geological Survey. 1991. *Geology of the United Kingdom, Ireland and the adjacent continental shelf (South Sheet).* 1:1 000 000 scale.

British Geological Survey. 1978. *Liverpool Bay Sheet. 53°N - 04°W, Solid Geology.* 1:250 000 series.

British Geological Survey. 1982. *Anglesey. Sheet 53°N - 06°W, Solid Geology.* 1:250 000 series.

British Geological Survey. 1982. *Cardigan Bay. Sheet 52°N - 06°W, Solid Geology.* 1:250 000 series.

British Geological Survey. 1988. *Bristol Channel. Sheet 52°N - 06°W, Solid Geology.* 1:250 000 series.

Geological Survey of Great Britain (England and Wales). 1972. *Swansea (Sheet 247), Drift Geology.* 1:50 000 scale.

Note that similar 1:50 000 scale sheets are available for much of coast of the region and further information may be obtained from the British Geological Survey, Keyworth, Nottingham.

B. Further reading

Challinor, J., & Bates, D. E. B. 1973. *Geology explained in North Wales.* Newton Abbot, David and Charles.

Owen, T. R. 1973. *Geology explained in South Wales.* Newton Abbot, David and Charles.

Owen, T.R., *ed.* 1974. *The Upper Palaeozoic and Post-Palaeozoic rocks of Wales,* 285-294. Cardiff, University of Wales Press.

George, T. N. 1970. *British Regional Geology: South Wales.* 3rd ed. London, HMSO.

Woodland, A. W. 1971. The Llanbedr (Mochras Farm) borehole. *Institute of Geological Sciences,* Report No. 71/18.

Detailed descriptions of Welsh Geological Conservation Review (GCR) sites can be found in published volumes of the Geological Conservation Review (eg: Campbell, S., & Bowen, D.Q. 1989. *Geological Conservation Review: Quaternary of Wales.* London, Chapman and Hall.). See also section 7.4 of this book for a discussion of the GCR sites in the region.

C. Contact names and addresses

Type of information	Contact address and telephone no.
Geological information for region and the whole of Britain	Coastal Geology Group, British Geological Survey, Keyworth, Nottingham NG12 5GG, tel: 0115 936 3100
GCR sites north Wales	*Senior Officer, CCW North Wales Region, Bangor, tel. 01248 372333
GCR sites mid-Wales	*Senior Officer, CCW Dyfed/Mid Wales Region, Aberystwyth, tel. 01970 828551
GCR sites south Wales	*Senior Officer, CCW South Wales Region. Cardiff, tel. 01222 485111

*Starred contact addresses are given in full in the Appendix

2.2 Offshore environment

Dr C.D.R. Evans

This section deals briefly with the geology of the rocks and sediments at, and below, the sea bed. The bulk of the information is shown on Maps 2.2.1 - 2.2.4, with some additional explanation provided by the text. Locations are shown on Map 1.2.1.

2.2.1 Bathymetry

The dominant bathymetric feature in the region is the wide trough, having a maximum depth in excess of 100 m, which runs the length of St George's Channel between Wales and Ireland. The Bristol Channel is less than 60 m deep and shallows to the east (Map 2.2.1).

Cardigan Bay is a shallow, smooth-floored embayment with the 60 m isobath close to shore off the Llyn Peninsula and west of Pembrokeshire. In the southern part of the bay, the 20 m isobath lies within a few kilometres of the coast. The northern part is shallower and its bathymetry is dominated nearshore by a series of shore-transverse ridges (sarnau), the crests of which locally dry at extreme low water.

Caernarfon Bay is shallow, but the zone of deeper water extends to within about 15 km of the north-west corner of Anglesey. Water depths reach 20 m within a few kilometres off the north Anglesey coast and the isobath continues towards the Great Orme, with shallower waters in Conwy Bay to the south.

2.2.2 Holocene sea-bed sediments

Sea-bed sediments are defined here as the unconsolidated sediments on the sea bed that have been laid down since the sea transgressed across the area during the early Holocene (Map 2.2.2).

In the Bristol Channel, tidal streams are especially strong and in general the Holocene sediments become coarser grained and thinner towards the east. In the centre of the channel, south of Gower, extensive areas of the sea bed are covered only by a thin veneer of gravel, and to the east, bedrock is widely exposed at the sea bed. Swansea Bay and Carmarthen Bay lie outside the main tidal steams, and as a result thicker sequences of fine grained Holocene sediments have accumulated within them. Sediments are generally thin and coarse grained off the Pembrokeshire coast. Within the outer part of Cardigan Bay the bulk of the sediments at the sea bed are gravelly, formed by the winnowing of finer material from a substrate of glacial till. Tidal currents have moved the finer sediment towards the coast, where thicker sands and, in Tremadog Bay, muds have accumulated.

A similar sediment distribution exists around Anglesey, with generally gravelly sediments offshore and thicker sands within Caernarfon Bay and Conwy Bay. Bedrock is extensively exposed at the sea bed north of the island.

2.2.3 Pleistocene geology

The Pleistocene is the period of time from about 1.6 million years to about 10,000 years before present during which the surface of the Earth was subject to a number of glacial and inter-glacial climatic cycles.

The last major ice sheet to cover Wales reached its maximum extent during the late Devensian, some 20,000 years ago. It extended southwards as far as Swansea Bay and Pembrokeshire. A separate tongue of ice flowing down St George's Channel extended southward into the Celtic Sea, possibly as far as the Isles of Scilly. Offshore the ice deposited a blanket of glacial till, which extends onshore to mantle many of the cliffs in the region.

This blanket of till (the Irish Sea Till) is extensive and over 10 m thick across much of Cardigan Bay. The till was produced in part by ice eroding the extensive areas of Triassic rocks underlying St George's Channel to the north and west, thereby producing a brownish-red deposit till with fewer boulders than its greyer, landward equivalent. In the centre of the main channel west of Anglesey the till is overlain by a thick succession of sands and muds, which were deposited during the melting of the ice sheet (see Map 2.2.3).

Offshore seismic and borehole evidence indicates that earlier, more extensive glaciations affected the region. The age of these events is uncertain but the consensus is that one such glaciation occurred about 150,000 years ago and was equivalent to the Wolstonian (Saalian) glaciation of East Anglia. Seismic evidence suggests that an even older, Anglian glaciation may have covered parts of the central Irish Sea. Some of these middle Pleistocene sediments crop out beneath Holocene sediments in the outer part of Cardigan Bay. The general thickness of the Pleistocene sediments, comprising both the glacial tills, glaciomarine sediments and inter-glacial deposits, exceeds tens of metres in parts of Cardigan Bay and St George's Channel, with a maximum in excess of 100 m. Raised beaches along the south and west coasts of Wales indicate that sea levels were higher than at present during parts of the Pleistocene.

2.2.4 Pre-Quaternary geology

Rocks formed before the start of the Quaternary Period (1.6 million years BP) are included by geologists in the category of 'solid geology'. Offshore in this region, these rocks are largely concealed by sea-bed sediments and palaeovalley infill sediments.

Sedimentary basins containing thick sequences of Mesozoic sediments surround the coasts of the region, but only at Mochras (where they are covered by Pleistocene deposits) do these sediments extend onshore (see Map 2.2.4). Elsewhere around this part of Wales the Precambrian and Palaeozoic rocks exposed at the coast extend at the sea bed for a few tens of kilometres offshore. The basins have a general synclinal form and, commonly, faulted margins.

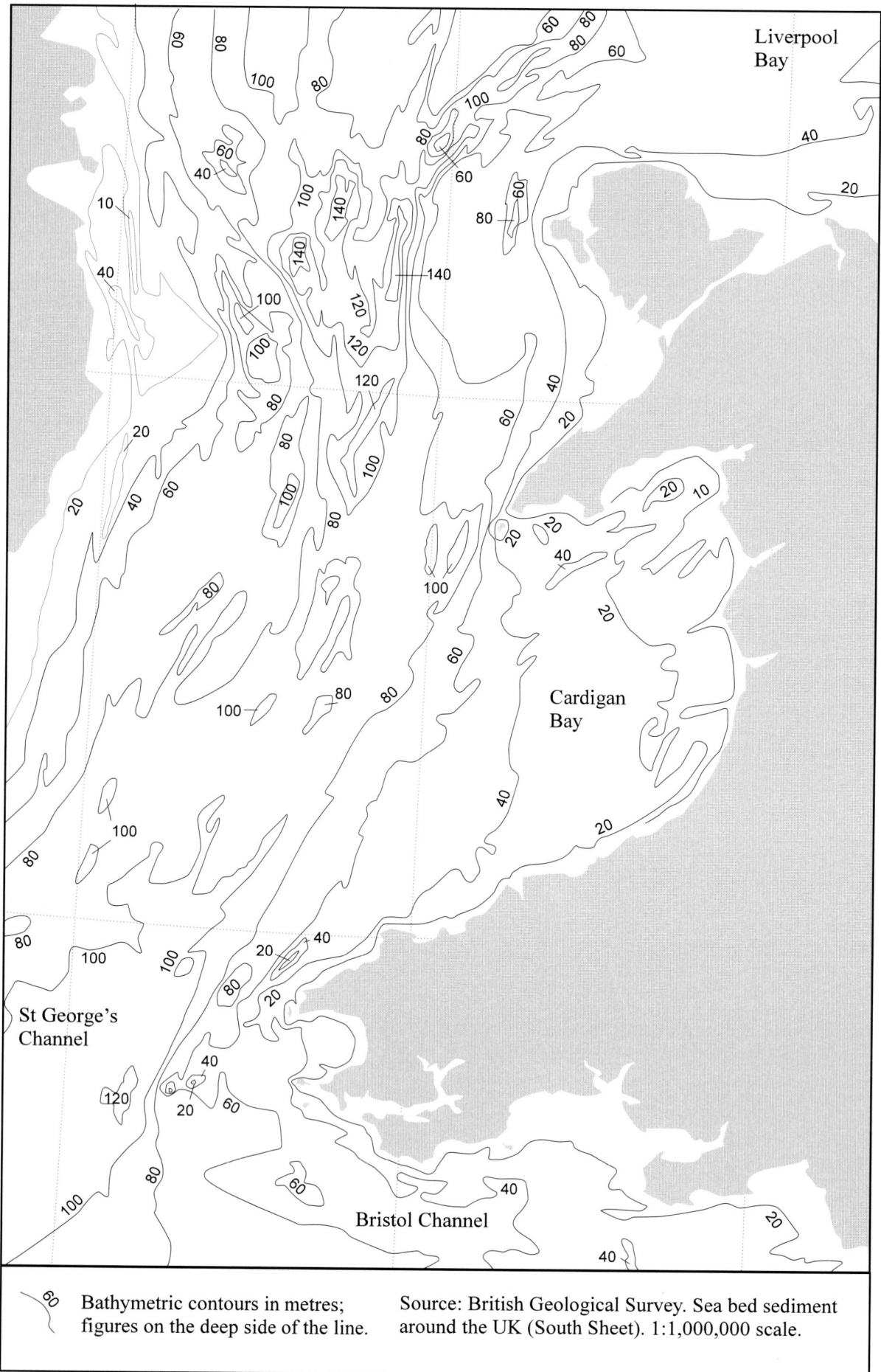

Liverpool Bay

Cardigan Bay

St George's Channel

Bristol Channel

60 Bathymetric contours in metres; figures on the deep side of the line.

Source: British Geological Survey. Sea bed sediment around the UK (South Sheet). 1:1,000,000 scale.

Map 2.2.1 Bathymetry

Liverpool
Bay

St George's Channel

Cardigan
Bay

Carmarthen Bay

Key to seabed sediment symbols

M	Mud	gS	Gravelly sand	
sM	Sandy mud	G	Gravel	
gM	Gravelly mud	mG	Muddy gravel	
S	Sand	msG	Muddy sandy gravel	
mS	Muddy sand	sG	Sandy gravel	
gmS	Gravelly muddy sand			

Areas of extensive boulder clay (till) at seabed

Areas of extensive rock at seabed

Source: British Geological Survey. Sediment classification modified after Folk, R.L. 1954. The distinction between grain-size and mineral composition in sedimentary rock nomenclature. Journal of Geology, 62, 344–359.

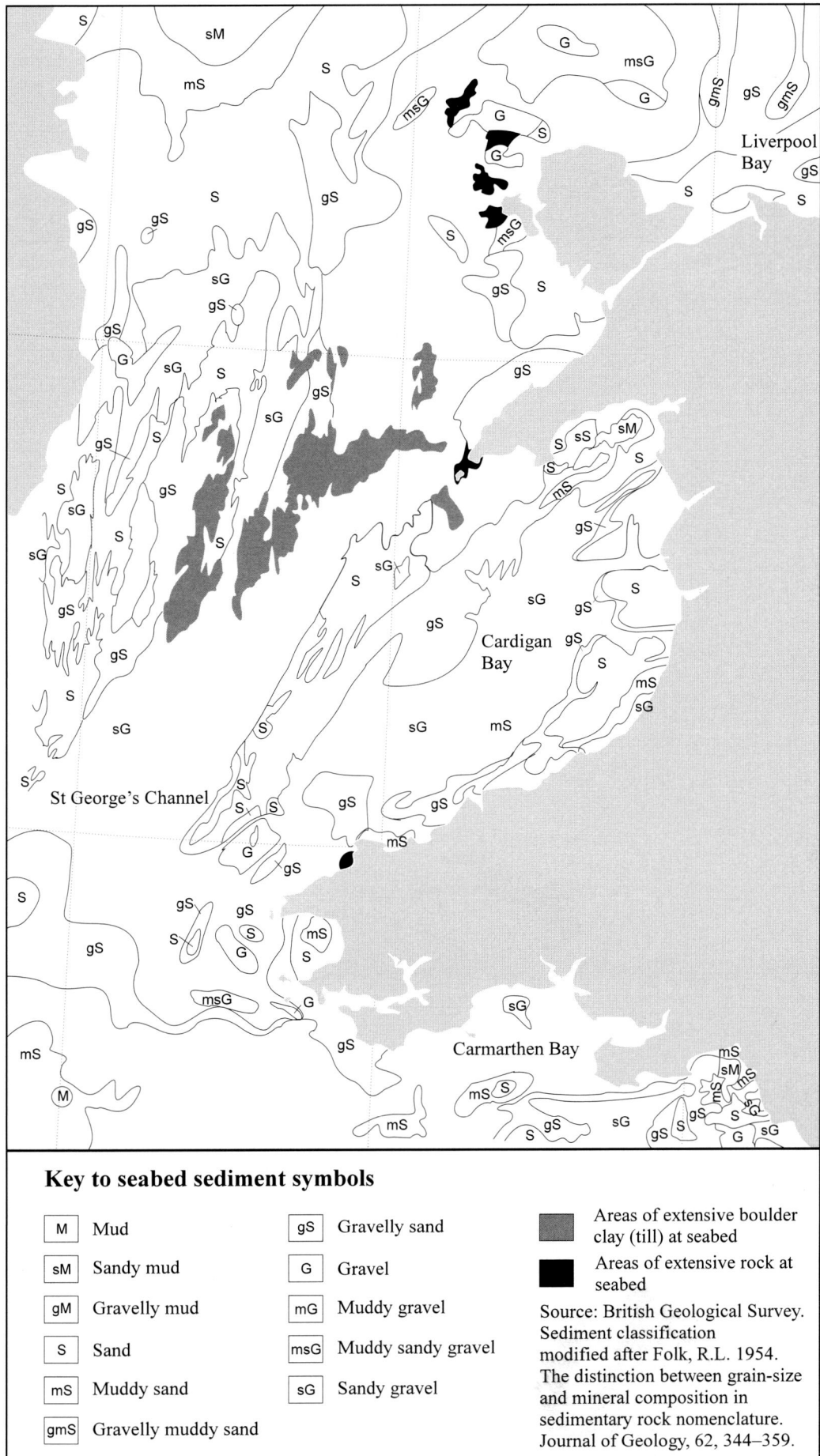

Map 2.2.2 Seabed sediments

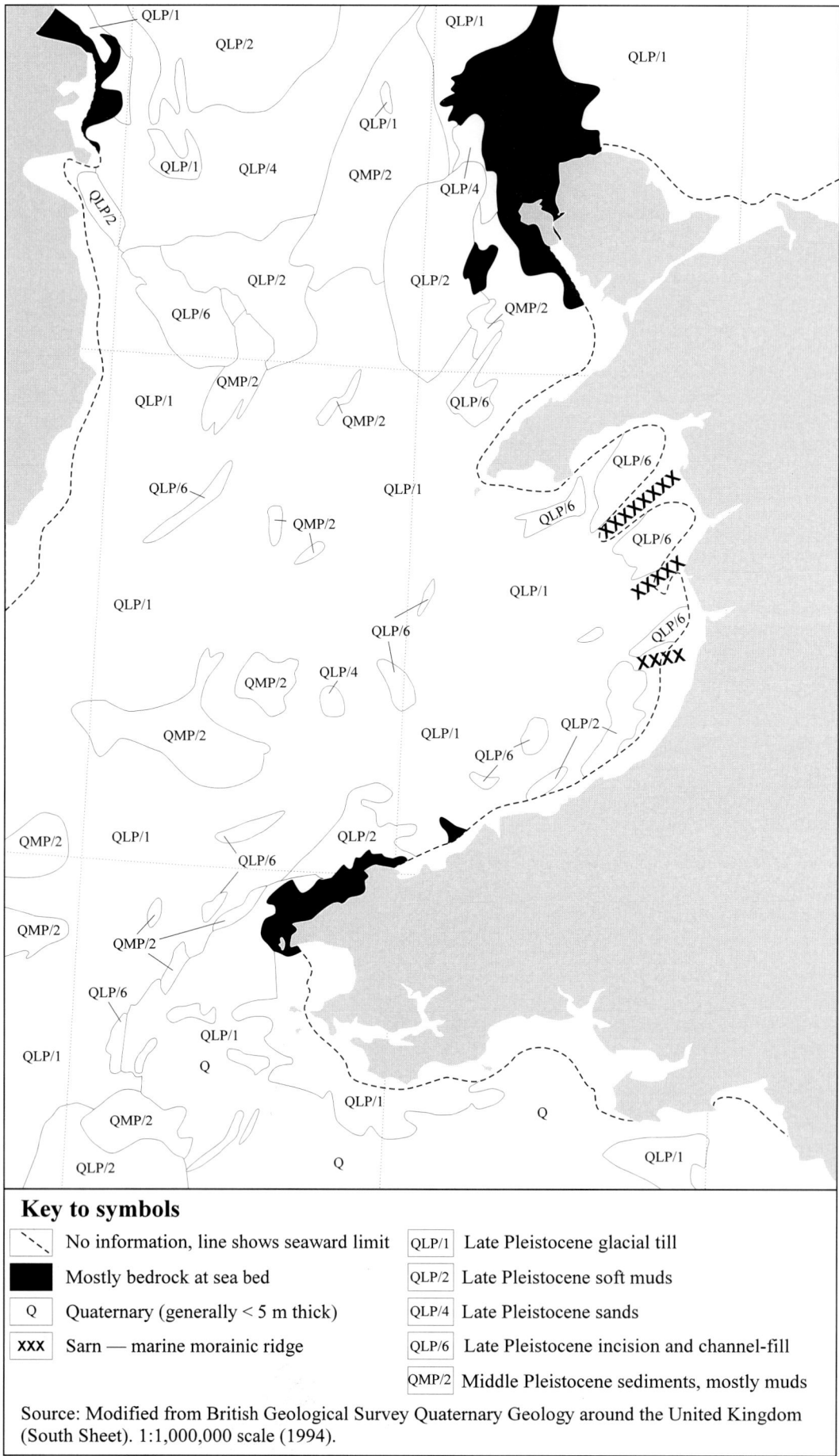

Key to symbols

	No information, line shows seaward limit
■	Mostly bedrock at sea bed
Q	Quaternary (generally < 5 m thick)
xxx	Sarn — marine morainic ridge

QLP/1	Late Pleistocene glacial till
QLP/2	Late Pleistocene soft muds
QLP/4	Late Pleistocene sands
QLP/6	Late Pleistocene incision and channel-fill
QMP/2	Middle Pleistocene sediments, mostly muds

Source: Modified from British Geological Survey Quaternary Geology around the United Kingdom (South Sheet). 1:1,000,000 scale (1994).

Map 2.2.3 Offshore Pleistocene deposits

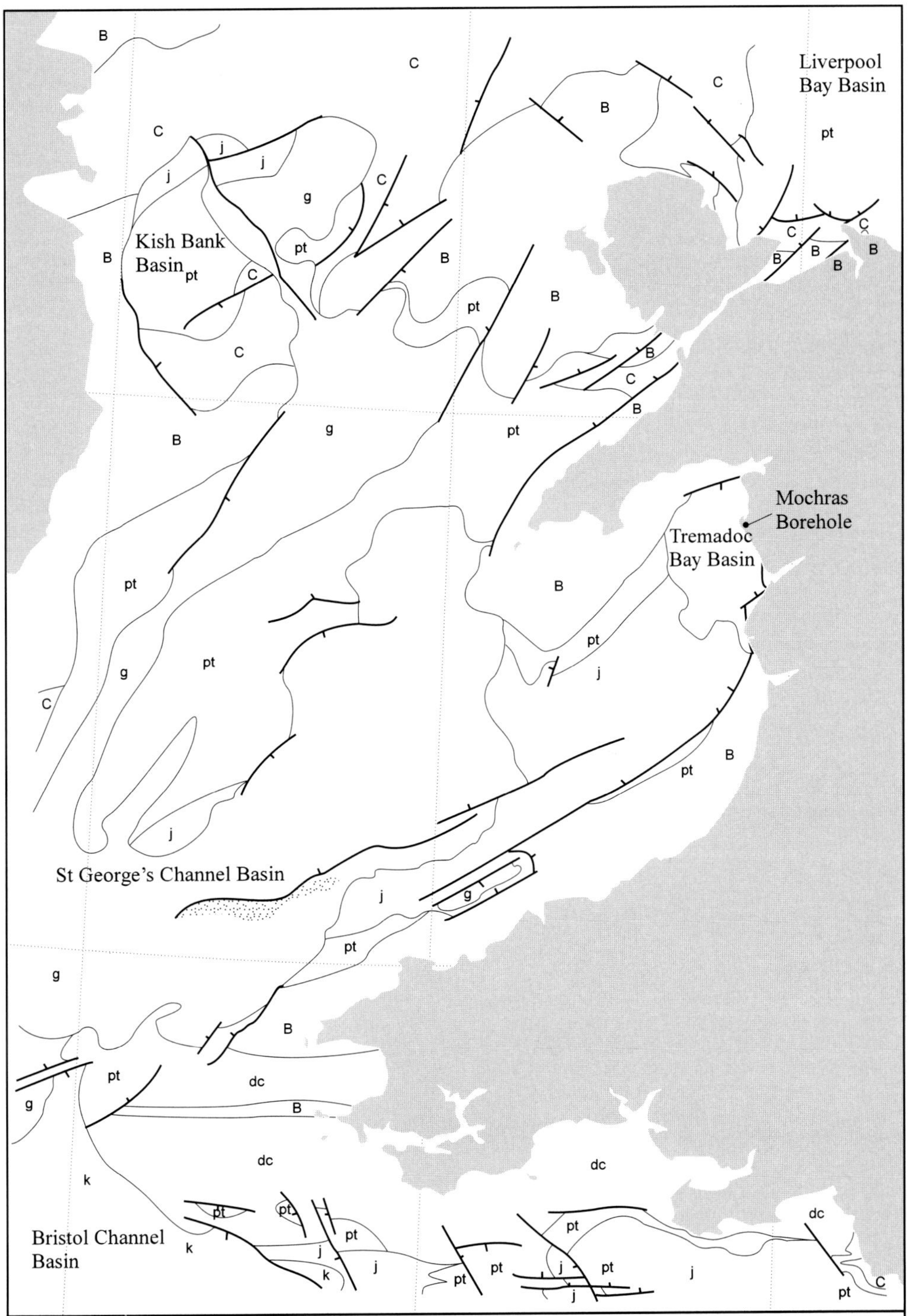

Stratigraphy

g	Tertiary
k	Cretaceous
j	Jurassic
pt	Permo-Triassic
C	Carboniferous
dc	Devonian and Carboniferous
B	Basement (Precambrian and Lower Palaeozoic)

Rock Types

Clays and sands

Chalk

Mudstones and limestones

Sandstones, siltstones and evaporites

Shales, limestones and sandstones

Sandstones and shales

Slates, volcanic and igneous rocks

Salt dome or wall

Fault, tick on downthrow side

Kish Bank Basin — Name and location of the major sedimentary basins

Source: British Geological Survey, Geology of the United Kingdom, Ireland and the adjacent continental shelf (South Sheet). 1:1,000,000 scale (1991).

Map 2.2.4 Offshore pre-Quaternary geology

West of the Pembrokeshire coast the St George's Channel Basin contains Mesozoic sediments that are over 5 km thick and include a thick Permo-Triassic salt unit. Locally, this salt has intruded into the heavier, overlying sediments to form an elongated salt wall some 20 km long and about a kilometre wide, which reaches the base of the overlying Pleistocene cover.

The Cardigan Bay Basin is aligned NE-SW, following the trend of Caledonian lines of structural weakness, whilst the Bristol Channel Basin follows an E-W Armorican trend. The basins formed over a long period of time by subsidence of the crust and infilling by sediment eroded off the adjacent basement rocks (mainland Wales). Major fault movement during early Tertiary time led to the formation of the Welsh uplands and subsidence in localised basins such as Tremadog Bay. The existence of thick mid-Tertiary sediments, deposited from rivers flowing off the Welsh landmass, was proved in the Tremadog Bay Basin by a borehole drilled at Mochras in 1969.

The deep Mesozoic sedimentary basins, especially in Cardigan Bay, have been of interest to the hydrocarbons industry since the late 1960s. Extensive seismic exploration took place in the early 1970s, and the first deep wells were drilled in 1974. Although source, reservoir and cap rocks have been identified in the basins, none of the wells drilled to date has proved the existence of economic hydrocarbon deposits.

2.2.5   Further sources of information

A. Maps

British Geological Survey. 1982. *Anglesey, Sheet 53°N-06°W, Solid Geology.* 1:250,000 series.

British Geological Survey. 1990. *Anglesey, Sheet 53°N-06°W, with part of Dublin, 53°N 08°W, Quaternary Geology.* 1:250,000 series.

British Geological Survey. 1982. *Anglesey, Sheet 53°N-06°W, with part of Dublin, 53°N 08°W, Seabed Sediments.* 1:250,000 series.

British Geological Survey. 1988. *Cardigan Bay, Sheet 52°N-06°W, including parts of Waterford, 52°N-08°W and Mid-Wales and the Marches, 52°N-04°W, Sea Bed Sediments.* 1:250,000 series.

British Geological Survey. 1982. *Cardigan Bay, Sheet 52°N-06°W, Solid Geology.* 1:250,000 series.

British Geological Survey. 1982. Cardigan Bay Sheet 52°N-06°W, with part of Waterford, 52°N 08°W, Quaternary Geology. 1:250,000 series.

British Geological Survey. 1983. *Lundy, Sheet 51°N-06°W, Sea Bed Sediments.* 1:250,000 series.

British Geological Survey. 1991. *North Celtic Sea including parts of the 1:250,000 series sheets Nymphe Bank, 51°N-08°W, Lundy 51°N-06°W, Labadie Bank, 50°N-10°W, Haig Fras 50°N-08°W and Lands End 50°N-06°W, Quaternary Geology.* 1:250,000 series.

British Geological Survey. 1983. *Lundy, Sheet 51°N-06°W, Solid Geology.* 1:250,000 series.

British Geological Survey. 1991. Geology of the United Kingdom, Ireland and the adjacent continental shelf (South Sheet). 1:1,000,000 scale.

British Geological Survey. 1994. Quaternary Geology around the United Kingdom (South Sheet). 1:1,000,000 scale.

British Geological Survey. 1987. Sea bed sediment around the United Kingdom (South Sheet). 1:1,000,000 scale.

B. References cited

Folk R.,L. 1954. The distinction between grain-size and mineral composition in sedimentary rock nomenclature. *Journal of Geology, 62:* 344-359.

C. Further reading

Banner, F. T., Collins, M. B., & Massie, K. S. 1980. *The north-west European shelf sea: the sea bed and the sea in motion. II. Physical and chemical oceanography, and physical resources.* Elsevier Oceanography Series. Cambridge, Elsevier.

Barne, J., Davidson, N.C., Hill, T.O., & Jones, M. 1994. *Coastal and Marine UKDMAP datasets: a user manual.* Peterborough, Joint Nature Conservation Committee.

Bowen, D. Q. 1973. The Pleistocene succession of the Irish Sea. *Proceedings of the Geologists' Association, 84:* 249-272.

Jackson, A. In press. *The geology of the Irish Sea.* HMSO. (British Geological Survey, Regional Offshore Report.)

Tappin, D. R. In press. *The geology of Cardigan Bay and the Bristol Channel.* HMSO. (British Geological Survey, Regional Offshore Report.)

D. Contact names and addresses

Type of information	Contact address and telephone no.
Geological information for region and the whole of Britain	Coastal Geology Group, British Geological Survey, Keyworth, Nottingham NG12 5GG, tel. 0115 936 3100
UKDMAP 1992. Version 2. United Kingdom digital marine atlas. Oceanographic maps	British Oceanographic Data Centre, Proudman Oceanographic Laboratory, Bidston Observatory, Birkenhead, Merseyside L43 7RA, tel. 0151 652 3950

2.3 Wind and water

Dr C.D.R. Evans

2.3.1 Wind

Parts of the coast of the region are among the windiest in the United Kingdom. The wind speeds at the coast exceed about 3.5 m/sec (about Force 3 on the Beaufort Scale) for 75% of the time. However for 0.1% of the time the wind speed along the coast of Pembrokeshire and the Llyn Peninsula exceeds 19 m/sec (Gale Force 8). These values are of mean hourly speeds, but for shorter intervals the maximum speed is considerably greater. Factors such as local topography and wind direction determine local conditions and extreme speeds, but these values are representative of the winds in coastal waters as they influence wave production.

The information on wind directions has been taken from the Admiralty Pilot, and the information for Holyhead and St Ann's Head is taken to be representative of the whole area (Anon 1960). The plot shows that the dominant winds are from the south-west and blow for some 20% of the time, while winds from the eastern sector blow for about 9% of the time (Maps 2.3.1 and 2.3.2 and Figure 2.3.1).

The Admiralty Pilot confirms that gales (force 8 or above) are more common in winter than in summer, averaging in December four days at Holyhead and five days at St Ann's Head. In July on average there are no gales at Holyhead and 0.1 days at St Ann's Head.

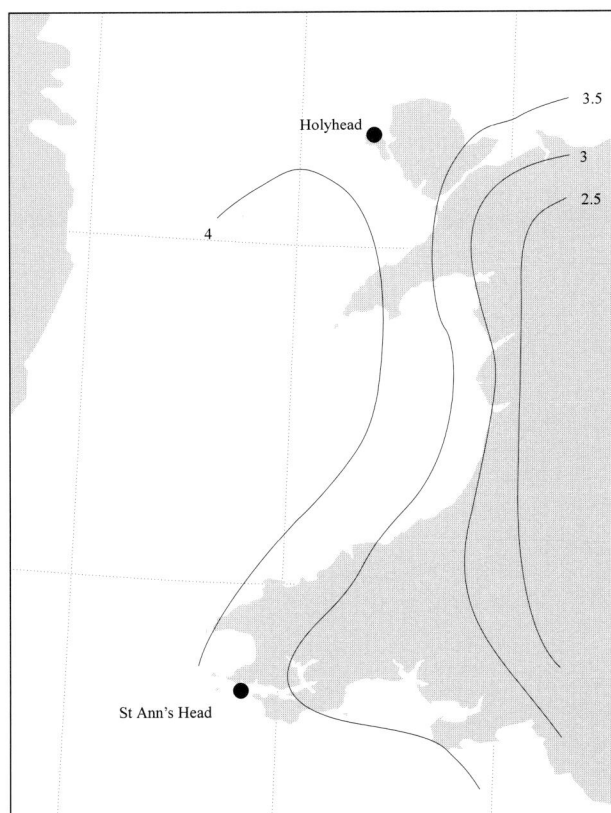

Map 2.3.2 Hourly mean windspeed in m/s exceeded for 0.1% of the time. Source: Caton (1976).

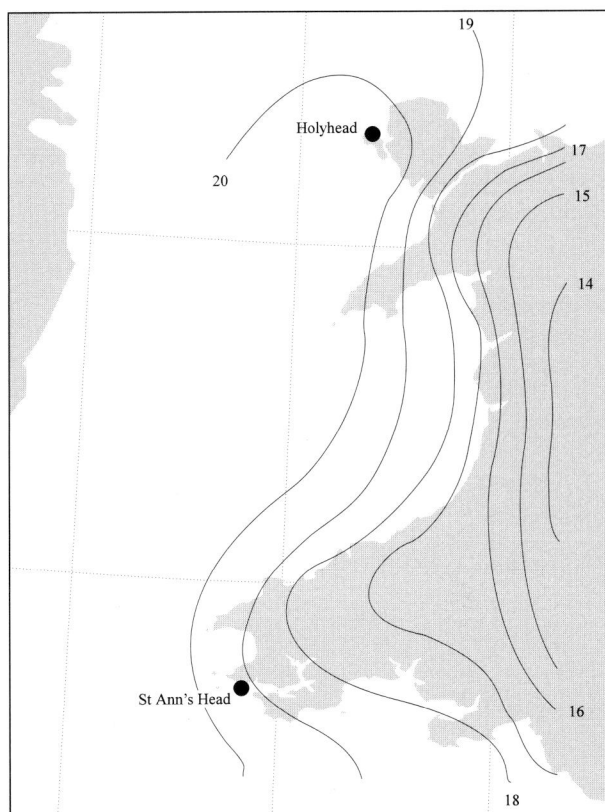

Map 2.3.1 Hourly mean windspeed in m/s exceeded for 75% of the time. Source: Caton (1976).

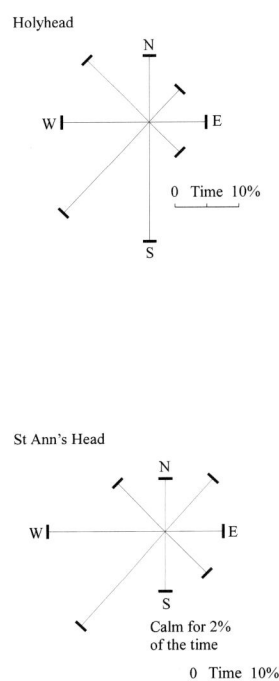

Fig 2.3.1 Wind directions at Holyhead and St Ann's Head shown as % of observations through the years 1916 - 1950. Source: Hydrographic Office (1960).

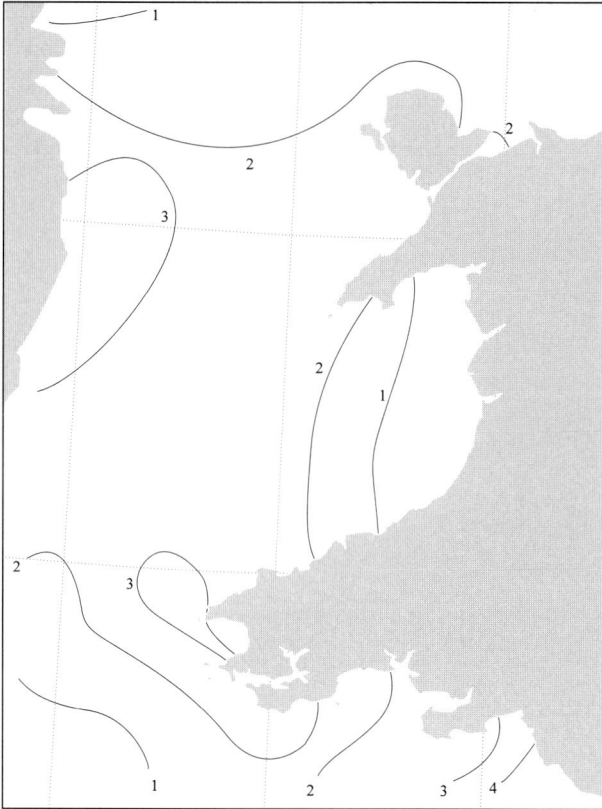

Map 2.3.3 Maximum tidal current (knots) at mean spring tides.
Source: Sager & Sammler (1968).

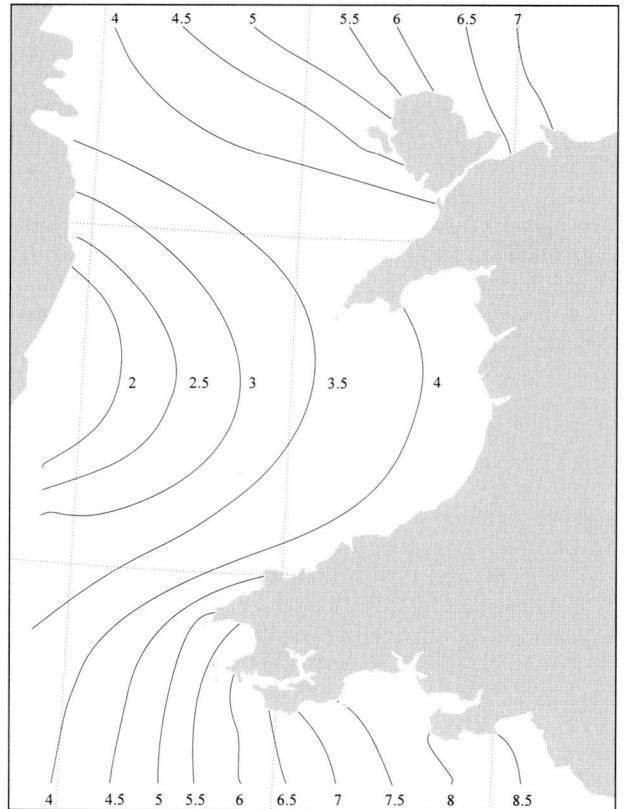

Map 2.3.4 Tidal range (m) at mean spring tides.
Source: Lee & Ramster (1981). © Crown copyright.

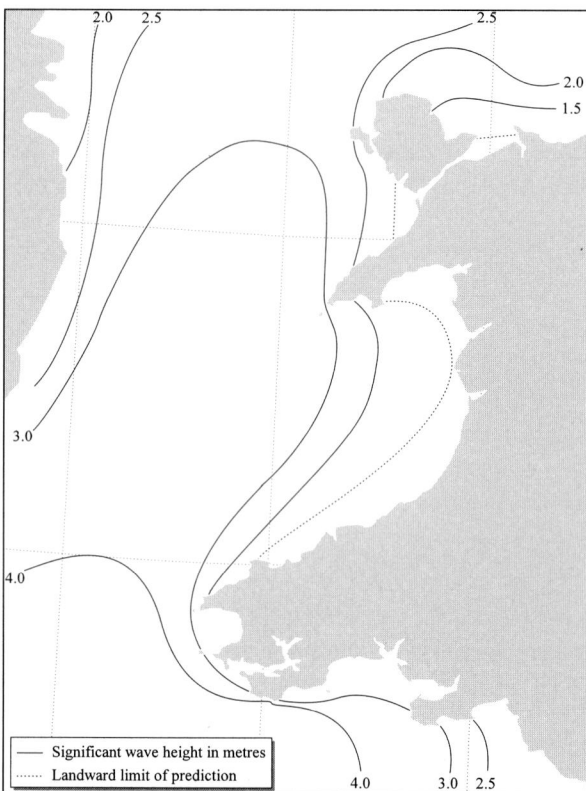

Map 2.3.5 Significant wave height (m) exceeded for 10% of the
winter (January, February and March).
Source: Draper (1992).

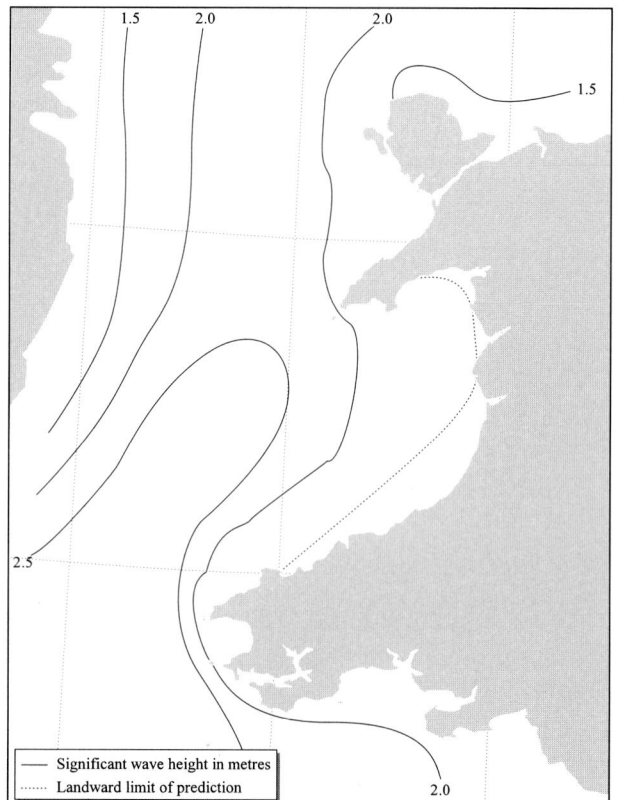

Map 2.3.6 Significant wave height (m) exceeded for 10% of the
Summer (July, August, September).
Source: Draper (1992).

2.3.2 Tidal currents

Tidal currents during mean spring tides (Map 2.3.3) are at their maximum of over 4 knots (2 m/sec) south of Swansea Bay. Values locally exceed 3 knots around the islands off the Pembrokeshire coast but decrease to less than a knot within the northeastern parts of Cardigan Bay. Maximum tidal currents along the northern coasts of the region are about 2 knots. Tidal currents nearshore are more variable, with swift-flowing races where the tides are constrained between narrow inter-island channels, for example off Skomer and in the Menai Strait.

2.3.3 Tidal range

The tidal range along the coasts of the area (Map 2.3.4) is generally high, ranging from a maximum of over 7 m in the eastern parts of Swansea Bay and off the Great Orme, to about 4 m in Cardigan Bay. The tidal range may be further modified by climatic effects, and the estimated 50-year storm surge may increase these values by over 1.5 m.

2.3.4 Wave exposure and sea state

Much of the coast of the region is open to the prevailing south-westerly winds, and locally, where deep water approaches the coast, it is subject to severe wave attack. During winter the significant wave height exceeded for 10% of the time varies from about 4 m off the western Pembrokeshire coast to less than 1.5 m in Conwy Bay east of Anglesey (Map 2.3.5). During the quieter summer months wave height exceeded about 2.5 m for 10% of the time off Pembrokeshire, while the value in Conwy Bay is similar to the winter value (Map 2.3.6). The predicted 50-year maximum wave height in open water is between 18 m and 16 m, being highest off south-west Pembrokeshire.

The wave heights quoted above are gross values, based on data from fully exposed sites, modified for water depth variations. At the coast there may be greater variation due to coastal orientation and nearshore bathymetry, which can have a significant effect on wave erosion and the residual drift of sediment.

A detailed study of wave climate was carried out in the eastern part of Swansea Bay by Heathershaw *et al.* (1980). They report that for 10% of the time at Port Talbot waves exceed a height of 1.6 m in winter and 1 m in summer. Local variations were predicted, depending on the orientation of the waves in relation to the protecting offshore sand banks.

2.3.5 Water characteristics

Most of the region is open to the flow of oceanic water from the Atlantic. Suspended sediment loads are greater where there is an influx of turbid flood water from a river and in parts of Swansea Bay at the seaward limit of the Severn Estuary turbid plume. The tidal flows in the region are strong enough to move sand grains along or near the sea bed and generate a range of bedforms such as sandwaves

and sand banks (Helwich Sand). See section 9.6 for a discussion of waste inputs and pollutants generated by human activities.

Temperature of sea water

The surface temperature of the sea water (Maps 2.3.7 and 2.3.8) varies with the seasons, being coldest in February/March at between 6° to 8.5°C, and warmest in August/September, when it varies between 14° and 16°C. The magnitude of this variation is greater in coastal waters (12°C) than in offshore waters (6°C). In winter, coastal waters are cooler than those offshore, and in summer they are warmer.

Gross flow

Summer warming of surface water encourages stratification of the water column so that warmer water overlies denser, colder water. Across most of the Irish Sea, energetic tidal streams ensure that most of the water column is mixed throughout the year. However to the west of the Isle of Man a two-layer system develops between April and October, the surface water being 20-30 m thick and up to 5° warmer than the bottom layer. A less pronounced stratification may form in Cardigan Bay during summer periods of calm weather. A 'front' some 5 to 10 km wide separates the stratified from the well-mixed regions. Biological activity may be high along this meandering front during spring when blooms of phytoplankton may occur (see section 4.3).

Flow through the Irish Sea averaged over a year (also termed residual flow) is northward from St George's Channel to the North Channel between Scotland and Ireland. The flow is weak, and water takes at least a year to traverse the full length of the Irish Sea. Thus in the long term discharges into the Bristol Channel form an input into the Irish Sea, and those from the north Irish Sea have a limited impact on the coast of this region. This flow is graphically illustrated by the distribution of radioactive materials from Sellafield within the waters of the Irish Sea. Caesium-137 on average shows a value five times higher along the coasts of Lancashire and Cumbria than around Cardigan Bay (see section 9.6).

Salinity of sea water

The salinity of the sea water varies slightly with the seasons, being generally greater in the summer than in the winter. Maps 2.3.9 and 2.3.10 show gross data with salinity values in summer ranging from 33‰ east of Anglesey to 35‰ at the mouth to St George's Channel. Greater variation occurs near the coast, especially near river mouths, where Atlantic water is diluted by river water. The input of fresh water from the rivers is unevenly distributed around the Irish Sea, with Cardigan Bay receiving an average 113 cu.m/sec. Rainfall into the Irish Sea contributes about one third of the riverine input. The freshwater input is small compared with the volume of the Irish Sea and is highly variable through the year and between years.

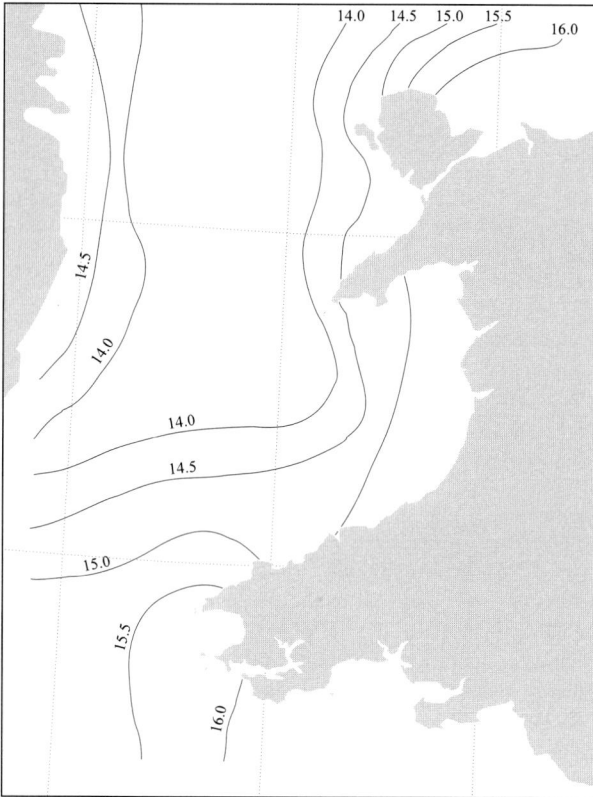

Map 2.3.7 Mean surface water temperature in summer (°C).
Source: Lee & Ramster (1981). © Crown copyright.

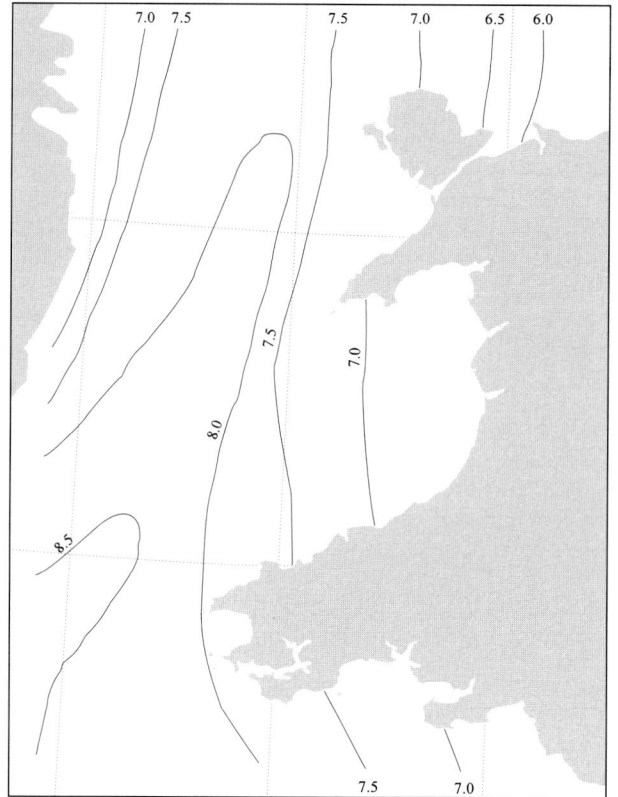

Map 2.3.8 Mean surface water temperature in winter (°C).
Source: Lee & Ramster (1981). © Crown copyright.

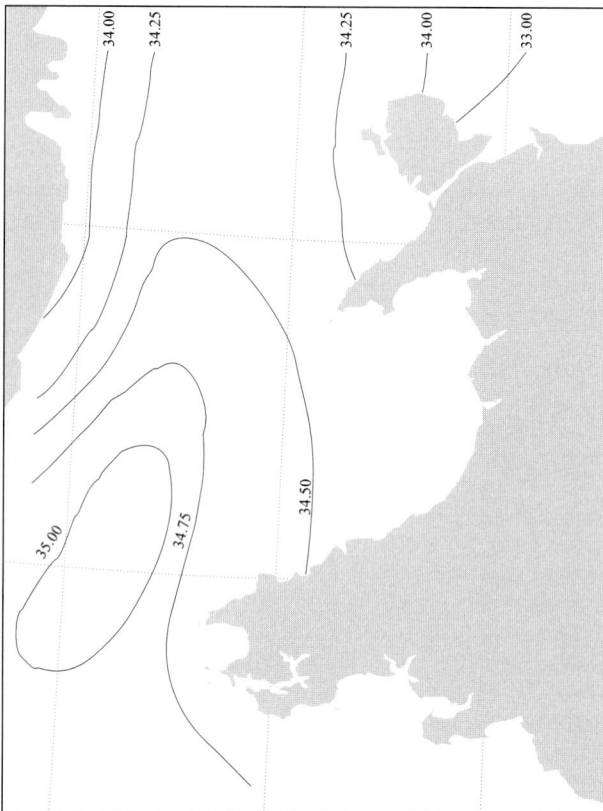

Map 2.3.9 Mean surface salinity of seawater in summer in g/kg of
total dissolved salt. Source: Lee & Ramster (1981).
© Crown copyright.

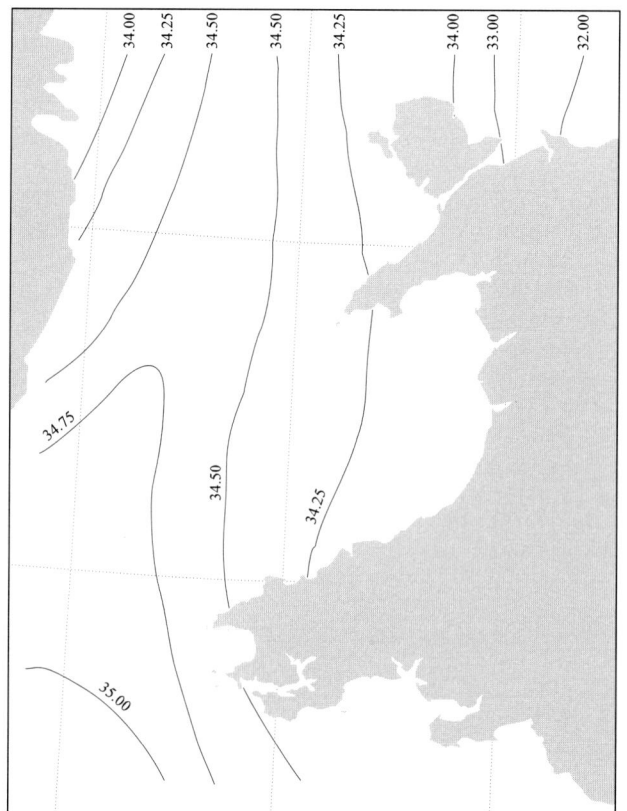

Map 2.3.10 Mean surface salinity of seawater in winter in g/kg of
total dissolved salt. Source: Lee & Ramster (1981).
© Crown copyright.

2.3.6 Further sources of information

A. References cited

Anon. 1960. *West coast of England pilot.* 10th ed. London,
    Hydrographic Office.
Heathershaw, A. D., Carr, A. P., & King, H. L. 1980. *Wave data:
    observed and computed wave climates.* Swansea Bay (Sker) Project:
    Topic Report: 5/Institute of Oceanographic Sciences Report No.
    99.
Orford, J.D., & Bowden, R. 1984. *Prediction of coastal erosion in
    southern Cardigan Bay.* Cardiff, Welsh Office (unpublished).
Caton, P.G. 1976. *Maps of hourly wind speed over the UK 1965 - 73.*
    Bracknell, Meteorological Office. (Climatological
    Memorandum No. 79.)
Draper, L. 1992. *Wave climate atlas of the British Isles.* Department of
    Energy. (Offshore Technology Report.)
Hydrographic Office. 1960. *West coast of England pilot.* Tenth ed.
    London, Hydrographic Office.
Lee, A. J., & Ramster, J. W. 1981. *Atlas of the seas around the British
    Isles.* Lowestoft, Directorate of Fisheries Research (MAFF).
Sager, G., & Sammler, R. 1968. *Atlas der Gezeitenströme für die
    Nordsee, den Kanal und die Irische See.* Rostock,
    Seehydrographischer Dienst der DDR.

B. Further reading

Barne, J., Davidson, N.C., Hill, T.O., & Jones, M. 1994. *Coastal and
    Marine UKDMAP datasets: a user manual.* Peterborough, Joint
    Nature Conservation Committee.
Collins, M. B., Banner, F. T., Tyler, P. A., Wakefield, S. J., & James, A.
    E. 1980. *Industrialised embayments and their environmental
    problems - a case study of Swansea Bay.* Pergamon Press.
Huckbody, A.J., Taylor, P.M., Hobbs, G., & Elliott, R. 1992.
    Caernarfon and Cardigan Bays: an environmental appraisal.
    London, Hamilton Oil Company.

C. Contact names and addresses

Type of information	Contact address and telephone no.
Windroses for rectangular areas defined by latitude and longitude for monthly/seasonal or annual periods, based on 10 or 20 year data from ships of passage.	Meteorological Office Marine Enquiry Service, Johnstone House, London Road, Bracknell RG12 2SY, tel: 01344 854979
UKDMAP 1992. Version 2. United Kingdom digital marine atlas. Oceanographic maps	British Oceanographic Data Centre, Proudman Oceanographic Laboratory, Bidston Observatory, Birkenhead, Merseyside L43 7RA, tel: 0151 652 3950

2.4 Sediment transport

Dr C.D.R. Evans

2.4.1 Description

The coasts of the region are subject to a wide range of wave and tidal energies, these being dependent on the orientation and morphology of each coastal sector. Motyka & Brampton (1993) divided the coast of England and Wales into a number of major littoral cells and sub-cells, each defining a section of coast within which sediment erosion and accretion are inter-related and largely independent of other cells. In this region there are parts of four major littoral cells and nine sub-cells (Map 2.4.1). Each cell is described below. Note that the sediment transport shown on the map is of sand and gravel 'bed load', not suspended sediments.

Margam – St David's Head

This stretch of coast is considered part of a cell which extends eastwards to Lavernock Point in Region 11. It is controlled by the strong tidal currents of the Bristol Channel and open to wave attack due to the predominantly south-westerly winds.

The sub-cell from Lavernock Point to Worms Head (8b) displays low to moderate littoral drift, which is variable in direction in the embayments but predominantly eastwards along the more open lengths of coast. Large-scale navigational dredging has modified the natural processes in the eastern part of Swansea Bay. Beach erosion is limited in this sub-cell to the upper parts of beaches under attack during south-westerly storms; these beaches largely repair themselves once the storm has abated. Helwick Sands, off Worms Head, may be an important part of the sand circulation budget of the immediate coastal area.

Carmarthen Bay, covered by a sub-cell from Worms Head to St Govan's Head (8c), is essentially a depositional embayment infilled with thick deposits of sand. Littoral drift is generally variable and low in volume, with movement into the Loughor, Gwendraeth and Twyi estuaries. Erosion is taking place at the major dune systems at both Pendine and Pembrey. Minor sections of coast show beach erosion (at Amroth) and accretion (at Burry Port).

The sub-cell covering St Govan's Head to St David's Head (8d) has a highly crenulate form and could be divided into even smaller units. Except for within St Bride's Bay and Milford Haven, there is limited sediment in the littoral zone and little interdependence between beaches. Wave action producing transient onshore/offshore movement in beach profiles is locally important. Cliff erosion continues along this stretch of coast but is so slow as to be difficult to quantify regionally.

Cardigan Bay

This cell (9) is divided into two in the north-eastern part of the bay, with Tremadog Bay acting as a sink for offshore fine sand and mud.

Within the sub-cell from St David's Head to the Glaslyn estuary (9a), the moderate littoral drift is to the north, though there is some drift reversal at estuary mouths. The northward prolongating spits on the southern shores of the

Dyfi, Mawddach and Glaslyn estuaries, along with Morfa Dyffryn, were produced by this longshore movement of sediment. The accreting sediment is supplied largely by erosion of the glacial till cliffs in the southern part of the bay. Erosion of beaches (at Aberystwyth, from Barmouth to Llanaber and in parts of Morfa Dyffryn) is also widespread in parts of the sub-cell.

Within the sub-cell from the Glaslyn estuary to Ynys Enlli (9b), littoral drift is to the east and increases in magnitude in that direction. Accretion of sand is taking place at Pwllheli, where shingle is also accreting across the harbour mouth. Widespread erosion occurs along the coast, of both the glacial till cliffs and the sand dune systems.

Llyn Peninsula – Great Orme

The cell from the north coast of the Llyn Peninsula to Great Orme (10) is divided into three sub-cells. The sub-cell covering the north coast of the Llyn (10a) has low, north-eastward littoral drift towards the Menai Strait. Erosion of rocky cliffs occurs at Nefyn and Trefor, and erosion of glacial till and shingle banks occurs at Dinas Dinlle. Accretion within the sub-cell is largely restricted to the northern end of Dinas Dinlle, but parts of this spit are also eroding.

Littoral drift within the sub-cell covering Anglesey (10b) is very low and variable in direction. Most of the beaches or embayments are themselves closed littoral cells, but little is known about the gross coastal processes around the island. Most of the erosion is taking place in the softer glacial till cliffs on the western side of the island. Accretion continues to take place locally along the coast of the sand dune complex at Newborough Warren.

The sub-cell embracing the Menai Strait and Conwy Bay experiences limited littoral drift, and there is little interaction of sediment between the two ends of the Strait. Minor erosion is taking place at the ends of the Strait (west of Caernarfon), on the shores of Conwy Bay (Llanfairfechan) and on the western shore of the Conwy estuary. Accretion is taking place locally on Lavan and Conwy Sands.

Great Orme eastwards

The Great Orme forms the western limit of the Liverpool Bay cell (11). Littoral drift is moderate across the limited part of the cell within this region, and is to the east. Much of this area is backed by limestone cliffs and erosion is limited, but littoral drift increases in importance to the east where the beaches are wider and backed by cliffs formed of softer sediments.

2.4.2 Further sources of information

A. References cited

Motyka, J. M., & Brampton, A. H. 1993. *Coastal management: Mapping of littoral cells.* HR Wallingford Report SR 328.

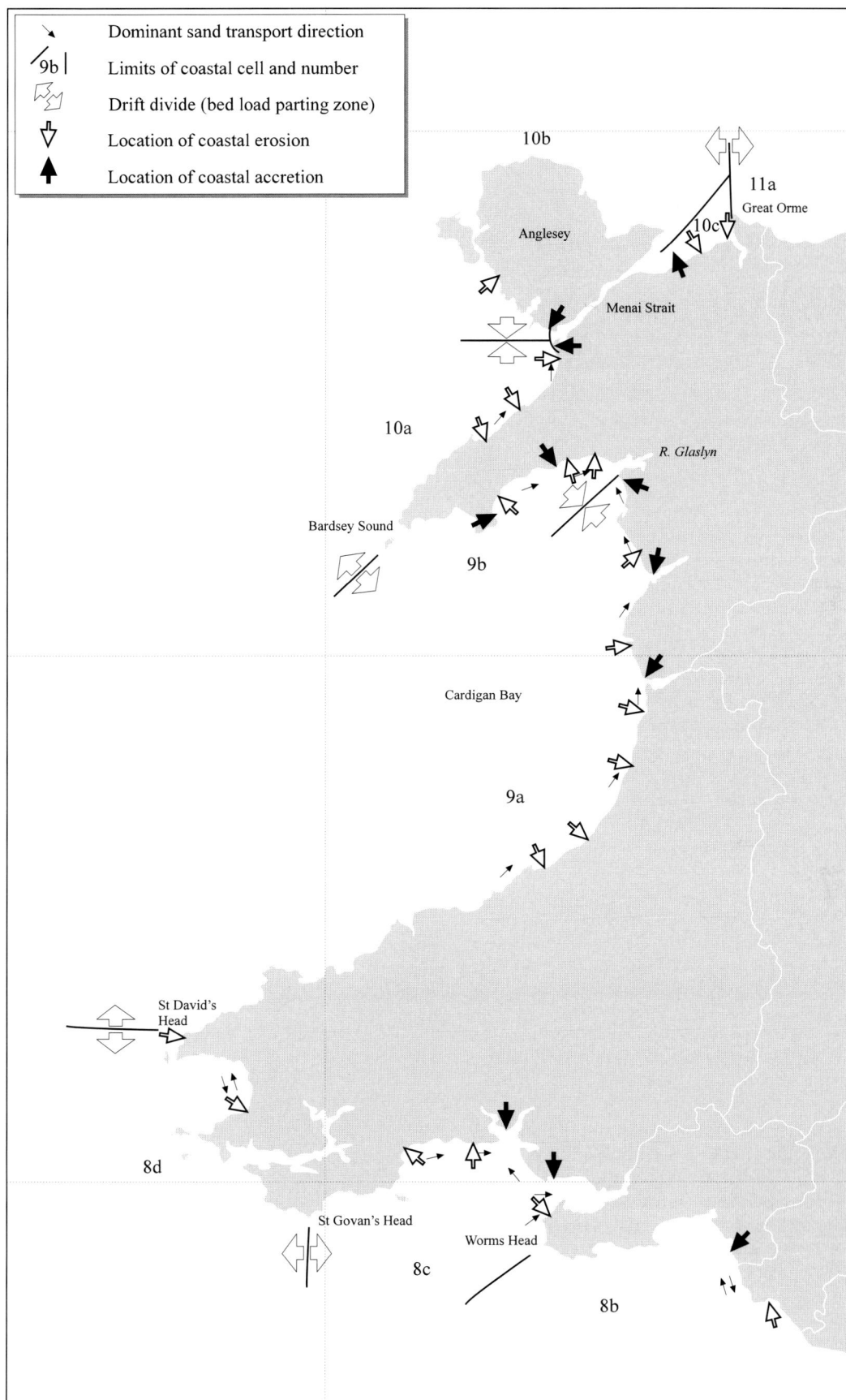

Map 2.4.1 Sediment transport and coastal cells. Source: Motyka & Brampton (1993). Adapted with permission from MAFF Flood and Coastal Defence Division.

B. Further reading

Carter, R. W. G. 1988. *Coastal environments.* London, Academic
    Press.
Rendel Geotechnics. 1995. *Coastal planning and management: a
    review of earth science information needs.* London, HMSO.

C. Contact names and addresses

Type of information	Contact address and telephone no.
Sediment cells	Ministry of Agriculture, Fisheries and Food (MAFF), Flood and Coastal Defence Division, Eastbury House, 30/34 Albert Embankment, London SE1 7TL tel: 0171 238 3000
Sediment cells	Institute of Hydrology, Crowmarsh Gifford, Wallingford, Oxfordshire OX10 8BB, tel. 01491 838800

2.5 Sea-level rise and flooding

Dr C.D.R. Evans

2.5.1 Description

Sea-level changes across the region are due to the combined effects of changes in global sea level and local changes in land level. The best estimates of recent sea-level change across the region are based on information from the tide gauges at Milford Haven, Holyhead and Dublin, with corroborative data from sites further afield. Sea level across the region is rising at at rate close to the global average, at about 1.5 to 2.0 mm/year, although a fall in sea level at Milford Haven measured on the tidal gauge is not yet understood. The data show no recent increase in this rate due to global warming, the effect of which can only be estimated from the predicted response of theoretical models of the oceans.

Evidence for land-level changes come from dating Holocene freshwater or marine sediments, such as the submerged forest beds located around the coast of the region. The evidence from the Dyfi estuary suggests that the area is sinking by about 0.1 mm/year, or 10 cm/1,000 years. In a British context a line from the Llyn to the Tees estuary separates areas to the south, which are subsiding, from areas to the north, which are rising. The change in land level is due to the isostatic rebound of the earth's crust following the melting of the continental late Devensian ice sheet (see also section 2.1.4).

The commonly cliffed nature of the coasts has restricted flooding in the region to the major estuaries and the major spit and sand dune complexes (Motyka & Brampton 1993) (Map 2.5.1). The low-lying land at the mouth of the Rivers Neath, Loughor, Taf and Towy is subject to flooding, along with some land south of Porthcawl and behind the storm beach at Newgale. The Dyfi and Mawddach estuaries in Cardigan Bay are areas of flood risk largely related to high river levels, especially when they coincide with high tide levels. Locally parts of Morfa Dyffryn and Morfa Harlech are inundated by the sea, as is low-lying land between Llanbedrog and Criccieth. Along the north coast of the region, parts of Dinas Dinlle and Malltraeth Marsh (although there is a cob to prevent inundation here) are also flood-risk areas. Local flooding occurs along the low-lying ground west of Caernarfon and east of Bangor. The low-lying Conwy Valley is especially liable to flooding when high river levels coincide with spring tides.

Storm surges raise sea level for a few hours and considerably increase the risk of flooding if they coincide with high water. The predicted 50-year storm surge for the Welsh coast varies in height from less than 1.25 m in the west to over 1.5 m in the east. Modelling techniques allow the location and duration of surges to be predicted some hours in advance.

2.5.2 Further sources of information

A. References cited

Motyka, J. M., & Brampton, A. H 1993. *Coastal management: mapping of littoral cells.* HR Wallingford. (Report SR 328.)

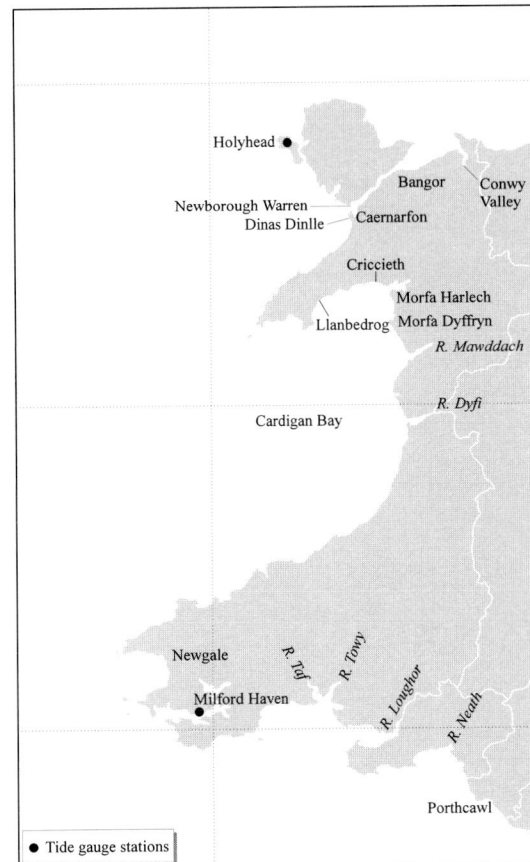

Map 2.5.1 Locations susceptible to flooding. Source: Motyka & Brampton (1993). Adapted with permission from MAFF Flood and Coastal Defence Division.

B. Further reading

Anon. 1992. *The Irish Sea Forum: global warming and climatic change - seminar report.* University of Liverpool Press.
Shennan, I. 1989. Holocene crustal movements and sea-level changes in Great Britain. *Journal of Quaternary Science,* 4: 77-89.
Shennan, I., & Woodworth, P. L. 1992. A comparison of late Holocene and twentieth-century sea-level trends from the UK and North Sea region. *Geophysical Journal International,* 109: 96-105.

C. Contact names and addresses

Type of information	Contact address and telephone no.
Flood defence (see also section 8.4)	*National Rivers Authority, Welsh Region, Cardiff, tel. 01222 770088
Flood defence	Ministry of Agriculture, Fisheries and Food (MAFF), Flood and Coastal Defence Division, Eastbury House, 30/34 Albert Embankment, London SE1 7TL, tel: 0171 238 3000
Tide gauge data	British Oceanographic Data Centre, Proudman Oceanographic Laboratory, Bidston Observatory, Birkenhead, Merseyside L43 7RA, tel. 0151 652 3950

* Starred contact addresses are given in full in the Appendix

2.6 Coastal landforms

Dr C.D.R. Evans

2.6.1 Introduction

This section describes the landforms of the coast, focusing on the areas subject to short and longer-term accretion and erosion (see also section 2.4). Along most of the region's coasts, which are predominantly rocky and cliffed, such changes are minimal on a historic timescale. However, along some sections of the coast, especially in northern Carmarthen Bay and northern Cardigan Bay, such changes are rapid and of economic significance. The coastal landforms of the region are typical of western Britain, and coastal change is generally not as rapid, nor as likely to endanger human life and property, as along the southern and eastern coasts of Britain. The major coastal landforms in the region are shown in Map 2.6.1.

2.6.2 Description

Swansea Bay – St Bride's Bay

Most of the land fringing Swansea Bay is built over, with only a few surviving remnants of the sand dunes that used to extend around its margins. The rivers Tawe and Neath drain into the bay, which is surrounded, at low tide, by a wide expanse of muddy sand.

The southern part of the Gower peninsula is a plateau surface at a height of about 70-90 m. Numerous raised beach levels are preserved in the cliffs where the plateau surface reaches the coast. Rare remains of Pleistocene flora and fauna have been found in beach sediments and caves associated with these levels. In contrast the eastward-facing sandy beaches within the bays at Oxwich and Port Eynon are backed by sand dunes and woods. Rhossili beach on the west coast of Gower faces the dominant wave direction and is a broad sandy beach backed by sand dunes. These dunes continue to the north at Whiteford Burrows, where they are built on a north-eastward-trending gravel spit. The wide Llanrhidian salt marshes along the northern coast of Gower pass northward into the channelled sand bank system of the Loughor estuary.

Carmarthen Bay from Burry Port to Amroth is surrounded by broad, gently-sloping, sandy beaches backed by extensive sand dune systems. Along this coast low cliffs of bedrock are exposed only around the Llanstephan peninsula.

Much of the Pembrokeshire coast from Amroth to south of Strumble Head is formed of steep cliffs falling from a plateau surface between 30 m and 130 m high. The variety of the rocks forming the cliffs has led to the formation of sea stacks, caves and natural bridges. The ria at Milford Haven, into which the Daugleddau drains, is one of the world's great natural harbours. It is fringed in its lower reaches by sandy coves, though industry has occupied lengths of the northern and southern shorelines.

Buried forests and peat beds are found at about low water mark in Swansea Bay, Amroth, Freshwater West and St Bride's Bay. Similar deposits are found in the Dyfi estuary and on the south Llyn coast.

Much of St Bride's Bay has a broad sandy beach, which is backed, in the northern part at Newgale, by a shingle storm beach. The attraction of the coastline is further enhanced by the rugged islands of Palaeozoic rocks off the Dale and St David's peninsulas. Many of the beaches, such as Marloes Sand, are of outstanding beauty and geological interest.

Cardigan Bay

From St Bride's Bay to Fishguard are a series of small pocket beaches alternating with steep and varied cliffs. Whitesand Bay forms the largest sandy beach along this section of coast, and many of the more exposed beaches such as Abermawr are backed by shingle storm ridges.

From Fishguard northward to the Dyfi estuary the coastline is generally cliffed, but in some places there are small estuaries such as the Teifi and Ystwyth and pocket beaches commonly related to glacial channels, such as at Mwnt. The cliffs are at their grandest at Dinas Head and Cemaes Head, where they reach nearly 200 m in height. Elsewhere they range from 100 m to 30 m in height. At Aberaeron the foreshore is formed of glacial till banked against an older cliff line to landward.

The northern shores of Cardigan Bay are dominated by depositional features, and the old cliff line lies some distance from the modern coast. The glacially over-deepened valleys of the Dyfi, Mawddach and Glaslyn rivers are now occupied by estuaries largely choked with sediment. These estuaries are surrounded by wide expanses of saltmarsh passing out into constantly changing channels with sand banks. Spits growing northwards, now covered by sand dunes, extend from the southern shores of the estuaries. The spits have led to the enclosure of mature marsh areas such as Borth Bog and Fairbourne Marshes.

Two major spit complexes have built out into Cardigan Bay between the Mawddach and Glaslyn estuaries. They indicate active sediment transport towards the north and east along this part of the coast. The southernmost spit, Morfa Dyffryn, has a linear shingle ridge at the coast passing landward into sand dunes and sandy pastures. The spit complex is over 3 km wide at its northern end near Mochras, a low island of glacial till marking the site of a moraine. The northernmost spit, Morfa Harlech, shows active accretion and northward extension of the seaward shingle ridge. Morfa Harlech passes northwards into the broad sandy expanse of Traeth Bach, which forms the southern part of the Glaslyn estuary. The estuary contains the dune complex of Morfa Bychan on its north-western margin and extensive enclosure of originally intertidal land in its upper part.

Extending seaward in a WSW direction from promontories in Cardigan Bay are five 'sarnau', causeways of boulders that are only exposed at low tide. The largest of these, Sarn Badrig, extends as a submarine feature for some 34 km, with up to 14 km exposed at lowest tides. Legends of buried villages (Cartref Gwaelod) have been attributed to the sarns, but it is likely that they were formed as morainic

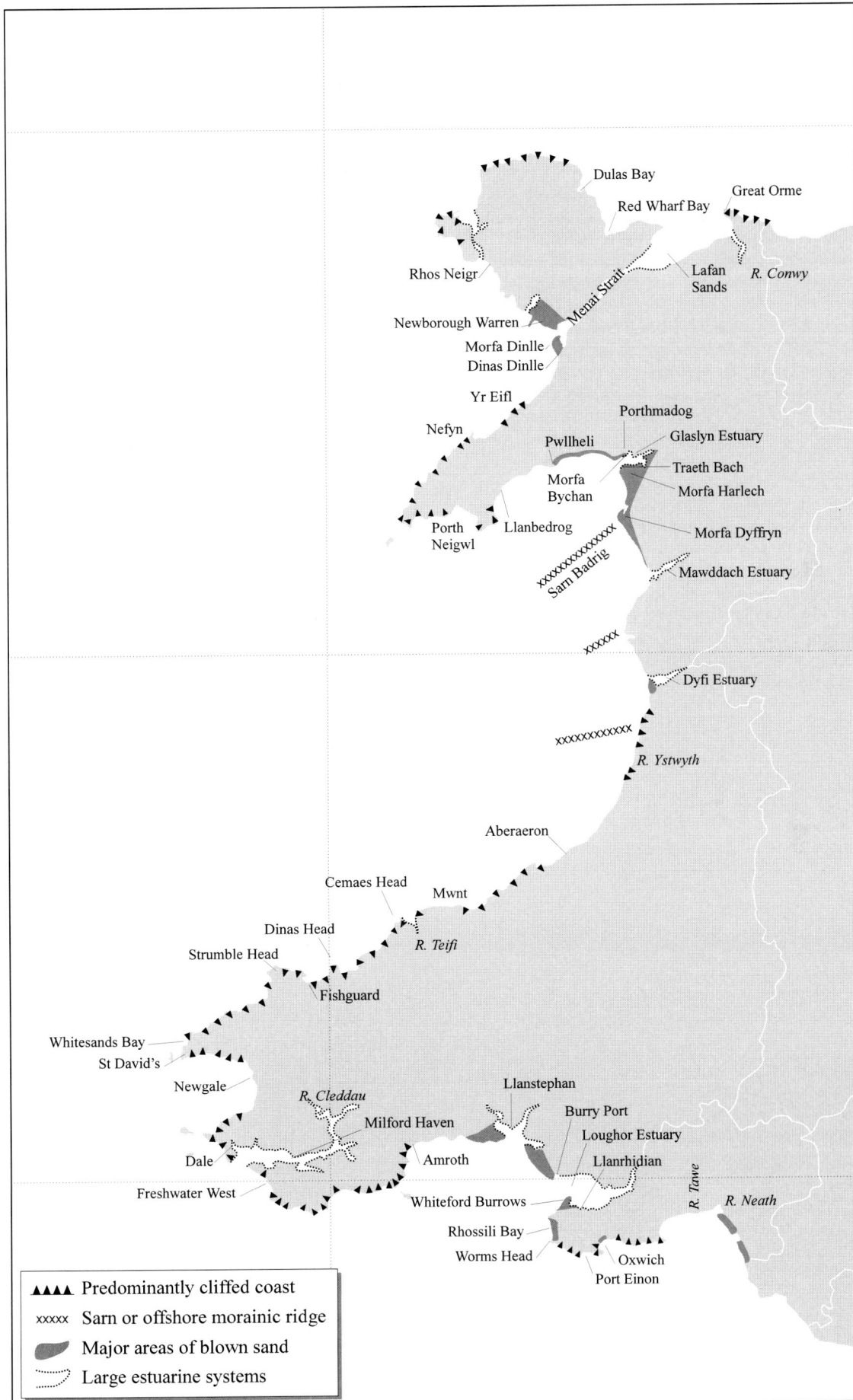

Dulas Bay

Red Wharf Bay

Great Orme

Rhos Neigr

Menai Strait

Lafan Sands

R. Conwy

Newborough Warren

Morfa Dinlle

Dinas Dinlle

Yr Eifl

Porthmadog

Glaslyn Estuary

Pwllheli

Nefyn

Morfa Bychan

Traeth Bach

Morfa Harlech

Porth Neigwl

Llanbedrog

Morfa Dyffryn

xxxxxxxxxxxxxx
Sarn Badrig

Mawddach Estuary

xxxxxx

Dyfi Estuary

xxxxxxxxxxxx

R. Ystwyth

Aberaeron

Cemaes Head

Mwnt

Dinas Head

R. Teifi

Strumble Head

Fishguard

Whitesands Bay

St David's

Newgale

R. Cleddau

Llanstephan

Burry Port

Milford Haven

Loughor Estuary

Dale

Llanrhidian

Amroth

R. Tawe

Freshwater West

Whiteford Burrows

R. Neath

Rhossili Bay

Worms Head

Oxwich

Port Einon

▲▲▲▲ Predominantly cliffed coast

xxxxx Sarn or offshore morainic ridge

Major areas of blown sand

Large estuarine systems

Map 2.6.1 Major coastal landforms. Source: British Geological Survey.

features during a period of ice retreat (see section 2.1).

Llyn Peninsula – Great Orme

The Llyn Peninsula has a complex glacial history, reflected in the variety of glacial landforms and deposits exposed at the coast. A smooth, sweeping series of sandy beaches backed by sand dunes extends from St Tudwal's peninsula eastwards to Porthmadog. The sweep is interrupted only by the limited outcrops of bedrock or till, as at Llanbedrog mountain. The coast to the west is more varied and includes the exposed, narrow shingle beach at Porth Neigwl, which is backed to the east by thick glacial till. High, rugged cliffs with minor pocket beaches dominate the south-western end of the peninsula. The cliffs of Precambrian rocks north-westwards to Nefyn are lower, though steep and irregular in form.

Extensive sections of glacial till are exposed along the coast from Nefyn to Dinas Dinlle. At Porth Dinllaen the till sections are over 30 m high, and display a range of sedimentary and glacial tectonic structures. Steeper cliffs are found at Yr Eifl, where the coast is formed of rugged acid intrusive rocks. Morfa Dinlle and Dinas Dinlle form a spit complex at the southwestern entrance to the Menai Strait. Opposite the former, on the northern shore of the strait, are the extensive sand dunes of Newborough Warren. Around Rhosneigr are low cliffs separated by a maze of sandy coves. Spectacular cliffs carved into a variety of rock types occur along the northern part of Holyhead island and the northern coast of Anglesey. A shingle bar beach at Cemlyn Bay impounds a shallow lagoon. Wide sandy beaches are formed in Lligwy Bay and Red Wharf Bay.

The Menai Strait is generally only a few hundred metres wide, with some gentle flanking, often wooded slopes, and some steeper, more rocky sections. The strait has been locally deepened by glacial action. Lavan Sands, at the eastern entrance, is a broad, sandy, intertidal belt linked to the mainland. To the east a narrow sandy coastal section extends to the Conwy estuary, where areas of sand dunes have formed along both sides of the river mouth.

Massive vertical cliffs almost encircle the Great Orme but along its southern side it passes into a low-lying area of recent marine sediment that joins it to the mainland. Between Great Orme and Little Orme shingle deposits are now mainly obscured by buildings and promenades.

2.6.3 Further sources of information

A. Further reading

Bowen, E. G., *ed.* 1957. *Wales: a physical, historical and regional geography*. London, Methuen.

Campbell, S., & Bowen, D.Q. 1989. *Geological Conservation Review: Quaternary of Wales*. London, Chapman and Hall.

Matley, C. A. 1938. The geology of the country around Pwllheli, Llanbedrog and Madryn. *Quarterly Journal of the Geological Society*, 94: 555-606.

Steers, J. A. 1969. *The coastline of England and Wales*. Cambridge University Press.

Chapter 3 Terrestrial coastal habitats

3.1 Cliffs and cliff-top vegetation

Dr T.C.D. Dargie

3.1.1 Introduction

The coast of West Glamorgan, Dyfed and Gwynedd contains much cliff and cliff-top habitat. Sea cliffs are generally steep slopes (>15 degrees), but in this region they show great diversity of form, from very tall vertical or near-vertical cliff faces, through long steep slopes with a vertical face restricted to the base, to low cliffs with a great variety of local slope forms. Geology and geological structure, with past environmental history (marine erosion (past and present) and glacial processes), determine cliff form (see also sections 2.1 and 2.4). The most distinctive cliff types are consolidated (hard cliffs developed from resistant bedrock) and unconsolidated (soft cliffs developed in easily-eroded, predominantly Quaternary deposits).

Cliff and cliff-top vegetation varies with slope angle, soil type, salt spray deposition and, locally around headlands, degree of exposure. The major natural and semi-natural cliff and cliff-top habitats in the region are: bare ground, spray-zone lichen-covered rock, rock crevice, cliff-ledge, sea-bird colony, maritime grassland and maritime heath. Seabird colonies may contribute a high level of nutrient enrichment, for example on Grassholm and Ynys Seiriol (Anglesey). Very sheltered cliffs and cliff-top sectors that receive little salt spray input are not here treated as coastal habitats. Of the twelve National Vegetation Classification (NVC) maritime cliff vegetation communities in the UK (Rodwell in prep.), ten are recorded for the region, the remaining two being confined to Scotland.

The large extent of cliffs and the great diversity of cliff and cliff-top habitats, which vary markedly even over short distances, make the region of great interest. This is reflected in the presence of 55 Sites of Special Scientific Interest (SSSIs) and seven National Nature Reserves (NNRs) containing cliffs. Most of the Pembrokeshire Coast National Park coastline is composed of sea cliffs and there are small lengths in the Snowdonia National Park. Outstanding cliffs are present in the Gower Area of Outstanding Natural Beauty and the Llyn Peninsula Environmentally Sensitive Area. The importance of the cliff features is also recognised in the fourteen Heritage Coasts, covering in total 472 km of regional coastline (40% of the region's total length), in which cliffs are the dominant landform (Heritage Coast Forum 1993). There is much overlap between Heritage Coast and land identified as SSSI, Environmentally Sensitive Area or National Park.

The region has a total cliff length of 492 km (Table 3.1.1 and Map 3.1.1) but the full extent of cliff-top habitat has not been surveyed. Most cliffs (over 60%) are high vertical cliffs, and most are in Dyfed. The total cliff length represents 12% of the British resource, the second largest length of any Coastal Directories region, and is therefore of great importance in the national context.

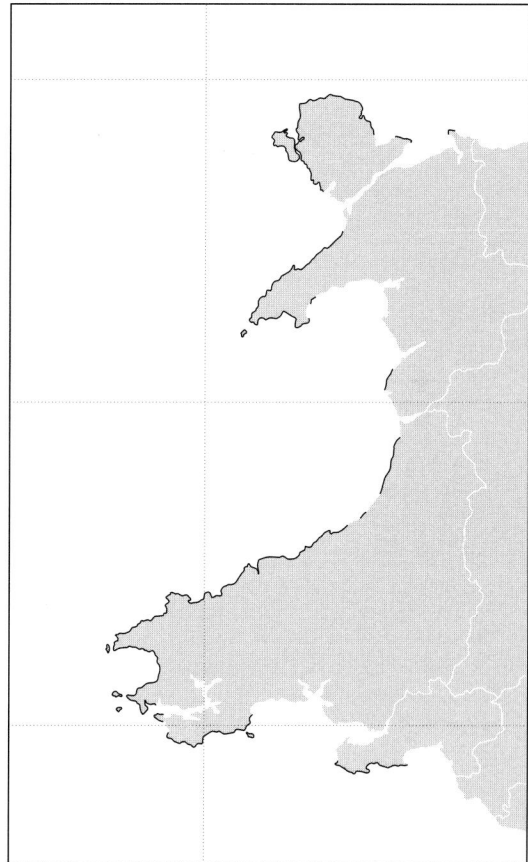

Map 3.1.1 Cliffs and cliff-top habitat. Marked sectors have >90% cliffed coast. Source: JNCC Coastal Database.

Table 3.1.1 Table of lengths (km) of cliff types

Cliff type	West Glam.	Dyfed	Gwynedd	Region 12	Wales	West Coast	Great Britain
Vertical >20 m height	4.5	241.5	59	305	328.5	724.5	1,325
Vertical <20 m height	0	14.5	24.5	39	45.5	438.5	818
Non-vertical >20m height	19.5	41	49	109.5	109.5	812.5	1,371
Non-vertical <20m height	0	5	33.5	38.5	38.5	284	545
Total	*24*	*302*	*166*	*492*	*522*	*2,259.5*	*4,059*
% in Region 12	*-*	*-*	*-*	*-*	*94*	*22*	*12*

Source: JNCC Coastal Resources Database.

3.1.2 Important locations and species

Cliffs in the region are extensive and exhibit great diversity in form. High, near-vertical cliffs >80 m in height are present around the Gower peninsula, at Dinas Head, Cemaes Head and the Great Orme, and on Ramsey, Bardsey and Holy Island. However, such sectors represent only a small proportion of the region's cliffs and most of the others are not as high as these. Long sectors of the south Pembrokeshire, Cardigan Bay, Llyn Peninsula and Anglesey coast, for example, have lower, near-vertical, 30 - 50 m cliffs. Cliffs <20 m height are uncommon in the region and make up only 16% of total cliffed coast. In a few places wind-blown sand has accumulated at the base of cliffs, forming climbing dunes (as at Gilter Point, for example).

The Gower peninsula coast and Stackpole (Pembroke Coast) contain some of the finest examples of limestone cliffs in Britain. Other large, high quality mainland cliff sectors include Castlemartin Cliffs, Druidston and Nolton Haven Cliffs, Saint David's Peninsula Coast, and Strumble Head - Llechdafad Cliffs (all on the Pembroke Coast), Glannau Ynys Gybi (Holy Island Coast) and the Great Orme. Many of the major islands of the region, particularly Skomer, Ramsey and Bardsey, have extensive cliffs. Tables 5.2.2 and 5.2.3, in section 5.2, list rare higher plants found on cliffs.

The lichens of maritime heath on climbing dunes over limestone cliffs at Stackpole are rated as the best of their type in Europe, and the maritime heaths on more acidic soils at Bardsey, Skomer, Aberdaron coast (Braich y Pwll, Pen y Cil), the Great Orme and Strumble Head are rated of national importance (James *et al*. 1979; Fletcher *et al*. 1984). Glannau Ynys Gybi, Anglesey, is also of national importance for its maritime heath.

The regional cliff fauna is notable, especially on islands (see also sections 5.4, 5.10 and 7.2). Important seabird colonies with Special Protection Area status (Stroud *et al*.1990) are present at Holy Island Coast (Gwynedd), Glannau Aberdaron/Ynys Enlli coast (Gwynedd), Grassholm (Dyfed), and Skokholm and Skomer (Dyfed); the Pembrokeshire Cliffs (Dyfed) are also of great importance for their seabird colonies. Chough *Pyrrhocorax pyrrhocorrax* breed on South Stack (Anglesey), Bardsey and Ramsey. The adder *Vipera berus* is moderately common in maritime heaths.

No systematic invertebrate survey of cliff and cliff-top habitats has been carried out, but because of their diversity these habitats support large numbers of species (Mitchley & Malloch 1991). Several sites in the region have long invertebrate lists, with many notable and rare (Red Data Book) species. Outstanding Invertebrate Site Register locations containing notable cliff habitat include Oxwich Bay (West Glamorgan), Stackpole to Castlemartin Cliffs, Gwbert Cliffs, Skokholm and Ynys Eidiol - Ynys Hir, Saint David's Peninsula Coast, Skomer Island (all Dyfed), and the Great Orme (Gwynedd) (see also section 5.3.2).

3.1.3 Human activities

Cliffs are among the least modified of terrestrial habitats, although the cliff-top zone, especially its inner sectors, has been affected by a variety of human impacts, sometimes leading to major habitat loss. Footpaths (notably the Pembrokeshire Coast long distance path) are heavily used in some parts of the region and local erosion is common, particularly on climbing dune sectors of the South Gower Coast, where visitor numbers are heavy (Dargie 1989). Rock

climbing on Great Orme has contributed to a serious rockfall, and a code of conduct based on marked routes has been introduced to minimise risk and erosion upon the site. Erosion is also present around climbing routes at Stackpole Head. Large sectors of cliff between Linney Head and Trevallen (near Stackpole, Dyfed) are used for military training, with tank erosion present in places. Quarries (many abandoned) are common, especially on the Llyn Peninsula, at Holyhead, and at Penmon (Anglesey). In general, visitor erosion, military activity and quarrying cause only local habitat loss and vegetation disturbance.

The most extensive influences upon cliff vegetation are grazing and burning, the major management techniques for cliff-top habitat (Mitchley & Malloch 1991). Rabbits, formerly managed in warrens, have a major influence on vegetation type: in areas affected by myxomatosis, grassland can grow rank quickly if ungrazed; where populations are allowed to grow out of control, rabbits can cause erosion and loss of species diversity. Grazing generally, particularly by sheep, cattle and horses (and feral goats on the Llyn Peninsula), is important for maintaining species richness and has been re-introduced by the National Trust for this reason into parts of the South Gower Coast. Burning encourages regrowth on grassland and heath and discourages gorse scrub, but accidental fires are a serious cause of local erosion. Scrub and weed control (particularly on Skomer Island) is often necessary at the rear of cliff-top sectors. Some stretches of cliff-top have been converted to arable land; grassland improvement using lime and fertiliser additions, together with re-seeding, has caused more serious modification of the habitat (Etherington & Clarke 1987). Former arable land at Stackpole is now reverting to grassland through grazing management by the National Trust.

3.1.4 Information sources used

NVC (National Vegetation Classification) surveys have been carried out at Stackpole, Strumble Head and Holyhead (Cooper 1988a,b,c), covering a total coastal length of 22 km (4.5% of the region's cliffs). The work was part of pilot study to assess the feasibility of mapping all cliff habitat in Britain. These surveys, all carried out in the summer of 1987, are detailed and use a consistent methodology. The data provide a sound baseline for future cliff vegetation studies and local management of the cliff resource. The National Trust have carried out NVC surveys on their properties, particularly on the Llyn Peninsula, and surveys of Skomer, Skokholm and Bardsey have been done by CCW and the Dyfed Wildlife Trust. The coastal heaths of Llyn and Anglesey have been surveyed by CCW. There is no survey information at all for the soft cliffs of the region, although the soft cliffs of Porth Neigwl have been studied for their invertebrates (Fowles 1994). Cliff lengths are derived from the JNCC's Coastal Resources Database, which records lengths and areas of coastal habitats in 10 km squares, measured at 1:50,000 scale.

3.1.5 Further sources of information

A. References cited

Cooper, E.A. 1988a. *Survey of sea-cliff vegetation of Great Britain. 1. Holyhead, Anglesey.* Peterborough, Nature Conservancy Council.

Cooper, E.A. 1988b. *Survey of sea-cliff vegetation of Great Britain. 5. Stackpole, Pembrokeshire.* Peterborough, Nature Conservancy Council.

Cooper, E.A. 1988c. *Survey of sea-cliff vegetation of Great Britain. 6. Strumble Head, Pembrokeshire.* Peterborough, Nature Conservancy Council.

Dargie, T.C.D. 1989. South Wales 1989 dune survey: regional report. *Nature Conservancy Council, CSD Report*, No. 1127.

Etherington, J.R., & Clarke, E. 1987. Impact of agriculture on the cliff vegetation of South Gower, West Glamorgan. *Nature Conservancy Council, CSD Report*, No. 731.

Fletcher, A., Coppins, B.J., Gilbert, O.L., James, P.W., & Lambley, P.W. 1984. Survey and assessment of lowland heathland lichen habitats. (Contractor: British Lichen Society.) *Nature Conservancy Council, CSD Report*, No. 522.

Fowles, A. 1994. *The invertebrates of Wales.* JNCC. Peterborough.

Heritage Coast Forum. 1993. *Heritage coasts in England and Wales: a gazetteer.* Manchester, Manchester Metropolitan University.

James, P., Crump, R., Leach, S., Holden, P., & Dyke, L. 1979. Stackpole Warren - Report 2. Lichen survey - preliminary report. *Nature Conservancy Council, CSD Report*, No. 361b.

Mitchley, J., & Malloch, A.J.C. 1991. *Sea cliff management handbook for Great Britain.* Lancaster, University of Lancaster.

Rodwell, J.S., *ed.* In prep. *British plant communities. Volume 5: maritime and weed communities.* Cambridge, Cambridge University Press.

Stroud, D.A., Mudge, G.P., & Pienkowski, M.W. 1990. *Protecting internationally important bird sites.* Peterborough, Nature Conservancy Council.

B. Further reading

Further details of coastal habitat sites, including cliffs, is available on the *Coastal & Marine UKDMAP datasets module* disseminated by JNCC Coastal Conservation Branch, Peterborough.

Barne, J., Davidson, N.C., Hill, T.O., & Jones, M. 1994. *Coastal and Marine UKDMAP datasets: a user manual.* Peterborough, Joint Nature Conservation Committee.

Davidson, N.C., Laffoley, D.d'A., Doody, J.P., Way, L.S., Gordon, J., Key, R., Drake, C.M., Pienkowski, M.W., Mitchell, R.M., & Duff, K.L. 1991. *Nature conservation and estuaries in Great Britain.* Peterborough, Nature Conservancy Council.

Gillham, M.E. 1955. Ecology of the Pembrokeshire Islands. III. The effects of grazing on the vegetation. *Journal of Ecology, 43*: 172-206.

Glading, P. 1984. *Ecological studies upon Carboniferous limestone vegetation in South Wales.* PhD Thesis, University of Wales.

Goldsmith, F.B. 1973. The vegetation of exposed sea-cliffs at South Stack, Anglesey. II. Experimental studies. *Journal of Ecology, 61*: 819-29.

Liddle, M.J. 1975. A selective review of the ecological effects of human trampling on natural ecosystems. *Biological Conservation, 7*: 17-36.

Mitchley, J. 1989. *A sea cliff bibliography.* Peterborough, Nature Conservancy Council. (Research and survey in nature conservation, No. 18).

Nature Conservancy Council. 1981. *Vegetation survey and monitoring on the hard coast areas of the South Gower Coast NNR site, West Glamorgan.* Unpublished report (Rep NC 203H). Bangor, Wales Field Unit.

Rodwell, J.S., *ed.* 1991a. *British plant communities. Volume 1: woodlands and scrub.* Cambridge, Cambridge University Press.

Rodwell, J.S., *ed.* 1991b. *British plant communities. Volume 2: mires and heaths.* Cambridge, Cambridge University Press.

Rodwell, J.S., *ed.* 1992. *British plant communities. Volume 3: grasslands and montane vegetation.* Cambridge, Cambridge University Press.

Rodwell, J.S., *ed.* In prep. *British plant communities. Volume 4: aquatic communities, swamps and tall herb fens.* Cambridge, Cambridge University Press.

Steers, J.A. 1964. *The coastline of England and Wales.* Cambridge, Cambridge University Press.

C. Contact names and addresses

Type of information	Contact address and telephone no.
Flora, fauna, habitat information, site reports, site management	*Coastal Ecologist, CCW HQ, Bangor, tel. 01248 370444
Issues, coastal zone management initiatives	*Projects Officer, Cardigan Bay Forum, Aberystwyth, tel. 01970 624471 ext 147
Recreation and access	*Arfordir Officer, CCW Aberystwyth, tel. 01970 828551
Cliff conservation	*Head of Coastal Conservation Branch, JNCC, Peterborough, tel. 01733 62626
Invertebrate fauna	*Invertebrate Site Register, Species Conservation Branch, JNCC, Peterborough, tel. 01733 62626

* Starred contact addresses are given in full in the Appendix

3.1.6 Acknowledgements

Assistance with sources was kindly provided by Cardigan Bay Forum and JNCC Species Conservation Branch.

3.2 Sand dunes

Dr T.C.D. Dargie

3.2.1 Introduction

The coast of West Glamorgan, Dyfed and Gwynedd contains a large number of sand dune systems associated with bays, estuaries and hard cliffs. The region has 45 dune sites (see Table 3.2.1 and Map 3.2.1) containing 7,172 ha of vegetated sand and other land cover. Together they represent 14% of the British sand dune resource (see Table 3.2.2), for which the region is therefore nationally important.

The large extent and diverse range of habitats (some very rare) make the sand dunes of the region of great interest. This is reflected in twenty Site of Special Scientific Interest designations, eight National Nature Reserves, and one Local Nature Reserve. Several sites fall within the Gower, Llyn and Anglesey Coasts Areas of Outstanding Natural Beauty; others are within the Pembrokeshire Coast and Snowdonia National Parks. Three sites are within the Llyn Peninsula Environmentally Sensitive Area.

Table 3.2.1 Sand dune sites in region

Code	Name	Grid ref	Area (ha)	Dune type	Conservation status
1	Margam Burrows	SS779839	101	Hindshore	SSSI
2	Baglan Bay	SS729917	78	Ness/foreland	
3	Crymlyn Burrows	SS714929	118	Ness/foreland, climbing	SSSI
4	Black Pill to Bryn Mill	SS637912	16	Bay	AONB
5	Pennard Burrows	SS543883	87	Bay, climbing	AONB
6	Penmaen Burrows	SS532880	17	Climbing	AONB
7	Nicholaston Burrows	SS520878	17	Spit, bay, climbing	SSSI, NNR, AONB
8	Oxwich Burrows	SS508871	76	Hindshore, spit	SSSI, NNR, AONB
9	Port-Eynon to Horton	SS473853	19	Bay	AONB
10	Hillend to Hills Tor	SS421920	224	Bay, climbing	AONB
11	Whiteford Burrows	SS438953	143	Spit	SSSI, NNR, AONB
12	Pembrey Coast	SN397033	1,559	Hindshore, spit	SSSI
13	Laugharne Burrows	SN286078	431	Spit	SSSI
14	Pendine Burrows	SN251076	173	Spit	SSSI
15	Tenby Burrows	SS127993	92	Bay, climbing	SSSI
16	Caldey Island	SS136967	3	Bay	NP
17	Lydstep Haven	SS092983	23	Bay, climbing	NP
18	Manorbier/Swanlake	SS053978	10	Bay	NP
19	Freshwater Bay East	SS018979	17	Bay, climbing	NP
20	Stackpole Warren	SR974945	179	Bay, climbing	SSSI, NNR, NP
21	Brownslade/Linney	SR898982	253	Bay, climbing	SSSI, NP
22	Broomhill Burrows	SM890003	183	Hindshore, climbing	SSSI, NP
23	Whitesand Bay	SM737268	28	Bay	NP
24	The Bennett	SN054404	20	Spit	NP
25	Poppit Sands	SN153485	11	Ness/foreland	NP
26	Towyn Warren	SN163489	30	Spit, climbing	SSSI
27	Ynyslas	SN607933	68	Spit	SSSI, NNR
28	Tywyn to Aberdovey	SN596978	111	Ness/foreland or spit	
29	Fairbourne	SH614134	15	Spit	
30	Morfa Dyffryn	SH564241	313	Spit	SSSI, NNR, NP
31	Morfa Harlech	SH573325	341	Ness/foreland, spit	SSSI, NNR, NP
32	Morfa Bychan	SH539372	169	Bay	SSSI, NWWT, ESA
33	Pwllheli/Pen Y Chain	SH407350	45	Bay	ESA
34	Traeth Crugan	SH365336	22	Bay, spit	
35	Tai Morfa	SH282264	20	Bay, climbing	SSSI, ESA, AONB
36	Morfa Dinlle	SH440594	67	Spit	
37	Newborough Warren	SH414634	1,257	Hindshore, spit	SSSI, NNR, AONB, ESA
38	Penhrhynoedd-Llangadwaladr	SH371657	25	Bay, climbing	SSSI, AONB, ESA
39	Aberffraw	SH367689	248	Hindshore	SSSI, AONB, ESA
40	Valley	SH314739	192	Bay, spit	ESA
41	Tywyn Gwyn	SH293814	17	Spit	AONB, ESA, SSSI
42	Traeth Dulas	SH488885	4	Bay	AONB, ESA, SSSI
43	Traeth Lligwy	SH494873	3	Bay	AONB, ESA
44	Red Wharf Bay	SH567807	6	Bay	AONB, ESA
45	Conwy/Deganwy	SH771798	75	Spit	
Total			*16,906*		

Source: Dargie (1995). Code refers to mapped site location (Map 3.2.1). Abbreviations: AONB Area of Outstanding Natural Beauty; ESA Environmentally Sensitive Area; LNR Local Nature Reserve; NNR National Nature Reserve; NP National Park; SSSI Biological Site of Special Scientific Interest; NWWT North Wales Wildlife Trust Reserve.

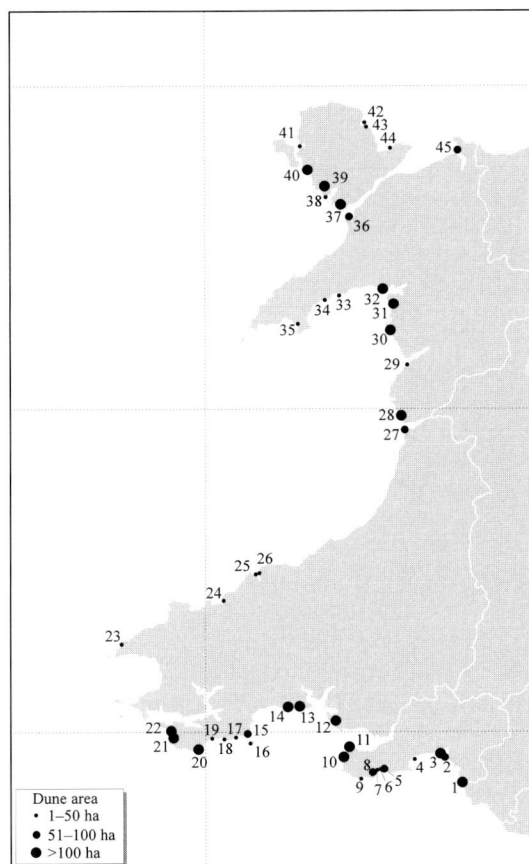

Map 3.2.1 Sand dune sites. Source: JNCC Coastal Database.

The major dune habitats are: strand and embryo dune; mobile and semi-fixed dune; acidic fixed dune grassland; neutral and calcareous fixed dune grassland; dune heath; dune slack; other dune wetland; dune woodland; transitions to saltmarsh; transitions to maritime cliff; other vegetation; and other land cover (e.g. bare ground, car park, caravan park). These are used here to set the dunes of the region in the context of counties and Wales (Table 3.2.2). Survey of dunes in Scotland is still in progress and it is not possible to

give detailed figures on extent for either the West Coast or Great Britain. An estimate of dune habitats for Scotland, based on a sample set of sites (Dargie 1993), is used here to allow some form of GB context to be indicated.

Some 90 National Vegetation Classification communities were recorded for all Welsh dunes, with a total of 156 types for communities and sub-communities combined. Wales is particularly notable in having the largest national areas of two rare dune slack communities (SD13 *Salix repens - Bryum pseudotriquetrum* slack and SD14 *Salix repens - Campylium stellatum* slack). Wales also has the largest area in Britain of non-dune scrub on its dunes, suggesting a lack of grazing in recent decades. There are also large expanses of dune grassland (SD8 *Festuca rubra - Galium verum* fixed dune), which are species-poor, an unusual feature for a community normally rich in species. Such areas are tall and rank, excluding many species typical of a grazed short sward, again suggesting insufficient grazing in recent years.

3.2.2 Important locations and species

The largest dunes are hindshore types (e.g. Margam Burrows, Pembrey Coast, Broomhill Burrows, Newborough Warren), developed above beaches with a good sand supply and an onshore prevailing wind, which drives sand inland as a series of dune ridges or mobile parabolic dunes. These are found in the most exposed sectors of the Welsh coast and in Swansea Bay, Carmarthen Bay, Cardigan Bay and Caernarfon Bay. Ness/foreland dunes develop on shores with sand supply coming from two directions, and they gradually extend seawards (e.g. Crymlyn Burrows, Morfa Harlech). Spit dunes (e.g. Whiteford Burrows, Morfa Dyffryn, Morfa Bychan) develop at the mouths of estuaries and depend strongly on river sediment for their sand supply. Bay dunes (e.g. Whitesand Bay) are very widespread in the region and develop upon sand trapped within the shelter of rock headlands. Climbing dunes (e.g. Penmaen Burrows) represent sand blown up on to terrain inland of the main dune system, in some cases covering

Table 3.2.2 Areas (ha) of dune vegetation types in the region

Dune vegetation type	West Glamorgan	Dyfed	Gwynedd	Region 12	Wales	West Coast	Great Britain**
Strand and embryo dune	43	24	58	125	136	*	340
Mobile and semi-fixed dune	307	593	719	1,619	1,961	*	8,504
Acidic fixed dune grassland	56	6	100	162	162	*	4,953
Neutral and calcareous fixed dune grassland	198	720	635	1,553	2,034	*	15,228
Dune heath and bracken	27	1	15	43	136	*	2,615
Dune slack	55	116	304	475	614	*	2,175
Other dune wetland	15	93	66	174	221	*	4,114
Dune woodland and scrub	112	1,308	855	2,275	2,364	*	8,965
Transitions to saltmarsh	6	29	21	56	59	*	836
Transitions to maritime cliff	-	9	6	15	21	*	64
Other vegetation types	2	79	38	119	123	*	540
Other land cover	98	253	205	556	652	*	1,866
Total	*919*	*3,231*	*3,022*	*7,172*	*8,483*	*31,298*	*50,200*
% in Region 12	-	-	-	-	*85*	*23*	*14*

Sources: Dargie (1993), Dargie (1995), Radley (1994), JNCC Coastal Resources Database. Key: *not available; **GB figures include estimates for Scotland.

large areas of steep cliff. The sand often forms only a thin veneer and there is a strong influence from the underlying geology. The larger dune systems in the region develop a fresh (or, rarely, brackish) watertable, which influences the vegetation of depressions, forming a distinct type of wetland termed dune slack. This habitat is common on hindshore dunes and the larger ness/foreland and spit dune types. It is rare or absent from most bay and climbing dunes.

In Great Britain, four nationally rare and thirteen nationally scarce higher plants are found mainly or exclusively on dunes. Only two of them, dune helleborine *Epipactis leptochila* (ssp. *dunensis)* and dune gentian *Gentianella uliginosa* (confined to Wales), are present in the region (see also Tables 5.2.2 and 5.2.3). Variegated horsetail *Equisetum variegatum*, sea stork's bill *Erodium maritimum*, Portland spurge *Euphorbia portlandica*, sea spurge *E. paralias*, and dune fescue *Vulpia membranacea* are nationally scarce plants found on dunes. Other nationally rare and scarce species more typical of other habitats also occur on dunes in the region, including sea stock *Matthiola sinuata*, striated catchfly *Silene conica*, fen orchid *Liparis loeselii*, sharp rush *Juncus acutus* and early sand-grass *Mibora minima*. Rare bryophytes (e.g. *Southbya nigrella, Pleurochaete squarrosa*) and lichens (e.g. *Fulgensia fulgens, Toninia caeruleonigricans*) also occur. Most dune site reports contain details of some of the notable species present.

Detailed ecological studies on animal populations are few (e.g. Miles (1983) at Ynyslas), but the invertebrate fauna of dunes in the region is well-studied. Many sites have long invertebrate lists, with many notable and rare (Red Data Book) species. Outstanding locations in the Invertebrate Site Register include Oxwich Burrows (as part of Oxwich Bay), Whiteford Burrows, Newborough Warren, Pembrey Coast, Ynyslas, Stackpole Warren, Morfa Harlech, Laugharne Burrows, Whitesand Bay, Morfa Dyffryn and Broomhill Burrows (see also section 5.3). Some dune wetlands (swamp, mire and open water habitats, rather than typical dune slack) are important for waterbirds (e.g. Laugharne and Pendine Burrows).

3.2.3 Human activities

In general sand dunes are among the least heavily modified of terrestrial habitats. However, the inner edge of many sand dune sites in the region has been strongly affected by a variety of human impacts, sometimes leading to major habitat loss or conversion to common vegetation lacking typical dune species (and thus of less interest). Most notable are the loss of large dune areas to industrial development around Swansea Bay and the afforestation of the Pembrey Coast and Newborough Warren (Doody 1989). Margam Burrows have been largely destroyed by sand-winning and tipping. Residential and recreational development has encroached on many sites, especially in south Wales, because of their high recreational amenity value. Car parks, caravan and camp sites and golf courses are very common on and adjacent to many sites. Military use is present on several sites but the total area of impact and damage is slight. Conservation is now a major activity in many locations, with many sites having one or more designations or forms of planning control (Table 3.2.1). Details of development for each site are given in Dargie (1995).

Management is now common on many sites. Recreational use is managed by car parking and the provision of hardened paths and boardwalks to reduce path erosion. Many sites in the Gower Area of Outstanding Natural Beauty, plus Morfa Bychan, show the effects of heavy visitor pressure. The most serious long-term problem is reduced grazing activity by stock and rabbits, leading to reduced floristic diversity as species-rich short grassland is replaced by taller, rank grassland and scrub (Hodgkin 1984). Several sites have required scrub removal (notably sea buckthorn *Hippophae rhamnoides*) and the reintroduction of grazing (a long-term monitoring programme has been initiated at Newborough Warren), with cutting in a few other sites. Coastal erosion is not a serious problem at most sites, but major measures were required at Port-Eynon to Horton following storms in March 1978, when sand movement resulted in the inundation of adjacent housing.

3.2.4 Information sources used

All 45 areas of vegetated sand dune in the region (Map 3.2.1 and Table 3.2.1) have been surveyed in recent years using the National Vegetation Classification (Rodwell 1991a, 1991b, 1992, in prep. a, in prep. b). This work was part of the Sand Dune Survey of Great Britain initiated by the Nature Conservancy Council in 1987 and continued after 1991 by the Joint Nature Conservation Committee.

These surveys, all carried out in the summer months, are very detailed and use a consistent methodology. One site was surveyed in 1986, thirteen in 1988 and all remaining sites in 1991. The vegetation is mapped and described, and information on coastal erosion and accretion, atypical vegetation and adjoining land use is also recorded. Individual site reports are available, as well as a national report for Wales (Dargie 1995). The data provide a sound baseline for future dune vegetation studies and both strategic and local management of the dune resource. All information presented here is derived from the national report.

No other comprehensive surveys exist for the region, though a small number of sites have specific information on invertebrates.

3.2.5 Further sources of information

A. *References cited*

Dargie, T.C.D. 1993. *Sand dune vegetation survey of Great Britain. Part 2 - Scotland.* Peterborough, Joint Nature Conservation Committee.

Dargie, T.C.D. 1995. *Sand dune vegetation survey of Great Britain. Part 3 - Wales.* Peterborough, Joint Nature Conservation Committee.

Doody, J.P. 1989. Conservation and development of the coastal dunes in Great Britain. *In: Perspectives in coastal dune management*, ed. by F. van der Meulen, P.D. Jungerius & J. Visser, 53-67. The Hague, SPB Academic Publishing.

Hodgkin, S.E. 1984. Scrub encroachment and its effects on soil fertility on Newborough Warren, Anglesey, Wales. *Biological Conservation*, 29: 99-119.

Miles, P.M. 1983. Terrestrial sand dune fauna at Ynyslas, Cardiganshire. *Nature in Wales New Series, 2 (1-2): 75-79.*

Radley, G.P. 1994. *Sand dune vegetation survey of Great Britain. Part 1 - England.* Peterborough, Joint Nature Conservation Committee.

Rodwell, J.S., *ed.* 1991a. *British plant communities. Volume 1: woodlands and scrub.* Cambridge University Press.

Rodwell, J.S., *ed.* 1991b. *British plant communities. Volume 2: mires and heaths.* Cambridge University Press.

Rodwell, J.S., *ed.* 1992. *British plant communities. Volume 3: grasslands and montane vegetation.* Cambridge University Press.

Rodwell, J.S., *ed.* In prep., a. *British plant communities. Volume 4: aquatic communities, swamps and tall herb fens.* Cambridge University Press.

Rodwell, J.S., *ed.* In prep., b. *British plant communities. Volume 5: maritime and weed communities.* Cambridge University Press.

B. Further reading

Further details of coastal habitat sites are given in the *Coastal & Marine UKDMAP datasets module*, available from JNCC Coastal Conservation Branch, Peterborough.

Barne, J., Davidson, N.C., Hill, T.O., & Jones, M. 1994. *Coastal and Marine UKDMAP datasets: a user manual.* Peterborough, Joint Nature Conservation Committee.

Atkinson, D., & Houston, J., *eds.* 1993. *The sand dunes of the Sefton coast.* Liverpool, National Museums & Galleries on Merseyside.

Brooks, A., & Agate, E. 1986. *Sand dunes: a practical conservation handbook.* Wallingford, British Trust for Conservation Volunteers.

Davidson, N.C., Laffoley, D.d'A., Doody, J.P., Way, L.S., Gordon, J., Key, R., Drake, C.M., Pienkowski, M.W., Mitchell, R.M., & Duff, K.L. 1991. *Nature conservation and estuaries in Great Britain.* Peterborough, Nature Conservancy Council.

Doody, J.P., *ed.* 1985. *Sand dunes and their management.* Peterborough, Nature Conservancy Council. (Focus on nature conservation, No. 13.)

Doody, J.P., *ed.* 1991. *Sand dune inventory of Europe.* Peterborough, Joint Nature Conservation Committee.

Hodgkin, S.E. 1981. *Scrub encroachment on Newborough Warren.* MSc Thesis, University College, London.

Radley, G.P., & Woolven, S.C. 1990. *A sand dune bibliography.* Peterborough, Nature Conservancy Council. (Contract Surveys, No. 122.)

Ranwell, D.S. 1972. *Ecology of salt marshes and sand dunes.* London, Chapman and Hall.

Ranwell, D.S., & Boar, R. 1986. *Coast dune management guide.* Huntingdon, Institute of Terrestrial Ecology.

Williams, A.T., & Randerson, P.F. 1989. Nexus: ecology, recreation and management of a dune system in South Wales. *In: Perspectives in coastal dune management*, ed. by F. van der Meulen, P.D. Jungerius & J. Visser, 217-227. The Hague, SPB Academic Publishing.

C. Contact names and addresses

Type of information	Contact address and telephone no.
Flora, fauna, habitat information, site management	*Coastal Ecologist, CCW HQ, Bangor, tel. 01248 370444
Issues, coastal zone management initiatives	*Projects Officer, Cardigan Bay Forum Aberystwyth, tel. 01970 624471 ext 147
National and international advice on dune conservation, sand dune survey site reports	*Coastal Conservation Branch, JNCC, Peterborough, tel. 01733 62626
Invertebrate fauna	*Invertebrate Site Register, Species Conservation Branch, JNCC, Peterborough, tel. 01733 62626

* Starred contact addresses are given in full in the Appendix

3.2.6 Acknowledgements

Assistance with sources was kindly provided by Cardigan Bay Forum and the Species Conservation Branch, JNCC.

3.3 Vegetated shingle structures and shorelines

Dr R.E. Randall

3.3.1 Introduction

'Shingle' means sediments coarser than sand but smaller than boulders; i.e. 2-200 mm in diameter. Shingle plant communities around Britain are distinctive (Sneddon & Randall 1993a), with some communities being widespread and others limited to a particular region or substrate.

Although much of the region's coast is bordered by shingle, the region contains only a small amount of the British shingle resource; there are few major shingle structures (Steers 1964), with few sites extending to over 7 ha. Nevertheless Cemlyn Bay, Aber Dysynni, Traeth Tanybwlch, Crabhall Saltings and Pwll du are significant for their large range of plant communities, from pioneer through to scrub, and the region as a whole has a wide representation of shingle vegetation communities. Several sites, particularly those on the Llyn Peninsula and Anglesey, are significant in having representative western communities. Pure shingle is uncommon in western Britain; Pwll du, Traeth Tanybwlch and Cemlyn Bay are important in this respect. Crabhall Saltings is a significant site for showing the influence of adjacent saltmarsh on shingle vegetation. Aber Dysynni is a good example of the influence of sand matrix on shingle.

Shingle sites covered here include both simple fringing beaches and also more complex structures where the shingle is vegetated yet not buried by more than 20 cm of sand (the depth at which the shingle ceases to influence the vegetation, as at e.g. Newborough Warren and Fairbourne (see section 3.2)).

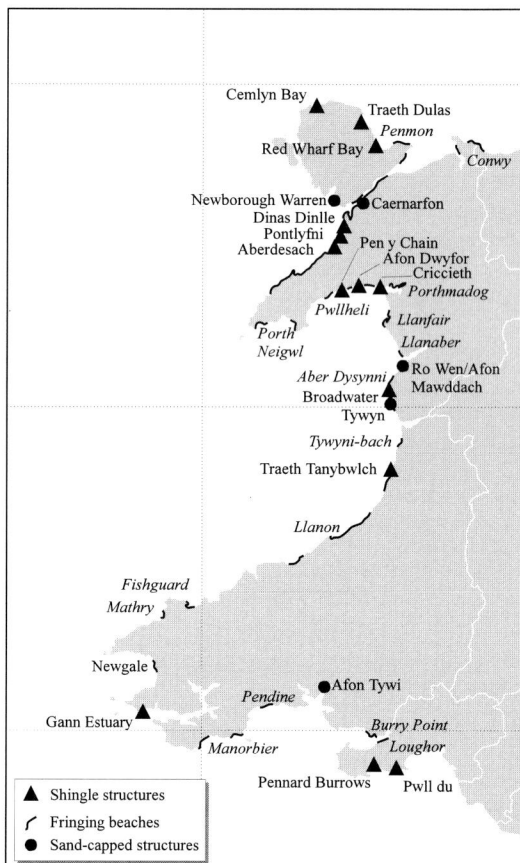

Map 3.3.1 Coastal shingle structures and fringing shingle beaches. Sources: JNCC Coastal Database and Randall (1989).

Table 3.3.1 Sand-capped shingle structures*		
Site name	*Location*	*Area (ha)*
Afon Tywi	SN31	15.5
Tywyn	SH50	7.0
Afon Mawddach (Fairbourne)	SH61	1.5
Caernarfon	SH46	34.5
Newborough	SH46	14.5
Total		**73.0**

Source: after Sneddon & Randall (1993b). *see also section 3.2

3.3.2 Important locations and species

Where the coast features shingle, it is often mixed with large amounts of sand, or sand dunes have developed on it. The major sand-capped shingle structures are listed in Table 3.3.1 and Table 3.3.2 lists the major fringing shingle beach sites in the region. Table 3.3.3 lists vegetated shingle structures surveyed by the Nature Conservancy Council in 1989 (Sneddon & Randall 1993b), giving the site type and conservation status. All sites are shown on Map 3.3.1.

Table 3.3.2 Fringing shingle beaches			
Site name	*10 km square*	*Area (ha)*	*Site type*
Loughor	SS59	2.0	sandy
Burry Point	SN40	0.5	sandy
Pendine	SN20	1.0	sandy
Manorbier	SS09	1.0	sandy
Newgale Sands	SM82	2.0	no vegetation
Mathry	SM83	0.5	no vegetation
Fishguard	SM93	0.5	no vegetation
Llanon	SN56	2.0	sandy
Twyni-bach	SN69	1.5	sandy
Llanaber	SH51	1.5	sandy
Llan fair	SH52	3.5	sandy
Porthmadog	SH53	1.0	sandy
Porth Neigwl	SH22	0.5	no vegetation
Penmon	SH68	0.5	sandy
Conwy	SH77	2.0	sandy
Total		**20.0**	

Most shingle sites are relatively small and contain high proportions of wind-borne sand. There is a three-ridge shingle beach at Pwll du, a small sandy spit at Pennard Burrows and a small but ecologically important pebble

Table 3.3.3 Vegetated shingle structures

Site name	Site type	Location	Area surveyed (ha)	Conservation status	Activities/ management disturbances
Pwll du	multiple ridge beach	SS 574875	2.6	SSSI/NT, AONB	light recreation
Pennard Burrows	sandy shingle spit	SS 540870	1.1	SSSI/NT	recreation
Crabhall Saltings/Pickleridge	spit	SM 817060	3.5	SSSI	light rabbit grazing
Traeth Tanybwlch	sandy shingle spit	SN 577800	5.6	SSSI	recreation
Aber Dysynni (Broadwater)	Complex spit with sand & saltmarsh	SH 582027	19.3	SSSI	rabbit grazing (light) recreation
Criccieth	multiple ridge	SH 525375	19.6	None	light grazing & recreation
Afon Dwyfor	spit	SH 475375	0.9	None	none
Pen-y-chain (Abersoch)	sandy multiple ridge shingle beach	SH 440355	6.3	None	grazing
Aberdesach	double ridge with sand matrix	SH 425515	1.4	None	recreation, construction
Pontlyfni	sandy shingle ridge	SH 433533	2.5	None	sewerage works, grazing
Dinas Dinlle	sandy foreshore and multiple ridge spit	SH 440580	4.0	None (partly in proposed MNR)	recreation, rabbit grazing
Cemlyn Bay	pebble bar	SH 331932	3.0	SSSI, NWWT, ESA,NT	past gravel extraction
Traeth Dulas	Shingle spit with sand overlay	SH 485888	3.2	SSSI, ESA	none
Red Wharf Bay	sandy calcareous spit	SH 545802	0.3	ESA	recreation
Total			73.3		

Source: after Sneddon & Randall (1993b). Key: NT: National Trust; NWWT: North Wales Wildlife Trust, ESA: Environmentally Sensitive Area; AoNB: Area of Outstanding Natural Beauty; MNR: Marine Nature Reserve.

ridge, the Pickleridge, fronting the Crabhall Saltings in Milford Haven. The Newgale shingle beach comprises 2 km of well-rounded shingle of local Cambrian sandstone and volcanics but is largely unvegetated. Northerly growing spits in Cardigan Bay have significantly vegetated shingle at Aber Dysynni and Traeth Tanybwlch. The latter is an almost pure shingle ridge deflecting the Ystwyth over 1 km north of its original course. The spit at Ro Wen is totally sand-capped. South Llyn has significant fluvioglacial sand and shingle structures. The shingle content increases eastward from Pwllheli, and there is a large shingle structure deposited at Pen-y-chain, where up to four storm ridges have built up. An almost pure shingle foreshore gives way to older ridges with over 20 cm depth of sand cap. Glacial cliffs at Criccieth also provide a shingle source. On the north of the Llyn coast, longshore drift has led to the northerly growth of Morfa Dinlle, a shingle spit with variable depths of sand capping. In Anglesey there are sandy/shingle spits at Red Wharf Bay and Traeth Dulas and a pure shingle bar at the head of Cemlyn Bay.

The sandy nature of the substrate at most of the west Wales shingle sites is strongly reflected in the vegetation. A common group near the water's edge on sandy shingle strands and structures is a cosmopolitan community dominated by sea sandwort *Honkenya peploides*, sea couch-grass *Elymus pycnanthus* and marram grass *Ammophila arenaria*, with sea holly *Eryngium maritimum* and sea spurge *Euphorbia paralias*. Further up the shore, the vegetation is frequently dominated by curled dock *Rumex crispus*, sea mayweed *Tripleurospermum maritimum* and yellow horned poppy *Glaucium flavum*, another cosmopolitan community. A more western community dominated by sea mayweed but with spear-leaved orache *Atriplex prostrata* and curled

dock occurs in some places. On pure shingle, communities dominated by sea beet *Beta maritima* are present and at Cemlyn there is a western community of sea campion *Silene vulgaris* subsp. *maritima* and sea kale.

Most Welsh shingle behind the backshore comprises grassland communities, with red fescue *Festuca rubra* subsp. *litoralis*, thrift *Armeria maritima* and buck's-horn plantain *Plantago coronopus* where there are saltmarsh influences and red fescue *Festuca rubra* subsp. *arenaria*, bird's-foot trefoil *Lotus corniculatus* and moss *Hypnum cupressiforme* communities where sand influences are strong. Elsewhere there are a range of communities based on creeping bent *Agrostis stolonifera* and red fescue, with a western open-grassland community based on red fescue - rest harrow *Ononis repens* - kidney vetch *Anthylis vulneraria* in a few places.

Heath communities are poorly represented on shingle in Wales, except at at Pwll du and Pen-y-chain, where ling *Calluna vulgaris* - lichen *Cladonia impexa* heath is present and wet heath with reed *Phragmites australis* and water mint *Mentha aquatica* also occurs. On the most inland parts of shingle sites there are communities based on gorse *Ulex europaeus* and in some sites communities dominated by blackthorn *Prunus spinosa* or bramble *Rubus fruiticosus*.

The most important shingle plant species in the region are sea kale *Crambe maritima*, which is declining in Britain, sea heath *Frankenia laevis*, which has its only western site in Britain on Anglesey (Roberts 1975), and Ray's bistort *Polygonum raii*, which occurs at Pickleridge on the Gann Estuary and a few fringing beaches in west and north-west Gwynedd.

There are tern colonies at Cemlyn Bay and Aber Dysynni. Rabbits and domestic livestock influence the vegetation at many sites. Cemlyn and Pickleridge are important for their invertebrates, for which other sites have not been fully surveyed.

3.3.3 Human activities

Many of the Welsh shingle sites have no national conservation status and can experience high levels of recreational pressure, including trampling, litter and the nutrient input from dogs (see Table 3.3.3). Recent construction and development have occurred at Dinas Dinlle, Pontlyfni and Aberdesach. Parts of Dinas Dinlle have been ploughed and Pontlyfni is also grazed, as are Criccieth and Pennard Burrows. Artificial reworking of the site has occurred over parts of Crabhall Saltings, Aber Dysynni and Criccieth. At Aber Dysynni, active wardening of the tern colony reduces trampling of the nest sites in the breeding season but increases the visitor pressure elsewhere on site. Traeth Dulas, Cemlyn Bay, Aber Dysynni, Traeth Tanybwlch, Crabhall Saltings, Pennard Burrows and Pwll du are Sites of Special Scientific Interest (SSSIs).

Several shingle structures in the region are heavily grazed by domestic stock. Here short swards occur with a poor range of plants.

3.3.4 Information sources used

All the shingle structures of the region were surveyed during the NCC's national shingle structures survey carried out between May and August 1989 (Tables 3.3.1 and 3.3.3). This survey used the National Vegetation Classification (NVC), applying a standard methodology (Sneddon & Randall 1993b). Unvegetated and minor sites were excluded. Many of the fringing beaches in Gwynedd were examined by the author in the early 1980s as part of a survey sponsored by British Petroleum (BP). These sites were examined only qualitatively (see Randall 1989). The Dale area has been surveyed by the Field Studies Council Research Centre over many years. Not all shingle sites are vegetated, especially not those on exposed high-energy coasts (e.g. Hell's Mouth - Porth Neigwl) or where disturbance is great (e.g. Pendine). These have not been surveyed.

3.3.5 Further sources of information

A. References cited

Randall, R.E. 1989. Geographical variation in British shingle vegetation. *Botanical Journal of the Linnean Society, 101*: 3-18.

Roberts, R.H. 1975. *Frankenia laevis* in Anglesey. *Watsonia, 10*: 291-292.

Sneddon, P., & Randall, R.E. 1993a. *Coastal vegetated shingle structures of Great Britain: main report*. Peterborough, Joint Nature Conservation Committee.

Sneddon, P., & Randall, R.E. 1993b. *Coastal vegetated shingle structures of Great Britain: Appendix I Wales*. Peterborough, Joint Nature Conservation Committee.

Steers, J.A. 1964. *The coastline of England and Wales*. London, Cambridge University Press.

B. Further reading

Further details of vegetated shingle sites may be found on the *Coastal & Marine UKDMAP datasets module,* available from JNCC Coastal Conservation Branch, Peterborough.

Barne, J., Davidson, N.C., Hill, T.O., & Jones, M. 1994. *Coastal and Marine UKDMAP datasets: a user manual*. Peterborough, Joint Nature Conservation Committee.

Chapman, V.J. 1976. *Coastal vegetation*. Oxford, Pergamon Press.

Ferry, B., *et al.* 1990. *Dungeness: a vegetation survey of a shingle beach*. Peterborough, Nature Conservancy Council. (Research and Survey in nature conservation, No.26.)

Fuller, R.M. 1987. Vegetation establishment on shingle beaches. *Journal of Ecology, 75*: 1077-1089.

Howarth, W.O. 1920. Notes on the habitats and ecological characters of three sub-varieties of *Festuca rubra*. *Journal of Ecology, 8*: 216-231.

National Trust. 1981. *Biological survey - Cemlyn, Anglesey*. Cheltenham (unpublished report).

Scott, G.A.M. 1963. The ecology of shingle beach plants. *Journal of Ecology, 51*: 517-527.

Scott, G.A.M., & Randall, R.E. 1976. Biological flora of the British Isles: *Crambe maritima* L. *Journal of Ecology, 64*: 1077-1091.

Sneddon, P., & Randall, R.E. 1989. *Vegetated shingle structures survey of Great Britain: Bibliography*. Peterborough, Nature Conservancy Council. (Research and Survey in nature conservation, No.20.)

C. Contact names and addresses

Type of information	Contact address and telephone no.
Pwll du / Pennard Burrows	*Chief Adviser Conservation, The National Trust HQ, Cirencester GL7 1QW, tel. 01285 651818
Pickleridge-Crabhall Saltings	Warden, Field Studies Council Research Centre, Dale Fort Field Centre, Dale, Pembroke SA62 3RD, tel. 01646 636205
Flora, fauna, habitat information, site management	*Coastal Ecologist, CCW HQ, Bangor, tel. 01248 370444
Site information, South Wales shingle	*District Officer, CCW Llandeilo, tel. 01558 822111
Site information, North Wales shingle	*North Wales Regional Officer, CCW, Bangor, tel. 01248 372333
Cemlyn Bay	*Conservation Officer, North Wales Wildlife Trust, Bangor, tel. 01248 351541

* Starred contact addresses are given in full in the Appendix

3.4 Coastal lagoons

Dr R.S.K. Barnes & Dr R.N. Bamber

3.4.1 Introduction

The term coastal lagoons is used here to include true lagoons, i.e. those wholly or partially separated from the sea by a natural sedimentary barrier, and also artificial brackish ponds and coastal pools, of a similarly restricted tidal range and often containing comparable lagoonal wildlife. Lagoons are commonly shallow, often with a varying salinity ranging from above to below normal sea-water levels (35‰). Freshwater systems are not considered.

Lagoons are a nationally rare habitat and a 'priority habitat type' under Annex 1 of the EU Habitats Directive.

The region is therefore significant in the national context even though it contains but one natural lagoon. The single semi-natural lagoon in the region (Cemlyn Lagoon, Anglesey - see Map 3.4.1) covers 12 ha, amounting to (a) 1% of Britain's total lagoonal resource, (b) 2% of that resource excluding the Fleet, Dorset (by far Britain's largest lagoon, comprising nearly 70% of the total resource) and (c) 19% of the lagoonal resource that was regarded by Barnes (1989) as being 'especially noteworthy in the national context', again excluding the Fleet (Tables 3.4.1, 3.4.2 and 3.4.3). Other lagoonal sites in the region are a small natural percolation pool of 0.1 ha at Morfa Gwyllt, Tywyn, Gwynedd, and behind the Pickleridge in the Gann Estuary (Crabhall Saltings).

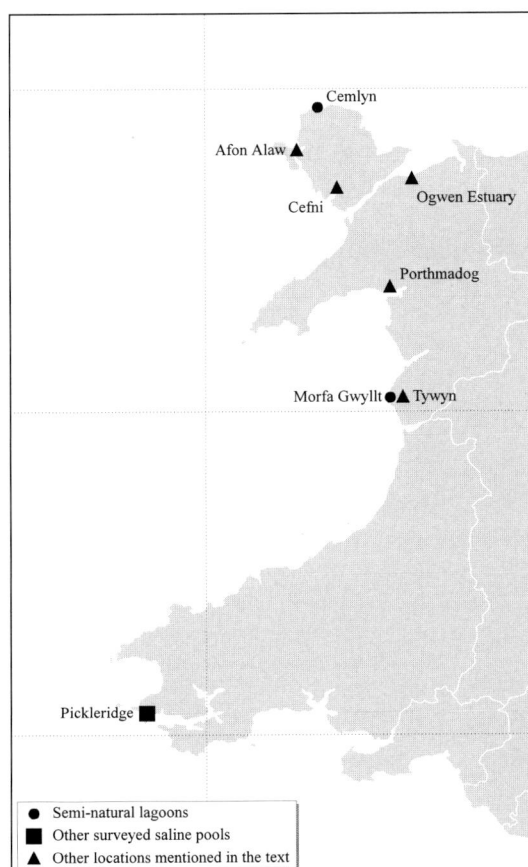

Map 3.4.1 Coastal lagoons

Table 3.4.1 Lagoons surveyed

Name	Grid ref.	Area (ha)	Type
Pickleridge, Dyfed	SM810070	4	Estuarine
Morfa Gwyllt, Gwynedd	SH565030	0.1	Percolation pool
Cemlyn, Gwynedd	SH330932	12	Semi-natural, typical

Note: others: none surveyed; individually small; <10 ha in total.

Table 3.4.2 Total lagoonal areas for region and country

Region	Lagoonal area (ha)	Overall % of GB total	% of GB total excluding the Fleet
Gwynedd	12	1	2
Other counties	0	0	0
Region 12	12	1	2
West Coast	98	8	13
North Sea coast	1,163	92	87
Great Britain	1,261		

Note: the residual unsurveyed resource of other than semi-natural 'lagoons' is unknown, but is less than a further 10 ha.

Table 3.4.3 'Nationally noteworthy' lagoonal areas for region and country

Region	Lagoonal area (ha)	Overall % of GB total	% of GB total excluding the Fleet
Gwynedd	12	2	19
Other counties	0	0	0
Region 12	12	2	19
West Coast	24	4	37
North Sea coast	521	96	63
Great Britain	545		

Source: after Barnes (1989)

3.4.2 Important locations and species

Apart from the Cemlyn lagoon and the pool at Morfa Gwyllt, there are a number of small percolation pools, artificial ponds and pools within estuarine systems throughout the region (see Map 3.4.1). They range in scale from a large low-tide pool on the Afon Alaw, Anglesey, which retains water at low tide but which is fully flushed on each high tide and is thus essentially estuarine, via excised meanders (Ogwen Estuary) and retained estuary pools (Cefni, Tywyn, Porthmadog), to a number of shingle pools, all very small and undoubtedly ephemeral, for example those within the Menai Straits. The cliff topography of most of the coastline generally precludes the development of lagoon-like features.

Many of these sites, being for example fully-flushed tidal pools, or too small to act as stable habitats, or now artificial boating lakes, are outside the present context of coastal lagoons. Estimates of the residual total resource are little more than guesswork.

There are no important plant species in lagoons in the region, although sea-kale *Crambe maritima* occurs on the enclosing shingle spit at Cemlyn. The seaweed *Fucus ceranoides* occurs in the artificial pool at Porthmadog. True lagoons support only three types of aquatic vegetation, namely stands of green algae (*Chaetomorpha, Ulva* and *Enteromorpha*), of sea-grasses and similar plants (predominantly *Ruppia* spp.) and, much more rarely, of stoneworts (especially *Lamprothamnium*). Much of the area of their beds, however, is in the form of bare sediment, devoid of vegetation cover. Fringing stands of reeds *Phragmites* spp., salt-marsh plants and/or sedges *Scirpus maritimus* are usual. All these communities, with the exception of the stoneworts, occur in Cemlyn Lagoon, although its fringing vegetation is poorly developed.

No protected lagoonal invertebrate species occur in the region, although the presence of the lagoonal snails *Hydrobia ventrosa* and *Littorina lagunae* and the bryozoan *Conopeum seurati* at Cemlyn is notable (see also section 5.4). This lagoon also supports waders and wildfowl, and is significant for the colonies of Sandwich, common and arctic terns that nest on its small islands (see also section 5.11).

The estuarine fauna of Pickleridge lagoon is typical of such habitats, being dominated by ragworm *Nereis diversicolor*, lugworm *Arenicola marina*, serpulid worms, the opposum shrimp *Praunus flexuosus* and the mud snail *Hydrobia ulvae*. None of these species is of conservation importance.

3.4.3 Human activities

Active management is applied to Cemlyn Lagoon itself, including regulating its water level with a weir, and it is maintained as a nature reserve (North Wales Wildlife Trust), largely for its birdlife.

No known ecological management exists for the other lagoons in the region.

3.4.4 Information sources used

All potential lagoons in the region were surveyed as part of the NCC's national lagoon survey in 1987 (Barnes 1991). Only Cemlyn Lagoon and Morfa Gwyllt have been the subject of specific and detailed lagoonal surveys. Other saline pools to have experienced incidental sampling are Pickleridge 'Lagoon', Gann Estuary, Dale, Dyfed (records in Crothers 1966) and the tidal-sluice-retained pool on the R. Glaslyn, Porthmadog (e.g. Gubbay 1988).

3.4.5 Further sources of information

A. References cited

Barnes, R.S.K. 1991. A survey of the coastal lagoons of North Wales (R. Clwyd - Aberystwyth), September 1987. *Nature Conservancy Council, CSD Report,* No. 1123.

Barnes, R.S.K. 1989. The coastal lagoons of Britain: an overview and conservation appraisal. *Biological Conservation, 49:* 295-313.

Crothers, J.H. 1966. Dale Fort marine fauna, 2nd ed. *Field Studies, 2:* Supplement, xxiv + 1-169.

Gubbay, S. 1988. *Coastal directory for marine nature conservation.* Ross-on-Wye, Marine Conservation Society.

B. Further reading

Barne, J., Davidson, N.C., Hill, T.O., & Jones, M. 1994. *Coastal and Marine UKDMAP datasets: a user manual.* Peterborough, Joint Nature Conservation Committee.

Bamber, R.N., Batten, S.D., & Bridgwater N.D. 1992. On the ecology of brackish water lagoons in Great Britain. *Aquatic Conservation: Marine and Freshwater Ecosystems, 2:* 65-94.

NERC. 1991. United Kingdom Digital Marine Atlas (UKDMAP). British Oceanographic Data Centre.

C. Contact names and addresses

Type of information	Contact address and telephone no.
Brackish lagoons of the region	Dr R.S.K. Barnes, St Catharine's College, Cambridge CB2 1RL, tel. 01223 336606
Cemlyn Lagoon	*Conservation Officer, North Wales Wildlife Trust, Bangor, tel. 01248 351541

* Starred contact addresses are given in full in the Appendix

3.4.6 Acknowledgements

We are grateful for information supplied by Ivor Rees, Andy Mackie and Dr Robin Crump.

3.5 Coastal grazing marsh

Dr H.T. Gee

3.5.1 Introduction

In this region, large areas of semi-natural coastal wet grassland have been lost through improvement or conversion to arable use. All the surviving resource is grazed, producing coastal grazing marsh. This is a distinctive habitat consisting of low-lying grassland drained by a series of ditches that may be either brackish or freshwater. No figures exist for the total area of grazing marsh or associated coastal wetland habitat in this region or the GB as a whole. In terms of total GB area the regional resource is relatively small: probably less than half of the Welsh total occurs in the region, although it has approximately three quarters of the Welsh coastline. Nevertheless, coastal grazing marsh is a widespread habitat and an important natural resource in this region, present in small pockets of land next to most of the region's estuaries, often in association with a range of other habitats such as saltmarsh, sand dunes, fen and reed swamp. Even the larger areas of grazing marsh in the region, such as Malltraeth Marsh on Anglesey (1,365.6 ha) and the grazing marshes associated with Carmarthen Bay and the Dyfi Estuary, are still relatively small when compared with the extensive grazing marshes of other regions. Grazing marsh forms part of a number of sites of designated conservation interest.

No sites are of importance because of their size. Many, however, contain unusual features, for example the grazing marsh adjacent to the Dyfi estuary and Glaslyn Marshes, or are part of a rich mosaic of habitats, indicating significant conservation interest. See Map 3.5.1 for major sites in the region.

The conservation value of most of the grazing marsh resource of this region is poorly known, although more comprehensive data do exist for its breeding waders and birds of associated wetland habitats. The ditch flora and fauna of Malltraeth Marshes are of significant conservation interest.

3.5.2 Important locations and species

Grazing marsh forms part of at least 12 Sites of Special Scientific Interest (SSSIs) in this region. Some of these sites are also designated as National Nature Reserves (NNRs) or North Wales Wildlife Trust Reserves, whilst there are also RSPB reserves on grazing marsh at Malltraeth Marsh and at Ynys Hir on the Dyfi estuary, and a Wildfowl and Wetlands Trust Reserve at Penclacwydd on the 'Llanelli Levels'. Further important areas of grazing marsh include the Dolgarrog Reed Bed on the Afon Conwy and the Aber Leri Fields and Penllyn Fields adjacent to Dyfi SSSI; others lie adjacent to a number of other SSSIs such as Pembrey Coast, Broadwater on the Afon Dysynni, Penmaenpool Reed-bed on the Afon Mawddach, Morfa Harlech and Foryd Bay. A list of grazing marsh sites in this region is given in Table 3.5.1.

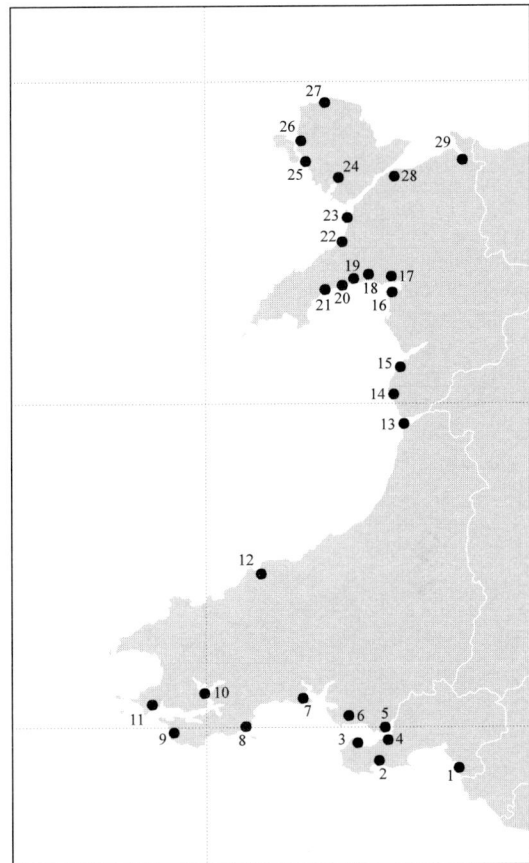

Map 3.5.1 Coastal grazing marsh sites. Numbers refer to Table 3.5.1.

Of particular note within the region are areas of atypical grazing marsh, where changing management practices, poor drainage or disuse have resulted in the development of other habitats, e.g. at Castlemartin Corse and Tre'r Gof, where reclamation of fen has been only partially successful; at Slebech Reed-bed and Carr, where the sea wall has been breached; and at Oxwich NNR, where the cessation of ditch maintenance has allowed the development of a freshwater marsh. Significant areas along the Carmarthen coast, at Pembrey - Kidwelly and at Pendine, have developed behind sand dunes.

Typically, the botanical interest is associated with the ditch systems rather than the fields between them. Where semi-improved grassland remains on grazing marsh it is usually National Vegetation Classification (NVC) MG5 *Cynosurus cristatus/Centaurea nigra* grassland. Exceptions to this include Dolgarrog Reedbeds, Glaslyn Marshes and Aber Leri Fields, where survey has shown the presence of saltmarsh communities that are interesting because of their brackish nature. Glaslyn Marshes includes an area of the nationally rare dwarf spike-rush *Eleocharis parvula* saltmarsh community (Rhind & Jones in press). At Aber Leri Fields there is an unusual transition from vegetation with saltmarsh character to acid bog. Other atypical sites include the fen meadows at Cors Penally, Castlemartin Corse and

Table 3.5.1 Grazing marsh sites shown on Map 3.5.1

No.	Site	Grid ref.	Conservation status of grazing marsh
W Glamorgan			
1	Margam Moor	SS783846	108 ha SSSI
2	Oxwich Bay	SS505870	reverted to fresh marsh SSSI and NNR
3	Cwm Ivy Marsh	SS442941	part of SSSI
4	Burry Inlet, W Glamorgan		adjacent to Burry Inlet SSSI, SPA and Ramsar site
Dyfed			
5	'Llanelli Levels'	SS535985	adjacent to Burry Inlet SSSI SPA and Ramsar site and Penclacwydd WWT Reserve
6	Pembrey-Kidwelly	SN410020	adjacent to Pembrey Coast SSSI
7	Pendine	SN300090	adjacent to Whitehill Down SSSI
8	Cors Penally	SS118989	part of SSSI
9	Castlemartin Corse	SM596998	part of marsh designated SSSI
10	Slebech Reedbed and Carr	SN053142	SSSI - grazing marsh reverting to reedbed
11	Gann Estuary	SM812070	SSSI - grazing marsh recolonised by saltmarsh
12	Teifi Marshes	SN165475	
13	Dyfi Estuary	SN608920	Hen Afon Leri SSSI
Gwynedd			
14	Afon Dysynni	SH585015	grazing marsh adjacent to Broadwater SSSI
15	Mawddach Estuary	SH709188 SH645147	grazing marsh adjacent to Penmaenpool SSSI and Arthog Bog SSSI
16	Glastraeth/Talsarnau marshes	SH610367	grazing marsh adjacent to Morfa Harlech SSSI and NNR
17	Glaslyn Marshes	SH582585 SH590393	SSSI and NWWT Reserve
18	Llyn Ystumllyn	SH526385	SSSI
19	Afon Dwyfor	SH526385	Glan y mor and Ty'ny Morfa NSSNCI
20	Morfa Abererch	SH420360	NSSNCI
21	Penrhos floodplain	SH357340	NSSNCI
22	Afon Llyfni	SH522529	Ynys and Trwyn maen Dylan NSSNCI
23	Afon Foryd	SH445575	adjacent to Foryd Bay SSSI, LNR
24	Malltraeth Marsh	SH440710	SSSI (1366.5ha), ESA, RSPB Reserve. ~2,000 ha of marsh
25	Afon Crigyll	SH325745	ESA
26	Bodlasan Groes	SH298818	ESA
27	Tre'r Gof	SH359936	SSSI, ESA
28	Traeth Lafan	SH613722	Aber Ogwen NWWT Reserve, LNR
29	Afon Conwy (Dolgarrog Reedbeds)	SH780665	(not protected)

Source: JNCC and CCW. Key: SSSI = Site of Special Scientific Interest; SPA = Special Protection Area; NNR = National Nature Reserve; Ramsar site = internationally important wetland; ESA = Environmentally Sensitive Area; NWNT = North Wales Wildlife Trust; NSSNCI = Non Statutory Sites of Nature Conservation Interest.

Tre'r Gof, where poor drainage has resulted in the retention of fenland communities.

Cors Penally supports a rich-fen example of the *Molinia/Myrica* community, rarely encountered in Britain. At Slebech Reed-bed and Carr SSSI on the Eastern Cleddau, the grazing marsh has reverted to a mixture of brackish marsh, reed-bed and carr because the site is periodically inundated by sea water. Margam Moor and the Llanelli Levels support fen meadows and ditch communities similar to the Gwent Levels and areas of grazing marsh in southern England.

Glaslyn Marshes support the nationally rare plants *Eleocharis parvula* and Welsh mudwort *Limosella australis*. Other species present at Glaslyn include the nationally scarce sharp rush *Juncus acutus*, small water pepper *Polygonum minus* and brackish water-crowfoot *Ranunculus baudotii*. The ditches on Castlemartin Corse support the nationally scarce fen pondweed *Potamogeton coloratus* and a number of locally uncommon species.

The flora of the ditches and ponds at Malltraeth is notably rich and supports the nationally rare pillwort *Pilularia globulifera* and locally uncommon plants such as

water violet *Hottonia palustris* and marsh stitchwort *Stellaria palustris* (Knott 1993). The ditches at Margam Moor support a range of species found widely on the Gwent Levels and generally typical of grazing marsh in southern England, including relatively uncommon species such as lesser water-plantain *Baldellia ranunculoides* and frogbit *Hydrocharis morsus-ranae*. See section 5.2 for more information on rare plants.

Grazing marsh is recognised as an important habitat for breeding waders, especially in lowland Britain, although it usually supports lower densities than saltmarsh (Davidson 1991) (see also section 5.11). Malltraeth Marsh and Llyn Ystumllyn are both potential nesting sites for species such as garganey, ruff, blacktailed godwit, marsh harrier and bittern. The management plan for Malltraeth Marsh produced by CCW (Knott 1993) is designed to encourage the establishment of breeding of these species. The management proposed by the Wildfowl and Wetlands Trust is likely greatly to increase the ornithological interest of Penclacwydd, which has already become important as a migration staging site for several waders including greenshank, spotted redshank and black-tailed godwit.

There are records for a number of invertebrate species from Margam Moor, including the nationally notable beetle *Haliplus mucronatus*. Morgan (1994) provided relatively extensive lists of invertebrate species that contain a number of species of conservation interest recorded from the 'Llanelli Levels'. Machynys Ponds - a site on these levels - support an outstanding assemblage of breeding dragonflies, including five species that are considered nationally notable (Morgan 1990). Another nationally notable species is present at Penclacwydd. Other invertebrate records for the Llanelli Levels include one vulnerable hoverfly *Parhelophilus consimilis* plus a further sixteen nationally notable species. Malltraeth supports two nationally notable dragonflies. Post-1980 records from the Welsh Peatland Invertebrate Survey (Holmes *et al.* 1992) for Dolgarrog Reedbed include one nationally rare insect and a further five nationally notable and 27 locally important invertebrate species (see section 5.3 for more detail on terrestrial invertebrates).

3.5.3 Human activities

Agricultural intensification has reduced the conservation value of many grazing marshes in the region. As in the rest of Britain, grazing marsh in West Glamorgan has suffered significantly from loss to industrial land claim, and Margam Moors SSSI (108 ha) are the last remnant of the once extensive levels in this county. In a few places grazing marsh has been lost to secondary natural habitats e.g. the freshwater marsh at Oxwich NNR, or the Gann Estuary, where the sea wall was breached in 1920 allowing the re-establishment of saltmarsh.

A number of grazing marsh sites, e.g. at Penclacwydd, Aber Leri Fields and Malltraeth Marsh, are now being managed in places to improve their ornithological interest. This involves raising water-levels and encouraging the establishment of extensive reedbeds, which may result in a significant change to the habitat and, in the case of some sites, loss of as yet undescribed conservation interest.

3.5.4 Information sources used

There is no survey of the total wet grassland resource in Wales comparable to that undertaken in England for English Nature (Dargie 1993). Although limited, Phase 2 information for lowland grasslands forms the most extensive botanical survey database and is available for eight sites (Wales Field Unit 1990). Surveys of ditch flora have been undertaken at Malltraeth Marsh (Smith & Humphreys 1986; Collonello, Graves & Wade 1992), and river corridor survey data exist for the grazing marshes of the Dyfi Estuary (NRA 1992). Botanical records for Cors Penally SSSI go back 130 years.

Survey data are probably most extensive for breeding birds and are available for Oxwich, Malltraeth Marsh and Dolgarrog Marsh. Grazing marsh sites were included in the survey of breeding redshank throughout Wales (Griffin, Saxton & Williams 1992), whilst those on Anglesey and the Llyn Peninsula were also surveyed as part of the breeding bird surveys for these parts of Wales (Seddon 1988).

A brief study of the Aber Leri fields was undertaken by Boyce in 1989 (Boyce 1990). An invertebrate survey has

been undertaken at Malltraeth Marsh where the aquatic coleoptera were surveyed by Foster & Bilton (1985) and the terrestrial invertebrate fauna was surveyed by Morgan (1992). The dragonfly fauna of Malltraeth Marsh, Oxwich Fresh Marsh and the 'Llanelli Levels' are well recorded, whilst there are also dragonfly records for the Dyfi Estuary and *ad hoc* invertebrate records for Margam Moor and the Llanelli Levels. A survey of the molluscs of Cwm Ivy Marsh, West Glamorgan, was undertaken by the Conchological Society of Great Britain. Information on particular sites may be held on the JNCC's Invertebrate Site Register, and some grazing marsh sites, including the Dolgarrog Reedbeds, were included in the Welsh Peatland Invertebrate Survey (Holmes, Boyce & Reed 1992).

Large areas of former grazing marsh are not likely to be included in any detailed surveys of grasslands in Wales, as many of the pastures are agriculturally improved, or turned over to arable farming.

Table 3.5.2 lists sites for which survey data are available.

Table 3.5.2 Selected survey data

Site	Survey data	Date
Margam Moors	list from CCW	
Oxwich Marsh	NCC Botanical & Hydrological Survey	1981
Dyfi Estuary	IDB Ditches River Corridor Survey	1992
Aber Leri Fields	Phase II CCW	1994
Penllyn Fields	Phase II CCW	1994
Morfa Harlech and Morfa Dyffryn	JNCC Phase II of dunes and associated marshes	1991
Glaslyn Marshes (adjacent to SSSI)	JNCC Phase II	1991
Llyn Ystumllyn	WFU Phase II	1990
Morfa Abererch	Phase II NVC Phase I survey with target notes	
Malltraeth Marsh	Botanical survey WFU	1986

3.5.5 Further sources of information

A. References cited

Boyce, D.C. 1990. Coleoptera recording in Ceredigion (VC 46) during 1989. *Dyfed Invertebrate Group Newsletter, 16:* 16-20.

Collonello, G., Graves, R., & Wade, P.M. 1992. *A survey and evaluation of ditch flora of Malltraeth Marsh SSSI, Anglesey, with recommendations on the management of the drainage system.* Loughborough University, International Centre of Landscape Ecology. (Report for CCW.)

Dargie, T.C. 1993. The distribution of lowland wet grassland in England. *English Nature Research Report*, No. 49.

Davidson, N.C. 1991. Breeding waders on British estuarine grasslands. *Wader Study Group Bulletin 61, Supplement:* 36-41.

Foster, G.N., & Biton, D.T. 1985. *A survey of the aquatic Coleoptera of the Malltraeth Marshes, Anglesey.* CCW (File SH47.5.1).

Griffin, B., Saxton, N., & Williams, I. 1992. *Breeding redshanks in Wales 1991.* RSPB unpublished report.

Holmes, P.R., Boyce, D.C., & Reed, D.C. 1992. *The Welsh peatland invertebrate survey: Meirionnedd.* Bangor, CCW.

Knott, H.A. 1993. *Malltraeth Marsh/Cors Ddyga management plan.* Bangor, CCW.

Morgan, I.K. 1990. Machynys Ponds - an important local wildlife site threatened by development. *Llanelli Naturalists' Newsletter,* summer 1990: 3-4.

Morgan, I.K. 1994. The Llanelli Levels. *The Llanelli Naturalists'
Society Bulletin*, 1: winter 1994-95.

Morgan, M.J. 1992. *Malltraeth Marsh SSSI invertebrate survey 1992.*
CCW (File SH47.5.1.)

National Rivers Authority Welsh Region. 1992. *River corridor survey
for IDD Ditches, Dyfi Estuary.* Unpublished.

Rhind, P.M., & Jones, A. In press. Brackish saltmarsh communities
in the Glaslyn Marsh Trust Reserve. *Field Studies.*

Sedden, A. 1988. *Breeding bird surveys of the Lleyn Peninsula and
Anglesey in 1986 and 1987.* RSPB unpublished report.

Smith, I.R., & Humphreys, E.A. 1986. *A botanical survey and
evaluation of drainage ditches on the Malltraeth Marsh SSSI, Ynys
Môn, Gwynedd.* Unpublished Wales Field Unit report to NCC.

Wales Field Unit. 1990. *WFU Wales lowland grassland survey draft
Phase II report - Glaslyn Marshes (north-west).* Unpublished
report to NCC.

B Further reading

Coleshaw, T. 1995. Rising to the water levels challenge. *Enact,
Vol. 3* No. 1: 7-9.

Harold, R. 1995. Creating wetlands at Holkham. *Enact, Vol. 3*
No. 1: 12-15.

Meade, R. 1982. *Botanical and hydrological survey of Oxwich Marsh,
1981.* Peterborough, NCC.

Scholey, G. 1995. Return of the "drowners". *Enact, Vol. 3* No. 1: 10-
11.

Thomas, G., José, P., & Hirons, G. 1995. Wet grassland in the
millenium. *Enact, Vol. 3* No. 1: 4-6.

C. Contact names and addresses

Type of information	Contact address and telephone no.
Breeding bird survey	*RSPB Wales, Newtown, tel. 01686 626678
Survey reports	*Grasslands Team, CCW HQ, Bangor, tel. 01248 370444
Invertebrate Site Register	*ISR, Species Branch, Joint Nature Conservation Committee, Monkstone House, Peterborough, tel. 01733 62626

* Starred contact addresses are given in full in the Appendix

3.5.6 Acknowledgements

Thanks are due to the District Officer Staff of CCW for
providing information on coastal grazing marsh in their
districts. Information was also received from Stephanie
Tyler of the RSPB, Peter Rhind of CCW headquarters and
Deborah Procter of the JNCC's Invertebrate Site Register.

3.6 Saltmarsh

Dr M.I. Hill

3.6.1 Introduction

The saltmarshes in Region 12 are largely estuarine, on both large and small sites. The largest areas occur in estuaries with extensive intertidal flats: the Burry Inlet, and 'Three Rivers' - Taf/Tywi/Gwendraeth and Dyfi. Both Snowdonia and Pembrokeshire Coast National Parks contain areas of saltmarsh, as does the proposed Menai Strait Marine Nature Reserve.

The total amount of saltmarsh in the region is 5,461 hectares - 24% of the area on the west coast of Britain, 12% of the British resource and 81% of that in Wales (Table 3.6.2). West Glamorgan contains the most, although there are more sites in Gwynedd. JNCC's Coastal Resources Database shows that 27% of the coastline (at Mean High Water) of West Glamorgan supports saltmarsh, compared with only 7% in Dyfed and 4% in Gwynedd. Compared with most other regions, much comprises mid to upper marsh communities (Table 3.6.1). This is because there has been less land claim of saltmarsh here than elsewhere, and so the saltmarsh succession is less often truncated by embankments. Common cord-grass *Spartina anglica* is the most extensive pioneer vegetation and has colonised substantial areas of intertidal flats since the 1930s and 1940s.

3.6.2 Important locations and species

Map 3.6.1 shows the locations of saltmarsh sites in the region (Burd 1989a). The largest saltmarshes in the region are on the Burry Inlet and the Three Rivers Estuary. The Burry Inlet is particularly noteworthy as it has the fourth largest saltmarsh area in Britain and has suffered little land claim. The landward transition is a natural one to sand dunes and a wide variety of plant communities are present. Elsewhere, the ria (drowned river valley) system of Milford Haven contains many pockets of saltmarsh. In addition, the estuaries and bays of mid and north Wales have significant areas of saltmarsh, with the Mawddach, Traeth Bach

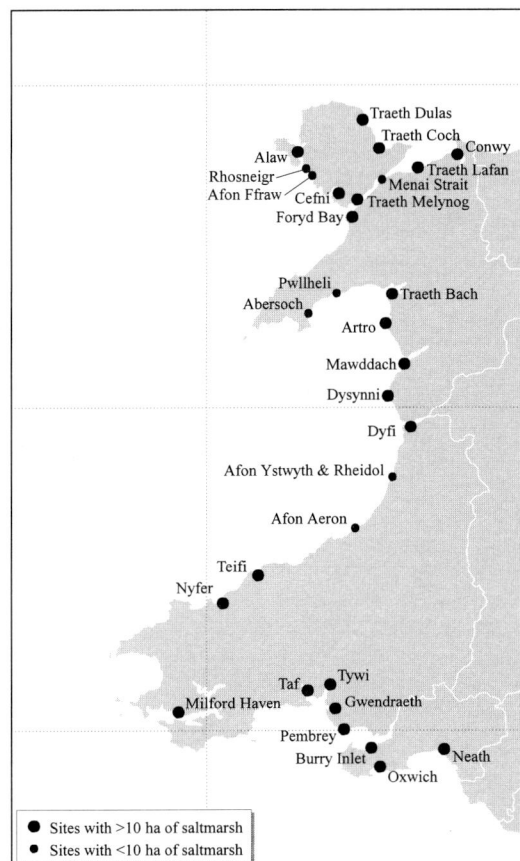

Map 3.6.1 Saltmarsh sites. Source: JNCC Coastal Database.

(estuaries of Glaslyn and Dwyryd), Foryd Bay, Cefni and Conwy all containing more than 100 ha. A particular feature of the region is the development of saltmarsh in the shelter of sand and shingle spits.

Saltmarshes in the region generally have a sandy substrate and are grazed, which greatly influences the type

Table 3.6.1 Areas (ha) of saltmarsh communities for region

	Spartina	Pioneer	Low-mid	Mid-upper	Drift-line	Upper Swamp	Transi-tions	Wet depression	Total	% of region total in county
West Glamorgan	404	302	581	981	1	19	7	0	2,296	42
Dyfed	660	40	523	495	5	85	43	0	1,850	34
Gwynedd	342	23	84	774	0	64	29	0	1,315	24
Region 12	1,406	364	1,188	2,250	6	168	79	0	5,461	-
										% of total in region
Wales	1,681	468	1,555	2486	267	202	89	0	6,748	81
West Coast	3,487	1,340	4,159	11,270	473	410	1,327	<1	22,582	24
GB	*6,948*	*3,470*	*12,353*	*16,042*	*1,824*	*1,475*	*1,670*	*2*	*44,370*	*12*

Source: Burd (1989a).

Table 3.6.2 Locations of saltmarsh in Region 12

Name	Grid ref.	Area (ha)
Sites with > 10 ha (to nearest ha)		
Neath Estuary	SS733942	159
Oxwich	SS510878	16
Burry Inlet, Loughor Estuary	SS500965	2121
Pembrey Burrows, Loughor Estuary	SS425999	66
Afon Gwendraeth (Carmarthen Bay)	SN385065	525
Afon Tywi (Carmarthen Bay)	SN375130	147
Afon Taf (Carmarthen Bay)	SN308107	238
Milford Haven (Cleddau)	SM916061	385
Afon Nyfer (Newport Sands)	SN058397	10
Afon Teifi	SN166475	46
Afon Dyfi	SN640955	556
Afon Dysynni (Tywyn Broadwater)	SH574025	22
Afon Mawddach	SH652170	219
Afon Artro (Morfa Dyffryn)	SH563267	54
Traeth Bach (Afon Glaslyn and Dwyryd)	SH590365	348
Foryd Bay	SH450600	123
Traeth Melynog (Afon Braint)	SH436630	66
Afon Cefni (Malltraeth Sands)	SH400675	111
Afon Alaw (Beddmanarch/ Cymyran)	SH275787	63
Traeth Dulas (Afon Goch)	SH480883	21
Traeth Coch (Afon Nodwydd)	SH540804	31
Traeth Lafan (Afon Ogwen)	SH630750	15
Afon Conwy	SH796765	105
Sites with < 10 ha (to nearest 0.1 ha)		
Afon Aeron	SN457628	0.3
Afon Ystwyth & Rheidol	SN584814	1.3
Pwllheli	SH377346	3.0
Abersoch	SH313282	1.2
Afon Ffraw	SH345685	1.5
Rhosneigr	SH322743	2.5
Menai Strait	SH524690	3.0
Total		*5,461*

Source: Burd (1989a). Some surveyed sites have been amalgamated

of vegetation. A typical zonation is from a pioneer zone of common cord-grass to a low-mid marsh of common saltmarsh grass *Puccinellia maritima*. However at some sites, such as Cefni on Anglesey, where rapid succession has been occurring, the lower saltmarsh is a mosaic of species such as thrift *Armeria maritima* and sea arrow grass *Triglochin maritima*, with common saltmarsh grass and red fescue *Festuca rubra*. In this region, *Festuca rubra* saltmarsh is the main mid to upper marsh vegetation type on grazed marshes. Sea rush *Juncus maritimus* saltmarsh is widespread and appears to reach lower levels on the shore than on the North Sea coast. Driftline vegetation and upper marsh swamps are usually dominated by species such as sea club-rush *Scirpus maritimus* and couch *Elymus repens*. More diverse upper marsh swamps, with species such as yellow iris *Iris pseudacorus,* are found in places such as Milford Haven and the Burry Inlet. Seagrasses *Zostera* spp. are present in intertidal and subtidal zones at many sites, although their presence is not well recorded (but see also section 4.2). In this region, *Zostera noltii* appears to be the least abundant of the three species.

Transitions from saltmarsh to other habitats, especially dunes, are a distinctive feature. Dune transitions occur e.g. at Traeth Melynog, in the Taf estuary, and at Pembrey Burrows. At Pembrey Burrows the transitional community, which contains rock sea lavender *Limonium binervosum* (usually a cliff species), is thought to occur in Britain only at this site.

The region contains some saltmarsh vegetation types and species that are scarce or near the edge of their range in Britain. Of particular interest are areas of dwarf spike-rush *Eleocharis parvula* saltmarsh, for which there are very few records in Britain. *Eleocharis parvula* is a nationally rare species, i.e. is present in only 1-15 10 km squares in Britain. In Wales, *Eleocharis parvula* saltmarsh as a vegetation type is thought to be present only in the Glaslyn/Dwyryd estuaries in Gwynedd. However, there are also records for the species in the Mawddach and Pwllheli harbour. Welsh mud-wort *Limosella australis* has been recorded at a few sites in Wales (several of them in the region, including the Glaslyn marshes, where it is often found in association with *Eleocharis parvula*) but nowhere else in Europe.

Sea wormwood *Artemisia maritima* saltmarsh, a mainly East Anglian and south coast vegetation type, is found in only a few, ungrazed, sites on the west coast, including several in the region, such as Pembrey Burrows and Milford Haven. The region is the southern limit of the flat sedge *Blysmus rufus* saltmarsh community, which is present in depressions in the upper marsh on Anglesey and in Traeth Bach. Individual plants occur as far south as the Burry Inlet and Afon Nyfer. Slender spike-rush *Eleocharis uniglumis* is a scarce and mainly northern saltmarsh community, found in small patches in the region's marshes, mainly north of the Dyfi.

Of the important species in the region, perennial glasswort *Salicornia perennis* is a nationally scarce species found mainly in south-east England but which has been recorded from the Artro and Mawddach estuaries. Sea heath *Frankenia laevis* occurs on sand or shingle margins of saltmarshes, also mainly in south-east England, and is also nationally scarce. There are only two Welsh records for this species, one in this region, at Rhosneigr on Anglesey. Marsh mallow *Althaea officinalis* is also a nationally scarce species, found at the upper edges of some saltmarshes in the south of the region, for example at Milford Haven and Burry Inlet.

Saltmarshes in the region provide breeding sites for waders such as redshank *Tringa totanus* and lapwing *Vanellus vanellus* (see also section 5.11). The 1985 RSPB survey showed that the Dyfi saltmarshes were one of the best sites in Britain in terms of total density of breeding waders. However, redshank had low nest densities or were absent from most sites in south Wales. The Dyfi marshes are also an important site for breeding lapwing. Compared with those in England, saltmarshes in this region support few breeding oystercatchers *Haematopus ostralegus*. A BTO/WWT survey of shelduck *Tadorna tadorna* in 1992 found many breeding pairs in the Dyfi, Cleddau, Teifi, and between the Pembrey and Pendine. Some no doubt use nest sites in the upper saltmarsh zones and transitions. As elsewhere, saltmarshes in this region provide roosting sites for shorebirds and food for wildfowl such as wigeon *Anas penelope* and pintail *Anas acuta*.

Many of the region's saltmarshes are within Sites of Special Scientific Interest (SSSIs); the 29 SSSIs containing saltmarsh are listed in Table 3.6.3.

3.6.3 Human activities

Most saltmarshes in the region have been stable or have accreted in the last 30 years (Pye & French 1993). Common cord-grass *Spartina anglica*, the main colonist of new mudflats, has spread widely since its introduction, and control measures have been attempted at several sites, including the Malltraeth Estuary. However, its spread seems to have slowed in many estuaries. No overall policy for *Spartina* management exists. Most saltmarshes in this region require management by grazing to maintain their existing vegetation. In general, current grazing levels appear to be sustainable.

3.6.4 Information sources used

Saltmarshes in this region were surveyed in 1982/3 as part of the NCC's national saltmarsh survey. This provided a intermediate level of detail between Phase 1 habitat survey and the National Vegetation Classification (NVC). It did not include all areas of transition to other habitats, such as sand dune, shingle and freshwater marsh. Areas of seagrasses *Zostera* spp. were not recorded, nor was saltmarsh in the embanked Glaslyn marshes and Dolgarrog flood plain (see Table 3.6.1 and 3.6.2). Detailed reports are available and results are summarised in Burd (1989a-d). Data presented here are derived from that database.

Other saltmarsh surveys in the region include those on the Burry Inlet (Kay & Rojanavipart 1977), Milford Haven (Dalby 1970), Afon Cefni (Packham & Liddle 1970; Jones 1990) and Conwy (Thorburn & Rees 1979). Surveys of *Spartina* have been carried out at many sites, e.g. Milford Haven (Baker *et al.* 1984; Wilson 1988), the Dyfi (Chater 1973), the Mawddach (Rughani 1985) and the Conwy (Institute of Terrestrial Ecology 1980). There have been few surveys using the National Vegetation Classification, except for Jones (1990) at Cefni and CCW in the Dolgarrog reedbeds of the upper Conwy and Glaslyn marshes (Jones 1990). The latter two sites contain saltmarsh vegetation, but are embanked and only partially tidal.

3.6.5 Further sources of information

A. References cited

Baker, J.M., Wilson, M., & Levell, D. 1984. *Dieback of the saltmarsh grass* Spartina *in Milford Haven*. Field Studies Council Report FSC/RD/5/84.

Burd, F. 1989a. *The saltmarsh survey of Great Britain*. Peterborough, Nature Conservancy Council. (Research & survey in nature conservation, No. 17.)

Burd, F. 1989b. *Saltmarsh survey of Great Britain. Regional Supplement No.9. North Wales*. Peterborough, Nature Conservancy Council.

Burd, F. 1989c. *Saltmarsh survey of Great Britain. Regional Supplement No.10. Dyfed Powys*. Peterborough, Nature Conservancy Council.

Burd, F. 1989d. *Saltmarsh survey of Great Britain. Regional Supplement No.11. South Wales*. Peterborough, Nature Conservancy Council.

Chater, D.H. 1973. Spartina in the Dyfi estuary. *In: A handbook for Ynyslas.*, ed. by E.E. Watkin. Nature Conservancy Council & School for Biological Sciences, Aberystwyth.

Dalby, D.H. 1970. The saltmarshes of Milford Haven, Pembrokeshire. *Field Studies*, 3:297-330.

Institute of Terrestrial Ecology. 1980. *Effects of proposed A55 tunnel works on the growth of* Spartina anglica *in the Conwy estuary*. Contract with R.Travers Morgan & Partners on behalf of Welsh Office. (ITE Project 600 Final Report.)

Jones, A.M. 1990. *An asssessment of changes in the vegetation of the Cefni saltmarsh 1966-90*. Bangor, University College of North Wales.

Kay, Q.O.N., & Rojanavipart, R. 1977. Saltmarsh ecology and trace-metal studies. *In: Problems of a small estuary*, ed. by A.Nelson-Smith & E.M. Bridges, 2:2/1 to 2:2/16. Swansea, Institute of Marine Studies.

Packham, J.R., & Liddle, M.J. 1970. The Cefni saltmarsh, Anglesey, and its recent development. *Field Studies*, 3:331-356.

Pye, K., & French, P.W. 1993. *Erosion and accretion processes on British saltmarshes*. (Contractor: Cambridge Environmental Research Consultants Ltd.) Report to Ministry of Agriculture, Fisheries & Food, London. (Contract No. CSA 1976.)

Rughani, P. 1985. Spartina *control programme for the Mawddach estuary*. Report to the Snowdonia National Park.

Thorburn, I.W., & Rees, E.I.S. 1979. *An ecological survey of the Conwy estuary*. Peterborough, Nature Conservancy Council. (CST Report 233. NCC Contract F3/03/99.)

Wilson, C.M. 1988. *A re-survey of the dieback of the saltmarsh grass* Spartina *in Milford Haven (1983-87)*. Field Studies Council Report FSC/OPRU/1/88.

B. Further reading

Further details of saltmarsh sites may be found in the *Coastal & Marine UKDMAP datasets module,* available from JNCC Coastal Conservation Branch, Peterborough.

Adam, P. 1990. *Saltmarsh ecology.* Cambridge University Press.

Barne, J., Davidson, N.C., Hill, T.O., & Jones, M. 1994. *Coastal and Marine UKDMAP datasets: a user manual.* Peterborough, Joint Nature Conservation Committee.

Ellis, R.G. 1983. *Flowering plants of Wales.* Cardiff, National Museum of Wales.

Rhind, P. In prep. *A conservation review of saltmarsh vegetation surveys in Wales.* Bangor, Countryside Council for Wales.

C. Contact names and addresses

Type of information	Contact address and telephone no.
Reports on the surveys of saltmarshes in the region. Management and site information	*Coastal Ecologist, CCW HQ, Bangor, tel. 01248 370444
Data from the National Saltmarsh Survey; Coastal Resource Database; UKDMA	*Coastal Conservation Branch, JNCC, Peterborough, tel. 01733 62626

* Starred contact addresses are given in full in the Appendix

3.6.6 Acknowledgements

Dr Peter Rhind of CCW kindly provided many references and survey reports.

Chapter 4 Marine and estuarine environments

4.1 Estuaries

Dr N.C. Davidson

4.1.1 Introduction

Estuaries are "partially enclosed tidal areas at least partly composed of soft tidal shores, open to saline water from the sea, and receiving fresh water from rivers, land run-off or seepage" (Davidson *et al.* 1991; Davidson & Buck in prep.). They comprise both aquatic (marine, brackish and fresh water) and terrestrial habitats, including adjacent sand dunes, saltmarshes, coastal grasslands and maritime heaths. All the estuaries discussed here were covered by the NCC Estuaries Review and have at least 2 km of tidal channel or 2 km of shoreline over 0.5 km wide at low tide, either now or historically. This section gives an overview of the main features of the estuarine resource in Region 12; for further details of habitats, species and human uses, refer to the relevant chapter sections.

The region is notable for the number (23 - see Map 4.1.1) and diversity of its estuaries. Most are small (ten being each less than 500 ha in total area) when compared with the generally large estuaries, embayments and firths of north-west England. However, they make an important contribution to the great diversity of size and form that is a key characteristic of UK estuaries. Region 12 estuaries are also important for their largely unspoilt nature (except in the south) and low level of nutrient enrichment. Overall, estuaries in the region form 6.7% by area of the total UK estuarine resource and 14.5% of the resource on the West Coast of Britain. Many are predominantly filled with intertidal sediments and the region holds a relatively large proportion of the country's estuarine intertidal area (8.1% of UK total) (Table 4.1.1). Since many Region 12 estuaries are long and narrow, total lengths of estuarine shoreline and tidal channels contribute around one-quarter of the West Coast total. The almost 39,000 ha of estuarine intertidal and

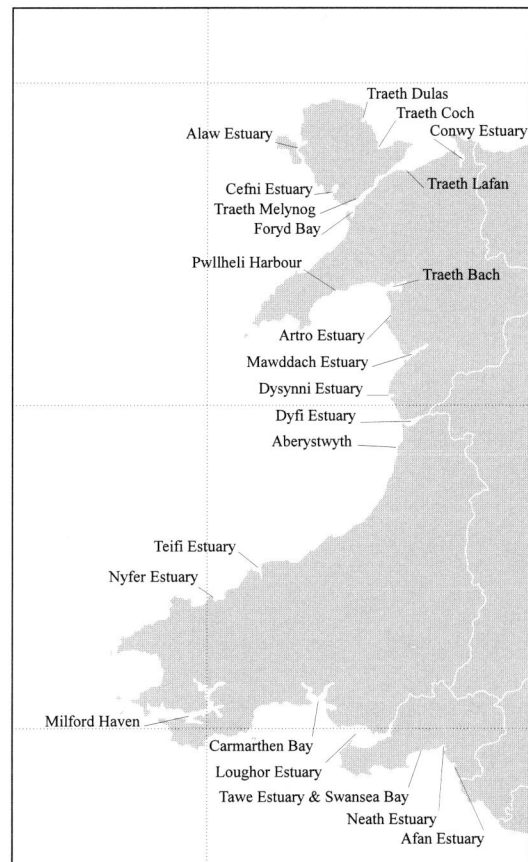

Map 4.1.1 Estuaries. Source: JNCC Coastal Database.

subtidal habitat in the region make up around 2% of the estuarine habitat of north-west Europe (Davidson *et al.* 1991).

Table 4.1.1 The percentage contributions of Region 12 estuaries to the wider resource

| | Total area | | | Intertidal area | | | Saltmarsh area | |
Geographical unit	% West Coast	% GB	% UK	% West Coast	% GB	% UK	% West Coast	% GB
W Glamorgan	4.3	2.2	2.0	4.9	2.6	2.5	11.4	5.7
Dyfed	9.6	4.9	4.4	9.0	4.8	4.6	19.8	9.9
Gwynedd	5.0	2.5	2.3	6.5	3.5	3.3	8.1	4.1
Region 12	*14.5*	*7.4*	*6.7*	*15.6*	*8.4*	*8.1*	*26.1*	*13.0*

Sources: Buck (1993); Davidson & Buck (in press). Note since each estuary is treated as a single site, percentages are given for all estuaries falling wholly or partly in each geographical unit. Where estuaries cross unit boundaries, regional percentages are therefore less than the sum of the county percentages. Areas of saltmarsh were not available for Northern Ireland and so estuarine saltmarsh area comparisons are not made for the UK. A small upper part of the Dyfi Estuary is in Powys.

4.1.2 Important sites, species and features

Within Region 12 much of the resource is in Dyfed, since the three largest estuaries are partly or wholly within the county: almost 60% of total estuary area in the region lies within Dyfed, as does over three-quarters of saltmarsh area. The four estuaries partly or wholly in West Glamorgan form almost 30% of the total regional area, mainly because this includes the large Loughor Estuary, whose major areas of saltmarsh lie on the southern (West Glamorgan) shore. In the north of the region, Gwynedd contains more than half of the region's estuaries, although these small, varied and largely unspoilt estuaries together form only 30-40% of areas and shoreline and channel lengths. Only a small part of the upper reaches of the Dyfi Estuary lies within Powys. Table 4.1.2 gives the total size of estuarine features in the region.

All the region's estuaries are macrotidal (i.e. their spring tidal range exceeds 4 m). Tidal ranges are greatest (over 8 m) in the south of the region and least around Cardigan Bay (4.0-4.5 m). Physical characteristics of each estuary are summarised in Table 4.1.3.

The largest estuaries in the region are in the south: the Loughor Estuary, Carmarthen Bay and Milford Haven are the only estuaries in the region larger than 5,000 ha; together they form almost 60% of the total estuary area in the region. They also contain by far the largest areas of saltmarsh and support nationally and internationally important numbers of wintering waterfowl. Further north are nine bar-built estuaries flowing into Cardigan Bay - predominantly sandy estuaries almost completely draining at low tide and closed by shingle spits and bars derived from offshore glacial deposits. Many of these spits are now capped by sand comprising some of the best examples in Britain of well-

Table 4.1.2 Total size of Region 12 estuaries

Geographical unit	Total area	Intertidal area	Saltmarsh	Shoreline length	Longest channel
	ha	*ha*	*ha*	*km*	*km*
W Glamorgan	11,476	8,398	2,346	139.3	49.8
Dyfed	25,641	15,417	4,085	457.5	131.4
Gwynedd	13,242	11,126	1,677	337.5	125.3
Region 12 total	*38,881*	*26,864*	*5,375*	*797.4*	*256.9*

Note: Since each estuary is treated as a single site, totals are given for all estuaries falling wholly or partly in each geographical unit. Where estuaries cross unit boundaries, regional totals are less than the sum of the county totals. Areas of saltmarsh were not available for Northern Ireland and so estuarine saltmarsh area comparisons are not made for the UK. A small upper part of the Dyfi Estuary is in Powys.

Table 4.1.3 Physical characteristics of Region 12 estuaries

Estuary	Centre grid reference	Geomorphological type	Total area	Inter-tidal area	Salt-marsh	Shore-line length	Main channel length	Spring tidal range	Sub tidal
			ha	*ha*	*ha*	*km*	*km*	*m*	*%*
W Glamorgan									
10. Afan Estuary	SS7588	Bar-built	38	18	0	4.9	2.5	8.6	52.6
11. Neath Estuary	SS7292	Ria	1,129	1,079	159	26.9	10.6	8.6	4.4
12. Tawe & Swansea Bay	SS6694	Embayment	785	748	0	22.8	6.5	8.6	4.7
W Glamorgan/Dyfed									
13. Loughor Estuary	SS4897	Coastal plain	9,524	6,553	2,187	84.7	30.2	7.1	31.2
Dyfed									
14. Carmarthen Bay	SN3408	Embayment	8,295	5,369	910	115.7	30.7	7.5	35.3
15. Milford Haven	SM9403	Ria	5,448	1,710	385	170.7	35.4	6.3	68.6
16. Nyfer Estuary	SN0540	Bar-built	100	75	10	6.1	3.1	4.0	25.0
17. Teifi Estuary	SN1648	Bar-built	302	181	46	21.0	10.0	4.1	40.0
18. Aberystwyth	SN5980	Bar-built	18	5	1	7.1	2.4	4.3	72.2
Dyfed/ Powys/Gwynedd									
19. Dyfi Estuary	SN6495	Bar-built	1,954	1,524	546	52.2	19.6	4.3	22.0
Gwynedd									
20. Dysynni Estuary	SH5802	Bar-built	117	69	22	9.9	4.4	4.3	41.0
21. Mawddach Estuary	SH6416	Bar-built	1,159	976	219	37.7	13.6	4.3	15.8
22. Artro Estuary	SH5725	Bar-built	120	114	10	7.4	1.7	4.4	5.0
23. Traeth Bach	SH5736	Bar-built	2,050	1,750	348	54.0	15.7	4.4	14.6
24. Pwllheli Harbour	SH3835	Bar-built	85	60	3	4.6	2.4	4.5	29.4
25. Foryd Bay	SH4559	Bar-built	343	285	123	9.4	4.5	4.7	16.9
26. Traeth Melynog	SH4364	Bar-built	365	314	66	10.9	5.4	4.7	14.0
27. Cefni Estuary	SH4067	Bar-built	744	614	111	26.1	12.7	4.7	17.5
28. Alaw Estuary	SH3081	Fjard	1,085	721	63	38.2	10.4	5.0	33.5
29. Traeth Dulas	SH4888	Bar-built	103	103	21	5.2	2.9	6.4	0.0
30. Traeth Coch	SH5380	Embayment	583	583	31	10.0	4.4	6.4	0.0
31. Traeth Lafan	SH6375	Linear shore	3,040	2,932	9	16.1	2.9	6.9	3.6
32. Conwy Estuary	SH7976	Coastal plain	1,494	1,081	105	55.8	24.7	7.1	27.6

Sources: Buck (1993); JNCC Integrated Coastal database. Note: Estuary numbers are those used in *An inventory of UK estuaries*. 'Geomorphological type' classifies estuaries into nine categories, described further in Chapter 5.7 of Davidson *et al.* (1991) and Chapter 4.5 of Davidson & Buck (in press). 'Spring tidal ranges' are for the closest station to the mouth of the estuary. Subtidal includes tidal channels remaining water-filled at mean low water.

Table 4.1.4 Human influences and water flows on Region 12 estuaries

Estuary	Centre grid reference	Human use type				Water quality	Catchment area km²	Average freshwater m³s⁻¹
		urban	industrial	rural	recreational			
10. Afan Estuary	SS7588	•	•			A	-	
11. Neath Estuary	SS7292	•	•			B(A)	321	13.4
12. Tawe & Swansea Bay	SS6694	○	•	•		A	246	13.1
13. Loughor Estuary	SS4897	○	○	•	•	A	262	5.6
14. Carmarthen Bay	SN3408			•	•	(B)A	1,849**	50.5**
15. Milford Haven	SM9403	○	•	•	•	A	550	18.5*
16. Nyfer Estuary	SN0540			•	•	A	-	
17. Teifi Estuary	SN1648			•	•	A	1,008	31.4
18. Aberystwyth	SN5980	•			•	A	193	6.5
19. Dyfi Estuary	SN6495			•	•	A	471	58.4
20. Dysynni Estuary	SH5802			•	•	A	75	4.6
21. Mawddach Estuary	SH6416			•	•	A	249	(11.2)
22. Artro Estuary	SH5725			•	•	A	-	-
23. Traeth Bach	SH5736	○		•	•	A(B)	192	(10.0)
24. Pwllheli Harbour	SH3835	•			•	-	-	-
25. Foryd Bay	SH4559			•	○	A	48	2.4
26. Traeth Melynog	SH4364			•	○	-	-	-
27. Cefni Estuary	SH4067			•	•	B(A)	-	-
28. Alaw Estuary	SH3081			•	•	A	-	-
29. Traeth Dulas	SH4888			•	○	-	-	-
30. Traeth Coch	SH5380			•	○	-	-	-
31. Traeth Lafan	SH6375	○		•	•	A	82	(4.1)
32. Conwy Estuary	SH7976	○		•	•	A(B)	345	17.8

Sources: Buck (1993) *An inventory of UK estuaries. Vol. 2. South-west Britain;* National Rivers Authority (1991); Hobbs & Morgan (1992); CCW (1993). Note: 'Human use types' are coded as major (•) or minor (○) use types. Where more than one 'water quality' code is shown, these are in downstream sequence, with brackets indicating a water quality referring in a small part of the estuary. * indicates median flow measure; ** excludes Gwendraeth; bracketed water flow figures are estimates.

developed sand-dune systems, notably at the mouths of the Dyfi Estuary and Traeth Bach, and also bordering Carmarthen Bay further south. In the northern part of the region are the bays and inlets forming parts of the Menai Strait and the largely unspoilt estuaries and bays around the coasts of Anglesey, including the shallow, sheltered glacial basin of the Alaw Estuary/Inland Sea.

There are sand dunes and saltmarshes of national conservation significance on several of the larger estuaries in the region, and some estuaries, notably Milford Haven and those in the Menai Strait, are important for their marine biological interest. Many, especially in south Dyfed and in Gwynedd, are of conservation importance for fish (notably shad and lamprey). A nationally rare plant (Welsh mudwort *Limosella australis*) is known in Britain only from the Dysinni Estuary and Traeth Bach; and three large estuaries in the region support internationally important waterfowl populations. All but one of the region's estuaries are at least in part Sites of Special Scientific Interest (SSSIs) for their geological or wildlife interest; four (Loughor Estuary, Carmarthen Bay, Dyfi Estuary and Lavan Sands) are designated as internationally important for their wetland habitat and the migratory waterfowl they support.

4.1.3 Human activities

Table 4.1.4 summarises the major human influences and water quality for estuaries in the region.

Estuaries in the south of the region have been much modified by past and present industrial use and are bordered at least in part by urban landscapes. In contrast, the estuaries of Dyfed and Gwynedd are predominantly rural and include some of the most unspoilt estuaries in southern Britain, although large parts of some, such as Traeth Bach, the Artro Estuary and Pwllheli Harbour, have been claimed or otherwise modified during the last 200 years. In the north-west of Region 12 the long narrow Conwy estuary has been extensively modified in its lower reaches by recent road tunnel construction. Although low-lying parts of most of the estuaries have sea-defences (usually low sea-walls), the often steeply rising or rocky shores mean than much of the shoreline is natural. Many estuaries in the west and north of the region are used extensively for recreation and there is widespread exploitation of natural resources, for instance through saltmarsh grazing, shellfisheries and bait collection.

Estuaries in this region, particularly those in Cardigan Bay, are generally very shallow and sandy and have low nutrient status, a consequence of their mountainous catchments with low intensity agriculture. The largest catchment areas discharge through Carmarthen Bay, Teifi Estuary and Milford Haven, with the largest freshwater discharges being through Carmarthen Bay, Dyfi Estuary and Teifi Estuary. Estuarine water quality is mostly rated good throughout the region, although the Conwy and some other estuaries (e.g. Traeth Dulas and the Mawddach Estuary) in the northern half of the region have high levels of heavy metals, derived from both natural leachate and former mine workings, in their river inflows.

Historically many of the region's estuaries were important ports, notably during Roman times for the transport of metals, and later for coal in the south and for slate in the north. Now there are important ports in the south, and Milford Haven is a major centre for oil transport and refining.

4.1.4 Information sources used

This chapter is summarised chiefly from JNCC's *An inventory of UK estuaries*, being published in six regional volumes along with an introduction and methods volume. All estuaries in Region 12 are included in *Volume 2. South-west Britain* (Buck 1993). Data presented in the inventory are drawn largely from material collected during 1989-90 (updated to 1993 where appropriate) for the NCC's Estuaries Review (Davidson *et al.* 1991). Saltmarsh data come originally from Burd (1989), whose surveys covered saltmarshes mostly >0.5 ha.

Hydrological data, for example on catchment areas and river flows, for some but not all estuaries as defined here, are available from sources including National Rivers Authority Catchment Management Plans (from early 1995 for the Tawe Estuary, Milford Haven, Menai Strait and Conwy Estuary). For other estuaries, information is readily available for only some parts of the catchment, often those upstream of tidal limits.

4.1.5 Further sources of information

A. References cited

Buck, A.L. 1993. *An inventory of UK estuaries. 2. South-west Britain.* Peterborough, Joint Nature Conservation Committee. (Covers all Region 12 estuaries. Copies of separately-bound individual site dossiers are also available from Coastal Conservation Branch, JNCC.)

Burd, F. 1989. *The saltmarsh survey of Great Britain.* Peterborough, Nature Conservancy Council. (Research & survey in nature conservation, No. 17.)

Countryside Council for Wales. 1993. *A review of Welsh estuaries.* Bangor, Countryside Council for Wales.

Davidson, N.C., Laffoley, D.d'A., Doody, J.P., Way, L.S., Gordon, J., Key, R., Drake, C.M., Pienkowski, M.W., Mitchell, R.M., & Duff, K.L. 1991. *Nature conservation and estuaries in Great Britain.* Peterborough, Nature Conservancy Council.

Davidson, N.C., & Buck, A.L. In prep.. *An inventory of UK estuaries. 1. Introduction and methods.* Peterborough, Joint Nature Conservation Committee.

Hobbs, G., & Morgan, C.I., eds. 1992. *A review of the environmental knowledge of the Milford Haven waterway.* Pembroke, Field Studies Council Research Centre.

National Rivers Authority. 1991. *The quality of rivers, canals and estuaries in England and Wales.* Bristol, National Rivers Authority. (Water Quality series, No. 4.)

B. Further reading

Further details of estuaries are in the *Coastal & Marine UKDMAP datasets* module (Barne *et al* 1994), available from JNCC Coastal Conservation Branch, Peterborough. A list of selected further reading for each estuary discussed in section 4.1 is given in Buck (1993) (above).

Barne, J., Davidson, N.C., Hill, T.O., & Jones, M. 1994. *Coastal and Marine UKDMAP datasets: a user manual.* Peterborough, Joint Nature Conservation Committee.

Davidson, N.C. 1991. *Estuaries, wildlife and man.* Peterborough, Nature Conservancy Council.

Davidson, N.C., & Buck, A.L. In prep. *An inventory of UK estuaries. 1. Introduction and methods.* Peterborough, Joint Nature Conservation Committee.

Noble, L., *ed.* 1993. *Estuaries and coastal waters of the British Isles. An annual bibliography of recent scientific papers. Number 17.* Plymouth, Plymouth Marine Laboratory and Marine Biological Association.

Peck, K. 1993. Estuaries Inventory - research towards a better understanding of the interactions between birds and human activities on UK estuaries. *RSPB Conservation Review 7*, 42-46.

Young, G.A. Undated. *The Menai Strait: a review and bibliography of literature from the Wolfson Library.* Unpublished report to CCW.

Marsh, T.J., & Lees, M.L., eds. 1993. *Hydrometric register and statistics 1986-90.* Wallingford, Institute of Hydrology.

C. Contact names and addresses

Type of information	Contact address and telephone no.
National database of estuaries;coastal habitats; statutory & non-statutory protected sites.	*Coastal Conservation Branch, JNCC, Peterborough, tel. 01733 62626
Statutory protected sites; detailed wildlife site information; coastal geomorphology. Numerical and some digitised data.	*Coastal & Marine Ecologists/ Coastal Scientist/Marine & Coastal Policy Officer, CCW HQ, Bangor, tel. 01248 370444
RSPB Estuaries Inventory: mapped and numerical information on land use and selected human activities for 57 major UK estuaries, including Loughor Estuary and Milford Haven in Region 12.	*Estuaries Inventory Project Officer, RSPB, Sandy, tel. 01767 680551
National River Flow Archive: catchments and river flows from upstream gauging stations; interpreted analyses for whole estuaries.	National Water Archive Manager, Institute of Hydrology, Maclean Building, Crowmarsh Gifford, Wallingford, Oxfordshire OX10 8BB, tel. 01491 838800

* Starred contact addresses are given in full in the Appendix

4.1.6 Acknowledgements

Thanks to John Barne for help in preparing data used in this chapter and to Dr Rod Jones (CCW) and Steve May (Dyfed County Council) for helpful comments.

4.2 The sea bed

R.A. Irving

4.2.1 Introduction

This section covers the occurrence and distribution of rare groups of species (communities) that live on the sea bed; the distribution and occurrence of indivually rare and scarce species in covered in section 5.4.

There are a large number of areas within this region that are of considerable conservation importance because of their marine biological interest, especially the Pembrokeshire coast, which has a particularly high density of such sites. Information on the precise extent of shore and sea bed types in a GB context is not yet available. However, the whole of the Milford Haven and Daugleddau estuary system is of national nature conservation importance as one of the best examples of a ria system (a flooded valley) in Britain, presenting a wide variety of habitats and communities (Davies 1991). The waters and intertidal areas of Skomer and the adjacent Marloes peninsula became Wales's first (and Britain's second) statutory Marine Nature Reserve in 1990. The Menai Strait and its adjacent areas have been put forward as a possible future Marine Nature Reserve, as has Ynys Enlli with part of the Llyn Peninsula. The Menai Strait and Bardsey Sound experience some of the strongest tidal streams in the Irish Sea, and the Menai Strait also provides extreme shelter from wave action. There are a number of biogeographic boundaries present within the region, at Swansea Bay (Hiscock 1979), St David's Head (Davies 1991), the Llyn Peninsula, and Carmel Head on Anglesey (Crisp & Knight Jones 1955).

A wide variety of both littoral (shoreline) and sublittoral habitats and their associated communities is represented. Shores range from exposed vertical rocky cliffs and boulder beaches to open sandy bays and sheltered muddy estuaries. Near-shore sublittoral habitats are also rich and varied. Sheltered areas of sand and mud are found within the region's estuaries and those bays not facing south-west. Coarser sediments, ranging from clean sand to pebbles and cobbles, occur off exposed bays and in tidal channels. In general, sheltered sites have greater conservation interest, as on exposed sites wave action increases the mobility of sediment, leading to reduced species richness and lower biomass in the communities present. Rocky substrates in the region are affected by a wide range of physical conditions including varying exposure to waves and tidal currents. A number of wrecks (ships, aircraft and other solid material) occur off the region's coast. They offer hard substrate in areas that may otherwise be largely sedimentary, providing habitats for opportunistic colonising species that otherwise would not be present.

4.2.2 Important locations and communities

Swansea Bay and Carmarthen Bays (including the Gower peninsula)

An extensive area of muddy sand borders much of Swansea Bay, with clean sand on the more exposed beaches of Margam Sands, Oxwich Bay and Rhossili Bay. The Gower peninsula exhibits some of the best moderately-exposed limestone shores in Britain, the whole of the peninsula being described by Powell *et al.* (1979) as of prime marine biological importance. The whole of the Burry Inlet is of regional conservation importance for its intertidal sediment communities and the tide-swept boulder and mussel scar communities at Whiteford Scar, which include rich algal communities (Moore 1989). Whiteford Sands were considered by Bishop & Holme (1980) to be of prime marine biological importance for their well-developed *Tellina* (a burrowing bivalve) community.

In the near-shore sublittoral, particularly rich animal communities have been recorded growing on vertical and overhanging surfaces of rock around the Gower peninsula (Hiscock 1979). The high turbidity of the water here restricts the depth to which algae can grow to no more than 3 m below chart datum.

Table 4.2.1 Locations (1 kilometre squares) of sites of importance mentioned in the text

Site no.	Name	Grid ref.
1	Margam Sands	SS7785
2	Oxwich Bay	SS5187
3	Rhossili Bay	SS4190
4	Whiteford Sands	SS4395
5	Whiteford Scar	SS4497
6	Caldey Island	SS1297
7	Greenala Point	SS0096
8	Stackpole Head	SR9994
9	Castlemartin peninsula	SR8899
10	West Angle Bay	SM8503
11	Angle Bay	SM8802
12	Pennar Gut / Pennar Mouth	SM9403
13	Pembroke River	SM9502
14	Lawrenny	SN0107
15	Stack Rock	SM8704
16	Dale / Gann Flats	SM8106
17	Marloes peninsula	SM70
18	Skokholm	SM7305
19	Broad Sound	SM7307
20	Skomer Island	SM7209
21	Grassholm	SM5909
22	St David's peninsula	SM72
23	Ramsey Sound	SM7124
24	Abereiddy Quarry	SM7931
25	Sarn Badrig	SH4720
26	Criccieth	SH5038
27	St Tudwall's Island	SH3426
28	Pen-y-Cil	SH1524
29	Ynys Enlli	SH2212
30	Bardsey Sound	SH2413
31	Porth Dinllaen	SH2741
32	Menai Strait	SH57
33	'Inland Sea', Anglesey	SH2779
34	Penrhyn Bay	SH8381

The Pembrokeshire coast: Tenby to Cardigan

A wide range of shore types is present along this dramatic stretch of coast, from exposed bedrock on headlands to sheltered sandy coves, and sheltered mud in the estuaries (e.g. the Pembroke River). On the north-west tip of Caldey Island rich shore communities were recorded by Warren & George (1988, in Davies (1991)). At the base of the exposed limestone cliffs of the Castlemartin peninsula are some of the finest examples of rocky shore communities in Wales (Powell *et al.* 1979).

At the mouth of Milford Haven, the shore platforms at West Angle Bay are of considerable importance, particularly for the algal communities within rockpools (Powell *et al.* 1979). Within the Haven, several sediment areas are of merit: Angle Bay has particularly rich infaunal communities (Powell *et al.* 1979); the embayment of the Pembroke River was considered by Rostron *et al.* (1986) to exhibit high species diversity, compared with other estuarine areas in the British Isles; sediment shores at Lawrenny had a rich polychaete community (Powell *et al.* 1979); and the 'Arenicola' and 'Pullastra' communities present at Dale/Gann Flats were considered by Bishop & Holme (1980) to be of prime marine biological importance. At Pennar Gut/Pennar Mouth, Little & Hiscock (1987) considered the sheltered bedrock and stable boulders to be regionally important, owing to their rich biota and some rarely encountered species. Beds of seagrass *Zostera* spp., providing a rarely encountered shallow-water habitat, are present in Angle Bay and in the embayment of the Pembroke River. The larger seagrass *Zostera marina* is present on shallow sublittoral sand/mud near Stack Rock, Milford Haven (Little & Hiscock 1987), with extensive beds occurring close by between the Esso and Amoco jetties. Important maerl beds (an unusual calcareous alga) have also been recorded near Stack Rock (Little & Hiscock 1987), and although scattered and broken, their algal communities were regarded as even richer than those found in the Fal estuary in Cornwall.

Outside Milford Haven, to the west, the rocky shores of the Marloes peninsula (and those of the St David's peninsula at the northern end of St Bride's Bay) are considered to be of primary marine biological importance (Powell *et al.* 1979). Skomer Island's rocky shores provide a wide variety of habitats and communities, as well as providing classic examples of extremely exposed shores (Bunker *et al.* 1983). A small bed of the seagrass *Zostera marina* occurs in North Haven. Well-developed rockpool communities have been identified at West Tump on Grassholm (Powell *et al.* 1979); and both Grassholm and Skokholm also exhibit good examples of very exposed rocky shores.

The near-shore sublittoral habitats and communities along much of the Pembrokeshire coast are also rich and varied. The communities present on limestone and sandstone bedrock from Greenala Point to Stackpole Head were considered by Hiscock (1981) to be of "outstanding scientific interest". Of special note here are the communities found on, and boring into, limestone. There are also rich sediment communities in this area, with dense populations of the heart urchin *Echinocardium cordatum* and razor-clams *Ensis* spp. (Davies 1991). In Milford Haven, the wave-sheltered bedrock and boulder habitats exposed to moderate tidal streams are considered to be of national conservation importance because of their highly distinctive 'ria' communities (Little & Hiscock 1987). Here there are few interesting algal communities

because of the shallowness of the water, but animal communities include large numbers of a small range of species characteristic of ria communities. Communities present in the Daugleddau are the best-developed and most extensive examples of their type known in south-west Britain (Davies 1991). The sublittoral sediment communities throughout Milford Haven have a strong southern influence, with many species reaching their northern distributional limit within the region (Rostron *et al.* 1983). The cobble and pebble habitat present off Lawrenny in the Daugleddau is of regional conservation importance (Little & Hiscock 1987).

Pembrokeshire's islands are also of considerable marine biological interest. Skomer Island exhibits an outstanding range of sublittoral habitats in a small area. The undisturbed bedrock and large boulders are of national marine nature conservation importance, and the communities on disturbed bedrock and boulders; medium and small boulders; stones and pebbles; and wrecks are regionally important (Bunker & Hiscock 1987). The circalittoral animal communities (especially of sponges) subject to tidal water movement within Broad Sound are particularly interesting. The sheltered sediments found at Skomer are of regional conservation importance (Bunker & Hiscock 1987). Though a similar range of habitats and communities exists at Grassholm and at Skokholm, the diversity is not as high as at the adjacent island of Skomer (Hiscock 1980, 1981). Ramsey Sound is an area of "outstanding scientific interest" (Hiscock 1981), the very strong tidal streams in the centre of the Sound giving rise to a distinctive community not encountered elsewhere in south-west Britain. The communities of southern St Bride's Bay are unusual for the large number of echinoderm species encountered (Hiscock 1980). Abereiddy Quarry is a disused slate quarry flooded with sea water, giving rise to an unusual sheltered habitat, thought to be unique in south-west Britain.

Cardigan Bay: Cardigan to Abersoch

The shores of Cardigan Bay range from rock, boulders and shingle (mostly found in the south), backed by low cliffs, to extensive sandy beaches (predominating in the north). Descriptions of littoral communities are extremely limited, though some sites in the south of the Bay were surveyed by Powell *et al.* (1979). At a number of locations, for example at Criccieth, patch reefs of the polychaete *Sabellaria alveolata* occur. The sandy estuarine sediments support few invertebrate species, in relatively now numbers.

In the near-shore sublittoral, shallow boulder reefs (known as 'sarnau') provide outcrops of hard substrata within the bay. These are subject to considerable wave exposure and strong tidal streams. In particular, Sarn Badrig, also known as St Patrick's Causeway, is a very impressive topographical feature (Hiscock 1986). Rising from a depth of 10 m, the jumble of boulders, cobbles and pebbles breaks the surface at low water at intervals along its length, up to 17 km offshore. Elsewhere, the sea bed is largely sandy sediment: there are extensive sand banks in the outer bay aligned in the direction of tidal streams. The marine fauna and flora of the bay is comparatively poorly-known.

The Llyn Peninsula, Anglesey and the Menai Strait

This stretch of coast again has a varied range of habitats, with rocky shores interspersed with small sandy bays and muddy inlets. The habitats present in a cave on St Tudwall's Island are of high conservation interest (Rostron 1984), as are those in a subtidal tunnel at Pen-y-Cil, opposite Ynys Enlli (Hiscock 1984). The wide variety of littoral communities present at Ynys Enlli are of conservation importance (Rostron 1984), and include good examples of exposed rocky shore communities and several rare algal species (see section 5.4). The tide-swept circalittoral communities on bedrock, boulders, cobbles and pebbles in Bardsey Sound are of considerable conservation importance (Hiscock 1984), as this habitat type is uncommon in southern Britain.

Extensive *Zostera marina* seagrass beds occur in the sheltered bay of Porth Dinllaen on the north of the Llyn coast, considerably larger than those found within the 'Inland Sea' on the west coast of Anglesey (I. Rees, pers. comm). The Inland Sea, a shallow partially enclosed sea area studied by Jones (1978, in Davies (1991)), has only a limited water exchange with the open sea, giving rise to an unusual tidal regime and consequent peculiarities in the zonation patterns of its biota. Hiscock (1976) described the fauna from 32 rocky sublittoral sites around Anglesey, identifying characteristic communities from the west, north and east coasts and the Menai Strait. West coast communities were typified by dense bryozoan cover with polyclinid tunicates, the hydroid *Nemertesia antennina* and the feather star *Antedon bifida*. Also present were the soft coral *Alcyonium digitatum*, the massive form of the sponge *Cliona celata* and the anemone *Actinothoe sphyrodeta*. On the north coast *Antedon bifida* and the brittlestar *Ophiothrix fragilis* were present in dense beds, with the sponges *Polymastia* spp. and *Suberites carnosus*. On the east coast, *Alcyonium digitatum* and the anemone *Metridium senile* dominated. The distribution of species was found to be related primarily to water quality and geographical location around Anglesey, and secondly to the degree of exposure to wave action and the strength of tidal streams.

The Menai Strait has been put forward by the Nature Conservancy Council (1988) and CCW (1992) as a Marine Nature Reserve. The shallow tide-swept communities present here (determined largely by the strength of the current they can tolerate) are of national marine nature conservation importance, owing in part to the wide range of habitats and species present. A summary of the biological interest of the Strait's littoral zone is provided by Jones (1983), and of the sublittoral zone by Lumb (1983). The Lafan Sands are extensive sediment flats at the northern entrance to the Menai Strait, whose invertebrate macrofauna was described by Eagle *et al.* (1974, in Davies (1991)). Beyond the peninsula of the Great Orme, a small area of peat beds (a rare intertidal habitat) is present at Penrhyn Bay, near Little Orme's Head.

Offshore

The offshore zone is taken to mean areas either more than 3 km offshore or greater than 50 m in depth. Far less recent information is available on benthic habitats and communities from offshore locations. The early pioneering work of Laurie & Watkin (1922) provided valuable records of Cardigan Bay's benthic fauna. More recently, the full results from benthic surveys of the southern Irish Sea by the National Museum of Wales were published in October 1994, following information published by Mackie (1990). Survey details for Caernarfon and Cardigan Bays can be found in Huckbody *et al.* (1992), where four communities are distinguished: the 'shallow Venus community' typical of clean, mobile sands, the 'deep Venus community' in deeper areas with muddier but coarser sands,

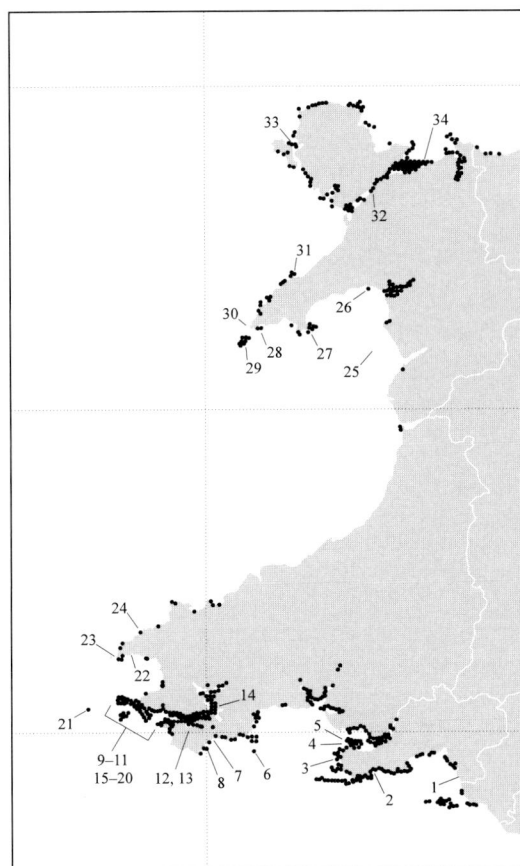

Map 4.2.1 Littoral surveys recorded on the MNCR database (source: JNCC) and key locations of marine biological importance described in the text.

and the 'Amphiura' and 'Abra' communities typical of more sheltered areas in Cardigan Bay. The paucity of information to the north and west of Anglesey is largely due to the hardness of the substrata, which cannot be sampled effectively using grabs.

An area approximately 10 km north of the tip of the Llyn Peninsula was surveyed in late 1992, as part of an environmental assessment study prior to proposed exploratory oil drilling; it found a substratum of tide-swept cobbles and pebbles embedded in a sediment matrix (Rees 1992).

4.2.3 Human activities

The human activities that affect sea-bed habitats and communities in the region are described in Sections 9.1 and 9.2.

4.2.4 Information sources used

JNCC's Marine Nature Conservation Review (MNCR) uses a standard recording methodology for littoral and sublittoral surveys, which describe both habitats and their associated communities (Hiscock 1990). Survey information from other sources may vary considerably in its methodology and coverage. Two major NCC resource surveys include coverage of this region: the South-west Britain sublittoral survey

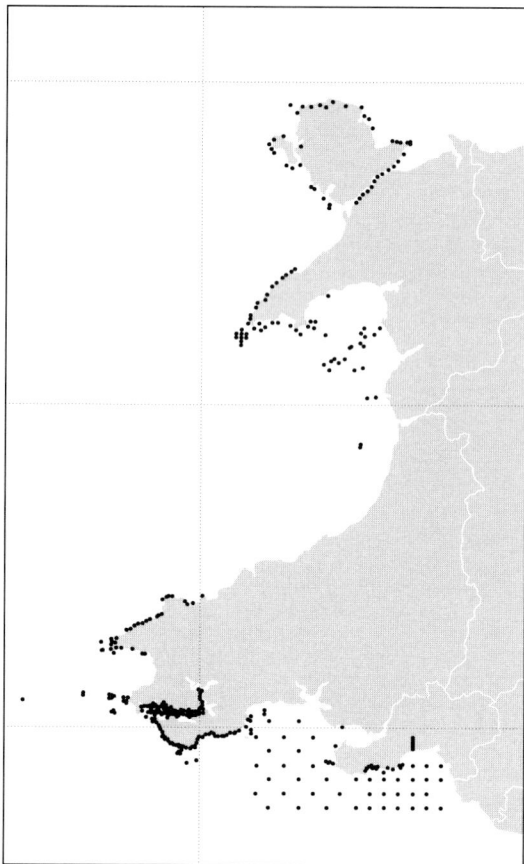

Map 4.2.2 Near-shore sublittoral surveys recorded on the MNCR database. Source: JNCC.

(1978-81); and the *Survey of harbours, rias and estuaries in southern Britain* (1985-89). The Smalls, a group of isolated rocky islets situated 25 km west of Skomer, were investigated by an MNCR diving team in August 1994. The MNCR will survey Cardigan Bay during 1995/96. Table 4.2.2 shows the number of sites with marine benthic (sea-bed) habitat and species information held on the MNCR database. Maps 4.2.1 and 4.2.2 show the locations of surveys recorded on the database. Note, however, that this information is not yet fully comprehensive. Records additional to those cited here may exist in sources that have yet to be consulted.

Anglesey's rocky shores are described in Lewis (1953) and

Table 4.2.2 Number of sites with marine benthic habitat and species information held on the MNCR database

Littoral	*Near-shore sublittoral*	*Offshore*	*Total*
237	314	0	551

its general marine biology in Jones (1990). The Marine Laboratories at Menai Bridge have been involved with many studies of the island's shores over the years (see section 4.2.5). By contrast, sublittoral areas are poorly recorded. A study of a population of the sea pen *Virgularia mirabilis* in Holyhead Harbour (SH2484) was reported by Hoare & Wilson (1977).

The Countryside Council for Wales (CCW) is currently undertaking an initial survey of littoral habitats of the whole Welsh coast. The sublittoral habitats and communities of Cardigan Bay are currently being investigated by sports divers as part of the Marine Conservation Society's 'Seasearch'

project. Additional information on biotope mapping (in central Cardigan Bay, on the north side of the Llyn Peninsula and the central Menai Strait) is being gathered by the BioMar project (see section 4.2.5). Other sources of information include Admiralty charts and British Geological Survey maps.

4.2.5 Further sources of information

A. References cited

Bishop, G.M., & Holme, N.A. 1980. Survey of the littoral zone of the coast of Great Britain. Final Report - part 1: The sediment shores - an assessment of their conservation value. (Contractor: Marine Biological Association/Scottish Marine biological Association, Plymouth.) *Nature Conservancy Council, CSD Report*, No. 326.

Bunker, F.St.P.D., & Hiscock, S. 1987. Sublittoral habitats, communities and species of the Skomer marine reserve - a review. (Contractor: Field Studies Council, Pembroke.) *Nature Conservancy Council, CSD Report*, No. 747. FSC Report, No. OFC/1/87.

Bunker, F.St.P.D., Iball, K., & Crump, R. 1983. Skomer Marine Reserve. Littoral survey. (Contractor: Field Studies Council Oil Pollution Research Unit, Pembroke.) *Nature Conservancy Council, CSD Report*, No. 901.

Countryside Council for Wales. 1992. *Menai Strait proposed Marine Nature Reserve.* Revised Consultative document. Bangor, CCW.

Crisp, D.J., & Knight Jones, E.W. 1955. Discontinuities in the distribution of shore animals in north Wales. *Report of Bardsey Bird and Field Observatory*, 2: 29-34.

Davies, J. 1991. *Benthic marine ecosystems of Great Britain: a review of current knowledge. Bristol Channel and approaches (MNCR Sector 9).* Peterborough, Joint Nature Conservation Committee, Marine Nature Conservation Review Report.

Hiscock, K. 1976. *The influence of water movements on the ecology of sublittoral rocky areas.* PhD thesis, University College of North Wales, Bangor.

Hiscock, K. 1979. South-west Britain sublittoral survey. Field surveys of sublittoral habitats and species along the Gower coast. June 25th to 30th, 1978. (Contractor: Field Studies Council Oil Pollution Research Unit, Pembroke.) *Nature Conservancy Council, CSD Report*, No. 274.

Hiscock, K. 1980. South-west Britain sublittoral survey. Field surveys of sublittoral habitats and species in west Pembrokeshire (Grassholm, Skomer and Marloes Peninsula). (Contractor: Field Studies Council Oil Pollution Research Unit, Pembroke.) *Nature Conservancy Council, CSD Report*, No. 301.

Hiscock, K. 1981. South-west Britain sublittoral survey. Final Report. (Contractor: Field Studies Council Oil Pollution Research Unit, Pembroke.) *Nature Conservancy Council, CSD Report*, No. 327.

Hiscock, K. 1984. Sublittoral survey of Bardsey and the Lleyn peninsula. 13-27 August, 1983. (Contractor: Field Studies Council Oil Pollution Research Unit, Pembroke.) *Nature Conservancy Council, CSD Report*, No. 612.

Hiscock, K. 1990. Marine Nature Conservation Review: Methods. *Nature Conservancy Council, CSD Report*, No. 1072. (Marine Nature Conservation Review Report, No. MNCR/OR/5.)

Hiscock, S. 1986. Sublittoral survey of the mid-Wales sarns (reefs): Sarn Badrig, Sarn-y-bwch and Cynfelin patches. July 2nd-9th 1986. *Nature Conservancy Council, CSD Report*, No. 696.

Hoare, R., & Wilson, E.H. 1977. Observations on the behaviour and distribution of *Virgularia mirabilis* O.F. Müller (Coelenterata: Pennatulaceae) in Holyhead harbour, Anglesey. *In: Biology of benthic organisms. 11th European Symposium on Marine Biology, Galway, October 1976*, ed. by B.F. Keegan, P.O. Céidigh and P.J.S. Boaden, 329-337. Oxford, Pergamon Press.

Huckbody, A.J, Taylor, P.M., Hobbs, G., & Elliott, R. 1992. *Caernarfon and Cardigan Bays - an environmental appraisal.* Aberdeen, Hamilton Oil Company Ltd.

Jones, W.E. 1983. Littoral hard substrata of the Menai Strait. (Contractor: University College of North Wales, Marine Science Laboratories, Menai Bridge.) *Nature Conservancy Council, CSD Report,* No. 486.

Jones, W.E. 1990. The marine biology of Anglesey. *In: A new natural history of Anglesey,* ed. by W.E. Jones, 109-133. Llangefni, Anglesey Antiquarian Society and Field Club. (Studies in Anglesey History, No. 8.)

Laurie, R.D., & Watkin, E.E. 1922. Investigations into the fauna of the sea floor of Cardigan Bay. A preliminary account of working the northern portion of a region between Aberystwyth and Newquay known as 'The Gutter'. *Aberystwyth Studies, 5:* 229-249.

Lewis, J.R. 1953. The ecology of rocky shores around Anglesey. *Proceedings of the Zoological Society of London, 123:* 481-549.

Little , A., & Hiscock, K. 1987. Survey of harbours, rias and estuaries in southern Britain: Milford Haven and the estuary of the rivers Cleddau. (Contractor: Field Studies Council, Oil Pollution Research Unit, Pembroke.) *Nature Conservancy Council, CSD Report,* No. 1002.

Lumb, C.M. 1983. Menai Strait sublittoral survey. (Contractor: University College of North Wales, Marine Science Laboratories, Menai Bridge.) *Nature Conservancy Council, CSD Report,* No. 467.

Mackie, A.S.Y. 1990. Offshore benthic communities of the Irish Sea. *In: The Irish Sea: an environmental review. Part 1: nature conservation,* ed. by Irish Sea Study Group, 169-218. Liverpool, Liverpool University Press for Irish Sea Study Group.

Mills, D.J.L. In prep. *Benthic Marine Ecosystems in Great Britain: a review of current knowledge. Cardigan Bay and north Wales (MNCR Sector 10).* Peterborough, Joint Nature Conservation Committee. (Marine Nature Conservation Review Report.)

Moore, J. 1989. Surveys of harbours, rias and estuaries in southern Britain: Loughor estuary incorporating the Burry Inlet. (Contractor: Field Studies Council Oil Pollution Research Unit, Pembroke.) *Nature Conservancy Council, CSD Report,* No. 1004.

Nature Conservancy Council. 1988. *Menai Strait proposed Marine Nature Reserve. Consultative document.* Peterborough, Nature Conservancy Council.

Powell, H.T., Holme, N.A., Knight, S.J.T., Harvey, R., Bishop, G., & Bartrop, J. 1979. Survey of the littoral zone of the coast of Great Britain. 4. Report on the shores of south west Wales. (Contractor: Scottish Marine Biological Association/Marine Biological Association Intertidal Survey Unit.) *Nature Conservancy Council, CSD Report,* No. 269.

Rees, E.I.S. 1992. *Environmental study of a proposed exploratory drilling location north of Bardsey Island: benthic habitats.* (Contractor: University College of North Wales, Unit for Coastal and Estuarine Studies, Menai Bridge.) Unpublished report to Hamilton Oil Company Ltd. (UCES Report, No. U92-6.)

Rostron, D. 1984. Littoral survey of Bardsey and the Lleyn Peninsula. 8-13 August 1983. (Contractor: Field Studies Council, Oil Pollution Research Unit, Pembroke.) *Nature Conservancy Council, CSD Report,* No. 540.

Rostron, D.M., Staggs, M., & Evans, L.J. 1983. *Biological survey of sediments within Milford Haven estuary. April 1982.* (Contractor: Field Studies Council Oil Pollution Research Unit, Pembroke.) Oil Companies Panel of the Institute of Petroleum.

Rostron, D.M., Little, D. I., & Howells, S.E. 1986. A study of the sediments and communities in Milford Haven, Wales. *Oil and Chemical Pollution, 3:* 131-166.

B. Further reading

Further details of marine survey sites are in the *Coastal & Marine UKDMAP datasets* module (Barne *et al.* 1994), available from JNCC Coastal Conservation Branch, Peterborough.

Barne, J., Davidson, N.C., Hill, T.O., & Jones, M. 1994. *Coastal and Marine UKDMAP datasets: a user manual.* Peterborough, Joint Nature Conservation Committee.

Bunker, F.St.P.D., Picton, B.E., & Morrow, C.M. 1992. *New information on species and habitats in the Skomer Marine Nature Reserve (and other sites off the Pembrokeshire coast).* Bangor, Countryside Council for Wales.

Conneely, M.E. 1988. *Swansea Bay benthic studies. Final Report.* Unpublished, Welsh Water Authority, Directorate of Scientific Services, Tidal Waters Unit. (Tidal Waters Report.)

Countryside Council for Wales (CCW). 1993. *Welsh estuaries review.* Bangor, Countryside Council for Wales. (Science Report.)

Davies, J. In prep. *Benthic marine ecosystems of Great Britain: a review of current knowledge. Bristol Channel and approaches (MNCR Sector 9).* Peterborough, Joint Nature Conservation Committee, Marine Nature Conservation Review Report.

Evans, R.G. 1947. The intertidal ecology of Cardigan Bay. *Journal of Ecology, 34:* 273-309.

Gilkes, L. 1994. A preliminary bibliography to the water and coast around Bardsey Island and the south-western Lleyn Peninsula.

Gubbay, S. 1988. *Coastal directory for marine nature conservation.* Ross-on-Wye, Marine Conservation Society.

Hobbs, G., & Morgan, C.I. 1992. *A review of the current state of environmental knowledge of the Milford Haven waterway.* (Contractor: Field Studies Council Research Centre, Pembroke.) Unpublished report to Milford Haven Environmental Monitoring Steering Group. (FSC Research Centre Report, No. FSC/RC/5/92.)

Mills, D.J.L., Hill, T.O., Thorpe, K., & Connor, D.W., eds. 1993. Atlas of marine biological surveys in Britain. *JNCC Report,* No. 167. (Marine Nature Conservation Review Report MNCR/OR/17.)

Moore, J. In prep. *Surveys of harbours, rias and estuaries in southern Britain. Final report and assessment of marine biological interest and nature conservation importance.* Peterborough, Joint Nature Conservation Committee. (Marine Nature Conservation Review Report.)

Nelson-Smith, A. 1974. The ecology of rocky shores around Swansea Bay. *In: Report on the working party on possible pollution in Swansea Bay.* Technical Report, No. 2, 55-70. Cardiff, Welsh Office.

Warwick, R.M., & Davies, J.R. 1977. The distribution of sublittoral macrofauna communities in the Bristol Channel in relation to the substrate. *Estuarine and Coastal Marine Science, 5:* 267-288.

Wood, E., *ed.* 1988. *Sea life of Britain and Ireland.* London, Immel. (Marine Conservation Society.)

Young, G.A. 1992. *The Menai Strait. A review and bibliography of literature from the Wolfston Library.* University College of North Wales (Bangor). Unpublished report to Countryside Council for Wales.

C. Contact names and addresses

Type of information	Contact address and telephone no.
Marine nature conservation Bangor, issues in Wales; mapping of littoral habitats	*Marine Ecologist, CCW HQ, tel. 01248 370444
Offshore survey information, southern Irish Sea	Andy Mackie, Department of Zoology, National Museum of Wales, Cathays Park, Cardiff CF1 3NP, tel. 01222 397951
Littoral & sublittoral studies in Swansea Bay, the Gower peninsula and environs	Dr Peter Dyrynda, School of Biological Sciences, University College of Wales, Singleton Park, Swansea SA2 8PP, tel. 01792 295456
Littoral & sublittoral studies, partic. in south-west Wales	Jon Moore, Field Studies Council Research Centre, Fort Popton, Angle, Pembroke, Dyfed SA71 5AD, tel. 01646 641404
Skomer MNR	*MNR Warden, CCW Skomer, tel. 01646 636736
General information on activities occurring within Cardigan Bay	*Projects Officer, Cardigan Bay Forum, Aberystwyth, tel. 01970 624471 x147
Various littoral studies (particularly of autecology) in Cardigan Bay, as listed in Mills (in prep.)	Dr John Fish, Institute of Biological Sciences, University College of Wales, Edward Llwyd Building, Aberystwyth, Dyfed SY23 3DA, tel. 01970 622321
MCS/JNCC Seasearch project: diving survey in Cardigan Bay	Francis Bunker, project co-ordinator, Marine Seen, Estuary Cottage, Bentlass, Hundleton, Dyfed SA71 5RN, tel. 01646 621277
Mapping of sublittoral benthic habitats (BioMar project)	Dr Bob Foster-Smith, project co-ordinator (Newcastle), Dove Marine Laboratory, Cullercoats, Tyne & Wear NE30 4PZ, tel. 0191 252 4850
Proposals for MNRs at Ynys Enlli (Bardsey) and Menai Strait	*Marine Conservation Officer, CCW North Wales Region, tel. 01248 372333
Littoral & sublittoral studies in the Menai Strait, Llyn peninsula and Anglesey. Also offshore information.	Ivor Rees, Senior Lecturer, School of Ocean Sciences, University of Wales (Bangor), Menai Bridge, Gwynedd LL59 5EY, tel. 01248 351151

* Starred contact addresses are given in full in the Appendix

4.2.6 Acknowledgements

The author acknowledges the considerable help of JNCC's Marine Nature Conservation Review team (particularly Dr Tim Hill) in compiling and presenting the information given here.

4.3 Plankton

Dr J.M.Colebrook and A.W.G. John

4.3.1 Introduction

Plankton include the bacteria (bacterio-), plant (phyto-) and animal (zoo-) plankton. This section discusses only the phyto- and zooplankton of the region. In temperate continental shelf seas, such as those in this region, the phytoplankton assemblage is dominated by diatoms and dinoflagellates, and the zooplankton, although containing representatives of most animal phyla at some stage, is dominated by crustaceans, principally copepods. The plankton's abundance is strongly influenced by factors such as depth, tidal mixing and temperature stratification, which determine the vertical stability of the water column. The distribution of species, here and elsewhere, is influenced directly by salinity and temperature (see section 2.3), by water flows into the area (see section 2.3) and by the presence of local benthic (bottom-dwelling) and littoral (shoreline) communities (see section 4.2 and Chapter 3). Many of the species of these communities, including commercially important fish and shellfish, have temporary planktonic larval forms (meroplankton). Tidal fronts (boundary zones between stratified and well-mixed water masses) in the region are likely to be of significant biological importance, since they are usually rich in plankton, which attracts other marine life. Phytoplankton blooms (transient, unsustainable growths, usually of single species and often associated with a visible discolouration of the water) are a normal feature in the seasonal development of plankton. Some blooms may reach exceptional proportions ($>10^6$ cells/l) or contain species (principally dinoflagellates) that could be toxic to humans and possibly have an important economic impact on mariculture, fisheries and tourism. There have been various such "red tide" events off West Wales, including one in St Bride's Bay in August 1994.

In Region 12, as elsewhere, the plankton has a fundamental role in the food chain of both benthic and pelagic (upper layers of open sea) wildlife. For both, the availability of food and nutrients, larval survival, maintaining populations and timing of egg production are highly dependent on the amount of phyto/zooplankton available. Any environmental stress on the plankton will have consequences throughout the food chain and may affect the amount of food available to fish, birds, marine mammals etc. In coastal management, plankton can also give early warning of adverse human impacts (e.g. the effects of eutrophication) and highlight different water masses.

Estimates of amounts of plankton produced in the Irish Sea are summarised in Savidge & Kain (1990); the values are very variable and none of the stations is actually in the region, but, by inference, values of 50-80 mg C m^{-2} day^{-1} in April rising to between 100-400 mg C m^{-2} day^{-1} in May and June might be anticipated. The overall production of phytoplankton in the region is determined less by the levels of production than by the relatively short season. The spring increase in the phytoplankton occurs at least a month later than is normal for other regions, and the productive season is short (Figure 4.3.1). St George's Channel and the Irish Sea are areas of relatively low plankton production, particularly of zooplankton: peak numbers of copepods are less than half of those for the Celtic Sea and the shelf area off the west coast of Scotland (Savidge & Kain 1990).

4.3.2 Important locations and species

The surveys indicate that the composition of the region's plankton is fairly typical of shallow and enclosed waters around the British Isles. The spring growth of phytoplankton is dominated by the diatom *Thalassiosira* spp. in April and May, followed by the dinoflagellates *Ceratium fusus* and *C. furca*. The main components of the zooplankton appear to be the mixed water copepods *Acartia clausi, Pseudocalanus elongatus* and *Temora longicornis*.

Compared with the offshore waters, in the inshore areas the larvae of benthic and littoral species are well represented for limited periods, particularly cirripedes in April and echinoderms in April and again in July/August. The Bristol Channel bays are generally similar, with the addition of more neritic (inshore) species: diatoms such as *Rhizosolenia hebetata, Leptocylindrus danicus, Coscinodiscus* spp. and *Biddulphia* spp., and in the zooplankton some mysids. There are also, in small numbers, species characteristic of more open waters, such as *Metridia lucens* and *Meganyctiphanes norvegica*.

Table 4.3.1 Details of plankton surveys (see map 4.3.1 for locations)

Identification in Map 4.3.1	Frequency	Period	Reference
LBS	Monthly	1905-1906	Scott 1906, 1907
IMER	Monthly	1973-1975	Williams & Collins 198
Mumbles Pier	Monthly	1970-1971	Isaac 1981
		1973-1974	Paulraj & Hayward 1981
Williamson	Occasional	1949-1952	Williamson 1952, 1956
CPR: 'IB' route	Monthly	1986 to present	
CPR: 'IN' route	Monthly	1970 to present	
CPR: 'IS' route	Monthly	1970-1985	
Milford Haven	Monthly	1958-1960,	Gabriel, Dias & Nelson-Smith 1975
		1970-1971	

Key: LBS: Liverpool Biological Society; IMER: Institute for Marine Environmental Research; CPR: Continuous Plankton Recorder

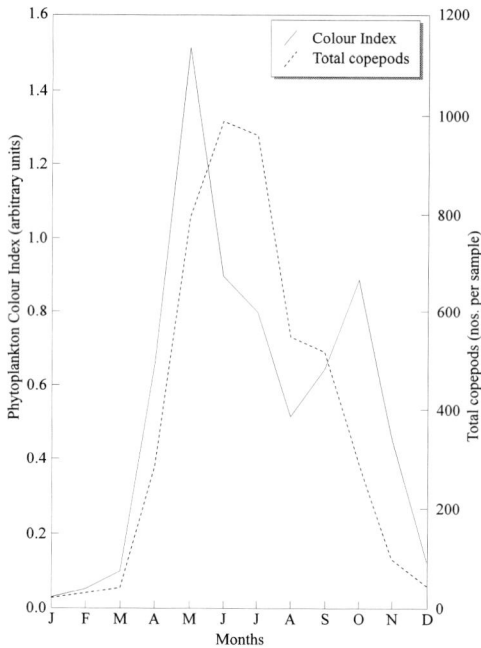

Fig 4.3.1 The seasonal cycles of an index of phytoplankton colour (a visual estimate of chlorophyll) and the numbers of copepods per sample (approximately 3 cubic metres of water filtered), derived from CPR data for 1958-1992.

Joint (1981) reports plankton production values of 340-410 mg C m^{-1} day^{-1} for Swansea Bay in August. Jones & Haq (1963) described a large bloom of *Phaeocystis* in the Menai Straits in the spring of 1957. Subsequent surveys showed that *Phaeocystis* occurs regularly in this area, but only occasionally is there a pronounced bloom. A series of stations worked in August 1973 from north to south, more or less along the midline of St George's Channel and into the Celtic Sea, demonstrated the presence of a pronounced tidal front at about 52°15′N (Savidge 1976). This front may be a regular feature and may extend from the coast of Ireland across into the Bristol Channel (Pingree & Griffiths 1978).

4.3.3 Information sources used

As is clear from Map 4.3.1 and Table 4.3.1, the coverage of survey data is poor and concentrated near the northern, southern and western boundaries. The only data from Cardigan Bay date from 1905 and 1906 (Scott 1906, 1907). The station locations are not specified and, while full monthly species lists are provided, the data record only presence or absence. The Continuous Plankton Recorder (CPR) surveys in this region are of particular importance because they contain long-term plankton data, which can be used to assess the effects of environmental variability and climatic changes on the marine biota. Isaac (1981) includes species lists for inshore communities found in Swansea Bay and details the medusae and the larvae of lamellibranchs, cirripedes and decapods.

4.3.4 Further sources of information

A. References cited

Gabriel, P.L., Dias, N.S., & Nelson-Smith, A. 1975. Temporal changes in the plankton of an industrialised estuary. *Estuarine and Coastal Marine Science*, 3: 145-151.

Isaac, M.J. 1981. The zooplankton of Swansea Bay. *In: Industrialised embayments and their environmental problems*, ed. by M.B.Collins, F.T.Banner, P.A.Tyler, S.J.Wakefield & A.E.James, 487-505. Oxford, Pergamon Press.

Joint, I.R. 1981. Phytoplankton production in Swansea Bay. *In: Industrialised embayments and their environmental problems*, ed. by M.B.Collins, F.T.Banner, P.A.Tyler, S.J.Wakefield & A.E.James, 469-479. Oxford, Pergamon Press.

Jones, P.G.W., & Haq, S.M. 1963. The distribution of *Phaeocystis* in the eastern Irish Sea. *Journal du Conseil Permanent International pour l'Exploration de la Mer, 28*: 8-20.

Paulraj, P.J., & Hayward, J. 1981. The phytoplankton of inshore Swansea Bay. *In: Industrialised embayments and their environmental problems*, ed. by M.B.Collins, F.T.Banner, P.A.Tyler, S.J.Wakefield & A.E.James, 481-486. Oxford, Pergamon Press.

Pingree, R.D., & Griffiths, D.K. 1978. Tidal fronts on the shelf seas around the British Isles. *Journal of Geophysical Research, 83*: 4615-4622.

Savidge, G. 1976. A preliminary study of the distribution of chlorophyll *a* in the vicinity of fronts in the Celtic and western Irish seas. *Estuarine and Coastal Marine Science, 4*: 617-625.

Savidge, G., & Kain, J.M. 1990. Productivity of the Irish Sea. *In: Irish Sea Study Group Report, part 3: exploitable living resources*, ed. by T.A. Norton & A.J. Geffen. Liverpool, The University Press.

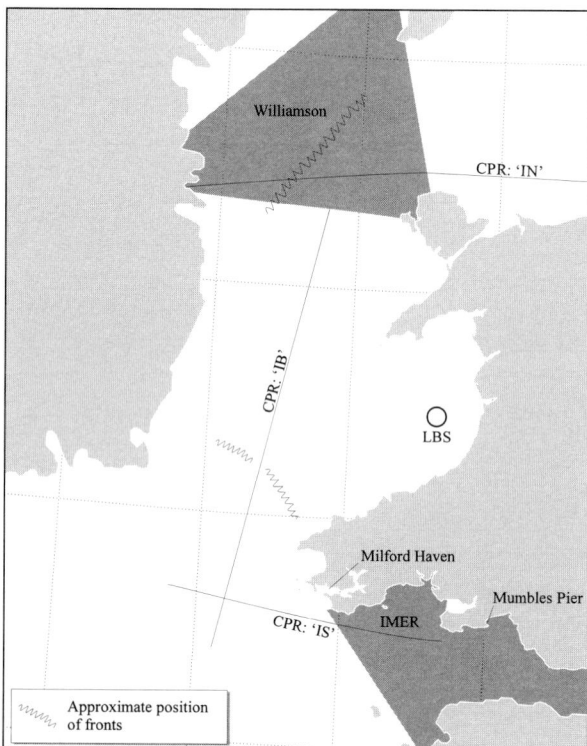

Map 4.3.1 Plankton surveys and 'fronts'. See Table 4.3.1 for details of surveys.

Scott, A. 1906. Report on the tow-nettings. *Proceedings and Transactions of the Liverpool Biological Society, 20*: 164-191.

Scott, A. 1907. Report on the tow-nettings. *Proceedings and Transactions of the Liverpool Biological Society, 21*: 137-191.

Williams, R., & Collins, N.R. 1985. *Zooplankton Atlas of the Bristol Channel and Severn Estuary*. Plymouth, Institute for Marine Environmental Research.

Williamson, D.I. 1952. Distribution of plankton in the Irish Sea in 1949 and 1950. *Proceedings and Transactions of the Liverpool Biological Society, 58*: 1-46.

Williamson, D.I. 1956. The plankton in the Irish Sea, 1951 and 1952. *Bulletins of Marine Ecology, 4*: 87-114.

B. Further reading

Dickson, R.R., *ed.* 1987. *Irish Sea status report of the Marine Pollution Monitoring Management Group*. Aquatic Environmental Monitoring Report, MAFF Directorate of Fisheries Research, Lowestoft, No.17, p 83.

Hobbs, G., & Morgan, C.I. 1992. *A review of the current state of environmental knowledge of the Milford Haven waterway*. Field Studies Council Research Centre Report No. FSC/RC/5/92, p 140.

Huckbody, A.J., Taylor, P.M., Hobbs, G., & Elliott, R., *eds.* 1992. *Caernarfon and Cardigan Bays: an environmental appraisal*. London, Hamilton Oil Company Ltd.

Norton, T.A., & Geffen, A.J., *eds.* 1990. Irish Sea Study Group Report, part 3: exploitable living resources. Liverpool, The University Press.

Comprehensive bibliographies are included in Dickson (1987) and Norton & Geffen (1990).

C. Contact names and addresses

Type of information	Contact address and telephone no.
IMER Bristol Channel data	Director, Plymouth Marine Laboratory, Prospect Place, The Hoe, Plymouth PL1 3DH, tel: 01752 222772
CPR survey data	Director, Sir Alister Hardy Foundation for Ocean Science, The Laboratory, Citadel Hill, Plymouth PL1 2PB, tel: 01752 222772
Ichthyoplankton (fish larvae)	MAFF Directorate of Fisheries Research, Fisheries Laboratory, Lowestoft, Suffolk NR33 0HT, tel: 01502 562244

4.3.5 Acknowledgements

The authors acknowledge the assistance of Dr P.C. Reid for commenting on the draft.

The gannet colony on Grassholm Island, Dyfed, is internationally important. The island has been designated a Special Protection Area for the more than 28,000 pairs of gannets that breed there. Photo: A. Webb, JNCC.

Chapter 5 Important species

5.1 Terrestrial lower plants

N.G. Hodgetts

5.1.1 Introduction

This section covers lichens, bryophytes (mosses and liverworts), stoneworts (a group of freshwater and brackish water algae) and fungi occurring in the coastal 10 km squares within the boundaries of the region. As it lies on the western seaboard of Britain, Region 12 is particularly important for lower plants with an oceanic distribution pattern. Many of these species have a very restricted international distribution, and several are almost confined to Britain and Ireland, where they grow only in strongly oceanic sites near the west coast.

The region is of national and international importance for its lower plants. About 63% of the British bryophyte flora and about 41% of the stonewort flora occur in the region. Similar figures are not available for the other groups, but a high percentage of both the lichen and fungus floras can be expected, as there is a great variety of habitats and an oceanic climate. Wales is particularly rich as there is a mixture of southern and northern species growing in close proximity.

Several of the region's habitat types support important lower plant communities. Dune systems, for instance, are important for bryophytes, lichens and fungi. Some bryophytes and many fungi are dune specialists. Many of the fungi are mycorrhizal with higher plants, with willow and marram grass apparently being important associates. Fungi are therefore probably instrumental in the process of dune stabilisation. Temporarily water-filled dune hollows can be important for stoneworts. The region has extensive dune systems, notably dune slacks, with good populations of the liverwort *Petalophyllum ralfsii* and a number of fungi that are restricted to sand dunes. The region has a high proportion of Britain's dune sites important for lower plants.

The extensive hard rock coasts of Wales are among the richest in Britain (and Europe) for coastal lichens. The area of exposed rock between high water mark and the clifftops on hard rock coasts is typically very important for lichens. Many distinctive species and communities grow on different rock types. Some lichens are distinctive components of the saxicolous vegetation in cliff bird roosts, where the rocks are enriched with bird droppings.

Important areas of coastal (usually clifftop) grassland and heath, in the region and elsewhere, usually have thin turf with complex vegetation mosaics rich in bryophytes, lichens and higher plants. The often extensive unstable areas are important in maintaining bare ground for colonisation by some of the rare ephemeral lower plants of this habitat. Calcareous grassland is usually richer than neutral or acidic grassland. Exposed rocks within the

grassland or health habitat are often good for southern warmth-loving species of bryophyte.

Oceanic woodlands and ravines, both in the region and elsewhere, are important for bryophytes, lichens and fungi, particularly myxomycetes (slime moulds). Many oceanic species (most notably small liverworts of the family Lejeuneaceae) are confined to this habitat. Fungi are important as wood decomposers. The few remaining oceanic woodlands in the region are of international importance. Western Scotland is much richer in oceanic woodlands, but the Welsh woodlands are somewhat different in lower plant species composition and are very important both phytogeographically and as places of high biodiversity. Some specialist aquatic species of all groups occur where there are streams and rivers. Reservoir and pool margins support important specialist bryophyte communities of bare mud exposed in drought years. The region's coastal bogs and flushes feature bryophytes,

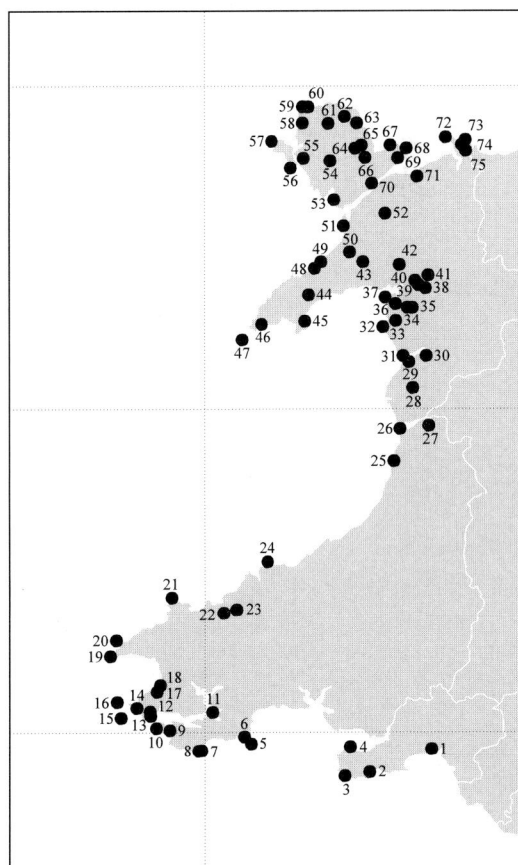

Map 5.1.1 Sites known to be important for lower plants. Site numbers refer to those in Table 5.1.2. Source: JNCC Red Data Book database.

75

particularly *Sphagnum* spp., which are often dominant or co-dominant. Some specialist fungi also occur. There are sometimes important stonewort communities where there is some open water associated with the site. The region's few remaining good quality bogs are amongst the richest in Britain for lower plants and are of international importance.

Important specialist bryophyte and lichen communities occur on sites contaminated with heavy metals, both here and elsewhere, with several species virtually confined to old mine-waste sites.

5.1.2 Important locations and species

The region contains a number of threatened species, some of which are given special protection under national and international legislation. Species protected under Annex II of the EC Habitats & Species Directive and Appendix I of the Bern Convention are: *Drepanocladus vernicosus* (moss) in base-rich upland and coastal flushes at numerous localities throughout Wales, some of which are in this coastal region; and *Petalophyllum ralfsii* (liverwort) on open damp dune slacks throughout the area. Additional species protected under Schedule 8 of the Wildlife & Countryside Act 1981 are *Caloplaca luteoalba* (lichen) on elm bark, Gwynedd; *Micromitrium tenerum* (moss) on mud at a reservoir margin, Anglesey; *Sematophyllum demissum* (moss) in a few oceanic woodlands in Gwynedd; and *Teloschistes flavicans* (lichen) on coastal rocks in Gwynedd and Dyfed. Additional Red Data Book species, excluding those with a status of Indeterminate, Insufficiently Known or Extinct (out of a total of 223 bryophytes, 17 stoneworts and 368 lichens on the British Red Lists) are listed in Table 5.1.1. For fungi there is insufficient information for a comprehensive count. The following very rare species listed by Ing (1992) occur on coastal dune systems in the area: *Coprinus ammophilae* (Gower), *Leucoagaricus pilatianus* (Gower), *Melanoleuca cinereifolia* (Gower, Ynyslas), *Tulostoma melanocyclum* (Gower).

In addition the region contains 127 of the 313 nationally scarce bryophytes and four of the six nationally scarce stoneworts; there is currently not enough information available to provide regional lists of nationally scarce lichens and fungi.

Table 5.1.1 Red Data Book lower plant species in Region 12

Liverworts	Locations	Lichens	Locations
Cephaloziella calyculata	Thin soil over limestone on Gower coast	*Arthonia astroidestra*	On smooth bark at two sites in Dyfed and Gwynedd
Cephaloziella massalongi	Copper-rich mine-waste in Gwynedd & Anglesey	*Bacidia herbarum*	On bryophytes in calcareous turf, Stackpole Warren, Dyfed
Gymnocolea acutiloba	Block scree in the Rhinog mountains (only British site)	*Blarneya hibernica*	Epiphytic in ancient woodland
Pallavicinia lyellii	Borth Bog and bog by Mawddach Estuary	*Caloplaca flavorubescens*	On tree in Glynlliffon Park, Gwynedd
Riccia huebeneriana	Exposed mud on reservoir margin in Anglesey	*Cladonia peziziformis*	Undisturbed peaty soil, Dowrog Common, Dyfed
Riccia nigrella	Thin soil over rocks at Harlech Castle	*Collema subnigrescens*	On nutrient-rich bark & rocks
Southbya tophacea	Calcareous dune grassland at Newborough, Anglesey	*Diploschistes gypsaceus*	On hard, calcareous rock, the Great Orme
		Fulgensia fulgens	Thin, calcareous soil, Stackpole area, Dyfed
Mosses		*Gyalidea subscutellaris*	Heavy metal-rich soil (untraced record near Aberystwyth)
Bryum calophyllum	Calcareous dune slacks in Gwynedd	*Heterodermia leucomelos*	Rocks or turf on exposed coastal cliffs, Anglesey
Bryum knowltonii	Calcareous dune slacks in Gwynedd		
Bryum marratii	Calcareous dune slacks in Gwynedd	*Lecanactis amylacea*	On ancient oak trees, Gower Coast
Bryum neodamense	Coastal fen in Gwynedd	*Lecania chlorotiza*	On shaded, basic bark, Coed More, Dyfed
Bryum warneum	Calcareous dune slacks in Gwynedd & Anglesey	*Lecanora strobilina*	On bark of conifers, Artro Valley, Gwynedd
Dicranum leioneuron	Borth Bog		
Dicranum undulatum	Borth Bog	*Leptogium diffractum*	On hard limestone, the Great Orme
Ditrichum plumbicola	Lead-mine spoil at sites in Gwynedd	*Nephroma tangeriense*	Exposed rocks and soil, two sites in Gwynedd and Dyfed
Fissidens algarvicus	Several sites on shaded soils on cliffs in Dyfed & Gwynedd	*Parmelia quercina*	On nutrient-rich bark, near Barmouth, Gwynedd
Fissidens monguillonii	Silty substrates by water at two sites in Dyfed & Anglesey	*Parmelia tinctina*	On sunny coastal boulders, Skomer
Fissidens serrulatus	Near Harlech	*Porocyphus kenmorensis*	On siliceous rocks by stream, Nant Gwynant, Gwynedd
Funaria pulchella	Thin soil over limestone on Great Orme's Head and Gower coast	*Protoparmelia atriseda*	On hard acid rocks, near Barmouth, Gwynedd
Grimmia arenaria	Crevices of slate walls in and around Ffestiniog	*Ramalina polymorpha*	On nutrient-enriched rocks, Grassholm and Skomer
Grimmia elongata	Acidic rocks on Yr Eifl, Gwynedd	*Roccella fuciformis*	On vertical coastal rocks, Skomer and adjacent mainland
Tortula cuneifolia	Bare soil near Barmouth, Gwynedd	*Staurothele rufa*	On dry limestone near Porthkerry, Glamorgan (only British site)
Weissia levieri	Thin soil over limestone on cliffs on the Gower coast	*Sticta canariensis*	Damp, shaded rocks and trees, Ynys Enlli and Bontddu Valley
Stoneworts		*Synalissa symphorea*	On limestone rocks, Penrhynside, Llandudno, Gwynedd
Nitella tenuissima	Cattle-poached calcareous pools, Anglesey		

Table 5.1.2 lists all the sites in the region that are known to be important for lower plants and that have had at least some degree of survey work, and their protected status. Many are large, in which case the grid reference given refers to a reasonably central point. Most of the sites in Table 5.1.2 are notified or designated at least partly on the basis of their bryophyte and lichen interest. Many of the others contain rare and scarce species and qualify for Site of Special Scientific Interest status on the basis of their lower plant flora (Hodgetts 1992). Locations are shown on Map 5.1.1.

5.1.3 Human activities

Current issues that may have a bearing on the lower plant flora of the region include the construction of (mainly small) hydro-electric and wind power schemes, road construction programmes and acid rain. Lowering of the water table may have an effect on wetland sites, particularly bogs and dune slacks. Some dune areas may be affected by holiday and leisure developments such as caravan sites and golf courses. Most of the old derelict mine sites rich in heavy metals and that are important for lower plants are at least potential targets for reclamation. Cliff-top grassland and heathland may be subject to erosion in some places. Pollution is a general problem and may be aggravated in some areas by new power stations, oil spillages, etc.

Table 5.1.2 Important lower plant sites

Site no. on Map 5.1.1	Site name	Grid ref.	Site status	Site no. on Map 5.1.1	Site name	Grid ref.	Site status
	West Glamorgan				**Gwynedd (cont.)**		
1	Crymlyn Bog	SS6994	NNR	35	Cwm Bychan	SH6431	SSSI
2	Oxwich	SS5087	NNR	36	Coed Llechwedd	SH5932	SSSI
3	Gower Coast	SS4286	NNR	37	Morfa Harlech	SH5634	NNR
4	Whiteford Burrows-Landimore Marsh	SS4495	NNR	38	Coed y Rhygen	SH6837	NNR
				39	Ceunant Llennyrch	SH6638	NNR
	Dyfed			40	Coed Camlyn	SH6539	NNR
5	Caldey Island	SS1396	not protected	41	Ceunant Cynfal	SH6941	SSSI
6	Tenby Cliffs	SS1198	SSSI	42	Hafod Garegog	SH6044	SSSI
7	Stackpole	SR9894	NNR	43	Cors Graianog	SH4945	SSSI
8	Stackpole to Castlemartin Cliffs & Bosherston Lake	SR9794	SSSI	44	Cors Geirch	SH3235	NNR
9	Broomhill Burrows	SM8800	SSSI	45	Cors Llyferin	SH3127	SSSI
10	Angle headland	SM8401	not protected	46	Glannau Aberdaron	SH1726	SSSI
11	Lawrenny Wood	SN0106	SSSI	47	Ynys Enlli	SH1121	NNR
12	Monk Haven	SM8206	not protected	48	Gallt y Bwlch	SH3443	SSSI
13	Dale Point only	SM8205	SSSI	49	Yr Eifl	SH3645	SSSI
14	Marloes Sands & Gateholm	SM7807	SSSI	50	Cors Gyfelog	SH4548	SSSI
15	Skokholm	SM7304	SSSI	51	Dinas Dinlle	SH4356	not protected
16	Skomer	SM7209	NNR	52	old lead mines in Llanberis area	SH5660	not protected
17	Goultrop Roads Cliffs & Musselwick Bay	SM8412	SSSI	53	Newborough Warren & Ynys Llandwyn	SH4064	NNR
18	Broad Haven to Settling Nose Cliffs	SM8514	SSSI	54	Cors Bodwrog	SH3976	SSSI
19	Ramsey Island	SM7023	SSSI	55	Llynnau Fali	SH3177	SSSI
20	St. David's Peninsula Coast	SM7228	SSSI	56	Rhoscolyn Coast	SH2774	SSSI
21	Strumble Head - Llechdafad Cliffs	SM8941	SSSI	57	Glannau Ynys Gybi	SH2182	SSSI
22	Preseli summits & Carningli Common (plus surrounding area outside SSSI)	SN0536	SSSI	58	Llyn Garreg-lwyd	SH3188	SSSI
23	Ty Canol	SN0937	NNR	59	Hen Borth	SH3193	SSSI
24	Creigiau Mwnt	SN1952	SSSI	60	Cemlyn Bay	SH3393	SSSI
25	Clarach Bay	SN5883	not protected	61	Llyn Hafodol	SH3988	SSSI
26	Dyfi a Cors Fochno	SN6093	NNR	62	Parys Mountain	SH4490	not protected
27	Cwm Einion	SN6994	not protected	63	Coed y Gell & Morfa Dulas	SH4888	SSSI
				64	Cors Erddreiniog	SH4780	NNR
	Gwynedd			65	Cors Goch	SH4981	SSSI
28	Craig-yr-Aderyn	SH6406	SSSI	66	Cors Bodeilio	SH5077	NNR
29	Arthog Bog	SH6314	SSSI	67	Bwrdd Arthur	SH5881	SSSI
30	Coed Abergwynant	SH6816	SSSI	68	Penmon Point	SH6380	not protected
31	Barmouth Hills	SH6116	SSSI	69	Baron Hill Park	SH6077	SSSI
32	Morfa Dyffryn	SH5525	NNR	70	Plas Newydd	SH5269	NT
33	Coed Lletywalter	SH5927	NNR	71	Coedydd Aber	SH6671	NNR
34	Rhinog	SH6331	NNR	72	Great Orme's Head	SH7583	SSSI, LNR,CP
				73	Little Orme's Head	SH8182	SSSI
				74	Gloddaeth	SH8081	SSSI
				75	Pydew	SH8179	SSSI

Sources: see Section 5.1.5A; also JNCC protected sites data. Key: NNR - National Nature Reserve; SSSI - Site of Special Scientific Interest; NT - National Trust site; LNR - Local Nature Reserve; CP - Country Park.

Many of the larger and more important sites in the region are National Nature Reserves and are therefore managed for nature conservation. Overgrazing in the important oceanic woodland sites has an effect on the lower plant communities in the long term, as the woods age. The spread of rhododendron has altered the character of many of these sites, where it should be controlled. Any insensitive burning of bog and moorland sites is damaging to the lower plant communities. Dune slacks important for bryophytes are vulnerable to scrub encroachment and eventual drying out, often the result of insufficient or no grazing. The same is true for coastal grassland sites, where grazing, often coupled with a certain amount of instability in the soil and a low level of nutrient input, is desirable.

5.1.4 Information sources used

Data for bryophytes and the larger lichens are generally good, but are less complete for fungi, algae and the smaller lichens.

Most important bryophyte sites in the region are well documented. The computerised database at the Biological Records Centre (BRC), Monks Wood, and the Red Data Book database at JNCC include recent records collected over decades by expert bryologists as well as important historical records. North Wales (Gwynedd and Dyfed north of Aberystwyth) is particularly well known because of the large number of expert bryologists who have lived there over the last thirty years and the systematic recording of its bryophyte flora (Hill 1988). Dyfed south of Aberystwyth and West Glamorgan is less comprehensively known, but data are still reasonably good and most important sites will have been identified.

Most important and potentially important coastal lichen sites have been identified in recent surveys (Fletcher 1984; James & Wolseley 1991). However, relatively few of these sites have been comprehensively surveyed, so there may be more lichen sites than appear in Tables 5.1.1 or 5.1.2. Many of the sites in these tables have only rather inadequate information for lichens, particularly microlichens. However, most of the larger and better-known sites and oceanic woodland sites have had at least some degree of lichen survey in recent years.

Data collation for fungi is still at a relatively early stage and it is not yet possible to incorporate fungi in the criteria for selecting sites for SSSI designation, except in rather an *ad hoc* fashion. All British Mycological Society foray data are currently being put onto a computer database at the International Mycological Institute under a JNCC contract. Important work on coastal dune fungi in the region has been done recently by Rotheroe (1986 *et seq.*). This has resulted in records of many rare and scarce species that are found only on relatively intact dune systems.

With the exception of stoneworts, algae are poorly known. Sites are not currently selected for designation on the basis of algae, except for stoneworts. Computerised stonewort data are held at BRC and JNCC. More information on other freshwater algae may be available from the Freshwater Biological Association.

5.1.5 Further sources of information

A. References cited

Fletcher, A. *ed.* 1984. Survey and assessment of lowland heath lichen habitats. *Nature Conservancy Council, CSD Report,* No. 522.

Hill, M.O. 1988. A bryophyte flora of North Wales. *Journal of Bryology 15*: 377-491.

Hodgetts, N.G. 1992. *Guidelines for selection of biological SSSIs: non-vascular plants.* Peterborough, Joint Nature Conservation Committee.

Ing, B. 1992. A provisional Red Data list of British fungi. *The Mycologist, 6*: 3. (British Mycological Society.)

James, P.W., & Wolseley, P.A. 1991. *A preliminary report of coastal lichen sites in England, Wales and Scotland.* Unpublished report to the NCC.

Rotheroe, M. 1986. *Ynyslas Mycoflora Survey, 1985.* Unpublished report to NCC.

Rotheroe, M. 1987. *A comparative survey of the Mycoflora of Welsh sand dunes, 1985, 1986 - a preliminary survey.* Unpublished report to NCC.

Rotheroe, M. 1989. *A comparative survey of the Mycoflora of Welsh sand dunes - report on 1988 survey work.* Unpublished report to the NCC.

Rotheroe, M., Hedger, J., & Savidge, J. 1987. The fungi of Ynyslas sand-dunes - a preliminary survey. *The Mycologist 1:1, January, 1987.* (British Mycological Society.)

B. Further reading

Hill, M.O., Preston, C.D., & Smith, A.J.E. 1991. *Atlas of the bryophytes of Britain and Ireland. Volume 1. Liverworts.* Colchester, Harley Books.

Hill, M.O., Preston, C.D., & Smith, A.J.E. 1992. *Atlas of the bryophytes of Britain and Ireland. Volume 2. Mosses (except Diplolepideae).* Colchester, Harley Books.

Hill, M.O., Preston, C.D., & Smith, A.J.E. 1994. *Atlas of the bryophytes of Britain and Ireland. Volume 3. Mosses (Diplolepideae).* Colchester, Harley Books.

Ratcliffe, D.A. *ed.* 1977. *A nature conservation review.* Cambridge, Cambridge University Press.

Rotheroe, M. 1990. *Welsh sand-dune Mycoflora survey, 1989.* Unpublished report to NCC.

Rotheroe, M. 1991. *Welsh sand-dune Mycoflora survey, 1990.* Unpublished report to NCC.

Schumacker, R. 1988. *Distribution maps of endangered bryophytes in Europe including Macaronesia with special attention to EEC countries.* Mont-Rigi, Station scientifique des Hautes-Fagnes. (Unpublished .)

C. Contact names and addresses

Type of information	Contact address and telephone no.
Lichens (hard rock coasts)	T. Duke, Sandrock, The Compa, Kinver, Staffs. DY7 6HS, tel. 01384 872798
Lichens (general coastal)	P.W. James, c/o Department of Botany, The Natural History Museum, Cromwell Road, London SW7 5BD, tel. 0171 938 9123
Lichens (woodland and general: British Lichen Society database)	Dr A. Fletcher, Leicester Ecology Centre, Holly Hayes, 216 Birstall Road, Birstall, Leicester LE4 4DG, tel. 0116 267 1950
Lichens (general Welsh)	R. Woods, Countryside Council for Wales, 3rd Floor, The Gwalia, Ithon Road, Llandrindod Wells, Powys LD1 6AA, tel. 01597 824661
Lichens (general; survey etc.)	A. Orange, Department of Botany, National Museum of Wales, Cardiff CF1 3NP, tel. 01222 397951
Fungi (general and sand dune)	M. Rotheroe, Fern Cottage, Falcondale, Lampeter, Dyfed SA48 7RX, tel. 01570 422041
Fungi (British Mycological Society database)	Dr P. Cannon, International Institute of Mycology, Bakeham Lane, Englefield Green, Egham, Surrey TW20 9TY, tel. 01784 470111
Bryophytes (general Welsh)	*T. H. Blackstock, CCW HQ, Bangor, tel. 01248 370444
Bryophytes (Dyfed)	*A. Hale, CCW Aberystwyth, tel. 01970 828551
Bryophytes (BRC database)	*C.D. Preston, Biological Records Centre, ITE, Monks Wood, tel. 01487 773381
Bryophytes (British Bryological Society herbarium)	A.R. Perry, Department of Botany, National Museum of Wales, Cardiff CF1 3NP, tel. 01222 397951
Lower plants (species status; Red Data Book Database; site register etc)	*N.G. Hodgetts, JNCC, Peterborough, tel. 01733 62626

* Starred contact addresses are given in full in the Appendix

5.2 Flowering plants and ferns

V.M. Morgan

5.2.1 Introduction

This section describes the importance of the region for vascular plants (i.e. flowering plants and ferns) occurring in the coastal 10 km squares within the boundaries of the region, particularly species that are rare or scarce in Great Britain. The region is of national importance for the many rare and scarce species it contains. Classic British botanical localities include the south Gower coast and the Great Orme. In addition to the key localities noted for rarities, shown in Map 5.2.1, there are many moderately species-rich sites throughout the region. Centres of plant biodiversity result from a combination of geology, climate and history. It is notable that four of the key localities include limestone cliffs, which typically support large numbers of rare and scarce plants; others have complex Pre-Cambrian and igneous rocks. The climate is characterised by mild winters, cool summers and a prolonged growing season of over 320 days per year. Many sites are also very exposed.

Some of Europe's most threatened species are present, including three listed on Annexes IIb and IVb of the EC Habitats Directive (of nine such species in Great Britain), and eight from Schedule 8 of the Wildlife and Countryside Act (1981) (107 in Great Britain). There are 27 species defined as nationally rare or 'Red Data Book' species (317 in Great Britain in 1983 (Perring & Farrell 1983)). 79 species are nationally scarce (known from up to 100 ten km squares in Great Britain), of 254 such species in Great Britain (Stewart, Pearman & Preston 1994). A number of taxa are endemic to the region, that is, they do not occur anywhere else; all of these are subspecies or species whose allocation to a taxon is difficult, such as rock sea-lavenders *Limonium* ssp., wild cotoneaster *Cotoneaster cambricus (C. integerrimus* var. *anglicus)* and field fleawort *Tephroseris integrifolia* ssp. *maritima*. Others, such as yellow whitlowgrass *Draba aizoides*, are not native elsewhere in Great Britain. Of the more widespread species, some such as hoary rockrose *Helianthemum canum* and sharp rush *Juncus acutus* have their stronghold in the region, whereas others occur as outliers of populations centred elsewhere, for example divided sedge *Carex divisa* and bulbous foxtail *Alopecurus bulbosus*. Table 5.2.1 lists the numbers of rare and scarce species by county.

Table 5.2.1 Number of rare and scarce coastal species

	Protected species	*Other Red Data Book species*	*Scarce species*
West Glamorgan	4	7	37
Dyfed	4	9	50
Gwynedd	5	7	64
Region 12	8	19	89

Source: JNCC rare plants database; Stewart *et al.* (1994); BRC database. Note: excludes known introductions and records from before 1970.

5.2.2 Important locations and species

Rare and scarce species grow in a wide range of habitats, but of particular importance in the region are limestone cliffs, raised beaches, muddy estuaries and dunes. It is rare for the associations of uncommon species to have been studied in detail and little information is available. A number of different geographical elements are found in the flora as a result of the region's geology, position and climatic history over the last 25,000 years (Ellis 1983). There are species characterised as 'Mediterranean', such as tree mallow *Lavatera arborea* and wild clary *Salvia verbenaca*; a few alpine elements such as yellow whitlow grass *Draba aizoides*; many oceanic western European species such as squinancy wort *Asperula occidentalis*, sea stork's-bill *Erodium maritimum* and Wilson's filmy-fern *Hymenophyllum wilsonii*; a continental component including marsh mallow *Althaea officinalis*; northern oceanic elements (some of them also known from North America), including grass-of-Parnassus *Parnassia palustris* and brown bent-grass *Agrostis vinealis*; and southern oceanic species such as bulbous foxtail *Alopecurus bulbosus*, small restharrow *Ononis reclinata* and subterranean clover *Trifolium subterraneum*. One species, Welsh mudwort *Limosella australis*, is more typically North American and is known from nowhere else in Europe.

Tables 5.2.2 and 5.2.3 list, respectively, protected and other rare species in the region.

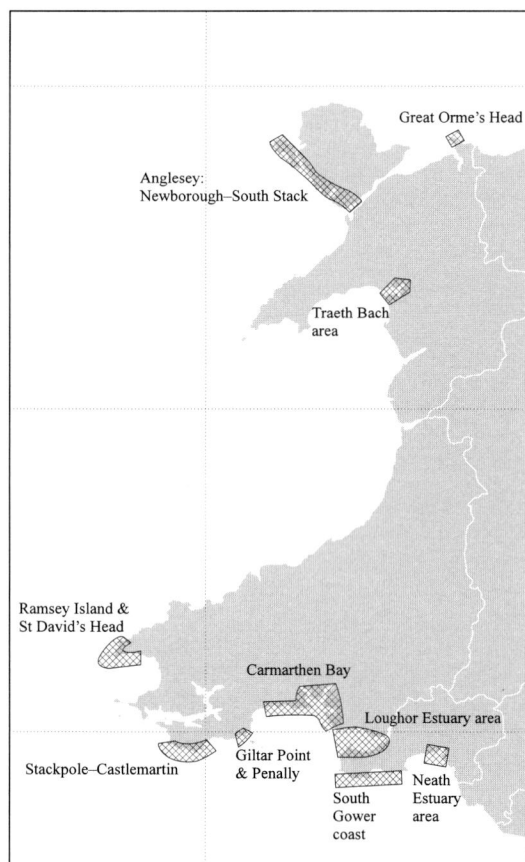

Map 5.2.1 Key localities for rare and scarce higher plants. Sites are listed in Table 5.2.4.

Table 5.2.2 Protected species

Schedule 8	Hab Dir + Bern	Species	Species present in			Key localities	Habitat
			Approx no. of sites in region	No. of coastal 10 km squares in region	Total no. of 10 km squares in GB		
✔		Wild cotoneaster *Cotoneaster cambricus* (*C.integerrimus* var. *anglicus*)	2	1	1	Gt Orme	cliffs
✔		Slender cottongrass *Eriophorum gracile*	3	3	6	Neath estuary area; Llyn Peninsula (SH23)*	bogs
		Dune gentian *Gentianella uliginosa*	9	5	7	south Gower coast; Loughor estuary area; Carmarthen Bay; Penally	dunes
✔		Welsh mudwort *Limosella australis*	8	6	6	Dysinni estuary (SH 50)* Traeth Bach area	mud
✔	✔	Fen orchid *Liparis loeselii*	1	1	7	Whiteford Burrows	dunes
✔	✔	Floating water-plantain *Luronium natans*	4	4	40	Ramsey Island; Anglesey	freshwater
		Small rest-harrow *Ononis reclinata*	8	6	8	south Gower coast; Giltar Pt; Lydstep (SS 09)*; Stackpole to Castlemartin	grassy cliffs
✔	✔	Shore dock *Rumex rupestris*	2	2	13	Newborough	dunes

Source: JNCC Rare Plants Database and rare plant survey reports. Key: Schedule 8 - listed for special protection in the Wildlife & Countryside Act (1981). Hab Dir + Bern - listed on Annexes IIb & IVb of EC Habitats Directive and Annex I of the Bern Convention. Numbers of 10 km squares - those in which the species has been recorded in GB since 1970. *Grid references are given for localities not shown in Map 5.2.1. Spiked speedwell *Veronica spicata* is listed on Schedule 8 of the Wildlife and Countryside Act (1981); however it has been excluded from this table, as the sub-species found in the region is *V. spicata* subsp. *hybrida,* which is scarce rather than nationally rare.

Areas that support two or more rare and/or many scarce species together with some notable species are listed in Table 5.2.4 and shown on Map 5.2.1.

5.2.3 Human activities

In the past some species have been threatened by collecting, particularly in the era of botanical exchange clubs around the end of the last century, when herbarium specimens were swapped amongst botanists. Apart from certain 'choice' horticultural species (possibly including yellow whitlow grass), this threat has passed.

Many sand and mud species depend on bare substrate for regeneration and do not thrive if a closed sward or scrub develops. Examples include fen orchid and early sand-grass. Closed vegetation can develop where such environments are artificially stabilised or where traditional grazing has ceased. Changes in land use such as afforestation or agricultural intensification can also affect populations of uncommon plants. Recreation may affect species, but some, such as dune gentian and early sand-grass *Mibora minima*, will benefit from moderate trampling and problems can often be overcome by careful design of footpaths and climbing routes. Aquatic species, such as floating water-plantain and pillwort *Pilularia globulifera*, are vulnerable to changes in water quality.

5.2.4 Information sources used

All the counties were covered by rare plant surveys between 1979 and 1988 and a series of detailed confidential reports were produced, now held by CCW and the JNCC. Scarce species were also surveyed in Gwynedd and parts of Dyfed in 1987. Further work has been carried out by CCW as part of their programme of monitoring. Records of Red Data Book species are kept in JNCC's rare plants database. The Botanical Society of the British Isles (BSBI) has recently compiled up-to-date records of scarce species, held at the Biological Records Centre and summarised in Stewart, Pearman & Preston (1994). Relationships within and between populations of rare and scarce species are now being studied by eco-geneticists (Kay & John 1993) and this work should shed light on the evolutionary history and conservation needs of individual species.

Table 5.2.3 *Other nationally rare species*

Species	Approx no. of sites in region	No. of coastal 10 km squares in region	Total no. of 10 km squares in GB	Key localities	Habitat
		Species present in			
Wild leek *Allium ampeloprasum*	1	1	4	near South Stack, Anglesey	waste ground
Wild asparagus *Asparagus officinalis* ssp. *prostratus*	3	3	9	south Gower coast; Giltar Point	raised beaches; cliff-tops
Goldilocks aster *Aster linosyris*	6	4	7	south Gower coast; St Govan's (SR 99) *- Castlemartin; Gt Orme's Head	grassy cliff-tops
Compact brome *Bromus madritensis*	5	4	17	Penally; Stackpole; Pembroke (SM 90)*, Carew (SM 00)* , West Williamston (SM 00)*	walls, waste ground
Perennial centaury *Centaurium scilloides*	1	1	5	Newport area (SN04)*	grassy cliffs
Yellow whitlowgrass *Draba aizoides*	7	2	2	south Gower coast	cliffs
Dwarf spike-rush *Eleocharis parvula*	6	3	5	Traeth Bach area	muddy estuaries
Nit-grass *Gastridium ventricosum*	7	2	20	south Gower coast	grassy slopes and cliffs
Hairy greenweed *Genista pilosa*	14	5	12	St Bride's Bay (SM82)* to St David's Head and Strumble Head	grassy cliffs
Toadflax-leaved St John's-wort *Hypericum linariifolium*	2	1	7	near Pwllheli (SH 33)*	cliffs
Spotted cat's-ear *Hypochoeris maculata*	1	1	9	Gt Orme's Head	grassland & cliffs
Rock sea-lavender *Limonium paradoxum*	1	1	1	St David's Head	cliffs
Rock sea-lavender *Limonium parvum*	1	1	1	Stackpole	rocky beach
Rock sea-lavender *L. transwallianum*	2	2	2	Giltar Pt; St Govan's	cliffs
Purple gromwell *Lithospermum purpurocaeruleum*	2	1	9	south Gower coast	scrub on cliffs
Sea stock *Matthiola sinuata*	4	3	5	Neath estuary area; Gower coast (some sites introduced)	dunes
Early sand-grass *Mibora minima*	9	5	6	Loughor estuary area; Anglesey: Newborough to Cymyran (SH 27)*	dunes
Yarrow broomrape *Orobanche purpurea*	1	1	17	Manorbier (SS 09)*	grassland
Spotted rock-rose *Tuberaria guttata*	7	4	4	Llyn Peninsula; Anglesey: Trearddur Bay (SH 27)*; South Stack; Clegir Mawr (SH 38)*	rocky heath

Source: JNCC Rare Plants Database and rare plant survey reports. Key: numbers of 10 km squares - recorded in GB since 1970, excluding known extinctions. *Grid references are for localities not shown in Map 5.2.1.

Table 5.2.4 Key localities for rare and scarce plants

Locality	Status	Species
Neath Estuary area	part SSSI, part NNR, part undesignated	2 Red Data Book species, plus Deptford pink *Dianthus armeria*, round-leaved wintergreen *Pyrola rotundifolia* ssp. *maritima*, sharp rush *Juncus acutus*, long-stalked orache *Atriplex longipes*, and 11 other scarce species.
South Gower coast	part SSSI, part NNR, part LNR, part undesignated	8 Red Data Book species, plus round-leaved wintergreen, spiked speedwell *Veronica spicata* ssp. *hybrida*, hoary rockrose *Helianthemum canum*, white horehound *Marrubium vulgare*, *Sorbus porrigentiformis*, western clover *Trifolium occidentale*, long-stalked orache, Isle of Man cabbage *Coincya monensis* ssp. *monensis*, sharp rush, and 17 other scarce species.
Loughor estuary area	SSSI, part NNR	3 Red Data Book species, plus sharp rush, white horehound, round-leaved wintergreen, long-stalked orache, Deptford pink, and 14 other scarce species.
Carmarthen Bay	part SSSI, part undesignated	2 Red Data Book species, plus maidenhair fern *Adiantum capillus-veneris*, long-stalked orache, sharp rush, marsh pea *Lathyrus palustris*, round-leaved wintergreen, three-lobed crowfoot *Ranunculus tripartitus*, and 17 other scarce species.
Giltar Point and Penally	part SSSI, part undesignated	5 Red Data Book species, plus galingale *Cyperus longus*, sharp rush, and 8 other scarce species
Stackpole to St Govan's to Castlemartin	SSSI, part NNR	5 Red Data Book species, plus white horehound, hoary rockrose, 10 other scarce species.
Ramsey Island and St David's Head	SSSI	3 Red Data Book species, plus chives *Allium schoenoprasum*, yellow centaury *Cicendia filiformis*, and 10 other scarce species.
Traeth Bach area	part SSSI, part NNR, part undesignated	2 Red Data Book species, plus galingale, sharp rush, round-leaved wintergreen, and 11 other scarce species.
Anglesey: Newborough to South Stack	part SSSI, part NNR, part undesignated	5 Red Data Book species, plus eight-stamened waterwort *Elatine hydropiper*, six-stamened waterwort *E. hexandra*, round-leaved wintergreen, and 19 other scarce species.
The Great Orme	SSSI, part LNR	2 Red Data Book species, plus hoary rock-rose, white horehound, spiked speedwell, and 13 other scarce species.

Source: Rare Plants Database; Stewart *et al.* (1994); SSSI citation sheets; BRC database. Note: scarce species may occur near to rather than within some localities. Only scarce species known from 16-30 10 km squares in GB are listed by name. Key: SSSI - Site of Special Scientific Interest; NNR - National Nature Reserve; LNR - Local Nature Reserve.

5.2.5 Further sources of information

A. References cited

Ellis, R.G. 1983. *Flowering plants of Wales*. Cardiff, National Museum of Wales.

Kay, Q.O.N., & John, R. 1993. Fragmented ranges and uncertain futures: population genetics, reproduction and dispersal in scarce grassland species. *BSBI News*, 63:51.

Perring, F.H., & Farrell, L. 1983. *British Red Data books: 1 Vascular plants*. 2nd ed. Nettleham, Lincoln, Royal Society for Nature Conservation.

Stewart, A., Pearman, D.A., & Preston, C.D. 1994. *Scarce plants in Britain*. Peterborough, Joint Nature Conservation Committee/Institute of Terrestrial Ecology/Botanical Society of the British Isles.

B. Further reading

Hutchinson, G., & Thomas, B.A. 1992. Distribution of Pteridophyta in Wales. *Watsonia*, 19(1): 1-19.

Hyde, H.A., Wade A.E., & Harrison, S.G. 1978. *Welsh ferns*. 6th ed. - 7th ed. in prep. Cardiff, National Museum of Wales. Keys, descriptions and illustrations with notes on habitat and distribution.

Stace, C. 1991. *New flora of the British Isles*. Cambridge University Press.

Stewart, A., Pearman, D.A., & Preston, C.D. 1994. *Scarce plants in Britain*. Peterborough, Joint Nature Conservation Committee.

C. Contact names and addresses

Type of information	Contact address and telephone no.
Species on SSSIs and NNRs, other protected areas, rare and scarce species, rare plant surveys, licensing and protected species.	*Coastal specialist, CCW HQ, Bangor, tel. 01248 370444
Distribution and history of plants in Wales, herbarium records, local 'flora's' and archives	Department of Botany, National Museum of Wales, Cardiff CF1 3NP, tel. 01222 397951
Local BSBI vice-county recorders' detailed records	Hon. Secretary, Welsh Committee, Botanical Society of the British Isles, c/o National Museum of Wales, Cardiff CF1 3NP, tel. 01222 397951
Database of rare and protected species	*Species Conservation Branch, JNCC, Peterborough, tel. 01733 62626

* Starred contact addresses are given in full in the Appendix

5.2.6 Acknowledgements

Thanks are due to J.H. Barne, G. Ellis, D. Evans, G. Hutchinson, R. John, A. Jones, M.A. Palmer, J. Ratcliffe, M.J. Wigginton, J. Wookey and the Biological Records Centre for their help in compiling this section.

5.3 Land and freshwater invertebrates

M.S. Parsons and A.P. Foster

5.3.1 Introduction

There are over 28,000 species in the better known groups of invertebrates in Great Britain (Kirby 1992). This chapter deals with most orders (although not all families) of free-living terrestrial and freshwater macro-invertebrates occurring in the coastal 10 km squares within the boundaries of the region.

The region's coast is very varied and its extensive range of habitats (described in other chapters) is known to support an impressive fauna, including many scarce and threatened species. There are several sand dune systems that are nationally important for invertebrates and which support many species that are restricted (or virtually so) to this region; these include Whiteford Burrows and Newborough Warren. Many of the coastal cliff sites, particularly to the south of the region, harbour a number of typically western and south-western species. Several of the coastal mires, such as Cors Fochno, have invertebrate communities that are important on a national scale, many of them supporting a mixture of both northern and southern species. The fauna of Crymlyn Bog, which has similarities to those of the East Anglian fens, is of national significance. The remaining habitats are less well studied, and further recording might reveal several more sites (particularly larger and ungrazed saltmarshes and soft-rock cliff sites) of national or regional importance.

Two species of insect, two molluscs and one leech listed on international Directives, Conventions or the Wildlife & Countryside Act 1981 (excluding Sale Only section) have been recorded within the region (Table 5.3.1). These are: the marsh fritillary butterfly *Euphidryas aurinia* (West Glamorgan, Dyfed and Gwynedd), the southern damselfly *Coenagrion mercuriale* (West Glamorgan, Dyfed and Gwynedd), an aquatic snail *Paludinella littorina*, two whorl snails *Vertigo angustior* (West Glamorgan) and *Vertigo geyeri* (Gwynedd) and the medicinal leech *Hirundo medicinalis* (West Glamorgan, Dyfed and Gwynedd). A few species or subspecies are found only in this region; others have their main national stronghold in the region. The region is of international importance for several species, e.g. the marsh fritillary butterfly, and also supports subspecies of moths not found outside Great Britain. The region is also nationally important for a range of individual species and assemblages of species. The butterflies *Hipparchia semele thyone* (a subspecies of the grayling) and *Plebejus argus caernensis* (a subspecies of the silver-studded blue) are not found outside Wales.

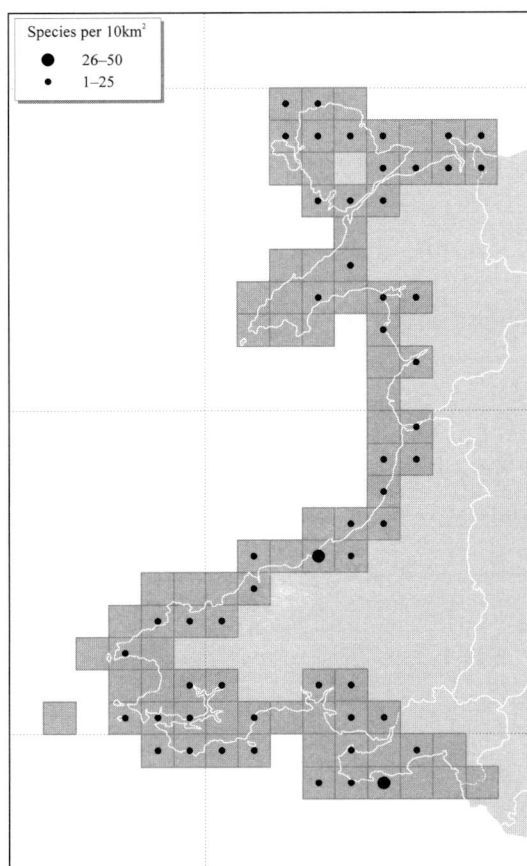

Map 5.3.1 Numbers of nationally rare (i.e. RDB) species of invertebrates recorded in coastal 10 km squares (all dates). Distribution may reflect differences in recording effort. Source Invertebrate Site Register, JNCC.

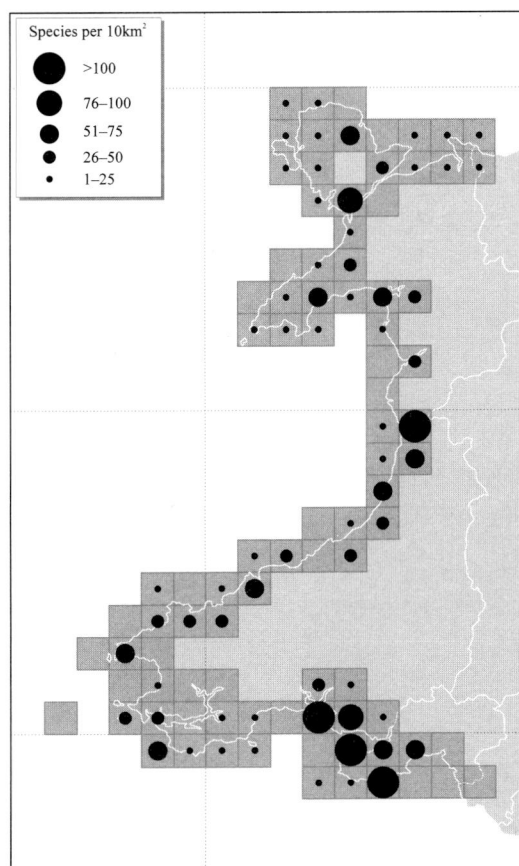

Map 5.3.2 Numbers of nationally scarce species of invertebrates recorded in coastal 10 km squares (all dates). Distribution may reflect differences in recording effort. Source Invertebrate Site Register, JNCC.

85

Table 5.3.1 Coastal Red Data Book (RDB) species in Region 12

Species	*Description and notes on recorded occurrence in the region*
RDB 1	
Aegialia rufa	Small beetle found amongst plant litter just below the sand surface of coastal dunes. Barmouth, Gwynedd*.
Agroeca lusatica	Coastal dune spider. Ynyslas Dunes, Dyfed.
Segmentina nitida	Ramshorn snail. Ponds and marsh drains, particularly when well oxygenated and with lush vegetation. An unconfirmed record from Stackpole to Castlemartin Cliffs, Dyfed.
Vertigo angustior	Small whorl snail found in permanently marshy grassland in dunes and lowland fens. IUCN threat category K (Insufficiently known) (Groombridge 1993). Whiteford Burrows and Oxwich Bay, West Glamorgan.
Proposed RDB 1	
Harpalus melancholicus	Phytophagous ground beetle associated with sand dunes. Sparsely vegetated sand at Stackpole to Castlemartin Cliffs, Dyfed.
Meloe brevicollis	Beetle found on heathland and coastal cliffs. Larvae parasitic, probably on bees. Coed cors y Gedol, Gwynedd.
Panagaeus cruxmajor	Red and black ground beetle found at the margins of standing or slow flowing water amongst rich vegetation. Pembrey Coast, Dyfed.
Pyrausta sanguinalis	Small pyralid moth inhabiting coastal dunes; larva feed from within a silken tube amongst the flowers of thyme. Oxwich Bay, West Glamorgan*.
RDB 2	
Andrena rosae	Mining bee associated with soft rock cliffs, coastal grasslands and heaths. Trefeiddan Moor, Dyfed..
Luperina nickerlii gueneei	Sub-species of the sandhill rustic moth; found only in North Wales. Larvae feed in the stems and root crowns of *Elymus farctus*. Morfa Conwy, Gwynedd.
Psen bicolor	Small black and red solitary wasp nesting in moist sandy soil, predatory on planthoppers. Oxwich Bay, West Glamorgan*.
Proposed RDB 2	
Cardiophorus erichsoni	Click beetle, in sandy soil on the coast. Larvae feed on grass roots. St. David's Peninsula Coast, Dyfed.
Cicindela hybrida	Bronze-purple tiger beetle that hunts over open ground, particularly sand and gravel. Usually a coastal species. Morfa Dyffryn, Gwynedd*.
Dicronychus equiseti	Click beetle of coastal dunes and cliffs. Larvae are root feeders. Several dune sites.
Gonomyia bradleyi	Cranefly of boulder clay coastal cliff seepages. Gwbert Cliffs, Dyfed.
Nephrotoma quadristriata	Dune cranefly found at the backs of mobile dunes, especially near the edges of dune slacks. Morfa Dyffryn, Tywyn Aberffraw, and Newborough Warren, Gwynedd.
RDB 3	
Cicindela germanica	Bronze-green tiger beetle that hunts on bare substrate associated with soft rock cliff sites. Wharley Point Cliffs, Dyfed*.
Clubiona genevensis	Spider associated with coastal cliffs and grassland. Found under stones and low vegetation. Skokholm, Dyfed*.
Coelioxys mandibularis	Cuckoo bee known only from coastal dunes sites. Several dune sites.
Colletes cunicularius	Mining bee, confined to the sand dunes of north-west England and Wales. Colonises old erosion hollows, forming dense colonies on steep inclines. Oxwich Bay, Whiteford Burrows and Penmaen Burrows, West Glamorgan.
Eubria palustris	Small black beetle associated with soft rock cliffs, fens and marshes. Cors Geirch & Cors Erddreiniog Gwynedd and Banc y Mwldan, Dyfed.
Graptodytes bilineatus	Water beetle associated with brackish water ditches. Unconfirmed record from Skomer Island, Dyfed.
Haematopota grandis	Horse fly associated with estuarine habitats. Ryers Down & Whiteford Burrows, W. Glam.; Pembrey, Dyfed and Morlais Colliery, Dyfed/West Glamorgan.
Limonia goritiensis	Cranefly found on seepages on coastal cliffs and rock faces. Several sites.
Lionychus quadrillum	Small bronze-black ground beetle associated with river and coastal shingle, sand or gravel. Several sites along the Afon Ystwyth and the Afon Rheidol, Dyfed.
Lycia zonaria	Belted beauty moth: associated with coastal dunes. Morfa Conwy, Gwynedd.
Monosynamma maritima	Plant bug associated with coastal dunes and shingle. Tywyn Aberffraw, Gwynedd.
Myopites eximia	Picture-winged fly occurring in saltmarshes and saline shingle banks where the larval foodplant, golden-samphire *Inula crithmoides*, thrives. Gower coast (Rhossili to Port Enyon Bay), West Glamorgan.
Ochthebius poweri	Very small black water beetle that lives in small seepages on cliff faces, especially those of Red Sandstone. Saint David's peninsula coast, Dyfed.
Odontoscelis fuliginosa	Burrowing shieldbug found in coastal dunes and the East Anglian breckland. Barafundle Bay, Dyfed.
Paludinella littorina	Small brackish-water snail found around the high water mark among moist rotting vegetation or in crevices high on the shore. Listed on schedule 5 of the Wildlife & Countryside Act 1981 (added in 1992). Stackpole to Castlemartin Cliffs, Dyfed.

Table 5.3.1 Coastal Red Data Book (RDB) species in Region 12 *(continued)*

Species	*Description and notes on recorded occurrence in the region*
Phlegra fasciata	Jumping spider found mainly on coastal dunes and sometimes shingle. Pennard Cliff, W. Glam.
Pionosomus varius	Groundbug associated with coastal dunes. Several dune sites.
Psen littoralis	Digger wasp that frequents marram dunes. Oxwich Bay, Penmaen Burrows, West Glamorgan, & Pembrey Country Park, Dyfed.
Trapezonotus ullrichi	Rare groundbug found on short grassland on clifftops. St David's peninsula coast, Dyfed.
Proposed RDB 3	
Agriotes sordidus	Click beetle of coastal and esturine habitats: banks of tidal rivers and beneath stones on a beach. Skokholm, Dyfed*.
Anthicus scoticus	Small beetle found within strand line debris on saltmarshes. Adults are flower feeders. Tywyn Aberffraw, Gwynedd.
Apion rubiginosum	Weevil associated with sheep's sorrel *Rumex acetosella* and with a preference for ruderal coastal habitats. Dolcniw, Pen Dinas and Penglais Quarry, Dyfed.
Dialineura anilis	Stiletto fly associated with sand dunes. Several dune sites.
Drapetis setigera	Fly recorded from coastal sand flats. Oxwich Bay, West Glamorgan*.
Hypocaccus metallicus	Predatory beetle occurring in dung and carrion on coastal dunes and shingle. Unconfirmed record for Whiteford Burrows, West Glamorgan.
Pamponerus germanicus	Robber fly frequenting sand dunes just behind the marram grass belt. Several dunes sites.
Tachytrechus ripicola	Fly associated with coastal sand near fresh water. Dyffryn, Gwynedd*, Dulas Bay, Gwynedd* and Oxwich Bay, West Glamorgan.
Thereva fulva	Fly associated with dunes and other sandy areas near the coast, apparently preferring areas of fixed sand with well-established vegetation and small open areas. Several dune sites.
RDB K	
Allomelita pellucida	Brackish-water amphipod recorded from harbours and ditch systems. Saltings of the river Tywi, Dyfed*.
Lithobius tenebrosus	Centipede known only from the cliffs at Aberystwyth, Dyfed.
Metatrichoniscoides celticus	Small woodlouse discovered new to science in 1979 on the Glamorgan coast. Now known from 7 sites along a 48 km stretch of the Glamorgan coast. IUCN threat category K (Insufficiently known) (Groombridge 1993).
Proposed RDB K	
Bibloplectus minutissimus	Small beetle known from coastal shingle and river margins. Glanyrafon (Afon Rheidol), Dyfed.
Calligypona reyi	Planthopper found on rushes *Juncus* and *Scirpus* spp. in coastal marshes. Saline swamp at Glynea, W. Glamorgan.
Ocyusa nitidiventris	Rove beetle found on sand dunes and in quarries and sand pits. Cors Goch, Anglesey and Cors Geirch, Gwynedd (unconfirmed).
Omalium rugulipenne	Exclusively maritime rove beetle found under dead seaweed on sandy coasts. Pembry Forest, Dyfed.
Phytosus nigriventris	Rove beetle reported from seaweed and egg capsules of the common whelk. Rhossili Down, West Glamorgan.
Thinobius brevipennis	Small black rove beetle found at coastal cliff and dune sites as well as fens. Newborough Warren, Gwynedd.
RDB I	
Philonthus pullus	Rove beetle associated with coastal sand dunes. Found at the roots of *Juncus* spp. and in depressions. Oxwich Bay, Llangennydd Burrows and Whiteford Burrows, West Glamorgan.

Key: Red Data Book categories: RDB 1 = endangered; RDB 2 = vulnerable; RDB 3 = rare; RDB K = insufficiently known; RDB I = indeterminate; p = Proposed species (as categorised in e.g. Hyman & Parsons 1992); *= Old records (before approx. 1970). Some records are doubtful (identified as 'unconfirmed'). For further description of RDB categories see Shirt (1987) and Bratton (1991).

Table 5.3.2 Important invertebrate sites in Region 12

Localities	Grid ref.	Status	Localities	Grid ref.	Status
West Glamorgan			Strumble Head to Llechdafad Cliffs	SM8835	SSSI, NT (in part)
Margam Moors	SS7884	SSSI	Good Hope	SM9140	NT
Pant-y-Sais	SS7194	SSSI	Goodwick Moor	SM9437	County Trust reserve
Crymlyn Bog	SS6994	NNR/SSSI, Ramsar site	Dinas Cliffs	SN0040	NT
			Cwm Dewi	SN0039	
Pwll Du Head & Bishopston Valley	SS5787	SSSI, NT	Gernos Cliffs	SN1248	NT
			Teifi Estuary	SN1549	
Penmaen Burrows / Nicholaston Burrows	SS5388	SSSI (in part), NT	Coedydd a chorsydd Aber Teifi	SN1845	SSSI
Nicholaston Woods	SS5187		Pentwd Marshes	SN1845	SSSI
Oxwich	SS5087	NNR/SSSI	Banc y Mwldan	SN1948	SSSI
Port-Eynon Point	SS4684	NT, County Trust reserve	Pen yr Ergyd	SN1648	SSSI
			Creigiau Gwbert	SN1550	
Port-Eynon Bay	SS4784	County Trust reserve	Cwm Byrlip a Chreigau Castell Bach	SN3657	SSSI, NT (in part)
Gower Coast: Rhossili to Port Eynon	SS4486	NNR/SSSI, NT (in part), Country Trust reserve (in part)	Rhos Rydd	SN5773	SSSI
			Coed nant Llolwyn	SN5877	SSSI
Horton	SS4785		Allt Wen a Traeth Tanybwlch	SN5779	SSSI
Rhossili Down	SS4289	SSSI, NT	Glandwr	SN6080	
Llangennith Burrows	SS4192		Glanyrafon	SN6180	
Whiteford Burrows	SS4595	NNR/SSSI, NT (in part)	Lovesgrove	SN6281	
			Cors Fochno	SN6391	NNR/SSSI, Ramsar site
Cefn Bryn and Broadpool	SS5090	SSSI, County Trust reserve			
Welsh Moor	SS5292	SSSI, NT	**Dyfed/Powys**		
			Dyfi (includes Ynys-Eidiol - Ynys-Hir)	SN6495	NNR/SSSI, Ramsar site, Biosphere reserve
Dyfed					
Techon Marsh	SS5499				
Machynys Ponds	SS5198		**Dyfed/Gwynedd**		
Stradey Estate	SN4801		Cwm Llyfnant	SN7297	
Ffrwd Farm	SN4202	SSSI, County Trust reserve	**Gwynedd**		
			Arthog Bog	SH6314	SSSI
Dyfed/West Glamorgan			Caerleon Reedbed	SH6417	SSSI
Pembrey Country Park (Pembrey Forest)	SN3901		Afon Mawddach	SH7119	
			Morfa Dyffryn	SH5525	NNR/SSSI
Dyfed			Morfa Harlech	SH5635	NNR/SSSI
Tywyn Gwendraeth & Cefn Sands	SN3705	SSSI	Coed Tremadog	SH5640	NNR
			Morfa Bychan	SH5436	SSSI, NT (in part), County Trust reserve (in part)
Cors Goch, Llanllwch	SN3618	SSSI			
Beacon Bog	SN3516				
Laugharne Burrows	SN3007	SSSI	Llyn Ystumllyn	SH5238	SSSI
Pendine Sands	SN2407		Porth Neigwl	SH2428	
Marros-Pendine Coast	SN2007	SSSI	Mynydd Penarfynydd	SH2226	SSSI, NT (in part)
Ritec (Cors Penally)	SN1101	SSSI	Glannau Aberdaron	SH1325	SSSI, NT (in part)
Freshwater East	SS0298		Cors Geirch	SH3136	SSSI
Stackpole to Castlemartin Cliffs (includes Bosherston Lake)	SR8899	NNR/SSSI, NT (in part)	Cors Gyfelog	SH4648	SSSI
			Cors Graianog	SH4945	SSSI
Castlemartin Range	SR9196		Newborough Warren	SH4461	NNR/SSSI
Broomhill Burrows	SM8800	SSSI, NT (in part)	Newborough Forest	SH4065	SSSI
West Williamston	SN0206	SSSI, NT (in part), County Trust reserve	Tywyn Aberffraw	SH3669	SSSI
			Tre Wilmot	SH2381	SSSI
Lawrenny Wood	SN0107	SSSI, NT	Glannau Ynys Gybi (includes South Stack)	SH2182	SSSI
Marloes Cliffs	SM7707	SSSI			
Marloes Mere & Deer Park	SM7708	SSSI, NT, County Trust reserve	Salbri	SH3788	SSSI
			Cors Clegyrog	SH3889	SSSI
Skokholm Island	SM7305	SSSI, County Trust reserve	Llyn Hafodol	SH3989	SSSI
			Cors Erddreiniog	SH4781	NNR/SSSI
Skomer Island	SM7209	NNR/SSSI	Cors Nant Isaf	SH4782	NNR/SSSI
Trefeiddan Moor	SM7325	SSSI	Cors Goch	SH4981	SSSI, County Trust reserve
St David's Peninsula Coast	SM7629	SSSI, NT (in part)			
St David's Airfield Heaths	SM7826	SSSI, NT (in part)	Cors Bodeilio	SH5077	NNR/SSSI
Dowrog Common	SM7727	SSSI, NT, County Trust reserve	Rhos-y-gad	SH5078	SSSI
			Coed Gorswen	SH7570	NNR/SSSI
Porthiddy Moor	SM8031	SSSI	Great Orme's Head	SH7683	SSSI, County Trust reserve (in part)
Ynys Barri	SM8032	SSSI (in part), NT			

Key: NNR - National Nature Reserve; NT - National Trust; SSSI - Site of Special Scientific Interest; SPA - Special Protection Area.

According to JNCC's Invertebrate Site Register there are 232 Red Data Book (RDB) species and 947 nationally scarce species recorded in the coastal 10 km squares of the region. As defined by Kirby (1994), there are 54 coastal RDB species and 242 coastal scarce species recorded in the region; coastal RDB species are listed in Table 5.3.1. Map 5.3.1 shows the distribution of all nationally rare (RDB) invertebrates recorded in coastal 10 km squares in the region; Map 5.3.2 shows that of nationally scarce invertebrates. Note that survey effort has not been equivalent throughout the region, so actual occurrence may differ from recorded distribution.

5.3.2 Important locations and species

Sites listed in Table 5.3.2 are those considered particularly important for invertebrate conservation. Nationally rare coastal species are listed in Table 5.3.1. Other nationally important species in the region include the ground beetle *Harpalus melancholicus,* which has recently been recorded from just a single site in Great Britain (Dyfed), and the rosy marsh moth *Eugraphe subrosea,* which is known from only a very few sites in Wales (Dyfed and Gwynedd). Several insects are largely restricted to this part of the country, including the ground bug *Pionosomus varius,* the click beetle *Dicronychus equiseti,* the Welsh subspecies of the sandhill rustic moth *Luperina nickerlii gueenei,* the cranefly *Nephrotoma quadristriata,* and the mining bee *Colletes cunicularis.* Several other species reach their northern limit in Great Britain along the coast of this region, e.g. the lesser cockroach *Ectobius panzeri.* Roesel's bush cricket *Metrioptera roeselii* is an example of a species with a disjunct distribution: most of its British distribution is along the Thames Estuary, but it is also known from the fringes of the Dyfi Estuary.

Table 5.3.1 shows that the nationally rare coastal species depend on a wide variety of the different coastal habitats of the region. Dune systems, here and elsewhere, have a range of microhabitats, all of which have their own distinctive invertebrate faunas. Undisturbed sandy strandlines have a characteristic invertebrate fauna which can include the ground beetle *Nebria complanata,* known from a few sites in the south of the region. Only a few species are found on the unstable fore dunes, but many of them are restricted to this habitat, for example the sand dart moth *Agrotis ripae.* Dune grassland can be important for a range of species, which can include in this region the marsh fritillary *Euphydryas aurinia,* and the compacted sand of the mature dunes is important for bees as it provides nesting sites and an abundance of nectar sources. The cuckoo bee *Coelioxys mandibularis* has been found on several dune sites in the region, in sunny and more sparsely vegetated areas, particularly those with a southern aspect. In the south of the region, damper areas in the slacks support characteristic species such as the hoverfly *Microdon mutabilis.* Wetter slacks, as at Morfa Harlech, can support important assemblages of wetland flies, and slacks dominated by creeping willow have their own distinctive faunas.

Cliff habitats fall broadly into two categories: hard-rock and soft-rock, which support different invertebrate faunas. Cliff paths provide suitable habitat for species that rely on areas of bare ground, for instance bees and wasps. Grassland associated with cliff sites, particularly when unimproved, can be important for a range of scarcer species,

which can include the pyralid moth *Dolicanthria punctalis.* Seepages and trickles are important for a number of species, such as the water-beetle *Octhebius poweri.* This species has been found on St David's Peninsula, where these trickles are within the reach of salt spray. Intertidal rocky shores support a distinctive, if limited, community that includes the ground beetles *Aepus robini* and *A. marinus.* Both of these beetles are known from several sites in the region. Calcareous habitats have a different range of species from those found on more acidic or neutral substrates, and can support significant bee populations. Coastal heathland is more usually found on cliff tops in the region. Some of these coastal heathlands, e.g. South Stack, Anglesey, have large populations of the silver-studded blue *Plebejus argus,* the larvae of which are attended by ants of the genus *Lasius.*

The soft-rock cliffs of the region, such as those at Porth Neigwl, support several nationally scarce species, e.g. the ground beetle *Tachys micros.* Species typical of this habitat tend to occupy less stable situations prone to slippages, which in this region are significant for their invertebrates.

Estuaries have a range of habitats, from tidal mud flats, through saltmarsh to areas of river shingle in their upper regions. All these habitats support their own specialist groupings of invertebrate species. The ground beetle *Bembidion laterale* is typical of tidal mudflats. The richest saltmarsh invertebrate communities are usually found where the upper saltmarsh has not been modified by grazing. Many saltmarsh invertebrates are more dependent on substrate conditions than on vegetation structure, and saltmarshes with a higher proportion of sandy material tend to hold more invertebrate species than those with siltier substrates. Banks of creeks provide suitable conditions for many species in the region, and saltpans and brackish ditches can contain a small, but distinctive, water-beetle fauna which includes *Enochrus bicolor* and *Octhebius auriculatus.* A scarce ground beetle, *Perileptus areolatus,* can be found in the more shingly habitats.

The region includes a number of coastal mires that are known to have nationally significant invertebrate assemblages and include the rosy marsh moth *Eugraphe subrosea* and the hoverfly *Lejogaster splendida.* Coastal fens, flooded brickpits and grazing levels in the region are all known to support distinctive faunas.

The invertebrate fauna of the coastal woodlands of this part of the coast is relatively poorly known. However, a range of interesting species have been recorded from several sites and Lawrenny Wood is known to support a regionally significant fauna of over-mature and dead wood habitats.

5.3.3 Human activities

Invertebrates occur in the full range of coastal microhabitats found in the region. Many use subtle features of vegetation structure, others areas of bare ground. As often as not, these features are overlooked even in site management for nature conservation, many species surviving by default. Invertebrates generally have annual life cycles and, hence, these features must be present in the right condition in each and every year. The management of coastal habitats for invertebrates is covered by Kirby (1992) and management for different Welsh habitats by Fowles (1994).

5.3.4   Information sources used

Data are scattered over a wide range of sources, including local records centres and literature. This report has largely been prepared from data from the Invertebrate Site Register (ISR). The ISR is a computerised database, which, although not comprehensive, includes data from many of the sources, specialists and surveys mentioned, as well as from the literature (such as entomological journals, *Nature in Wales* etc.) and local biological records centres. It is the most complete data set available on the scarcer species occurring in the region, having records for just over 700 of its coastal sites, although some of these are subsites of larger areas. Most are the habitats of nationally scarce species and many support RDB species. Provisional distribution maps have been published for a wide range of invertebrates, including many for which this region is important (e.g. Heath & Emmet (1979, 1983, 1990) for several Lepidoptera species, Drake (1991) for flies, Mendel (1990) for click beetles and Stubbs (1992) for crane flies).

The level of recording varies over this region, between orders and even between families of invertebrates. Consequently, the data are patchy compared with those for some other regions. Despite this, there is available a wealth of information, which is being continually added to and updated. Several large-scale invertebrate surveys in recent years have covered many of the region's coastal sites. The Nature Conservancy Council's Welsh Peatland Invertebrate Survey covered several coastal mire sites, and the National Trust has undertaken a biological survey of many of its holdings in Wales. This survey includes many invertebrate data on coastal sites. The Butterfly Monitoring Scheme also has data from two sites within the region (Pollard, Hall & Bibby 1986). The Dyfed Invertebrate Group and North Wales Invertebrate Group have both recently formed, and each group holds field meetings within the region. There are national recording schemes for a wide range of invertebrate groups with records from this part of the coast. Most are co-ordinated by specialists with assistance from the Biological Records Centre. Fowles (1994) gives a review of the invertebrates of Wales and provides a further discussion on the invertebrate interest of the region's coastline.

Most of the major groupings of invertebrates have been studied, especially the more popular groups, such as the Coleoptera (beetles) and the Lepidoptera (butterflies and moths). However discoveries continue to be made and more work is needed, particularly along little-known stretches of the coast. The dune systems, hard-rock cliffs and coastal mires are comparatively well known, but many other habitats (other than a few favoured localities) are less well studied.

5.3.5 Further sources of information

A. References cited

Bratton, J.H., *ed.* 1991. *British Red Data Books: 3. Invertebrates other than insects.* Peterborough, Joint Nature Conservation Committee.

Fowles, A.P. 1994. *Invertebrates in Wales: a review of important sites and species.* Peterborough, Joint Nature Conservation Committee.

Groombridge, B., *ed.* 1993. *The 1994 IUCN red list of threatened animals.* Gland, Switzerland and Cambridge. IUCN.

Heath, J., & Emmet, A.M., *eds.* 1979. *The moths and butterflies of Great Britain and Ireland.* London, Curwen Press. (Volume 9.)

Heath, J., & Emmet, A.M., *eds.* 1983. *The moths and butterflies of Great Britain and Ireland.* Colchester, Harley Books. (Volume 10.)

Heath, J., & Emmet, A.M., *eds.* 1990. The butterflies of Great Britain and Ireland. *In: The moths and butterflies of Great Britain and Ireland.* Colchester, Harley Books. (Volume 7, part 1.)

Kirby, P. 1992. *Habitat management for invertebrates: a practical handbook.* Sandy, Royal Society for the Protection of Birds / Joint Nature Conservation Committee / National Power.

Kirby, P. 1994. *Habitat fragmentation; species at risk.* Peterborough, English Nature. (English Nature Research Reports, No. 89.)

Pollard, E., Hall, M.L,. & Bibby, T.J. 1986. *Monitoring the abundance of butterflies 1976-1985.* Peterborough, Nature Conservancy Council. (Research & survey in nature conservation, No. 2.)

Shirt, D.B., *ed.* 1987. *British Red Data Books: 2. Insects.* Peterborough, Nature Conservancy Council.

B. Further reading

Abbot, A. 1992. *Reconnaissance survey of aculeate hymenoptera habitat on South Gower coast.* CCW Contract Science 19. Bangor, CCW.

Chalmers-Hunt, J.M. 1989. *Local lists of Lepidoptera.* Uffington, Hedera Press.

Colvin, M., & Reavey, D. 1993. *A directory for entomologists.* 2nd edition. Middlesex Amateur Entomologists Society. (Pamphlet no. 14.)

Drake, C.M. 1991. *Provisional atlas of the larger Brachycera (Diptera) of Britain and Ireland.* Huntingdon, Biological Records Centre.

Falk, S. 1991. *A review of the scarce and threatened bees, wasps and ants of Great Britain.* Peterborough, Nature Conservancy Council. (Research & survey in nature conservation, No. 35.)

Falk, S. 1991. *A review of the scarce and threatened flies of Great Britain (part 1).* Peterborough, Nature Conservancy Council. (Research & survey in nature conservation, No. 39.)

Foster, A.P. 1983. *National review of non-marine Molluscs.* London, Nature Conservancy Council. (Chief Scientist's Team Report, No.4490 (unpublished).)

Fowles, A.P. 1988. *The moths of Ceredigion.* Peterborough, Nature Conservancy Council. (Research & survey in nature conservation, No. 8.)

Fowles, A.P., & Morris, M.G. 1994. *Apion (Helianthemapion) aciculare* Germar (Col., Apionidae), a weevil new to Britain. *Entomologists' Monthly Magazine, 130:* 177-181.

Hammond, C.O. (revised by Merritt, R.) 1983. *The dragonflies of Great Britain and Ireland.* 2nd edition. Colchester, Harley Books.

Harding, P.T., & Sutton, S.L. 1985. *Woodlice in Britain and Ireland: distribution and habitat.* Huntingdon, Institute of Terrestrial Ecology.

Harrison, T.D. 1994. Notable Coleoptera from the Angle Peninsula, Pembrokeshire including *Harpalus melancholicus* Dejean (Carabidae). *Entomologist's Monthly Magazine, 130:* 148.

Hyman, P.S., & Parsons, M.S. 1992. *A review of the scarce and threatened Coleoptera of Great Britain. Part 1.* Peterborough, Joint Nature Conservation Committee. (UK Nature Conservation, No. 3.)

Hyman, P.S., & Parsons, M.S. 1994. *A review of the scarce and threatened Coleoptera of Great Britain. Part 2.* Peterborough, Joint Nature Conservation Committee. (UK Nature Conservation, No. 12.)

Kirby, P. 1992. *A review of the scarce and threatened Hemiptera of Great Britain.* Peterborough, Joint Nature Conservation Committee. (UK Nature Conservation, No. 2.)

Marshall, J.A., & Haes, E.C.M. 1988. *Grasshoppers and allied insects of Great Britain and Ireland.* Colchester, Harley Books.

Mendel, H. 1990. *Provisional atlas of the click beetles (Coleoptera: Elateroidea) of the British Isles.* Huntingdon, Biological Records Centre.

Merrett, P. 1990. *A review of the nationally notable spiders of Great Britain.* Peterborough, Nature Conservancy Council. (Contract surveys, No. 127.)

Parsons, M.S. 1993. *A review of the scarce and threatened pyralid moths of Great Britain.* Peterborough, Joint Nature Conservation Committee. (UK Nature Conservation, No. 11.)

Plant, C.W. 1994. *Provisional atlas of the lacewings and allied insects (Neuroptera, Megaloptera, Raphidioptera and Mecoptera) of Britain and Ireland.* Huntingdon, Biological Records Centre.

Smith, K., & Smith, V. 1983. *A bibliography of the entomology of the smaller British offshore islands.* Faringdon, E.W. Classey.

Stubbs, A.E. 1992. *Provisional atlas of the long-palped craneflies (Diptera: Tipulinae) of Britain and Ireland.* Huntingdon, Biological Records Centre.

Thomas, J., & Lewington, R. 1991. *The butterflies of Britain and Ireland.* London, National Trust/Dorling Kindersley.

Waring, P., in prep. A review of the scarce and threatened macrolepidoptera of Great Britain. Peterborough, Joint Nature Conservation Committee.

C. Contact names and addresses

Type of information	Contact address and telephone no.
Occurrence of land and freshwater invertebrates in Britain and Ireland	*Biological Records Centre, ITE, Monks Wood, tel. 01487 773381
Conservation of butterflies and moths in Great Britain	Butterfly Conservation, South Wales Branch, 31 Drummau Road, Birchgrove, Swansea SA7 9QA, tel. 01792 813600
Invertebrate conservation in Wales	*Invertebrate Zoologist, CCW HQ, Bangor, tel. 01248 370444
Invertebrates in Dyfed	*Dyfed Invertebrate Group, c/o CCW Aberystwyth, tel. 01970 828551
Invertebrates in Dyfed	*Dyfed Wildlife Trust (Vice County recorders), Dyfed, Haverfordwest, tel. 01437 765462
National inventory of invertebrate conservation sites; records of local, scarce and threatened species	*Invertebrate Site Register, JNCC, Peterborough, tel. 01733 62626
Invertebrate interest of the National Trusts holdings	*The National Trust HQ, Cirencester, tel. 01285 651818
Invertebrates in Pembrokeshire	Pembrokeshire Biological Records Centre, Scolton House and Museum, Spittal, Haverfordwest, Pembrokeshire SA62 5QL tel. 01437 731328
Dragonflies in Glamorgan	Glamorgan Dragonfly Survey Group, Kenfig Reserve Centre, Ton Kenfig, Pyle, Mid Glamorgan CF33 4PT
North Wales invertebrates	North Wales Invertebrate Group, North Wales Biological Records Centre, School of Animal Biology, University College of North Wales, Bangor, Gwynedd LL57 2UW, tel. 01248 351151

* Starred contact addresses are given in full in the Appendix

5.3.6 Acknowledgements

Most of the data used in this section came from the Invertebrate Site Register, and thanks are due to D. A. Procter and Dr S.G. Ball (JNCC) for help with this. Thanks are also due to Dr K.N.A. Alexander (National Trust) for additional records and to Mr A.P. Fowles (CCW).

5.4 Rare sea-bed species

Dr W.G. Sanderson

5.4.1 Introduction

This section considers rare and scarce marine benthic (sea-bed) species, excluding fish. The occurrence and distribution of benthic communities is discussed in section 4.2. 'Nationally rare' marine benthic species in this section are those native organisms that occur in seven or fewer of the 10 km squares (of the Ordnance Survey national grid) containing sea within the three-mile territorial limit for Great Britain. 'Nationally scarce' are those that occur in 45 or fewer. This methodology and these criteria are analogous to those used for other groups of organisms in British Red Data Books (e.g. Bratton 1991) and by the International Union for Conservation of Nature and Natural Resources (IUCN) (see Mace *et al.* 1993). The development of the current criteria and the choice of study area for rarity assessment in the marine benthos of Great Britain are discussed by Sanderson (in prep.). Species considered in this chapter are those conspicuous and readily identifiable in the field by the Marine Nature Conservation Review (MNCR) and similar techniques or where taxonomic experts consider that sufficient data exist on a national basis to warrant their inclusion. Some species classed here as rare or scarce may also be present in deeper water beyond the study area. In addition, species at the limit of their global distribution ('northern' or 'southern' species) may be rare

only within Great Britain's territorial seas. A species described here as 'nationally rare' or 'nationally scarce' is therefore not necessarily endangered. The analysis in this section represents the first attempt to quantify rarity of marine benthic species and to summarise the distributions of rare and scarce species. As more data become available or populations change, the status of species listed in this chapter will require re-evaluation.

Nineteen rare and 24 scarce marine benthic species have been recorded in Region 12. Maps 5.4.1 and 5.4.2 summarise the current known occurrence of rare and scarce marine benthic species in the region. The Menai Strait/Anglesey, Ynys Enlli and Skomer areas apparently contain more rare and scarce marine benthic species than other parts of the region. Skomer Island has more than twice as many rare and scarce marine benthic species recorded than any other area in Region 12. These appearances may be somewhat misleading, however, since survey effort in Region 12 is uneven (see also section 4.2) and has tended to focus on known areas of marine importance.

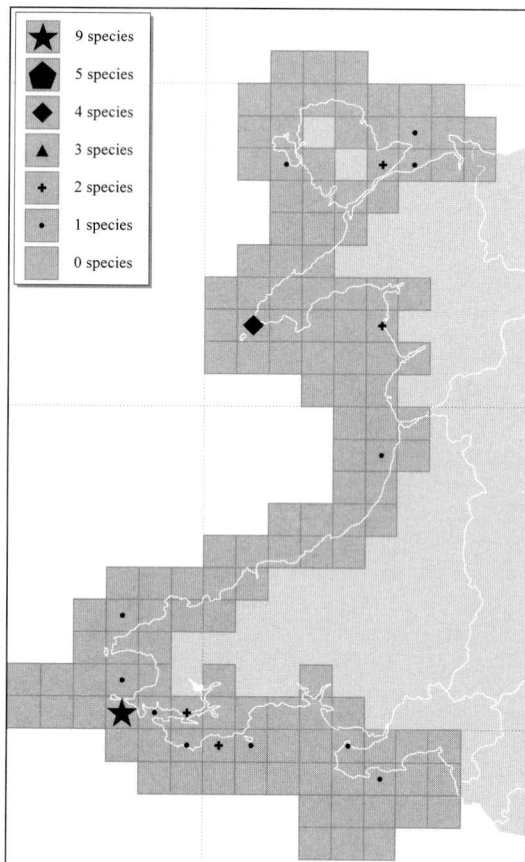

Map 5.4.1 Numbers of rare marine benthic species recorded in 10 km squares within the 3 mile limit.

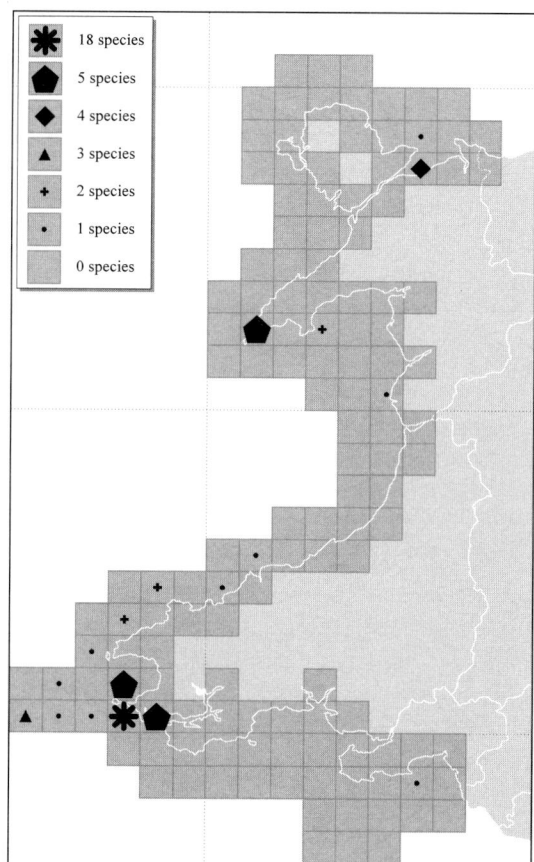

Map 5.4.2 Numbers of scarce marine benthic species recorded in 10 km squares within the 3 mile limit.

5.4.2 Important locations and species

Table 5.4.1 shows important marine benthic species and occurrences in Region 12. The species codes given (after Howson 1987) are often used in marine conservation and survey work. Most of the species are identified by scientific name and group only, as very few have common names.

Within this region certain species are nationally rare or scarce because they are 'southern' (Mediterranean-Atlantic) species at the margins of their distributions. Rare and scarce southern species found in Region 12 include: the sponge *Axinella damicornis*, the hydroid *Aglaophenia kirchenpaueri*, the anthozoans (e.g. 'corals', sea fans and anemones) *Balanophyllia regia*, *Caryophyllia inornata*, *Hoplangia durotrix*, *Eunicella verrucosa*, *Parazoanthus axinellae* and *Parerythropodium coralloides*, the sea slugs and snails *Caloria elegans*, *Doris sticta*, *Greilada elegans*, *Thecacera pennigera*, *Trapania maculata*, *Tritonia nilsodhneri* and *Paludinella littorina*, the bryozoan *Amathia pruvoti*, the sea squirt *Phallusia mammillata* and the alga *Carpomitra costata* (see e.g. Picton 1985; Graham 1988; Manuel 1988; Ackers, Moss & Picton 1992; Picton & Morrow 1994). The distributions of the sponge *Stelletta grubii* and the bryozoan *Hincksina flustroides* are also known to include the Mediterranean. Populations of many sessile (non-mobile) southern species are often long-lived and recruit

Table 5.4.1 Nationally rare* and nationally scarce marine benthic species found in Region 12 and their known distribution

Species code	Species	Common name/group	Area(s) of occurrence
C0150	*Stelletta grubii*	Sponge	West Anglesey, Ynys Enlli, S. Llyn Peninsula, Skomer Island
C0156	*Stryphnus ponderosus**	Sponge	NW Puffin Island (Menai Strait), Skomer Island
C0207	*Thymosia guernei**	Sponge	Ynys Enlli, off Abereiddy (North Pembrokeshire), Skomer Island, Skokholm Island
C0351	*Axinella damicornis*	Sponge	Grassholm Island, Skomer Island, St. Ann's Head
C0445	*Tethyspira spinosa**	Sponge	Menai Strait, Ynys Enlli, Skomer Island
C0842	*Plocamilla coriacea**	Sponge	Menai Strait, Skomer Island
D0589	*Tamarisca tamarisca*	Hydroid	Menai Strait
D0715	*Hartlaubella gelatinosa*	Hydroid	Menai Strait
D0720	*Laomedea angulata*	Hydroid	Menai Strait, Skomer Island
D0552	*Aglaophenia kirchenpaueri*	Hydroid	The Smalls, Skomer Island, Skokholm Island
D1030	*Parerythropodium coralloides*	Soft coral	North Pembrokeshire (inc. Cardigan Island), Skomer Island
D1043	*Eunicella verrucosa#*	Sea fan	The Smalls, Skomer Island, Strumble Head
D1115	*Parazoanthus axinellae*	Yellow trumpet anemone	Ynys Enlli, N. Pembrokeshire, Skomer Island
D1121	*Isozoanthus sulcatus*	Anemone	Llyn Peninsula/Ynys Enlli, Sarn-y-Bwch (N. Cardigan Bay), Skomer Island, SW. Pembrokeshire
D1303	*Halcampoides elongatus**	Burrowing anemone	Skomer Island, Stackpole Quay
D1314	*Mesacmaea mitchellii*	Burrowing anemone	Skomer Island
D1371	*Caryophyllia inornata**	Cup coral	Ynys Enlli, Skomer Island
D1386	*Hoplangia durotrix**	Carpet coral	Skomer Island
D1404	*Balanophyllia regia*	Gold and scarlet star coral	N. Pembrokeshire, Ramsey Island, Skomer Island
P1689	*Ophelia bicornis**	Worm	Llandidian sands, Three Cliffs Bay (Gower)
S0522	*Nannonyx spinimanus**	Amphipod	Menai Strait
S0783	*Pectenogammarus planicrurus**	Amphipod	Aberystwyth
W0379	*Paludinella littorina*#*	Sea snail	Broad Haven, Caldey Island (S. Pembrokeshire)
W0732	*Simnia patula*	Sea snail	The Smalls, Skomer Island
W1245	*Tritonia nilsodhneri*	Sea slug	Skomer Island
W1302	*Okenia elegans**	Sea slug	Skomer Island, Stackpole Quay
W1313	*Trapania maculata**	Sea slug	Off Shell Island (Sarn Badrig)
W1367	*Greilada elegans*	Sea slug	Skomer Island, Milford Haven
W1376	*Thecacera pennigera*	Sea slug	Skomer Island
W1397	*Doris sticta*	Sea slug	Skomer Island
W1442	*Hero formosa*	Sea slug	Menai Strait
W1536	*Caloria elegans**	Sea slug	Off Shell Island (Sarn Badrig)
Y0243	*Amathia pruvoti**	Bryozoan	Milford Haven
Y0715	*Hincksina flustroides**	Bryozoan	Ynys Enlli
ZB0184	*Stichastrella rosea*	Starfish	Menai Strait
ZD0092	*Polysyncraton lacazei**	Colonial sea squirt	Skomer Island
ZD0159	*Phallusia mammillata**	Sea squirt	Ynys Enlli
ZD0258	*Molgula oculata*	Sea squirt	Ynys Enlli, Skomer Island
ZM0230	*Gelidiella calcicola*##*	Red seaweed	Milford Haven
ZM0559	*Schmitzia hiscockiana*	Red seaweed	Ynys Enlli, N. Pembrokeshire, Skomer Island, Milford Haven
ZM0618	*Gigartina pistillata*	Red seaweed	Skomer Island, Gower
ZM0701	*Cruoria cruoriaeformis##*	Red seaweed	St. Tudwal's Island & Ynys Gwylan-fawr (Llyn Peninsula), Milford Haven
ZR0485	*Carpomitra costata*	Brown seaweed	Skomer Island

Note: Species codes are after Howson (1987). Key: * nationally rare; # protected under Wildlife & Countryside Act 1981; ## - occurs in association with the maerl species *Phymatolithon calcareum* and *Lithothamnion corallioides*, both listed on the EC Habitats Directive 1992.

(≈ reproduce) slowly here; they are therefore particularly vulnerable to even the most minor, infrequent damage. This makes these communities particularly important as reference sites for monitoring the marine environment (Fowler & Laffoley 1993).

In contrast to the Mediterranean species, the distribution of the hydroid *Tamarisca tamarisca* is known to extend to the Arctic, and the sponge *Stryphnus ponderosus*, the hydroid *Hartlaubella gelatinosa* and the anemones *Isozoanthus sulcatus* and *Mesacmaea mitchellii* all have broader distributions to the north and south of Great Britain. The worm *Ophelia bicornis* and the starfish *Stichastrella rosea* are known from other Atlantic coasts in Europe (see e.g. Hayward & Ryland 1990; Picton 1993).

The sponge *Stryphnus ponderosus* is known to have a wide depth range, and so may be rare only in the near-shore sea area which is the focus of this analysis.

The rare colonial sea squirt *Polysyncraton lacazei*, although reasonably distinctive, may be more under-recorded than other listed species (B.E. Picton *pers. comm.*), and although scarce on a national basis, some sea slugs and algae are recorded only sporadically; populations are prone to fluctuate from year to year. Such short-lived organisms may require more regular re-evaluation of their occurrence. In addition, other species, e.g. *Pectenogammarus planicrurus*, *Mesacmaea mitchellii* and *Schmitzia hiscockiana*, although rare or scarce in terms of their areas of occurrence, may not be uncommon where they do occur.

Many rare and scarce marine benthic species in Region 12 occur on sublittoral rock: the sponges *Axinella damicornis*, *Plocamilla coriacea*, *Stelletta grubii*, *Stryphnus ponderosus*, *Tethyspira spinosa* and *Thymosia guernei*, the hydroids *Aglaophenia kirchenpaueri* and *Hartlaubella gelatinosa*, the anthozoans *Balanophyllia regia*, *Caryophyllia inornata*, *Eunicella verrucosa*, *Hoplangia durotrix*, *Isozoanthus sulcatus*, *Parazoanthus axinellae* and *Parerythropodium coralloides*, the bryozoan *Hincksina flustroides*, the sea squirts *Phallusia mammillata* and *Polysyncraton lacazei* and the algae *Carpomitra costata*, *Gelidiella calcicola*, *Gigartina pistillata* and *Schmitzia hiscockiana* (see e.g. Picton 1985; Manuel 1988; Dixon & Irvine 1977; Ackers, Moss & Picton 1992). Of these, *Caryophyllia inornata*, *Hoplangia durotrix*, *Phallusia mammillata*, *Polysyncraton lacazei* and *Stelletta grubii* tend to favour sheltered localities, whereas *Gigartina pistillata*, *Stichastrella rosea*, *Tethyspira spinosa* and *Thymosia guernei* prefer wave-exposed coasts and *Plocamilla coriacea* and *Thymosia guernei* favour flowing water conditions. The sponge *Stryphnus ponderosus*, the hydroid *Obelia bidentata* and the anthozoans *Isozoanthus sulcatus* and *Parazoanthus axinellae* may also be found on other substrata, such as shells and wrecks and, in the case of *Stryphnus ponderosus* and *Obelia bidentata*, on sand. *Hincksina flustroides* is commonly found on shell. *Isozoanthus sulcatus* and *Parazoanthus axinellae* sometimes occur on organic substrata as well although records from this region are mostly from rock (F.St.P.D. Bunker *pers. comm.*). The hydroid *Laomedea angulata* grows on eel grass and the bryozoan *Amathia pruvoti* is often found tangled in a turf of other organisms.

Halcampoides elongatus, *Mesacmaea mitchellii* and *Molgula oculata* are found in sediments, where they are nevertheless usually partially exposed. The polychaete worm *Ophelia bicornis*, however, lives buried in loose-packed intertidal

sand and the amphipod *Pectenogammarus planicrurus* lives intertidally in clean shingle beaches (Hayward & Ryland 1990). *Paludinella littorina* can be found high on the shore in crevices or amongst rotting vegetation (Bratton 1991); see also Table 5.3.1.

Several of the species in this region are often associated with other benthic organisms. The sponge *Stelletta grubii* is associated with a variety of epifaunal organisms (growing attached), which can cover it over (Ackers, Moss & Picton 1992). Despite this it is still safe to regard it as scarce rather than as inconspicuous and so under-recorded (D. Moss pers. comm.). The sponges *Plocamilla coriacea* and *Stryphnus ponderosus* also have other sponges growing on them. *Axinella damicornis*, however, is sometimes found partly hidden by bryozoan and hydroid undergrowth. Another rare species of sponge in Region 12, *Thymosia guernei*, is regularly associated with *Polydora* worms, and juvenile brittlestars *Ophiothrix fragilis* also often occur in the same location (Ackers, Moss & Picton 1992).

The alga *Gelidiella calcicola* is at the northern limit of its distribution at Milford Haven, and, as with *Cruoria cruoriaeformis*, it is found associated with maerl (Hiscock *in prep.*).

Nudibranchs (sea slugs) are predatory and many are very specialist predators. The rare nudibranch *Okenia elegans*, found around Skomer, feeds on the sea squirt *Polycarpa rustica* and is often found partially buried into the body of the prey animal (Picton & Morrow 1994). For the same reason *Greilada elegans* and *Thecacera pennigera* are often found in association with bryozoans (*Bugula* spp.); *Tritonia nilsodhneri* on the sea fan *Eunicella verrucosa*; and *Trapania maculata* with small invertebrates on the surface of bryozoans, sponges, and hydroids. The foods of the sea slugs *Caloria elegans*, *Doris sticta* and *Hero formosa* are not known but they have all been found on the hydroids *Nemertesia*, *Plumularia* and *Halecium*. The food of *Simnia patula*, however, is known to be coelenterates (e.g. 'corals', anemones and hydroids) such as *Alcyonium*, *Eunicella* and *Tubularia*.

5.4.3 Information sources used

The sites of littoral (shore) and sublittoral benthic surveys used in the present work for Region 12 are those mapped in section 4.2. A large proportion of the available data originates from MNCR survey work and former NCC-funded surveys, many of which are available as JNCC reports. Other available published sources have been used as well as the personal records of taxonomic experts. It has only been possible to list recent and review publications in the further reading section. This list, as well as the references cited in section 4.2, will allow access to the literature on which the analysis for the current section is based.

MNCR survey work uses a consistent methodology to assess conspicuous species (Hiscock 1990). Not all the data available from other studies in this region are as broad in scope, and sometimes they have not included less common species or those less familiar to the specialist worker, thus reducing the data available for rarity assessment.

Some areas within Region 12 have a long history of study; for example, records for the Menai Strait go back to the 19th century. Data from reports more than 30 years old have not been used in this section. Elsewhere in this region, particularly some areas in Cardigan Bay, suitable information is lacking. The MNCR of Great Britain is at present incomplete but in future will substantially increase the quality and evenness of distribution of the available data. This will almost certainly expand our knowledge of the 'nationally rare' species in Region 12, making the re-evaluation of their status necessary and possibly also requiring the addition of further species. A re-evaluation of status will be more likely with certain faunal and floral groups that are less well understood, for example hydroids and bryozoans.

5.4.4 Further sources of information

A. References cited

Ackers, R.G., Moss, D., & Picton, B.E. 1992. *Sponges of the British Isles ('Sponge V') - a colour guide and working document.* 5th ed. Ross-on-Wye, Marine Conservation Society.

Bratton, J.H., ed. 1991. *British Red Data Books: 3. Invertebrates other than insects.* Peterborough, Joint Nature Conservation Committee.

Dixon, P.S., & Irvine, L.M. 1977. *Seaweeds of the British Isles. Vol. 1. Rhodophyta. Part 1. Introduction, Nemaliales, Gigartinales.* London, British Museum (Natural History).

Fletcher, R.L. 1987. *Seaweeds of the British Isles. Vol. 3 Fucophyceae (Phaeophyceae).* London, British Museum (Natural History).

Fowler, S., & Laffoley, D. 1993. Stability in Mediterranean-Atlantic sessile epifaunal communities at the northern limits of their range. *Journal of Experimental Marine Biology & Ecology,* 172: 109-127.

Graham, A. 1988. *Molluscs: Prosobranch and pyramellid gastropods. Keys and notes for the indentification of the species.* 2nd ed. Leiden, E.J. Brill/Dr W. Backhuys for Linnean Society of London/Estuarine and Brackish-water Sciences Association. (Synopses of the British Fauna (New Series), No. 2).

Hayward, P.J., & Ryland, J.S., eds. 1990. *The marine fauna of the British Isles and north-west Europe.* 2 Vols. Oxford, Clarendon Press.

Hiscock, K. 1990. Marine nature conservation review: methods. *Nature Conservancy Council, CSD Report,* No. 1072. (Marine Nature Conservation Review Report, No. MNCR/OR/5.)

Hiscock, K., ed. In prep. *Surveys of harbours, rias and estuaries in southern Britain. Final report and assessment of marine biological interest and nature conservation.* Peterborough, Joint Nature Conservation Committee (Marine Nature Conservation Review Report).

Howson, C.M., ed. 1987. *Directory of the British marine fauna and flora. A coded checklist of the marine fauna and flora of the British Isles and its surrounding seas.* 1st ed. Ross-on-Wye, Marine Conservation Society.

Mace, G., Collar, N., Cooke, J., Gaston, K., Ginsberg, J., Leader-Williams, N., Maunder, M., & Milner-Gulland, E.J. 1993. *The development of new criteria for listing species on the IUCN Red List.* Unpublished IUCN article.

Manuel, R.L. 1988. *British Anthozoa (Coelenterata: Octocorallia and Hexacorallia); keys and notes for the identification of the species.* 2nd ed. Leiden, Linnean Society of London/Estuarine and Brackish Water Sciences Association.

Picton, B.E. 1985. *Ascidians of the British Isles. A colour guide.* Ross on Wye, Marine Conservation Society.

Picton, B.E. 1993. *A field guide to the shallow-water echinoderms of the British Isles.* London, IMMEL Publishing, for Marine Conservation Society.

Picton, B.E., & Morrow, C.C. 1994. *A field guide to the nudibranchs of the British Isles.* London, Immel Publishing.

Sanderson, W.G. In prep. *Rare marine benthic fauna and flora in Great Britain: the development of criteria.* Peterborough, Joint Nature Conservation Committee.

B. Further reading

Bunker, F.St.P.D., & Hiscock, S. 1987. Sublittoral habitats, communities and species of the Skomer Marine Reserve - a review. (Contractor: Field Studies Council, Pembroke.) *Nature Conservancy Council, CSD Report,* No. 747. (FSC Report, No. (OFC)/1/87.)

Bunker, F.St.P.D., Picton, B.E., & Morrow, C.M. 1992. *New information on species and habitats in the Skomer Marine Nature Reserve (and other sites off the Pembrokeshire coast).* (Contractor: Marine Seen/Ulster Museum, Belfast.) Unpublished report to Countryside Council for Wales.

Davies, J. 1991. Benthic marine ecosystems of Great Britain: a review of current knowledge. Western Channel and the Bristol Channel and approaches (MNCR coastal sectors 8 & 9). *Nature Conservancy Council, CSD Report,* No. 1173.

Killeen, I.J., & Light, J.M. 1994. *A survey of the prosobranch mollusc Paludinella littorina on the Pembrokeshire coast.* Unpublished, Countryside Council for Wales. (CCW Science Report, No. 62.)

Maggs, C.A., & Guiry, M.D. 1987. *Gelidiella calcicola* sp. nov. (Rhodophyta) from the British Isles and northern France. *British Phycological Journal,* 22: 417-434.

Maggs, C.A., & Guiry, M.D. 1989. A re-evaluation of the crustose red algal genus *Cruoria* and the family Cruoriaceae. *British Phycological Journal,* 24: 253-269.

Maggs, C.A., & Hommersand, M.H. 1993. *Seaweeds of the British Isles. Volume 1: Rhodophyta. Part 3A: Ceramiales.* London, HMSO, for Natural History Museum, London.

Mills, D.J.L. 1991. Benthic marine ecosystems in Great Britain: a review of current knowledge. Cardigan Bay, north Wales, Liverpool Bay and the Solway (MNCR Coastal sectors 10 and 11). *Nature Conservancy Council, CSD Report,* No. 1174.

Rees, E.I.S. 1992. *Environmental study of a proposed exploratory drilling location north of Bardsey Island: benthic habitats.* (Contractor: University College of North Wales, Unit for Coastal and Estuarine Studies, Menai Bridge.) Unpublished report to Hamilton Oil Company Ltd. (UCES Report, No. U92-6.)

C. Contact names and addresses

Type of information	Contact address and telephone no.
Rhodophycean algae	Dr J. Brodie, Bath College of Higher Education, Newton Park, Newton Street, Loe, Bath BA2 9BN, tel: 01225 873701
Tunicates	*D.W. Connor, Marine Conservation Branch, JNCC, Peterborough, tel: 01733 62626
Phaeophycean algae	Dr F.L. Fletcher, University of Portsmouth, Marine Laboratory, Ferry Road, Hayling Island, Hants PO11 0DG, tel: 01705 876543
Pectenogammarus	Dr J.D. Fish, University College of Wales, Institute of Biological Science, Edward Llwyd Building, Aberystwyth, Dyfed SY23 3DA, tel: 01970 623111
Ophelia	Dr T. Harris, Department of Biological Sciences, University of Exeter, Hatherly Laboratories, Prince of Wales Road, Exeter EX4 4PS, tel: 01392 263263
Bryozoans	Dr P.J. Hayward, School of Biological Sciences, University College Swansea, Singleton Park, Swansea, West Glamorgan SA2 8PP, tel: 01792 205678
Molluscs	J. Light, 88 Peperharow Road, Godalming, Surrey GU7 2PN, tel: 01483 417782
Rhodophycean algae	Dr C.A. Maggs, School of Biology & Biochemistry, Queen's University of Belfast, Belfast BT7 1NN, tel: 01232 245133
Amphipods	Prof. P G Moore, University Marine Biological Station, Millport, Isle of Cumbrae KA28 0EG, tel: 01475 530581
Sponges	D. Moss, Department of Mathematics, University of Manchester, Manchester M13 9PL, tel: 0161 275 2000
Echinoderms, nudibranchs, hydroids, sponges.	B.E. Picton, BioMar, Environmental Science Unit, University of Dublin, Trinity College, Dublin 2, Republic of Ireland, tel: 010 353 167 72941

* Starred contact addresses are given in full in the Appendix

5.4.5 Acknowledgements

The author is grateful for the assistance of the JNCC Marine Conservation and Coastal Conservation Branches, as well as for the expert advice of Dr J. Brodie, Mr F.St.P.D. Bunker, Mr D.W. Connor, Dr M.J. Costello, Dr R.L. Fletcher, Dr J.D. Fish, Dr J. Hall-Spencer, Dr . T. Harris, Dr P.J. Hayward, Dr K. Hiscock, Mrs J. Light, Dr C.A. Maggs, Prof. P.G. Moore, Mr D. Moss, Dr J.D. Nunn, Mr B.E. Picton, Dr S.M. Smith and Dr R. Williams. Data from the Marine Nature Conservation Review database and the Northern Ireland Biological and Earth Sciences Record Centre have been invaluable.

5.5 Exploited sea-bed species

Dr M.G. Pawson and C.F. Robson

5.5.1 Introduction

This section describes the distribution of large populations of species that live on, near, or in the bottom sediments of the sea bed (the benthos) and that are routinely exploited by humans, mainly for human food The exploitation itself is described in sections 9.1 and 9.2. Many of these species also provide an essential food source for other species, such as fish and birds, for example migrant and wintering waders and wildfowl. Most of the species discussed have planktonic larvae; the dispersal of planktonic larvae and the interrelation between populations of the same species can only be inferred from studies on movements of water masses. Their distributions are often determined by water temperature (see section 2.3) and available habitat/substrate type (see section 4.3). The species described may also be found elsewhere in the region, but in smaller numbers.

All species apart from *Nephrops* are referred to by their common names in the text. The scientific names of the species are given in Table 5.5.1.

5.5.1 Table of species names

Common name	Scientific name
Lobster	*Homarus gammarus*
Edible crab	*Cancer pagurus*
Spider crab	*Maja squinado*
Crawfish, spiny lobster	*Palinurus elephas*
Dublin Bay prawn, scampi, Norway lobster or langoustine	*Nephrops norvegicus*
Deep water prawn (or shrimp - referred to as both)	*Pandalus borealis*
Brown shrimp	*Crangon crangon*
Pink prawn (or shrimp - referred to as both)	*Pandalus montagui*
Cockle	*Cerastoderma edule*
Mussel	*Mytilus edulis*
Native oyster	*Ostrea edulis*
Pacific oyster (non-native)	*Crassostrea gigas*
Periwinkle	*Littorina littorina*
Scallop	*Pecten maximus*
Queen scallop	*Chlamys opercularis*
Whelk	*Buccinum undatum*
Lugworm	*Arenicola marina*
Ragworm	*Nereis* spp.
Maerl	*Lithothamnion* spp.
Laver weed	*Porphyra* spp.

In the region there are exploitable populations of crawfish and spider crab which are of national importance. Lobster and edible crab, though important in the region, are also important in most other parts of Great Britain and the Isle of Man. Compared with other areas there are only small quantities of *Nephrops* and brown shrimp. Although mussels and cockles are present elsewhere, the region's sites for these species, for example Burry Inlet for cockles and the Menai Strait for mussels, sustain nationally significant shellfisheries.

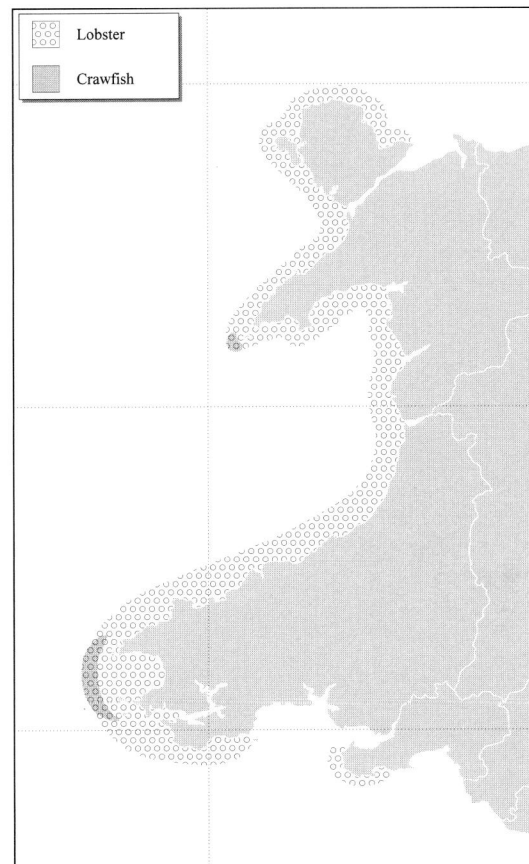

Map 5.5.1 Distribution of exploited crustacea: lobster and crawfish. Copyright of the Shellfish Resource Group, MAFF Directorate of Fisheries Research (Lowestoft).

5.5.2 Important locations and species

Crustacea: Relatively small stocks of lobster are distributed throughout the region wherever there is suitable habitat, such as rocky reefs with crevices for protection. Crawfish have a more limited distribution in the region and are found off the Pembrokeshire peninsula and to a lesser extent off Ynys Enlli. The broad-scale distributions of lobster and crawfish in the region are shown in Map 5.5.1. Edible crabs are found along exposed or rocky shorelines throughout most of the region, often on softer sediments (ranging from sand/gravel to rock) than lobsters. Juveniles tend to be found inshore and adults further offshore (Rees & Dare 1993). Spider crabs are mainly present south from Cemaes Head around the Pembrokeshire islands as far as, and including, Carmarthen Bay. The distribution of *Nephrops* is determined by its preference for a sea bed of muddy sand, into which it burrows, and in this region it is restricted to small populations occurring between the Smalls and Milford Haven. Deep-water prawns and brown shrimps are not found in exploitable quantities in the region, although some pink prawns are found around Cardigan Bay. The broad-scale distributions of edible crabs and spider crabs in the region are shown in Map 5.5.2.

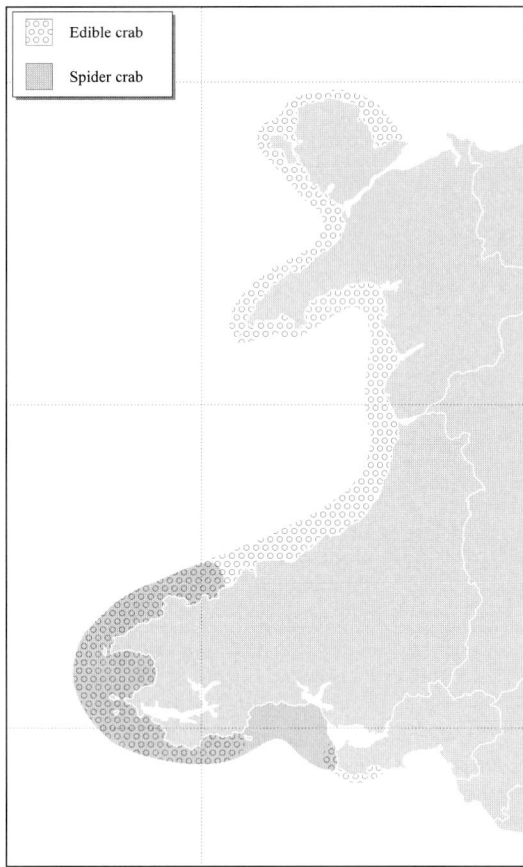

Map 5.5.2 Distribution of exploited crustacea: edible crab and spider crab. Copyright of the Shellfish Resource Group, MAFF Directorate of Fisheries Research (Lowestoft).

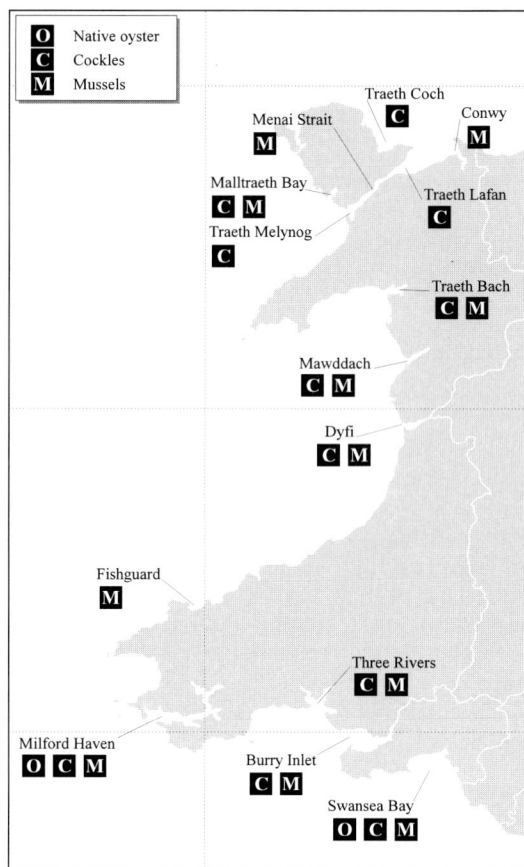

Map 5.5.3 Main locations of exploited mollusc species: inshore and estuarine. Copyright of the Shellfish Resource Group, MAFF Directorate of Fisheries Research (Lowestoft).

Molluscs - inshore and estuarine: Cockles are found in the intertidal zones of many sandy estuaries and other sheltered sites in this region, but the main locations of commercial significance are the Burry Inlet, the Dyfi estuary, Traeth Bach and Traeth Lafan, and to a lesser extent Swansea Bay, the Three Rivers estuary, Milford Haven, the Mawddach estuary, Traeth Melynog, Maltraeth Bay and Traeth Coch. Cockles in the Burry Inlet appear to be a self-sustaining population, but there is no comparable information for other areas in the region (SWSFC pers. comm.). Mussels are found from the mid shore to the subtidal zone in water of normal or variable salinity and in areas exposed to water currents. They attach themselves using 'byssus threads' to sand, gravel or pebble substrata or other mussels and empty shells, effectively binding the substratum. Mussel stocks are widely distributed around coastal sites in the region, with the main areas in the Menai Strait (where yield is enhanced using husbandry techniques - see section 9.2) and Conwy. The main locations at which exploitable populations of cockles, mussels and native oyster are found in the region are shown in Map 5.5.3.

The native or flat oyster develops on the lower shore of the intertidal zone and subtidally, on a wide range of substrata from mud to bedrock, but is now considered to be quite rare. Native oyster beds have normally developed in sheltered conditions in estuaries and their decline around Britain has been attributed to various factors, including overfishing, the failure of 'spatfall' (spat are newly settled metamorphosed juveniles), disease (*Bonamia ostreae*) and cold winters (Spencer 1990). In a few locations in the region commercially exploitable populations are present - in

Milford Haven and offshore from Swansea. The Pacific oyster is a non-native species, introduced to encourage oyster farming (see section 9.2); it does not develop naturally in the region. However, small spatfalls of the non-native Pacific oyster have been recorded in the Menai Strait, probably owing to the warm summers of 1989 and 1990 (Spencer *et al.* 1994). This species is now farmed in preference to the native oyster, because it grows to a marketable size faster and is resistant to the pest *Bonamia ostreae* (Spencer 1990) (see section 9.2).

Perwinkles live on algae growing on rocky shorelines throughout the region.

Molluscs - offshore: Scallops and queen scallops live on sandy/gravely areas of sea bed. Scallops are found north of Anglesey and in the south of Cardigan Bay. Queen scallops are also found in the south of Cardigan Bay, though stocks have declined there since the 1970s and it is not known whether exploitable populations survive (NW & NWSFC pers. comm.). Whelks are probably widely dispersed throughout the region but concentrations exist in two areas: in the north of Cardigan Bay and to the east of Anglesey. The broad-scale distributions of scallops, queen scallops and whelks in the region are shown in Map 5.5.4.

Polychaetes: The intertidal and subtidal zones in the region's estuaries support populations of polychaetes, such as the lugworm and ragworm, which are commonly dug by anglers for rod and line bait (see section 9.1). Lugworms are common in less exposed areas where there is a higher organic content in the substratum. They occur elsewhere in a wide range of sediment types, from almost pure mud to clean sand (Davidson *et al.* 1991).

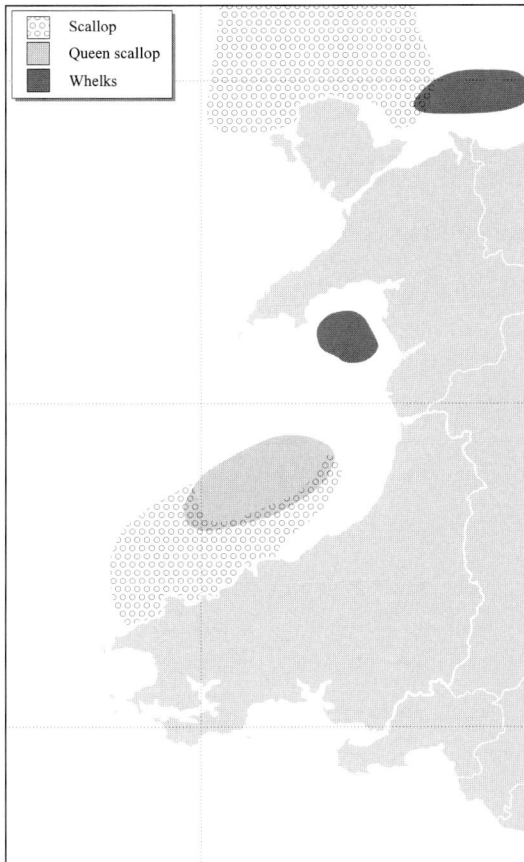

Map 5.5.4 Main locations of exploited mollusc species: offshore. (Queen scallop may not be present in commercial quantities throughout area shown.) Copyright of the Shellfish Resource Group, MAFF Directorate of Fisheries Research (Lowestoft).

Others: Maerl (see also section 4.2) is a collective name given to various species of calcareous algae within the Rhodophyta (red seaweeds) that in this region live unattached on the substratum in sheltered areas in Milford Haven (Gubbay 1988) (see also section 4.2). Laver weed is common on exposed bedrock in intertidal areas in south and west Wales.

5.5.3 Human activities

The exploitation by fisheries of the species covered in this section is described in Section 9.1, and by mariculture in Section 9.2. There are two issues relating to the shellfish industry in the region: firstly, the general levels of exploitation, unregulated except for crustacea (currently lobster and crab minimum sizes) and the restrictions placed on the exploitation of cockles and mussels through Regulating Orders (see sections 9.1.2 & 9.1.4); and, secondly, the possible effects of mechanical harvesting on the benthos, feeding birds and cockle stocks (Evans & Clark 1993). Both mobile and, to a lesser extent, static gears damage and/or modify sea-bed habitats and their associated animal and plant communities by direct physical impact. For example in 1985, scallop dredging was shown to cause significant habitat, community and species damage in the then proposed Skomer Marine Nature Reserve (Bullimore 1985),

and it is now prohibited within the Marine Nature Reserve under SWSFC Byelaws.

Bait collection, especially digging, can have major localised effects on intertidal habitats and communities and can also cause disturbance to birds, when concentrated in estuaries and embayments. These issues are explored in the references given in section 5.5.5.

Industrial effluents, domestic sewage and estuarine run-off are sources of chemical pollutants (e.g. PCBs, heavy metals) and pathogenic organisms and can elevate nutrient levels or increase the oxygen demand; these can all impact directly on exploited sea-bed species.

5.5.4 Information sources used

The four maps in this section show schematically the known broad-scale distribution of the main species of interest, based on current knowledge from MAFF scientists and fishery officers on the location of the species and their fisheries. Barring substantial climate change or over-exploitation, these distributions and relationships are likely to remain stable over several decades. The seaward boundaries on the maps are only indicative, and because only large, exploitable populations are described, the species may also be found elsewhere in the region, but in smaller numbers. There is supporting information in the form of catch statistics for commercial landings, biological samples of crustacea collected at the main ports and some secondary ports, and intertidal surveys for molluscs in selected areas. These data provide some information about the location of spawning and nursery areas, but to establish the links between individual spawning, nursery and adults areas would require specific research vessel investigations on the planktonic stages, the hydrography, and the movement (or otherwise) of juveniles and adults.

5.5.5 Further sources of information

A. *References cited*

Bullimore, B. 1985. *An investigation into the effects of scallop dredging within the Skomer Marine Reserve.* A report to the Nature Conservancy Council from the Skomer Marine Reserve Subtidal Monitoring Project (unpublished).

Davidson, N.C., Laffoley, D.d'A., Doody, J.P., Way, L.S., Gordon, J., Key, R., Drake, C.M., Pienkowski, M.W., Mitchell, R., & Duff, K.L. 1991. *Nature conservation and estuaries in Great Britain.* Peterborough, Nature Conservancy Council.

Evans, J., & Clark, N.A. 1993. *Disturbance studies on Swansea Bay and the Burry Inlet in relation to bird populations.* Thetford, British Trust for Ornithology (Research Report No. 107).

Gubbay, S. 1988. *A coastal directory for marine nature conservation.* Ross-on Wye, Marine Conservation Society.

Rees, H.L., & Dare, P.J. 1993. *Sources of mortality and associated life-cycle traits of selected benthic species: a review.* Lowestoft, MAFF. (Directorate of Fisheries Research, Fisheries Research Data Report No. 33.)

Spencer, B.E. 1990. *Cultivation of Pacific oysters.* Lowestoft, MAFF. (Directorate of Fisheries Research Laboratory Leaflet No. 63.)

Spencer, B.E., Edwards, D.B, Kaiser, M.J., & Richardson, C.A. 1994. Spatfall of the non-native Pacific oyster *Crassostrea gigas* in British waters. *Aquatic Conservation: Marine and Freshwater Ecosystems,* 4: 203-217.

B. Further reading

Further details of marine survey sites are in the *Coastal & Marine UKDMAP datasets* module (Barne *et al.* 1994), available from JNCC Coastal Conservation Branch, Peterborough.

Barne, J., Davidson, N.C., Hill, T.O., & Jones, M. 1994. *Coastal and Marine UKDMAP datasets: a user manual.* Peterborough, Joint Nature Conservation Committee.

Cadman, P.S. 1989. Environmental impact of lugworm digging. (Contractor: University College of Swansea, Marine, Environmental and Evolutionary Research Group.) *Nature Conservancy Council, CSD Report,* No. 910.

Chatfield, J. 1979. Marine molluscs in Wales. *Journal of Conchology, 30:* 1-34.

Clark, P.F. 1986. North-east Atlantic crabs; an atlas of distribution. Ross-on-Wye, Marine Conservation Society.

Coates, P.J. 1983. *Fishing bait collection in the Menai Strait and its relevance to the potential establishment of a Marine Nature Reserve with observations on the biology of the main prey species, the ragworm* Nereis virens. MSc thesis, Centre for Environmental Technology, Imperial College of Science and Technology, University of London.

Cook, W. 1991. *Studies on the effects of hydraulic dredging on cockle and other macroinvertebrate populations 1989 - 1990.* North Western and North Wales Sea Fishery Committee.

Countryside Council for Wales. 1994. *A preliminary bibliography to the water and coast around Bardsey Island and the southwestern Lleyn Peninsula.* Unpublished draft.

Cryer, M., Whittle, G.N., & Williams, R. 1987. The impact of bait collection by anglers on marine intertidal invertebrates. *Biological Conservation, 42:* 83-93.

Eno, N.C., *ed.* 1991. *Marine conservation handbook.* 2nd ed. Peterborough, English Nature.

Ferns, P.N., & Siman, H.Y. 1993. Effects of mechanised cockle harvesting on bird feeding activity in the Burry Inlet. *Countryside Council for Wales Science Report,* No. 34.

Franklin, A., Pickett, G.D., & Connor, P.M. 1980. *The scallop and its fishery in England and Wales.* Lowestoft, MAFF. (Directorate of Fisheries Research Laboratory Leaflet No. 51.)

Hancock, D.A. 1971. The role of predators and parasites in a fishery for the mollusc *Cardium edule* L. *In: Dynamics of populations,* ed. by P.J. den Boer & G.R. Gradwell. Proceedings of the Advanced Study Institute, Oosterbeck, 1970, Centre for Agric. Publ. and Documentation, Wageningen.

Huggett, D. 1992. *Foreshore fishing for shellfish and bait.* Sandy, Royal Society for the Protection of Birds.

McLusky, D.S., Anderson, F.E., & Wolfe-Murphy, S. 1983. Distribution and population recovery of *Arenicola marina* and other benthic fauna after bait digging. *Marine Ecology Progress Series, 11:* 173 - 179.

Moore, J. 1991. *Studies on the impact of hydraulic cockle dredging on intertidal sediment flat communities.* Final report to NCC from the Field Studies Council Research Centre. (FSC/RC/4/91.)

Norton, T.A., & Geffen, A.J. 1990. *Exploitable living resources.* Liverpool University Press. (Irish Sea Study Group Report Part 3.)

Olive, P.J.W. 1993. Management of the exploitation of the lugworm *Arenicola marina* and the ragworm *Nereis virens* (Polychaeta) in conservation areas. *Aquatic Conservation: Marine and Freshwater Ecosytems, 3:* 1-24.

Rostron, D.M. 1993. The effects of tractor towed cockle dredging on the invertebrate fauna of Llanrhidian Sands, Burry Inlet. *Countryside Council for Wales Science Report,* No. 36. Bangor, Countryside Council for Wales.

Seaward, D.R. 1990. *Distribution of the marine molluscs of north-west Europe.* Peterborough, NCC, for Conchological Society of Great Britain and Ireland.

Seaward, D.R. 1993. Distribution of the marine molluscs of north-west Europe (1990). Additions and amendments. *JNCC Report,* No. 165.

Simpson, A.C. 1961. A contribution to the bionomics of the lobster *Homarus vulgaris* (Edw.) on the coast of North Wales. MAFF Fishery Invest., Lond., Ser II, 23 (7).

Young, G.A. 1992. *The Menai Strait: a review and bibliography of literature from the Wolfson Library.* Unpublished report to Countryside Council for Wales. (Contractor: University College of North Wales, Bangor.)

C. Contact names and addresses

Type of information	Contact address and telephone no.
Fish stocks and fisheries advice to assist with management and policy decisions for the coastal zone	Director, MAFF Directorate of Fisheries Research, Fisheries Laboratory (Conwy), Benarth Road, Conwy, Gwynedd LL32 8UB, tel: 01492 593883
Assessment and provision of advice on the conservation of commercial fish and shellfish stocks. Publications leaflet.	Director, MAFF Directorate of Fisheries Research, Fisheries Laboratory (Lowestoft), Pakefield Road, Lowestoft, Suffolk NR33 OHT, tel: 01502 562244
Reviews and bibliography. Information and advice on marine conservation issues in Wales	*Marine and Coastal Section, CCW HQ, Bangor, tel: 01248 370444. Also Regional Offices.
Benthic surveys: (Marine Nature Conservation Review Database)	*Marine Conservation Branch, JNCC, Peterborough, tel: 01733 62626
Library and scientific advice	Director/Librarian, University College of North Wales, School of Ocean Sciences, Menai Bridge, Gwynedd LL59 5EY, tel: 01248 716367
Reports and publications from work undertaken	Director, Field Studies Council Research Centre, Oil Pollution Research Unit, Fort Popton, Angle, Pembroke, Dyfed SA71 5AD, tel: 01646 641404
Milford Haven monitoring studies and reports produced for and compiled by the Steering Group	Trevor D. Lloyd, Milford Haven Waterway Environmental Monitoring Steering Group, Civil Protection Planning Unit, Dyfed County Council, Hill House, Picton Terrace, Carmarthen, Dyfed SA31 3BS, tel: 01267 236651
Information and advice on marine conservation issues in the Skomer Marine Nature Reserve	*Warden, CCW Skomer, Haverfordwest, tel: 01646 636736
Marine Fisheries Task Group paper and advice on marine conservation issues	*Marine Advisory Officer, Marine Conservation Branch, JNCC, Peterborough, tel: 01733 62626
Information and advice on marine conservation issues in Wales	*Marine and Coastal Section, CCW HQ, Bangor, tel: 01248 370444
Information and advice on marine conservation issues	*Marine Conservation Officer, RSPB Sandy, tel: 01767 680551
Information and advice on marine conservation issues	*Fisheries Officer, Marine section, WWF-UK, Godalming, tel. 01483 426444
Information and advice on marine conservation issues	*Conservation Officer, Marine Conservation Society, Ross-on-Wye, tel: 01989 566017
Information and advice on issues in Cardigan Bay	*Projects Officer, Cardigan Bay Forum, Aberystwyth, tel: 01970 624471
Information on issues in Irish Sea Study Group area	*Chairman, Irish Sea Forum, University of Liverpool, tel: 0151 794 4089
Information and advice on marine conservation issues	Administrator, The Marine Forum for Environmental Issues, Department of Zoology, The Natural History Museum, Cromwell Road, London SW7 5BD, tel: 0171 938 9114

* Starred contact addresses are given in full in the Appendix

5.5.6 Acknowledgements

Thanks to R.C.A. Bannister (Shellfish Resource Group, MAFF Directorate of Fisheries Research, Lowestoft) and Blaise Bullimore (CCW) for their helpful comments and additional written sections.

5.6 Amphibians and reptiles

Dr M.J.S. Swan

5.6.1 Introduction

All nine of the widespread species of amphibian and terrestrial reptile and two species of marine turtle have been recorded in the coastal 10 km squares that fall within the boundaries of this region. They are the amphibians: common frog *Rana temporaria*, common toad *Bufo bufo*, smooth newt *Triturus vulgaris*, palmate newt *T. helveticus* and great crested newt *T. cristatus*; the terrestrial reptiles: slow-worm *Anguis fragilis*, common lizard *Lacerta vivipara*, grass snake *Natrix natrix* and adder *Vipera berus*; and the marine turtles: leatherback *Dermochelys coriacea* and loggerhead *Caretta caretta*. There are also unconfirmed 1970s reports of sand lizards *Lacerta agilis*. All the region's amphibian and reptile species have some national and international protection, and three - sand lizard, loggerhead turtle and leatherback turtle - have particular international significance. The number of records for reptiles and amphibians in the region is summarised in Table 5.6.1.

Frogs and toads are widely, but patchily, distributed along the region's coastline, occurring in 87% and 79% of surveyed 10 km squares, respectively. They have also been recorded on relatively barren offshore islands. The smooth newt and great crested newt are rare or virtually absent from Dyfed (5% and 0% of 10 km squares respectively), although both species are quite well represented in Gwynedd (24% and 27%

Table 5.6.1 Total and mean numbers of amphibian and reptile records per 10 km square

	Total no. of individual records		Mean no. individual records 10 km square	
	amphibians	reptiles	amphibians	reptiles
W. Glamorgan	36	34	5.1	4.8
Dyfed	107	200	4.9	6.1
Gwynedd	509	300	15.4	9.4
Region 12	*652*	*534*	*10.5*	*7.4*
GB West Coast	3,383	1,536	10.2	5.1
GB coast	7,524	3,138	11.3	5.7
Whole GB	27,182	8,803	12.1	4.7

Source: Biological Records Centre, Monks Wood.

respectively). Survey coverage in West Glamorgan is insufficient to comment on species' distributions or status (see section 5.6.4). Gwynedd contains a high diversity of amphibian species, with 69% of surveyed 10 km squares containing at least three species (Map 5.6.1), comparing favourably with the entire British west coast (49%), the GB coast (also 49%) or Great Britain as a whole (22%).

Note that survey effort has not been equivalent throughout the region, so actual occurrence may differ from recorded distribution.

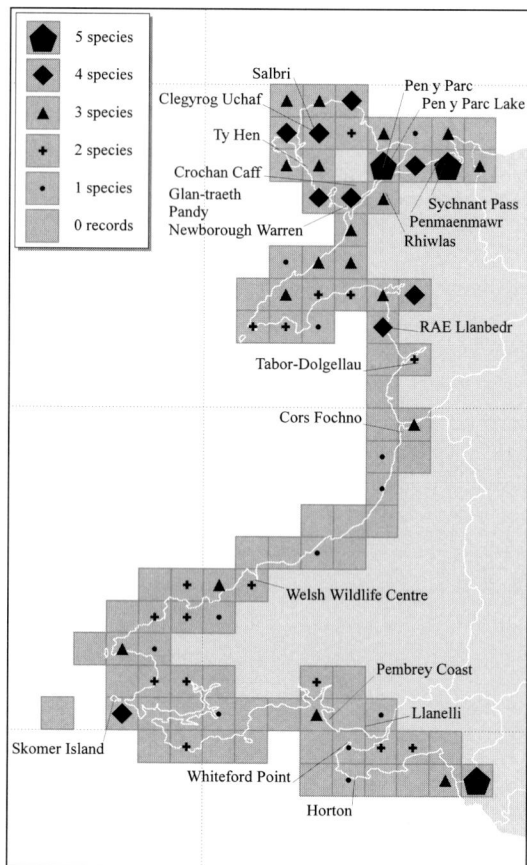

Map 5.6.1 Numbers of amphibian species recorded in coastal 10km squares and known key localities for amphibians. Source: Biological Records Centre, ITE Monks Wood.

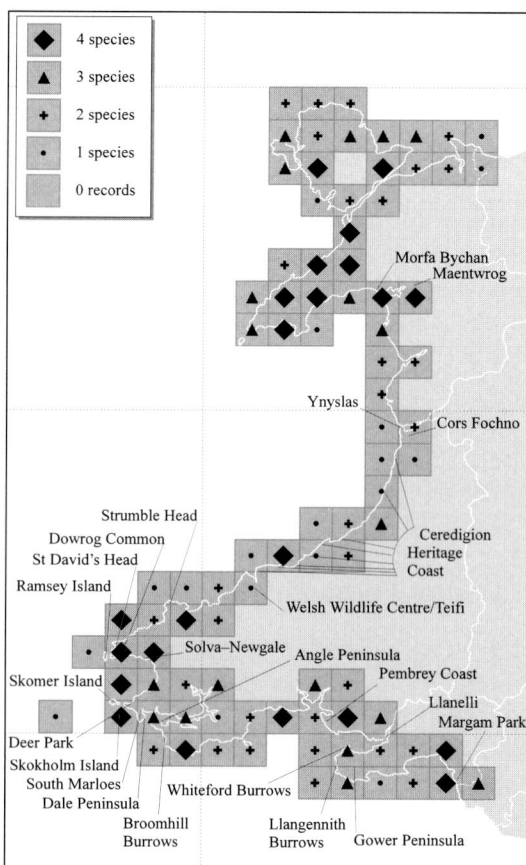

Map 5.6.2 Numbers of reptile species recorded in coastal 10km squares and known key localities for reptiles. Source Biological Records Centre, ITE Monks Wood.

Table 5.6.2 Important sites for amphibians

Site name	Grid ref.	Species	Information
Horton, Gower (farm pond - only recorded breeding site in W. Glamorgan)	SS4786	great crested newts	qualitative
Whiteford Point (dune slack)	SN4595	frog, palmate newt	qualitative
Llanelli (dune slack)	SN5-9-	frog, palmate newt	qualitative
Pembrey Coast (dune slack)	SN3-0-	frog, palmate newt	qualitative
Skomer Island	SM725096	frog, toad, palmate newt	*
Welsh Wildlife Centre/Teifi Estuary (marsh)	SN1845	frog, toad, palmate newt	qualitative
Cors Fochno (raised mire)	SN6292	frog, toad, palmate newt	qualitative
Tabor-Dolgellau	SH747176	frog, toad, palmate newt	*
RAF Llanbedr (50 m from Morfa Dyffryn)	SH564257	great crested newts	
Glan-traeth SSSI	SH415665	great crested newts (large population)	
Pandy	SH412658	frog, toad, palmate newt	*
Newborough Warren NNR/SSSI (4 locations)	SH392648	great crested newts (moderate population)	
	SH398651	great crested newts (moderate population)	
	SH404637	great crested newts (moderate population)	
	SH404651	great crested newts (moderate population)	
Crochan Caffo	SH436692	frog, toad, palmate newt	*
Ty Hen Farm	SH327734	frog, toad, palmate newt	*
Clegyrog Uchaf (100 m from Llyn Hafodol and Cors Clegyrog SSSI)	SH386888	great crested newts	
Salbri (200 m from Salbri SSSI)	SH376890	great crested newts	
Pen y Parc	SH586752	frog, toad, palmate newt, great crested newt, smooth newt	*
Pen y Parc Lake	SH585753	frog, toad, palmate newt, great crested newt	*
Rhiwlas	SH583661	frog, toad, palmate newt	*
Sychnant Pass SSSI	SH755766	great crested newts (moderate population)	

Sources: Welsh Wildlife Trusts, CCW, Vice-county recorders, National Park, National Nature Reserve (NNR), Heritage Coast and Sites of Special Scientific Interest (SSSI) managers, Swan & Oldham (1993a,b). Note: * = important sites, based on NCC amphibian community scoring system described in Swan & Oldham (1989).

This region contains a slightly higher percentage of 10 km squares supporting at least three reptile species (50%) (Map 5.6.2) than the west coast (44%), the GB coast (43%) or Great Britain as a whole (45%). Coastal habitats in the region may provide a stronghold for reptiles, which are particularly abundant on some clifftops and areas of coastal heath and grassland. A national pilot study (Corbett 1994) has identified several sand dune systems in the region as potential sand lizard re-introduction sites. Common lizards and adders are widely distributed along the coast, occurring in over 70% of recorded squares in each county. Slow-worms are also present throughout the region but have been observed less frequently (47% of surveyed 10 km squares), possibly because of their more secretive nature. Slow-worms also occur on the offshore islands of Skokholm, Skomer and Ramsey. Grass snakes have been recorded more frequently on the south-facing than the west-facing coasts of each of the three counties and generally in wetter, lusher areas (e.g. Winterton Marsh, Dyfed) than the other reptiles. Adders and common lizards are particularly abundant on the Pembrokeshire coast.

5.6.2 Important locations and species

This region contains one of only nine SSSIs in Britain notified for their great crested newt populations. Great crested newts in the region are concentrated in Gwynedd, being apparently absent from Dyfed and recorded so far in only one site in West Glamorgan. The region also supports 11% (see Table 5.6.2) of the best amphibian community assemblage sites in Great Britain. Table 5.6.2 lists important sites for great crested newts and other amphibian species.

The mainly narrow coastal strip between farmland and the shoreline provides habitat for adders and common lizards - sand dunes, coast paths, short grassland, heathland (wet and dry) and exposed bare rocks. The region's dune slacks and coastal scrub are also excellent amphibian habitat.

Fewer quantitative data are available for the identification of prime reptile sites than for amphibian sites, so most of the information presented is anecdotal. Reptile presence in most of the named areas, if not their level of abundance, is confirmed by National Amphibian and Reptile Surveys (NARS) data. Important reptile areas are listed in Table 5.6.3.

Five species of marine turtle have been recorded in British waters, two of which, the leatherback turtle *Dermochelys coriacea* and the loggerhead turtle *Caretta caretta*, have been recently reported in the region. In 1991 two stranding incidents were recorded: a loggerhead and an unidentified turtle were found at Newgale and at Tenby beaches, respectively. The loggerhead was still alive when found, but died within days of rescue. In 1993, a leatherback was found at Hell's Mouth on the Llyn Peninsula, entangled in lobster pot lines, and in 1994 an unidentified turtle was found at Rhosneigr.

Table 5.6.3 Important areas for reptiles

Site/area	Grid ref.	Habitat	Species
W. Glamorgan			
Margam Park	SS7887		grass snake, slow worm, adder
Gower Peninsula		coastal grassland, wet heath	common lizard, grass snake, slow worm, adder
Llangennith Burrows	SS4291	sand dunes	common lizard, grass snake, adder
Whiteford Burrows	SS4595	sand dunes	common lizard, grass snake, slow worm, adder
Dyfed			
Llanelli	SS5-9-	sand dunes	slow worm, common lizard, grass snake, adder
Pembrey Coast	SS3-0-	sand dunes	slow worm, common lizard, grass snake, adder
Broomhill Burrows	SM8900	sand dunes, shingle	adder
Angle Peninsula	SM8603	path, cliff grassland, exposed rocks, heath	slow worm, common lizard, grass snake (uncommon), adder (particularly abundant)
Dale Peninsula	SM8205	path, cliff grassland, exposed rocks, heath	slow worm, common lizard, grass snake (uncommon), adder (particularly abundant)
South Marloes Coast	SM7808	path, cliff grassland, exposed rocks, heath	slow worm, common lizard, grass snake (uncommon), adder (particularly abundant)
Deer Park	SM7509	path, cliff grassland, exposed rocks, heath	slow worm, common lizard, grass snake (uncommon), adder (particularly abundant)
Skokholm Island	SM7305	heath, grassland	slow worm
Skomer Island	SM7209	heath, grassland	slow worm
Solva to Newgale	SM8223	path, cliff grassland, exposed rocks, heath	slow worm, common lizard, grass snake (uncommon), adder (particularly abundant)
Ramsey Island	SM7023	heath, grassland	slow worm
St David's Head	SM7629	path, cliff grassland, exposed rocks, heath	slow worm, common lizard, grass snake (uncommon), adder (particularly abundant)
Dowrog Common	SM7727	wet heath	common lizard, adder
Strumble Head	SM9141	path, cliff grassland, exposed rocks, heath	slow worm, common lizard, grass snake (uncommon), adder (particularly abundant)
Teifi Estuary/Welsh Wildlife Centre	SN1945	slate quarry, woodland, low cliff, grazing marsh, reed bed	common lizard, slow worm, adder, probably grass snake
8 locations along coastal strip between Towyn Warren and Brynbala	SN1648 to SN5987	path, shingle, cliff, cliff grassland, heath	common lizard, slow worm, adder
Cors Fochno	SN6393	raised mire	slow worm, common lizard, grass snake, adder
Ynyslas	SN6094	sand dunes	common lizard, sand lizard*
Gwynedd			
Maentwrog	SH6540	woodland, wetland, scrub, heath	slow worm, common lizard, grass snake, adder
Morfa Bychan SSSI	SH5436	sand dune, reed bed	slow worm, common lizard, grass snake, adder

Sources: Welsh Wildlife Trusts, CCW, Vice-county recorders, National Park, Nature Reserve, Heritage Coast and SSSI wardens, Swan & Oldham (1993a,b). * - not reported since 1970s.

5.6.3 Human activities

Currently, few land-use issues affect the herpetofauna of this region. In Gwynedd, only 10% of potential amphibian breeding sites are thought to be affected by harmful human activities, compared with 35% of recorded sites nationally (Swan & Oldham 1993a,b). Coastal reptile habitats subject to visitor pressure are being damaged, but those relatively remote from human population centres are not thought to be at risk.

5.6.4 Information sources used

Of the coastal 10 km squares in Britain, 69% have been surveyed for amphibians and reptiles. Table 5.6.4 indicates the percentage of 10 km squares which have been surveyed for herpetofaunal species throughout Great Britain and in 10 km coastal squares nationally, along the west coast of Britain, the coastline of Wales and of each of the counties of

this region. Overall, therefore, the coast of Wales has been well recorded, especially Gwynedd. Reptile recording effort in Dyfed is also high but for amphibians is low; West Glamorgan, however, is a particularly under-recorded county for both amphibian and reptile species. Records of reptiles and amphibians are concentrated in the north and south-west of the region, largely reflecting recording effort. However, anecdotal evidence suggests that the paucity of records from the centre of the region could also be due to a shortage of small water-bodies and to the narrowness of the undisturbed coastal strip, relative to areas to the north and south.

National distribution data after 1970 for amphibians and terrestrial reptiles were provided by the Biological Records Centre (BRC) at Monk's Wood (Arnold 1983; Arnold in prep.). These include all the data collected during the National Amphibian and Reptile Surveys (NARS) undertaken by De Montfort University for English Nature (Oldham & Nicholson 1986; Swan & Oldham 1989, 1993 a, b). Qualitative information was provided by the

Table 5.6.4 Percentage of 10 km squares surveyed for amphibians and reptiles

	Total 10 km squares	%10 km squares surveyed		
		Any herp species	Amphibians	Reptiles
W Glamorgan	12	67	58	58
Dyfed	44	75	50	75
Gwynedd	38	87	87	84
Region 12	*90*	*82*	*69*	*80*
GB West Coast	620	63	53	49
GB coast	1,124	69	59	49
Whole GB	2,862	84	79	66

Source: Biological Records Centre, Monks Wood.

Countryside Council for Wales (CCW), the Welsh Wildlife Trusts, vice-county recorders of amphibians and reptiles and staff of coastal Country Parks, Heritage Coasts and local authorities, as well as being extracted from the NARS databases. Turtle information was supplied by the Natural History Museum and Southampton University. CCW and the Welsh Wildlife Trusts hold lists of recorded great crested newt and other amphibian breeding sites throughout Wales.

5.6.5 Further sources of information

A. References cited

Arnold, H.R., *ed.* 1983. *Distribution maps of the amphibians and reptiles of the British Isles.* Huntingdon, Biological Records Centre.

Arnold, H.R., *ed.* In prep. *Atlas of amphibians and reptiles in Britain and Ireland.* Huntingdon, Biological Records Centre.

Corbett, K. 1994. Pilot study for sand lizard UK recovery programme. *English Nature Research Report,* No 102. (Contractor: Herpetological Conservation Trust.)

Oldham, R.S., & Nicholson, M. 1986. *Status and ecology of the warty newt* Triturus cristatus. *Final Report.* (Contractor: Leicester Polytechnic.) Peterborough, unpublished report to the Nature Conservancy Council.

Swan, M.J.S., & Oldham, R.S. 1989. *Amphibian communities, final report.* Peterborough, unpublished report to the Nature Conservancy Council. (Contractor: Leicester Polytechnic.)

Swan, M.J.S., & Oldham, R.S. 1993a. Herptile sites. Volume 1: National amphibian survey. *English Nature Research Report,* No. 38. (Contractor: De Montfort University.)

Swan, M.J.S., & Oldham, R.S. 1993b. Herptile sites. Volume 2: National reptile survey. *English Nature Research Report,* No. 39. (Contractor: De Montfort University.)

Whitten, A.J. 1990. *Recovery: A proposed programme for Britain's protected species.* Peterborough, Nature Conservancy Council.

B. Further reading

British Herpetological Society. 1990. *Save our reptiles.* (Advisory leaflet issued by the BHS Conservation Committee.)

British Herpetological Society. 1990. *Surveying for amphibians.* (Advisory leaflet issued by the BHS Conservation Committee.)

British Herpetological Society. 1990. *Garden ponds as amphibian sanctuaries.* (Advisory leaflet issued by the BHS Conservation Committee.)

Corbett, K. 1990. *Conservation of European reptiles and amphibians.* London, Christopher Helm.

Mallinson, J.J. 1990. Turtle rescue. *Marine Conservation, Winter 1990/91:* 8-9.

Mallinson, J.J. 1991. Stranded juvenile loggerheads in the United Kingdom. *Marine Turtle Newsletter, 54:* 14-16.

Wisniewski, P.J. 1984. Distribution of amphibians and reptiles in Glamorgan, South Wales. *British Herpetological Society Bulletin, 9:* 29-34.

C. Contact names and addresses

Type of information	Contact address and telephone no.
Conservation and captive breeding of herptiles	The British Herpetological Society, c/o The Zoological Society of London, Regent's Park, London NW1 4RY, tel. 0181 452 9578
Conservation of threatened reptiles and amphibians	Conservation Officer, The Herpetological Conservation Trust, 655A Christchurch Road, Boscombe, Bournemouth, Dorset BH1 4AP, tel. 01202 391319
Amphibian and reptile conservation and recording groups (national secretariat)	Common Species Co-ordinator, Herpetofauna Groups of Britain and Ireland, c/o HCIL, Triton House, Bramfield, Halesworth, Suffolk IP19 9AE, tel. 0198 684 518
Herpetological conservation in Britain (lead conservation agency)	Lowlands Team, English Nature, Northminster House, Peterborough PE1 1UA, tel. 01733 340345
National distribution data and recording schemes	*Biological Records Centre, ITE Monks Wood, tel. 01487 773381
Turtles	Dr Colin McCarthy, Natural History Museum, Cromwell Road, London SW7 5BD, tel. 0171 938 9123
as above	Dept of Oceanography, Southampton University, Highfield, Southampton SO9 5NH, tel. 01703 595000
Amphibians and reptiles in Wales	*Phase 1 Coordinator, CCW North Wales Region, Bangor, Gwynedd, tel. 01248 372333
as above	University of Wales - Llysdinam Field Centre, Newbridge-on-Wye, Llandrindod Wells, Powys LD1 6NB, tel. 0159 789308
as above	*Vice-county recorders for Pembrokeshire, Ceredigion and Carmarthen, c/o Dyfed Wildlife Trust, Haverfordwest, tel. 01437 765462
as above	*North Wales Wildlife Trust, Bangor, tel./fax. 01248 351541
as above	*Glamorgan Wildlife Trust, Tondu, tel. 01656 724100
Herptiles on the West Glamorgan Coast	*CCW South Wales Region, Cardiff, tel. 01222 485111
Herptiles on the Ceredigion Heritage Coast	Planning Department, Cyngor Dosbarth Ceredigion, Penmorfa, Aberaeron, Dyfed SA46 0AT, tel. 01545 571115
Herptiles on the Pembrokeshire Coast National Park	National Park Ecologist, County Offices, St Thomas's Green, Haverfordwest, Pembrokeshire SA61 1QZ, tel. 01437 764591
Herptiles in the Welsh Wildlife Centre/Teifi Marshes	Welsh Wildlife Centre, Aberteifi, Cilgerran, Cardigan, Dyfed SA43 2TB, tel. 01239 621600
Herptiles in Ynyslas NNR	*Ynyslas NNR Warden, CCW North Wales Region, Bangor, tel. 01248 372333
Herptiles on the Pembrokeshire Coast	*CCW Fishguard, tel. 01348 874602
Herptiles on the Cardigan Coast, Stackpole	*CCW Aberystwyth, tel. 01970 828551

* Starred contact addresses are given in full in the Appendix

5.6.6 Acknowledgements

The author thanks the following people for providing information and for commenting on drafts: Liz Allan, Henry Arnold, Sue Byrne, Ian Callan, Jo Exell, Jim Foster, Jane Garner, Holly Harris, Jane Hodges, Robin Howard, Liz Howe, Alan Lewis, Gordon Lumby, Jenny Mallinson, Colin McCarthy, Morgan Parry and Annie Poole.

5.7 Fish: exploited sea fish

Dr M.G. Pawson and C.F. Robson

5.7.1 Introduction

This section describes the distributions of sea fish species that are of interest because they are exploited by people, mainly for food. Their exploitation through fisheries is described in section 9.1 and through mariculture in section 9.2. Sea fish described as pelagic (Table 5.7.1) are most commonly found in shoals swimming in midwater; they typically make extensive seasonal movements or migrations between sea areas. 'Demersal' fish are those found living at or near the bottom of the sea. For this report, all sea fish that are not 'pelagic' are termed 'demersal', the latter term thus including bass and grey mullet. Demersal species are here divided into four groups: elasmobranchs (sharks, skates and rays), gadoids (the cod family), flatfish, and other demersal fish (Table 5.7.2). Most demersal species gather in late winter or spring on persistent and recognisable spawning grounds, to release millions of minute free-floating eggs. From these hatch larvae, which feed on and move with the plankton, often for a hundred miles or more, before metamorphosing into tiny fish, which recruit to inshore nursery grounds.

The distribution of each exploited sea fish species can be mapped from expert analysis of catch data, but this is outside the scope of this report. This description of their distribution covers only their occurrence at identifiable localities during particular phases of their life history, and the three maps are restricted to showing the known spawning areas (Map 5.7.1 and 5.7.2) and nursery areas (Map 5.7.3) of key species in the region. Barring substantial climate change, or complete over-exploitation, these distributions and relationships will remain stable over several decades.

5.7.2 Important locations and species

Mackerel is the region's most abundant pelagic fish. They spawn along the edge of the continental shelf from February to July, after which the majority of adult fish migrate to the area around the north of Scotland, although shoals of

Table 5.7.1 Pelagic species and their protected status in region

Species	Protected status
Mackerel *Scomber scombrus*	QM and gear restrictions in southern margin of the region
Horse mackerel *Trachurus trachurus*	QM/MLS
Herring *Clupea harengus*	QM/MLS and mesh regulations on pelagic trawls and gill nets
Sprat *Sprattus sprattus*	-
'Whitebait' - juvenile sprat *Sprattus sprattus* and herring *Clupea harengus*	Limits on proportion of herring permitted in catch

Key MLS = minimum landing size; QM = catch quota management.

Table 5.7.2 Demersal species and their protected status in region

Species	Protected status
Elasmobranchs	
Spurdog *Squalus acanthias*	-
Thornback ray *Raja clavata*	-
Small-eyed ray *Raja microocellata*	-
Gadoids	
Cod *Gadus morhua*	MLS/QM
Whiting *Merlangius merlangus*	MLS/QM
Ling *Molva molva*	-
Pollack *Pollachius pollachius*	MLS/QM
Saithe *Pollachius virens*	MLS/QM
Hake *Merluccius merluccius*	MLS/QM
Flatfish	
Plaice *Pleuronectes platessa*	MLS/QM
Dab *Limanda limanda*	MLS
Sole *Solea solea*	MLS/QM
Turbot *Psetta maxima*	MLS
Brill *Scophthalmus rhombus*	MLS
Megrim *Lepidorhombus whiffiagonis*	MLS/QM
Flounder *Platichthys flesus*	MLS
Other demersal fish	
Bass *Dicentrarchus labrax*	Nursery areas, MLS and mesh size in gill nets
Grey mullets *Chelon labrosus*, *Liza ramada* and *Liza aurata*	MLS (mesh size in gill nets)
Monkfish (angler) *Lophius piscatorius*	QM
Conger eel *Conger conger*	MLS
Gurnards *Triglidae* spp.	-
Wrasse *Labridae* spp.	-
Sandeels *Ammodytes* spp.	-

Key MLS = minimum landing size; QM = catch quota management.

smaller fish occur in coastal waters of the region throughout the summer. Herring are locally abundant and are found around the Pembrokeshire coast. There are no autumn/winter spawning areas in the region, but local spring spawning occurs in Milford Haven (Hobbs & Morgan 1992). Sprat are widely dispersed throughout the region and their main egg and larval distribution covers the whole region apart from Cardigan Bay. Juvenile sprats are often found mixed with young herring in inshore areas, when they are known as 'whitebait'.

All elasmobranch species produce relatively small numbers of live young (10-100 per annum, sometimes fewer in big sharks) or lay large eggs on the sea bed close to their nursery areas. Several species of shark occur at low numbers during their summer migrations off the west coast, but only the spurdog is found regularly in sufficient abundance to be exploited. Another elasmobranch, the thornback ray, is also important locally, especially *en route* to its spring spawning grounds in shallow bays around the region. A number of other ray species are patchily distributed in the area, for example the small-eyed ray off the Gower Peninsula.

Of the gadoids, cod and whiting are abundant and

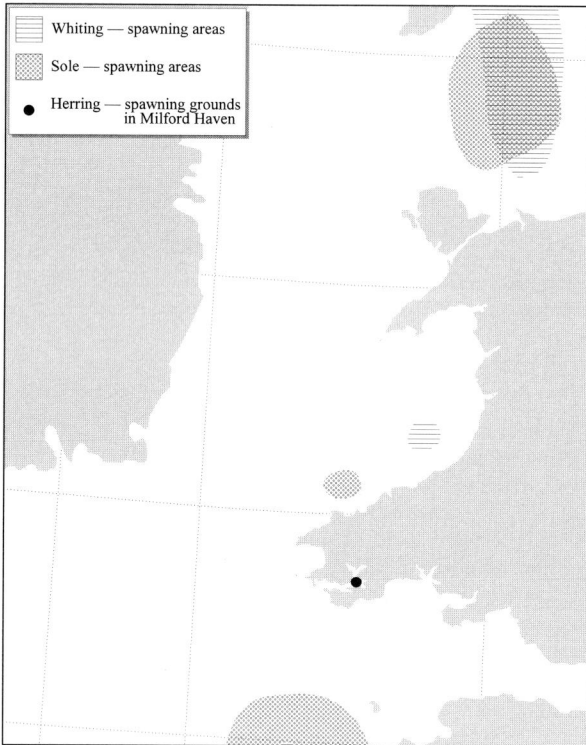

Map 5.7.1 Whiting, sole and herring spawning areas. Source: Lee & Ramster (1981). (c) Crown copyright.

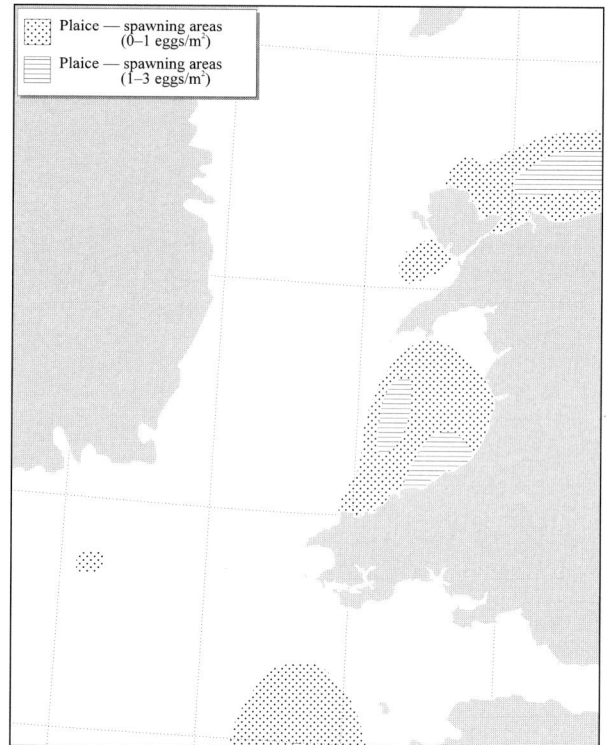

Map 5.7.2 Plaice spawning areas. Source: Lee & Ramster (1981). (c) Crown copyright.

widely distributed in the region. There is a more pronounced aggregation of cod for spawning during February and March at the entrance to the Bristol Channel to the south of the region, and cod have more clearly defined seasonal migrations associated with feeding and spawning than are observed with whiting. Cod congregate for spawning during February and March at the entrance to the Bristol Channel to the south of the region, and their seasonal migrations for feeding and spawning are more clearly defined than those for whiting. There are recognisable whiting spawning areas in the region (Map 5.7.1): one in Cardigan Bay and one off north Wales; the latter only just enters the region and extends north past the Isle of Man. Ling, pollack and saithe are less abundant and more locally distributed, being found particularly around rocky reefs and wrecks. Hake - strictly not a gadoid but included here - is found in the deeper water of the Celtic sea, where the main part of its population lies beyond coastal waters towards the edge of the continental shelf.

The most abundant flatfish in the region's coastal waters are plaice and dab, though much more is known about the life history of the plaice. These species occur on sandy bottoms throughout the area, the juveniles living close to the shore and gradually moving to deeper water as they grow. The knowledge of plaice spawning areas (Map 5.7.2) is obtained from the distribution of newly spawned eggs. Plaice nursery areas in the region are in Carmarthen and Swansea Bays in south Wales and along the coast of north Wales (Map 5.7.3). Sole, which have a similar lifestyle to plaice and dab, spawn in the early summer (April to June) in three known areas within the region (Map 5.7.1). The young sole may spend up to two years in the same inshore nursery areas used by plaice (Map 5.7.3). Turbot and brill are much less abundant but have a similar lifestyle to plaice, dab and sole. There is a nursery area for turbot and brill in

Cardigan Bay (Map 5.7.3). None of these species exhibits extensive migrations, though flatfish larvae can drift for 100 miles or more from offshore spawning grounds to inshore nursery areas, and some juveniles making the transition to the adult phase may move from the Irish Sea into the Bristol Channel, and vice versa. Megrim tend to be found only in the deepest water of this region. All along the coast of the region, flounders migrate between inshore, estuarine and even riverine nursery areas, and spawn up to 20 or 30 miles offshore in late winter; however, there appears to be little longshore coastal movement other than in the egg or larval phase. Important estuarine nursery areas in the region are the Burry Inlet and Milford Haven, and the Dyfi, Dwyryd, Traeth Melynog, Maltraeth and Conwy estuaries.

Bass and the grey mullets are seasonally abundant inshore and in estuaries, and move south along the coast in the autumn to overwintering areas, before spawning offshore and returning north to feeding grounds in the spring. These species use estuaries and sheltered inshore waters as nursery areas. Known bass nursery areas (Kelley 1988) in the region are shown on Map 5.7.3. The nursery areas that are protected by the Bass (Specified Sea Areas) (Prohibition of Fishing) Order 1990: SI 1990 No.1156 are given in section 5.7.3 (MAFF & WO 1990).

Monkfish (angler) spawn in deep water along the shelf edge, but juveniles and non-spawning adults occur throughout the coastal seas. Other demersal species of minor commercial importance are conger eel and various gurnards and wrasse species. Sandeels are distributed widely throughout the region and provide an important food source for many other fish species, including other exploited fish, and for seabirds (see section 5.10). They are also the basis of a minor bait industry.

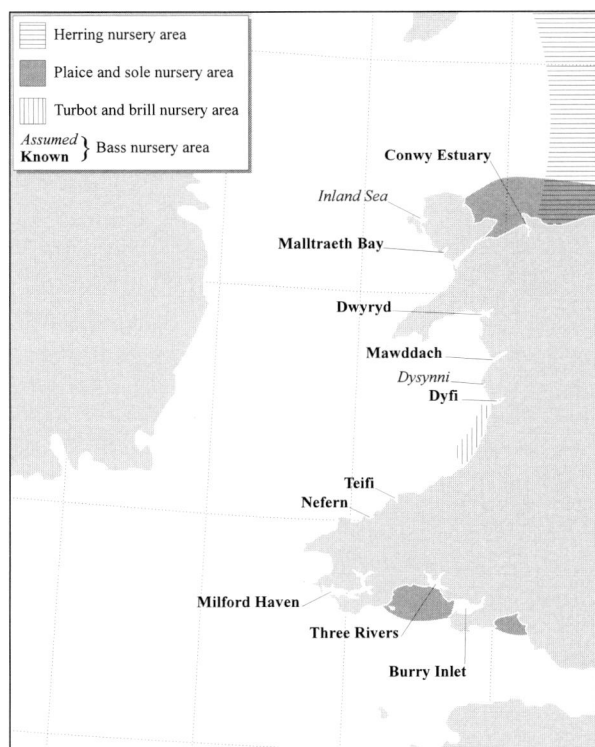

Map 5.7.3 Pelagic and demersal fish species nursery areas. Source: Lee & Ramster (1981). (c) Crown copyright.

5.7.3 Human activities

A feature of all fish stocks, and the primary reason for their fluctuation, is the variability of recruitment of juvenile fish to the exploited populations. This variability, the causes of which are not fully understood, is determined largely by environmental conditions at the time of spawning and in the subsequent larval survival. Exploitation of fish stocks may increase the extent of these fluctuations.

Efforts are made to conserve stocks of pelagic and demersal species by giving them categories of protected status (see Tables 5.7.1 and 5.7.2) reflecting their commercial importance or state of exploitation. Management measures are applied, including minimum landing sizes (MLS), closed fishing areas and seasons, mesh size regulations and quantitative controls on catches (QM) or fishing effort (further explained in section 9.1.3). Their implementation means that species caught below minimum landing size or for which the quota is exhausted may be discarded at sea, and this may affect the exploited species fish stocks as well as other fish species, birds and species that live on the sea bed.

Spawning and nursery areas may be vulnerable to other human activities and their effects occurring in the coastal zone, such as sewage sludge dumping, dredging and dredge spoil dumping and the development of infrastructure, such as barrages and pipelines. MAFF is a statutory consultee for activities such as these, in which the distributions of exploited fish populations and their spawning and nursery areas have to be taken into account before permission is granted.

Out of 34 established bass nursery areas in England and Wales, there are seven in this region, at Burry Inlet, Three Rivers Estuary (Carmarthen Bay), Milford Haven, River Dyfi, River Mawddach, Dwyryd and Glaslyn Estuary, and

the River Conwy (MAFF & WO 1990). They are located where juvenile bass usually predominate and are more easily caught, particularly during the summer. The legislation prohibits fishing for bass from any vessel during the close season, which in these nursery areas is from 1 May to 31 October, and although fishing from the shore is not covered, anglers are expected to return to the sea any bass caught from within the nursery area.

The elasmobranch species have no protected status and are potentially vulnerable because they take a relatively long time to reach reproductive maturity and produce only small numbers of young. Elasmobranchs, particularly rays, have been declining in catches from Cardigan and Carmarthen Bays.

5.7.4 Information sources used

Whereas the life histories of the exploited crustacean and mollusc species can largely be observed at or near the sites at which they are harvested, the distributions of fish populations can change considerably between juvenile and adult phases and with seasonal migrations. Therefore the information used in this section is based on the distribution and relative abundance of fish species revealed by fisheries catch statistics obtained from recorded commercial landing figures. In addition, information is used from research vessel catch data and data from biological sampling during fishing surveys. Data from these surveys on the occurrence of spawning fish and juveniles can be used to identify spawning and nursery areas. However, this information is sometimes limited and there may therefore be other areas in addition to those described or shown on the maps where the species might also occur. Research surveys involving plankton sampling, hydrographic studies, fishing and tagging are required to establish the links between spawning groups and specific nursery areas, and between growing juveniles there and the adult populations to which they eventually recruit. Lee & Ramster (1981) has been extensively used as a source for the maps.

5.7.5 Further sources of information

A. References cited

Hobbs, G., & Morgan, C.I. 1992. *A review of the current state of environmental knowledge of the Milford Haven Waterway.* Commissioned by the Milford Haven Waterway Environmental Steering Group. FSC/RC/5/92.

Kelley, D.F. 1988. The importance of estuaries for sea-bass *Dicentrarchus labrax* (L.). *Journal of Fish Biology, 33* (Supplement A): 25-33.

Lee, A.J., & Ramster, J.W. 1981. *Atlas of the seas around the British Isles.* MAFF, Lowestoft.

Ministry of Agriculture, Fisheries and Food & Welsh Office Agriculture Department. 1990. *Bass nursery areas and other conservation measures.* London, Ministry of Agriculture, Fisheries and Food.

B. Further reading

Barne, J., Davidson, N.C., Hill, T.O., & Jones, M. 1994. *Coastal and Marine UKDMAP datasets: a user manual.* Peterborough, Joint Nature Conservation Committee.

Earll, R.C., *ed.* 1992. *Shark, skate and ray workshop.* Ross-on-Wye, Marine Conservation Society. (Report for Joint Nature Conservation Committee.)

Fowler, S.L., & Earll, R.C., *eds.* 1994. *Proceedings of the second European Shark and Ray Workshop, 15-16 February 1994. Tag and Release Schemes and Shark and Ray Management Plans.* Unpublished report, Peterborough, JNCC.

Norton, T.A., & Geffen, A.J. 1990. *Exploitable living resources.* Liverpool University Press. (Irish Sea Study Group Report Part 3.)

Pawson, M.G., & Pickett, G.D. 1987. *The bass* Dicentrarchus labrax *and management of its fishery in England and Wales.* Lowestoft, MAFF Directorate of Fisheries Research. (Laboratory Leaflet No. 59.)

5.7.6 Acknowledgements

Thanks to the following for providing information Steve May (FSCRC & Dyfed CC), Phil Coates (South Wales Sea Fisheries Committee), Bill Cook (NW & NWSFC), Blaise Bullimore (CCW) and David Rye (Milford Port Health Authority).

C. Contact names and addresses

Type of information	Contact address and telephone no.
Advice to assist with management and policy for the coastal zone	Head of Laboratory, MAFF Directorate of Fisheries Research, Fisheries Laboratory (Conwy), Benarth Road, Conwy, Gwynedd LL32 8UB, tel: 01492 593883
Assessment and advice on the conservation of commercial fish stocks. MAFF Databases e.g. young fish and ground fish surveys, commercial landing statistics. Publications leaflet.	Director, MAFF Directorate of Fisheries Research, Fisheries Laboratory (Lowestoft), Pakefield Road, Lowestoft, Suffolk NR33 OHT, tel: 01502 562244
UKDMAP software with maps showing distributions of selected sea fish	Project Manager, British Oceanographic Data Centre, Proudman Oceanographic Laboratory, Bidston Observatory, Birkenhead, Merseyside L43 7RA, tel: 0151 652 3950
Library and scientific advice	Director/Librarian, University College of North Wales, School of Ocean Sciences, Menai Bridge, Gwynedd, North Wales LL59 5EY, tel: 01248 716367
Information and advice on marine conservation issues in the Skomer Marine Nature Reserve	*Warden, CCW Skomer, Haverfordwest, tel: 01646 636736
Marine Fisheries Task Group papers and advice on marine conservation issues	*Marine Advisory Officer, Marine Conservation Branch, JNCC, Peterborough, tel: 01733 62626
Information and advice on marine conservation issues in Wales	*Marine and Coastal Section, CCW HQ, Bangor, tel: 01248 370444
Information and advice on marine conservation issues	*Marine and Coastal Policy Officers, Conservation Policy Division, RSPB Sandy, tel: 01767 680551
Information and advice on marine conservation issues	*Fisheries Officer, Marine section, WWF-UK, Godalming, tel. 01483 426444
Information and advice on marine conservation issues	*Conservation Officer, Marine Conservation Society, Ross-on-Wye, tel: 01989 566017
Information and advice on issues in Cardigan Bay	*Projects Officer, Cardigan Bay Forum, Aberystwyth, tel: 01970 624471
Information issues in Irish Sea Study Group area	*Chairman, Irish Sea Forum, University of Liverpool, tel: 0151 794 4089
Information and advice on marine conservation issues	Administrator, The Marine Forum for Environmental Issues, Department of Zoology, The Natural History Museum, Cromwell Road, London SW7 5BD, tel: 0171 938 9114

* Starred contact addresses are given in full in the Appendix

5.8 Fish: salmon, sea trout and eels

Dr M. Aprahamian and C.F. Robson

5.8.1 Introduction

Diadromous fish migrate between fresh water and the sea. The three diadromous fish species covered in this section because they are exploited for human consumption - the Atlantic salmon, sea trout and eel - are widespread in British waters, and all are present in this region. (Twaite shad is also diadromous but is included in section 5.9, as it is not routinely exploited.) The salmonids (salmon and sea trout) spawn in fresh water and then migrate out to sea to mature, but eels mature in fresh water and reproduce at sea. Sea trout and brown trout are the same species, but the latter is a freshwater form and is therefore not covered in this section. Information on the life-cycles of these fish can be found in Jones (1959), Mills (1971, 1989), Moriarty (1978), Shearer (1992), Sinha & Jones (1975) and Tesch (1977). Table 5.8.1 gives the protected status of salmon, sea trout and eels in the region.

Table 5.8.1 Species and their protected status

Species name	Protected status
Atlantic salmon *Salmo salar*	Habitats Directive Annexes IIa, Va (freshwater only); close season
Sea trout *Salmo trutta*	Minimum landing size, close season
Eel *Anguilla anguilla*	None

5.8.2 Important locations

Salmon, sea trout and eels have a widespread distribution in British waters, and most of the rivers and coastal seas within the region support populations. The principal rivers that are known from NRA catch statistics to contain salmon and sea trout are shown on Map 5.8.1. Distribution of these species in rivers is controlled by natural factors, such as water levels and the presence of impassable falls or man-made barriers that may limit the extent to which they can go upstream. Sea trout generally have a westerly distribution in Britain and have a modest stronghold in Welsh rivers, which are particularly noted for large fish (i.e. fish that have spawned in a number of successive years). Eels probably occur in all river systems in the region, as elsewhere in Britain.

5.8.3 Human activities

Under the 1991 Water Resources Act, the Welsh Region of the NRA has a duty to maintain, improve and develop salmon, trout, freshwater fish and eel fisheries. Its authority extends from the rivers to coastal waters out to the 6 nautical mile limit, and it shares this responsibility with the two Sea Fisheries Committees of the region (see section 9.1). The NRA uses a variety of techniques, such as

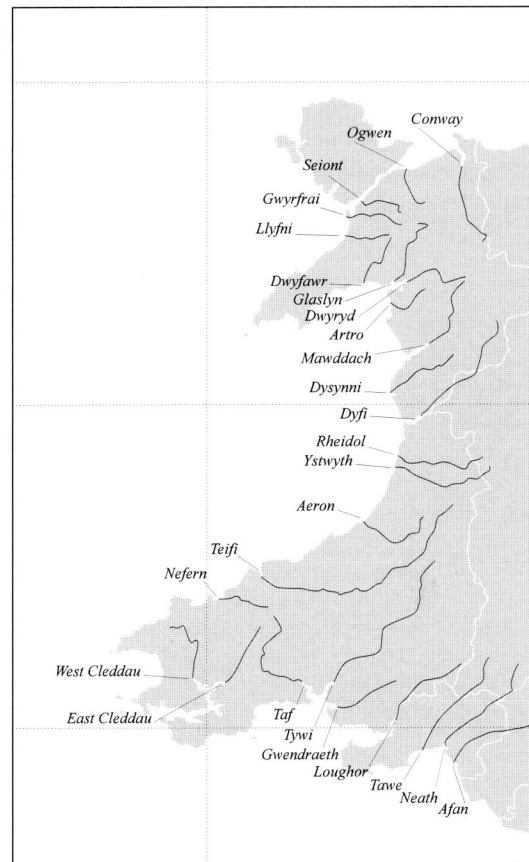

Map 5.8.1 Salmon and sea trout rivers. Source: NRA. River names are as used by NRA for catch statistics.

netting, electric fishing and monitoring of angling catches, to assess fish stocks of salmon and sea trout. They are currently working on a 'Fisheries Classification Scheme' where fisheries will be allocated a quality class on the basis of fish and river habitat data. The NRA construct fish passes around barriers such as falls, or make them passable by fish in other ways. This has been done at the Conwy Falls, with the construction of the longest rock tunnel fish pass in Britain. The NRA also undertakes habitat improvement by, for example, creating pools and adding spawning gravels, riffles and trees for cover.

The effects of exploitation, especially by the different catch methods, i.e. the use of rod and line or nets (MAFF/SO 1991), is an issue for salmon and sea trout stocks. Catch statistics of salmon and sea trout from the region's rivers compared with those for the rest of Great Britain are presented in section 9.1.5. Maitland & Campbell (1992) list the possible effects of a variety of factors on freshwater fish. Issues mentioned which are of relevance in the region include the possible effect of acid deposition on fish stocks (Edwards & Stoner 1990) and the effects of obstructing rivers with amenity and tidal barrages (Dyrynda 1991).

5.8.4 Information sources used

The rivers shown in Map 5.8.1 either support net fisheries or have mean annual rod catches in excess of 30 salmon or 100 sea trout (NRA 1994); some small rivers selected by the Welsh Region of the NRA are also included. Tributaries and minor rivers with a shared estuary are included under the main river, and any remaining rivers in each NRA region are recorded separately in the 'others' category. Diadromous fish are therefore probably also present in rivers not shown. NRA Welsh Region counts fish on the Rivers Usk and Conwy, yielding information on the number of salmon and sea trout migrating upstream.

5.8.5 Further sources of information

A. References cited

Dyrynda, P. 1991. *Tawe Estuary Barrage monitoring Phase 1. Assessment of the existing environment prior to impoundment.* WWF UK (Worldwide fund for Nature).

Edwards, R.W., & Stoner, J.H., *eds.* 1990. Acid waters in Wales. *Monographiae Biologicae*, Vol. 66. Kluwer Academic Publishers.

Jones, J.W. 1959. *The salmon.* London, Collins.

MAFF/SO. 1991. *Salmon net fisheries: report of a review of salmon net fishing in the areas of the Yorkshire and Northumbria regions of the National Rivers Authority and the salmon fishery districts from the River Tweed to the River Ugie.* Presented to Parliament by the Minister of Agriculture, Fisheries and Food, and the Secretary of State for Scotland, pursuant to section 39 of the Salmon Act 1986. London, HMSO.

Maitland, P.S., & Campbell, R.N. 1992. *Freshwater fishes of the British Isles.* Harper Collins. (New Naturalist Library.)

Mills, D.H. 1971. *Salmon and trout: a resource, its ecology, conservation and management.* Edinburgh, Oliver and Boyd.

Mills, D.H. 1989. *Ecology and management of Atlantic salmon.* London, Chapman and Hall.

Moriarty, C. 1978. *Eels.* Newton Abbot, David and Charles.

National Rivers Authority. 1994. *Salmonid and freshwater fisheries statistics for England and Wales, 1992.* London, HMSO & NRA.

Shearer, W.M. 1992. *The Atlantic salmon: natural history, exploitation and future management.* Oxford, Blackwell Scientific.

Sinha, V.R.P, & Jones, J.W. 1975. *The European freshwater eel.* Liverpool, University of Liverpool press.

Tesch, F.W. 1977. *The eel: biology and management of anguillid eels.* London, Chapman and Hall.

B. Further reading

Davidson, N.C., *et al.* 1991. *Nature conservation and estuaries in Great Britain.* Peterborough, Nature Conservancy Council. (Contains a review of fish found in estuaries.)

Jenkins, D., & Shearer, W.M. 1986. *The status of the Atlantic salmon in Scotland.* NERC Institute of Terrestrial Ecology symposium No.15. Banchory Research Station, 13 and 14 February 1985.

National Rivers Authority. 1992. *Sea trout in England and Wales.* NRA, Fisheries Technical Report No. 1.

National Rivers Authority. 1992. *Sea trout literature review.* NRA, Fisheries Technical Report No. 3.

National Rivers Authority. 1992. *The feasibility of developing and utilising gene banks for sea trout* Salmo trutta *conservation.* NRA, Fisheries Technical Report No. 4.

C. Contact names and addresses

Type of information	Contact address and telephone no.
Regional scientific information and advice	*Regional Fisheries Manager, National Rivers Authority - Welsh Region, Cardiff, tel. 01222 770088
Scientific advice and policy. Information on Fisheries Classification Scheme	*Head of Department, National Rivers Authority - Fisheries Department, Bristol, tel. 01454 624400
General enquiries including publications	*Public Relations Officer, National Rivers Authority - Public Relations Department, address as above
Advice on a range of environmental services and scientific advice on its programme of research into freshwater habitats and species	The Director, Institute of Freshwater Ecology - Head Office, Windermere Laboratory, Far Sawrey, Ambleside, Cumbria LA21 0LP, tel. 015394 42468.
Conservation of wild salmon; salmonid research	The Director, The Atlantic Salmon Trust, Moulin, Pitlochry PH16 5JQ, tel. 01796 473439

* Starred contact addresses are given in full in the Appendix

5.8.6 Acknowledgements

Thanks are due to Catherine Smith (JNCC) for compiling information for Map 5.8.1. The following commented on drafts: Steve May (Field Studies Council Research Centre), David Rye (Milford Port Health Authority), Mark Tasker (JNCC), Mike Pawson (MAFF Directorate of Fisheries Reasearch), Phil Coates (SWSFC), John Barne (JNCC) and Richard Howell (NRA - Welsh Region).

5.9 Fish: other species

Dr G.W. Potts and S.E. Swaby

5.9.1 Introduction

The estuaries and coastal waters of the region have rich and diverse fish fauna. 166 fish species have been recorded: one hagfish and two lampreys (Agnatha), 26 sharks and rays (elasmobranchs) and 137 bony fishes (teleosts) (Potts & Swaby 1994b). The region contains a great variety of marine habitats. It is affected by the North Atlantic Drift and the Lusitanian Current, and so the species found include some more characteristic of southern and Mediterranean areas. All seven of Britain's protected fish species occur here. They are the lampern *Lampetra fluviatilis*, the sea lamprey *Petromyzon marinus*, the sturgeon *Acipenser sturio*, the allis and twaite shads *Alosa alosa* and *A. fallax*, and the sand and common gobies *Potamoschistus minutus* and *P. microps*. The sturgeon is now considered a vagrant in British waters and the two gobies are common and not considered threatened in the UK and Europe. The lampreys and shad have been recorded throughout the region, particularly around Gwynedd and, especially, south Dyfed (see Maps 5.9.1 and 5.9.2). The estuaries that feed into the Bristol Channel contain the only known viable populations of shad in the UK and some significant populations of lamperns and sea lampreys (Potts & Swaby 1993b). For this reason the region is of national importance.

5.9.2 Important locations and species

West Glamorgan is popular with anglers, and many species have been recorded. Swansea, Blackpill and the Mumbles are regular angling sites, as is Oxwich Bay on Gower. Important records from Oxwich Bay include increasing numbers of triggerfish *Balistes carolinensis*, which have been recorded from wrecks by anglers, and the first confirmed capture of the blackfish *Centrolophus niger*. In 1985 an angler made the first confirmed catch in Wales of a Cornish blackfish *Schedophilus medusophagus*, off Cefn Sidan Sands, Dyfed.

The River Twyi and the estuaries of the Gwendraeth and Taf are important for allis and twaite shad, as recent records suggest they hold viable populations of both species. Carmarthen Bay and the coasts off Saundersfoot, Tenby and Lydstep are angled frequently. Milford Haven is a centre for boat hire for angling trips, which operate out to approximately 30 miles. Several sunfish *Mola mola* were sighted in 1993 during a survey carried out from Skomer by the Dyfed Wildlife Trust. Non-exploited species caught in Cardigan Bay are occasionally landed at Milford Haven, Fishguard, New Quay and Aberystwyth, including the first Welsh record of the bogue *Boops boops*, which was landed at New Quay in 1985. The first recorded Spanish mackerel

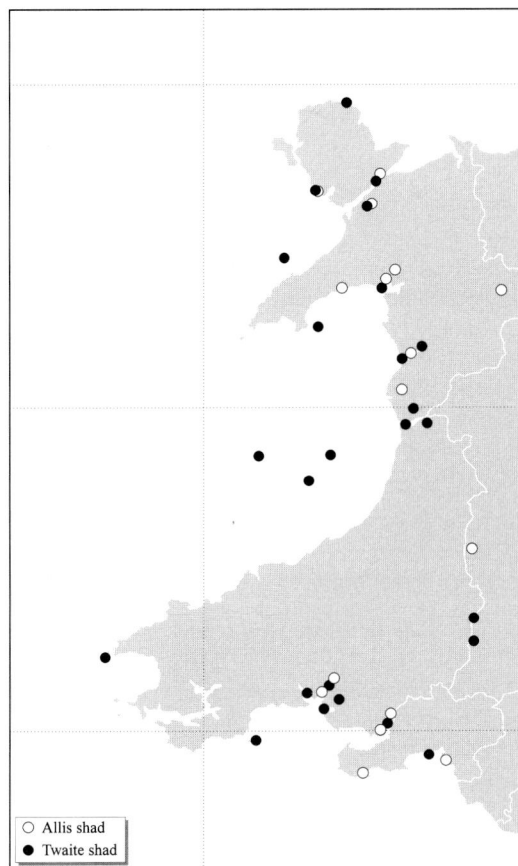

Map 5.9.1 Distribution records on the British Marine Fishes Database of sea lamprey *Petromyzon marinus* and lampern *Lampetra fluviatilis*. After Potts & Swaby (1993a).

○ Sea lamprey
● Lampern

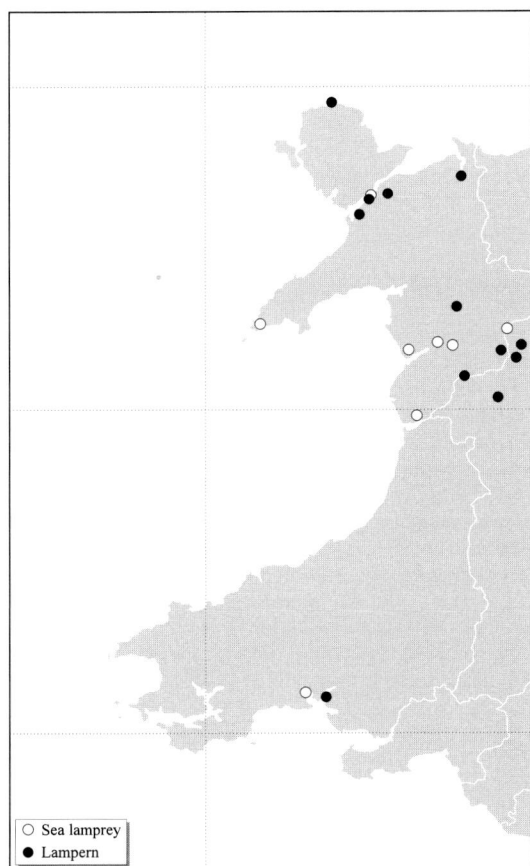

Map 5.9.2 Distribution records on the British Marine Fishes Database of allis shad *Alosa alosa* and twaite shad *Alosa fallax*. After Potts & Swaby (1993a).

○ Allis shad
● Twaite shad

Scomber japonicus was netted off Aberporth.

Gwynedd is an important county for three protected species: the sturgeon and the allis and twaite shads. The Dyfi, Mawddach, and Glaslyn/Dwyryd estuaries all have records of allis and twaite shads and there are more sturgeon records from Gwynedd than from either Dyfed or West Glamorgan (Potts & Swaby 1993b). North Cardigan Bay, including Tremadog Bay, is renowned for unusual fish records, including the only Welsh records for the dentex *Dentex dentex*, from Pwllheli in 1905, and a yellowfin tuna *Thunnus albacares* from Portmerion in 1972. Caernarfon Bay is a commercial fishing ground frequented by many species of ray, including some less common species, e.g. the electric ray *Torpedo nobiliana*, starry ray *Raja radiata* and sting ray *Dasyatis pastinaca*. Sturgeon were once regularly recorded in the Conwy but have declined since the 1950s.

The associations of fish with habitats in Wales are given in Potts & Swaby (1993c). Major marine habitat types identified include estuarine, littoral, sublittoral, offshore and specialist habitats (symbiotic and other relationships), further divided by substrate type (mud, sand, gravel and particulate substrate, bedrock or boulders (reef)) and water column, where appropriate. However, many fish occupy several habitats during different phases of their life-cycles.

5.9.3 Human activities

Human activities affecting estuaries and adjacent coasts are summarised in Buck (1993), and many of these activities affect the abundance and distribution of fishes. Human activities in the region include the following: urban and industrial development and agricultural pollution, which have been shown to have a detrimental impact on the estuarine environment; dams, weirs and barrages, which can impede the passage of migratory fish, for example on the Tawe estuary (Dyrynda 1991); salmon 'passes', which allow some selected species to migrate up or down rivers and estuaries but provide obstacles to the majority of fish, which are unable to reach spawning and feeding grounds; and the disposal of untreated sewage in estuaries, which results in a reduction in dissolved oxygen, to which fish are particularly sensitive (they leave the area, returning only when sewage levels are reduced and oxygen levels increase (Potts & Swaby 1993a)). An additional activity which may have a detrimental effect on the fish fauna is power generation, for example at Wylfa Power Station on Anglesey (Spencer 1989).

5.9.4 Information sources used

The Factsheet Book (Potts & Swaby 1994b) and the further reports (Potts & Swaby 1993a & b, 1994a) give the distribution of all marine and estuarine fish recorded from Welsh waters, including this region, based on a recent survey (1993/4) by the Marine Biological Association for the Countryside Council for Wales (CCW). The survey was the most comprehensive on fish in the UK and is part of the British Marine Fishes Database. The information was gathered from a variety of sources, including universities, NRA, MAFF, Sea Fisheries Committees, anglers and fishermen. The Factsheet Book provides a baseline of

information against which to measure changes in the distribution of fishes and also environmental changes. However, more field surveys are needed, as is still greater involvement of the fishing community and those organisations responsible for the inshore environment.

Surveys of different parts of the region have been carried out by the National Rivers Authority (NRA), universities and other research institutes. Swansea University records coastal and estuarine fishes; Aberystwyth University keeps records of fishes in Cardigan Bay; the University of North Wales keeps records of fish in the Menai Strait area; and all three act as recording centres for the Welsh rod-caught Fish Committee. Fish lists are available for Swansea Bay and Gower (Cox & King 1987). The Menai Strait is regularly surveyed by the University of North Wales. Wylfa Power Station has been surveyed for fishes caught on the intake screens (Spencer 1989). MAFF Fisheries Laboratory have records of the fish in Conwy Bay and the surrounding rivers and estuaries, including non-commercial species taken during their sampling programmes, conducted throughout the Bristol Channel and Irish Sea. The information obtained from these sources has been collated on the British Marine Fishes Database (see below).

This region is covered by an ongoing monitoring programme to identify the impact of environmental change on fish populations. A network of those with a professional or personal interest in fish in Wales has been established, providing the basis of the recording scheme, managed by the British Marine Fishes Database.

5.9.5 Further sources of information

A. References cited

Buck, A.L. 1993. *An inventory of UK estuaries. Volume 2. South-west Britain.* Peterborough, Joint Nature Conservation Committee.

Cox, J.H.S., & King, P.E. 1987. Marine fish of Gower. [Checklist including first records for 18 species]. *Gower, 38:* 37-44.

Dyrynda, P. 1991. *Tawe Estuary Barrage monitoring Phase I. Assessment of the existing environment prior to impoundment.* Godalming, WWF UK.

Potts, G.W., & Swaby, S.E. 1993a. *Review of the status of estuarine fishes.* Peterborough, English Nature. (English Nature Research Reports No. 34.

Potts, G.W., & Swaby, S.E. 1993b. *Marine fishes on the EC Habitats and Species Directive.* Confidential report to the JNCC. Peterborough, JNCC.

Potts, G.W., & Swaby, S.E. 1993c. *Marine and estuarine fishes of Wales. The development of the British Marine Fishes Database and monitoring programme for Wales.* Bangor, Countryside Council for Wales.

Potts, G.W., & Swaby, S.E. 1994a. *Marine and estuarine fishes of Wales. Review of the monitoring programme and 1993/94 results.* Bangor, Countryside Council for Wales.

Potts, G.W., & Swaby, S.E. 1994b. *Marine and estuarine fishes of Wales. Factsheet Book.* 2nd ed. Bangor, Countryside Council for Wales.

Spencer, B, J.F. 1989. *The impingement of fish, invertebrates and weed on the cooling water screens of Wylfa Power Station, September 1985 - September 1987.* National Power. (Research Report. ESTD/L/0076/R89.)

B. Further reading

Jones, G. 1992. *Shad - their status and exploitation in Welsh region.* National Rivers Authority, internal report.

Rees, E.I.S., & Grove, D.J. 1973. Some recent rare and unusual marine fish in north Wales. *Nature in Wales, 13:* 226-228.

Shackley, S.E., King, P.E., & Rhydderch, J. 1979. *Fish and fisheries in Greater Swansea Bay. In:* Industrial embayments and their environmental problems. A case study of Swansea Bay, ed. by M.B. Collins, F.T. Banner, P.A. Tyler, S.J. Wakefield & A.E. James, 555-563. Oxford, Pergamon Press.

C. Contact names and addresses

Type of information	Contact address and telephone no.
British Marine Fishes Database	Prof. Geoffrey W Potts or Miss Silja E Swaby, Marine Biological Association UK, Citadel Hill, Plymouth PL1 2PB, tel: 01752 222772, or British Marine Fishes Database, FREEPOST PY 1767, Plymouth PL1 2BR
Conservation	*Marine Ecologist, CCW HQ, Bangor, tel: 01248 370444
Fisheries	Director, Ministry of Agriculture, Fisheries and Food, Fisheries Laboratory, Benarth Road, Conwy, Gwynedd LL32 8UB, tel: 01492 593883

* Starred contact addresses are given in full in the Appendix

5.9.6 Acknowledgements

The authors wish to thank Dr Mandy Richards (CCW) for her help in compiling this section.

5.10 Seabirds

M.L. Tasker

5.10.1 Introduction

This section deals with seabirds both at their colonies on land and while at sea. It covers not only those species usually regarded as seabirds (see species list in Table 5.10.1), but also divers, grebes and seaducks - i.e. birds reliant for an important part of their life on the marine environment.

This region is important for seabirds in both national and international contexts. The greatest concentrations of birds at sea in this region occur near the colonies during the breeding season. Breeding seabirds require habitat that is free from predatory mammals, so nearly all colonies are on offshore islands or cliffs (Map 5.10.1). The islands of Skomer, Skokholm and Grassholm support the most important seabird colonies in the region. Numbers of Manx shearwater, gannet and lesser black-backed gull all exceed 1% of the world population. The tern population using three sites around Anglesey is also of international importance. Several other sites support nationally important breeding populations. Cormorant, herring gull, guillemot, razorbill and puffin breeding in the region also all occur in internationally important numbers in the region as a whole (Table 5.10.1). The three islands off south-west Wales and the tern colonies of Anglesey are Special Protection Areas (SPAs) under the EC Birds Directive for their seabird populations. There are at present no protected sites at sea in the region.

Map 5.10.1 Colonies holding at least 1% of the GB population of any seabird species. Numbers are those listed in Table 5.10.3. Source: JNCC Seabird Colony Register.

Table 5.10.1 Total numbers and importance of breeding seabird populations in the region

Species	Total in region	% GB	% Europe
Fulmar *Fulmarus glacialis*	3,125	<1	<1
Manx shearwater *Puffinus puffinus*	141,416	56	46
Storm petrel *Hydrobates pelagicus*	500+	n/a	n/a
Gannet *Morus bassanus*	28,600	18	13
Cormorant *Phalacrocorax carbo*	1,658	24	1.9
Shag *Phalacrocorax aristotelis*	677	1.8	<1
Black-headed gull *Larus ridibundus*	397	<1	<1
Lesser black-backed gull *Larus fuscus*	30,760	37	16
Herring gull *Larus argentatus*	10,082	6.7	1.0
Great black-backed gull *Larus marinus*	277	1.5	<1
Kittiwake *Rissa tridactyla*	8,394	1.7	<1
Sandwich tern *Sterna sandvicensis*	441	3.1	<1
Roseate tern *Sterna dougallii*	16	20	2.1
Common tern *Sterna hirundo*	295	2.3	<1
Arctic tern *Sterna paradisaea*	871	2.0	<1
Little tern *Sterna albifrons*	6	<1	<1
Guillemot *Uria aalge*	36,338*	3.5	1.2
Razorbill *Alca torda*	9,685*	6.6	1.6
Black guillemot *Cepphus grylle*	35*	<1	<1
Puffin *Fratercula arctica*	21,000*	2.3	<1

Key: All counts are of pairs, except those marked *, which are of individuals. n/a - data not available. Source: figures for Britain from Walsh *et al.* (1994); for Europe from Lloyd *et al.* (1991). Regional totals are compiled from the most recent available good-quality counts up to 1993.

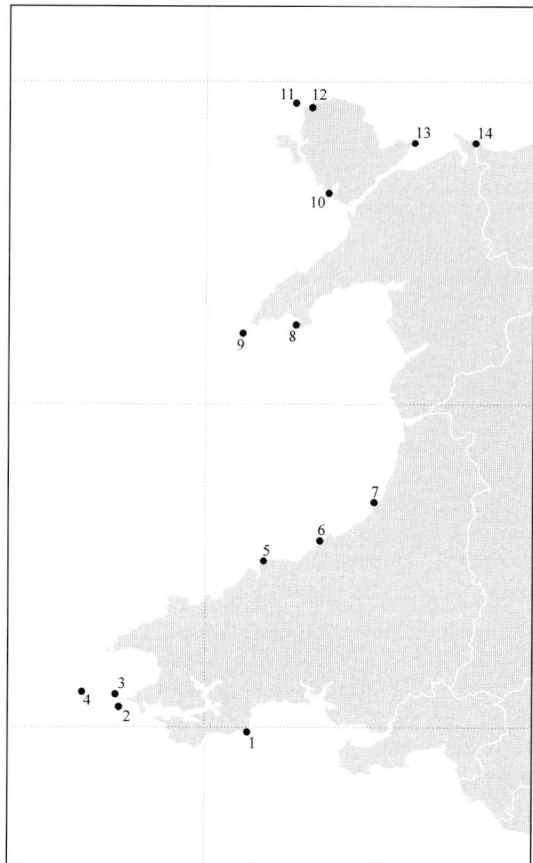

Map 5.10.2 shows the importance of the region's seas for seabirds, in terms of their vulnerability. Seabird vulnerability is calculated from the abundance of birds in the rectangles shown on the map and a factor derived from the amount of time spent on the water, the overall population size and the rate at which the species recruits new individuals to the population (for discussion of vulnerability see Carter *et al.* 1993; Webb *et al.* in prep.).

Table 5.10.2 relates numbers of wintering waterfowl at sea in the region to British and north-west European totals.

5.10.2 Important locations and species

Nine colonies hold numbers of at least one seabird species at or above 1% of the EU total population for that species (Table 5.10.3, Map 5.10.1). A further five colonies are important at the Great Britain level. Both Skomer and Skokholm hold more than one population of international importance. The Marine Nature Reserve at Skomer will help safeguard some seabirds, but it was not established primarily for their conservation. The feeding areas of birds from these colonies are as important as the island itself. Research in 1990 and 1992 indicated that most auks raising chicks at the colonies feed within 30 km of Skomer and

Table 5.10.2 Peak numbers of wintering waterfowl at sea in three areas in relation to British and north-west European populations

Species	Peak numbers	1% GB	1% NW Europe
Northern Cardigan Bay			
Red-throated diver *Gavia stellata*	960	50	750
Great crested grebe *Podiceps cristatus*	380	100	1,000+
Common scoter *Melanitta nigra*	c. 6,000	230	8,000
Red-breasted merganse *Mergus serrator*	210	100	1,000
Southern Conwy Bay			
Great crested grebe *Podiceps cristatus*	156	100	1,000+
Red-breasted merganser *Mergus serrator*	441	100	1,000
Carmarthen Bay			
Common scoter *Melanitta nigra*	2,500	230	8,000

Peak numbers from Green & Elliott (1993), Kirby *et al.* (1993), Owen *et al.* (1986) and JNCC Birds database; 1% GB from Waters & Cranswick (1993); 1% NW Europe from Rose & Scott (1994).

Map 5.10.2 Relative importance of 15'N x 30'W rectangles for seabirds

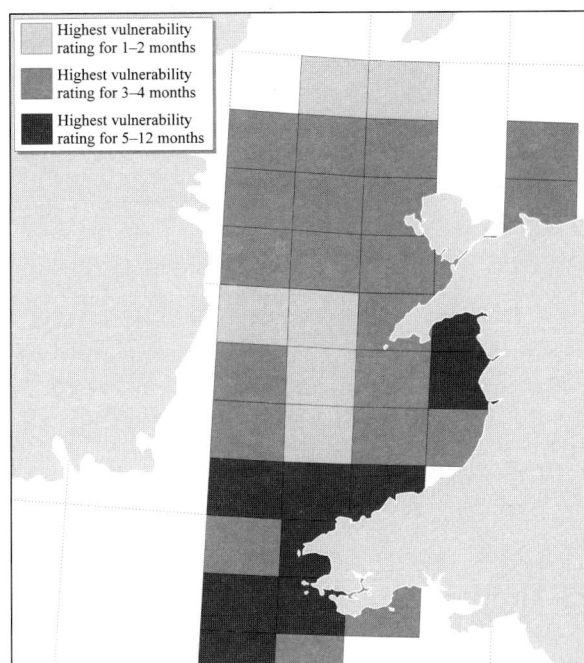

Map 5.10.2 Relative importance of region and adjacent seas for seabirds. The grid is of 15'N x 30'W rectangles; see text for explanation of vulnerability ratings. Source: JNCC Seabirds at Sea Team.

Skokholm (Stone *et al.* 1992). Gannets and lesser black-backed gulls forage frequently near fishing fleets. There is no particular area where auks feed.

At sea, seabirds food sources range from zooplankton to small fish and waste from fishing fleets. Habitats that concentrate any of these foods are preferred. Zooplankton can be concentrated in zones where water masses meet, or where tides converge around islands or over some seabed features (see section 4.3). Many seabirds feed on sandeels *Ammodytes* spp.: offshore sandbanks are the preferred habitat for these fish, and so the waters over them are important for seabirds. Common scoter feed on a range of small or immature shellfish and are likely to prefer areas with high spatfalls of these species. In general, scoters, divers and grebes tend to be found in areas with less than about 20 m water depth.

Table 5.10.3 Counts of seabird colonies in the region holding more than 1% of the European Union (EU) or 1% of the Great Britain total for particular species

Site no. on Map 5.10.1	Colony	OS ref	Species	Year	Count	1%	SPA/SSSI
1	St. Margaret's Island	SS122972	Cormorant	1993	320	**	SSSI
2	Skokholm	SM736050	Manx shearwater	1969	35,000	**	SPA
			Lesser b.-b. gull	1993	4,652	**	
3	Skomer	SM725095	Manx shearwater	1981	100,000	**	SPA
			Lesser b.-b. gull	1992-93	15-20,000	**	
			Razorbill	1993	3,676	**	
			Puffin	1984	7,250	**	
4	Grassholm	SM598093	Gannet	1987	28,535	**	SPA
5	Cardigan Island	SN160516	Lesser b.-b. gull	1993	3,541	**	
6	Trwyn-Crov - Cwntydu	SN341563	Cormorant	1987	92	*	
7	Penderi	SN545725	Cormorant	1993	86	*	SSSI
8	Trwyn Cilan	SH287240	Cormorant	1986	85	*	
9	Ynys Enlli	SH120216	Manx shearwater	1986	4,250	**	SSSI
10	Cwningar Bodowen	SH373656	Lesser b.-b. gull	1989	964	*	SSSI
11	Ynysoedd y Moelrhoniaid	SH269949	Arctic tern	1994	803	*	SPA, SSSI
			Lesser b.-b. gull	1994	926	*	
12	Cemlyn	SH331933	Sandwich tern	1993	564	**	SPA,SSSI
13	Ynys Seiriol	SH650820	Cormorant	1993	400	**	SSSI
14	Creigiau Rhiwledyn	SH814826	Cormorant	1993	279	**	SSSI

Source: JNCC/Seabird Group Seabird Colony Register. Note: A single asterisk in the 1% column indicates count ≥1% of the GB total (nationally important population), while two asterisks indicates ≥1% of the EU total (internationally important). The final column indicates whether a site receives any formal conservation protection as a Site of Special Scientific Interest (SSSI) or Special Protection Area (SPA). For most species the most recent available good-quality count is presented. For terns (whose numbers may fluctuate markedly from year to year, reflecting inter-colony movements), the highest count from the period 1989-93 is presented. Recent reappraisal of Manx shearwater colonies indicates no major changes in size.

Most of the birds from the south-west Wales islands feed to the south-west of the islands, but nearshore areas to the north of the islands are also important for auks. The northern part of Cardigan Bay supports at least nationally important wintering populations of red-throated diver, great crested grebe, red-breasted merganser and common scoter (Green & Elliott 1993). At times, the populations of red-throated diver and common scoter may be of international importance. In autumn and early winter the southern part of Cardigan Bay is important for Manx shearwater, guillemot and razorbill (Stone *et al.* in prep.). Carmarthen Bay has held very large numbers of common scoter in the past (25,000 in 1974, 10,600 in 1986/87), and up to 11,000 have been counted in recent winters. This bay is, however, difficult to census. In the past, the area off Traeth Lafan has been nationally important for great crested grebes and red-breasted mergansers (Owen *et al.* 1986). Seabird surveys have recorded large, probably nationally important, common scoter flocks further offshore. The offshore waters of the region are populated by moderate densities of fulmars, kittiwakes, auks, gannets and Manx shearwaters.

5.10.3 Human activities

Seabirds can be particularly affected by marine oil pollution. Spills near the main colonies during the breeding season could be particularly damaging. There was concern that offshore oil exploration in the area would add to the risks of oil spillage, but so far there have been no major spills from this source. The risk of accidents from tankers serving the Milford Haven terminals has been recognised and offshore routeing schemes are in operation off south-west Wales (see Map 8.3.3). Spills can also occur from non-tanker shipping movements; the major shipping route from the west and south-west into Liverpool passes close to coastlines in this area.

Land management raises issues for seabirds. Burrow-nesting seabirds require about 0.5 m of soil to dig into; excessive burrowing into slopes (by rabbits, for instance), coupled with grazing animals, can lead to erosion and eventual abandonment of colonies. This is believed to have happened in the past on Grassholm. Introduction of rats and cats onto islands presently free of these mammals would damage their seabird populations.

5.10.4 Information sources used

All seabird colonies in the region were counted or reappraised between 1984 and 1987. These counts, and all those made since 1979, are held on the JNCC/Seabird Group Seabird Colony Register. Numbers and breeding performance of several species are evaluated annually at colonies throughout the region, particularly on Skomer, which is one of the UK Seabird Monitoring Programme's key sites. Surveys of birds at sea and around the islands of south-west Wales have been carried out by JNCC's Seabirds at Sea Team. The Team's survey effort from ships has been greatest off south-west Wales and near Anglesey. Waters at 2 km and 5 km from the shore have been surveyed from the air by SAST on a bi-monthly basis over one year. Few surveys have taken place in the past in Cardigan Bay,

particularly the northern half, apart from some from small vessels in recent years. Coverage of Carmarthen Bay has been irregular, and counts of common scoter within the Taf/Twyi estuaries may be duplicates, both between themselves and with the larger offshore concentration in Carmarthen Bay. Coverage, from the land, of most nearshore waters in the region has been generally poor.

5.10.5 Further sources of information

A. References cited

Carter, I.C., Williams, J.M., Webb, A., & Tasker, M.L. 1993. *Seabird concentrations in the North Sea: an atlas of vulnerability to surface pollutants.* Aberdeen, Joint Nature Conservation Committee.

Green, M., & Elliott, D. 1993. Surveys of wintering birds and cetaceans in northern Cardigan Bay, 1990-93. (Contractor: Friends of Cardigan Bay.) *Countryside Council for Wales, Contract Science Report,* No. 60.

Kirby, J.S., Evans, R.J., & Fox, A.D. 1993. Wintering seaducks in Britain and Ireland: populations, threats, conservation and research priorities. *Aquatic Conservation: Marine and Freshwater Ecosystems,* 3:105-137.

Lloyd, C.S., Tasker, M.L., & Partridge, K. 1991. *The status of seabirds in Britain and Ireland.* London, Poyser.

Owen, M, Atkinson-Willes, G.L., & Salmon, D.G. 1986. *Wildfowl in Great Britain.* 2nd ed. Cambridge, Cambridge University Press.

Rose, P.M., & Scott, D.A. 1994. *Waterfowl population estimates.* Slimbridge, International Waterfowl and Wetlands Research Bureau. (IWRB publication No.29).

Stone, C.J., Webb, A., Barton, T.R., & Gordon, J.R.W. 1992. Seabird distribution around Skomer and Skokholm Islands, June 1992. *JNCC Report,* No. 152.

Stone, C.J., Webb, A., Barton, C., Ratcliffe, N., Reed, T.C., Tasker, M.L., & Pienkowski, M.W. In prep. *An atlas of seabird distribution in north-west European waters.* Peterborough, Joint Nature Conservation Committee.

Walsh, P.M., Brindley, E., & Heubeck, M. 1994. *Seabird numbers and breeding success in Britain and Ireland, 1993.* Peterborough, Joint Nature Conservation Committee. (UK Nature Conservation, No. 17.)

Waters, R.J., & Cranswick, P.A. 1993. *The wetland bird survey 1992-93: wildfowl and wader counts.* Slimbridge, British Trust for Ornithology/The Wildfowl & Wetlands Trust/Royal Society for the Protection of Birds/Joint Nature Conservation Committee.

Webb, A., Stone, C.J., Stronach, A., & Tasker, M.L. In prep. *Vulnerable concentrations of seabirds south and west of Britain.* Peterborough, Joint Nature Conservation Committee

B. Further reading

Donovan, J. & Rees, G. 1994. *Birds of Pembrokeshire.* Dyfed Wildlife Trust.

Prater, A.J. 1981. *Estuary birds of Britain and Ireland.* Calton, Poyser.

Webb, A., Harrison, N.M., Leaper, G.M., Steele, R.D., Tasker, M.L., & Pienkowski, M.W. 1990. *Seabird distribution west of Britain.* Peterborough, Nature Conservancy Council.

C. Contact names and addresses

Type of information	Contact address and telephone no.
Seabird colonies	*Co-ordinator, Seabird Colony Register, JNCC, Aberdeen, tel: 01224 642863
Seabirds at sea	*Head, Seabirds at Sea Team, JNCC, Aberdeen, tel: 01224 642863
Birds database	*Head, Vertebrate Ecology and Conservation Branch, JNCC Peterborough, tel: 01733 62626
Nearshore waterfowl	*The Wildfowl & Wetlands Trust HQ, Slimbridge, tel: 01453 890333

* Starred contact addresses are given in full in the Appendix

5.11 Other breeding birds

D.M. Craddock and D.A. Stroud

5.11.1 Introduction

The region's coastal breeding birds other than seabirds (which are covered in section 5.10) are very varied. In a national and international context, the region is particularly important for breeding chough *Pyrrhocorax pyrrhocorax*, with a significant proportion (*c.* 26%) of the total (entirely cliff-breeding) British population resident on the region's coast. The main areas of importance for chough, and for peregrine falcon *Falco peregrinus* (the other principal breeding species of national importance occurring on this coastline) are cliffs and cliff-top low-intensity farmland, associated generally with areas of high importance for seabirds. There are notable concentrations of choughs on Anglesey and in Pembrokeshire. The 1991 survey of breeding peregrines found that coastal breeding birds account for 28% of the Welsh population. Numbers on the Pembrokeshire coast (36 pairs in 1991 - Williams 1992) are especially notable. There are also a few notable concentrations of breeding waders on saltmarshes within the region, such as on the Dyfi Estuary.

Table 5.11.1 Sites of international importance for breeding (and wintering) chough

Site	Status	Number of breeding pairs	% British population
Glannau Ynys Gybi	SPA	6	2
Glannau Aberdaron and Ynys Enlli	SPA	15	5
Pembrokeshire Cliffs	-	50	19

Source: after Pritchard *et al.* (1992). Key: SPA - Special Protection Area

5.11.2 Important locations and species

Maps 5.11.1 and 5.11.2 show the incidence in coastal 10 km squares of confirmed breeding of selected species characteristic of two typical coastal habitats: wet grassland (teal *Anas crecca*, lapwing *Vanellus vanellus*, redshank *Tringa totanus*, mallard *Anas platyrhynchos*, snipe *Gallinago gallinago*, pintail *Anas acuta*) and shingle, sand dune and other dry grasslands (ringed plover *Charadrius hiaticula*, oystercatcher *Haematopus ostralegus*, shelduck *Tadorna tadorna*). The largest number of species in each of the habitats occurs in the northern part of the region, north of the Dyfi.

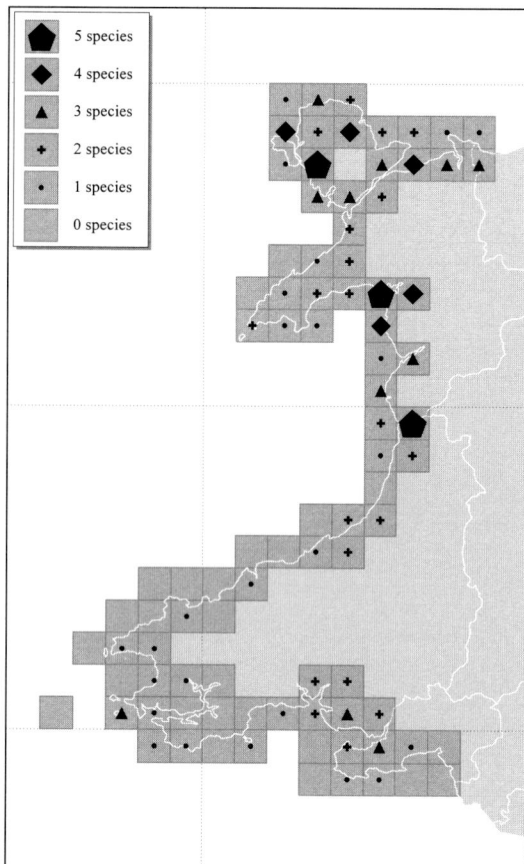

Map 5.11.1 *Number of confirmed breeding species characteristic of wet grassland (redshank, snipe, lapwing, teal and pintail) in coastal 10 km squares. Based on Gibbons, Reid & Chapman (1993).*

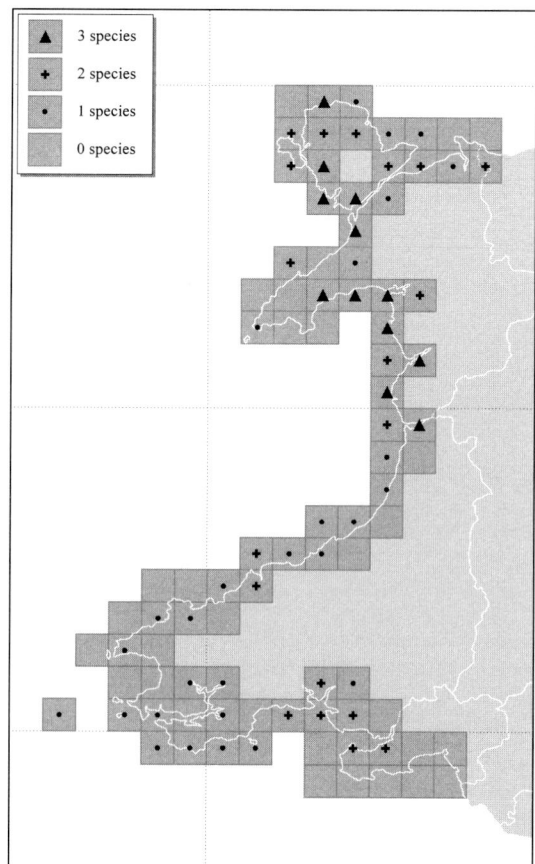

Map 5.11.2 *Number of confirmed breeding species characteristic of shingle, sand dunes and other dry grasslands (ringed plover, oystercatcher and shelduck) in coastal 10 km squares. Based on Gibbons, Reid & Chapman (1993).*

Table 5.11.2 Densities of breeding waders on a sample of saltmarshes surveyed in 1985

Site	Oystercatcher (pairs/km²)	Redshank (pairs/km²)	Lapwing (pairs/km²)	Breeding waders (all) (pairs/km²)	Welsh ranking
Gorseinon, West Glamorgan		11		11	9
Gowerton, West Glamorgan		15		15	7
Whiteford, West Glamorgan		23	11	34	4
Loughor Bridge, Dyfed	7	22		29	5
Trostre, Dyfed		12	2	14	8
Pembrey, Dyfed		10		10	10
Ynys-hir, Dyfed	6	65		71	1

Source: Data from Allport *et al.* (1986). Note that other saltmarshes in the region were not surveyed, so this is *not* a comprehensive listing. More recent data are available for redshank from a survey in 1991 (Griffin, Saxton & Williams 1992).

Within the region there are a number of coastal Sites of Special Scientific Interest (SSSIs) important for land birds, containing both cliff and estuarine habitats. In addition there are RSPB reserves at Grassholm, Ramsey Island, Ynys-hir (on Dyfi Estuary), South Stack cliffs and Valley Lakes (Anglesey). Two internationally important sites (Glannau Ynys Gybi (Holy Island Coast), and Glannau Aberdaron and Ynys Enlli (Aberdaron Coast and Bardsey Island), are designated as Special Protection Areas (SPAs) for their chough populations (Pritchard *et al.* 1992) (Table 5.11.1), and the Pembrokeshire cliffs also hold internationally important numbers of breeding choughs. The chough population is faring well, maintaining its numbers and increasing very slightly in coastal areas (Green & Williams 1993). Since 1990 they have recolonised the Gower peninsula, and in 1992 they nested on Skokholm for the first time since 1928.

Much of the southern coast of Cardigan Bay (from Aberystwyth to Pembrokeshire) is cliff-bound or rocky (see section 3.1) and is attractive to cliff-nesting birds. There are few extensive areas of coastal grassland or saltmarsh, so much is therefore unsuitable for some groups of species, such as breeding waterfowl. Maps 5.11.3 - 6 show the incidence in coastal 10 km squares of breeding chough, ringed plover, shelduck and peregrine falcon. The last named now occurs along most of the coast with significant densities along the cliffs of southern Cardigan Bay, where they prey on seabirds and rock doves *Columba livia*.

There are important cliff-top bird communities along much of the coast - birds of gorse *Ulex* spp., scrub and coastal heath, such as stonechat *Saxicola torquata*, linnet *Carduelis cannabina*, whitethroat *Sylvia communis*, yellowhammer *Emberiza citrinella* and grasshopper warbler

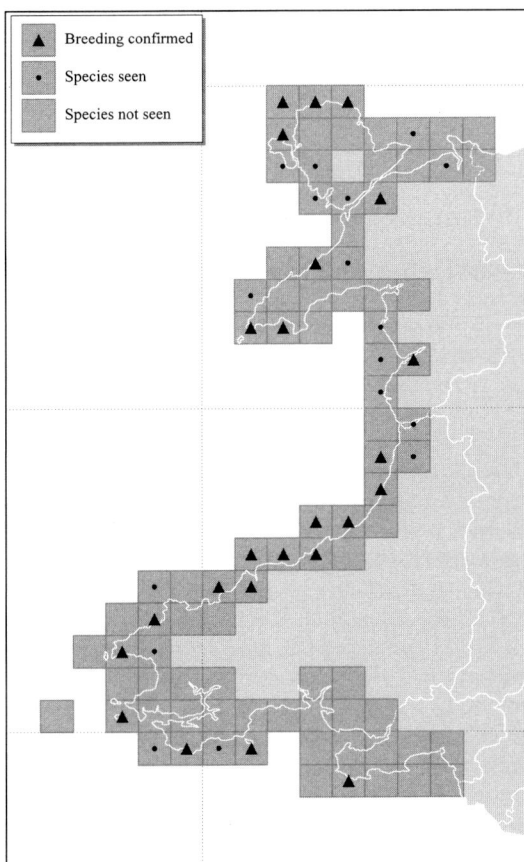

Map 5.11.3 Distribution of breeding chough in coastal 10 km squares. Based on Gibbons, Reid & Chapman (1993).

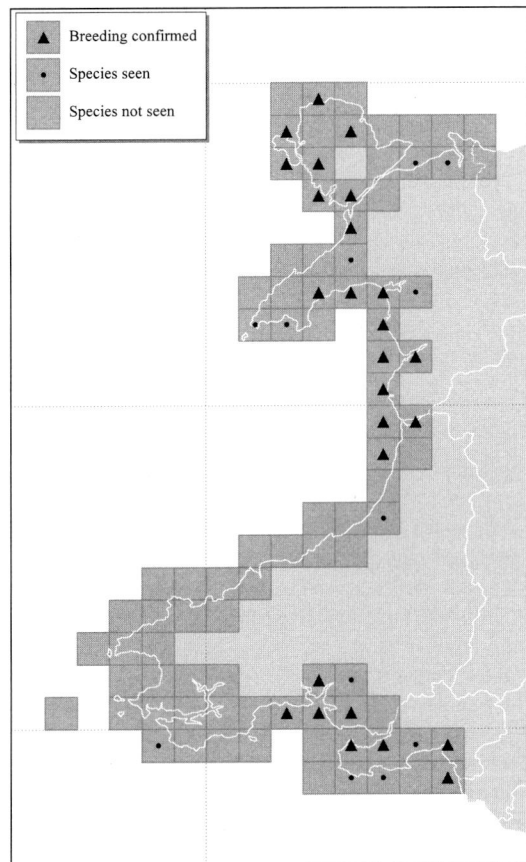

Map 5.11.4 Distribution of breeding ringed plover in coastal 10 km squares. Based on Gibbons, Reid & Chapman (1993).

121

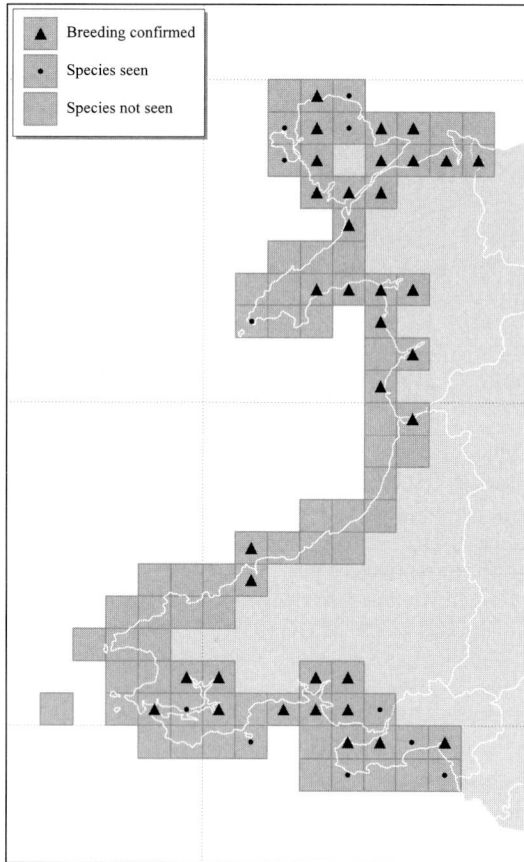

Map 5.11.5 Distribution of breeding shelduck in coastal 10 km squares. Based on Gibbons, Reid & Chapman (1993).

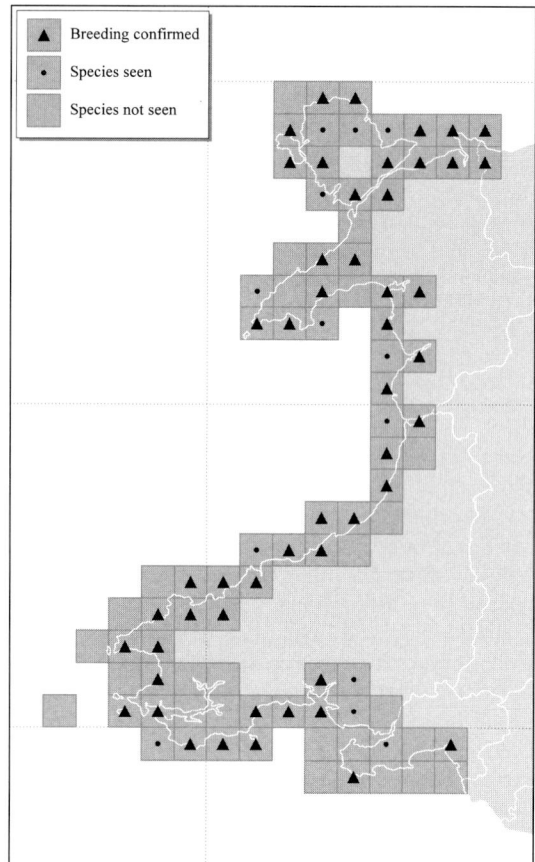

Map 5.11.6 Distribution of breeding peregrine falcon in coastal 10 km squares. Based on Gibbons, Reid & Chapman (1993).

Locustella naevia. Some of these species are scarce or localised elsewhere in Wales.

Wet grassland, although now limited in extent (see section 3.5), contains small but significant numbers of breeding waterfowl. Numbers (and species diversity) of breeding waders on saltmarshes (Table 5.11.2) and coastal dry grasslands are low in the region, compared with other parts of Britain (Davidson 1991; Davidson *et al.* 1991). The Dyfi Estuary, however, has significant populations of several grassland waders (particularly redshank), whose breeding is encouraged by positive conservation management within the SSSI (Griffin, Saxton & Williams 1992). Oystercatchers occur at low density along much of the coast, becoming more abundant in northern Wales. The highest density of breeding ringed plover occurs in the northern part of Cardigan Bay and especially on the Llyn Peninsula (Prater 1989). Both the national survey of 1984 (Prater 1989) and the atlas surveys of 1988-91 (Gibbons, Reid & Chapman 1993) found this species patchily distributed elsewhere (Map 5.11.4).

Other breeding waterfowl are variably located. A significant number of breeding teal occur on the Dyfi (Fox 1987) as well as elsewhere around northern Cardigan Bay, and there is a nationally significant concentration of breeding red-breasted mergansers *Mergus serrator* in this area. Breeding mallard occur in small numbers along the whole non-cliff coastline, whilst mute swans *Cygnus olor* breed in small numbers in suitable wetland habitats. Breeding shelduck occur along much of coastal Wales (Map 5.11.5) with particularly dense populations on the Gower peninsula and along the coast of north Wales (Gibbons *et al.* 1993).

In south and west Wales, the coastal woodlands of sessile oak *Quercus petraea* support a characteristic assemblage of passerines, including pied flycatcher *Ficedula hypoleuca*, as well as dense populations of buzzard *Buteo buteo* and sparrowhawk *Accipiter nisus*.

5.11.3 Human activities

For choughs, appropriate low-intensity agricultural land management is critically important in the areas they use throughout the year (see e.g. papers in Bignal & Curtis 1989). The withdrawal of stock from coastal land can affect choughs as ungrazed land is unsuitable for them. In particular, 'support ground' for non-breeders and juvenile birds is crucial for maintaining a healthy chough population (Bignal, Bignal & Curtis 1989). Breeding birds, including chough and peregrine falcon, can be disturbed by tourists, walkers and climbers on the coast, and this disturbance influences their feeding and breeding success (Owen 1989). The British Mountaineering Council have produced guidance for rock-climbers, and there are local schemes in some parts of Wales where certain cliffs are wardened to reduce climbing disturbance in the breeding season, as well as some voluntary bans. Chough and peregrine nests on the Castlemartin coast in south Pembrokeshire have benefited from such cooperation and wardening.

The correct agricultural and hydrological management of wet grassland is of crucial importance for breeding waterfowl populations (see e.g. Coleshaw 1995; Harold 1995; Scholey 1995; Thomas *et al.* 1995), which have been in national decline for several decades (see papers in Hötker 1991).

5.11.4 Information sources used

Lovegrove, Williams & Williams (1994) provide a comprehensive summary of the status of each breeding bird species in Wales. However, the most recent and comprehensive overview of the status of breeding birds throughout Britain and Ireland is provided by Gibbons *et al.* (1993). This summarises the results of a national breeding bird census undertaken between 1988 and 1991. The atlas presents the data on a 10 x 10 km square basis and also maps breeding density derived from them. Data were collected at a tetrad (2 x 2 km) scale and are held by the British Trust for Ornithology (see section 5.11.5). The new atlas compares distributions at the 10 x 10 km square level with those reported in the first breeding bird atlas of 1968-1972 (Sharrock 1976). Whilst the data are one of the best sources for comparisons at county, regional or national scales, care should be taken with their use to assess individual sites or 10 km squares. This is because the tetrad coverage of each 10 km square was not always the same, there may be greatly varying amounts of land within each square, and some distributions may have changed since the survey period.

Extensive survey work has also been undertaken for a number of species, by volunteers or as part of a joint CCW/RSPB bird monitoring programme, usually as part of wider British surveys. Often the Welsh results have also been written up in more detail (e.g. for peregrine falcons (Williams 1992) and chough (Bullock *et al.* 1983; Green & Williams 1993). There have also been some Welsh national surveys, such as that for redshank in 1991 (Griffin, Saxton & Williams 1992).

5.11.5 Further sources of information

A. *References cited*

Allport, G., O'Brien, M., & Cadbury, C.J. 1986. Survey of redshank and other breeding birds on saltmarshes in Britain 1985. *Nature Conservancy Council, CSD Report*, No. 649.

Bignal, E.M., & Curtis, D.J., eds. 1989. *Choughs and land use in Europe.* Paisley, Scottish Chough Study Group.

Bignal, E.M., Bignal, S., & Curtis, D.J. 1989. Functional unit systems and support ground for choughs - the nature conservation requirements. *In: Choughs and land use in Europe,* ed. by E.M. Bignal & D.J. Curtis, 102-109. Paisley, Scottish Chough Study Group.

Bullock, I.D., Drewett, D.R., & Mickleburgh, S.P. 1983. The chough in Wales. *Nature in Wales (New Series)*, 4: 46-57.

Coleshaw, T. 1995. Rising to the water levels challenge. *Enact, Vol. 3* No. 1: 7-9.

Davidson, N.C. 1991. Breeding waders on British estuarine wet grasslands. *Wader Study Group Bulletin, 61, Supplement:* 36-41.

Davidson, N.C., Laffoley, D d'A., Doody, J.P., Way, L.S., Gordon, J., Key, R., Drake, C.M., Pienkowski, M.W., Mitchell, R.M., & Duff, K.L. 1991. *Nature conservation and estuaries in Great Britain.* Peterborough, Nature Conservancy Council.

Fox, A.D. 1987. The breeding teal *Anas crecca* of a coastal raised mire in central Wales. *Bird Study, 33:* 18-23.

Gibbons, D.W., Reid, J.B., & Chapman, R. 1993. *The new atlas of breeding birds in Britain and Ireland 1988-1991.* London, T. & A.D. Poyser.

Green, M., & Williams, I. 1993. The status of the chough *Pyrrhocorax pyrrhocorax* in Wales in 1992. *Welsh Bird Report,* No. 6 1992, 77-84.

Griffin, B., Saxton, N., & Williams, I. 1992. *Breeding redshank in Wales, 1991.* Newtown, RSPB Report.

Harold, R. 1995. Creating wetlands at Holkham. *Enact, Vol. 3 No. 1:* 12-15.

Hötker, H., ed. 1991. Waders breeding on wet grassland. *Wader Study Group Bulletin,* 61, Supplement.

Lovegrove, R., Williams, G., & Williams, I. 1994. *Birds in Wales.* Poyser, London.

Owen, D.A.L. 1989. Vigilance by foraging choughs in relation to tourist disturbance. *In: Choughs and land use in Europe,* ed. by E..M. Bignal & D.J. Curtis, 57-62. Paisley, Scottish Chough Study Group.

Prater, A.J. 1989. Ringed plover *Charadrius hiaticula* breeding population of the United Kingdom in 1984. *Bird Study,* 36: 154-159.

Pritchard, D.E., Housden, S.D., Mudge, G.P., Galbraith, C.A., & Pienkowski, M.W., eds. 1992. *Important bird areas in the UK including the Channel Islands and the Isle of Man.* Sandy, RSPB.

Scholey, G. 1995. Return of the "drowners". *Enact, Vol. 3 No. 1:* 10-11.

Sharrock, J.T. 1976. *The Atlas of Breeding Birds in Britain and Ireland.* British Trust for Ornithology and Irish Wildbird Conservancy. Bath, T. & A.D. Poyser.

Thomas, G., José, P., & Hirons, G. 1995. Wet grassland in the millenium. *Enact, Vol. 3 No. 1:* 4-6.

Williams, I. 1992. The breeding population of the peregrine *Falco peregrinus* in Wales in 1991. *Welsh Bird Report,* No. 5 1991: 62-69.

B. *Further reading*

The annual series *Welsh Bird Report,* published by the Welsh Ornithological Society, contains occasional review papers of significance, in addition to annual status summaries for breeding and other birds. A detailed account of the breeding (and wintering) birds of Wales, their past and current status and population trends, is given by Lovegrove, Williams & Williams (1994), cited above. With its extensive bibliography, it is a particularly useful introduction to further relevant literature.

Tyler, S. 1992. A review of the status of breeding waders in Wales. *Welsh Bird Report,* No. 5 1991: 74-86.

C. *Contact names and addresses*

Type of information	*Contact address and telephone no.*
Breeding atlas data	Head of Development Unit, The British Trust for Ornithology, The Nunnery, Nunnery Place, Thetford, Norfolk IP24 2PU, tel: 01842 750050
Site designations	*CCW HQ, Bangor, tel: 01248 370444

* Starred contact addresses are given in full in the Appendix

5.11.6 Acknowledgements

Thanks are due to David Cole and George Boobyer for help in compiling this section. Early drafts were improved by comments from Nick Davidson, John Barne and Mark Tasker (JNCC), Steve Parr and Barry Long (CCW), Alister Scott and Clive Morgan (Cardigan Bay Forum), and Stephen Evans (CCW) and Steve May (FSCRC & Dyfed CC).

5.12 Migrant and wintering waterfowl

D.M. Craddock and D.A. Stroud

5.12.1 Introduction

Waterfowl are defined as waders and wildfowl (ducks, geese and swans together with coot *Fulica atra*). This section details the importance of the region to these birds during their non-breeding period. The importance of offshore areas for wintering sea duck species, divers, grebes and cormorant *Phalacrocorax carbo* is outlined in section 5.10. Large stretches of the coast are cliff-bound, especially Gower and Pembrokeshire in the south and around the Llyn Peninsula in the north. These areas are of generally low importance for waterfowl.

Table 5.12.1 gives the total January 1993 waterfowl count for this coastal region as a proportion of the totals (coastal and inland) for Wales and for British coastal sites. It should be noted that such comparisons can give only a rough approximation of relative regional importance, however, since the data are uncorrected for coverage - some areas of Britain are better counted for waterfowl than others.

Table 5.12.1 Overall coastal waterfowl count of Region 12 related to the total waterfowl count for Wales and Great Britain in January 1993

	Total waterfowl count in January 1993	Number of sites counted	Region 12 coastal waterfowl total as a percentage of the comparison area
Coastal sites in Region 12	79,738	29	
All counted Welsh coastal sites	131,642	33	60.4
All counted Welsh wetlands (coastal and inland)	276,129	122	28.9
All counted British coastal sites	2,060,961	214	3.8

Sources: Data from Waters & Cranswick (1993) and Rose & Taylor (1993).

Although absolute numbers of wintering waterfowl in Welsh coastal areas are often small, the restricted extent of inland wetlands in Wales, including in this region, means that the coastal areas are of special significance in maintaining national distributions for many waterfowl. There are sites of importance in Welsh, UK and international contexts although the region as a whole is not one of the most important areas of coastal Britain for wintering waterfowl. Map 5.12.1 shows the distribution of the main concentrations of wintering intertidal waterfowl in the region. The region lies on a major migratory flyway, and many birds moving to and from other wintering areas on the African, Mediterranean and south-west European coasts to arctic breeding grounds pass through and stage on its estuaries and coasts. The region can increase in importance in periods of severe cold weather further east in Britain or Europe, since it is on the relatively mild west coast of the British mainland. Under these conditions, there may be major influxes of waterfowl, such as wigeon *Anas penelope*

and teal *Anas crecca*, from other coastal regions or inland areas (Ridgill & Fox 1990). Locally some sites also act as cold weather refuges: the sheltered embayments of the Cleddau estuarine system freeze more slowly than other coastal and inland wetlands in south Wales, and thus provide open-water feeding when conditions make other sites unavailable (Owen, Atkinson-Willes & Salmon 1986).

Table 5.12.2 Overall densities of wintering waders on non-estuarine coasts in the region

(birds/km)	Number of wader species recorded	Total number of waders	Extent of non-cliff, non-estuarine coast in county (km)	Extent of coast (surveyed) (km)	Overall wader density (birds/km coast)
Gwynedd	15	13,042	339.1	337.1	38.7
Dyfed	15	7,760	148.0	140.4	55.3
Glamorgan	14	6,505	106.4	106.4	61.1

Source: Data from Winter Shorebird Count (Moser & Summers 1987).

5.12.2 Important locations and species

Three coastal wetlands (Burry Inlet, Lavan Sands and Carmarthen Bay) are internationally important for their wintering waterfowl populations, although the latter has yet to be designated as either a Ramsar site or Special Protection Area (SPA) (see section 7.2). The Dyfi Estuary has been designated as a Ramsar site (but largely on habitat grounds) as well as being a Biosphere Reserve (see section 7.2). The Dyfi Estuary is especially important as the sole remaining regular wintering site for Greenland white-fronted geese *Anser albifrons flavirostris* in Wales and England (Fox & Stroud 1985; Fox *et al.* 1994). The Burry Inlet qualifies as an internationally important wetland by holding over 20,000 waterfowl (an average of 37,600 in the period 1988/89 - 1992/93), in addition to being of international importance for wintering populations of pintail *Anas acuta* and oystercatcher *Haematopus ostralegus*. The Cleddau Estuary holds five populations of waterfowl of importance at a Great Britain level, whilst the Cefni Estuary is also of British importance for two species. Densities of wintering waders on non-estuarine coasts (Table 5.12.2) are generally low to moderate, compared with other areas of Great Britain (Moser & Summers 1987)).

The areas of sheltered soft coastline in the region, particularly the estuaries, and especially in south Wales and to a lesser extent in the general shelter of Anglesey, give ideal conditions for wintering waterfowl and for some migrant waterfowl in spring and autumn. Densities of wintering waders on non-estuarine coasts are higher on the more sheltered coasts of South Glamorgan than on the coasts of Dyfed and Gwynedd, which are exposed to the Irish Sea (see Table 5.12.2). Other western-facing estuaries of Cardigan Bay (such as the Teifi, Dyfi and Mawddach estuaries) are more exposed and sandy, with generally smaller over-wintering waterfowl populations. Sheltered

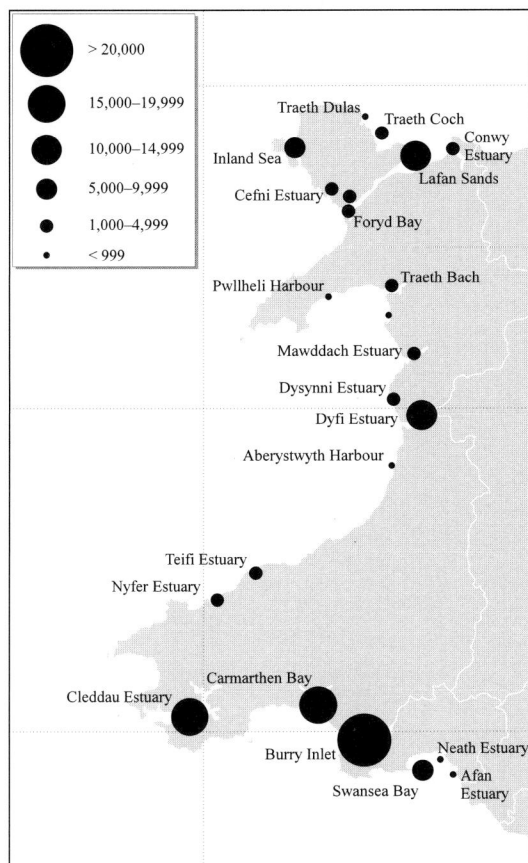

Map 5.12.1 Distribution of main concentrations of wintering estuarine waterfowl. Size of circle is proportional to the 5-year mean of waterfowl numbers, from Waters & Cranswick (1993). Offshore sea-duck concentrations are not shown (see Fox & Roderick (1990); Kirby, Evans & Fox (1993) and section 5.10), nor is the distribution of those waterfowl, mainly waders, wintering on the non-estuarine coast (see Moser & Summers (1987)).

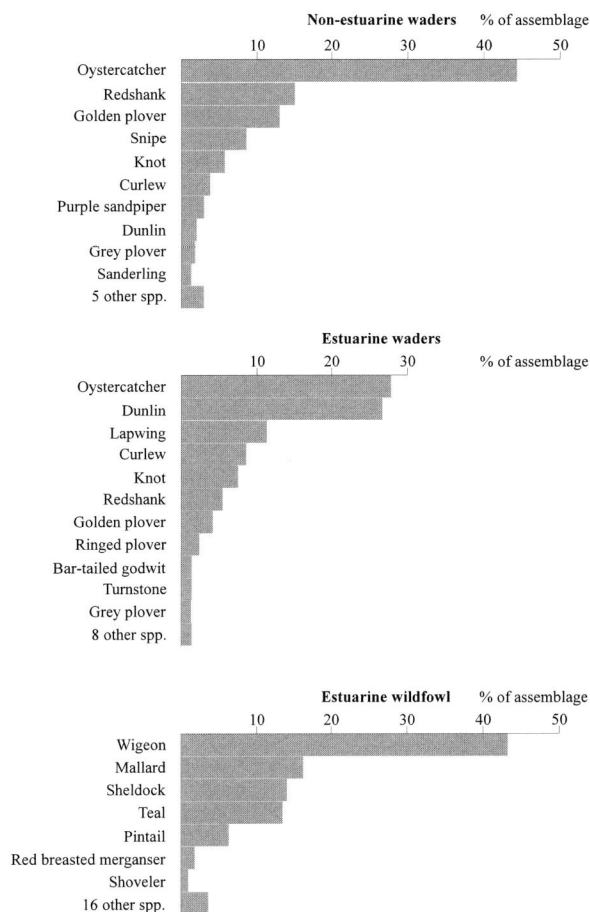

Fig 5.12.1 Relative species composition of non-breeding waterfowl on coastal areas of the region. Estuarine waterfowl data from Prater (1981), non-estuarine wader data from Moser & Summers (1987).

muddy substrates (such as occur in the Inland Sea and parts of the Cleddau Estuary) are especially attractive to dunlin *Calidris alpina*, whilst sandier estuaries and embayments hold larger numbers of oystercatchers and curlews *Numenius arquata* (e.g. the Mawddach Estuary). On non-estuarine shores (Figure 5.12.1), oystercatcher is the most abundant species, followed in order of decreasing abundance by redshank *Tringa totanus*, golden plover *Pluvialis apricaria*, snipe *G. gallinago*, knot and curlew (Moser & Summers 1987).

Table 5.12.3 lists sites important for wintering waterfowl. There are two species that occur at levels of international importance on at least one estuary, and a further eleven species that occur at levels of national (i.e. Great Britain) importance. Of particular significance are the numbers of oystercatchers on the coast of south Wales, whilst there are nationally important numbers of curlew on at least three sites (Burry Inlet, Carmarthen Bay and Cleddau Estuary) and of shelduck at two sites (Burry Inlet and the Cleddau). The small Cefni Estuary is notable for its nationally important populations of pintail and black-tailed godwit.

At nearly all regularly-counted estuaries, the wintering waterfowl assemblage is dominated by a small number of species occurring in varying proportions according to the characteristics of the habitat. Figure 5.12.1 shows that the most abundant estuarine waders in the region are oystercatcher and dunlin, whilst the estuarine wildfowl assemblage is dominated by wigeon *Anas penelope*. Sites dominated by wigeon typically have extensive areas of saltmarsh or grazing marsh close to inter-tidal areas. These are also attractive to lapwing *V. vanellus*, curlew and golden plover (as at Dulas Bay and the Dyfi Estuary), as they provide a wide range of feeding opportunities. Such sites include all the larger sites (e.g. the Cleddau, Mawddach and Dyfi estuaries) as well as some smaller sites (e.g. the Artro, Dysynni and Braint estuaries). On the majority of estuaries, however, oystercatcher is the most frequently occurring wader, and at some sites it is also the most abundant waterfowl species (e.g. Cefni Estuary, Traeth Lafan and Carmarthen Bay).

Other regularly-occurring waterfowl include pintail, teal *Anas crecca*, mallard *A. platyrhynchos*, shelduck *T. tadorna*, dunlin, lapwing, curlew, golden plover and redshank. Common scoter *Melanitta nigra* occur offshore in important numbers in Cardigan Bay and Carmarthen Bay (see section 5.10, and Kirby, Evans & Fox (1993). Less frequently occurring waders include knot *Calidris canutus* and bar-tailed godwit *Limosa lapponica*, which occur at only a few sites.

125

Table 5.12.3 Wintering waterfowl numbers (including seaducks, divers and grebes) on estuaries and other coastal areas in the region

Estuary/area	Site protection status	Five year mean wintering waterfowl numbers	1992/93 peak waterfowl numbers	1992/93 peak wildfowl numbers	1992/93 peak wader numbers	Species occurring at levels of national or international* importance
Burry Inlet	SPA & Ramsar	**37,614	27,777	5,497	22,280	Pintail*, Oystercatcher*, Black-tailed godwit, Shelduck, Shoveler, Dunlin, Curlew,
Carmarthen Bay		19,083	26,058	933***	25,125	Common scoter, Sanderling, Golden plover, Oystercatcher
Cleddau Estuary		17,254	15,769	7,314	8,455	Shelduck, Wigeon, Teal, Curlew, Redshank
Lavan Sands	SPA	11,769	10,297	2,314	7,983	Oystercatcher, Curlew
Dyfi Estuary	Ramsar, Biosphere Reserve	10,232	9,780	6,046	3,734	Wigeon
Inland Sea		5,812	7,187	2,018	5,169	
Swansea Bay		5,204	3,950	124	(3,826)	
Traeth Bach		4,205	2,699	2,396	1,303	
Foryd Bay		3,901	4,304	2,744	1,560	
Conwy Estuary		3,717	3,297	1,074	3,223	
Cefni Estuary		3,305	3,041	1,147	1,894	Pintail, Black-tailed godwit
Red Wharf Bay		2,704	2,245	589	1,656	
Braint Estuary		2,519	1,378	256	1,122	
Mawddach Estuary		2,032	1,612	873	739	
Dysynni Estuary		1,855	2,737	1,842	895	
Teifi Estuary		1,320	1,215	634	581	
Nyfer Estuary		1,029	548	194	354	
Dulas Bay		948	782	81	701	
Artro Estuary		648	805	346	349	
Afan Estuary		239	239	83	156	

Key: * - Species occurring in internationally important numbers, i.e. ≥1% of the international total for the species: other species are nationally important (≥1% of the British population); ** - sites holding ≥20,000 waterfowl are of international importance by virtue of absolute numbers; *** - Number used to determine national importance excludes common scoter. Bracketed figures are incomplete counts. SPA = Special Protection Area; Ramsar = site classified as internationally important under the Ramsar Convention. Note: Estuaries arranged in descending order of average waterfowl numbers for the period 1988/89 to 1992/93. Sources: WeBS data from Waters & Cranswick (1993), to which refer for further detail on interpretation of counts and limitations of data. The winter season used by WeBS is November to March for waders and September to March for wildfowl. Protected status follows Pritchard *et al.* (1992).

5.12.3 Human activities

Wintering waterfowl are potentially affected by a wide range of human activities, either directly or indirectly. Wildfowling occurs, especially in estuaries, although it is generally well regulated (see also section 9.3). On the National Nature Reserves (NNRs) of the Dyfi, Traeth Bach (Morfa Harlech NNR), and Cefni (Newborough/Ynys Llanddwyn NNR), the impacts and regulation of wildfowling have been reviewed by Owen (1992). Permit systems generally operate and there is close liaison in the regulation of wildfowling between local shooting clubs, the BASC and CCW local staff. On the Dyfi, a voluntary shooting ban on Greenland white-fronted geese is in operation. This has been instrumental in the survival of this once declining stock, which in the late 1970s had reached critically small numbers (Fox & Stroud 1985).

Incremental land claim, including barrage schemes, can affect waterfowl populations through loss of feeding habitat. In sensitive areas, coastal windfarm developments also have the potential to be highly disruptive to wintering waterfowl (Crockford 1992).

There has been a long history of conflict between commercial cockle fisheries and oystercatchers on the Burry Inlet. In the early 1970s, cockle fishermen claimed that

natural predation on cockles by oystercatchers greatly reduced commercial catches, and 11,000 oystercatchers were shot under licence between 1972 - 1974. Conservation organisations have not accepted that numbers of oystercatchers are the major determinant of cockle numbers (see review in Prater 1981).

Shellfish collection and bait digging from inter-tidal sediments could limit waterfowl access to feeding areas through disturbance. The significance of this disturbance for birds and that from other sources varies not only from site to site but also with the time of year: especially in cold periods, it is crucial for the survival of wintering waterfowl that they are able to feed for extended periods when the sediments are exposed. Further information is needed on the extent of such disturbance and its significance for waterfowl populations (see Davidson & Rothwell 1993 and papers therein).

Oil pollution is well known as a serious potential threat to wintering waterfowl in areas where high densities of birds occur. In areas of the highest risk, however, such as around the Milford Haven oil refinery, there are well-developed contingency plans for dealing with accidental spillages.

5.12.4 Information sources used

As with other areas of the UK, migrant and wintering waterfowl are well surveyed by the Wetland Bird Survey (WeBS - organised by the British Trust for Ornithology, The Wildfowl & Wetlands Trust, the Royal Society for the Protection of Birds and the JNCC), which collates monthly counts from coastal and inland wetlands through the UK. Coastal coverage is generally good for Welsh estuaries, although the open coast is not thoroughly surveyed on an annual basis. The whole Welsh coastline was surveyed for wintering waders during the Winter Shorebird Count of 1984/85 (Moser & Summers 1987), and there are current WeBS plans for a repeat national survey, possibly in 1995/96. Sites in the region for which WeBS information is already available are Swansea Bay, Burry Inlet, Carmarthen Bay, Cleddau Estuary, Dyfi Estuary, Mawddach Estuary, Artro Estuary, Glaslyn/Dwyryd/Foryd Bay and Lavan Sands. The non-estuarine coast of Cardigan Bay is particularly poorly counted (Waters & Cranswick 1993). More detailed studies of the wintering waterfowl of the Cleddau Estuary and of Carmarthen Bay have been undertaken by Prys-Jones (1989) and Prys-Jones & Davis (1990) respectively.

5.12.5 Further sources of information

A. References cited

Crockford, N.J. 1992. A review of the possible impacts of windfarms on birds and other wildlife. *JNCC Report,* No. 27.

Davidson, N.C., & Rothwell, P.I. 1993. Disturbance to waterfowl on estuaries: the conservation and coastal management implications of current knowledge. *Wader Study Group Bulletin,* 68: 97-105.

Fox, A.D., & Roderick, H.W. 1990. Wintering divers and grebes in Welsh coastal waters. *Welsh Bird Report, 1989,* 53-60.

Fox, A.D., & Stroud, D.A. 1985. The Greenland white-fronted goose in Wales. *Nature in Wales* (New Series), 4: 20-27.

Fox, A.D., Norriss, D.W., Stroud, D.A., & Wilson, H.J. 1994. *Greenland white-fronted geese in Ireland and Britain 1982/83 - 1993/94 - the first twelve years of international conservation monitoring.* National Parks and Wildlife Service and Greenland White-fronted Goose Study Report.

Kirby, J.S., Evans, R.J., & Fox, A.D. 1993. Wintering seaducks in Britain and Ireland: populations, threats, conservation and research priorities. *Aquatic conservation: marine and freshwater ecosystems, 3:* 105-137.

Moser, M., & Summers, R.W. 1987. Wader populations on the non-estuarine coasts of Britain and Northern Ireland: results of the 1984-85 Winter Shorebird Count. *Bird Study, 34:* 71-81.

Owen, M. 1992. An analysis of permit systems and bag records on NNRs. *JNCC Report,* No. 68.

Owen, M., Atkinson-Willes, G.L., & Salmon, D.G. 1986. *Wildfowl in Great Britain.* 2nd ed. Cambridge, Cambridge University Press.

Prater, A.J. 1981. *Estuary birds in Britain and Ireland.* Carlton, Poyser.

Pritchard, D.E., Housden, S.D., Mudge, G.P., Galbraith, C.A., & Pienkowski, M.W., eds. 1992. *Important bird areas in the UK including the Channel Islands and the Isle of Man.* Sandy, RSPB. (Summarises data on the important bird populations and habitats of each site.)

Prys-Jones, R.P. 1989. The abundance and distribution of wildfowl and waders on the Cleddau (Milford Haven). *Nature Conservancy Council, CSD Report,* No. 964.

Prys-Jones, R.P., & Davis, P.E. 1990. The abundance of wildfowl and waders on Carmarthen Bay (Taf/Tywi/Gwendrath). *Nature Conservancy Council, CSD Report,* No. 1053.

Ridgill, S.C., & Fox, A.D. 1990. *Cold weather movements of waterfowl in western Europe.* Slimbridge, IWRB. (IWRB Special Publication No. 13.)

Rose, P.M., & Taylor, V. 1993. *Western Palearctic and south-west Asia waterfowl census 1993. Mid-winter waterfowl counts, January 1993.* Slimbridge, IWRB.

Waters, R.J., & Cranswick, P.A. 1993. *The Wetland Bird Survey 1992-1993: wildfowl and wader counts.* Slimbridge, BTO/WWT/RSPB/JNCC. (Annual summary report on species trends, based on counts at wetlands throughout the UK).

B. Further reading

The WeBS waterfowl count scheme is the primary source of information on wintering and migrant waterfowl in the UK. The annual reports (most recently Waters & Cranswick 1993) can only summarise what are very detailed data, and in summary form such counts may be subject to misinterpretation for a number of reasons. Detailed count data for sites can be provided by WeBS, as detailed below, and inspection of these data is recommended for any planning-related activity. A detailed account of the wintering (and breeding) birds of Wales, their past and current status and population trends is given by Lovegrove, Williams & Williams (1994). With its extensive bibliography, it is a particularly useful introduction to further relevant literature. Buck (1993) summarises the wintering waterfowl assemblage on each estuary in the region. Davidson *et al.* (1991) provides a detailed analysis of British migrant and overwintering waterfowl on estuaries.

Buck, A.L. 1993. *An inventory of UK estuaries. Volume 2, South-west Britain.* Peterborough, JNCC.

Davidson, N.C., Laffoley, D d'A., Doody, J.P., Way, L.S., Gordon, J., Key, R., Drake, C.M., Pienkowski, M.W., Mitchell, R.M., & Duff, K.L. 1991. *Nature conservation and estuaries in Great Britain.* Peterborough, Nature Conservancy Council.

Lovegrove, R., Williams, G., & Williams, I. 1994. *Birds in Wales.* London, Poyser.

C. Contact names and addresses

Type of information	Contact address and telephone no.
High tide and low tide counts of wintering and migrant wildfowl (WeBS)	WeBS National Organiser (wildfowl), The Wildfowl & Wetlands Trust, Slimbridge, Gloucestershire GL2 7BX, tel: 01453 890333
High tide counts of wintering and migrant waders (WeBS)	WeBS National Organiser (waders), British Trust for Ornithology, The Nunnery, Nunnery Place, Thetford, Norfolk IP24 2PU, tel: 01842 750050
Low tide counts of wintering and migrant waders (WeBS)	WeBS National Organiser (Low Tide Counts), British Trust for Ornithology, address as above
Site designations	*CCW HQ, Bangor, tel: 01248 370444

* Starred contact addresses are given in full in the Appendix

5.12.6 Acknowledgements

Thanks to Dave Cole, George Boobyer, Humphrey Crick, Eric Steer and Simon Delany for providing unpublished shelduck data. Early drafts were improved by comments from Nick Davidson, John Barne and Mark Tasker (JNCC), Steve Parr and Barry Long (CCW), and Peter Cranswick (WWT).

5.13 Land mammals

Dr C.E. Turtle

5.13.1 Introduction

This section covers land mammals that occur in the coastal 10 km squares within the region, concentrating on those species that are truly coastal, such as otters, and those that occur on the coast for reasons of shelter and foraging, such as the greater horseshoe bat. Other mammals - common and widespread throughout Britain, feral or recently introduced - are not considered in any detail.

Large parts of the coastal area are dominated by semi-natural habitats, particularly the coastal strip (see section 2.6 and Chapter 3). The water quality of both coastal and estuarine waters is good throughout most of the region (National Rivers Authority 1991). The quality of the coastal habitat and rivers is partly reflected in the incidence and distribution of terrestrial mammals, with several nationally rare species occurring. The frequently cliffed coast limits the occurrence of some lowland species.

There are no reliable estimates of the numbers of mammals in the region or in Britain that could be used to assess the relative importance of the region in national terms. Using the data from Arnold (1993), an assessment has been made for the frequency of occurrence of mammals within the coastal area, but some of the records are anecdotal (see Table 5.13.1). On this assessment, the region is important for some of the nationally important mammal

Table 5.13.1 Records of protected mammal species distribution

Protected species	Estimate of occurrence in the region
Greater horseshoe bat	Stronghold in south-west (England and Wales)
Lesser horseshoe bat	Frequent; predominantly Welsh and south-west distribution
Whiskered/Brandt's bats	Widespread
Whiskered bat	Rare
Natterer's bat	Widespread
Daubenton's bat	Frequent; roosts rare
Noctule	Rare
Pipistrelle	Frequent
Brown long-eared bat	Frequent
Red squirrel	Rare
Dormouse	Rare
Pine marten	Rare
Polecat	Common; predominantly Welsh distribution
Otter	Frequent

Adapted from Arnold (1993). Note: all the above species are listed on Schedule 5 of the Wildlife & Countryside Act 1981, except the polecat (Schedule 6).

species, most of which are vulnerable and declining (Morris 1993). The Skomer vole *Clethrionymus glareolus skomerensis* is endemic to the island. Ten of the fourteen species of British bats are recorded for this region (Arnold 1993), of which the two horseshoe bats are the most important, owing to their limited national distribution and declining numbers. All of the other species listed on Schedule 5 of the Wildlife and Countryside Act 1981 (except the wildcat) are recorded from this region. They are the red squirrel *Sciurus vulgaris*, pine marten *Martes martes*, common dormouse *Muscardinus avellanarius* and otter *Lutra lutra*. Of note is the stronghold in Wales of the polecat *Mustela putorius*, which is protected under Schedule 6 of the Wildlife and Countryside Act. All British bats are listed under Appendix II of the Bern Convention, and the dormouse and red squirrel are listed under Appendix III.

5.13.2 Important locations and species

Otters are extinct or endangered over most of mainland Britain except the north-west (Morris 1993). The Welsh population is important because of its size and genetic diversity. The otter is the terrestrial mammal which uses coastal areas most frequently. Three surveys of otters in Wales, in 1977-78 (Crawford *et al.* 1979), in 1984-85 (Andrews & Crawford 1986) and in 1991 (Andrews, Howell & Johnson 1993), have all demonstrated the importance of the region for otters. Although the species was formerly found throughout the coastal region (Map 5.13.1), according to Arnold (1993) it was not recorded from Anglesey during the 1991 survey. That survey showed that positive signs of otters are widely but patchily distributed: signs of otters were found on none of the surveyed sites on Anglesey but 78% of those in the Cleddau area near Pembroke. Their

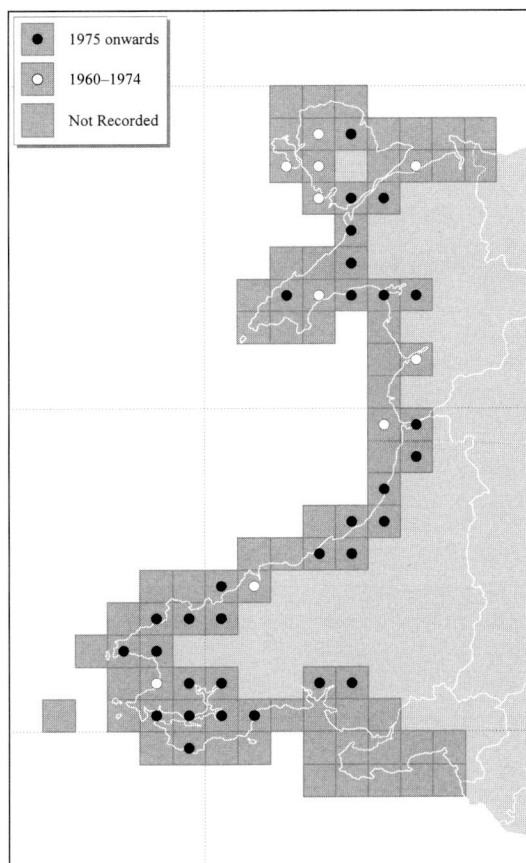

●	1975 onwards
○	1960–1974
▨	Not Recorded

Map 5.13.1 Recorded coastal distribution of otters by coastal 10 km square. Source: Arnold (1993).

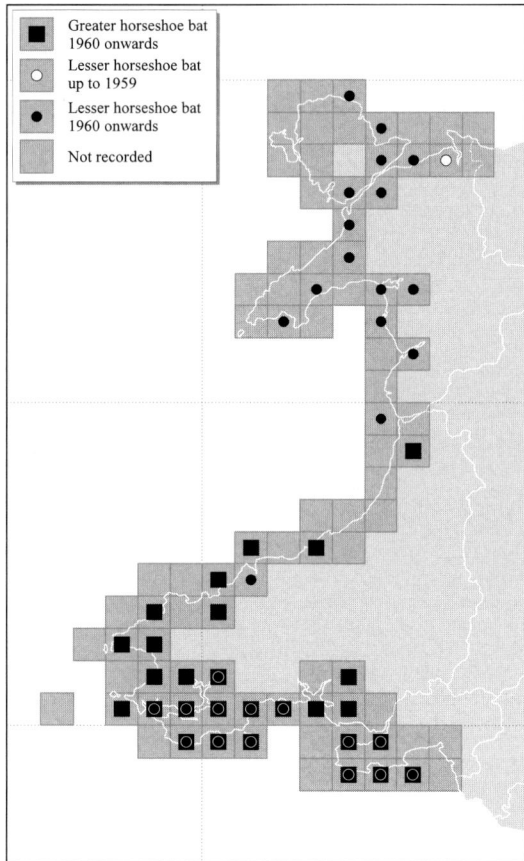

Map 5.13.2 Recorded coastal distributions of horseshoe bats by coastal 10 km square. Source: Arnold (1993), Dyfed Bat Group (1995 data).

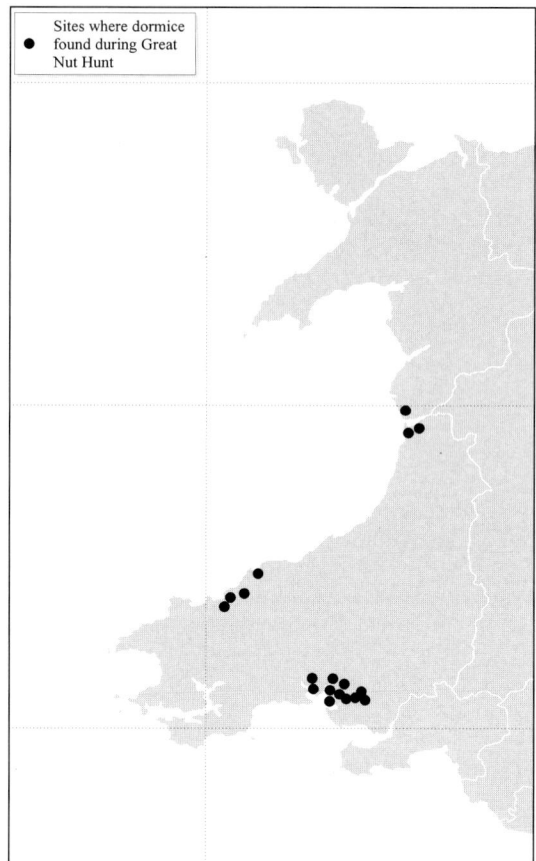

Map 5.13.3 Recorded coastal distribution of dormice. Source: Morris, Bright & Mitchell-Jones (in prep.).

range has expanded since the previous survey (Andrews & Crawford 1986) in some areas, for instance where water quality and habitat have improved. The coast in this region is important because otters use most of the rivers down to the coast and move between estuaries using the coastline. Coastal sightings have been reported at Skomer, Milford Haven and the Teifi estuary (Andrews & Crawford 1986). However, unlike the situation in Scotland, it is believed that otters no longer breed on the coast, because of disturbance particularly by tourists (Crawford pers. comm.).

Linear landscape features such as coastlines and streams are important to bats for navigation, and all species may hibernate in crevices in coastal cliffs. Some bat species also use the coast for foraging, and decaying seaweed seems to be an important source of insects on which bats feed (T. McOwat, pers. comm.). In addition, the maritime climate may help bats to be more active in winter. The notification for Whiteford Burrows Site of Special Scientific Interest (SSSI) includes unnamed bat species (the Bat Sites Register identifies the species concerned). Map 5.13.2 shows the distribution of greater and lesser horseshoe bats in the region, based on BRC data but updated by Dyfed Bat Group data.

The greater horseshoe bat *Rhinolophus ferrumequinum* occurs in the southern Palaearctic from Britain to Japan and is endangered worldwide (Stebbings & Griffith 1986). The northern boundary of its range is south-west England and south-west Wales, and the Welsh population is of national importance. The greater horseshoe bat is normally associated with semi-natural areas such as pastureland,

scrub and woodland. Its distribution and that of the lesser horseshoe bat often correlates with limestone areas, which support cave and mine systems which may house important hibernacula (T. McOwat pers. comm.). Unimproved coastal habitat may be an important feeding ground. This species will cross to islands such as Caldey and Skomer. The known roost sites for this and other bat species in Britain are recorded on English Nature's Bat Sites Register, which lists several important coastal cave systems in the region (Mitchell-Jones in press).

The lesser horseshoe bat *Rhinolophus hipposideros* is restricted to south-western areas of Britain (Arnold 1993), where it is on the northern edge of its range in Europe. It is classified as endangered worldwide (Stebbings & Griffith 1986). This bat is associated with areas of semi-natural habitat and particularly ancient woodlands. Where there is suitable habitat, the region's coast is important for this species, and records are concentrated in the north-west and south of the region (Map 5.13.2). There are important populations on Gower and also around Tremadoc Bay, where there are reports of this species foraging on saltmarshes and river banks. The species is also found in Pembrokeshire within one mile of good nursery roosts.

The red squirrel is extinct over much of England and Wales (Morris 1993) and has a patchy distribution where it remains. Red squirrels are dependent on large conifer plantations with good seed crops and relatively low tree densities. There are a few records from within this region, such as at the pine plantation at Newborough Warren, Anglesey, probably partly because grey squirrels do not have such an advantage over reds in this habitat.

In Britain the dormouse is on the western edge of its range in Europe (Corbet & Harris 1991), and although there are only low numbers in this region, they are of importance because they are close to the northern edge of the British range. Dormice are associated with ancient semi-natural woodland and edge habitats, such as broadleaved trees on the edge of forestry plantations or mature, diverse hedgerows. Isolated areas of suitable habitat are unlikely to hold viable populations if they are less than 20 ha in extent (Bright, Mitchell & Morris 1994). In 1993 English Nature coordinated the Great Nut Hunt, a volunteer survey covering the whole of England and Wales, which recorded the incidence of nut shells nibbled in characteristic dormouse fashion. Its preliminary findings have shown that dormice occur in north Wales, although not on the coast (Morris, Bright & Mitchell-Jones in prep.). Records of dormice in Dyfed (see Map 5.13.3) are likely to be associated with suitable habitat occurring on the coast, rather than coastal habitats themselves, such as sea cliffs and saltmarshes.

The pine marten is extinct over most of England and Wales and there are few reliable records within this region (Arnold 1993); actual numbers are likely to be low. Pine martens depend on large, mixed conifer plantations, although the more mature plantations are less valuable (Corbet & Harris 1991). Some areas of suitable habitat in the region might be selected for re-introduction programmes. Records do suggest the presence of pine martens at some coastal sites, and these may be verified by the latest (as yet unpublished) survey.

Wales holds most of the known British polecat population, and some are recorded throughout the region from the coastal strip. Polecats are recorded from a variety of habitats, particularly farmland that is not intensively managed. They are known to use coastal dunes, for example at Ynyslas, and strips of remnant semi-natural habitat between farmland and the coast, such as occur in Pembrokeshire; these support high rabbit populations, important to the local polecat population (J. Birks pers. comm.).

5.13.3 Human activities

Disturbance on the coast during the holiday season deters otters from breeding in these areas. This is particularly true of leisure activities such as 'coastaleering' (cliff scrambling), which may also disturb important bat roosts. Industrial development resulting in habitat loss and poor water quality has an adverse effect on the otter population and prevents recolonisation. Oil spills could result in the death of otters using the coastal area. The increasing numbers of polecat deaths on roads may be significant for the species.

Intensification of farming, especially pesticide use, has an adverse effect on all species of bat. The removal of hedgerows and woodland is particularly significant, as bats rely heavily on shelter and good insect populations to survive; this will also have a severe effect on dormice, especially where hedgerows link two woods. Fragmentation or inappropriate management of ancient woodlands within coastal areas would also reduce local dormouse populations. The decline in the rate of softwood planting in large areas may contribute to both the decline of the red squirrel and the extinction of the pine marten in Wales. The control of predators and pests can result in the decline of other species. For instance, incidental poisoning and trapping during the control of rodents, mink and grey squirrel have affected polecat populations in the past.

5.13.4 Information sources used

There have been no specifically coastal mammal surveys within this region, and therefore even the nationally comprehensive surveys, such as for otters, have their limitations when assessing the importance of the coast. Nor have there been any nationally comprehensive surveys that cover coastal and inland areas equally for red squirrels, dormice, polecats or any of the bats, although there are recent records of all of these species (Biological Records Centre (BRC) data). Therefore Arnold (1993) has been used here to provide a guide to the occurrence of mammals in the region. As a general observation, mammal surveys are not recorded with the same intensity as botanical ones and the occurrence of mammals within 10 km squares is not enough to establish the status of species (Morris 1993).

The known roosts of the greater and some of the lesser horseshoe bats have been monitored regularly, and there are recent records for many sites (BRC data); the commoner bats, however, are under-recorded.

5.13.5 Further sources of information

A. References cited

Andrews, E., & Crawford, A.K. 1986. *Otter survey of Wales 1984-85.* London, The Vincent Wildlife Trust.

Andrews, E., Howell P., & Johnson K. 1993. *Otter survey of Wales 1991.* London, The Vincent Wildlife Trust.

Arnold, H.R. 1993. *Atlas of mammals in Britain.* London, HMSO. (ITE research publication No. 6.)

Bright, P.W., Mitchell, P., & Morris, P.A. 1994. Dormouse distribution: survey techniques, insular ecology and selection of sites for conservation. *Journal of Applied Ecology, 31:*329- 339.

Corbet, G.B., & Harris, S.H., *eds.* 1991. *The handbook of British mammals.* 3rd ed. Oxford, Blackwell Scientific Publications.

Crawford, A.K., Evans, D., Jones, A,. & McNulty, J. 1979. *Otter survey of Wales 1977-78.* Nettleham, Lincoln, Society for the Promotion of Nature Conservation.

Mitchell-Jones, A.J. In press. The status and conservation of horseshoe bats in Britain. *Myotis, Vol 32.*

Morris, P.A. 1993. *A red data book for British mammals.* London, The Mammal Society.

Morris, P.A., Bright, P.W., & Mitchell-Jones, A.J. In press. *The Great Nut Hunt.* Peterborough, English Nature.

National Rivers Authority. 1991. *The quality of rivers, canals and estuaries in England and Wales: Report of the 1990 survey.* National Rivers Authority, Water Quality Series No 4.

Stebbings, R.E. & Griffith, F. 1986. *Distribution and status of bats in Europe.* Huntingdon, Institute of Terrestrial Ecology, Monks Wood Experimental Station.

B. Further reading

Bright, P.W. Undated. *Distribution, status and conservation requirements of the dormouse* Muscardinus avellanarius *in Wales: a preliminary review.* Report to the Countryside Council for Wales.

Chanin, P.R.F. 1985. *The natural history of otters.* London, Croom Helm.

Cresswell, P., Harris, S., & Jefferies, D.J. 1990. *The history, distribution, status and habitat requirements of the badger in Britain.* Peterborough, Nature Conservancy Council.

Hurrell, E., & McIntosh, G. 1984. Mammal Society dormouse survey, January 1975 - April 1979. *Mammal Review, 14*: 1-18.

MacDonald, S.M., & Mason, C.F. 1983. Some factors influencing the distribution of otters *Lutra lutra. Mammal Review, 13*: 1-10.

MacDonald, S. M. 1983. The status of the otter *Lutra lutra* in the British Isles. *Mammal Review, 13*: 11-23.

Neal, E. 1986. *The natural history of badgers.* London, Croom Helm.

Schober W., & Grimmberger, E. 1987. *A guide to bats of Britain and Europe.* London, Hamlyn.

Strachan, R., & Jefferies, D.J. 1993. *The water vole* Arvicola terrestris *in Britain 1989-90: its distribution and changing status.* Vincent Wildlife Trust.

Stebbings, R.E. 1988. *Conservation of European bats.* London, Christopher Helm.

Verlander, K.A. 1983. *Pine marten survey of England, Scotland and Wales 1980-1982.* London, Vincent Wildlife Trust.

C. Contact names and addresses

Information held	Contact address and telephone no.
Local site and species information	*Conservation Officer, Dyfed Wildlife Trust, Haverfordwest, tel: 01437 765462
as above	*Conservation Officer, Glamorgan Wildlife Trust, Tondu, tel: 01656 724100
as above	*Conservation Officer, North Wales Wildlife Trust, Bangor, tel: 01248 351541
Bats	T. McOwat, Dyfed Bat Group, 19 Parc Puw, Drefach, Velindre Llandyssul SA44 5UZ, tel: 01559 370846
Bat Sites Register	*Mammal Ecologist, English Nature HQ, Peterborough, tel: 01733 340345
Otters in Wales project	Geoff Liles, Llwyn Ffynnon, Harfod, Pwmpsaint, Llanwrda, SA19 8DJ, tel: 01267 223571
Polecats	Johnny Birks, 3 Knell Cottages, Harcourt Road, Mathan, Nr. Malvern, Worcestershire, WR13 5PG tel: 01684 575876
Coordinates national recording schemes and collates biological data from throughout UK	*Biological Records Centre, ITE Monks Wood, tel: 01487 773381
Species monitoring, protected sites	*CCW HQ, Bangor, tel: 01248 370444
General mammal information	The Mammal Society, Unit 15, Cloisters House, Cloisters Business Centre, 8 Battersea Park Road, London SW8 4BG, tel: 0171 498 4358
as above	Gower Countryside Service, Planning Department, Swansea City Council, Guildhall, Swansea SA1 4PH, tel: 01792 301301

* Starred contact addresses are given in full in the Appendix

5.13.6 Acknowledgements

The author would like to thank all those people cited in the text for their valuable information and their time. The Biological Records Centre, Monks Wood, and Thomas McOwat, Dyfed Bat Group, provided recent data for the area.

5.14 Seals

C.D. Duck

5.14.1 Introduction

Grey seals *Halichoerus grypus* occur throughout the region; they haul-out on the remote parts of the coast. Breeding occurs on beaches inaccessible to humans and in caves around Anglesey, the Llyn Peninsula, the Pembroke coast and its off-lying islands. The breeding season is prolonged in comparison with that of colonies in Scotland and on the east of England; pups are born from late July until mid-December and occasionally outside this period. Outside the breeding season, the numbers of grey seals at haul-out sites are unpredictable and can vary greatly from day to day. Therefore this section refers mainly to grey seal distribution during the breeding season.

Pup production in the region in 1993 represented approximately 5% of the British total. There are no breeding sites in Mid or West Glamorgan; over 92% of the pups born in the region are from Dyfed; the remainder are born in Gwynedd. Table 5.14.1 gives the numbers of seals in the region in relation to the rest of Great Britain.

Table 5.14.1 Grey seal pup production and population size for Region 12 in relation to GB

Location	Pup production (to nearest 50)	Associated population ≥ 1 yr old (to nearest 50)	% of GB population
Dyfed	1,400	4,800	4.1
Gwynedd	100[1]	350[1]	0.3
Region total	1,500	5,150	4.4
South-west Britain (Regions 10 - 12)	1,650[1]	5,650[1]	4.9
GB total	*33,700*	*115,650*	

[1] Estimated pup production and associated total population figures. Sources: Dyfed Wildlife Trust (DWT), Bardsey Bird Observatory, Countryside Council for Wales (CCW), Sea Mammal Research Unit (SMRU).

Common seals *Phoca vitulina* very rarely visit and do not breed in the region. There are anecdotal accounts of single or pairs of animals that have remained around the Menai Straits or on Ynys Enlli for some months at a time.

Both grey and common seals are listed in Appendix III of the Berne Convention and Annexes II and V of the Habitats Directive. The Conservation of Seals Act 1970 makes it an offence to kill or take seals at certain times of the year or by the use of certain prohibited means. SSSIs have been designated at the following locations, in part because of seal conservation concerns: Skomer Island and Middleholm; Deer Park, Marloes; St. David's Peninsula Coast; Ramsey Island; Bishops and Clerks Islands; Strumble Head; Cemaes Head; Creigiau Pen y graig (Dyfed); and at Ynys Enlli (Gwynedd). In this region the close season for grey seals is between 1 September and 31 December and for common seals 1 June to 31 August.

5.14.2 Important locations

The Dyfed coast, from Caldey Island to Aberystwyth, together with the islands of Ramsey and Skomer, accounts for over 90% of the pups born in the region. Ynys Enlli has a small breeding population. Main grey seal breeding sites in Dyfed are listed in Table 5.14.2, with figures for their pup production in 1993, and their distribution is shown on Map 5.14.1.

Table 5.14.3 lists breeding and non-breeding grey seal sites in Gwynedd; the numbers show the locations of these sites as indicated on Map 5.14.1.

Table 5.14.2 Grey seal pup production at the main breeding sites in the region in 1993

Breeding location	Grid ref.	Numbers of pups born	% of region total
Skomer	SM730090	190	12.7
Ramsey	SM700420	467	31.1
North Pembroke Coast (Porth Clais to Cardigan)	SM743237 to SN147493	625	41.7
Ceredigion Coast (Cardigan to Aberystwyth)	SN155515 to SN575795	30	2.0
Ynys Enlli	SH120220	5	0.4
Llyn Peninsula and Anglesey	SH521374 to SH832815	95[1]	6.3
Total		*1,412*	

[1] Estimated pup production for Gwynedd, excluding Ynys Enlli.
Sources: DWT, Bardsey Bird Observatory, CCW.

5.14.3 Human activities

Although the Welsh grey seal population does not make a great contribution to the British total, it is important in terms of the range of this species in Great Britain, as the region has the largest breeding colony in south-west GB. Some of the main colonies in the region attract considerable local interest and are important tourist attractions. Visits are either through commercially-operated boat tours or by walkers visiting nature reserves. At two sites (Ramsey and Skomer Islands), reserve management schemes provide tourists with information on how best to minimise disturbance to seals, particularly during the breeding season. At Ramsey Island (a significant pupping site), 'potentially damaging operations' listed on the SSSI notification seek to control recreational activities or the use of vehicles or craft which may affect seal behaviour, and the killing and removal of any wild animal. Human disturbance has been identified as possibly one of the main

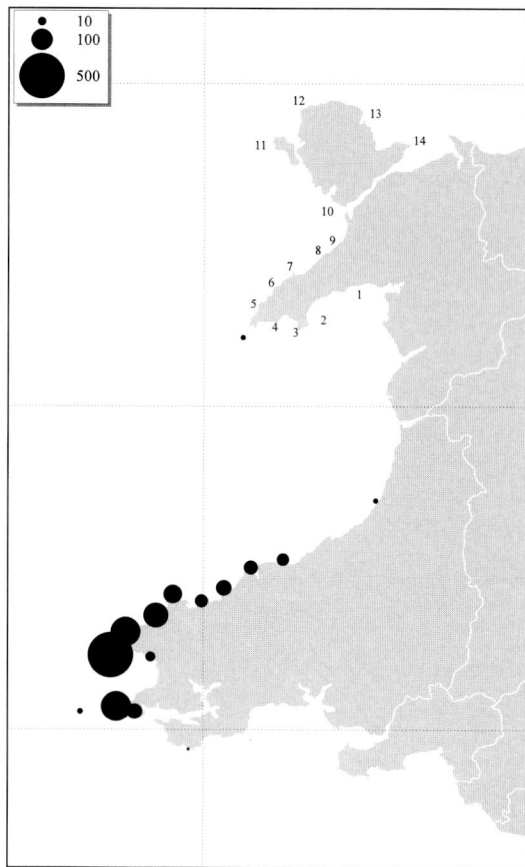

Map 5.14.1 Grey seal pup production. Circles represent the numbers of pups born along sections of the coast (as defined by Dyfed Wildlife Trust). Figures around Gwynedd refer to locations in Table 5.14.2. Data from DWT, CCW and Bardsey Bird Observatory; Anderson (1977); Baines *et al.* (1994); Rees (1973) and Thomas (1993).

factors affecting the distribution of sites used for breeding (Baines & Pierpoint 1993; Baines 1993). Tour boat operators are co-operating with local conservation organisations (Countryside Council for Wales (CCW), Dyfed Wildlife Trust (DWT), Royal Society for the Protection of Birds (RSPB)) in defining the most instructive and least disturbing methods for approaching colonies (Baines 1993; Thomas 1994). The Skomer Marine Nature Reserve, encompassing Skomer and the Marloes Peninsula, is managed by the CCW under byelaws and a voluntary code of conduct. The code, which is not legally enforceable, advises that breeding and haul-out sites should not be approached within 100 m between 1 September and 28 February. Though no byelaws explicitly relate to seals, a general byelaw provides that either a permit from CCW or a reasonable excuse is required before any animal may be disturbed. The effects of human disturbance are currently being studied in conjunction with DWT's breeding season survey of grey seals in west Wales.

Throughout the region the use of leisure craft (particularly jet-skis, inflatables and sea-kayaks) has recently increased and may increase the disturbance to seals.

There is a locally important inshore coastal fishing industry in the region (see section 9.1). Fishing methods vary from recreational sea angling to gill, tangle and trammel netting. Studies of interactions with fisheries have shown that a small number of seals drown in tangle and gill nets, and occasionally some are shot (Thomas 1992, 1993).

Concern has been expressed about the potential effects on marine mammals of oil-related developments in the region. Richardson *et al.* (1989) conclude, from a literature review, that they are relatively minor. The risk to seals from contamination with oil also appears to be small. There has been one report of small numbers of grey seal pups dying as a result of severe oiling (Davies & Anderson 1976), but such events appear to be rare. The air-gun arrays used in seismic surveys generate high levels of low frequency sound. Most of the energy in the output from these arrays is outside the known hearing range of seals and is unlikely to disturb

Table 5.14.3 Sites in Gwynedd used by breeding and non-breeding grey seals

Location (see Map 5.14.1)	Grid ref.	Rees (1973)	Anderson (1977)	Breeding in 1993?	Non-breeding haul-out
Llyn Peninsula					
1. Criccieth - Afon Wen	SH455372	yes	no	? no	yes
2. St Tudwal's Islands	SH340250	yes	?	? no	yes
3. Pencilan Head	SH290235	yes	no	? no	?
4. Porth Cadlan -Ynys Gwylan	SH183245	yes	yes	? yes in 1991	?
5. Porthor - Penrhyn Mawr	SH165315	?	n/a	? yes	? yes
6. Porth Gwylan	SH216366	?	n/a	? yes	? yes
7. Aber Geirch - Porth Dinllaen	SH265405	?	no	? yes	? yes
8. Trefor - Penrhyn Glas	SH348455	yes	no	? no	?
9. Gored - Clynnog	SH415505	?	no	? no	?
Anglesey					
10. Ynys Llanddwyn	SH385620	yes	?	? no	?
11. Holy Island (west coast)	SH210950	yes	yes	? yes	? yes
12. The Skerries	SH270950	yes	yes	yes	yes
13. Ynys Dulas	SH502902	yes	?	yes	yes
14. Puffin Island	SH650820	yes	?	? no	yes

Sources: Anderson (1977), Rees (1973), Thomas (1993); CCW, RSPB, UCNW (Bangor). Note: Many sites have not been officially surveyed since 1974. Key: n/a - not covered in this source.

them. There is a very small risk of injury to seals in the immediate vicinity of a vessel conducting seismic surveys.

5.14.4 Information sources used

Pup production around the Pembroke and Ceredigion coast, from Caldey Island to Aberystwyth, has been systematically monitored throughout each breeding season since 1991 by DWT (Baines 1992, 1993, 1994; Baines, Earl & Strong 1994), under contract to CCW, with funding from the Pembrokeshire Coast National Park, Welsh Water and others; most of the information presented here was summarised from those reports. The most recent breeding survey of the entire region was carried out between 20 September and 11 October 1974 (Anderson 1977). Most breeding sites were visited once, and counts of pups were obtained from inflatable boats and by swimmers. A survey of breeding sites on Anglesey and the Caernarfonshire (Gwynedd) coast was made by Rees (1973). Pup production on Ynys Enlli is monitored by Bardsey Bird Observatory. Pup production on Skomer has been monitored annually since 1983.

Information on seal distribution outside the breeding season is collected routinely at a number of sites: on Ynys Enlli by Bardsey Bird Observatory; on The Skerries (north-west Anglesey from mid-May to mid-August) by the RSPB; on the north Pembroke coast (DWT and CCW); on Ramsey (RSPB); and on Skomer (DWT). There are anecdotal accounts from haul-out sites elsewhere, particularly round the Gwynedd coast (Table 5.14.2).

5.14.5 Further sources of information

A. References cited

Anderson, S.S. 1977. The grey seal in Wales. *Nature in Wales, 15*: 114-123.
Baines, M.E. 1992. *West Wales grey seal census - report on the 1991 survey.* Unpublished report to the Countryside Council for Wales from the Dyfed Wildlife Trust.
Baines, M.E. 1993. *West Wales grey seal census - report on the 1992 season.* Unpublished report to the Countryside Council for Wales from the Dyfed Wildlife Trust.
Baines, M.E. 1994. Grey seals in west Wales. *British Wildlife, 5*: 341-348.
Baines, M.E., Earl, S.J., & Strong, P.G. 1994. *West Wales grey seal census - interim report on the 1993 season.* Unpublished report to the Countryside Council for Wales from the Dyfed Wildlife Trust.
Baines, M.E., & Pierpoint C.J.L. 1993. *Ramsey Island grey seal census 1992.* Unpublished report to Dyfed Wildlife Trust.
Davies, J.D., & Anderson S.S. 1976. Effects of oil pollution on breeding grey seals. *Marine Pollution Bulletin, 7*: 115-118.
Rees, S. 1973. *Survey of grey seal breeding sites on the Anglesey and Caernarfonshire coasts.* Unpublished internal Nature Conservancy Report (held by the Countryside Council for Wales, Bangor).
Richardson, W.J., Hickie, J.P., Davis, R.A., & Thomson, D.H. 1989. *Effects of offshore petroleum operations on cold water marine mammals: a literature review.* American Petroleum Institute Publication No. 4485.
Thomas, D. 1992. *Marine wildlife and net fisheries around Wales.* RSPB/CCW Report.
Thomas, D. 1993. *Marine wildlife and net fisheries in Cardigan Bay.* RSPB/CCW Report.
Thomas, D. 1994. *Observations on disturbance to breeding seals on Ramsey, 1993.* Unpublished report to Dyfed Wildlife Trust.

B. Further reading

Cullen, M.S. 1978. The stock of grey seal *Halichoerus grypus* off Pembrokeshire, Dyfed. 1977. *Nature in Wales, 16*: 20-24.
Evans S.B. 1979. *Oil pollution of west Wales by the CHRISTOS BITAS 12 October to 20 November, 1978.* Unpublished NCC Report (Held by CCW).
Gubbay, S. 1988. *A coastal directory for marine nature conservation.* Ross-on-Wye, Marine Conservation Society.
McGillivray, D. 1995. Seal conservation legislation in the UK: past, present and future. *International Journal of Marine and Coastal Law, 10*: 19-52.

C. Contact names and addresses

Type of information	Contact address and telephone no.
Seals on Ynys Enlli	The Warden, Bardsey Bird and Field Observatory, Aberdaron, Pwllheli, Ynys Enlli LL53 8DE, Gwynedd
Seals on West Hoyle Bank, a major haul-out site just outside the region	Dee Estuary Ranger, Hilbre Reserve, c/o The Post Office, Grange Road, West Kirby, Wirral L46 4HA
Seals around the Dyfed coast	*DWT Seal Survey Team, Dyfed Wildlife Trust, Haverfordwest, tel: 01437 765462
Seals around the Gwynedd coast	*North Wales Wildlife Trust, Bangor, tel: 01248 351541
Seals in the region's SSSIs	*CCW Fishguard, tel: 01348 874602, or CCW HQ Bangor, tel: 01248 370444
Seals around Skomer MNR	*CCW Skomer, tel: 01646 636736
Licences to kill seals	Welsh Office Agriculture Department, Cathays Park, Cardiff CF1 3NQ, tel: 01222 823176
Seals on The Skerries, Anglesey	The Warden, RSPB Office, Swn-y-Mor, South Stack, Holy Island, Anglesey, Gwynedd OL65 3HB, tel: 01407 764973
Seals on Ramsey Island	The Warden, RSPB, 'Tegfan', Caerbwdi, St Davids, Dyfed SA62 6QT, tel: 01437 720065
Seal numbers and distribution around the UK	Callan Duck, Sea Mammal Research Unit, High Cross, Madingley Road, Cambridge CB3 0ET, tel: 01223 311354

* Starred contact addresses are given in full in the Appendix

5.14.6 Acknowledgements

Kim Atkinson and the Bardsey Bird Observatory; Sally Budd, Steve Evans, Michael Gash and Peter Hope Jones of CCW; Mick Baines, Margaret Brooke and David Saunders of DWT; Vicky Seager, Ranger for the Dee Estuary; Ian Bullock, Alistair Moralee and Dave Thomas of the RSPB and Ivor Rees of UCNW (Bangor) kindly provided information on seal distributions. On seal conservation law, grateful thanks are due to Donald McGillivray, Kent University, for information and comments, and to Mick Baines, Dyfed Wildlife Trust; Amanda Richards and Caroline Naylor, CCW, and Caroline Robson and Rob Keddie, JNCC, for help in gathering information on protected sites.

5.15 Whales, dolphins and porpoises

Dr P.G.H. Evans

5.15.1 Introduction

Fourteen species of cetaceans have been recorded since 1980 along the coasts or in nearshore waters (within 60 km of the coast) of the region. In terms of the diversity of regularly occurring cetacean species, the region is not particularly rich, with less than 25% (six out of 26 species) of the UK cetacean fauna recorded regularly in the region since 1980 (Table 5.15.1). These six species - harbour porpoise, common dolphin, bottlenose dolphin, killer whale, long-finned pilot whale and Risso's dolphin - are either present throughout the year or are recorded annually as seasonal visitors. The region is, however, nationally important for having the only recognised resident community of bottlenose dolphins in England and Wales. The population numbers at least 130 individuals (and probably many more, although only a proportion of these are likely to be resident), and at least some individuals occur in several months of the year (Evans 1992; Arnold 1993; Lewis & Evans 1993). The harbour porpoise and bottlenose dolphin are both listed in Annex II of the Habitats Directive as species whose conservation requires the designation of Special Areas of Conservation. Maps 5.15.1 - 4 show the distribution of sightings of common dolphins, harbour porpoise and bottlenose dolphins in the region.

Other cetacean species recorded in the region include fin whale *Balaenoptera physalus*, minke whale *B. acutorostrata*, humpback whale *Megaptera novaeangliae*, pygmy sperm whale *Kogia breviceps*, Blainville's beaked whale *Mesoplodon densirostris* (only British record, and only of stranded specimens), striped dolphin *Stenella coeruleoalba*, Atlantic white-sided dolphin *Lagenorhynchus acutus*, and white-beaked dolphin *L. albirostris*. For geographical comparisons of sightings rates for various cetacean species, see Evans (1990, 1992) and Northridge *et al.* (in prep.).

5.15.2 Important locations and species

Most nearshore cetacean sightings in the region are of bottlenose dolphin or harbour porpoise, although populations of the latter are small compared with those in northern Britain. Both species typically occur in the shallow seas bordering the North Atlantic. The species most frequently recorded offshore is the common dolphin.

Along the West Glamorgan coast, conditions do not favour concentrations of food fishes and so cetaceans are uncommon (Evans 1987).

The coastal waters of Dyfed support a number of different cetacean species at various times, as follows. Harbour porpoises are reported throughout the year around the islands of Skomer, Skokholm and Ramsey, but particularly between June and October, and there is a locally important concentration in St Bride's Bay. In coastal waters around Strumble Head, the Teifi Estuary and Cardigan Island and also off the series of headlands (Mwnt, Pen Peles, Aberporth, Ynys Lochtyn) reaching up to Newquay, they occur in small numbers throughout the year but particularly between late July and September. In Cardigan Bay, harbour porpoises are seen in greatest numbers between July and October over sandbanks and undersea mounts, notably the Patches, Sarn y Bwch and Sarn Badrig.

Bottlenose dolphins are most commonly seen within ten miles of the coast between Cardigan and Borth, from April to October, although they are also seen off Skokholm and Skomer and sometimes off Strumble Head, especially between July and September. Headlands at Mwnt, Pen Peles, Aberporth, Ynys Lochtyn and New Quay are particularly favoured feeding areas for bottlenose dolphins. Like harbour porpoises, they are also seen in significant numbers further north in Cardigan Bay, especially in shallower water.

Table 5.15.1 Cetacean species regularly recorded in the region

Species name	Status	Distribution/seasonal occurrence
Harbour porpoise *Phocoena phocoena*	Fairly common	All months of the year but with greatest numbers April - November, particularly early September. Widely distributed, particularly around the Pembrokeshire islands and offshore sand banks and sea mounts.
Common dolphin *Delphinus delphis*	Common	Offshore in the Irish Sea & St George's Channel. All months of the year but with greatest numbers July - September.
Bottlenose dolphin *Tursiops truncatus*	Common	All months of the year, but peak numbers August - December, with possible spring (late April - May) and autumn (October - November) influxes. Nearshore waters, particularly between Cardigan and New Quay (but extending north to Criccieth) and around several offshore sand banks and sea mounts in central and northern Cardigan Bay.
Killer whale *Orcinus orca*	Uncommon	Mainly off the Dyfed coast, April - September.
Long-finned pilot whale *Globicephala melas*	Fairly common	Mainly offshore. All months of the year but most sightings and greatest numbers August - December.
Risso's dolphin *Grampus griseu*	Uncommon	Nearshore waters, with most sightings around the Pembrokeshire islands and western end of the Llyn Peninsula, including Ynys Enlli, mainly April - September.

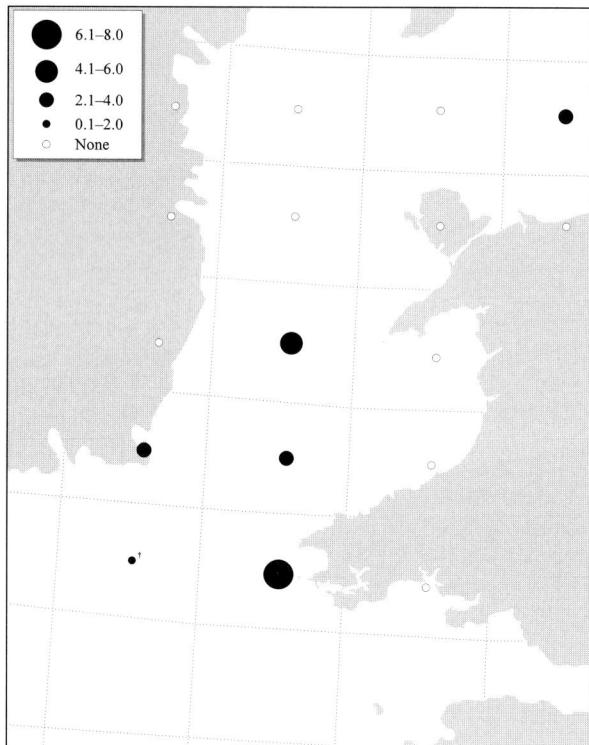

Map 5.15.1 Sightings of common dolphins, summer 1992. Number of sightings per 1,000 km travelled (from 'platforms of opportunity'). Source: Evans (1992).

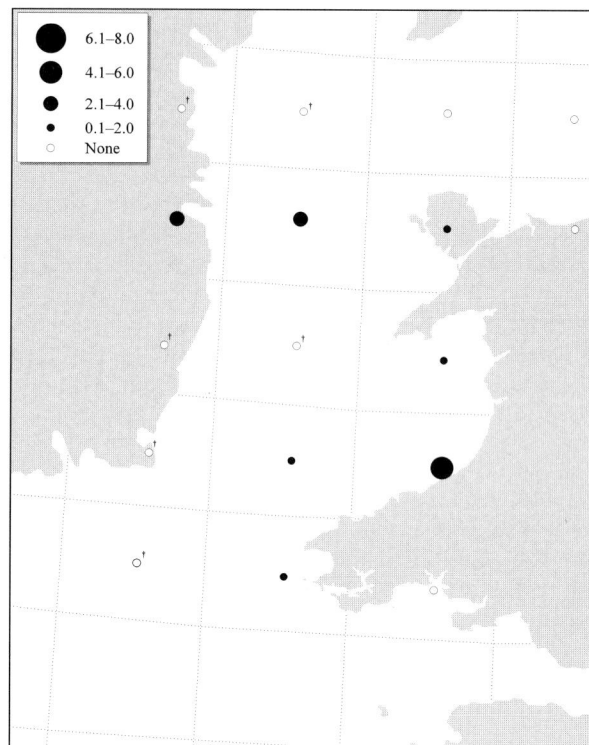

Map 5.15.2 Sightings of harbour porpoise, summer 1992. Number of sightings per 1,000 km travelled (from 'platforms of opportunity'). Source: Evans (1992).

Common dolphins are also seen off Skokholm and Skomer (as are Risso's dolphins) but are more typically encountered further offshore in the Irish Sea and St George's Channel. In the summer a frontal system develops in the Irish Sea (see section 4.3), with concentrations of plankton, fish and squid, which attracts feeding concentrations of cetaceans otherwise found only in the open sea, such as long-finned pilot whales and baleen whales, as well as the common dolphins. Other species sometimes recorded far offshore include fin whale (October - December) and minke whale (July - September).

Cetaceans have been sighted in coastal waters around Gwynedd, particularly in Caernarfon Bay. Harbour porpoises occur around Ynys Enlli and Holy Island, Anglesey, from at least June to October. Other species recorded in small numbers include Risso's dolphin and bottlenose dolphin.

Off the north coast of Gwynedd, coastal waters are again infrequently visited by cetaceans.

5.15.3 Human activities

Cetaceans in the region face three main pressures from human activities: conflicts with fisheries (either by competition for a common food resource, or accidental capture in fishing gear), habitat degradation (mainly from untreated sewage, but possibly other contaminants), and disturbance (from underwater sounds).

Tangle nets set for demersal fish in Caernarfon and Cardigan Bays have been reported accidentally catching harbour porpoises (Thomas 1992). Although local sources of pollution (besides untreated sewage) have not been identified, two bottlenose dolphins found stranded on the Dyfed coast in 1988 and 1992 respectively contained high levels of PCBs (max. 290 ppm), DDT (max. 150 ppm), and mercury (max. 190 ppm) (Morris *et al.* 1989; Law *et al.* 1992). It is not known how these dolphins ingest these levels in comparatively unpolluted waters.

Recreational activities (speedboats, jet skis, etc.) around resorts such as Cardigan, Aberporth, New Quay and Borth, pose threats of disturbance from the high frequency (>1 kHz) noise generated by these vessels (Evans *et al.* 1992). Negative responses (vessel avoidance and increased dive times) by both bottlenose dolphins and harbour porpoises to such sounds have been reported by Evans *et al.* (1992; in press). Other underwater sounds from seismic activities (as part of oil and gas exploration) are at lower frequencies, and therefore are most likely to affect baleen whales, which communicate primarily at these frequencies (20-500 Hz), although Baines (1993) reported a possible temporary negative correlation between porpoise presence off Strumble Head and seismic activities, during summer 1993. Results obtained during seismic surveys by Marathon and Hamilton oil companies (Evans *et al.* 1993) were inconclusive and experimental evidence remains lacking.

5.15.4 Information sources used

Information on cetacean status and distribution comes primarily from the national sightings database (1973 - present) maintained by the Sea Watch Foundation (SWF) and the strandings scheme organised by the London Natural History Museum (1913-present). In addition, dedicated surveys for bottlenose dolphins and harbour

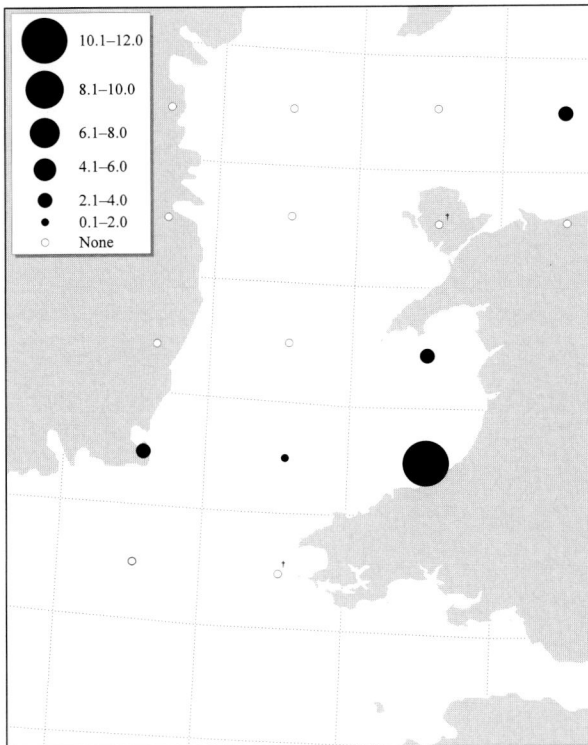

Map 5.15.3 Sightings of bottlenose dolphins, summer 1992. Number of sightings per 1,000 km travelled (from 'platforms of opportunity'). Source: Evans (1992).

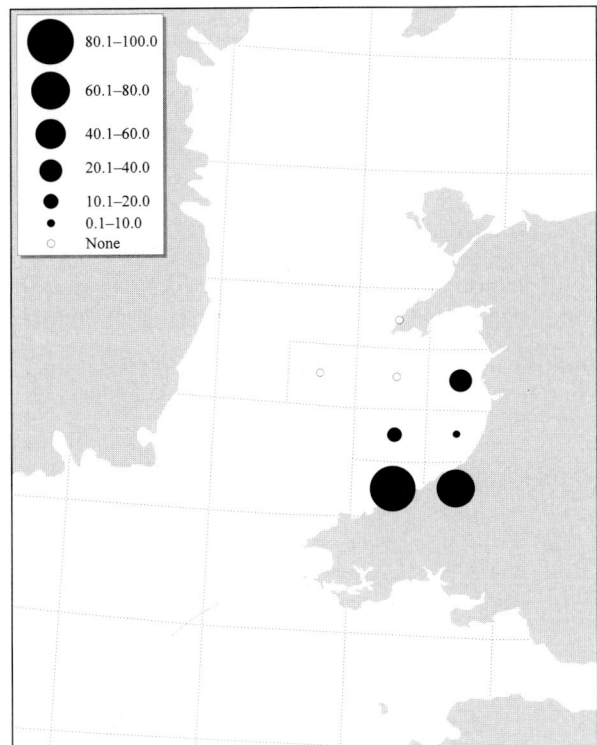

Map 5.15.4 Sightings of bottlenose dolphins in Cardigan Bay, summers 1991 and 1992. Number of sightings per 1,000 km travelled (from dedicated cruises). Source: Evans (1992).

porpoises have been carried out in recent years in Cardigan Bay, mainly between June and September, by the Sea Watch Foundation (see Lewis & Evans 1993), the University of Aberdeen and Greenpeace (Arnold 1993). Systematic land-based watches have been carried out by the wardens of Skomer and Skokholm Islands, and Ynys Enlli, and by members of Dyfed Wildlife Trust, Friends of Cardigan Bay, and other volunteers at Strumble Head, overlooking Ramsey Sound, at Newquay and Holy Island. Offshore effort-related data are also collected by trained observers aboard various sea-angling vessels operating between May and October; Sea Link ferries operating throughout the year between Rosslare and Cherbourg, passing down the centre of the southern Irish Sea; seabird surveys of the Irish Sea by JNCC's Seabirds at Sea Team, mainly between 1986 and 1990; and a survey of the Irish Sea utilising yachts, ferries, and the Royal Navy, between May and September 1992. As part of surveillance of seismic exploration activities, cetacean observations were collected during systematic surveys of the southern Irish Sea, with Marathon Oil (May-June 1993), and Hamilton Oil (January 1994).

Survey effort remains patchy, with some areas poorly covered (e.g. West Glamorgan and north Gwynedd), and effort is highest between the months of July and September when sea conditions also tend to be most favourable. Although the list of important sites partly reflects the fact that they are better known, other systematic data support their regional importance.

5.15.5 Further sources of information

A. References cited

Arnold, H. 1993. Distribution, abundance and habitat use of bottle-nosed dolphins in Cardigan Bay, Wales, 1992. *In: European research on cetaceans: 7*, ed. by P.G.H. Evans, 63-66. Cambridge, European Cetacean Society.

Baines, M.E. 1993. Marine mammal monitoring during the seismic exploration of block 107/21 in Cardigan Bay, Autumn 1993. Haverfordwest, Dyfed Wildlife Trust.

Evans, P.G.H. 1987. *The natural history of whales and dolphins.* London, Christopher Helm.

Evans, P.G.H. 1990. Whales, dolphins and porpoises. The order Cetacea. *In: Handbook of British mammals*, ed. by G.B. Corbet & S. Harris, 299-350. Oxford, Blackwell.

Evans, P.G.H. 1992. *Status review of cetaceans in British and Irish waters.* Oxford, Sea Watch Foundation. (Report to the UK Dept. of the Environment, London.)

Evans, P.G.H., Canwell, P.J., & Lewis, E.J. 1992. An experimental study of the effects of pleasure craft noise upon bottle-nosed dolphins in Cardigan Bay, West Wales. *In: European research on cetaceans - 6*, ed by P.G.H. Evans, 43-46. Cambridge, European Cetacean Society.

Evans, P.G.H., Lewis, E.J., & Fisher, P. 1993. *A study of the possible effects of seismic testing upon cetaceans in the Irish Sea.* Oxford, Sea Watch Foundation. (Report to Marathon Oil UK.)

Evans, P.G.H., Carson, Q., Fisher, P. Jordan, W., Limer, R., & Rees, I. In press. A study of the reactions of Harbour Porpoises to various boats in the coastal waters of SE Shetland. *In: European research on cetaceans - 8*, ed. by P.G.H. Evans. Cambridge, European Cetacean Society.

Law, R.J., Jones, B.R., Baker, J.R., Kennedy, S., Milne, R., & Morris, R.J. 1992. Trace metals in the livers of marine mammals from the Welsh coast and the Irish Sea. *Marine Pollution Bulletin*, 24: 296-304.

Lewis, E.J., & Evans, P.G.H. 1993. Comparative ecology of bottle-nosed dolphins *Tursiops truncatus* in Cardigan Bay and the Moray Firth. *In: European research on cetaceans: 7*, ed. by P.G.H. Evans. 57-62. Cambridge, European Cetacean Society.

Morris, R.J., Law, R.J., Allchin, C.R., Kelly, C.A., & Fieleman, C. 1989. Metals and organochlorines in dolphins and porpoises of Cardigan Bay, West Wales. *Marine Pollution Bulletin, 20:* 512-523.

Northridge, S., Tasker, M.L., Webb, A., & Williams, J.M. 1995. Seasonal distribution and relative abundance of harbour porpoises *Phocoena phocoena* (L.), white-beaked dolphins *Lagenorhynchus albirostris* (Gray) and minke whales *Balaenoptera acutorostrata* (Lacepède) in the waters around the British Isles. *ICES Journal of marine Science.*

Thomas, D. 1992. *Marine wildlife and net fisheries around Wales.* Newtown and Bangor, Royal Society for the Protection of Birds/Countryside Council for Wales.

B. Further reading

Evans, P.G.H. 1990. European cetaceans and seabirds in an oceanographic context. *Lutra, 33:* 95-125.

Mayer, S., Arnold, H., & Evans, P.G.H. 1991. Preliminary findings from a photo-identification study of bottle-nosed dolphins *Tursiops truncatus* in Cardigan Bay, Wales, UK, during 1990. *In: European research on cetaceans: 5*, ed. by P.G.H. Evans, 45-46. Cambridge, European Cetacean Society.

Natural History Museum. 1990-present. *Annual Reports.* London, Natural History Museum.

Pierpoint, C., Earll, S., & Baines, M.E. In press. Observation of harbour porpoise in West Wales, 1993. *In: European research on cetaceans: 8*, ed. by P.G.H. Evans. Cambridge, European Cetacean Society.

C. Contact names and addresses

Type of information	Contact address and telephone no.
Cetacean strandings	Dr D. George & Mr A. Muir, Natural History Museum, Cromwell Road, South Kensington, London SW7 5BD, tel: 0171 938 8861
Cetacean strandings	R. Penrose, Welsh Strandings Co-ordinator, Penwalk, Llechryd, Cardigan, Dyfed SA43 2PS, tel: 01348 875000/875281
Cetacean sightings and surveys	Dr P.G.H. Evans, c/o Dept. of Zoology, University of Oxford, South Parks Road, Oxford OX1 3PS, tel: 01865 727984
Cetacean sightings	*JNCC Seabirds & Cetaceans Branch, Aberdeen tel: 01224 642863
Cetacean organochlorine and heavy metal levels	Dr R.J. Law, MAFF Fisheries Laboratory, Remembrance Avenue, Burnham-on-Crouch, Essex CM0 8HA, tel: 01621 782658
Cetacean bycatches in Cardigan and Caernarfon Bays	*D. Thomas, RSPB Wales, tel: 01686 626678
Conservation issues facing cetaceans in Cardigan Bay	*M. Taylor, Cardigan Bay Forum, tel: 01970 624471
Cetacean surveys in southern Cardigan Bay	M.E. Baines, Dyfed Wildlife Trust, Cefn Garth, Cilgerran, Cardigan, SA61 1NF, tel: 01239 682548
Studies of bottlenose dolphins; effects of sound disturbance	Dr P.G.H. Evans & E.-J. Lewis, c/o Zoology Department, University of Oxford, South Parks Road, Oxford OX1 3PS, tel: 01865 72798
Bottlenose dolphin studies	H. Arnold, c/o Aberdeen University Lighthouse Field Station, Cromarty, Ross-shire IV11 8YJ, tel: 01381 600548
Harbour porpoise watches	C. Pierpoint, 7 Parkway, Wallasey, Merseyside L45 3HU, tel: 0151 639 3813
Dolphin acoustic studies around New Quay	Dr R.J. Morris, 38b Old Burleigh Road, Surfers Paradise, Queensland, Australia 4217

* Starred contact addresses are given in full in the Appendix

5.15.6 Acknowledgements

Thanks are due to J. Heimlich-Boran and E.-J. Lewis for help in the preparation of the maps, and to the following persons for contributing valuable sightings data: M.E. Baines, T. Bristow, B. Bullerose, P. Dare, J. Durrant, P. Fisher, M. Green, J. Hagan, S. Hartley, N. Hughes, I. Hutchin, P.H. Jones, R.J. Law, E.-J. Lewis, S. Mayer, M. Morgan-Jenks, G. Reading, S. Sutcliffe, D. Taylor, M. Taylor, D. Thomas, A. Webb and T. Wenden.

Chapter 6 Archaeology and human history

A.B. Gale

6.1 Introduction

This chapter provides a brief introduction to the archaeological evidence which is an integral part of the coastal resource.

Archaeology can be broadly defined as the study of the past through physical evidence. It uses a wide variety of scientific techniques to record and analyse the available evidence. As for other areas of Britain, there is a growing interest in the archaeology and history of the coast of this region, which arises from an increasing awareness of the potential to recover high quality information from archaeological sites in the intertidal and sub-tidal zones.

This coastal region, although narrow, broadening out only in Pembrokeshire and across Anglesey, has been a major focus for human activity in all periods. This low-lying land and the tidal river valleys provide a more fertile area for habitation than the hills and mountains of the interior, which also form a barrier to communication. The coastal strip has, however, been constantly changing: contracting through erosion and inundation, widening through accretion and land claim. There is an increasing interest in reconstructing past environments and correlating them with evidence for sea-level change. Instances of marine and intertidal archaeological material associated with evidence indicative of terrestrial palaeo-environments demonstrate the potential of sites in this region to extend current knowledge hitherto based solely on terrestrial sites.

Map 6.2.1 shows some of the principal locations mentioned in the text.

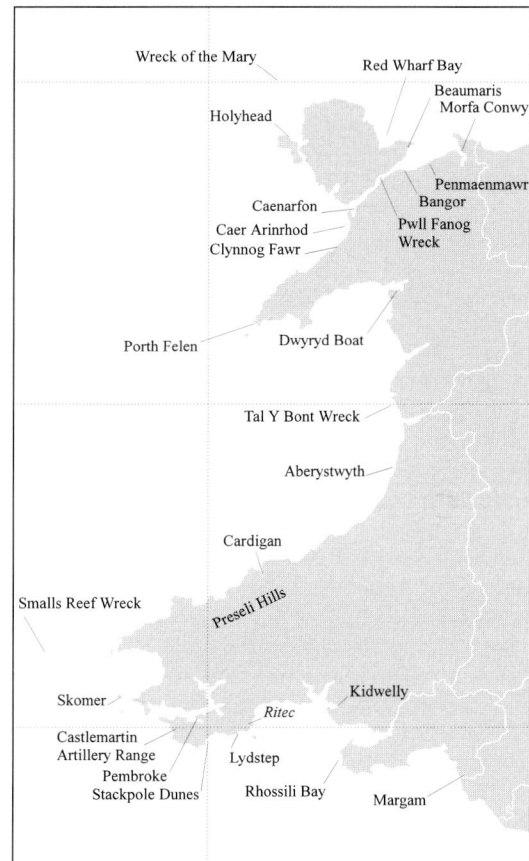

Map 6.2.1 Archaeology: locations mentioned in the text.

6.1.1 History and archaeology of the region

Hunters, gatherers and early farmers (Mesolithic and Neolithic): During the last Ice Age sea-level was about 40 m lower than today and Britain was joined to continental Europe. The coastal plain of Wales was much more extensive than now and was occupied by roaming bands of Mesolithic peoples (hunter-gatherers with stone tools). Communication with the Cornish Peninsula was easier as the Bristol Channel was then a river valley (Wainwright 1963). The ice-sheets began melting around 10,000 years ago, and since then the coastal plain has been much narrowed by rising sea-level.

The present intertidal area lies at the landward limit of the former coastal plain. Sites can be anticipated, therefore, on the seabed and in inundated rias as well as sealed beneath alluvial deposits. Mesolithic artefacts found are characterised by 'limpet scoops' indicative of fish eating. Submerged forests and peat have been recorded since the 19th century, during the construction of Swansea Docks for example. Similar palaeo-environmental deposits are now being recorded from around the whole region. Flint tools and animal debris have been found in the submerged forests, particularly in Carmarthen Bay and on the coast of Pembrokeshire. Material from Lydstep included the skeleton of a boar containing the microlith (flint tip) from a Mesolithic weapon (Lewis 1991).

Prehistoric landsurfaces have not only been submerged: they have also been sealed beneath massive accumulations of sand dunes. These are known on the coasts of West Glamorgan and Dyfed, with notable sites at Rhossili, Stackpole Dunes and the River Ritec near Tenby.

The Neolithic population, who cleared land for farming, often occupied sites once used by Mesolithic peoples. Their characteristic polished stone axes were made from the igneous rocks found in the Preseli Hills (Dyfed) and Penmaenmawr (Gwynedd) (McCough & Cummins 1988). Occupation of the coast is indicated by long barrows, especially gallery graves, which occur in the former counties of Pembrokeshire, Caernarfonshire, Anglesey, Merioneth and Denbighshire. Such burial sites might have provided navigation markers during crossings of the Irish Sea (Corcoran 1972).

Metal-working peoples (Bronze Age and Iron Age): The Bronze Age people also occupied coastal sites. Their settlements, too, are marked by burial mounds, and also by circular huts and defended enclosures. Coastal mineral resources, particularly copper and lead, were exploited and traded overseas up to the middle ages. The Great Orme had some of the largest copper mines in Europe. Rich hoards from the Iron Age have been found, including evidence of the use of horses and wheeled vehicles. Strongholds were built on high ground, especially on headlands (promontory forts) in Pembrokeshire and the Llyn Peninsula. Field systems surviving on Skomer, for example, show that offshore islands also came into occupation.

The Roman province: The Roman army crossed the Menai Strait into Anglesey in AD 60 and defeated the Welsh tribes. They controlled the region, with its important mineral reserves, from legionary bases at the ports of Caerleon and Chester. They probably relied on sea communications, as there were auxilliary fortresses within the region on the rivers Taf, Neath, Dyfi, Seiont and Conwy (Cleere 1978). The presence of Black-Burnished ware from Dorset (Webster 1990) suggests a south Wales/south-west England trade link which is apparent in the later historic period. The exploitation of Welsh copper was increased, along with lead, gold and slate. These heavy materials could best be carried by sea and Roman ships navigated around the region. One, in negotiating the Llyn Peninsula, lost an anchor, the lead stock of which was found off Porth Felen (Boon 1977).

Roman departure to Norman conquest: In comparison with the quantity of material from Roman Wales, little survives from the subsequent 700 years. Yet this "was the time when almost everything which is today considered characteristically Welsh took shape - language, place-names, religion, geographical boundaries..." (Moore 1972). Biographies of early saints reveal the coastal orientation of Christianity in Wales. The initial missionary thrust established small island monasteries, such as Caldey. There followed major coastal establishments (Thomas 1994). Many of the 450 surviving Welsh inscribed memorial stones of early Christians derive from the coast (Bowen 1972). The Scandinavian raiders of the 9th and 10th centuries sacked coastal settlements and monasteries before finally settling in southern Pembrokeshire and the Vale of Glamorgan.

The medieval period: Religious institutions provided a spur to activity in the region. Large numbers of pilgrims journeyed to the shrines of Celtic saints, particularly St David's, St Beuno at Clynnog Fawr and Ynys Enlli. Coastal towns such as St David's and Bangor grew up as many settlements developed around monastic churches. Monasteries were also associated with exploitation of the sea. A surviving 13th century stone fish trap in Caernarfon Bay (Momber 1991) was probably made by local monks. Such fish traps are characteristic of the region, especially around Caernarfon Bay and the Menai Strait.

Edward I (1272-1307) dominated Wales by controlling the coast and sea communications. His castles at Caernarfon and Beaumaris were designed to be supplied by sea; 30 boats brought materials to build Beaumaris (Johnson 1978). These and other castles, such as Kidwelly, Pembroke, Aberystwyth and Cardigan also provided a focus for the development of coastal settlements and ports.

The sea routes around the region were familiar to 15th-century mariners. One of the earliest descriptions of sailing on the British coast includes the Skerries, Holyhead and seventeen islands in the Severn Estuary (Burwash 1969). In the early 16th century Leland described the hazards to ships entering the ports of Carmarthen Bay caused by enlarging sand banks.

Modern times: Wales lies between Liverpool and Bristol,

the two ports which until recently dominated foreign trade from western Britain. The sea routes around this region were travelled by foreign-going ships, while its ports were mainly engaged in coastwise shipping of minerals and other raw materials. From the 17th century, Swansea, Neath, Llanelli, Burry and Milford Haven expanded rapidly as they began to export coal to south-west England. Links with the Cornish peninsula were strong, especially after imports of tin and copper ore became established in the early 18th century. Using these resources Swansea became the major copper smelting centre in Britain and a worldwide exporter of coal.

The ports of Cardigan Bay and the Menai Strait also exported raw materials, supplying slate for roofs and hearths across Britain. By the late 19th century Welsh slate accounted for over 75% of the total national output (David 1987). This provided shipping employment, with small harbours such as Porthmadog supporting an international trade and building many ships. Other minerals provided a stimulus for individual ports: for example, prior to 1750, Aberdovey was the only port in the region to ship lead (Willan 1967).

Pembroke Dockyard, founded as a shipbuilding yard, was the only Royal Naval Dockyard to be established in Britain in the 19th century.

The importance of the shipping routes around the region and the dangers of the coast are indicated by the numerous lighthouses, particularly around the Smalls, Pembrokeshire and Anglesey.

6.1.2 Types of archaeological evidence in the region

Since the late 18th century a large body of information on land-based archaeological sites in the region has been built up. The region contains known surviving sites, sites that have been investigated but since destroyed, and sites that have been located but never investigated, such as burial mounds which have been ploughed out since being photographed during RAF reconnaissance flights, or villages described in documents but now covered by sand dunes or lost to the sea.

Historically, discoveries in the intertidal zone have tended to be finds of artefacts. In this region these include pottery and flint implements, eroded from either cliffs or beach deposits. In recent years archaeological surveys in the intertidal zone have focused on *in situ* features. These include both sites with a maritime function, such as fish weirs, slipways, abandoned boats, and shipwrecks, and those sites which do not have a maritime function but which have been inundated by rising sea-level. Peat and forest deposits in the sub-tidal and intertidal zones are now recognised as the submerged landscapes of earlier periods.

Archaeological investigation of sea-bed sites has only been possible since the development of SCUBA. Traditionally, work has focused on individual wreck sites but there is a now a commitment to create a comprehensive record of sea-bed sites for this region. Most located shipwrecks around Britain are metal ships which have sunk this century. These usually stand proud of the seabed and can be located using remote-sensing equipment. Known examples of much earlier shipwrecks show, however, that wooden hulls can also survive in the seabed. Judging by the numbers of ships recorded as lost, the region may hold many as yet undiscovered shipwrecks. Records of losses are comprehensive for the 19th century, relatively complete for the 18th, and patchy for the 14th to 17th centuries. For earlier periods it is necessary to examine documentary evidence for sea-borne trade and extrapolate the opportunities for ship losses by considering the hazards to navigation. This process has then to be extended into the prehistoric period by looking at archaeological evidence for trade and seafaring.

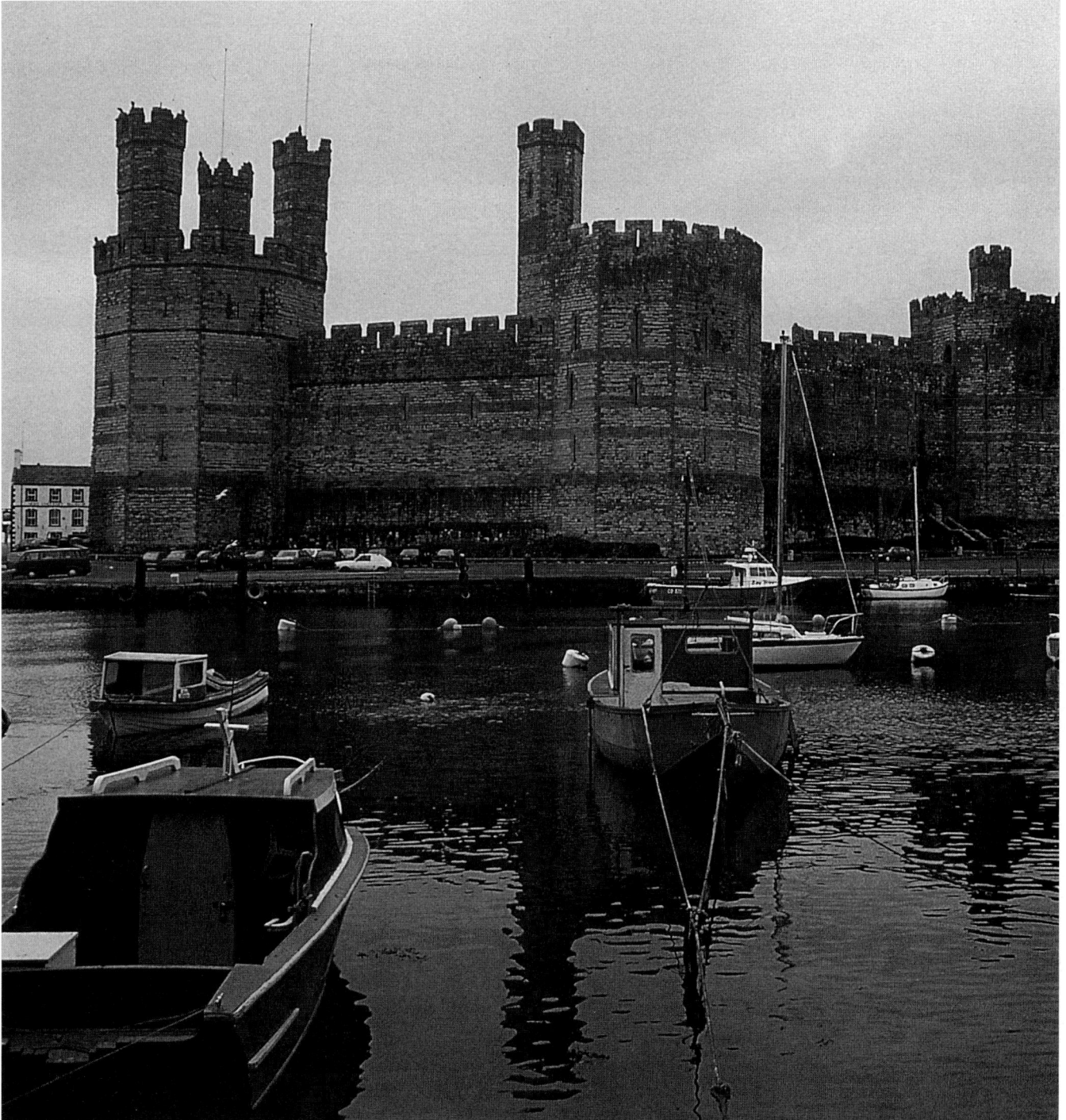

Originally a Norman stronghold, Caernarfon Castle (Gwynedd) was rebuilt in the late 13th century by Edward I as the seat of his court in Wales. It dominates a natural harbour important since at least Roman times. Photo: N.C.Davidson.

6.2 Important locations

In Wales, three statutory designations are intended to protect *in situ* remains of archaeological or historic importance: the Ancient Monuments & Archaeological Areas Act 1979 (AMAA) provides for Scheduled Ancient Monuments; the Planning (Listed Buildings and Conservation Areas) Act 1990 provides for Listed Buildings; and the Protection of Wreck Act 1973 provides for Historic Wreck Sites.

Many sites in the region, particularly promontory forts and burial monuments, are among the 2,700 Scheduled Ancient Monuments in Wales. For England and Wales there is a published list of criteria for determining the national importance of a monument (Welsh Office 1991); the number of scheduled sites is expected to increase following current review programmes. Table 6.2.1 shows the numbers of Scheduled Monuments in England, Scotland and Wales. Cadw (see section 6.3.3) inspects monuments, assists owners by drawing up management agreements which are supported by grants, and directly manages those monuments in Guardianship.

Table 6.2.1 Numbers of scheduled monuments

Country	No. of scheduled monuments	No. of monuments in Guardianship
Wales	2,700	125
England	13,000	400
Scotland	5,300	330

Source: Breeze (1993)

The AMAA definition of monument includes sites both on land and in UK territorial waters, including remains of vehicles, vessels and aircraft. In practice, however, scheduling has only been applied above low water mark in England and Wales (Firth 1993). There is a presumption against the destruction of Scheduled Monuments: prior consent is necessary for any works which will destroy, damage, repair or remove such a monument.

Buildings considered of special architectural or historic importance may be Listed. Listed Buildings in the region include maritime structures such as docks, dock gates, warehouses and lighthouses. There is no presumption against the destruction of Listed Buildings, but consent is required prior to any demolition, alteration or extension (Suddards 1993).

There are four Historic Wrecks designated in the region (Table 6.2.2). Shipwrecks that are considered of archaeological, historical or artistic importance may be designated; there are no standard criteria for designation but Cadw receives guidance from the Advisory Committee on Historic Wreck. Fewer than 45 wrecks have been designated for the whole of Britain: these do not form a representative sample of the total seabed resource. Designation usually applies to an area of seabed in which the wreck is considered to lie. Except under licence from Cadw, it is illegal to tamper with or remove material, to use diving or salvage equipment, or to deposit anything which may damage or obliterate the wreck (Firth 1993). Sites may be inspected on behalf of Cadw by the Archaeological Diving Unit, which is contracted by the Department of National Heritage (DNH) to provide field inspection.

Information on designated sites in Wales is available from Cadw. Guidance notes for finders of historic wreck are available from DNH.

Table 6.2.2 Historic wrecks designated in the region

Site name & designation order	Location	Grid ref.	Description
Smalls wreck site (1991 No. 2 1991/2746)	Smalls Reef, Dyfed	SM464087	300 m radius around find spot. Hiberno-Norse sword guard c.AD 1100.
Tal-y-Bont wreck site (1979 No.1 1979/31) Amendment Order 26.10.1989 (1989/1766)	Off Barmouth, Dyfed	SH566222	300 m radius of wreck carrying marble blocks. Also called Bronze Bell wreck.
Pwll Fanog wreck site (1978 No.1 1978/199)	Menai Strait, Gwynedd	SH534707	150 m radius of wreck carrying slates. Medieval or later.
Mary (1974 No.4 1974/58)	Anglesey, Gwynedd	SH265947	Yacht given to Charles II in 1660. Lost 1675. Radius 100 m.

Source: Department of National Heritage

6.3 Human activities

6.3.1 Activities and processes affecting the archaeological resource

The archaeological resource does not consist solely of discrete sites such as intact wrecks: many sites are scattered, and palaeo-environmental deposits can be extensive, crossing the boundaries between the terrestrial, intertidal and subtidal zones.

Terrestrial activities: Coastal sites experience both natural and human influences. Cliff erosion can threaten sites such as promontory forts and the scatters of flints worked by prehistoric man. Trampling causes erosion, particularly on long distance coastal paths. Erosion has been recorded in Dyfed (Dyfed Archaeological Trust (DAT) 1994) and in Gwynedd (Smith 1993). Developments such as caravan parks and car parks can also affect archaeological sites, as can the extension of agriculture to the cliff edge. Rising sea level may affect the integrity of sites, as might any coastal protection and flood defence works.

Many docks and harbours of the region are being redeveloped to support economic regeneration. There are large-scale initiatives such as the Llanelli Coast Venture and the barrage projects, and changes to smaller ports such as Aberyswyth and Cardigan. Redevelopment often involves remodelling of the coast edge and landscape features. Such projects require skilful planning to provide new uses while retaining the fabric and character of historic buildings and structures. Demolition and rebuilding can both reveal and destroy fragile remains of earlier waterfronts sealed beneath existing structures. Medieval and earlier waterfront structures may survive in locations which were not favoured by nineteenth century developers.

Intertidal activities: Foreshore deposits are sensitive to erosive or depositional action of the sea. Remodelling or protection of the coast in one area may threaten archaeological deposits in another. Developments which directly impinge on the intertidal area such as sewage outfalls and oil and gas pipelines can disturb archaeological sites, as can individual activities such as bait digging.

Sub-tidal activities: The influence of human activities on the subtidal resource is poorly understood because so little survey work has been done. There is clearly scope for activities to directly damage or destroy sites, for example through salvage diving, dredging or the use of fishing gear which is in contact with the seabed. Chemical or physical change of the marine environment may also alter the stability of sites.

6.3.2 Development control

Terrestrial and intertidal development: To landward of mean low water mark archaeology is considered within the unified system of development control provided by the planning system. The Welsh Office has issued guidance notes (Welsh Office 1991) explaining the requirements on planning authorities and developers regarding archaeological remains. In essence there is a presumption in favour of the preservation *in situ* of archaeological remains and their settings. They therefore recommend that it is in the interest of developers, as

part of their research, to make an initial assessment of whether the site is known or likely to contain such remains. The Sites and Monuments Records (SMRs - see section 6.3.3) provide information on the location of archaeological sites and should be consulted at an early stage.

Planning decisions should take into account the more detailed policies which appear in Development Plans. Thus the Structure Plans for the counties of West Glamorgan, Dyfed, and Gwynedd, and the Local Plans for their constituent districts, all contain policies on archaeology. Where county boundaries extend beyond low water mark, for example on the coast of West Glamorgan, these policies may apply to seabed sites.

Further policies and information related to archaeology appear in a variety of management plans. The policies deal with the resource generally and not specifically with coastal archaeology. Heritage Coast Plans exist for parts of Gower, the Ceredigion coast and parts of the Llyn Peninsula (see also section 7.3). The existence of the seabed archaeological resource is recognised in the draft Pembrokeshire Coast National Park plan, as is the lack of inventory and survey (Pembrokeshire Coast National Park 1994).

For certain types of development (listed in Schedules 1 and 2 to the Town & County Planning (Assessment of Environmental Effects) Regulations 1988) formal Environmental Assessments (EA) may be necessary. The EA should include information on any effects on the cultural heritage.

Subtidal development: To seaward of low water mark there is a sectoral approach to development control (Department of the Environment 1993). Regulation, including the requirement for EA, is divided between a range of government departments and agencies. Until recently, the lack of databases and management structures for archaeology in the subtidal zone has precluded its consideration by many authorities. For example, the procedure (under review) by which the Crown Estate Commissioners consider licences for survey and extraction of aggregates only specifies the need to weigh the impact on designated wrecks. However growing awareness of marine archaeology is leading to voluntary consideration of the archaeological resource and a Code of practice for seabed developers (Joint Nautical Archaeology Policy Committee 1995) has been published by the Joint Nautical Archaeology Policy Committee (see section 6.5 C).

6.3.3 Key organisations and their responsibilities

'Cadw: Welsh Historic Monuments' (known as Cadw) executes the responsibilities of the Secretary of State for Wales in respect of the Ancient Monuments and Archaeological Areas Act (1969) and the Protection of Wrecks Act (1973). Cadw funds rescue archaeology and survey work.

The Royal Commission on the Ancient and Historical Monuments of Wales (RCAHMW) has a statutory responsibility for survey and inventory of archaeological sites in Wales. Since 1964 it has maintained a card index of terrestrial sites as part of the National Monuments Record (NMR). In 1992 new Royal Warrants extended the remit of

RCAHMW to the territorial seas. An officer has been appointed to create a Maritime Section of the NMR. RCAHMW is now the lead agency responsible for overseeing and grant-aiding the local inventories known as Sites and Monuments Records (SMRs).

The Region is covered by three SMRs, maintained respectively by Glamorgan-Gwent Archaeological Trust (GGAT), Dyfed Archaeological Trust (DAT) and Gwynedd Archaeological Trust (GAT). These Trusts were created in the 1970s in reponse to the increasing threat to the archaeological resource. Their role has recently been restated as the maintenance of the SMRs and "therefore provision of advice to local planning authorities and the implementation of schemes to mitigate the archaeological consequences of development" (Welsh Office 1991).

RCAHMW, in collaboration with the Trusts, and in association with Cadw and bodies such as the National Trust and National Park authorities, is working towards an integrated information system. This will provide a computerised version of elements of the NMR and SMRs in a single national index for Wales (ENDEX).

Management initiatives within the Heritage Coasts, the National Trust, the RSPB, Wildlife Trusts and the National Park authorities all provide for consideration of the archaeological resource. Schemes such as Tir Cymen (see section 7.4) (CCW 1992), on the Gower peninsula, provide further scope for archaeological conservation in agricultural areas. The study of historic landscapes being undertaken by the Countryside Council for Wales (CCW) and Cadw may provide management options; the six proposed pilot Tir Cymen schemes in Dyfed, for example, include intertidal and sub-tidal areas of archaeological significance.

Archaeological representation on management and advisory bodies is important: for example, DAT is represented on the Range Advisory Committee for Castlemartin Royal Artillery Range, and the voluntary North Wales Marine Study Group (NWMSG) is a member of Cardigan Bay Forum.

6.3.4 Reporting archaeological information

RCAHMW and the SMRs are the accepted reporting points for new archaeological information. The only legal requirement to report archaeological and historical artefacts arises when the objects fall within the laws on Treasure Trove or Salvage. The law of Treasure Trove is used to secure important treasures for the nation (Longworth 1993). Objects of gold or silver found on land must be reported to the National Museum of Wales, the police or the coroner. Should a coroner's inquest then declare the objects Treasure Trove, the National Museum of Wales may retain them and, in return, provide an *ex gratia* payment to the finder. The National Museum may waive its right in favour of another museum.

The Merchant Shipping Act (1894) requires any recovered wreck to be reported to the Receiver of Wreck. Wreck is defined as any ship, aircraft, hovercraft or parts of these, their cargo, or equipment, found in or on the shores of the sea, or any tidal water. The Receiver advertises reported wreck, regardless of age, in order that owners may claim their property. After one year, unclaimed wreck becomes the property of the Crown and is disposed of in order to pay the expenses of the Receiver and any salvage awards. During the statutory year, such items may be lodged with an appropriate museum or conservation facility with suitable storage conditions. Finders are often allowed to keep unclaimed wreck in lieu of a salvage award.

There is a policy of offering unclaimed wreck of historic, archaeological or artistic interest to registered museums. The responsibility of the Receiver to the finder, with regard to salvage awards, remains regardless of the historic character of the wreck.

The Receiver is preparing new forms for reporting wreck. These include a form which finders may use to volunteer to the RCAHMW information on the identity and condition of wreck sites.

6.4 Information sources

6.4.1 Terrestrial surveys

Few surveys have specifically addressed coastal sites within the region. However, some studies of economic activities, such as coal and lime production, include surveys of extant coastal sites (Moore-Colyer 1988).

RCAHMW includes 260 buildings in the Industrial: Maritime category of their index. The new Industrial Archaeology Section has recently published Hague's Welsh lighthouse survey (Hughes 1994) and has undertaken a survey of the industrial area of Swansea including the docks. Cadw have funded a number of the survey projects mentioned below by county. Their in-house Scheduling Enhancement Programme has included a review of caves containing archaeological deposits.

There has been no formal programme of survey in West Glamorgan. A member of Glamorgan-Gwent Archaeological Trust (GGAT) has, however, examined changing sea levels and the sealing of palaeo-environments by sand dunes in historic and prehistoric periods (Toft 1993).

In Dyfed individual research interests have focused attention on the potential for archaeological sites to be preserved through natural changes to the coastline, e.g. by being covered by sediments or wind-blown sand (James 1991). There have been a number of thematic surveys in the county: Dyfed Archaeological Trust (DAT) has undertaken a survey of coastal promontory forts (DAT 1994), and the Pembrokeshire Coast National Park has commissioned studies of historic buildings, including a survey of military buildings which described 431 sites with extant 19th and 20th century structures (Thomas 1994). Many of these defensive structures lie on the coast. DAT has also studied individual locations in response to management requirements, for example, the land use of south-east Llanelli (James 1993), the Ministry of Defence Castlemartin Range (DAT 1993), Skomer Island, and the coastline of Carmarthen Bay.

Gwynedd Archaeological Trust (GAT) has completed a survey of the coastal resource on a 139 km stretch from the Llyn Peninsula to the Great Orme (Smith 1993). Fieldwalking of the foreshore and a 150 m strip inland tripled the number of sites in the Sites and Monuments Records (SMRs) for this area from 45 to 130.

6.4.2 Intertidal surveys

Knowledge of intertidal sites in West Glamorgan has only arisen as a result of chance discoveries. For instance, Glamorgan-Gwent Archaeological Trust (GGAT) have recently recorded a prehistoric trackway on peat deposits in Swansea Bay (GGAT 1993).

Dyfed Archaeological Trust (DAT) has carried out a pilot project for the Royal Commission on the Ancient and Historical Monuments of Wales (RCAHMW) recording intertidal and maritime sites in Carmarthen Bay. The existing Dyfed SMR records 11 wrecks in the intertidal sands off Carmarthen. Similar wrecks appear in Rhossili Bay, West Glamorgan, which are not included in the SMR. The survival of wrecks in areas with many documented ship losses indicates the potential for surveys to reveal more sites.

Individual research projects have examined aspects of the intertidal area. These include studies of fish traps in Caernarfon Bay and the Menai Strait (Jones 1982; Summers 1990; Momber 1991); an investigation of palaeo-environmental evidence from submerged forests in Pembrokeshire; and a preliminary consideration of the potential of submerged material as an adjunct to excavation of cliff-top Mesolithic material (David, 1990).

Chance finds on beaches, such as at Margam, Newgale, Whitesands, Borth and Rhyl, have been the subject of detailed investigation by the Department of Archaeology and Numismatics of the National Museum of Wales. One ongoing study is that of 16th century finds from Margam, possibly derived from the 'Anne Francis' (wrecked in 1583). The museum is also surveying the hulk of a mid-19th century barque on the Taf in cooperation with local divers through the Nautical Archaeological Society training scheme.

In Gwynedd the coastal survey by GAT (Smith 1993) included the foreshore. The area is also studied by the North Wales Marine Study Group (NWMSG). Members work in association with the Extra-Mural and History Departments of the University College of Wales, Bangor. Fieldwork has focused on a few vessels, such as a boat engulfed in the marsh of the Dwyryd River, Porthmadog, hulks in Bangor harbour and wrecks on the shore (Table 6.4.1). Some members of NWMSG are currently looking at submerged forest sites with members of the Great Orme Exploration Society (Jones pers. comm.).

Table 6.4.1 Some intertidal ship and boat sites examined in the Bangor area

Site	Location	Grid ref.	Description
Dwyryd Boat	Dwyyrd River	SH604368	Heavily built boat, possibly used for loading slates to ships in river mouth.
Eliza Goddard	Bangor Harbour	SH588727	Hulk of schooner. Built 1858, Rhuddlan.
Unknown	Near Holyhead	SH285799	Wrecked 1930s possibly Scandinavian/ Baltic origin.
William	Red Wharf Bay	SH544812	Built 1866. Wrecked 1906. Ketch in coal trade.

6.4.3 Subtidal surveys

The Royal Commission on the Ancient and Historical Monuments of Wales (RCAHMW) Maritime Section of the National Monuments Record (NMR) will include documented ship losses, located wreck sites and submerged terrestrial sites. The initial record will be formed in collaboration with the Royal Commission on the Historical Monuments of England, drawing on the Wreck Index of the Admiralty's Hydrographic Department and records of private researchers. It is estimated that the record will grow to around 15,000 entries.

The Wreck Index of the Admiralty Hydrographic Department is primarily concerned with shipwrecks as hazards to navigation and contains predominantly 20th century wrecks. For Cardigan Bay there are records of 165 wreck sites (Huckbody *et al.* 1992). However the number of ships wrecked far exceeds those recorded in the Wreck Index, especially prior to 1900 when there were many more ships in service than now.

No reference to general archaeological survey of the seabed has been found for West Glamorgan or Dyfed. However, local researchers have collected details of wrecks (James pers. comm.). The National Museum of Wales has investigated individual sites with the cooperation of diving clubs, including the Smalls Viking sword site and the Porth Felen anchor stock site.

The North Wales Marine Study Group (NWMSG) is active in this region looking both at wrecks and inundated sites. Individual members have built up large records of seabed features, particularly in Cardigan Bay (Bowyer pers. comm.). The many legends of inundation around the Gwynedd coast have prompted a study of Caer Arianrhod, which is said to have been a fortress lost to the sea (Jones 1993).

6.4.4 Further sources of information

A. References cited

Boon, G. 1977. The Porth Felen anchor-stock. *International Journal of Nautical Archaeology.* 6 (3): 239-241.

Bowen, E.G. 1972. *Britain and the western seaways.* London, Thames & Hudson.

Breeze, D.J. 1993. Ancient monuments legislation. *In: Archaeology resource management in the UK - an introduction,* ed. by J. Hunter & I. Ralston, 56-65. Stroud, Alan Sutton.

Burwash, D. 1969. *English merchant shipping 1460 - 1540.* Newton Abbot, David & Charles.

Cleere, H. 1978. Roman harbours in Britain south of Hadrian's Wall. *In: Roman shipping and trade: Britain and the Rhine provinces,* ed. by J. du Plat Taylor & H. Cleere, 36-40. London, Council for British Archaeology (CBA Research Report No. 24.)

Corcoran, J.X.W.P. 1972. Multi-period construction and the origin of chambered long cairns in western Britain and Ireland. *In: Prehistoric man in Wales and the west,* ed. by F. Lynch & C. Burgess, 31-63. Bath, Adams & Bart.

Countryside Council for Wales. 1992. *Tir Cymen - a farmland stewardship scheme.* Bangor, Countryside Council for Wales.

David, R. 1987. The slate quarrying industry in Westmoreland: part one: the valleys of Troutbeck. *Transactions of the Cumberland and Westmoreland Antiquarian and Archaeological Society, LXXVII:* 215-233.

David, A. 1990. *Palaeolithic and Mesolithic settlement of Wales with particular reference to south-west Dyfed.* PhD Thesis. St David's University College, Lampeter.

Department of the Environment. 1993. *Development below low water mark. A review of regulations in England and Wales.* London, HMSO.

Dyfed Archaeological Trust. 1993. *Castlemartin RAC Range Electrification Scheme. Report on Archaeological Monitoring.* (Contractor Dyfed Archaeological Trust.) Unpublished Report to Secretary of State for Defence, Defence Land Agent, Barracks, Brecon, Powys.

Dyfed Archaeological Trust. 1994. *Dyfed coastal promontory forts assessment.* (Contractor: Dyfed Archaeological Tust.) Unpublished report for Cadw.

Firth, A. 1993. The management of underwater archaeology. *In: Archaeology resource management in the UK - an introduction,* ed. by J. Hunter & I. Ralston, 65-76. Stroud, Alan Sutton.

Gwent-Glamorgan Archaeological Trust. 1993. *Archaeological field evaluation of Brynmill peat shelf Swansea Bay 1993.* (Contractor: Gwent-Glamorgan Archaeological Trust.) Unpublished report for Cadw.

Huckbody, A.J, Taylor, P.M., Hobbs, G. & Elliott, R. 1992. *Caernarfon and Cardigan Bays: an environmental appraisal.* Hamilton Oil Company.

Hughes, S. 1994. *Lighthouses of Wales. Their architecture and archaeology.* Aberystwyth, RCAHMW.

James, H. 1993. *Past land use of Llanelli.* (Contractor: Dyfed Archaeological Trust.)

James, T. 1991. Where sea meets land: the changing coast of Carmarthenshire. *In: Sir Gad Studies in Carmarthenshire history,* ed. by H. James, 143-166. Carmarthen, Carmarthenshire Antiquarian Society. (Monograph Series Volume, No.4.)

Johnson, P. 1978. *The National Trust book of British castles.* London, National Trust and Weidenfeld & Nicholson.

Joint Nautical Archaeology Policy Committee. 1995. *Code of practice for seabed developers.* Swindon, Joint Nautical Archaeology Policy Committee.

Jones, C. 1982. Walls in the sea - the goradau of Menai. *International Journal of Nautical Archaeology, 11,* 4:1-7.

Jones, C. 1993. *Caer Arianrhod, a reef in Caernarfon Bay.* Unpublished report.

Lewis, M. 1991. *A palaeo-environmental investigation of submerged forests in south west Wales with particular reference to Mesolithic settlement.* PhD Thesis, St David's University College, Lampeter.

Longworth, I. 1993. Portable antiquities. *In: Archaeology resource management in the UK - an introduction,* ed. by J. Hunter & I. Ralston, 56-65. Stroud, Alan Sutton.

Lynch, F. & Burgess, C., eds. 1972. *Prehistoric man in Wales and the west.* Bath, Adams & Bart.

McClough, T.H. & Cummings, W.A. 1988. *Stone axe studies volume II.* London, Council for British Archaeology. (Council for British Archaeology Research Report, No. 67.)

Momber, G. 1991. Gorad Beuno: investigation of an ancient fish-trap in Caernarfon Bay, N. Wales. *International Journal of Nautical Archaeology, 20,* 2: 95-110.

Moore, D. 1972. *Monuments of early christianity in Wales.*

Moore-Colyer, R.T. 1988. Of lime and men: aspects of the coastal trade in lime in south west Wales in the eighteenth and nineteenth centuries. *Welsh History Review, 14:* 54-77.

Pembrokeshire Coast National Park. 1994. *Draft National Park Plan.*

Savory, H.N. 1980. *Guide catalogue to the Bronze Age collections.* Cardiff, National Museum of Wales.

Smith, G. 1993. *Coastal erosion survey Aberdaron Bay to Great Orme.* (Contractor: Gwynedd Archaeological Trust.) Unpublished report to Cadw.

Suddards, R,W. 1993. Listed buildings. *In: Archaeology resource management in the UK - an introduction,* ed. by J. Hunter & I. Ralston, 77-88. Stroud, Alan Sutton.

Summers, M. 1990. *A study of the variations in design and function between coastal riverine and estuarine fish weirs through ancient, medieval and modern times, with particular reference to the coastal fish weirs of Aberarth beach and the Isle of Rhe.* Undergraduate dissertation, University of Lampeter, Department of Archaeology.

Thomas, C. 1994. *And shall these mute stones speak?* University of Wales Press.

Toft, L. 1993. Roman quays and tide levels. *Britannia, 23:* 249-254.

Wainwright, G.J. 1963. A reinterpretation of the Mesolithic industries of Wales. *Proceedings of the Prehistoric Society, 29:* 99-132.

Webster, P. 1990. Pottery and trade in Roman Wales. *In: Conquest, co-existence and change: recent work in Roman Wales,* ed. by B. Burnham & J. Davies, 138-149. (Trivium, No.25.)

Welsh Office. 1991. *Planning policy guidance note 16: archaeology and planning.* Cardiff, Welsh Office.

Willan, T.S. 1967. *The English coasting trade 1600 - 1750.* Manchester, Manchester University Press.

B. Further reading

Archaeological Diving Unit. 1994. *Guide to the historic wreck sites designated under the Protection of Wrecks Act 1973.*

Davies, P.N., & McBride, P.W.J. 1973. The Mary Charles II yacht. *International Journal of Nautical Archaeology, 2,* 1: 59-74.

Jones, C. 1977. A relic of the slate trade on the Menai Strait. *Maritime Wales, 2:* 13-15.

Jones, C. 1978. The Pwll Fanog - a slate cargo in the Menai straits. *International Journal of Nautical Archaeology, 7,* 2: 152-159.

Ilsley, J.S. 1982. Admiral Lord Edward Russell and the building of St Paul's Cathedral. *Mariners Mirror, 68,* 3: 305-315.

Lynch, F. 1991. *Prehistoric Anglesey.* Anglesey Antiquarian Society. 2nd edition.

Redknap, M. 1992. Remarkable Viking find in a remote site. *Amguedda, 9.*

Roberts, O.T.P. 1979. Pwll Fanog wreck, Menai Strait, North Wales. *International Journal of Nautical Archaeology, 8,* 3: 249-54.

Thomas, R.J.C. 1994. *Survey of 19th and 20th century military buildings of Pembrokeshire.* Pembrokeshire Coast National Park.

C. Contact names and addresses

Type of information	Contact address and telephone no.
Historic wreck sites	The Secretary, The Advisory Committee on Historic Wreck Sites, Department of National Heritage, Room 306, 2-4 Cockspur Street, London, SW1Y 5DH, tel. 0171 211 6369 or 6367
Sub-tidal sites	Archaeological Diving Unit, Insitute of Maritime Studies, University of St Andrews, St Andrews, Fife, Scotland, KY16 9AJ, tel. 01334 62919 (contracted to the above)
Code of practice for seabed developers	Secretary, Joint Nautical Archaeology Policy Committee, National Monuments Record - Maritime Section, Kemble Drive, Swindon, SN2 2GZ, tel. 01793 414713
National Monuments, designated Historic Wrecks, Scheduled Monuments, Listed Buildings	Royal Commission on the Historic & Ancient Monuments of Wales, Crown Building, Plas Crug, Aberystwyth, Dyfed, SY23 1NL, tel. 01970 621200.
Statutory body responsible for archaeological conservation. Funding of rescue archaeology and survey	Inspector of Ancient Monuments, Cadw, Brunel House, 2 Fitzalan Road, Cardiff, CF2 1UY, tel. 01222 500200
Maintains sites and monuments records for Dyfed	Principal Archaeological Officer (Heritage Management), Dyfed Archaeological Trust Ltd, Shire Hall, Carmarthen Street, Llandeilo, Dyfed, SA19 6AF, tel. 01558 823121
As above for Glamorgan	Development Control Officer, Glamorgan-Gwent Archaeological Trust Ltd, Ferryside Warehouse, Bath Lane, Swansea, West Glamorgan, SA1 1RD, tel. 01792 655208
As above for Gwynedd	Principal Archaeological Officer (Curatorial), Gwynedd Archaeological Trust Ltd, Garth Road, Bangor, Gwynedd, LL57 2SE, tel. 01248 352535
Nautical archaeological survey	Department of History, University College of North Wales, College Road, Bangor, Gwynedd, LL5 2DG, tel. 01248 351151
As above	Department of Extra-Mural Studies, address as above
As above	Secretary, North Wales Marine Study Group, address as above c/o Department of Extra-Mural Studies
Nautical archaeology training	Training Officer, Nautical Archaeology Society, c/o 19 College Road, HM Naval Base, Portsmouth, PO1 3LJ, tel. 01705 818419

| Reporting point for recovered wreck | Receiver of Wreck, Coastguard Agency, Spring Place, 105 Commercial Road, Southampton, S015 1EG, tel. 01703 329474 |
| Advice on finds; reporting point for treasure in trove in Wales | National Museum of Wales, Department of Archaeology and Numismatics, Cathys Park, Cardiff, CF1 3NP, tel. 01222 397951 |

6.4.5 Acknowledgements

Particular thanks go to Valerie Fenwick for help in preparing this chapter. Thanks are also due to the staff of all the organisations mentioned in the text, who gave their time to provide information, and to Dr Ben Ferrari for his advice in developing the chapter.

Chapter 7 Protected coastal sites

7.1 Introduction

R.G. Keddie

7.1.1 Chapter structure

This chapter incorporates statutory and non-statutory site protection mechanisms operating at international, national and local level, including those administered by voluntary bodies and other organisations who own land. It covers only the various types of site protection mechanism currently found within this region, giving a brief description for each category and listing sites and their locations. For the purposes of this chapter, any site that is wholly or partly intertidal, and any terrestrial site at least partly within 1 km of the Mean High Water Mark, or any tidal channel as depicted on 1:50,000 Ordnance Survey maps, is included as 'coastal'. Where a site straddles the boundaries of two Coastal Directories Project regions and there is no easy way of calculating the percentage of the site lying in each, the site area has been halved, one half being included in each region. Data included in this section are correct as at October 1994, unless otherwise stated.

Statutory protected sites are those notified, designated or authorised under European Directives and/or implemented through British legislation (most notably the Wildlife and Countryside Act 1981) by a statutory body, thereby having recognised legal protection. 'Non-statutory sites' include a wide variety of kinds of site not directly protected by legislation but which are either identified by statutory bodies or owned, managed or both by non-statutory organisations for their nature conservation or aesthetic value. Note that the categories of conservation protection (e.g. National Nature Reserve, RSPB Reserve) are not mutually exclusive. In many localities several different types of protected site overlap, since they have been identified for different wildlife and landscape conservation purposes. Patterns of overlap are often complex, since site boundaries for different categories of site are not always coterminous.

Further explanation of the various site protection mechanisms can be found in Davidson *et al.* (1991). For England, Planning Policy Guidance Note (PPG) 9 - Nature Conservation (DOE 1994) also gives useful summaries of existing site protection mechanisms. It also includes copies of the Ramsar Convention, the Birds Directive and the Habitats Directive (including lists of important species and habitat types). However, at the time of writing, no comparable Welsh Office guidance has yet been issued.

The following types of protected site have not been included in this chapter:

- Archaeological designations and protected sites, covered in Chapter 6.
- Special Areas of Conservation (SACs), one of the tools to be used to implement the Habitats Directive. They are areas considered to be important for habitat and non-avian species interest in a European context. A list of possible SACs was announced by the Government on 31 March 1995. There are ten SACs proposed for their coastal/marine interest in Region 12, from a total of 71 in GB (see JNCC (1995) for more information). The protection measures for SACs are based around a series of six annexes: Annexes I & II require the designation of SACs for certain habitats and species; Annex IV prohibits the taking of certain species; Annex V requires the taking of certain species to be monitored; Annex VI prohibits some means of capture or killing of mammals and fish. In the UK the Directive will be implemented through the Habitats etc. Regulations 1994.

'Sites of Importance for Nature Conservation' (SINCs): a general term for the variously-named non-statutory sites identified by local authorities and wildlife trusts as having special local value for nature conservation but not currently managed for nature conservation; the most common are Sites of Nature Conservation Importance. For more information, see Collis & Tyldesley (1993).

Non-site based measures contained in conventions and directives aimed at broad species and habitat protection, such as the Bonn Convention, CITES, parts of the EC Birds Directive and parts of the EC Habitats Directive, are also not covered. For further information, see references in section 7.1.3A.

This chapter is divided into five sections. A regional summary of all categories of site is given in section 7.1.2. Section 7.2 covers those site-based protection measures falling under international conventions or European directives. Section 7.3 discusses sites identified under national statute, whereas section 7.4 covers sites without statutory protection but which are identified, owned or managed by statutory bodies; and finally, section 7.5 describes other types of sites (i.e. those identified, owned or managed by charities, trusts etc.). For each category of protected site, a list of coastal sites is given (clockwise around the coast), showing their type, area/length and location, with an accompanying map. Each section concludes with further information sources and contact points relevant to the region.

Table 7.1.1 Summary of site protection in Region 12

	Total number in region	Total number on West Coast	Number % of West Coast total in region	Total number on GB coast	% of GB coast total in region	Total area in region (ha)	Total area on West Coast (ha)	Area % of West coast area in region	Total area on GB coast (ha)	% of coastal area in region
Biosphere Reserves	1	6	16.7	8	12.5	2,097	21,142	9.9	27,243	7.7
Ramsar sites	3	19	15.8	47	6.4	9,418	71,424	13.2	238,075	4.0
Special Protection Areas	7	31	22.6	71	9.9	10,735	80,759	13.3	252,880	4.2
Environmentally Sensitive Areas	3	10	30.0	17	17.7	238,300	1,114,254	21.4	1,393,732	17.1
Geological Conservation Review	141	543	26.0	1,077	13.1	n/a[a]	n/a[a]	n/a[a]	n/a[a]	n/a[a]
National Nature Reserves	12	39	30.8	77	15.6	6,792	51,538	13.2	84,340	8.1
Sites of Special Scientific Interest	176	631	27.9	1,182	14.9	38,229	369,189	10.4	701,517	5.5
Marine Nature Reserves	1	2	50.0	2	50.0	1,500	2,890	51.9	2,890	51.9
Areas of Special Protection	2	9	22.2	23	8.7	n/a[b]	n/a[b]	n/a[b]	n/a[b]	n/a[b]
The Ministry of Defence	12	45	26.7	111	10.8	5,746	18,960	30.3	53,409	10.8
National Parks	2	4	50.0	6	33.3	272,600	571,100	47.7	745,000	36.6
Heritage Coasts	13	27.5**	47.3	45	28.9	472*	864*	54.6*	1,525*	30.9*
Areas of Outstanding Natural Beauty	3	9.5**	31.6	23	13.0	57,000	185,100	30.8	880,400	6.5
Local Nature Reserves	8	25	32.2	94	8.5	3,045	4,605	66.1	13,336	22.8
Country Parks	4	14	28.6	34	11.8	798	1,498	53.3	4,383	18.2
The National Trust & The National Trust for Scotland	88	257	34.3	446	19.7	6,840	45,258	15.1	62,648	10.9
Royal Society for the Protection of Birds	8	26	30.8	78	10.3	1,603	13,736	11.7	37,032	4.3
The Wildfowl & Wetlands Trust	1	3	33.3	6	16.7	82	1,113	7.4	1,585	5.2
The Wildlife Trusts	38	108	35.2	219	17.3	1,128	13,724	8.2	23,380	4.8
Woodland Trust	7	29	24.1	64	10.9	141	363	38.8	1,458	9.7

Source: JNCC Coastal Conservation Branch. Key: n/a[a] = not applicable; n/a[b] = not available; * = length in kilometres; ** only half of the area/length is included, as the sites straddle the region's boundaries (see section 7.1.1). Notes: Site types not currently found in the region: World Heritage (Natural) Sites, Biogenetic Reserves. In this table any site that is wholly or partly intertidal, and any terrestrial site at least partly within 1 km of the Mean High Water Mark, or any tidal channel as depicted on 1:50,000 Ordnance Survey maps, is included as 'coastal'.

7.1.2 Importance of the region

The region contains a large proportion of the Heritage Coasts, National Parks and Marine Nature Reserves of Britain: respectively 31%, 37% and 52% by area/length. In many other site categories the region contains between 10% and 20% of the number of sites, but a smaller proportion if calculated by area, implying that sites in the region are mostly smaller than the national average. Table 7.1.1 summarises site protection in the region, showing the numbers and areas of each type of site and comparing these with West Coast and British coastal totals.

7.1.3 Further sources of information

A. References cited

Collis, I., & Tyldesley, D. 1993. *Natural assets: non-statutory Sites of Importance for Nature Conservation.* Newbury, Local Government Nature Conservation Initiative.

Davidson, N.C., Laffoley, D.d'A., Doody, J.P., Way, L.S., Gordon, J., Key, R., Drake, M.C., Pienkowski, M.W., Mitchell, R., & Duff, K.L. 1991. *Nature conservation and estuaries in Great Britain.* Peterborough, Nature Conservancy Council.

Department of the Environment. 1994. Planning Policy Guidance Note 9 - Nature Conservation. HMSO.

Joint Nature Conservation Committee, 1995. *Council Directive on the Conservation of natural habitats and wild fauna and flora (92/43/EEC) – the Habitats Directive: a list of possible Special Areas of Conservation in the UK. List for consultation (31 March 1995).* Peterborough (unpublished report to the Department of the Environment).

B. Further reading

Countryside Council for Wales. 1995. European Habitats Directive. Bangor.

Countryside Council for Wales. 1995. The EC Habitats Directive: Marine Special Areas of Conservation. Bangor.

Doody, J.P., Johnston, C., & Smith, B. 1993. *The directory of the North Sea coastal margin.* Peterborough, JNCC.

Gubbay, S. 1988. *A Coastal directory for marine conservation.* Ross-on-Wye, Marine Conservation Society.

Hatton, C. 1992. *The Habitats Directive: time for action.* Godalming, WWF UK (World Wide Fund for Nature).

7.1.4 Acknowledgements

The author wishes to thank all the staff of JNCC Coastal Conservation Branch, and particularly Nick Davidson and John Barne, for help in compiling this chapter.

7.2 Sites designated under international conventions and directives

This section describes those types of site designated under international conventions to which the UK is a contracting party, and sites designated under UK statute to implement EC Directives concerning wildlife and landscape conservation. Sites protected by domestic legislation only are covered in section 7.3.

7.2.1 Biosphere Reserves

Biosphere Reserves are non-statutory protected areas representing significant examples of biomes - terrestrial and coastal environments, throughout the world - protected for conservation purposes. They have particular value as benchmarks or standards for the measurement of long-term changes in the biosphere as a whole. They were devised by UNESCO as project number 8 of their Man and the Biosphere (MAB) ecological programme, and were launched in 1970. Criteria and guidelines for selection of sites were produced by a UNESCO task force in 1974.

There is one Biosphere Reserve (2,097 ha) in Region 12, at the Dyfi Estuary (see Table 7.2.1 and Map 7.2.1). This compares with a total of eight coastal Biosphere Reserves (27,243 ha) in Great Britain, six of which (21,142 ha) are on the West Coast. Britain has thirteen Biosphere Reserves (44,258 ha), all of them designated in 1976 and 1977. All these sites are also National Nature Reserves (data provided by International Policy Branch, JNCC).

7.2.2 Wetlands of international importance (Ramsar sites)

Ramsar sites are statutory areas designated by the UK government on the advice of the conservation agencies under the 'Ramsar Convention' (the Convention on wetlands of international importance especially as waterfowl habitat). Contracting parties (of which the UK is one) are required to designate wetlands of international importance and to promote their conservation and 'wise use'. Ramsar sites are thus designated for their waterfowl populations, their important plant and animal assemblages, their wetland interest or a combination of these. So far, most Ramsar sites in Britain have been designated for their waterfowl, although two of the sites in this region (Crymlyn Bog and Cors Fochno & Dyfi) are designated partly for, respectively, wetland habitats and rare species. There are three coastal Ramsar sites (9,418 ha) in Region 12 (see Table 7.2.1 and Map 7.2.1). This compares with a total of 47 coastal Ramsar sites (238,075 ha) in Great Britain, of which nineteen (71,424 ha) are on the West Coast. There are currently 82 designated Ramsar sites (342,019 ha) in Great Britain, as at November 1994 (data provided by Vertebrate Ecology and Conservation Branch, JNCC). Sections 5.10, 5.11 and 5.12 describe the importance of these sites for the region's birds.

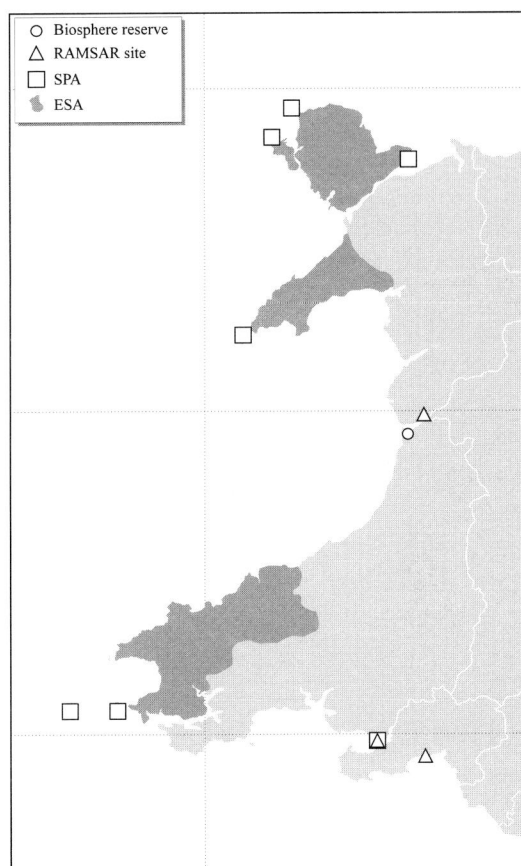

Map 7.2.1 Coastal Biosphere Reserves, Environmentally Sensitive Areas, Ramsar sites and Special Protection Areass. Source: JNCC, WOAD.

7.2.3 Special Protection Areas

The 1979 EC Directive on the Conservation of Wild Birds (the Birds Directive) requires member states to take conservation measures particularly for certain rare or vulnerable species and for regularly occurring migratory species of birds. In part this is achieved through the designation of statutory Special Protection Areas (SPAs) by the UK government on the advice of the statutory conservation agencies. This designation is implemented through the Wildlife and Countryside Act 1981; all SPAs must first be notified as SSSIs.

There are seven coastal SPAs (10,735 ha) in Region 12 (see Table 7.2.1 and Map 7.2.1). This compares with a total of 71 coastal SPAs (252,880 ha) in Great Britain, of which 31 (80,759 ha) are on the West Coast. There are currently 96 (292,878 ha) designated SPAs in Britain, as at November 1994 (data provided by Vertebrate Ecology and Conservation Branch, JNCC). Again, sections 5.10, 5.11 and 5.12 describe the importance of these sites for the region's birds.

153

Table 7.2.1 Internationally important sites

Site name	Grid ref.	Area (ha)	County	Date designated
Biosphere Reserve				
Dyfi Estuary	SN630910	2,097	Dyfed/Gwynedd/Powys	1977
Ramsar				
Crymlyn Bog (including Pant-y-Sais Fen)	SS695945	267	W. Glamorgan	1993
Burry Inlet	SS500970	6,654	Dyfed/W. Glamorgan	1992
Cors Fochno & Dyfi	SN6595	2,497	Dyfed/Gwynedd/Powys	1976
Total		*9,418*		
SPA				
Burry Inlet	SS500970	6,654	Dyfed/W. Glamorgan	1992
Skokholm & Skomer*	SM725095	422	Dyfed	1982
Grassholm	SM598093	9	Dyfed	1986
Glannau Aberdaron & Ynys Enlli	SH120220	513	Gwynedd	1992
Holy Island Coast	SH210820	351	Gwynedd	1992
Cemlyn Bay & Skerries	SH2694	87	Gwynedd	1992
Traeth Lafan (Conwy Bay)	SH630750	2,700	Gwynedd	1992
Total		*10,735*		
ESA				
Preseli	-	120,900	Dyfed	1994
Llyn Peninsula	-	45,400	Gwynedd	1988
Ynys Mon	-	72,000	Gwynedd	1993
Total		*238,300*		

Source: CCW, JNCC, WOAD. Key: * extended to include Skokholm and Middleholm. Note: In this table any site that is wholly or partly intertidal, and any terrestrial site at least partly within 1 km of the Mean High Water Mark, or any tidal channel as depicted on 1:50,000 Ordnance Survey maps, is included as 'coastal'.

7.2.4   Environmentally Sensitive Areas

European Community authorisation for Environmentally Sensitive Areas (ESAs) is derived from Article 19 of Council Regulation (EEC) No. 797/85 - National Aid in Environmentally Sensitive Areas. ESAs are statutory areas in which the Government seeks to encourage environmentally sensitive farming practices, prevent damage that might result from certain types of agricultural intensification, and restore traditional landscapes, for which member states are allowed to make payments to farmers.

There are three ESAs (238,300 ha) that include areas in Region 12 (see Table 7.2.1 and Map 7.2.1). This compares with a total of seventeen coastal ESA sites (1,393,732 ha) in Great Britain, of which ten (1,114,254 ha) are on the West Coast. 22 ESAs (3,101,200 ha) have been designated in England, seven in Wales and ten in Scotland (data from Parliamentary News (1994), English Nature (EN), Welsh Office Agriculture Department (WOAD), and Scottish Office Agriculture and Fisheries Department (SOAFD)).

7.2.5 Further sources of information

A. References cited

Parliamentary News. 15/03/94. Environmentally Sensitive Areas (in a report on the House of Lords debate on the proposed merger of English Nature and the Countryside Commission).

B. Further reading

Davidson, N.C., Laffoley, D.d'A., Doody, J.P., Way, L.S., Gordon, J., Key, R., Drake, M.C., Pienkowski, M.W., Mitchell, R., & Duff, K.L. 1991. *Nature conservation and estuaries in Great Britain.* Peterborough, Nature Conservancy Council.

Goodier, R., & Mayne, S. 1988. United Kingdom Biosphere Reserves: opportunities and limitations. *Ecos, 9:* 33-39.

IUCN. 1979. *The Biosphere Reserve and its relationship with other protected areas.* Morges, International Union for the Conservation of Nature and Natural Resources.

IUCN. 1982. *The world's greatest natural areas. An indicative inventory of natural sites of World Heritage quality.* IUCN Commission on National Parks and Protective Areas for World Heritage Committee.

Ministry of Agriculture, Fisheries and Food. 1989. *Environmentally Sensitive Areas.* London, HMSO.

Nature Conservancy Council. 1988. *Internationally important wetlands and Special Protection Areas for birds.* Peterborough, Nature Conservancy Council.

Stroud, D.A., Mudge, G.P., & Pienkowski, M.W. 1990. *Protecting internationally important bird sites. A review of the EEC Special Protection Area network in Great Britain.* Peterborough, Nature Conservancy Council.

Von Droste, B., & Gregg, W.P. 1985. Biosphere Reserves: demonstrating the value of conservation in sustaining society. *Parks, 10:* 2-5.

C. Contact names and addresses

Type of information	Contact address and telephone no.
Biosphere Reserves	*European International Affairs Officer, Science and Policy Development Directorate, CCW HQ, Bangor, tel: 01248 370444
Ramsar sites, SPAs, Special Areas of Conservation in Gwynedd	*Senior Officer, CCW North Wales Region, Bangor, tel: 01248 372333
Ramsar sites, SPAs, Special Areas of Conservation in Dyfed	*Senior Officer, CCW Dyfed/Mid Wales Region, Aberystwyth, tel: 01970 828551
Ramsar sites, SPAs, Special Areas of Conservation in W. Glamorgan	*Regional Officer, CCW South Wales Region, Cardiff, tel: 01222 485111
Ramsar sites, SPAs	*Conservation Officer, RSPB Wales Office, Newtown, tel: 01686 626678
Environmentally Sensitive Areas	*Agriculture Section, Planning, Land Use and Landscape Designation Branch, CCW HQ, Bangor, tel: 01248 370444
Environmentally Sensitive Areas	WOAD, Welsh Office Agriculture Department, Trawsgoed, Aberystwyth, Dyfed SY23 4HT, tel: 01974 261301
Special Areas of Conservation	European Wildlife Division, DoE, Room 9/03B, Tollgate House, Houlton Street, Bristol BS2 9DJ, tel: 0117 9878811 ext. 8341

* Starred contact addresses are given in full in the Appendix.

7.2.6 Acknowledgements

Thanks are due to Alan Law and International Policy Branch (JNCC), Siaron Hooper (EN), Site Safeguard Team (CCW) and Welsh Office Agriculture Department (WOAD).

7.3 Sites established under national statute

Included in this section are the eight types of site identification made under national legislation relating to wildlife, landscape and amenity value. Identifications are made by the statutory conservation agencies (in this region the Countryside Council for Wales), local authorities or the government acting on advice from these bodies.

7.3.1 National Nature Reserves

National Nature Reserves (NNRs) contain examples of some of the most important natural and semi-natural ecosystems in Great Britain. They are managed to conserve their habitats, providing special opportunities for scientific study of the habitats, communities and species represented within them (Marren 1994). They are statutorily declared by the country agencies (in this region by the Countryside Council for Wales) under section 19 of the National Parks and Access to the Countryside Act 1949, or section 35 of the Wildlife and Countryside Act 1981.

There are twelve National Nature Reserves (NNRs) (6,792 ha) in Region 12 (see Table 7.3.1 and Map 7.3.1). This compares with a total of 77 coastal NNRs (84,340 ha) in Great Britain, of which 39 (51,538 ha) are on the West Coast. As at March 1994, the total number of NNRs in Britain was 269 (187,210 ha) (data provided by CCW, EN, SNH and Biotopes Conservation Branch, JNCC).

Table 7.3.1 NNRs in Region 12

Site name	Grid ref.	Area (ha)	Date last declared
W.Glamorgan			
Oxwich	SS506870	289	1963
Gower Coast	SS383876	47	1958
Whiteford	SS450955	782	1964
Dyfed			
Stackpole	SR882996	199	1981
Skomer Island	SM725095	307	1959
Dyfed/Gwynedd			
Dyfi	SN640955	2,262	1969
	SN633910		
Gwynedd			
Morfa Dyffryn	SH550250	202	1962
Morfa Harlech	SH650350	884	1958
Coed Camlyn	SH661399	64	1959
Ynys Enlli - Bardsey	SH120220	180	1986
Newborough Warren & Ynys Llanddwyn	SH410630	1,507	1955
Coed Dolgarrog	SH769665	69	1986
Total		**6,792**	

Note: In this table any site that is wholly or partly intertidal, and any terrestrial site at least partly within 1 km of the Mean High Water Mark, or any tidal channel as depicted on 1:50,000 Ordnance Survey maps, is included as 'coastal'.

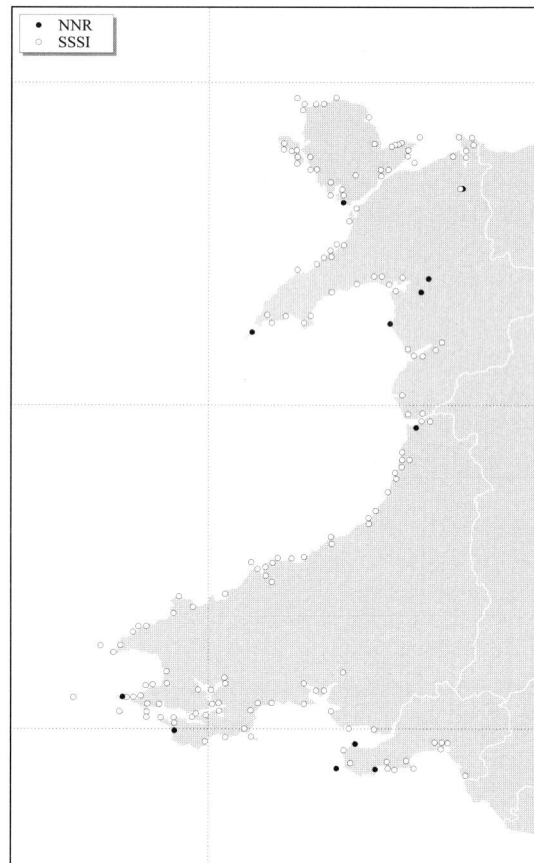

Map 7.3.1 Coastal National Nature Reserves and Sites of Special Scientific Interest. Source: CCW, JNCC Note: a single symbol may represent more than one site in close proximity.

7.3.2 Sites of Special Scientific Interest

Sites of Special Scientific Interest (SSSIs) are statutorily notified under the Wildlife and Countryside Act 1981. They are intended to form a national network of areas, representing in total the parts of Britain in which the natural features, especially those of greatest value for wildlife or earth science conservation, are most highly concentrated or of highest quality. Within the area of an SSSI the provisions of the Wildlife & Countryside Act 1981 and its 1985 amendments aim to ensure that actions damaging to the wildlife interest of the area are not carried out, unless appropriately consented.

There are 176 coastal Sites of Special Scientific Interest (SSSIs) (38,229 ha) in Region 12, as at September 1994 (see Table 7.3.2 and Map 7.3.1). This compares with a total of 1,182 coastal SSSIs (701,517 ha) in Great Britain, of which 631 (369,189 ha) are on the West Coast. The total number of SSSIs in Britain as at June 1994 was 6,055 (1,920,527 ha), or 7.98% of the total land mass, with 3,794 (871,066 ha) in England, 1,371 (846,869 ha) in Scotland and 890 (202,592 ha) in Wales (data provided by CCW, EN, SNH and Biotopes Conservation Branch, JNCC).

Of the 176 coastal SSSIs in the region, almost two-thirds include intertidal land to mean low water mark; only one

Table 7.3.2 SSSIs in Region 12

Site name	Grid ref.	Area (ha)	Date last notified	Site name	Grid ref.	Area (ha)	Date last notified
W.Glamorgan				**Dyfed (cont.)**			
Margam Moors	SS783846	108	1984	Slebech Reed-Bed & Carr	SN053142	16	1985
Earlswood Road Cutting and Ferryboat				Little Castle Head	SM855065	3	1990
Inn Quarries	SS729946	4	1987	Gann Estuary	SM812070	97	1986
Pant-y-Sais	SS716942	20	1983	Dale Point	SM818053	13	1986
Crymlyn Burrows	SS712927	244	1987	St. Ann's Head	SM805029	2	1986
Crymlyn Bog	SS695945	244	1983	Marloes Sands and			
Oystermouth Old Quarry	SS615883	1	1986	Gateholm	SM780076	75	1987
Blackpill	SS623878	467	1984	Skokholm	SM736050	106	1986
Bracelet Bay	SS629872	6	1986	Marloes Mere	SM775082	18	1985
Caswell Bay	SS579872	69	1983	Deer Park, Marloes	SM757090	35	1993
Pwll-Du Head &				Skomer Island &			
Bishopston Valley	SS574875	181	1983	Middleholm	SM725095	316	1986
Minchin Hole	SS555869	2	1986	Grassholm	SM598093	9	1985
Penard Valley	SS541883	32	1987	Musselwick Sands	SM787092	3	1986
Oxwich Bay	SS506870	427	1987	Millhaven Cliffs	SM817125	2	1986
Gower Coast: Rhossili -				Goultrop Roads Cliffs &			
Porteynon	SS383876	346	1986	Musselwick Bay	SM837129	22	1986
Rhossili Down	SS423895	334	1988	Broadhaven to Settling			
Broughton Bay	SS416930	10	1987	Nose Cliffs	SM861139	30	1985
Cwm Ivy Marsh,				Druidston & Nolton			
Dunes & Tor	SS442941	76	1982	Haven Cliffs	SM860168	100	1986
Whiteford Burrows -				Ramsey	SM702238	277	1987
Landimore Marsh	SS450955	842	1984	Bishops & Clerks Islands	SM667255	17	1985
Burry Inlet and Loughor				Trefeiddian Moor	SM733252	20	1984
Estuary	SS435985	5,898	1981	Saint David's Peninsula			
				Coast	SM766297	634	1954*
Dyfed				Abereiddi-Castell Coch			
Pyllau Machynys				Cliffs & Llanfyrn			
(Machynys Ponds)	SS512980	6	1993	Quarries	SM790308	33	1987
Pembrey Coast	SN316054	3,180	1984	Abereiddi-Trwyncastell			
Glan Pibwr Stream Section	SN417179	1	1985	Cliffs & the Blue			
Creigiau Llansteffan	SN351100	3	1990	Lagoon	SM795315	7	1987
Craig Ddu - Wharley				Portheiddy Moor	SM808314	10	1987
Point Cliffs	SN320102	43	1987	Aber Mawr	SM883346	4	1986
Whitehill Down	SN290135	46	1987	Strumble Head -			
Laugharne and				Llechdafad Cliffs	SM910410	204	1988
Pendine Burrows	SN290070	1,581	1983	Creigiau Abergwaun			
Marros - Pendine Coast	SN183073	188	1989	(Fishguard Cliffs)	SM958375	7	1987
Amroth to Wiseman's				Newport Cliffs	SN054407	50	1986
Bridge Cliffs	SN155066	48	1986	Cemaes Head	SN132500	17	1985
Saundersfoot Cliffs	SN139043	2	1954*	Poppit Beach & Cliffs	SN146489	6	1985
Cors Penally				Netpool Wood	SN170462	1	1988
(Penally Marsh)	SS118989	10	1984	Coedydd a Chorsydd			
St. Margaret's Island	SS122973	11	1985	Aber Teifi	SN183458	102	1981
Tenby Cliffs	SS046978	401	1954*	Pen yr Ergyd	SN165488	45	1981
Stackpole Quay-Trewent	SR989952-			Creigiau Traeth y Mwnt	SN194519	2	1989
Point	SS016975	63	1993	Creigiau Mwnt	SN200522	4	1981
Stackpole	SR980948	315	1993	R.A.E. Aberporth Cliffs	SN244526	67	1982
Castlemartin Corse	SR896998	30	1985	Creigiau Penbryn	SN286520	22	1979*
Castlemartin Cliffs &	SR885997 -			Cwm Byrlip a Chreigiau			
Dunes	SR977935	756	1993	Castell-bach	SN366578	30	1988
Broomhill Burrows	SM890004	201	1987	Craig yr Adar (Birds Rock)	SN376599	17	1979*
West Angle Bay	SM851034	20	1989	Coed Allt Craig Arth	SN495625	56	1983
Angle Bay	SM883025	157	1993	Creigiau Aberarth Morfa	SN491649	24	1987
Pembroke River and				Traeth Llanon	SN509673	27	1990
Pwllcrochan Flats	SM940025	360	1993	Creigiau Pen y graig	SN552734	22	1981
Cosheston Pill	SM990036	54	1993	Creigiau Cwm-Ceriw a			
Carew and Cresswell				Ffos-las (Morfa Bychan)	SN560763	32	1989
Rivers	SN025055	283	1993	Allt Wen A Traeth			
West Williamston Quarries	SN026060	19	1986	Tanybwlch	SN572788	37	1981
Lawrenny Wood	SN010069	36	1986	Gweunydd Pendinas	SN586807	8	1981
Daugleddau	SN003116	672	1993	Hen Afon Leri	SN609820	7	1983
Hook Wood	SM973114	13	1986	Craigyfulfran & Clarach	SN585834	25	1987
Minwear Wood	SN042138	14	1985	Creigiau Glan-y-mor	SN585843	3	1979*

157

Table 7.3.2 SSSIs in Region 12 (continued)

Site name	Grid ref.	Area (ha)	Date last notified	Site name	Grid ref.	Area (ha)	Date last notified
Dyfed (cont.)				Rhosneigr Reefs	SH313727	27	1987
Dyfi	SN640955	2,785	1985	Rhosneigr	SH317734	4	1991
Ynys-Eidiol-Ynys-Hir	SN676957	93	1982	Ynys Feurig	SH305737	25	1985
				Llynnau y Falin: Valley			
Gwynedd				Lakes	SH310770	101	1986
Coed y Gofer	SN640967	25	1987	Rhoscolyn Reedbed	SH275753	15	1989
Craig y Don	SN611960	1	1987	Rhoscolyn Coast	SH269746	54	1987
Broadwater	SH582027	263	1982	Pant yr Hyman	SH262764	13	1985
Arthog Bog	SH633145	64	1983	Porth Diana	SH254781	1	1984
Arthog Hall Woods	SH647144	12	1988	Glannau Ynys Gybi: Holy			
Cregennen	SH655145	11	1983	Island Coast	SH237796	351	1987
Coedydd Abergwynant	SH682165	88	1982	Tre Wilmot	SH230817	63	1986
Penmaenpool Reedbed	SH703188	93	1982	Beddmanarch-Cymyran	SH275790	911	1986
Barmouth Hillside	SH615164	66	1983	Clegir Mawr	SH299900	10	1986
Morfa Dyffryn	SH550250	506	1982	Carmel Head	SH293928	8	1985
Morfa Harlech	SH560350	1,536	1983	The Skerries	SH269949	17	1984
Glaslyn Marshes	SH582385	54	1985	Henborth	SH321931	11	1989
Morfa Bychan	SH542365	346	1988	Cemlyn Bay	SH331933	45	1985
Llyn Ystumllyn	SH526385	154	1988	Tre'r Gof	SH359936	10	1987
Criccieth Coastal Section	SH507381	5	1987	Llanbadrig-Dinas Gynfor	SH372941	28	1986
Glanllynnau	SH459373	42	1990	Traeth Lligwy	SH491884	26	1993
Penmaen	SH363348	1	1985	Coed y Gell and Morfa			
Cors Llyferin	SH311271	32	1986	Dulas	SH483880	19	1985
Porth Ceiriad	SH290252	233	1987	Trwyn Dwlban	SH512817	17	1985
Mynydd Penarfynnydd	SH225265	160	1986	Fedw Fawr	SH573808	68	1992
Ynysoedd y Gwylanod:				Bwrdd Arthur	SH586815	17	1985
Gwylan Islands	SH184245	5	1984	Tandinas Quarry[a]	SH585821	14	1994
Glannau Aberdaron	SH167263	358	1985	Fedw Fawr - Caeau Ty			
Ynys Enlli: Bardsey Island	SH120220	201	1984	Cydwys[a]	SH606819	31	1994
Porth Dinllaen	SH270410	32	1987	Puffin Island: Ynys Seiriol	SH650820	32	1984
Carreg y Llam	SH334437	14	1984	Lleiniog	SH619787	18	1988
Gallt y Bwlch	SH345440	18	1985	Baron Hill Park	SH605770	113	1985
Yr Eifl	SH365447	423	1986	Cadnant Dingle	SH558735	19	1985
Coed Elernion	SH378461	17	1985	Menai Straits Shore	SH538737	26	1957*
Gwydir Bay	SH391481	56	1989	Coedydd Afon Menai	SH536707	22	1986
Coed Cwmgwared	SH413481	30	1992	Traeth Lafan	SH630750	2,700	1984
Dinas Dinlle	SH437562	27	1986	Friars Road Shore	SH610774 -		
Foryd Bay	SH450600	283	1979*		SH630790	71	1949*
Newborough Warren-Ynys				Coed Dolgarrog	SH769665	69	1986
Llanddwyn	SH410630	1,552	1990	Sychnant Pass	SH747773	109	1983
Newborough Forest	SH400650	702	1986	Benarth Wood	SH788770	22	1982
Glan -traeth	SH416667	14	1989	Deganwy Quarries and			
Malltraeth Marsh				Grasslands	SH785791	7	1982
(Cors Ddyga)	SH440710	1,367	1992	Great Orme's Head	SH767833	321	1982
Penrhynoedd				Gloddaeth	SH803810	90	1983
Llangadwaladr	SH365655	180	1990	Little Orme's Head	SH814826	25	1960*
Tywyn Aberffraw	SH365690	364	1985	**Total**		**38,229**	
Llyn Maelog	SH 326729	36	1991				

Source: data from CCW, JNCC. Key: [a]= 1995 data. * Sites notified before the 1981 Wildlife and Countryside Act and not yet renotified are not afforded protection under this Act: these sites may later be renotified. Note: In this table any site that is wholly or partly intertidal, and any terrestrial site at least partly within 1 km of the Mean High Water Mark, or any tidal channel as depicted on 1:50,000 Ordnance Survey maps, is included as 'coastal'.

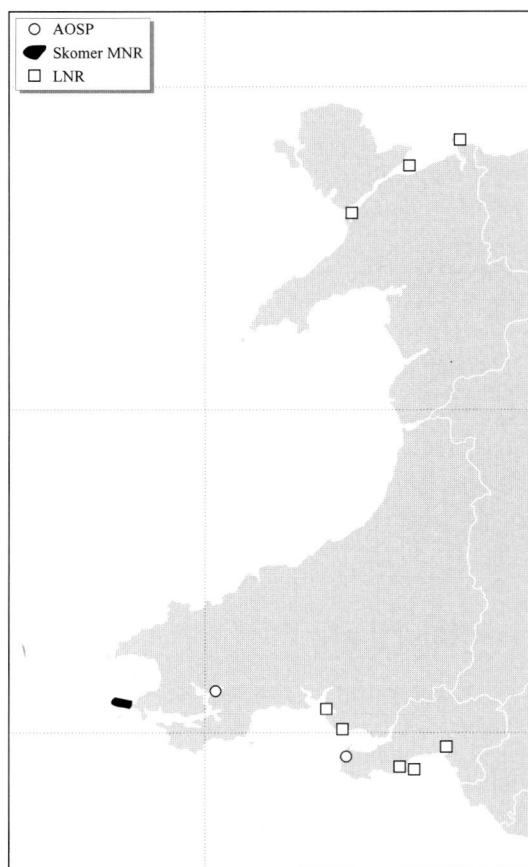

Map 7.3.2 Coastal Local Nature Reserves, Marine Nature Reserves and Areas of Special Protection. Source: CCW, DoE.

Map 7.3.3 Landscape designations. Source: Countryside Commission, CCW.

quarter are purely terrestrial. More than three-quarters were selected at least partly for their biological interest and more than one third at least partly for their geological or geomorphological interest. Of the total, nearly a quarter have both biological and earth science interest. Examples of a very wide range of habitats and species occur within the SSSIs in this region, the most frequently occurring habitats being grassland, woodland, maritime heath, cliffs, saltmarsh

and tidal flats, all of which occur in more than 15% of sites. SSSIs in the region include many sites of interest for their lower and higher plants, terrestrial invertebrates, breeding seabirds, other birds and migrant and wintering waterfowl. In addition, at least 15% of sites have important marine biological interest.

7.3.3 Local Nature Reserves

Local Nature Reserves (LNRs) are statutorily designated by local authorities, under Section 21 of the National Parks and Access to the Countryside Act 1949, for the same purposes as NNRs, but because of the local rather than the national interest of the site and its wildlife. Local authorities have powers to issues bylaws to protect LNRs. There are eight coastal LNRs (3,045 ha) in Region 12, as at March 1994 (see Table 7.3.3 and Map 7.3.2). This compares with a total of 94 coastal LNRs (13,336 ha) in Great Britain, of which 25 (4,605 ha) are on the West Coast. There are a total of 396 LNRs (21,513 ha) in Britain (data provided by EN, CCW and SNH).

Table 7.3.3 Local Nature Reserves

Site name	Grid ref.	Area (ha)	Date designated
W. Glamorgan			
Pant-y-Sais Fen	SS716942	20*	1987
Mumbles Hill	SS625875	21	1989
Bishops Wood	SS592880	14	1976
Dyfed			
Swansea Canal	SS438996	4	1987
Pembrey Burrows & Saltings	SN361054	208	1993
Gwynedd			
Y Foryd (Foryd Bay)	SH450600	283	1993
Traeth Lafan	SH630750	2,200	1979
Great Orme's Head	SH767833	195	1981
Total		*3,045*	

Source: CC, CCW, 1994 data (*1995 data). Note: In this table any site that is wholly or partly intertidal, and any terrestrial site at least partly within 1 km of the Mean High Water Mark, or any tidal channel as depicted on 1:50,000 Ordnance Survey maps, is included as 'coastal'.

7.3.4 Marine Nature Reserves

Marine Nature Reserves (MNRs) are created by statute (under the Wildlife and Countryside Act 1981) to conserve marine flora and fauna and geological or physiographical features of special interest, while providing opportunities for study of the systems involved. MNRs may be established within 3 nautical miles of the coast or, by an Order in Council, to the limits of UK territorial waters; they include both the sea and the sea bed. MNRs can be protected by bye-laws. There is one Marine Nature Reserve in Region 12: Skomer (1,500 ha), off south-west Wales (Countryside Council for Wales 1992) (see Table 7.3.4 and Map 7.3.2), and only one other statutory designated Marine Nature Reserve in Britain - Lundy Island.

Table 7.3.4 Skomer Marine Nature Reserve (MNR) and Areas of Special Protection (AoSPs)

Site name	Grid ref.	Area (ha)	Date designated
MNR			
Skomer, Dyfed	SM725095	1,500	1990
AoSP			
Burry Estuary (No. 1795),			
W. Glam.	SS449947	na[a]	1969
Cleddau (No. 72), Dyfed	SN005115	na[a]	1970

Source: CCW, DOE. Key: na[a] = not available. Note: In this table any site that is wholly or partly intertidal, and any terrestrial site at least partly within 1 km of the Mean High Water Mark, or any tidal channel as depicted on 1:50,000 Ordnance Survey maps, is included as 'coastal'.

7.3.5 Areas of Special Protection

'Area of Special Protection' (AoSP) is a statutory protection mechanism replacing Bird Sanctuary Orders under the 1954 to 1967 Protection of Birds Acts, which were repealed and amended under the Wildlife and Countryside Act 1981. It aims to prevent the disturbance and destruction of the birds for which the area is identified, by making it unlawful to damage or destroy either the birds or their nests and in some cases by prohibiting or restricting access to the site. There are two AoSPs in Region 12 (Table 7.3.4 and Map 7.3.2), compared with a total of 23 sites identified as coastal in Great Britain, nine of them located on the West Coast. So almost two-thirds of great Britain's 38 AoSPs are coastal (data supplied by DoE, European Wildlife Division).

7.3.6 Areas of Outstanding Natural Beauty

The primary purpose of the Area of Outstanding Natural Beauty (AONB) designation is to conserve natural beauty, but account is taken of the need also to safeguard agriculture, forestry and other rural industries, and of the economic and social needs of local communities (Countryside Commission 1994). AONBs are statutorily designated, in England by the CC and since 1991 in Wales by CCW, under the National Parks and Access to the Countryside Act 1949. There are three coastal Areas of Outstanding Natural Beauty (AONBs) (57,000 ha) in Region

12 (Table 7.3.5 and Map 7.3.3). This compares with a total of 23 (880,400 ha) that include coastal areas in Great Britain, of which nine whole sites and part of one other, together covering 185,100 ha, are on the West Coast. In 1993 the total area covered by AONBs (2,104,200 ha) represented nearly 14% of the countryside of England and Wales (Countryside Commission 1994).

Table 7.3.5 Areas of Outstanding Natural Beauty (AONB)

Site name	Area (ha)	Date designated
Gower, W.Glamorgan	18,800	1956
Lleyn, Gwynedd	16,100	1957
Anglesey, Gwynedd	22,100	1967
Total	*57,000*	

Source: CC,CCW. Note: In this table any site that is wholly or partly intertidal, and any terrestrial site at least partly within 1 km of the Mean High Water Mark, or any tidal channel as depicted on 1:50,000 Ordnance Survey maps, is included as 'coastal'.

7.3.7 National Parks

The purpose of National Parks is to preserve and enhance the most beautiful, dramatic and spectacular expanses of countryside in England and Wales (Countryside Commission 1993), while promoting public enjoyment of it, and having regard for the social and economic well-being of those living within it. National Parks in England and Wales were statutorily designated by the National Parks Commission and confirmed by the Government between 1951 and 1957, and one area with similar status, The Broads, was established in 1989. The Countryside Commission (England) and CCW (Wales) advise government on National Parks, each of which is administered by a Park Authority. There are two National Parks (272,600 ha) in Region 12 (Table 7.3.6 and Map 7.3.3). This compares with a total of six identified National Parks (745,000 ha) that include coastal areas in Great Britain, of which four sites (571,100 ha) are on the West Coast.

Table 7.3.6 National Parks

Site name	Area (ha)	Date designated
Pembrokeshire Coast, Dyfed	58,400	1952
Snowdonia, Gwynedd	214,200	1951
Total	*272,600*	

Source: CC,CCW. Note: In this table any site that is wholly or partly intertidal, and any terrestrial site at least partly within 1 km of the Mean High Water Mark, or any tidal channel as depicted on 1:50,000 Ordnance Survey maps, is included as 'coastal'.

7.3.8 Country Parks

Country Parks are primarily intended for recreation and leisure opportunities close to populations and do not necessarily have any nature conservation interest. Nevertheless, many are in areas of semi-natural habitat and so form a valuable network of locations at which informal recreation and the natural environment co-exist. They are statutorily declared and managed by local authorities under section 7 of the Countryside Act 1968. There are four coastal

Country Parks (798 ha) in Region 12 (see Table 7.3.7 and Map 7.3.3). This compares with a total of 33 coastal Country Parks (4,383 ha) in Great Britain, of which fourteen (1,498 ha) are on the West Coast. There are total of 281 Country Parks in Britain, with a total area of approximately 35,150 ha (data provided by the CC, CCW and from Countryside Commission for Scotland (1985)).

Table 7.3.7 Country Parks

Site name	Grid ref.	Area (ha)	Date opened
Clyne Valley, W. Glam.	SS617908	280	1980
Pembrey, Dyfed	SN396003	211	1980
Breakwater Quarry, Gwynedd	SH227832	16	1990
Great Orme, Gwynedd	SH767834	291	1977
Total		798	

Source: CC, CCW, 1993 data. Note: In this table any site that is wholly or partly intertidal, and any terrestrial site at least partly within 1 km of the Mean High Water Mark, or any tidal channel as depicted on 1:50,000 Ordnance Survey maps, is included as 'coastal'.

7.3.9 Further sources of information

A. *References cited*

Countryside Commission. 1993. *The National Park Authority - purposes, powers and administration: a guide for members of National Park Authorities*. Cheltenham, Countryside Commission and Countryside Council for Wales.

Countryside Commission. 1994. *AONBs in England and Wales (CCP276)*. Rev. ed. Cheltenham, Countryside Commission.

Countryside Commission for Scotland. 1985. *Scotland's Country Park register*. Countryside Commission for Scotland.

Countryside Council for Wales. 1992. *Skomer Marine Nature Reserve - an introduction with map*. Bangor, Countryside Council for Wales.

Marren, P.R. 1994. *England's National Nature Reserves*. Newton Abbot, David and Charles.

B. *Further information*

Further details of SSSIs may be found on the *Coastal & Marine UKDMAP datasets module* (Barne *et al.* 1994), disseminated by JNCC Coastal Conservation Branch, Peterborough.

Barne, J., Davidson, N.C., Hill, T.O., & Jones, M. 1994. *Coastal and Marine UKDMAP datasets: a user manual*. Peterborough, Joint Nature Conservation Committee.

Countryside Commission. 1992. *Directory of Areas of Outstanding Natural Beauty*. Cheltenham, Countryside Commission.

Countryside Commission. 1994. *Areas of Outstanding Natural Beauty - a guide for members of Joint Advisory Committees (CCP246)*. Cheltenham, Countryside Commission.

Countryside Commission. 1994. *Countryside planning file*. Cheltenham, Countryside Commission.

Countryside Commission. 1994. *United Kingdom protected environment map*. Southampton, Ordnance Survey.

Countryside Commission for Scotland. 1978. *Scotland's scenic heritage*. Perth, Countryside Commission for Scotland.

Davidson, N.C., Laffoley, D.d'A., Doody, J.P., Way, L.S., Gordon, J., Key, R., Drake, M.C., Pienkowski, M.W., Mitchell, R., & Duff, K.L. 1991. *Nature conservation and estuaries in Great Britain*. Peterborough, Nature Conservancy Council.

Mullard, J. 1994. *Coastal management in a designated area-the Gower Area of Outstanding Natural Beauty and Heritage Coast*. Centre for Coastal Zone Management, University of Portsmouth. (Paper from a conference on management techniques in the coastal zone, October 1994.)

Nature Conservancy Council. 1984. *Nature conservation in Great Britain*. Peterborough, Nature Conservancy Council.

Nature Conservancy Council. 1989. *Guidelines for selection of biological SSSIs*. Peterborough, Nature Conservancy Council.

Nature Conservancy Council. 1989. *Local Nature Reserves*. Peterborough, Nature Conservancy Council (Library information sheet No. 6).

C. *Contact names and addresses*

Type of information	Contact address and telephone no.
NNRs, SSSIs, National Parks, AONBs, LNRs in Gwynedd, Marine Nature Reserves under consideration for Ynys Enlli and Menai Strait	*Senior Officer, CCW North Wales Region, Bangor, tel. 01248 372333
NNRs, SSSIs, Marine Nature Reserve, National Parks, LNRs in Dyfed	*Senior Officer, CCW Dyfed/Mid Wales Region, Aberystwyth, tel: 01970 828551
NNRs, SSSIs, AoSPs, AONBs, LNRs in W. Glamorgan	*Senior Officer, CCW South Wales Region, Cardiff, tel. 01222 485111
Skomer Marine Nature Reserve	*Marine Conservation Officer, CCW Skomer, Haverfordwest, tel. 01646 636736
Local authority involvement in coastal site management	*Arfordir Officer, CCW Aberystwyth, tel. 01970 828551
Areas of Special Protection	European Wildlife Division, DoE, Room 9/03B, Tollgate House, Houlton Street, Bristol BS2 9DJ, tel. 0117 9878811
Country Parks	*Recreation and Tourism Policy Officer, CCW HQ, Bangor, tel. 0248 370444
National Parks	Council for National Parks, Boughrood House, 97 The Struet, Brecon, Powys LD3 7LS, tel. 01874 622446

* Starred contact addresses are given in full in the Appendix

7.3.10 Acknowledgements

Thanks are due to, in particular, Ray Woolmore (Countryside Commission), Carol Thornley and Site Safeguards Team (CCW), Roger Bolt and Earth Sciences Branch (JNCC), Sylvia White and Phillip Biss (EN), Kathy Duncan and Natasha O'Connel (SNH), Neale Oliver (DoE), Ade Adeyoe, Brian Choun (MAFF), and Neil Sinclair (SOAFD).

7.4 Sites identified by statutory agencies

This section covers sites which, although not protected by statute, have been identified by statutory agencies as being of nature conservation or landscape importance.

7.4.1 Nature Conservation Review sites

There are 953 confirmed Nature Conservation Review (NCR) sites (approximately 1,500,000 ha) in Britain. NCR sites are non-statutory sites identified by statutory conservation bodies. As defined by Ratcliffe (1977), whose definition differs from that adopted in this chapter (see section 7.1.1), there are 149 'coastal' NCR sites (approximately 360,000 ha) in Region 12 (data provided by Biotopes Conservation Branch, JNCC). Coastal NCR sites include sites supporting nationally and internationally important bird populations, as well as sites holding the best representative examples of vegetative habitats. The NCR series helps to identify suitable candidates for biological NNR designation.

7.4.2 Geological Conservation Review sites

Geological Conservation Review (GCR) sites are non-statutory sites identified by the statutory conservation agencies; they are sites of national and international earth science importance. The GCR selection process describes and assesses key sites in the context of an aspect of the geology, palaeontology, mineralogy or geomorphology; GCR sites are the earth science equivalent of NCRs. GCR site descriptions are being published as a series of volumes, each covering sites selected for one aspect of earth science interest. Several volumes describe some Welsh sites, including Campbell & Bowen (1989), which deals with the Quarternary in Wales (see also Chapter 2). Almost 3,000 individual GCR Single Interest Localities (SIL) have been identified, of which 1,077 are coastal; 543 of them are on the West Coast (data provided by the JNCC Earth Sciences Branch). The 141 GCR SILs within Region 12 are listed in Table 7.4.1, with an indication of whether they were selected for their geological or their coastal geomorphological interest (see also Map 7.4.1).

7.4.3 Heritage Coasts

Heritage Coasts are areas selected for having a coastline of exceptionally fine scenic quality, exceeding one mile in length, substantially undeveloped and containing features of special significance and interest. This non-statutory protection is agreed between local authorities and (in Wales) CCW, as a aid to local authorities in planning and managing their coastlines. There are thirteen Heritage Coasts (472 km)

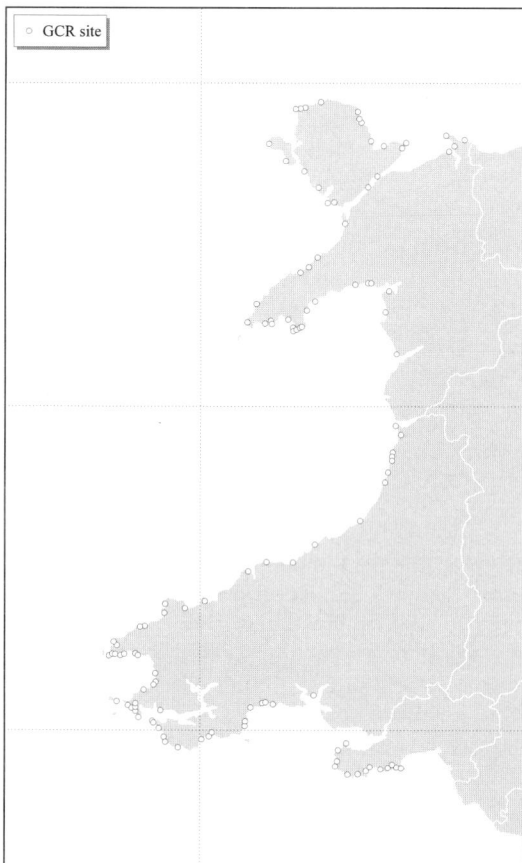

Map 7.4.1 Coastal Geological Conservation Review sites. Source: CCW, JNCC Note: a single symbol may represent more than one site in close proximity.

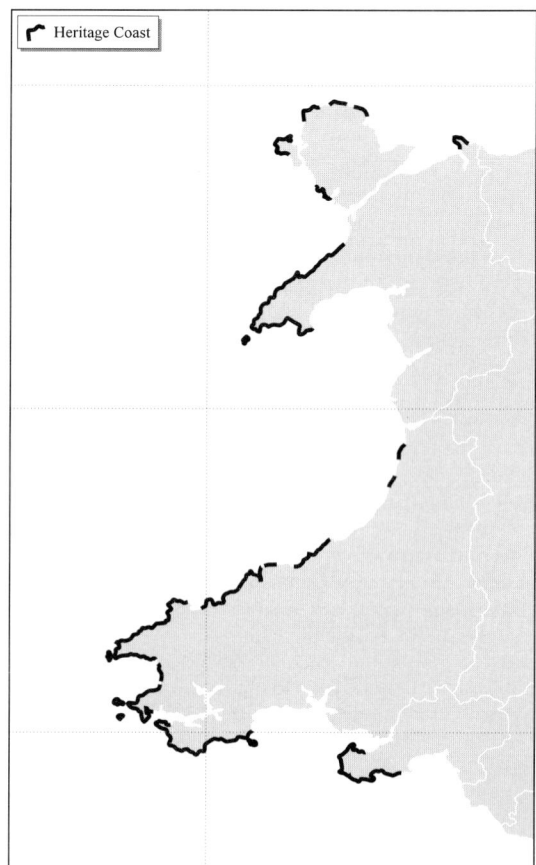

Map 7.4.2 Heritage Coasts. Source: Countryside Commission.

Table 7.4.1 GCR Single Interest Localities (SILs)

Site name	Site name
	Castell Coch-Trwyncastell
West Glamorgan	Llanvirn-Abereiddy
Oystermouth Old Quarry	Abermawr
Bracelet Bay (2)	Pen Caer
Rotherslade	Abergwaun
Caswell Bay (2)	Dinas and Esgyrn Bottom
Pwll-Du*	Poppit
Pwll Du Head	Mwnt
Hunts Bay	Traeth Penbryn
Bacon Hole (2)	Cwmtudu
Bosco's Den	Aberarth-Morfa
Minchin Hole (2)	Morfa Bychan
Three Cliffs Bay	Allt - Wen
Oxwich Bay*	Craig y Fulfran
Eastern and Western Slade	Clarach
Horton	North Clarach
Longhole Cave	Ynyslas and Borth
Long Hole	Ynyslas*
Worms Head	**Gwynedd**
Rhosili Bay	Barmouth Hillside
Broughton Bay	Morfa Dyffryn*
West Glamorgan/Dyfed	Morfa Harlech*
Burry Inlet* (Landimore, Llanrhidian and Berthlwyd)	Rhiw-for-fawr
Dyfed	Morannedd
Craig y Fulfran	Glanllynnau
Llanstephan	Llanbedrog
Carmarthen Bay*	Pen Benar
Marros	Porth Ceiriad (2)
Wiseman's Bridge - Amroth Coast	Trwyn-llech-y-doll
Tenby - Saundersfoot Coast	Trwyn Carreg-y-tir
Freshwater East	Porth Neigwl* (2)
Tenby Beach	Mynydd Penarfynydd
Freshwater East (Dyfed/S. Pembrokeshire)	Benallt
Tenby Cliffs (2)	Nant y Gadwyn
Freshwater East	Wig Bach
Stackpole Quarry	Braich y Pwll to Parwyd
South Pembroke Cliffs*	Porth Oer
Freshwater West (South)	Penrhyn Nefyn foreshore section
Blucks Pool - Bullslaughter Bay	Penrhyn Bodeilas
Freshwater West (North)	Trywyn-y-Gorlech to Yr-eifl Quarries
West Angle Bay	Dinas Dinlle
West Angle Bay (North)	Llanon
Little Castle Head	Cadnant Cutting
St Ann's Head	Deganwy Quarries
Marloes (2)	Bwlch Mine
Albion Sands and Gateholm Island	Great Orme
Marloes Sands to Albion Sands	Little Orme
Skomer Island	Newborough Warren*
Deer Park	Llanddwyn Island
Musselwick Sands	Tywyn Aberffraw
Mill Haven	Rhosneigr
Musselwick Bay	Rhoscolyn
Broadhaven to Settling Nose	South Stack
Druidston	Carmel Head (2)
Druidston Haven	Hen Borth
Nolton Haven Coast	Llanbadrig area
Solfach*	Ogof Gynfor-Hells Mouth
Solva Harbour	Ogof Gynfor
Dwrhyd Pit	Rhosmynach-Fawr
Porth y Rhaw	Porth y Mor
St Noris-Caerfai Bay	Lligwy Bay
Trywyn Cynddeiriog	Lligwy Bay
Porth Clais	Red Wharf Bay
Marros	Trwyn Dwlban
Aber Mawr-Porth Lleuog	Tandinas Quarry
Ogoffhen	Flagstaff Quarry
St David's Coast (Preseli)	Lleiniog
St David's Head	Marquis of Anglesey's Column
White Sands Bay	

Source: CCW, JNCC. Key: * Sites selected wholly or partly for their coastal geomorphological interest (all other sites geological). (2) = two SILs at this location. Note: In this table any site that is wholly or partly intertidal, and any terrestrial site at least partly within 1 km of the Mean High Water Mark, or any tidal channel as depicted on 1:50,000 Ordnance Survey maps, is included as 'coastal'.

in Region 12 (see Table 7.4.2 and Map 7.4.2). This compares with a total of 45 Heritage Coasts (1,525 km) on the English and Welsh coasts, as at May 1993. The Heritage Coast coastline in this region is predominantly cliffed or rocky, with sandy bays. In Wales 37% by length of the Heritage Coasts is protected by the National Trust (Heritage Coast Forum 1993).

Table 7.4.2 Heritage Coasts			
Site name	*Grid ref.*	*Length (km)*	*Date designated*
W. Glamorgan			
Gower Coast	SS520954-SS593876	59	1973
Dyfed			
South Pembrokeshire	SS125983-SM871029	62	1974
Marloes and Dale	SM815055-SM852128	46	1974
St. Bride's Bay	SM860143-SM854204	7	1974
St. David's Peninsula	SM845225-SM955394	83	1974
Dinas Head	SM961375-SN045398	15	1974
St. Dogmael's and Molygrove	SN054407-SN160485	19	1974
Ceredigion Coast	SN159501-SN218524	34	1982
	SN278517-SN386605		
	SN532702-SN556746		
	SN586842-SN602886		
Gwynedd			
Lleyn (Lyn)	SH424514-SH324266	90	1974
Aberffraw Bay	SH378654-SH339674	8	1973
Holyhead Montain	SH243796-SH224837	12	1973
North Anglesey	SH300892-SH491911	30	1973
Great Orme*	SH768823-SH783832	7	1976
Total		**472**	

Sources: CC, CCW. All Heritage Coasts are laterally defined (boundary defines extent of coast along shore) except for that marked *, which is completely defined (i.e. also has a defined landward boundary).

7.4.4 Tir Cymen

The Countryside Council for Wales has set up a non-statutory pilot scheme, Tir Cymen, which expands upon the concept of Environmentally Sensitive Areas (ESAs). It requires farmers to follow a simple code of environmental good practice (the Tir Cymen code) over the whole farm for a 10 year period, in return for financial incentives. It encourages appropriate environmental management for various habitat types, including one defined as 'coastal land'. It emphasises enjoyment of the countryside coupled with positive environmental management, including the use of traditional methods, a reduction of pollution and a move to organic fertilisers. Two of the three pilot regions, Meirionnydd and Abertawe Swansea, contain areas within Region 12.

7.4.5 Further sources of information

A. References cited

Campbell, S., & Bowen, D.Q. 1989. *Quaternary of Wales.* Peterborough, Nature Conservancy Council.
Heritage Coast Forum. 1993. *Heritage Coasts in England and Wales; a gazetteer.* Manchester, Heritage Coast Forum.
Mullard, J. 1994. *Coastal management in a designated area-the Gower Area of Outstanding Natural Beauty and Heritage Coast.* Centre for Coastal Zone Management, University of Portsmouth. (Paper from a conference on management techniques in the coastal zone, October 1994.)
Ratcliffe, D.A, *ed.* 1977. *A nature conservation review.* Cambridge, Cambridge University Press.

B. Further reading

Countryside Commission. 1970. *The coastal heritage. A conservation policy for coasts of high quality scenery.* London, HMSO.
Countryside Commission. 1992. *Heritage Coasts in England, policies and priorities 1992.* Cheltenham, Countryside Commission.
Countryside Council for Wales. 1992. *Tir Cymen - a farmland stewardship scheme.* Bangor, Countryside Council for Wales.
Davidson, N.C., Laffoley, D.d'A., Doody, J.P., Way, L.S., Gordon, J., Key, R., Drake, M.C., Pienkowski, M.W., Mitchell, R., & Duff, K.L. 1991. *Nature conservation and estuaries in Great Britain.* Peterborough, Nature Conservancy Council.

C. Contact names and addresses

Type of information	*Contact address and telephone no.*
NCRs, GCRs in Gwynedd	*Senior Officer, CCW North Wales Region, Bangor, tel: 01248 372333
NCRs, GCRs in Dyfed	*Senior Officer, CCW Dyfed/Mid Wales Region, Aberystwyth, tel: 01970 828551
NCRs, GCRs in W. Glamorgan	*Regional Officer, CCW South Wales Region, Cardiff, tel: 01222 485111
Tir Cymen	*Tir Cymen Officer, Headquarters, CCW Bangor, tel: 01248 370734

*Starred contact addresses are given in full in the Appendix

7.4.6 Acknowledgements

Thanks are due to, in particular, Ray Woolmore (Countryside Commission), Carol Thornley and Site Safeguards Team (CCW), Roger Bolt and Earth Sciences Branch (JNCC), Sylvia White and Phillip Biss (EN), Kathy Duncan and Natasha O'Connel (SNH) and David Masters (Heritage Coast Forum).

7.5 Other types of protected site

7.5.1 The National Trust

The National Trust (NT) is an independent charity that is currently the largest private landowner in Britain. The National Trust owns about 230,000 ha of land in England, Wales and Northern Ireland, and over 200 buildings of outstanding importance. It has also accepted or bought covenants, which protect against development, for a further 31,600 ha of land and buildings. Many of the tenanted properties have individual intrinsic value; when viewed cumulatively, they protect large areas of unique landscape and countryside. The National Trust has statutory powers to protect its properties, under an Act of Parliament (1907) which declares its holdings of land and buildings inalienable; these properties cannot be sold or mortgaged. In addition, National Trust properties can be protected by bye-laws. In 1985 the National Trust relaunched its 1965 campaign 'Enterprise Neptune' to raise funds for the purchase of coastal areas. A total of 850 km of coast are now protected by the National Trust (National Trust 1993). The National Trust is currently in the process of preparing a coastal strategy for Wales.

There are 88 National Trust sites (6,840 ha) in Region 12 (see Table 7.5.1 and Map 7.5.1). This compares with a total in Britain of 446 coastal sites (62,648 ha) under the protection of the National Trust or National Trust for Scotland (NTS), of which 257 sites (45,258 ha) are on the West Coast. The National Trust (England and Wales) has 426 coastal sites (37,478 ha) (data extracted from National Trust (1992)); the National Trust for Scotland has nineteen coastal sites (25,170 ha) (data extracted from National Trust for Scotland (1993)).

7.5.2 The Royal Society for the Protection of Birds

The Royal Society for the Protection of Birds (RSPB) has substantial non-statutory reserve holdings and currently manages over 130 reserves (over 84,000 ha) in Britain (RSPB 1993). Wherever possible, reserves are purchased, so that the level of safeguard for the wildlife and its habitats is high. Where reserves are leased, the RSPB aims to acquire long leases (longer than 21 years) with appropriate management rights. There are eight RSPB reserves (1,603 ha) in Region 12 (see Table 7.5.2 and Map 7.5.2). This compares with a total of 78 coastal RSPB reserves (37,032 ha) in Great Britain, of which 26 (13,736 ha) are on the West Coast (data extracted from RSPB (1993) and RSPB (*in litt.*)). Reserves in the region include several islands and cliffed coasts with major seabird colonies, including large populations of breeding choughs and peregrine falcons; estuarine habitats; coastal fringing woodland, and coastal freshwater wetlands.

Map 7.5.1 Coastal National Trust sites. Source: National Trust.
Note: a single symbol may represent more than one site in close proximity.

Table 7.5.2 RSPB reserves

Site name	Grid ref.	Area (ha)	Date acquired
Dyfed			
Grassholm	SM599093	9	1948
Ramsey Island	SM700237	253	1992
Ynys-hir	SN686956	424	1985
Gwynedd			
Mawddach Valley	SH660175	521	1983
Ynys Feirig island	SH304735	2	1975
Valley Lakes	SH310775	61	1983
South Stack Cliffs	SH205823	316	1977
The Skerries	SH269949	17	1983
Total		*1,603*	

Source: RSPB (1993, 1994 and *in litt.*). Note: In this table any site that is wholly or partly intertidal, and any terrestrial site at least partly within 1 km of the Mean High Water Mark, or any tidal channel as depicted on 1:50,000 Ordnance Survey maps, is included as 'coastal'.

Table 7.5.1 National Trust sites

Site name	Grid ref.	Area (ha)	Date acquired	Description
W.Glamorgan				
Bishopston Valley	SS575894	62	1954	coastal wooded valley
Notthill	SS535885	2	1955	coastal hill
Pennard Cliff	SS534875	100	1954-63	cliff
Nicholaston Burrows	SS530877	113	1967	cliffs, beach and sand burrows
Penmaen Common	SS527887	15	1967	common land
Port Eynon Point	SS468845	18	1964	headland
Paviland Cliff	SS442856	32	1939	cliff
Pitton Cliff	SS427865	16	1939	cliff
Thurba Head	SS421869	22	1933	cliffland
Worms Head, Rhossili Beach & Mewslade	SS383878	406	1967	headland, cliffs, island, foreshore and beach
Raised Terrace	SS415886	14	1986	coastal plateau
Rhossili Down	SS420900	215	1967	coastal hill
Whitford Burrows	SS445951	271	1965	saltmarsh and sand burrows
Llanrhidian Marsh	SS490932	514	1967	saltmarshes
Dyfed				
Tregoning Hill	SN362087	8	1962	cliffs and fields
Wharley Point	SN340093	156	1983	cliff and farmland
The Colby Estate	SN155080	394	1980	coastal farmland and woodland
Lydstep Headland	SS090976	22	1936	headland
Manorbier Cliff	SS065971	20	1965	cliffs
Stackpole	SR977963	806	1976	cliffs, beaches, dunes, woods and farmland
Williamston Park	SN030057	21	1978	rocky promontory
Kete	SM800045	68	1967	coast
Marloes: West Hook, Trehill & Runwayskiln Farms	SM775085	212	1942	headland and coastal farmland
Marloes: The Deerpark and Middleholm and Gateholm Islands	SM758091	30	1981	headland and two islands
St Elvis	SM810240	112	1967	beaches and cliffs
Upper Solva to Cwm Bach	SM802238	82	1937-73	cliffs, beaches, farmland
Llanunwas	SM787245	57	1987	coastal farmland
Carn Nwchwn to Nine Wells	SM775242	45	1940-45	coastal farmland and rough grassland
Lower Treginnis Farm	SM725240	102	1984	coastal farmland
Whitesands Bay to Porth-clais	SM725245	33	1937-40	cliffs and farmland
St David's Head	SM721278	211	1974-80	coastal headland
Pwll Caerog Farm	SM786302	98	n/a	coastal farmland
Ynys Barri	SM805320	81	1985	coastal farmland
Long House Farm	SM853337	61	1988	coastal farmland and islands
Treseissylt Farm	SM892354	64	n/a	coastal farmland
Good Hope	SM912407	39	1987	coastal outcrop and ancient pastures
Dinas Island Farm	SN010404	168	1988	coastal farmland
Cippin Fach and Gernos	SN122488	43	1989	coastal promontory
Mwnt	SN193520	40	1963-71	coastal farmland
Ty Hen	SN285520	17	1987	coastal scrub and pasture
Llanborth Farm	SN295519	39	1967	coastal farmland
Pencwm	SN292524	12	1987	coastal wooded valley
Lochtyn, Llandranog	SN315545	86	1965	beach, cliffs, islands and farmland
Penparc Farm	SN354574	49	1990	coast
Caerllan Farm	SN355577	30	1968	coastal farmland
Pen-y-Graig Farm	SN360582	31	1991	coastal farm, island, beach
Cwm Soden	SN365584	22	1984	coastal valley and woodland
Coybal	SN369589	15	1986	coast
Craig-yr-Adar	SN378601	10	1987	cliffs
Gwynedd				
Dinas Oleu and Cae Fadog	SH615158	8	1895-80	cliffland
Llandanwg	SH570270	10	1983	medieval church
Coed Cae Fali	SH635403	109	1984-85	coastal mixed woodland
Ynys Towyn	SH572385	1	1956	coastal rocky knoll
Morfa Bychan	SH550368	35	1960	dunes and golf course
Ynysgain	SH480375	80	1961	foreshore, coast and farmland
Tywyn-Y-Fach (Sandburrows), Abersoch	SH317292	8	1957	sandhills and scrub
Pant Farm, Abersoch	SH312249	9	1990	coastal farmland
Llanengan	SH290249	28	1950-58	cliffs

Table 7.5.1 National Trust sites (continued)

Site name	Grid ref.	Area (ha)	Date acquired	Description
Gwynned (cont.)				
Penrallt Neigwl	SH248287	4	1966	cliff and farmhouse
Plas-yn-Rhiw	SH237282	168	1950-66	coastal estate
Mynydd-y-Graig	SH230270	81	1955	coastal summit
Penarfynydd, Rhiw	SH217265	99	1974	clifftop rough and farmland
Porth Ysgo	SH208266	9	1967	beach, cliffs, waterfall
Cwrt Farm, Aberdaron	SH159259	96	1990	coastal farmland
Pen-Y-Cil, Aberdaron	SH158240	12	1968	clifftop and common land
Mynydd Bychestyn	SH158240	19	1981-84	common land
Braich-Y-Pwll	SH140254	49	1948	coast
Porth Llanllawen	SH145265	17	1980	cliffs and coastland
Mynydd Anelog	SH150275	49	1981	common land
Porth Orion	SH156285	4	1961	cliffland
Dinas Fawr and Dinas Bach	SH156285	17	1981	islands and cliffland
Carreg Farm, Aberdaron	SH162292	58	1986	headland
Porthor (Whistling Sands)	SH166298	30	1990	beach, cliffs and farmland
Porth Gwylan	SH215365	22	1982	harbour and coast
Porthdinllaen	SH275415	9	1994	coastal village, cliffs and beach
Pistyll Farm, Nefyn	SH325421	109	1990	coastal farmland
Pen-Y-Graig	SH303897	4	1985	coastal farmland
Mynachdy	SH295920	167	1987	coastal farmland
Clegir Mawr	SH315913	61	1978	coastal farmland
Cemlyn	SH325933	130	1968	farmland and nature reserve
Felin Cafnan and Trwyn Pencarreg	SH340937	15	1982	headland
Dinas Gynfor	SH392951	2	1913	cliffland
Llangoed	SH603818	19	1982	common land
Plas Newydd	SH521696	68	1976	coastal estate and woodland
Glan Faenol	SH530695	127	1985	coastal wood and farmland
Cae Glan-Y-Mor	SH546718	5	1938-80	coast
Ynys Welltog	SH549717	1	1982	island
Penrhyn Castle	SH603720	19	1951	castle and grounds
Total		**6,840**		

Source: The National Trust. Key: n/a - not available.. Note: In this table any site that is wholly or partly intertidal, and any terrestrial site at least partly within 1 km of the Mean High Water Mark, or any tidal channel as depicted on 1:50,000 Ordnance Survey maps, is included as 'coastal'.

7.5.3 The Wildfowl & Wetlands Trust (WWT)

As well as their wildfowl collections, used extensively for education, The Wildfowl & Wetlands Trust (WWT - formerly the Wildfowl Trust) has established non-statutory reserves in a number of key wintering areas for migrant wildfowl. The level of protection afforded to such sites is high, since the land is either owned or held on long leases. There is one coastal WWT site (82 ha) in Region 12 (see Table 7.5.3 and Map 7.5.2). This compares with a total of six coastal WWT sites (1,585 ha) in Great Britain, of which three (1,113 ha) are on the West Coast (data provided by WWT).

Table 7.5.3 Wildfowl and Wetlands Trust sites

Site name	Grid ref.	Area (ha)	Date acquired
Llanelli, Dyfed	SS530984	82	1991

Source: WWT 1994 data. Note: In this table any site that is wholly or partly intertidal, and any terrestrial site at least partly within 1 km of the Mean High Water Mark, or any tidal channel as depicted on 1:50,000 Ordnance Survey maps, is included as 'coastal'.

7.5.4 The Wildlife Trusts

The Wildlife Trusts have been established to promote non-statutory nature conservation at a local level in both the marine and terrestrial environments. They own, lease and manage (by agreement with owners) over 1,800 nature reserves, covering more than 52,000 ha. In most areas one trust covers a whole county or group of counties, although both Scotland and the Isle of Man each have a single Trust. The Trusts in the region are the North Wales Wildlife Trust, the Dyfed Wildlife Trust and the Glamorgan Wildlife Trust. There are 38 coastal Wildlife Trust sites (1,128 ha) in the region (see Table 7.5.4 and Map 7.5.2). This compares with a total of 219 coastal Wildlife Trust sites (23,380 ha) in Great Britain, of which 108 (13,724 ha) are on the West Coast. Of the 220 coastal sites in Britain covering the coast, there are 26 Scottish sites (13,805 ha), 189 English/Welsh sites (9,280 ha) and six Isle of Man sites (14 ha). The Wildlife Trusts were revising their databases at the time this section was collated; 1990 data on English/Welsh Wildlife Trust Sites have therefore been utilised, except where indicated otherwise in Table 7.5.4.

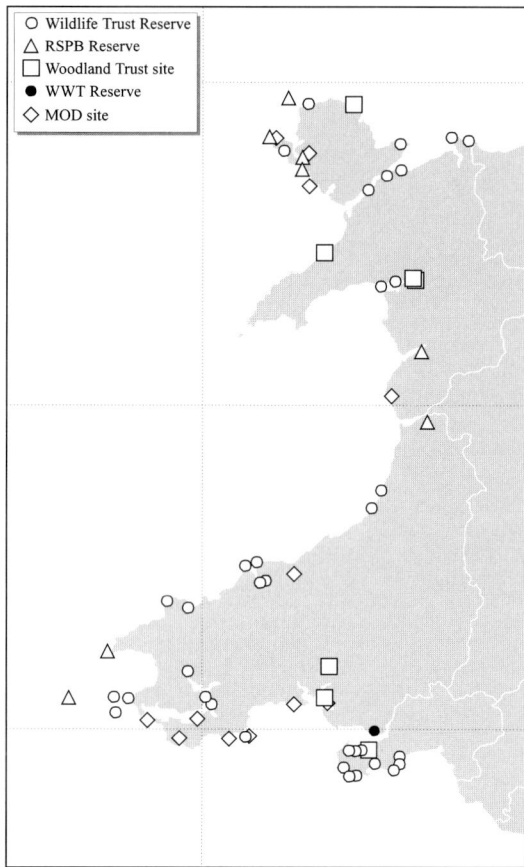

Map 7.5.2 Other voluntary and private sites. Source: Ministry of Defence, Wildlife Trusts, RSPB, Woodland Trust, Wildfowl & Wetlands Trust (NB not all sites are shown if several are located very close together).

Table 7.5.4 Wildlife Trusts sites

Site name	Grid ref.	Area (ha)	Date acquired
Glamorgan Wildlife Trust			
Ridgewood Park Mayals	SS611906	1	1962
Peel Wood	SS607883	1	1969
Redley Cliff	S589875	4	1970
Redden Hill Wood	SS539894	1	1979
Segders Bank	SS470844	35	1966
Port Eynon/Overton	SS465845	34	1964
Long Hole Cave Cliff	SS450850	21	1970
Deborah's Hole Cliff	SS435862	7	1972
Cwm Ivy Woods	SS443938	6	1964
Castle Wood Field	SS472931	1	1968
Hambury Wood	SS472929	5	1977
LLanrhidian Hill	SS495922	3	1976
Dyfed Wildlife Trust			
St Margaret's Island	SS120973	6	1950
West Williamston	SN027060	19	1979
Sam's Wood	SN004093	12	1985
Old Mill Grounds	SM953165	3	1973
Brunt Hill	SM816074	3	1982
Skokholm	SM735050	100	1948
Marloes Mere	SM775083	11	1969
Skomer Island	SM725095	292	1959
Llangoffan Fen[a]	SM894397	13	1984
Goodwick Moor	SM946377	15	1975
Cemaes Head	SN132500	16	1984
Teifi Marshes[a]	SN185450	370	1968
Teifi Foreshore	SN187457	14	1968
Cardigan Island	SN160515	16	1944
Aber Stinchell Lime Kilns[a]	SN519684	1	1993
Penderi [a]	SN550732	12	1966
North Wales Wildlife Trust (Gwynedd)			
Traeth Glaslyn[a]	SH587384	36	1974
Morfa Bychan	SH548367	11	1964
Porth Diana	SH254781	2	1979
Cemlyn[a]	SH331932	16	1971
Mariandyrys	SH604812	6	1980
Coed Porthamel[a]	SH508679	3	1982
Nantporth[a]	SH567718	14	1969
Spinnies Aberogwen	SH613722	3	1983
Gogarth, Great Orme	SH760832	3	1972
Rhiwledyn[a]	SH813821	5	1995
Total		**1,128**	

Source:- The Wildlife Trust. Key: [a] data correct at 1995; otherwise data correct at 1990. Note: In this table any site that is wholly or partly intertidal, and any terrestrial site at least partly within 1 km of the Mean High Water Mark, or any tidal channel as depicted on 1:50,000 Ordnance Survey maps, is included as 'coastal'. Some sites in this table are very close together; they have been represented on Map 7.5.2 by a single dot.

7.5.5 The Woodland Trust

The Woodland Trust was established in 1972 with the aim of conserving, restoring and re-establishing trees (particularly broad-leaved) and woodland plants and wildlife in the United Kingdom. There are seven non-statutory Woodland Trust sites (141 ha) in Region 12 (Table 7.5.5 and Map 7.5.2). This compares with a total of 64 coastal Woodland Trust sites (1,458 ha) in Great Britain, of which 29 (363 ha) are on the West Coast (data extracted from Woodland Trust (1993)).

Table 7.5.5 The Woodland Trust sites

Site name	Grid ref.	Area (ha)
W.Glamorgan		
Common Wood	SS508926	16
Dyfed		
Beech Hill Wood	SN365095	1
Coed Ystrad	SN395189	12
Gwynedd		
Coed Friog	SH657390	3
Coed Felinrhyd	SH657390	88
Coed Elernion	SH378462	20
Coed Avens	SH476923	1
Total		*141*

Source: Woodland Trust (1993). Note: In this table any site that is wholly or partly intertidal, and any terrestrial site at least partly within 1 km of the Mean High Water Mark, or any tidal channel as depicted on 1:50,000 Ordnance Survey maps, is included as 'coastal'.

7.5.6 The Ministry of Defence

As at August 1994, the Ministry of Defence (MOD) owned, leased or used under licence landholdings covering some 320 km of coastline around the UK, not all of it significant for its nature conservation value. The MOD gives high priority to nature conservation on the Defence Estate, subject to the overriding importance of military training. The restrictions to public access on some sites mean that they can be amongst the most pristine areas of wildlife habitat in the region. There are twelve coastal Ministry of Defence (MOD) sites (5,746 ha) in Region 12 (see Table 7.5.6 and Map 7.5.2). This compares with a total of 111 identified MOD coastal sites (approximately 53,409 ha) around the UK, of which 45 sites (approximately 18,960 ha) are on the West Coast of Britain (data provided by MOD).

Table 7.5.6 MOD sites

Site name	Area (ha)*	Habitats	Protected status
Dyfed			
Pembrey	614	saltmarsh and sand dune	SSSI
Pendine	1,928	sand dunes	SSSI
Penally	86	cliffs	SSSI, NP
Manorbier	42	cliffs	SSSI, NP
Castlemartin	2,390	sand dunes and cliffs	SSSI, NP
Angle	19	cliffs	SSSI, NP
Pembroke Dock	15	foreshore of mud	-
Aberporth	224	cliffs	-
Gwynedd			
Tywyn	0.4	estuary bank	NP
Ty Croes	25	rocky foreshore	AONB
Holyhead RAF Valley	399	sand dunes	SSSI, AONB
Holyhead RAF Craft Unit	4	rock outcrops	-
Total	*5,746*		

Source: Ministry of Defence. Key: * All areas are approximate and not definitive and include land leased or used under licence. SSSI = Site of Special Scientific Interest; NP = National Park; AONB = Area of Outstanding Natural Beauty. Note: In this table any site that is wholly or partly intertidal, and any terrestrial site at least partly within 1 km of the Mean High Water Mark, or any tidal channel as depicted on 1:50,000 Ordnance Survey maps, is included as 'coastal'.

7.5.7 Further sources of information

A. References cited

National Trust. 1992. *Properties of the National Trust.* National Trust.
National Trust. 1993. Enterprise Neptune - saving our unspoiled coastline. *Coastline 1993*, No.2: 1-11.
National Trust for Scotland. 1993. *Guide to over 100 properties.* The National Trust for Scotland.
Royal Society for the Protection of Birds. 1993. *Nature Reserves - information for visitors.* Sandy, RSPB.
Woodland Trust. 1993. *Directory of Woodland Trust properties 1993.* The Woodland Trust.

B. Further reading

Davidson, N.C., Laffoley, D.d'A., Doody, J.P., Way, L.S., Gordon, J., Key, R., Drake, M.C., Pienkowski, M.W., Mitchell, R., & Duff, K.L. 1991. *Nature conservation and estuaries in Great Britain.* Peterborough, Nature Conservancy Council.

C. Contact names and addresses

Type of information	Contact address and telephone no.
National Trust sites in GB	*Coast and Countryside Adviser, The National Trust HQ, Cirencester, tel. 01285 651818
National Trust sites in north Wales	*Land Agent, The National Trust North Wales Office, Llandudno, tel. 01492 860123
National Trust sites in south Wales	*Area Manager, The National Trust South Wales Office, Llandeilo, tel. 01558 822800
Royal Society for the Protection of Birds sites	*Regional Officer, RSPB Wales Office, Newtown, tel. 01686 626678
Wildfowl and Wetlands Trust site	*Dr G.Proffitt, The Wildfowl and Wetlands Trust, Llanelli, tel. 01554 741087
North Wales Wildlife Trust sites	*Conservation Officer, NWWT, Bangor, tel. 01248 351541
Dyfed Wildlife Trust sites	*Director and Marine Conservation Officer, DWT, Haverfordwest, tel. 01437 765462 / 767062
Glamorgan Wildlife Trust sites	*Conservation Officer, GWT, Tondu, tel. 01656 724100
Woodland Trust sites	The Woodland Trust, Autumn Park, Dysart Road, Grantham, Lincolnshire NG31 6LL, tel. 01476 74297
MOD sites	Conservation Officer, MOD Conservation Office, B2/3, Government Buildings, Leatherhead Road, Chessington, Surrey KT9 2LU, tel. 0181 391 3028/9

* Starred contact addresses are given in full in the Appendix

7.5.8 Acknowledgements

The author wishes to thank Andrea Firth for MOD text and data, Jo Burgon and Richard Offen (The National Trust), Dr J. Fenton (National Trust for Scotland), Bob Scott (RSPB), Mark Pollitt (Wildfowl and Wetlands Trust), Sarah Hawkswell (The Wildlife Trusts), Dr A. Somerville (Scottish Wildlife Trust), Meryl Eales (Manx Trust for Nature Conservation), Andrew Johnson (Manx Natural Heritage), The Woodland Trust, and Martin Mathers (WWFN).

Chapter 8 Land use, infrastructure and coastal defence

8.1 Introduction

M.J. Dunbar, S.J. Everett and S.L. Fowler

This chapter is divided into three sections: land use, covering agriculture and woodlands; infrastructure, covering population distribution, industry, ports, harbours and shipping lanes, road and rail communications, airfields and airports, ferries, pipelines, cables and power generation; and coastal defence, including sea defence and coast protection.

Most of the coastal land in the region is in agricultural use. There are, however, three main urban and industrial areas. In the south, the Swansea/Port Talbot area is dominated by residential, port and industrial uses. On the west coast, the Milford Haven waterway is bordered by several major industrial sites, mainly associated with the oil refining industry. And to the north, much of the Gwynedd coast north-east of Caernarfon is also urbanised.

Dyfi National Nature Reserve, on the Dyfed/Gwynedd border. Railways run alongside the sea in several parts of the region, here hugging the north shore of the Dyfi estuary. Photo: P. Wakely, English Nature.

171

8.2 Land use

M.J. Dunbar, S.J. Everett and S.L. Fowler

8.2.1 Introduction

Agriculture is the region's most widespread land use. The regional proportion of tilled land (see Map 8.2.1) is broadly comparable to that for agricultural coastal areas elsewhere on the west coast and on much of the south coast of England. Arable farming and horticulture is most widespread on the south coast of the region, in south-east Gower and south-west Dyfed, where there is a high proportion of cultivated land and intensive dairying. Most of the coastal land is grades 3 or 4 (MAFF grades), with smaller areas of grade 2 land. In the coastal plain of south-east Gower there is some mixed farming and horticulture on grade 2 and a small amount of grade 1 land.

In the west and north of the region, arable farming is a much less important activity and the emphasis is on livestock production, with coastal farmed areas dominated by grazing on managed grassland land and semi-natural rough grassland and heath. The whole of the Welsh coast is important for livestock production. A large amount of the British extent of managed coastal grassland is located in the region, particularly in south and south-west Dyfed and on Anglesey (Map 8.2.2). The map does not differentiate between land used for dairying (mainly along the south coast of the region) and beef or sheep rearing (on the west

and north coasts). In contrast to this region, the North Sea coast of England and Scotland has limited amounts of managed grassland.

Most of the woodlands in Wales are located away from the coast, with the exception of some conifer plantations on areas of sand dune. Those ancient semi-natural and mixed woodlands on or near the coast are often located on steep slopes and alongside estuaries, streams and rivers. Wooded areas are listed in Table 8.2.1 and shown on Map 8.2.3.

8.2.2 Effects of agriculture and forestry

In parts of the Pembrokeshire Coast National Park, land has been agriculturally improved and cultivated up to the cliff edge, leaving only a very narrow margin of semi-natural vegetation. Set-aside and agri-environment projects are also likely to have an impact on agriculture on the coastal fringe. Many farms are trying to develop farm tourism as a source of alternative income. See Chapter 7 for more details of Environmentally Sensitive Areas and the Tir Cymen initiative.

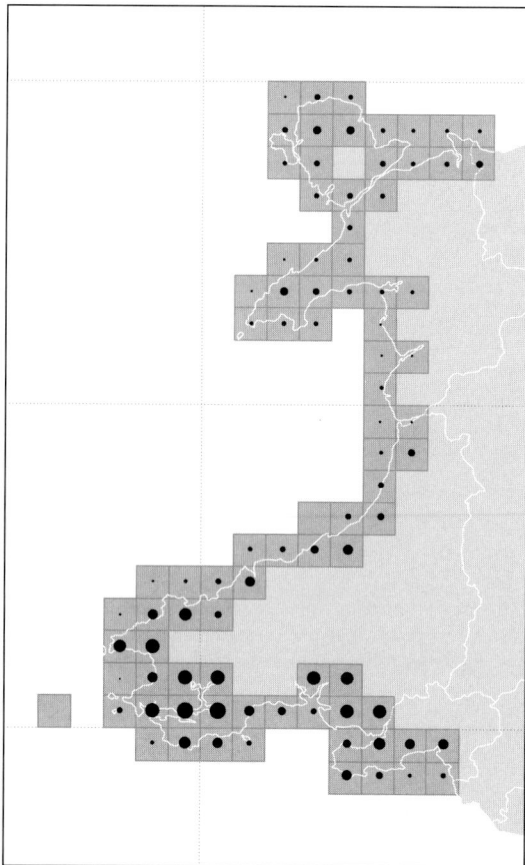

Map 8.2.1 Tilled land. Note: area of circle indicates the area of this land cover type in the 10 km square. Source: Countryside Survey (1990), ITE Monks Wood.

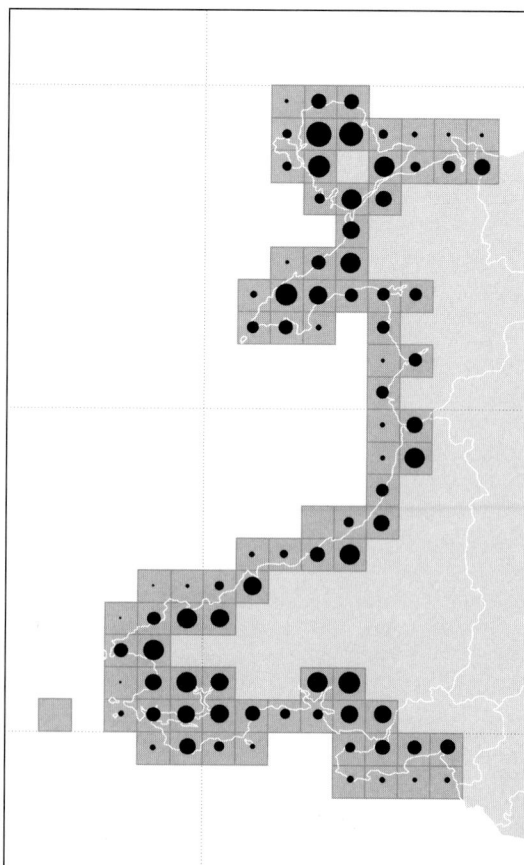

Map 8.2.2 Mown/grazed turf. Note: area of circle indicates the area of this land cover type in the 10 km square. Source: Countryside Survey (1990), ITE Monks Wood.

Table 8.2.1 Main areas of coastal woodland in Region 12

	Location	Grid ref.	Details
	W Glamorgan		
1	Nicholaston Woods	SS5188	Broadleaved strips on steep slopes adjacent to coast
2	Oxwich	SS5086	Broadleaved strips on steep slopes to sea
3	Whiteford Burrows	SS4494	Small blocks of mature conifer plantation on sand dunes
	Dyfed		
4	Pembrey Forest	SS3802	Conifer plantation covering 897 ha of sand dunes
5	Benton Wood	SN0006	Conifer plantation on steep slopes of Daugleddau. Broadleaved woodland on east bank slopes
6	Dyfi Estuary	SN6495	Extensive wooded slopes along south and north banks of the estuary: coniferous, mixed and broadleaved.
	Gwynedd		
7	Mawddach Estuary (both sides)	SH6615	Extensive mixed & coniferous woodland on steep banks
8	Morfa Harlech	SH5732	Conifer plantation on 14 ha of sand dunes
9	Newborough Forest, Anglesey	SH4063	Conifer plantation covering 741 ha of sand dunes
10	Myndd Llwydiarth	SH5479	Conifer plantation abutting Red Wharf Bay (but mostly extending inland) over approx. 3 km^2
11	Menai Straits, Anglesey	SH5270	Coastal woodland fringe along approx. 2.5 km west of Pont Britannia
12	Menai Straits (south bank)	SH5370	Mixed woodland over approx 0.5 km^2
13	Menai Straits (both banks)	SH5471	Mixed woodland for approx. 2 km west of suspension bridge (south bank); a small block on Anglesey near Pont Britannia.
14	Penrhyn	SH6072	Mixed woodland along approx. 1 km of coast east of Bangor

Note: location numbers refer to sites shown on Map 8.2.3.

Some saltmarsh areas such as at Burry Inlet and Llanridian Marsh are heavily grazed (see section 3.6 and 9.3): the agricultural use of the latter site combined with its relative remoteness from urban centres has helped to protect it from other developments. Other vegetation types used in the region for rough grazing and which are mapped in ITE (1993) but not presented in this chapter are rough grass/marsh, moorland grass, bracken and open shrub heath/moor. Agricultural intensification has destroyed parts of the major dune systems (see section 3.2). Today, many such areas lie under arable fields, as in parts of Morfa Harlech (Gwynedd), or are permanent pastures. See section 9.3 for further details of grazing on saltmarsh and sand dunes.

Afforestation has affected large areas of sand dune. Of the thirteen major dune afforestation schemes in Britain identified by Doody (undated), three are in this region, at Pembrey, Morfa Harlech and Newborough Warren.

8.2.3 Information sources

The main source of information for this section was the Countryside Survey 1990 (ITE 1993), which is based primarily on high resolution satellite images. These images show the dominant land cover for each 25 m x 25 m area (pixel) of Great Britain, classified into 17 key types. Field surveys of randomly selected areas were used to 'ground-truth' the results. The Countryside Information System can provide data on a 1 km square framework, but this level of detail was not considered appropriate here. More detailed information on agricultural land use is held by the Pembrokeshire Coast National Park Plan, local plans and Agricultural Development Advisory Service (ADAS) (e.g. information on set-aside targets).

Information on forestry was obtained from the 1:50,000 scale Ordnance Survey Landranger maps, which distinguish between coniferous, mixed and broadleaved woodland. The NCC's inventory of ancient woodlands (Spencer & Kirby 1992) may provide another source of comparative data for the region, and the Forestry Commission is able to provide maps of forestry areas throughout the country.

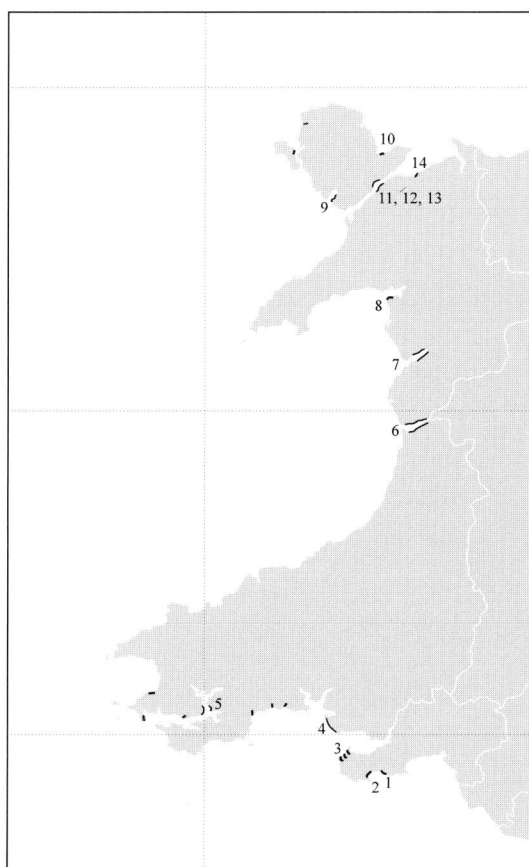

Map 8.2.3 Coastal woodland. Larger (numbered) sites are those listed in Table 8.2.1. Source: Ordnance Survey Landranger maps. © Crown copyright.

173

8.2.4 Further sources of information

A. References cited

Doody J.P. Undated. *Coastal habitat change - a historical review of man's impact on the coastline of Great Britain.* Peterborough, Joint Nature Conservation Committee (unpublished draft).

Institute of Terrestrial Ecology. 1993. *Countryside survey 1990: main report.* London, Department of the Environment.

Spencer, J.W., & Kirby, K.J. 1992. An inventory of ancient woodland for England and Wales. *Biological Conservation* 62: 77-93.

B. Further reading

Etherington, J.R, & Clark, E.A. 1987. Impact of agriculture on the cliff vegetation of South Gower, West Glamorgan. *Nature Conservancy Council, CSD Report*, No 731.

Welsh Office. 1993. *Environmental Digest for Wales. No. 7, 1992.* Cardiff, Welsh Office.

C. Contact names and addresses

Type of information	Contact address and telephone no.
Land use, grades, set-aside (MAFF/ADAS Land Service)	MAFF, Whitehall Place, London SW11 2HH, tel: 0171 270 3000
	ADAS, Oxford Spire Business Park, The Boulevard, Kidlington, Oxford OX5 1NZ, tel: 01865 842742
Countryside Survey 1990	Department of Rural Affairs, Department of the Environment, Room 919, Tollgate House, Houlton Street, Bristol BS2 9DJ, tel: 0117 9218811
as above	*Land Use Group, ITE Merlewood, tel: 01539 532264
as above	*Environmental Information Centre, ITE Monks Wood, tel: 01487 773381
Woodland extent, ownership, management	Chief Conservator, Forestry Commission Wales Conservancy, North Road, Aberystwyth, Dyfed SY23 2EF, tel: 01970 612367
Ancient Woodland Inventory	*Woodland Ecologist, CCW HQ, Bangor, tel: 01248 370734

* Starred contact addresses are given in full in the Appendix

8.2.5 Acknowledgements

Thanks to Robin Fuller, ITE Monks Wood for providing information on the Countryside Survey.

8.3 Infrastructure

M.J. Dunbar, S.J. Everett, S.L. Fowler, C.A.

8.3.1 Introduction

This section summarises the infrastructure of the region, including population distribution, industry, ports, harbours and shipping lanes, road and rail communications, airfields and airports, ferries, pipelines, cables and power generation, and land claim for these developments. Oil and gas exploration and development are covered in section 9.6.

This is one of the least densely populated regions in southern Britain, with a total population in West Glamorgan, Dyfed and Gwynedd of only 960,000 (1991 figure from Cook 1993) - 5% of the UK's population - although much of this total is concentrated along the coast. Residential development on the south and north coasts of the region is as intensive as in the more heavily populated areas of England, whereas on the west coast it is more akin to that along the National Park coasts of the Lake District and North York Moors.

The main centres of population in the region are on the south coast, from Swansea Bay to Llanelli and Milford Haven, and on the north coast, where there are several towns and the small city of Bangor. Aberystwyth is the only sizeable town on the west coast. Most of the industrial areas in the region are situated along estuaries or other marine inlets. Industries generally take the form of locally-based undertakings mainly dealing with the processing of local agricultural output or related regional crafts (Smith & Geffen 1990). The most important ports in the region include Port Talbot, Swansea and Milford Haven/Pembroke Dock in the south and Holyhead in the north. Except for around Swansea and Milford Haven, industrial areas in the region are mainly of only regional or local importance.

The region is a net energy exporter (Countryside Council for Wales 1992). Energy is produced here by a variety of methods, including nuclear, conventional, hydro-electric and wind-derived methods. The diversity and locations of production methods reflect the variety of sources of power available. Pembroke Power station accounts for 1.2% of the conventional power output in the UK. Only 3% of the total UK energy production in 1990 was from renewable sources, of which only 5% is accounted for by wind energy (Country-side Council for Wales 1992). The wind farm in this region accounts for 4.5 % of the UK's wind energy output capacity of 160 MW. In 1989, of the 2,570 MW of hydro power energy being produced in Wales, 82% was produced with the help of imported electricity at off-peak times for pumping of water to storage (Countryside Council for Wales 1992).

8.3.2 Important locations

Residential development

Apart from the main populations centres in the north and south and Aberystwyth in the west, there are numerous smaller towns that house considerable populations during the summer tourist season but whose permanent populations are smaller (<5,000). These include include Mumbles, Tenby, Fishguard, Cardigan, Aberdyfi, Barmouth, Portmadog, Pwllheli and Abersoch (see Map 8.3.1). Table 8.3.1 lists the main towns and cities in the region and their populations.

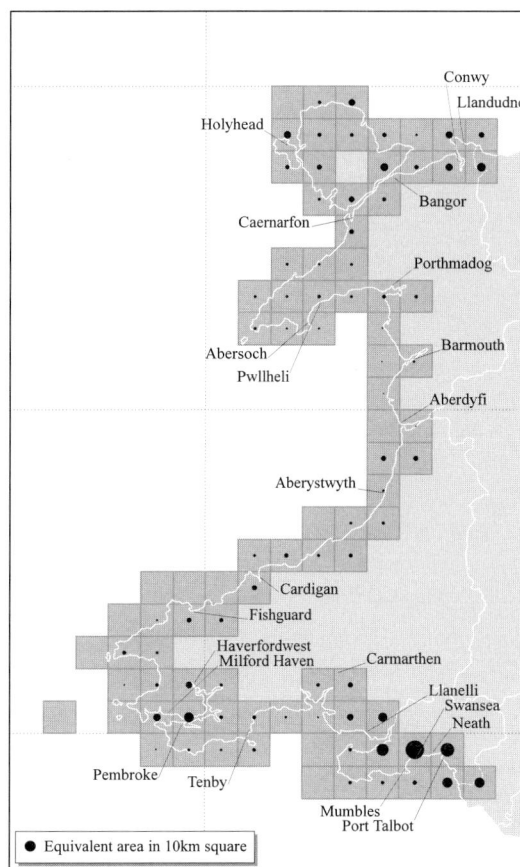

Map 8.3.1 Urban, suburban and rural development. Note: area of circle indicates the combined area of these land cover types in the 10 km square. Major towns and cities are also shown. Source: Countryside Survey (1990); ITE Monks Wood.

Table 8.3.1 Main coastal towns and cities in Region 12

Town or city	Population
Port Talbot	51,300
Neath	66,000
Swansea	187,600
Llanelli	75,300
Pembroke	15,600
Milford Haven	13,900
Aberystwyth	8,700
Caernarfon	9,500
Holyhead	10,500
Bangor	12,100
Conwy	13,000
Llandudno	19,000

Source: Cook (1993)

175

Table 8.3.2 Major areas of coastal industrial development

	Site/area	Location	Details
1	Port Talbot, Margam and Baglan Bay, Glamorgan	SS78	>10 km² industrial area, including steel works at Margam Docks and chemical works at Baglan Bay.
2	Llandarcy, nr. Neath, Glamorgan	SS7295	2 km² area oil refinery and oil storage
3	Swansea	SS69	3 km² area of docks, petrochemical storage along coast to east of docks, motor works (1 km²)
4	Llanelli	SS5199	1 km² area of works at Trostre, dock, 50 ha of other works.
5	Burry Port	SN4401	Power station, 50 ha.
6	BP Angle Bay Ocean Terminal, Milford Haven	SR9003	Reception and storage facility, >100 km oil pipeline to Llandarcy near Swansea. Closed 1985, jetty now operated by Texaco
7	Texaco Refinery, Rhoscrowther, Milford Haven	SR9203	Opened 1964, catalytic cracker built in 1982.
8	Pembroke Power Station, Milford Haven		2 km² of land occupied by four 500 MW fuel oil units and three 25 MW gas turbine generators. Plans to convert to Orimulsion
9	Pembroke Dock, Milford Haven	SR9604	Land fill associated with dock developments.
10	Gulf Refinery, Waterston, Milford Haven	SM9305	Opened 1968. Shares catalytic cracker at Rhoscrowther with Texaco.
11	Elf Refinery, Milford Haven	SM8808	1 km² in area, located 2 km inland. Opened in 1973, with catalytic cracker built 1981.
12	Former Esso Refinery, jetties, Milford Haven	SM8706	3 km² area on coast occupied by oil refinery, opened in 1960, closed in 1983 and dismantled. Jetty now operated by Milford Haven Port Authority.
13	Penrhyndeudraeth, near Portmadog, Gwynedd	SH6139	Explosives works
14	Menai Straits, north east of Caernarfon, Gwynedd	SH4965	Bricks and plastics works, around 10 ha.
15	Holyhead, Anglesey	SH2583	Aluminium smelting works, (25 ha) and other small industries
16	Wylfa, Anglesey	SH3534	Nuclear power station
17	Amlwch, Anglesey	SH4594	Chemical works (Associated Octel), former Anglesey offshore marine terminal, now decommissioned.

Industrial development

The region's significant industries are listed in Table 8.3.2 and the main industrial areas are shown on Map 8.3.2.

In total, about 22 km² of land in the region is occupied by heavy industrial activity, with over 60% of this industry (1,300 ha) located in West Glamorgan, in the Port Talbot, Neath and Swansea area. There are about 200 ha of land in industrial use around Llanelli and Burry Port, and 625 ha on the shores of Milford Haven. Other industrial areas in the region each occupy around 10-25 ha at most.

The industrial area around Swansea Bay is the most important, initially developed in parallel with the nearby south Wales coal fields. The Swansea-Neath-Port Talbot complex has economically important metal refining industries and other heavy industries (e.g. plastics), which now rely heavily on imports of raw materials. There is a large British Steel works at Margam, where there are extensive ore importation facilities, although some of the former industrial land has now been converted into a country park (Clyne Valley Country Park - see section 7.3.8). Several modern industrial estates are also being developed in this area, taking advantage of the proximity of the M4 motorway. There is a British Petroleum refinery at Llandarcy (Neath), chemical works and oil storage facilities at Baglan Bay (Port Talbot) and a Ford works at Jersey Marine, Neath. The Lower Swansea Valley has historically been a metallurgical industrial area. The 'Five Parks' initiative, including the designation of an Enterprise Zone, was developed in the early 1980s to tackle the problems of industrial dereliction.

Llanelli is a significant industrial and commercial centre, with its importance again originally stemming from the coal

mining industry. Heavy industry includes steel and tinplate works, manufacturing of machinery and metal casting. There is a chemical works at nearby Bynea.

Another major centre of industrial activity is situated around Milford Haven and at Pembroke Dock, where there are oil refineries, extensive oil storage facilities, facilities for catalytic cracking of hydrocarbons and other petrochemical-based industries. The Milford Haven waterway is an ideal deep water port, taking tankers of up to 250,000 tonnes, and although it has a long history of industrial activity (Hobbs & Morgan 1992), it has largely been developed since 1960 to serve the oil refining industry. At one stage there were four major oil refineries and an oil terminal on or very close to the shores of the other parts of the Haven, but the first refinery built and the terminal have since been dismantled. Four oil refineries are now located in the region, two at Milford Haven, one at Pembroke and one at Llandarcy. These deal with crude oil bought in by tanker. Section 9.6 describes oil and gas exploration and developments in the region, and Map 9.6.1 shows the locations of the region's refineries, also shown as locations 2, 7, 10 and 11 on Map 8.3.2.

There are a few other locally important areas of industry on the west coast, such as the explosives works at Penrhyndeudraeth near Portmadog and a brick and plastics works along the Menai Straits north-east of Caernarfon. Anglesey has an aluminium smelting works at Holyhead and a chemical works (Associated Octel) at Amlwch. An oil terminal and transhipping jetty nearby have now been decommissioned.

Enterprise Zones, lasting ten years and designed to promote the rejuvenation of employment and the encouragement of new industry, were designated by the government covering the Lower Swansea Valley (March

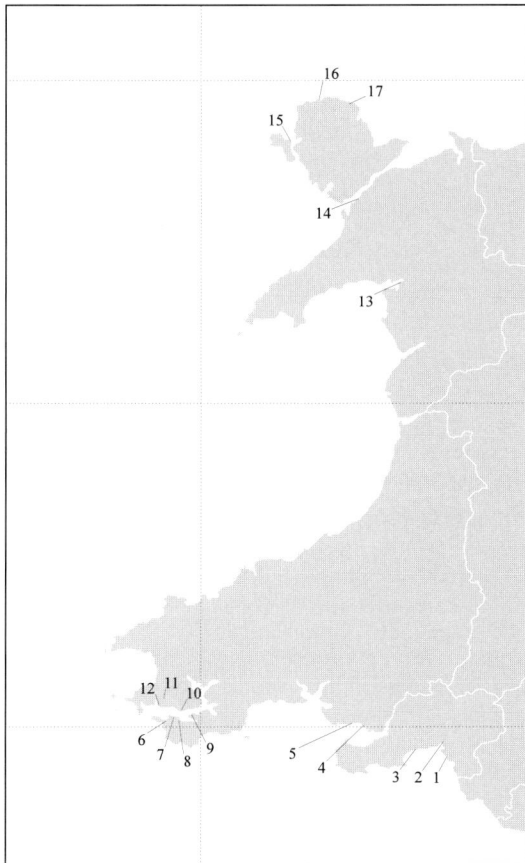

Map 8.3.2 Industrial infrastructure. Numbered locations refer to those listed in Table 8.3.2.

Llanelli and Burry Port are no longer used for commercial traffic.

As well as extensive oil terminal infrastructure, there are general port facilities at Milford Docks. The port can service tankers up to 250,000 tonnes. There are four very large jetties constructed for oil tanker use, 'ro-ro' (roll on, roll off) and container facilities. Milford Haven is also an important white fish port (see section 9.1), and trawlers are built and maintained here. Pembroke Dock, formerly an important Admiralty dockyard, is a large ferry port with services to Cork and Rosslare in Ireland. The area around the Smalls and Grassholm is a voluntary tanker exclusion zone (International Maritime Organisation).

Fishguard, owned by Sealink Harbours Ltd, is a general cargo and ferry port with 'ro-ro' facilities. There is a small general port at Caernarfon. Holyhead has regular ferries to Dublin and Dun Laoghaire, 'ro-ro' and general harbour facilities. Amlwch, a small port on the north coast of Anglesey, is now used for pilot launches for Liverpool and occasionally by leisure craft. Port Penrhyn (Bangor) at the eastern end of the Menai Strait, has facilities for 'ro-ro' freight and sand and gravel. It is also the centre for the landing of mussel catches from the Strait (see sections 9.1 and 9.2). Traffic separation schemes, which segregate north- and south-bound shipping in the more congested waters off Pembrokeshire and Anglesey, are shown on Map 8.3.3.

1985) and Milford Haven Waterway (April 1984). The latter zone includes sites in the Royal Dockyard, Pembroke Dock and the Milford Haven Docks, with three other sites also having water frontage. Deep water quays have been newly constructed in the Milford Haven Enterprise Zone for cargo handling.

Ports, harbours and shipping lanes

Apart from Port Talbot, Swansea, Pembroke Dock, Milford Docks and Holyhead there are a number of smaller ports in the region. These are Llanelli, Burry Port, Tenby, Fishguard, Aberystwyth, Aberdyfi, Barmouth, Porthmadog (associated in the past with coal and slate export, now discontinued), Pwllheli, Abersoch, Caernarfon, Port Dinorwic, Amlwch, Port Penrhyn (Bangor) and Conwy. Most of these also have modest fishing fleets (see section 9.1) and are used by recreational craft. All are shown on Map 8.3.3 and their facilities listed in Table 8.3.2. Port Talbot is a high capacity port with a well-protected harbour of 186 ha, but it is not currently used as a general freight port. Some of the old port area has been converted to provide warehousing and distribution facilities. It is used by British Steel for importing raw materials, handling over seven million tonnes per year. It comes under the control of the Associated British Ports (ABP) Swansea office. The River Neath is a commercial waterway navigable as far as Neath Abbey Wharfs. Swansea is a well-developed container port with ships sailing to and from all parts of the world, but particularly to Ireland and western Europe. It also has facilities for bulk liquid cargoes (and can pump these to the nearby BP refineries and chemical works) and aggregates.

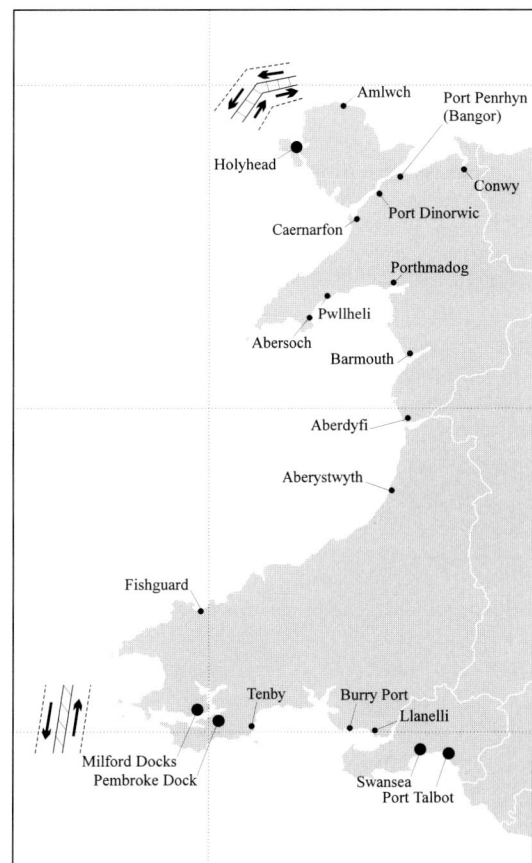

Map 8.3.3 Ports and harbours; traffic separation schemes off Pembrokeshire and Anglesey.

Map 8.3.4 Coastal power stations and wind farms.

Road and rail communications

These are most highly developed around the significant industrial and urban areas of this region, notably in the Port Talbot/Swansea area and to a lesser extent around Llanelli and Burry Port in the south, and in the north between Menai Bridge, Bangor and Conwy. All the major centres on the south coast, from Port Talbot to Llanelli, have good road links with the M4.

Elsewhere, larger towns and industrial areas are served by trunk roads and occasionally by railways. The railway from Borth to Dyfi crosses former tidal marshland, truncating the remaining saltmarsh to the north for a length of some 8 km. There is a long railway crossing over the Mawddach estuary at Barmouth, and the railway also runs along the coast south of Harlech and near Criccieth and Pwllheli. Toll roads cross the Glaslyn estuary east of Porthmadog and at Penrhyndeudraeth, the former alongside the Ffestiniog railway. There is also a toll bridge close to the upper tidal limit on the Mawddach estuary.

On the north coast, there are major crossings from Bangor to Anglesey and from Anglesey to Holy Island (both have one shared road and rail bridge and a second smaller road bridge). The A55 and the Crewe-Bangor railway line run along an artificial length of shoreline between Bangor and Conwy for about 8 km. There is a road and rail bridge at Conwy and a new 'cut and cover' road tunnel beneath the Conwy estuary to Llandudno Junction.

Airfields and airports

There are no international airports in this coastal region. In Dyfed, all the small airfields are situated on high land above cliffs. However, Valley Airfield (Anglesey) is situated in an area of low-lying coastland and was partly constructed on nearby dunes. The airfield at Morfa Dinlle is similarly situated.

Ferries

Apart from the major ferry ports described above, there are smaller, local ferries operating around the coast, some running only during the summer tourist season. Local ferries operate across the Mawddach from Barmouth; day trips also run in summer to the islands of Skomer, Skokholm and Grassholm from Martin's Haven and Dale, and from St Justinian to Ramsey Island. A hovercraft passenger ferry (summer only) takes people between Aberystwyth, Borth and Aberdyfi, and there are cruises on the Menai Strait from Caernarfon, from where infrequent informal services also run to Ynys Enlli.

Pipelines and cables

There is a pipeline from the Angle Bay refinery in Milford Haven to Llandarcy near Swansea, and another from Crymlyn to Port Talbot across the Neath Estuary. One active submarine cable comes ashore on the west coast of Holy Island, and there are several abandoned cables on the north coast, including four to Morfa Nefyn on the north coast of the Llyn, two to Aberffraw on the west Anglesey coast, two running from Ireland into Holyhead, one from the Isle of Man to the north Anglesey coast, and two to Conwy from the Isle of Man and Blackpool. There are no sub-sea pipelines in the region.

Power generation

There is one nuclear power station on the region's coast at Wylfa (Anglesey), with an output of 840 MW. It discharges liquid wastes into the Irish Sea within the authorised limits recommended by the International Commission on Radiological Protection (ICRP). There is one oil fired power station in this region, on the coast at Pembroke, with an output of 500 MW. Thermal and other discharges from the power station are monitored by the NRA. Map 8.3.4 shows all power stations on the region's coastline.

No offshore wave power energy production operations exist in this region and none are planned. However, there are several macrotidal estuaries in the region that could be suitable for generating renewable tidal energy. No energy-generating barrages have yet been constructed in Britain, although a barrage with a power generating capacity of up to 50 MW (Eno 1991) was proposed for the Conwy. The only operational coastal wind farm in this region is at Rhyd-y-Groes on Anglesey; it has 24 turbines and a capacity of 7.2 MW.

8.3.3 Effects of human activities

The populations of the Gwynedd and Dyfed coastal towns are predicted to increase by around 5% from 1985-2001 (Evans & Thomason 1990). Land use policies are now increasingly geared to strengthening the identities of existing towns and restricting countryside development. For example, all the County Councils have policies to minimise urban expansion into agricultural land. There are also increasing efforts being put into stemming the decline of the rural population, particularly in Dyfed and Gwynedd (see also Tir Cymen - section 7.4.4).

The scale and impacts of industrial land-claim in the region and elsewhere in Britain are discussed in Davidson *et al.* (1991) and Buck (1993). Doody (undated) has investigated the impacts of industrial land claim on the coastline of south Wales, measuring the loss of semi-natural habitat at fourteen sites on the industrialised south Wales coast by comparing Ordnance Survey maps from 1889 and 1985. The sites were: Port Talbot/Margam, Baglan Burrows, River Neath, Crymlyn Burrows, Crymlyn Bog, Swansea Bay, Swansea Docks, Pennard Burrows, Whiteford/Broughton Burrows, Loughor Bridge, Loughor River, Llanelli Harbour, Burry Port and Pembrey Burrows. He found that, out of an original area of 4,330 ha of semi-natural habitat, there had been a total loss of 2,689 ha of sand dune, saltmarsh, 'marsh', bog, intertidal flats and coastal grassland as a result of human developments, including industry, docks, forestry, agriculture and housing.

8.3.4 Information sources used

The information on population statistics comes from Cook (1993), who uses data from population censuses from a number of dates, including the 1981 census; some figures may therefore be slightly out of date. Map 8.3.1 is based on the ITE (1993) Countryside Survey 1990 database and areas shown include both continuous urban areas and suburban/rural developments.

Industrial development data came from Buck (1993), Cook (1993), Ordnance Survey Landranger 1:50,000 maps, Bown (1990), Dyfed County Council (1980, 1987), Gwynedd County Council (1991), Hobbs & Morgan (1992), West Glamorgan County Council (1993), and Doody (undated).

Areas of coastal industrial developments in Table 8.3.2 and Map 8.3.2 are as shown on OS 1:50,000 Landranger maps; however some of these sites will undoubtedly have since been abandoned (as indicated by Hobbs & Morgan 1992 for Milford Haven). Up to date information is held by local planning authorities (see Appendix). Most of the information on ports was derived from the two national handbooks for the British Ports Federation (BPF) (undated) and Sutton (1989), which may be incomplete or out of date. In 1991 the BPF was replaced by the British Ports Association and the UK Major Ports Group. Lord Donaldson (1994) records that there is little clear information available on where ships go within UK waters.

Most of the information on road and rail links, bridges, ferries and airfields was derived from 1:50,000 Land Ranger Ordnance Survey maps. Cables and pipelines are shown on the UKDMAP and Admiralty Charts. It is not always clear from these sources which of these communications infrastructures are still in use.

8.3.5 Further sources of information

A. References cited

Bown, D.P. 1990. Coastal resources and proposed developments. *In: The Irish Sea, an environmental review. Part 4. Planning, development and management,* ed. by H.D. Smith & A.J. Geffen. Liverpool, Irish Sea Study Group, Liverpool University Press.

British Oceanographic Data Centre, Proudman Laboratory. 1991. *UKDMAP (United Kingdom Digital Marine Atlas). Version 2.* Computer software. British Oceanographic Data Centre, Proudman Laboratory, Birkenhead.

British Ports Federation. Undated. *UK member ports directory.* London, British Ports Federation.

Buck, A.L. 1993. *An inventory of UK estuaries. Volume 2. South-West Britain.* Peterborough, Joint Nature Conservation Committee.

Cook, C. 1993. *Pears cyclopaedia 1993-1994.* London, Penguin Books Ltd.

Countryside Council for Wales. 1992. *Energy: policy and perspectives for the Welsh countryside* (policy document) (CCC031). Bangor.

Davidson, N.C., Laffoley, D.d'A., Doody, J.P., Way, L.S., Gordon, J., Key, R., Drake, M.C., Pienkowski, M.W., Mitchell, R., & Duff, K.L. 1991. *Nature conservation and estuaries in Great Britain.* Peterborough, Nature Conservancy Council.

Doody, J.P. Undated. *Coastal habitat change - a historical review of man's impact on the coastline of Great Britain.* Peterborough, Joint Nature Conservation Committee (unpublished draft).

Dyfed County Council. 1980. *Dyfed county structure plan written statement.* Carmarthen, Dyfed County Council.

Dyfed County Council. 1987. *Dyfed county structure plan proposals for alteration.* Carmarthen, Dyfed County Council.

Eno, N.C., ed. 1991. *Marine conservation handbook.* 2nd ed. Peterborough, English Nature.

Evans D.M., & Thomason, H. 1990. Tourism and recreational developments. *In: The Irish Sea, an environmental review. Part 4. Planning, development and management,* ed. by H.D. Smith & A.J. Geffen. Liverpool, Irish Sea Study Group, Liverpool University Press.

Gwynedd County Council. 1991. *Gwynedd county structure plan written statement.* Caernarfon, Gwynedd County Council.

Hobbs, G., & Morgan, C.I. 1992. A review of the current state of environmental knowledge of the Milford Haven Waterway. *Report to the Milford Haven Waterway Environmental Monitoring Steering Group.* Field Studies Council Research Centre, 5/92. Pembroke.

Institute of Terrestrial Ecology. 1993. *Countryside survey 1990: main report.* London, Department of the Environment.

Lord Donaldson. 1994. *Safer seas, cleaner ships. Report of Lord Donaldson's Inquiry into the prevention of pollution from merchant shipping.* CM2560. HMSO, London.

Smith, H.D., & Geffen, A.J., eds. 1990. *The Irish Sea: an environmental review. Part 4. Planning, development and management.* Liverpool, Liverpool University Press. (Irish Sea Study Group.)

Sutton, G, ed. 1989. *ABP '89, A guide to the ports and shipping services of Associated British Ports Holdings plc.* King's Lynn, Charter International Publications Ltd.

Welsh Office. 1993. *Environment digest for Wales. No.7, 1992.* Cardiff, Welsh Office.

West Glamorgan County Council. 1993. *West Glamorgan structure plan.* Swansea, West Glamorgan County Council.

B. Further reading

ACOPS. 1990. *Survey of oil pollution around the coasts of the United Kingdom.* Advisory Committee on Pollution of the Sea. Annual Report.

Barne, J., Davidson, N.C., Hill, T.O., & Jones, M. 1994. *Coastal and Marine UKDMAP datasets: a user manual.* Peterborough, Joint Nature Conservation Committee.

British Ports Association. 1994. *British Ports Association 1994.* King's Lynn, Charter International.

Chris Blandford Associates. 1994. *Wind turbine power station construction monitoring study.* Chris Blandford Associates, in association with University of Wales, Bangor. (A report commissioned by the Countryside Council for Wales.)

Countryside Council for Wales. 1992. *Wind turbine power stations* (policy document CCC031). Bangor.

Department of the Environment. 1992. *Enterprise zones.* London, Department of the Environment.

Department of Transport. 1991. *Port statistics 1990.* Department of Transport & British Ports Federation.

European Sea Ports Organisation. 1994. *Environmental Code of Practice.* Brussels.

Huckbody, A.J, Taylor, P.M., Hobbs, G., & Elliott, R. 1992. *Caernarfon and Cardigan Bays: an environmental appraisal.* London, Hamilton Oil Company.

Institute of Petroleum Information Service. 1993. *UK petroleum industry statistics: consumption and refinery production.* London, Institute of Petroleum.

Irish Sea Study Group. 1990. *The Irish Sea; an environmental review.* Liverpool, Liverpool University Press.

North Sea Task Force. 1993. North Sea Quality Status Report 1993. Oslo and Paris Commissions, London.

Scottish Office. 1993. *The Scottish environment - statistics, No. 4 1993.* Edinburgh, The Government Statistical Service.

Taylor, P.M., & Parker, J.G., eds. 1993. *The coast of north Wales and north-west England: an environmental appraisal.* London, Hamilton Oil Company Ltd.

Technica. 1995. *Shipping routes in the area of the United Kingdom continental shelf.* Prepared by Technica for the Department of Energy. London, HMSO.

C. Contact names and addresses

Type of information	Contact address and telephone no.	Type of information	Contact address and telephone no.
Industrial development, Enterprise Zones, oil terminals	David Gleave, Department of the Environment, 2 Marsham Street, London SW1P 3EB, tel. 0171 276 6166	Swansea Bay Port Health Authority	Swansea Bay Port Health Authority, Kings Dock Lock, Swansea SA1 8RU, tel. 01792 653523
Lower Swansea Valley Enterprise Zone	John Weston, Lower Swansea Valley Enterprise Zone, Swansea City Council, Guild Hall, Swansea SA1 4PH, tel. 01792 302748	Milford Haven Port	Milford Haven Port Authority, PO Box 14, Milford Haven, Pembrokeshire, Dyfed SA73 3ER, tel. 016462 3091/4
Milford Haven Waterway Enterprise Zone	Economic Development Officer, Milford Haven Waterway Enterprise Zone, Economic Development Unit, South Pembrokeshire District Council, Pier House, Pier Road, Pembroke Dock SA72 6TR, tel. 01646 684914	Milford Docks	The Milford Docks Company, The Docks, Milford Haven, Dyfed SA73 3AF, tel. 016462 2271/3
Oil and gas development policy	Public Relations Officer, Department of Trade and Industry, 1 Palace Street, London SW1E 5HE, tel: 0171 238 3214	Milford Haven Port Health Authority	Milford Haven Port Health Authority, Gorsewood Drive, Hakin, Milford Haven, Pembs. SA73 3EP, tel. 01646 69486
Oil refinery environmental problems and general marine environmental issues (Milford Haven)	The Chairman, Milford Haven Waterway Environmental Monitoring Steering Group, County Civil Protection Planning Unit, Hill House, Picton Terrace, Carmarthen, Dyfed SA31 3BS, tel: 01267 236651	Fishguard Harbour	Sealink Harbours Ltd, Fishguard Harbour, Dyfed SA64 0BU, tel. 01348 872220
		Caernarfon Harbour	Caernarfon Harbour Trust, Harbour Office, Slate Quay, Caernarfon, Gwynedd LL55 2PB, tel. 01286 2118
Oil transportation and terminals	Technical Adviser, Oil Companies International Marine Forum (OCIMF), OCIMF, 15th Floor, 96 Victoria Street, London SW1E 5JW, tel: 0171 828 7966	Holyhead Harbour	Sealink Harbours Ltd, Sealink House, Turkey Shore Road, Holyhead, Gwynedd, tel. 01407 2304
		Power generation	
Oil developments and general issues	*Projects Officer, Cardigan Bay Forum, Aberystwyth, tel: 01970 624471	Energy production general	Department of Energy, 1 Palace Street, London SW1E 5HE, tel. 0171 238 3000
as above	*Secretary, Carmarthen Bay Forum, Whitland, Dyfed, tel: 01994 419313	Energy production general	Secretary, Institute of Energy, 18 Devonshire Street, London W1N 2AU, tel. 0171 580 7124
as above	*Chairman, North Wales Coastal Forum, Pwllheli, tel. 01758 83423	Wave and hydro power	Project Director, Energy Systems Group, Department of Electrical, Electronic and Systems Engineering, Priory Street, Coventry CV1 5FB, tel. 01203 838861
Research on local issues	The Director, Field Studies Council Research Centre, Fort Popton, Angle, Pembroke, Dyfed SA71 5AD, tel: 01646 641404		
Ports, harbours and shipping lanes		Hydro, solar, tidal, wave and wind power	Business Development Manager, Energy Technology Support Unit (ETSU), Building 156, Harwell, Oxfordshire OX11 0RA, tel. 01235 43317
International Maritime Organisation	4 Albert Embankment, London SE1 7SR, tel. 0171 735 7611	Offshore wind farms	The Senior Lecturer, School of Ocean Sciences, University of Wales, Menai Bridge, Bangor, Gwynedd LL59 5EY, tel. 01248 351151
Associated British Ports; Port Talbot Harbour	Associated British Ports (Swansea), Harbour Office, Adelaide Street, Swansea, West Glamorgan SA1 1QR, tel. 01792 650855		
British Ports Association	British Ports Association, Africa House, 64-78 Kingsway, London WC2B 6AH, tel. 0171 242 1200	Wind energy- general	Chairman, British Wind Energy Associateion (BWEA), 4 Hamilton Place, London W1V 0BQ, tel. 0171 499 3515
The UK Major Ports Group Ltd	The UK Major Ports Group Ltd, 150 Holborn, London EC1N 2LR, tel. 0171 404 2008	Wind farms - general	Public Information Officer, Coastal Geology Group. British Geological Survey, Kingsey Dunham Centre, Keyworth, Nottingham NG12 5GG, tel. 01602 363100
Neath Harbour Commissioners	Bankside, The Green, Neath, tel. 01639 633486		

C. Contact names and addresses (continued)

Type of information	Contact address and telephone no.	Type of information	Contact address and telephone no.
Energy resources	Energy Officer, Welsh Development Agency, Ash Road North, Wrexham Industrial Estate, Wrexham, Clwyd LL13 9FU, tel. 01978 661011	Nuclear power (Wylfa NPS)	Public Relations Officer, Wylfa NPS, Nuclear Electric, Cemaes Bay, Anglesey, Gwynedd LL67 0DH, tel. 01407 733733
Conventional power Station	Public Relations Officer, Pembroke production/Pembroke Power Station, Pembroke, Dyfed Power SA71 5SF, tel. 01646 661011	Radioactive discharges	Information Officer, National Radiological Protection Board (NRPB), Chilton, Didcot, Oxfordshire OX11 0RQ, tel. 01235 831600
Pollution from energy production (Wales)	Her Majesty's Inspectorate of Pollution (HMIP), Public Registry, Brunel House, Cardiff CF2 1SH, tel. 01222 495558	General energy issues	*Projects Officer, Cardigan Bay Forum, Aberystwyth, tel. 01970 624471
Pollution from energy production (Wales)	Pollution Control Officer, NRA (Welsh Region), Glan Teifi, Barley Mow, Lampeter, Dyfed SA48 7BY, tel. 01570 422455	as above	*Secretary, Carmarthen Bay Forum, Whitland, Dyfed, tel. 01994 419313
		as above	*Chairman, North Wales Coastal Forum, Pwllheli, tel. 01758 83423
Pollution from conventional power production (Pembroke power station)	Pollution Control Officer, National Rivers Authority (NRA), Llys Afon, Hawthorne Rise, Haverfordwest, Dyfed SA71 2BQ, tel. 01437 760081	Nuclear issues - general	Secretary-General, British Nuclear Forum, 22 Buckingham Gate, London SW1E 6LB, tel. 0171 828 0166

* Starred contact addresses are given in full in the Appendix

8.3.6 Acknowledgements

Thanks to Colin Macduff-Duncan (Esso), for providing information and commenting on drafts.

8.4 Coastal defence

M.J. Dunbar, S.J. Everett and S.L. Fowler

8.4.1 Introduction

Coastal defence covers two types of works: coast protection and sea or flood defence. Coast protection works prevent or slow the erosion of land and encroachment by the sea, and are generally the responsibility of District Councils. Sea or flood defence works are built to protect low-lying land from flooding by high tides and are the responsibility of the National Rivers Authority, although Internal Drainage Boards and local authorities can also undertake flood defence works. Some coastal defences are owned and maintained privately or by other bodies such as the MoD. Railtrack (formerly British Rail) maintains some important stretches of coastal defence alongside railway lines.

The hard rock and rugged nature of much of the Welsh coast greatly reduces the requirement for coast protection in the region. Here such works are built mainly to protect coastal settlements, industrial areas or historic sites, and are also located alongside bridges or road and rail embankments. Sea defences in the region are built mainly in low-lying estuaries and inlets, or where natural coastal habitats such as sand dunes have been lost or damaged through man's activities. Sand dune systems are important for providing natural dynamic coastal defences (see section 3.2). Where human activities have caused erosion or dunes have been used for housing and industrial purposes, this natural form of defence is lost and artificial defences become necessary. This has occurred in the region, especially along lengths of the south and north coasts.

Flood defences are common in the region where areas of former intertidal land have been claimed from the sea for agricultural or industrial use. They usually take the form of artificial embankments bordering areas of land claim. Apart from on estuaries, there are not many areas of land claim in the region that are vulnerable to flooding. However, in some parts of the region, for example Swansea Bay, the extremely high tidal range contributes to the land's susceptibility to flooding.

Although coastal protection works are generally on a small scale compared with other parts of the UK, their impacts may be locally significant. For example, the 'Cob' embankment and road/rail bridge at Porthmadog dramatically changed the form of the Glaslyn estuary when it was built in the 19th century.

8.4.2 Important locations

The coastal defence works in the region are shown on Map 8.4.1 (adapted from undated Welsh Office map) and are found mainly on the open coast, but occasionally within estuaries and inlets. In some areas, notably around Swansea Bay, the shoreline is completely artificial for several kilometres. Several ports have large breakwaters, for example Port Talbot, Fishguard and Holyhead.

The scattered flood defence works in the region are located chiefly along the Loughor Estuary, in Carmarthen Bay, in the Dyfi, Mawddach and Glaslyn estuaries and Malltraeth Bay on Anglesey. In some of the mid-Wales estuaries the shoreline is completely artificial for several kilometres, and virtually all estuaries have been altered to some extent as a result of flood defence works, land claim, dredging or canalisation. More details on coastal defence works in estuaries may be found in Buck (1993).

The results of a recent coast protection survey by the Welsh Office are given in Table 8.4.1.

8.4.3 Information sources

The Welsh Office have compiled the results of the 1994 coast protection survey into a database. British Rail (now Railtrack) have also surveyed their coastal works.

More detailed information on flood defences can be obtained from the NRA, who carried out a sea defence

Table 8.4.1 Lengths of defended and undefended coastline in the region by district (km)

District	Coast protection	Sea defence	'Soft' natural coastline	'Hard' natural coastline	Total length of coastline
Port Talbot	9.1	0	3.6	0	12.7
Neath	3.5	0	3.0	0	6.5
Swansea	13.9	2.2	35.1	32.4	83.6
Lliw Valley	0	0	3.0	0	3.0
Llanelli	9.3	5.3	20.9	2.0	37.5
Carmarthen	3.1	4.7	18.0	7.2	32.9
S. Pembrokeshire	12.0	0.1	6.3	72.0	90.4
Preseli	12.3	1.5	8.6	145.1	167.6
Ceredigion	14.6	11.2	19.3	51.3	96.4
Meirionnydd	27.7	27.5	28.7	13.8	97.7
Dwyfor	16.4	10.0	43.6	60.5	130.5
Arfon	16.7	5.1	22.5	4.3	48.5
Anglesey	32.4	1.9	43.8	127.9	205.9
Aberconwy	23.4	2.4	17.0	8.2	51.0
Region total	*137.7*	*34.4*	*194.5*	*450.4*	*817.0*

Source: Welsh Office 1995. 'Hard' natural coastline includes sections of cliff and rocky coast; other sections are 'soft'.

Ynys Enlli–Llandudno
Coastal Group

Liverpool Bay
Coastal Group

Cardigan Bay
Coastal Group

Carmarthen Bay
Coastal Group

Swansea Bay
Coastal Group

★ Sea defence (NRA)
● Coast protection (LAs)
○ Other defences (e.g. MOD, BR)

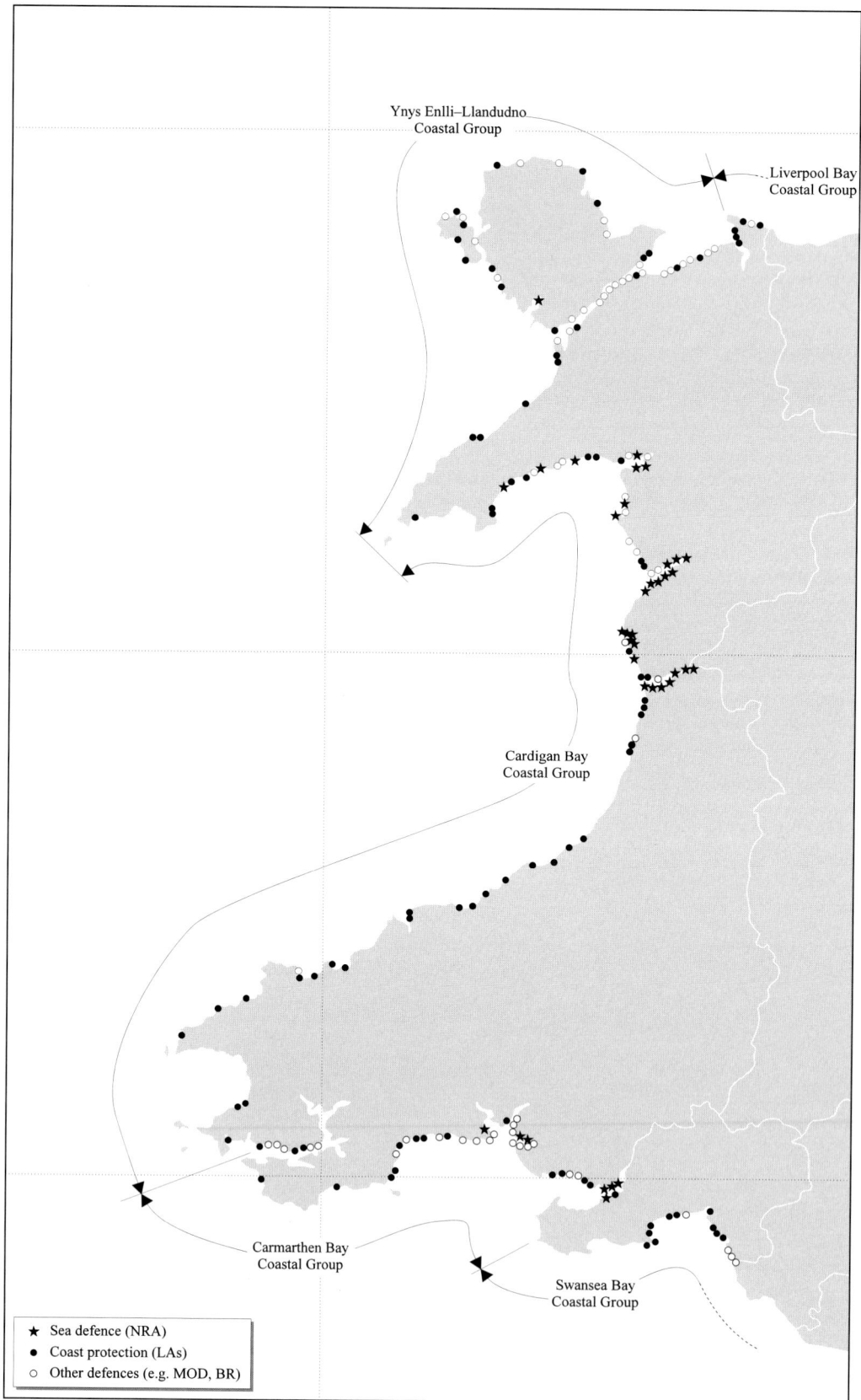

Map 8.4.1 Coastal defences and lengths of coast covered by Coastal Groups (see also section 10.3). Source: Welsh Office. © Crown copyright.

survey in 1991. The results of this are held in a proprietary database cross-referenced to maps, and may be viewed at regional NRA offices by prior arrangement. This survey includes coast protection structures in areas where wave splash-over would also cause flooding.

8.4.4 Further sources of information

A. *References cited*

Buck, A.L. 1993. *An inventory of UK estuaries. 3. South-west Britain.* Peterborough, Joint Nature Conservation Committee.

B. *Further reading*

Barber, P.C., & Thomas, R.C. 1989. Case study at Carmarthen Bay. *In: Coastal management, proceedings of ICE Conference, May 1989.* Thomas Telford.
Bullen and Partners. 1994. *Swansea Bay Sea Defence Assessment.* Bristol. Unpublished report to the NRA.
Bullen and Partners & James and Nicholas, Consulting Engineers. 1993. *Coastline response study: Worms Head to Penarth Head.* Unpublished report to local authorities group, NRA and CCW.
House of Commons. 1992. *Environment Select Committee report on coastal zone protection and planning.*
Hydraulics Research Ltd. 1991. A summary guide to the selection of coast protection works for geological Sites of Special Scientific Interest. *Nature Conservancy Council, CSD Report,* No. 1245. (Unpublished report.)
Ministry of Agriculture, Fisheries and Food. 1993. *Coastal defence and the environment: a guide to good practice.* London, MAFF.
Ministry of Agriculture, Fisheries and Food. 1993. *Coastal defence and the environment: a strategic guide for managers and decision makers in the National Rivers Authority, local authorities and other bodies with coastal responsibilities.* London, MAFF.
Ministry of Agriculture, Fisheries and Food. 1993. *Flood and coastal defence project appraisal guidance note.*
Ministry of Agriculture, Fisheries and Food/Welsh Office. *Flood and coastal defence strategy for England and Wales.*
National Rivers Authority. 1993. *NRA flood defence strategy.* London, NRA.
Rendel Geotechnics. 1995. *Coastal planning and management: a review of earth science information needs.* London, HMSO.

C. *Contact names and addresses*

Type of information	Contact address and telephone no.
Responsibility for coastal defence policies & provision of grants. Coastal defence survey database (1994).	Hugh Payne, Environment Division, Welsh Office (Y Swyddfa Gymreig), Parc Cathays, Cardiff CF1 3NQ, tel: 01222 823176
Coast protection. Power to carry out works to protect land from erosion and encroachment by the sea and to prevent the flooding of non-agricultural land.	Responsibility of Maritime District Councils (see Appendix).
Flood defence	National Rivers Authority, Welsh Region, Rivers House, Cardiff CF3 0LT, tel. 01222 770088
Co-operation between parties responsible for coastal defences, identification of research needs and promotion of strategic planning of coastal defences	Welsh Coastal Groups Forum, Welsh Office Environment Division, Parc Cathays, Cardiff CF1 3NQ
as above	Swansea Bay Coastal Group, Chairman: M E Thomas, Chief Technical Officer, Ogwr Borough Council, P.O. Box 4, Civic Offices, Angel Street, Bridgend, Mid Glamorgan CF31 1LX, tel. 01656 643643
as above	Carmarthen Bay Coastal Group, Chairman: R Paul Thomas, *Llanelli Borough Council, tel. 01554 741100
as above	Cardigan Bay Coastal Group, Chairman: Martin Wright, *Meirionnydd District Council, tel. 01341 422341
as above	Ynys Enlli to Llandudno Coastal Group, Chairman: M F Davies, National Rivers Authority, Bryn Menai, Holyhead Road, Bangor, Gwynedd LL57 2EF, tel. 01248 370970
as above	Liverpool Bay Coastal Group, Chairman: A M Rhodes, Borough Engineer, Metropolitan Borough of Wirral, Town Hall, Bebington, Wirral L63 7PT, tel. 0151 645 2080
Wildlife and landscape conservation issues and advice	*Coastal Scientist, CCW HQ, Bangor, tel: 01248 370734
Coastal Engineering Advisory Panel	Secretary: Anne-Marie Ferguson, Institute of Civil Engineers, Great George Street, London SW1P 3AA, tel. 0171 222 7722

* Starred contact addresses are given in full in the Appendix

8.4.5 Acknowledgements

Thanks to Hugh Payne (Welsh Office), the Cardigan Bay
Forum and the University of Greenwich for their kind
assistance in obtaining information for this region.

Chapter 9 Human activities

9.1 Fisheries

C.F. Robson

9.1.1 Introduction

This section gives an overview of the main fishing activities in the coastal waters and rivers of the region. There are fisheries for pelagic and demersal fish (demersal fish live on or near the sea bed; pelagic fish do not), marine shellfish species, and diadromous fish - salmon, sea trout and eels - which spend part of their lives in fresh water and part at sea. The section also covers sea angling and bait collection. For this section, West Coast figures include figures for the Isle of Man, except where stated otherwise. For more information about the species concerned, see sections 5.5, 5.7 and 5.8.

Milford Haven is now the only port with a substantial market and is the single 'major port' (as identified in MAFF (1994b) from fish landings) in the region (Map 9.1.1). Map 9.1.1 also shows the 25 other smaller ports where landings are made in the region and are recorded by the Ministry of Agriculture, Fisheries and Food (MAFF). The fishing industry is important to many sectors of the local economy but its development is limited in many areas in the region by poor road and rail links with major markets. The tonnage of shellfish and pelagic and demersal fish landed reflects this fact (see Table 9.1.1). Of all recorded landings of fish and shellfish species in GB and the Isle of Man, the proportions landed in this region are below average for regions in GB and very small compared with those for some regions, for example in Scotland. Nevertheless, the region is of major importance for certain demersal species (see section 9.1.2).

The northern and southern coasts of the region are the most important for fin fish (i.e. pelagic, demersal and diadromous species) landings, with Milford Haven in particular being an important landing centre for fish caught locally, in the Bristol Channel and to the south and west of Ireland.

Holyhead is an important landing centre for both fin fish and shellfish. In the central part of the region, from Pembroke to the Llyn Peninsula, the fishery is predominantly for a wide range of shellfish species taken by local boats close to their home base. For shellfish species such as cockles, lobster and whelk, the landing figures in the region are important in the national context.

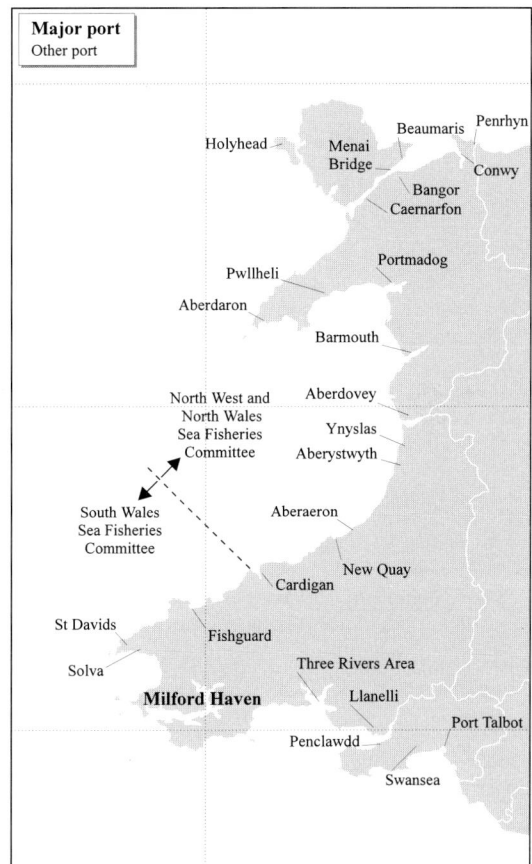

Map 9.1.1 Landing ports and coverage of the region by Sea Fisheries Committees.

Table 9.1.1 Total tonnages of pelagic and demersal fish and shellfish landed in the region in 1992

Species group totals	Tonnage landed in region	Tonnage landed in West Coast (includes Isle of Man)	Tonnage landed in England and Wales	Total tonnage landed in GB and Isle of Man	% of West Coast total landed in region	% of GB and Isle of Man total landed in region
Pelagic	28	68,029	23,809	252,339	<0.1	<0.1
Demersal	4,936	47,409	81,237	275,476	10.4	1.8
Shellfish	3,411	42,987	55,360	104,926	7.9	3.3
All groups	*8,375*	*158,425*	*160,406*	*632,741*	*5.2*	*1.3*

Sources: Scottish Office Agriculture and Fisheries Department (1993), Ministry of Agriculture, Fisheries and Food (1994a,b,c) and Isle of Man Department of Agriculture, Fisheries & Forestry. Note: Amounts landed are rounded up to the next whole tonne. Interpretation of the figures in this table is complex: refer to section 9.1.4.

Three diadromous species - salmon, sea trout and eel - support both net and rod-and-line fisheries in the region, the most important of which are for sea trout, salmon and grilse (young salmon that have spent not more than one winter at sea before maturing). Table 9.1.2 shows that the region's average recorded catch of salmon and grilse in the five years from 1989 to 1993 represents only a small proportion of the GB and West Coast averages. For sea trout the region's average recorded catch for the five years is more significant. The eel catch for 1992 for this region was approximately 1-2 tonnes (catches from both fresh and sea water combined). Most are however, caught within fresh water, though there is some fishing for eel along the coast.

Table 9.1.2 Average catch of salmon and grilse and sea trout 1989 - 1993

	Salmon and grilse	*Sea trout*
Total region	2,773	12,270
Total West Coast	58,582	37,024
Total England & Wales	67,347	76,337
Total GB	254,829	141,813
% of West Coast total in region	4.7%	33.1%
% of GB total in region	1.1%	8.7%

Source: Department of Agriculture and Fisheries (1990); National Rivers Authority (1991, 1992, 1993, 1994a & 1994b) and Scottish Office (1991, 1992, 1993 & 1994). Note: Amounts landed are rounded up to the next whole tonne. Interpretation of the figures in this table is complex: refer to section 9.1.4. The total for the 'West Coast' in this table does not include figures for the Isle of Man.

9.1.2 The fisheries

Pelagic: Seasonal fisheries for pelagic species attract a relatively small amount of effort in the region as demand is low. Mackerel are targeted in the summer and herring in the winter/early spring months, from south-west Wales as far north as Anglesey. Pelagic trawls are sometimes used to catch sprat and herring off Swansea and the Gower Peninsula, and gill nets are used to target herring off the Gower Peninsula. Table 9.1.3 gives the tonnages of pelagic species landed in the region in 1992.

Demersal: Landings of demersal fish include not only those from local inshore trawlers but also a major contribution from Spanish-owned vessels registered in Milford Haven. In addition to the major landing centre in Milford Haven, landings by local vessels are also made at Holyhead, Swansea, Caernarfon and Conwy. Demersal species are also taken by smaller inshore netters from a number of centres in south, mid and north Wales, both as prime fish for human consumption and as bait for the shellfish pot fishery. Bass are caught in the summer and autumn months by drift netters and commercial rod and line anglers.

Table 9.1.4 shows that the tonnage of demersal species landed in the region in 1992 represents only a small percentage of the total tonnage landed in GB and the Isle of Man. However, significant landings were made in the region of several demersal species such as conger eel, dogfish, hake, skates and rays and species in the 'others' category. Recent trends in demersal fisheries in the region have seen a decline in the inshore trawl fisheries, with an increase in netting activity, particularly trammel netting for flatfish and tangle netting for ray species and angler fish (see Gray 1994 for a description of the different types of fishing gear).

Shellfish: The inshore fishermen of the region exploit local populations of cockles, mussels and oysters, found in and around estuaries, and work inshore along the rocky coastline for lobsters, brown crabs and crawfish, or fish offshore for scallops and whelks. An important shellfish industry operates from Milford Haven for crustaceans, including lobster and crab, which are distributed to markets in the UK, Spain and France by merchants operating vivier (watertank) lorries. The tonnages of shellfish species landed in the region in 1992 (Table 9.1.5) represent only a small percentage of the total tonnages landed in GB and the Isle of Man. However, the totals are the highest of all the species group totals in the region, and for several species the proportions of GB totals landed in the region are significant.

Table 9.1.3 Pelagic species landing data for 1992

Species group totals	Tonnage landed in region	Tonnage landed in West Coast (includes Isle of Man)	Tonnage landed in England and Wales	Total tonnage landed in GB and Isle of Man	% of West Coast total landed in region	% of GB and Isle of Man total landed in region
Argentines	0	43	0	179	0	0
Herring	1	10,944	915	85,652	<0.1	<0.1
Horse mackerel	7	125	1,026	1,500	5.6	0.5
Mackerel	20	55,360	9,142	150,728	<0.1	<0.1
Pilchard	0	0	4,244	4,244	0	0
Sprat	0	1,554	8,478	10,033	0	0
Whitebait	0	0	1	1	0	0
Others	0	0	3	3	0	0
Total	*28*	*68,026*	*23,809*	*252,339*	*<0.1*	*<0.1*

Source: Ministry of Agriculture, Fisheries and Food (1994a,b,c); Scottish Office Agriculture and Fisheries Department (1993) and Isle of Man Department of Agriculture, Fisheries & Forestry. Note: Amounts landed are rounded up to the next whole tonne. Interpretation of the figures in this table is complex: refer to section 9.1.4.

Table 9.1.4 Demersal species landing data for 1992

Species group totals	Tonnage landed in region	Tonnage landed in West Coast (includes Isle of Man)	Tonnage landed in England and Wales	Total tonnage landed in GB and Isle of Man	% of West Coast total landed in region	% of GB and Isle of Man total landed in region
Brill	10	126	392	445	7.9	2.3
Catfish	0	39	557	1,935	0	0
Cod	477	6,084	23,530	59,525	7.8	0.8
Conger eel	68	411	403	508	16.5	13.4
Dab	5	198	456	1,214	2.5	0.4
Dogfish	1,581	5,899	3,625	13,348	26.8	11.9
Flounder	1	106	269	274	0.9	0.4
Gurnard	15	253	589	622	5.9	2.4
Haddock	14	4,365	3,706	53,587	0.3	<0.1
Hake	307	3,031	1,621	3,619	10.1	8.5
Halibut	0	28	80	196	0	0
Halibut, Greenland	0	18	117	136	0	0
Lemon sole	7	569	3,000	5,573	1.2	0.1
Ling	88	1,433	1,708	6,027	6.1	1.5
Megrim	135	2,658	1,471	4,038	5.1	3.3
Monkfish/angler	132	4,865	3,102	14,679	2.7	0.9
Plaice	189	3,138	15,970	23,887	6.0	0.8
Pollack (lythe)	45	1,102	1,734	3,022	4.1	1.5
Redfish	P	56	581	774	-	-
Saithe	44	1,570	2,284	12,600	2.8	0.3
Sand eels	0	0	0	4,152	0	0
Skates and rays	941	4,011	4,142	7,827	23.5	12.0
Sole	82	855	2,812	2,875	9.6	2.9
Torsk (tusk)	P	42	13	209	-	-
Turbot	11	181	545	743	6.1	1.5
Whiting	191	4,322	5,088	41,055	4.4	0.5
Whiting, blue	0	0	0	6,531	0	0
Witch	5	576	192	1,980	0.9	0.3
Others	588	1,415	3,151	3,835	41.6	15.3
Fish roe	0	48	99	244	0	0
*Total**	*4,936*	*47,409*	*81,237*	*275,476*	*10.4*	*1.8*

Source: Ministry of Agriculture, Fisheries and Food (1994a,b,c); Scottish Office Agriculture and Fisheries Department (1993) and Isle of Man Department of Agriculture, Fisheries & Forestry. Key: P = species landed in the region in small quantities (here <0.5 tonnes); - = % not calculated; * = total values include figures for all species landed, including those given as P. Note: Amounts landed are rounded up to the next whole tonne. Interpretation of the figures in this table is complex: refer to section 9.1.4.

Table 9.1.5 Shellfish species landing data in the region for 1992

Species group totals	Tonnage landed in region	Tonnage landed in West Coast (includes Isle of Man)	Tonnage landed in England and Wales	Total tonnage landed in GB and Isle of Man	% of West Coast total landed in region	% of GB and Isle of Man total landed in region
Cockles	1,853	5,848	29,501	32,047	5.8	31.7
Crabs	640	7,853	9,453	16,971	3.8	8.2
Lobsters	67	447	504	1,073	6.3	15.0
Mussels	309	1,690	3,488	6,555	4.7	18.3
Nephrops	30	11,257	1,918	19,627	0.2	0.3
Periwinkles	0	1,592	70	1,908	0	0
Queen scallops	141	9,066	2,989	11,272	1.7	1.6
Scallops	99	3,771	2,589	8,291	1.3	2.6
Shrimps	P	128	563	743	-	-
Squids	17	623	919	2,007	0.9	2.7
Whelks	230	488	1,535	2,393	9.6	47.1
Others	25	207	1,831	2,026	1.2	12.1
*Total**	*3,411*	*42,987*	*55,360*	*104,926*	*3.4*	*7.9*

Source: Ministry of Agriculture, Fisheries and Food (1994a,b,c); Scottish Office Agriculture and Fisheries Department (1993) and Isle of Man Department of Agriculture, Fisheries & Forestry. Key: P = species landed in the region in small quantities (here <0.5 tonnes); - = % not calculated; * = total values include figures for all species landed, including those given as P. Note: Amounts landed are rounded up to the next whole tonne. Interpretation of the figures in this table is complex: refer to section 9.1.4.

Table 9.1.6 presents the tonnages of certain shellfish species landed to some of the ports in the region in 1992.

Table 9.1.6	Tonnages of selected shellfish species landed in 1992 to ports/areas within the jurisdiction of the South Wales Sea Fisheries Committee (SWSFC)	
Species	*Port/landing area*	*Tonnes*
Mussels	Three Rivers	13
Cockles	Burry Inlet	1,827
	Three Rivers	238
Lobster	Swansea	6
	Burry Inlet	<1
	South Pembrokeshire	7
	Milford Haven and surrounds	23
	North Pembrokeshire	16
Crawfish	South Pembrokeshire	<1
	Milford Haven and surrounds	11
	North Pembrokeshire	<1
Edible crab	Swansea	5
	Burry Inlet	<1
	South Pembrokeshire	18
	Milford Haven and surrounds	199
	North Pembrokeshire	241
Spider crab	Swansea	1
	Burry Inlet	<1
	South Pembrokeshire	12
	Milford Haven and surrounds	98
	North Pembrokeshire	14

Source: SWSFC. Note: 'Swansea' includes vessels fishing from Porthcawl. 'South Pembrokeshire' includes Saundersfoot, Tenby and Freshwater East; 'north Pembrokeshire' includes Solva, Porthclais, Abereiddy, Porthgain, Abercastle, Fishguard and Newport and includes vessels fishing from Port of Cardigan. Amounts landed are rounded up to the next whole tonne. Interpretation of the figures in this table is complex: refer to section 9.1.4. Figures often vary markedly from year to year. Information was not available for ports in the north of the region (see section 9.1.3).

The flat or native oyster is exploited by dredging under permit from the South Wales Sea Fisheries Committee (SWSFC) as an occasional natural fishery in Milford Haven. The fishery is permitted for a limited period of approximately six weeks commencing in November. The annual production of the native oyster in Milford Haven in 1992 (contained in the shellfish 'others' category in Table 9.1.5) was approximately 10.2 tonnes (SWSFC pers. comm.). Although a small quantity, this is about 2% of the GB total of approximately 500 tonnes (Shellfish Association of GB, pers. comm.).

There is a growing fishery for mussels at Conwy (where there is a Regulating Order - see section 9.1.3 and Table 9.1.8) and in the Menai Strait (where there is a Several Order - see section 9.1.3 - and yield is enhanced using husbandry techniques - see section 9.2.2). Mussels are collected increasingly in the Burry Inlet area and the Three Rivers area. There is a fishery for mussels near Swansea and in a number of estuaries such as the Dyfi and Mawddach.

The fishery for cockles is important in the Burry Inlet, where there is a Regulating Order (see section 9.1.3 and Table 9.1.8). Cockles are also periodically important to the fishery in the Three Rivers area, the Dyfi and Dwyryd estuaries and at Traeth Lafan. Landing totals for cockles fluctuate from year to year, but in 1993 over 7,500 tonnes of cockles were landed from the combined area of Burry Inlet and the Three Rivers alone and 1,100 tonnes were landed from Traeth Lafan. At

Traeth Lafan in recent years (1989, 1990 and 1993) the North Wales and North Western Sea Fisheries Committee (NW & NWSFC) have issued authorisation for a limited period of three months for vessel-borne suction dredging over varying areas. Landings from Traeth Lafan are recorded by NW & NWSFC only for these authorised operations: no authorisation was issued in 1991, 1992 and 1994. A smaller, unrecorded, amount of cockles is also taken in the area by hand gatherers.

Whelks are caught using pots twelve miles or further offshore in the northern part of Cardigan Bay and off the north of Anglesey. Scallops are dredged mainly north of Pembrokeshire.

The lobster fishery operates mostly from late spring to early autumn, from most ports in the region. Most lobsters are taken by potting from small inshore vessels, the scale of operations ranging from part-time fishermen with only a few pots to professional operators using up to 800 - 1,000 pots. Lobster fishing effort in Cardigan Bay, although greatest close inshore, can extend twelve miles or further offshore. Crawfish are taken between Govan and Strumble Heads by potting and tangle netting, and also around Ynys Enlli by tangle netters and occasionally by commercial divers.

Edible crabs are caught throughout the region, and an important autumn fishery for this species exists between Fishguard and Cardigan. Spider crabs are landed at and around Milford Haven and also around north Pembrokeshire, with smaller amounts landed in south Pembrokeshire and Swansea.

Other species fished in the region include pink prawns, caught by potters operating from Pembroke and Cardigan Bay, and there is a developing fishery for velvet swimming crabs in the south of the region. Green (or shore) crabs have been fished commercially in Milford Haven and the Menai Strait. Squid are present off the east of Gower and are fished in September and October. Periwinkles are exploited when situated in dense aggregations on accessible shores. Razor shells are also exploited locally around Milford Haven.

Diadromous fish: Table 9.1.7 lists the locations in the region (shown on Map 5.8.1) from which salmon, grilse and sea trout catches have been recorded, details the catch methods used and gives five-year average catch statistics for 1989-1993. Note that rods are used mainly by game fishermen; rod angling is the most widespread method of catching in the region. On fourteen estuaries from the Three Rivers area north to the Conwy a variety of nets are used, and most of the region's catch is from rivers where nets are used in addition to rods. Coracles remain in use by fishermen on several estuaries in the region, including the Tywi, Taf and Teifi. The overall salmon and grilse catch is highest on the Tywi and Teifi, with large catches also on the Conwy, Ogwen, Mawddach and Dyfi. Large catches of sea trout are more widespread but again are largest on the Tywi. Eels are exploited from the time they enter fresh water as elvers, during their stay in fresh and estuarine water and as they migrate to sea as silver eels. The main areas of exploitation of eels in the region are in the lakes of North Wales.

Sea angling: Sea angling has three main forms: angling from the shore, inshore fishing within about 5 km of the shore and deep sea fishing. It is distinguished from two other types of sport fishing: game fishing, for salmon, sea trout, brown and rainbow trout (the first two are discussed above), and coarse fishing (for freshwater fish species - not covered here). Sea angling is a popular and widespread pastime in the region and is practised by over two million people in Great Britain

Table 9.1.7 Methods used to catch salmon, grilse and sea trout in 1993 for each river/fishery in the region and the five-year average (1989 - 1993) of catch (as numbers of fish reported to NRA)

River/fishery	Method used in 1993, and no. of net licences issued for salmon & grilse	Five year average (1989 - 1993) for salmon & grilse	Five year average (1989 - 1993) for sea trout
Afan	rod	5	138
Neath	rod	12	152
Tawe	rod	45	281
Loughor	rod	7	133
Gwendraeth	rod	0	105
Tywi	rod, seine (7) & coracle (10) nets	550	725
Taf	rod, coracle (1) & wade (1) nets	48	175
SW Coastal	wade (11) nets	17	85
E+W Cleddau	rod, compass nets (8)	68	549
Nevern	rod, seine nets (1)	29	304
Teifi	rod, seine (3) & coracle (10) nets	530	518
Aeron	rod	5	356
Ystwyth	rod	8	111
Rheidol	rod	35	175
Dyfi	rod, seine nets (2)	258	409
Dysynni	rod, seine net (1)	25	343
Mawddach	rod, seine nets (2)	201	384
Artro	rod	5	73
Dwyryd	rod	20	132
Glaslyn	rod, seine net (2)	62	482
Dwyfawr	rod, seine nets (2)	83	549
Llyfni	rod	14	93
Gwyrfai	rod	4	5
Seiont	rod	47	88
Seiont/Gwyrfai	seine nets (1)	139	75
N.Anglesey	last year 1990	0	3
Ogwen	rod, seine nets (1)	200	89
Conwy	rod, seine nets (4) & basket trap (1)	356	218
Total region	*68**	*2,773*	*12,270*
Total England & Wales	*780**	*67,347*	*76,337*

Source: Department of Agriculture and Fisheries (1990); National Rivers Authority (1991, 1992, 1993, 1994a & 1994b) and Scottish Office (1991, 1992, 1993 & 1994). Key: * = total number of licences issued (net methods). Note: interpretation of the figures in this table is complex: refer to section 9.1.4. The total for the 'West Coast' in this table does not include figures for the Isle of Man. 'Sea trout' here includes all migratory trout. 'Nets' are defined as instruments other than rod and line. Rivers with very small recorded catches have been excluded from this table, so the distribution of the fishing methods may be more widespread than appears here. Map 5.8.1 shows the locations of rivers in this table.

(Fowler 1992). The governing body of sea angling in the region, the Welsh Federation of Sea Anglers, has approximately 62 affiliated clubs with approximately 4,000 individual members, many in this region.

Bait collection: Many sea anglers normally collect their own live bait locally, and this activity occurs in many areas in the region, although some areas are targeted more than others and may attract commercial collectors, who travel in teams to suitable shores. Many species are collected in this region, mainly by digging and boulder turning, including ragworm, lugworm, peeler crabs (moulting shore crabs), mussels, cockles, limpets and razor shells. Different bait species are collected according to the fish being targeted as well as the location and time of year. Baitdigging, especially for lugworms, is carried out over the lower part of muddy and sandy shores around the time of low water. Fowler (1992) identified that the exploitation of bait species was taking place in the region at locations in south Wales, e.g. Milford Haven, Pendine Beach, along the South Gower coast, Swansea Bay and at Penclawdd in the Burry inlet. Occasional small-scale digging also occurs in the Dyfi and Dwyryd estuaries and at Morfa Harlech. In north Wales, areas such as Holy Island, Red Wharf Bay and the Menai Strait experience larger numbers of diggers.

9.1.3 Management and issues

Responsibility for the management of fisheries in coastal waters, extending from low water mark, rests with the Commission for the European Union, who delegate it to member states under the Common Fisheries Policy. This policy seeks to manage stocks of fish in EU waters on a biological basis (MAFF 1994b) by setting agreed annual Total Allowable Catches (TACs) for particular stocks. The Common Fisheries Policy came into effect in 1983 and was subject to a mid-term review in 1993, with a full review planned for 2002. Under the Common Fisheries Policy, fishing in this region is restricted to national boats in an area of up to 12 nautical miles from the coast, in order to protect the interests of local fishermen. Outside this 12 mile limit, all European Union member countries have equal access to the Exclusive Fishing Zone, whereas under European, national and local byelaw legislation, non-member countries are only allowed to fish by agreement. The coastal waters of the region are part of the 'Irish box', which has historically excluded Spanish vessels. However, as of 1 January 1996 Spanish vessels will be allowed access (MAFF 1994c).

For the purpose of stock management, the UK coastal waters have been designated by the International Council for the Exploration of the Sea (ICES) into statistical areas. The coastal seas around this region are part of three 'divisions': VIIa (Irish Sea), VIIf (Bristol Channel) and VIIg (East Celtic Sea). ICES provides scientific advice on the management of all the important commercial species of fin fish and some shellfish stocks in all areas of the north-east Atlantic. This work is summarised in the annual report of the Advisory Committee on Fishery Management, which is responsible for providing scientific advice on TACs and other conservation measures. The TACs and catch quotas themselves are decided by the European Council of Ministers on the basis of this advice, and having taken socio-economic considerations into account. The TACs, UK quotas and 'uptake' for 1991 and 1992 for each species in the three ICES statistical divisions in the region are given in MAFF (1994b). Further restrictions applying in the region, on minimum landing sizes, annual quotas and mesh sizes for the important pelagic and demersal species, are listed in Tables 5.7.1 and 5.7.2.

In this region the North Wales and North Western Sea Fisheries Committee (NW & NWSFC) and the South Wales Sea Fisheries Committee (SWSFC) manage the inshore fisheries from the high water mark out to 6 nautical miles (3 nautical miles until October 1993) offshore from the UK baselines (as defined by the Territorial Water Order in Council 1964). The boundary between these two Sea Fisheries Committees (SFCs) lies between the Districts of Preseli Pembrokeshire and Ceredigion (Map 9.1.1). The Welsh Region of the National Rivers Authority (NRA) has joint responsibility with the Sea Fisheries Committees (SFCs) for the fishery for diadromous fish in coastal waters in the region.

There are two Regulating Orders in this region (in the Burry Inlet and the Conwy estuary - Table 9.1.8), covering around 5,300 ha, out of eight (covering 94,584 ha) in GB, as at July 1994. Regulating Orders are granted in Wales by the Welsh Office to a responsible body to enable it to regulate the natural fishery. The specified shellfish may be taken only in accordance with the terms of the order and any regulations made under it.

The SWSFC operates a crustacean authorisation scheme for the commercial exploitation of lobster, crawfish, edible and spider crabs. The NW & NWSFC operated a similar scheme in 1992, but only for lobster in the Aberystwyth area. SWSFC also operate an authorisation scheme for cockles in the Burry Inlet (where most of the south Wales cockles are taken), under their Regulating Order. 47 permits were issued in 1992. These measures prohibit the unauthorised collection of the species concerned and limit the authorised catch.

MAFF's Directorate of Fisheries Research (DFR) Laboratory at Lowestoft is responsible for collecting and collating information on fish stocks exploited by UK vessels. The MAFF DFR Fisheries Laboratory at Conwy is the

Directorate's centre for assessing the implications of non-fisheries activities and coastal zone usage on fish stocks and fisheries. MAFF DFR databases are described in Flatman (1993). Local MAFF fishery officers based in Milford Haven deal with quota management, enforcement of UK and EU fisheries legislation and licensing of fishing vessels.

Issues relating to the fisheries for pelagic, demersal and shellfish species and sea angling and bait collection are closely linked to wildlife conservation in several ways. Issues include the effects on target species as major components in marine ecosystems, the changed availability of food for predators, the effects on non-target fish species (due to multi-species fisheries, especially those directed at demersal species), and effects on species and habitats of nature conservation interest. These issues are under consideration by the 'Marine Fisheries Task Force', an inter-agency team of the statutory nature conservation organisations (the Countryside Council for Wales, English Nature, Scottish Natural Heritage and the Department of the Environment (Northern Ireland), together with the JNCC). A consultation draft paper prepared by the group, entitled *Developing an action programme for sea fisheries and wildlife* (Marine Fisheries Task Force 1994), identifies the main areas where marine fisheries (broadly defined to encompass the exploitation of all living marine resources) affect wildlife and identifies any action needed.

Further information relating to fisheries issues is given in sections 5.5.3, 5.7.3, 5.8.3 and 9.2.3.

9.1.4 Information sources used and their interpretation

Inshore fisheries review of England, Scotland and Wales, 1992/1993 (Gray 1994) has been used extensively in compiling this section. It gives details of the numbers of boats operating from ports in the region, the amount of fishing effort involved by various methods and which species or species groups are targeted during the different seasons. Figures given in Tables 9.1.1 and 9.1.3 - 9.1.5 come from three sources and the method of their adaptation is described below.

Pelagic, demersal and shellfish: Statistics given here are for landings recorded in the region, not estimated catches made in the region. Some fish caught in the region may not be landed in the region's ports or even in the UK; other fish are landed in the region but are caught outside it; and until 1993, boats under 10 m were not obliged to register their landings. The tonnages of various pelagic, demersal and shellfish species (fresh and frozen) landed at the major ports in England and Wales by UK vessels come from *UK sea fisheries statistics for 1991 and 1992* (MAFF 1994b): this applies to Milford Haven, the single 'major port' in the region. A total for

Table 9.1.8 Regulating Orders in the region

Title	Species	Grid ref.	Location	Grantee	Approx. area (ha)	Expiry date
Burry Inlet Cockle Fishery Order 1965	Cockles	SS449968 to SS436998; and SS560980 to SS564978	Llanelli,Dyfed, W. Glamorgan	SWSFC	4,528	2025
Conwy Mussel Fishery Order 1912	Mussels	SH763801	Gwynedd	NW & NWSFC	777	2008

Source: MAFF (1994a) and Grantees. Note: Several Orders are listed in Table 9.2.2.

the 'other' smaller ports (see Map 9.1.1), was provided by the MAFF Fisheries Statistics Unit. These data have been combined to give the 'tonnage landed in region' column in Tables 9.1.1, 9.1.3, 9.1.4 and 9.1.5. The 'tonnage landed in England and Wales' column was obtained by adding together all of the MAFF data for England and Wales, and the 'total tonnage landed in GB and Isle of Man' column was obtained by combining MAFF, SOAFD and Isle of Man data. Because MAFF and SOAFD do not use the same categories, fish landings in some of their categories have been added to the 'others' columns in the tables in this section. Also, SOAFD publish the weight of fish as 'standard landed weight' (gutted fish with head on), whereas MAFF publish them as 'nominal live weight' (whole fish). These two are the same for pelagic and shellfish species, but converted data from SOAFD were used for all demersal species, apart from sandeels (which are not gutted), so that all the data presented are in 'nominal live weight'. The 'total landed in West Coast' column was calculated by adding together all the landings data for the six regions in the GB West Coast and the Isle of Man.

A specialist subset of the electronic mapping system UKDMAP (see 'Core reading list' - section A3 in the Appendix), called SHELLMAP, is being prepared by the MAFF Shellfish Division in Weymouth, to meet the requirements of the EC shellfish harvesting and hygiene directives (section 9.2.3; see also Ramster *et al.* in press). The software includes charts of all coastal areas (principally estuaries) which support known molluscan shellfisheries, showing all details of the production areas and their classification.

Diadromous: NRA reported catches for salmon, grilse and sea trout vary in accuracy from year to year, as they represent only declared catches by individuals with a net or rod and line licence; in addition, catches themselves fluctuate, and so the relationship between catch and stock is not straightforward. Further, in 1992, changes to the catch recording system may have resulted in a reduced level of recording: there is evidence to suggest that catches were higher than shown in Table 9.1.7. Therefore the figures given in Table 9.1.7 should be used only as an indication of the pattern of the catch in the region. The annual NRA *Salmonid and freshwater statistics for England and Wales* (National Rivers Authority 1991, 1992, 1993, 1994a & 1994 b) contain more detailed information.

Bait collection: Information on bait collection comes from a survey around the coast of Britain in 1985 (Fowler 1992). A survey of bait digging was carried out in 1993 around Milford Haven by Palmer (1993), in conjunction with the Milford Port Health Authority and the Field Studies Council Research Centre (Milford Haven Waterway Environmental Monitoring Steering Group 1994).

9.1.5 Further sources of information

A. *References cited*

Department of Agriculture and Fisheries. 1990. *Scottish salmon and sea trout catches: 1989.* (DAFS Statistical Bulletin 1/90.)

Fowler, S.L. 1992. Survey of bait collection in Britain. *JNCC Report,* No.17.

Gray, M. 1994. *Inshore fisheries review of England, Scotland and Wales, 1992/1993.* World -Wide Fund for Nature, Godalming.

Marine Fisheries Task Force. 1994. *Developing an action programme for sea fisheries and wildlife.* Peterborough, JNCC. (Draft consultation paper by the Marine Fisheries Task Group.)

Milford Haven Waterway Environmental Monitoring Steering Group. 1994. *Report of the Milford Haven Waterway Environmental Monitoring Steering Group.* Civil Protection Planning Unit, Dyfed County Council (unpublished report).

Ministry of Agriculture, Fisheries and Food. 1994a. *List of Orders in England and Wales.* MAFF (unpublished).

Ministry of Agriculture, Fisheries and Food. 1994b. *UK sea fisheries statistics 1991 and 1992.* London, HMSO.

Ministry of Agriculture, Fisheries and Food. 1994c. *Spanish fishermen to be controlled in Irish Box.* London (News Release 22 December 1994).

National Rivers Authority. 1991. *Salmonid and freshwater fisheries statistics for England and Wales, 1989.* Almondsbury, NRA.

National Rivers Authority. 1992. *Salmonid and freshwater fisheries statistics for England and Wales, 1990.* Almondsbury, NRA.

National Rivers Authority. 1993. *Salmonid and freshwater fisheries statistics for England and Wales, 1991.* Almondsbury, NRA.

National Rivers Authority. 1994a. *Salmonid and freshwater fisheries statistics for England and Wales, 1992.* London, HMSO & NRA.

National Rivers Authority. 1994b. *Salmonid and freshwater fisheries statistics for England and Wales, 1993.* London, HMSO & NRA.

Palmer, T. 1993. *Bait digging in Milford Haven.* Bangor, University College of North Wales MSc thesis.

Ramster, J.W., Tabor, A.R., Lockwood, S.J., & Sheehan R. In press. Access to coastal zone information: a possible common approach for the UK. *In: Proceedings of the conference on management techniques in the coastal zone, University of Portsmouth: October 24-25 1994.* Portsmouth, University of Portsmouth.

Scottish Office Agriculture and Fisheries Department. 1993. *Scottish sea fisheries statistical tables 1992.* Edinburgh, Scottish Office.

Scottish Office. 1991. *Scottish salmon and sea trout catches: 1990.* Edinburgh, Scottish Office. (Scottish Office Statistical Bulletin, Fisheries Series.)

Scottish Office. 1992. *Scottish salmon and sea trout catches: 1991.* Edinburgh, Scottish Office. (Scottish Office Statistical Bulletin, Fisheries Series No. Fis/1992/1.)

Scottish Office. 1993. *Scottish salmon and sea trout catches: 1992.* Edinburgh, Scottish Office. (Scottish Office Statistical Bulletin, Fisheries Series No. Fis/1993/1.)

Scottish Office. 1994. *Scottish salmon and sea trout catches: 1993.* Edinburgh, Scottish Office. (Scottish Office Statistical Bulletin, Fisheries Series No. Fis/1994/1.)

B. *Further reading*

Bergman, M.J.N, Fonds, M., Hup, W., & Uyl, D. den. 1990. Direct effects of beam trawling fishing on benthic fauna. *In: Effects of beam trawl fishery on the bottom fauna in the North Sea. Beleidgericht Ecologisch Onderzoek Norddzee - Wadenzee. Rapport, 8:* 33 - 57.

Boon, M.J. 1992. *Landings into England and Wales from the UK demersal fisheries of the Irish Sea and Western Approaches, 1979 - 1990.* Lowestoft, MAFF Directorate of Fisheries Research. (Fisheries Research Data Report No. 26.)

Bullimore, B. 1985. *An investigation into the effects of scallop dredging within the Skomer Marine Reserve.* A report to the Nature Conservancy Council from the Skomer Marine Reserve Subtidal Monitoring Project.

Fowler, S.L. 1989. *Nature conservation implications of damage to the seabed by commercial fishing operations.* Peterborough, Nature Conservancy Council (unpublished report).

Flatman, S. 1993. MAFF Fisheries Databases. *In: The Irish Sea: an environmental review. Part five.* Liverpool University Press.

Franklin, A. Pickett, G.D., & Connor, P.M. 1980. *The scallop and its fishery in England and Wales.* Lowestoft, MAFF Directorate of Fisheries Research. (MAFF Laboratory Leaflet No. 51.)

Huggett, D. 1992. *Foreshore fishing for shellfish and bait.* Sandy, Royal Society for the Protection of Birds.

Irish Sea Forum/Marine Forum. 1993. *Managing marine fisheries: a case study of the Irish Sea. Joint Seminar Report, Liverpool, 16/17 September 1993.* Liverpool University Press.

Kaiser, M.J., & Spencer, B.E. 1993. *A preliminary assessment of the immediate effects of beam trawling on a benthic community in the Irish Sea.* Copenhagen, Denmark, International Council for the Exploration of the Sea (ICES).

Lucas, M.C., Diack, I.,& Laird, L. 1991. *Interactions between fisheries and the environment. Proceedings of the Institute of Fisheries Management 22nd Annual study course, 10-12th September 1991.* University of Aberdeen.

Lutchman, I. 1992. *A general overview of European and UK fisheries.* WWF International.

Ministry of Agriculture, Fisheries and Food. 1992. *Directorate of Fisheries Research, Fisheries Laboratory, Conwy: Handout 4.* MAFF, Lowestoft.

Mason, J. 1987. *Scallop and queen fisheries in the British Isles.* Farnham, Fishing News Books for Buckland Foundation.

Norton, T.A., & Geffen, A.J. 1990. *Exploitable living resources. The Irish Sea: an environmental review. Part three.* Liverpool University Press.

Pawson, M.G., & Rogers, S.I. 1989. *The coastal fisheries of England and Wales. Part ii: A review of their status in 1988.* Lowestoft, MAFF Directorate of Fisheries Research. (Internal Report No.19.)

C. Contact names and addresses

Type of information	Contact address and telephone no.
Central contact for the local Sea Fisheries Committees and advice on general policy issues	Chief Executive, Association of Sea Fisheries Committees, Buckrose House, Commercial Street, Norton, Malton, North Yorkshire YO17 9HX, tel: 01653 698219
Affiliated angling clubs	Secretary, Welsh Federation of Sea Anglers, 46 Lydstep Crescent, Gabalf, Cardiff CF4 2RA, tel: 01222 621795
Scientific advice on the management of the most important fish and shellfish stocks. Leaflets and publications list.	General Secretary, International Council for the Exploration of the Sea (ICES), Palaegade 2 -4, DK-1261 Copenhagen K, Denmark, tel: (+45) 33157092
Assessment of implications of non-fisheries activities and coast usage on fish stocks and fisheries; advice to assist with management and policy decisions for the coastal zone	Head of Laboratory, MAFF Directorate of Fisheries Research, Fisheries Laboratory, Benarth Road, Conwy, Gwynedd LL32 8UB, tel: 01492 593883
Fish stocks exploited by UK vessels; assessment and advice on their conservation. MAFF Publications leaflet.	Director, MAFF Directorate of Fisheries Research, Fisheries Laboratory, Pakefield Road, Lowestoft, Suffolk NR33 OHT, tel: 01502 562244.
Additional statistics other than in publications (available from HMSO)	MAFF Fisheries Statistics Unit, Nobel House, 17 Smith Square, London SW1P 3JR, tel: 0171 238 6000
Local fisheries information, quota management, licensing of fishing vessels and enforcement and advice on UK and EC legislation	District Inspector, MAFF Sea Fisheries Inspectorate, Fisheries Office, 5 Hamilton Terrace, Milford Haven, Dyfed SA73 2AL, tel: 01646 693412
Bivalve molusc production areas, the classification of shellfish waters and shellfish diseases; preparation of SHELLMAP (a subset of UKDMAP)	Director, MAFF Shellfish Division, Fish Diseases Laboratory, Barrack Road, The Nothe, Weymouth, Dorset DT4 8UB, tel: 01305 206600
Local inshore fisheries information and advice on byelaws, National and EC legislation	Clerk and Chief Fisheries Officer, North Wales and North Western Sea Fisheries Committee (NW & NWSFC), University of Lancaster, Bailrigg, Lancaster, Lancashire LA1 4XY, tel: 01524 68745
Local inshore fisheries information and advice on byelaws, National and EC legislation	Director, South Wales Sea Fisheries Committee (SWSFC), Queens Buildings, Cambrian Place, Swansea, West Glamorgan SA1 1TW, tel: 01792 654466
Details of planned projects and national NRA fisheries policy; salmonid and freshwater statistics for England and Wales.	*NRA Head Office - Fisheries Department, Bristol, tel: 01454 624400
Regional information and advice on diadromous fisheries; salmonid and freshwater statistics for Wales	*Regional Fisheries Officer, NRA Welsh Region, Cardiff, tel: 01222 770088

C. Contact names and addresses (continued)

Type of information	Contact address and telephone no.
Commercial advice on fin fish	Technical Director, Sea Fish Industry Authority, Seafish Technology Division, Sea Fish House, St Andrew's Dock, Hull, North Humberside HU3 4QE, tel: 01482 27837
Publications and shellfish production information	Director, Shellfish Association of the UK, Fishmongers Hall, London Bridge, London EC4R 9EL, tel: 0171 6263531
Administration of fisheries and mariculture in Wales	Welsh Office Agriculture Department, Fisheries Department, Division 2B, New Crown Buildings, Cathays Park, Cardiff CF1 3NQ, tel: 01222 823567.
Game fishing	Director, Salmon and Trout Association, Fishmongers Hall, London Bridge, London EC4R 9EL, tel. 0171 2835 838
Monitoring studies and reports produced for Milford Haven	Trevor D. Lloyd, Milford Haven Waterway Environmental Monitoring Steering Group, Civil Protection Planning Unit, Dyfed County Council, Hill House, Picton Terrace, Carmarthen, Dyfed SA31 3BS, tel. 01267 236651
Fisheries Task Group paper and advice on interaction between fisheries and non-fisheries conservation issues	*Marine Advisory Officer, JNCC Peterborough, tel. 01733 62626
Information and advice on interaction between fisheries and non-fisheries conservation issues in the Skomer Marine Nature Reserve	*Marine Conservation Officer, CCW Skomer, Haverfordwest, tel. 01646 636736
Information and advice on interaction between fisheries and non-fisheries conservation issues in Wales	*Marine and Coastal Section, CCW HQ, Bangor, tel. 01248 370444
Information and advice on interaction between fisheries and non-fisheries conservation issues	*Marine Policy Officer, RSPB HQ, Sandy, Beds., tel. 01767 680551
Information and advice on interaction between fisheries and non-fisheries conservation issues	*Fisheries Officer, WWF-UK, Godalming, tel. 01483 426444
Information and advice on interaction between fisheries and non-fisheries conservation issues	*Conservation Officer, Marine Conservation Society, Ross-on-Wye, tel. 01989 566917
Information and advice on interaction between fisheries and non-fisheries conservation issues in Cardigan Bay	*Projects Officer, Cardigan Bay Forum, Aberystwyth, tel. 01970 624471
Information on fisheries and non-fisheries conservation issues in the Irish Sea Study Group area	*Chairman, Irish Sea Forum, University of Liverpool, tel. 0151 794 4089
Information and advice on interaction between fisheries and non-fisheries conservation issues	Administrator, The Marine Forum for Environmental Issues, Department of Zoology, The Natural History Museum, Cromwell Road, London SW7 5BD, tel. 0171 938 9114

* Starred contact addresses are given in full in the Appendix

9.1.6 Acknowledgements

The author thanks the following members of the 'Fisheries Working Group' for their contributions and comments: Stephen Lockwood (MAFF DFR), Mike Pawson (MAFF DFR), Miran Aprahamian (NRA North-West Region), Bill Cook (NW & NWSFC), Phil Coates (SWSFC), Russell Bradley (Association of SFCs), Paul Knapman (English Nature), Blaise Bullimore (Countryside Council for Wales), Indrani Lutchman (WWF UK), Clare Eno (JNCC), Mark Tasker (JNCC) and Nancy Harrison (RSPB). Martin Dufty (MAFF Statistics Unit), Derek Murison (SOAFD Marine Laboratory), Dave Dunkely (SOAFD Montrose Field Station) and Terry Holt (Port Erin, Isle of Man) have also provided information. Catherine Smith, Rob Keddie and Jenni Mitchell (JNCC) helped to compile the tables and map, and thanks are due to the many other individuals who have commented on drafts.

9.2 Mariculture

C.F. Robson

9.2.1 Introduction

Mariculture is the cultivation of marine species in coastal waters. In Region 12 only shellfish are cultivated. This activity is concentrated in the Menai Strait and Milford Haven, with significant production also in the Conwy Estuary, the Inland Sea and Burry Inlet (see section 5.5 for a description of the distribution of exploited species). The potential for rearing scallops is being explored in Milford Haven, where there is also the potential for cultivating fish species such as salmon and rainbow trout (see section 9.2.2 and 5.8).

9.2.2 Locations and species

The locations of commercial mariculture areas in the region and the species that are cultivated are presented on Map 9.2.1. Table 9.2.1 lists the main native and non-native species that are under commercial cultivation in the region and in Great Britain and the Isle of Man.

Table 9.2.1 Main species cultivated in the region and in GB and Isle of Man

	Native or non-native	Cultivated in region?
Salmonids		
Atlantic salmon *Salmo salar*	Native	
Rainbow trout *Oncorhynchus mykiss*	Non-native	
Non-salmonids		
Turbot *Psetta maxima*	Native	
Halibut *Hippoglossus hippoglossus*	Native	
Shellfish: bivalve molluscs		
Common mussel *Mytilus edulis*	Native	√
Pacific oyster *Crassostrea gigas*	Non-native	√
Native oyster *Ostrea edulis*	Native	
Hard-shelled clam *Mercenaria mercenaria*	Non-native	√
Manila clam *Tapes philippinarum*	Non-native	√
Palourde *Tapes decussatus*	Native	√
Scallop/queen scallop *Pecten maximus/Chlamys opercularis*	Native	
Polychaetes		
King ragworm *Nereis virens*	Native	

Salmonids: Although there is currently no cultivation of salmonids in this region, the potential of Milford Haven as a site has been established: the 'Warrior' fish farm, with 36 cages, is capable of producing an estimated 300 tonnes of sea trout and rainbow trout a year, but has not been stocked since 1989. A salmon farm based at Cosherton Trot in Milford Haven closed in 1990.

Shellfish: Mussels are cultivated on sub-tidal ground lays ('relaying') in the Burry Inlet, Menai Strait and the Conwy estuary; in the Conwy, production comes from six different mussel beds. The raft culture of mussels on long

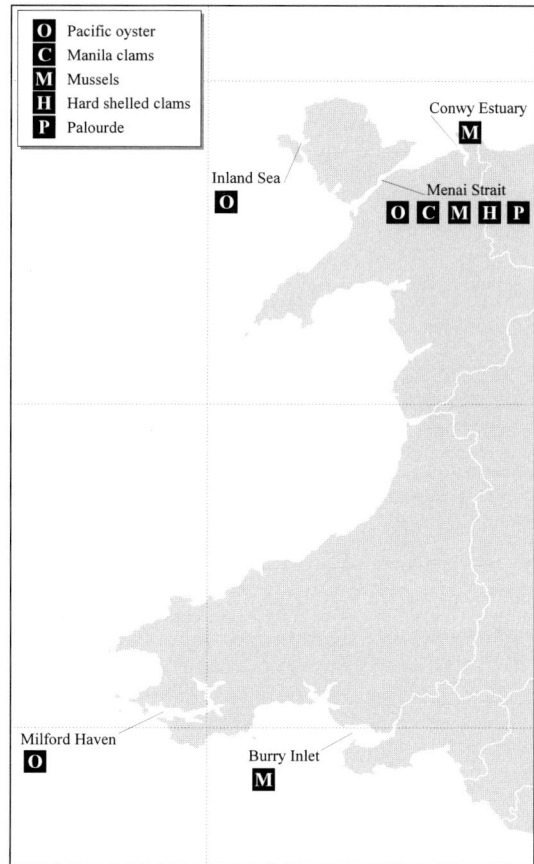

Map 9.2.1 Location of mariculture areas and the species in culture.

lines is currently being developed in Milford Haven and is being tried out in the Burry Inlet and in Swansea Bay, where an application has been made to the Welsh Office for a Several Order (see section 9.2.3).

The Pacific oyster is reared, using seed from commercial hatcheries, in trays on trestles at the level of low water of spring tides in three sheltered areas of this region. The main production occurs in Milford Haven, where the annual production is 100 tonnes per year (Carew Oysters, pers. comm.), about 20% of the estimated British production of 500 tonnes (Shellfish Association of the UK, pers. comm.). There are also smaller quantities reared in the Menai Strait and the Inland Sea.

Clams (hard-shell clam, Manila clam and palourde) are reared commercially in small quantities in the Menai Strait. A selection of species, including these clams and the New Zealand oyster *Tiostrea lutaria* and the American oyster *Crassostrea virginica*, are kept in the Menai Strait as broodstock for experimental hatchery use. The University College of North Wales (UCNW) School of Ocean Science Laboratory at Menai Bridge also keeps various species for experimental use. An experimental hatchery at the MAFF Fisheries Laboratory, Conwy, produces native and non-native species in support of the shellfish industry.

A large-scale experiment is being carried out in Cardigan Bay by the North Western and North Wales Sea Fisheries Committee (NW & NWSFC) to evaluate the enhancement of lobster stocks using hatchery-reared juveniles. Between September 1984 and October 1988 a total of 19,957 tagged juvenile lobsters, reared by NW & NWSFC at the hatchery at UCNW School of Ocean Sciences Laboratory, were released into the sea off Aberystwyth. Early results were encouraging and may lead to large-scale restocking of lobster grounds or to ranching of the species (Cook, Fish & Sankey 1989). Beard & Wickins (1992) summarise the rearing and tagging aspects of this work.

9.2.3 Management and issues

In the areas where mariculture occurs in the region and which also have high human population densities, there is concern about the effects of sewage discharges on exploited species - both on stocks that are fished (see section 9.1) and those that are cultivated. The Food Safety (Live Bivalve Molluscs) Regulations (implementing European Council Directives) require that all waters from which bivalve molluscs are taken for human consumption are classified by MAFF, and depending on the resulting category (A - D), restrictions may be imposed (Milford Haven Waterway Environmental Monitoring Steering Group 1994). Samples are taken regularly and the classification can change.

The consent of the owners or managers of the sea bed is required and a lease may be needed before structures for mariculture can be erected on the sea bed. In many areas consent must be sought from the Crown Estate, since it owns or manages 55% of the foreshore and the same proportion of the beds of tidal rivers between mean high and low water in GB, together with virtually the entire territorial sea bed. If the structures are potentially hazardous to navigation the Department of Transport must also authorise their construction, and if they are to be above mean low water mark planning permission must be sought from the local authority. Within Milford Haven maricultural activities are concentrated in or near SSSIs and within a National Park, so nature conservation and landscape considerations also apply. The former also apply in the Menai Strait, which is proposed as a Marine Nature Reserve.

Several Orders granted under section 1 of the Sea Fisheries (Shellfish) Act 1967 are administered in the region by the Welsh Office. They are granted to an individual, a co-operative or a responsible body to cultivate the sea bed within a designated area and to conserve and develop stocks of molluscan shellfish. Out of a total of 22 shellfish Several Orders in GB there are two in this region (Table 9.2.2), both granted to the North Wales and North West Sea Fisheries Committee, who have leased the rights to others, with the consent of the Welsh Office.

The introduction of non-native shellfish species for

cultivation has caused concern over their potential to establish self-sustaining populations and so affect marine ecosystems. Since January 1993 there have been new, less stringent, requirements for the control of shellfish disease in Great Britain and for the 'deposit' and importation of molluscan shellfish and lobsters, under the EC Fish Health Directive (Directive 91/67). Under this legislation, only the deposit of shellfish originating from areas in which *Bonamia ostreae* occurs is now controlled. (*Bonamia* is a parasite that infects the blood cells of native oysters, causing high mortalities of infected oysters.) These changes in the legislation have caused concern that the transfer of molluscan shellfish may be accompanyied by accidental releases of associated non-native predators, pests, parasites and diseases. Shellfish and fish farms in the region have to be registered with MAFF and the Welsh Office Agriculture Department, under the Fish Farming and Shellfish Farming Business Order 1985. Registration is designed to assist MAFF in dealing with any outbreaks of pests and diseases.

Mariculture and its effects are limited in this region compared with some other parts of Britain, and concerns at current cultivation levels in the region are generally site-specific. Issues relating to the cultivation of marine species are closely linked to marine nature conservation interests, particularly the possible effects on species and habitats of nature conservation interest. These issues are under consideration by the 'Marine Fisheries Task Force', an inter-agency team of the statutory nature conservation organisations (the Countryside Council for Wales, English Nature, Scottish Natural Heritage and the Department of the Environment (Northern Ireland) together with the JNCC). A consultation draft paper prepared by the group, entitled *Developing an action programme for sea fisheries and wildlife* (Marine Fisheries Task Force 1994), identifies the main areas where marine fisheries (broadly defined to encompass the exploitation of all living marine resources and which therefore includes mariculture) affect wildlife and identifies any action needed.

9.2.4 Information sources used

Addison & Bannister (1994) review lobster stock enhancement generally, and results from experiments in other parts of the UK are summarised by Burton (1993) and Bannister *et al.* (1994). For details of the current classification categories in the Designated Bivalve Mollusc Production Areas in the region, reference should be made to the relevant Port Health or Local Authority. A specialist subset of the electronic mapping system UKDMAP (see 'Core reading list', section A3 in the Appendix), called SHELLMAP, is being prepared by the MAFF Shellfish

Table 9.2.2 Several Orders in the region

Title	Species covered	Grid ref.	Location	Grantee	Approx. area (ha)	Year of expiry
Menai Strait Oyster and Mussel Fishery Order 1962	Oysters and mussels	SH600740	Bangor, Gwynedd	NW & NWSFC	780	2022
Menai Strait (West) Oyster, Mussel and Clam Fishery Order 1978	Oysters, mussels and clams	SH479652 and SH515674	Bangor, Gwynedd	NW & NWSFC	96	2008

Source: MAFF (1994) and Grantees. Note: Regulating Orders are presented in Table 9.1.8.

Division in Weymouth in order to meet the requirements of the EC shellfish harvesting and hygiene directives (Ramster *et al.* in press). The software gives charts of all coastal areas (principally estuaries) that support known molluscan shellfisheries, showing all details of the production areas and their classification.

9.2.5 Further sources of information

A. *References cited*

Addison, J.T., & Bannister, R.C.A. 1994. Re-stocking and enhancing clawed lobster stocks: a review. *Crustaceana, 67* (2): 131-155. (Proceedings of the Fourth International Workshop on Lobster Biology and Management, Sanriku, Japan.)

Bannister, R.C.A., Addison, J.T., & Lovewell, S.R.J. 1994. Growth, movement, recapture rate and survival of hatchery-reared lobsters *Hommarus gammarus* Linnaneus, 1758, released into the wild on the English east coast. *Crustaceana, 67* (2): 156-172. (Proceedings of the Fourth International Workshop on Lobster Biology and Management, Sanriku, Japan.)

Beard, T.W., & Wickins, J.F. 1992. *Techniques for the production of juvenile lobsters* Homarus gammarus. Lowestoft, MAFF. (Fisheries Research Technical Report No. 92.)

Burton, C.A. 1993. The United Kingdom lobster stock enhancement experiments. *In: Proceedings of the 1st British conference on artificial reefs and restocking. Stromness, Orkney. 12 September, 1992, 22-35.*

Cook, W., Fish, J.D., & Sankey, S.A. 1989. *Lobster stock enhancement experiments in Cardigan Bay - an interim report 1984 - 1988.* Mimeo, North Western and North Wales Sea Fishery Committee.

Ministry of Agriculture, Fisheries and Food. 1994. List of Orders in England and Wales (unpublished).

Marine Fisheries Task Force. 1994. *Developing an action programme for sea fisheries and wildlife.* Peterborough, JNCC. (Draft consultation paper by the Marine Fisheries Task Group.)

Milford Haven Waterway Environmental Monitoring Steering Group. 1994. *Report of the Milford Haven Waterway Environmental Monitoring Steering Group.* Civil Protection Planning Unit, Dyfed County Council (unpublished report).

Ramster, J.W., Tabor, A.R., Lockwood, S.J., & Sheehan R. In press. Access to coastal zone information: a possible common approach for the UK. *In: Proceedings of the conference on management techniques in the coastal zone, University of Portsmouth: October 24-25 1994.* Portsmouth, University of Portsmouth.

B. *Further reading*

Cobham Resource Consultants. 1987. *An environmental assessment of fish farms.* Final report to Countryside Commission for Scotland, Crown Estate Commissioners, Highlands and Islands Development Board and Scottish Salmon Growers Association.

Dixon, F. 1986. *Development of the bottom culture mussel industry in the UK.* Sea Fish Authority Industrial Development Unit. (Internal Report Number 1271.)

Frid, C.L.J., & Mercer, T.S. 1989. Environmental monitoring of caged fish farming in macrotidal environments. *Marine Pollution Bulletin, 20*: 379-383.

Ministry of Agriculture, Fisheries and Food. 1982. Bonamia, *a new threat to the native oyster fishery.* Lowestoft, MAFF. (Directorate of Fisheries Research Fisheries Notices Number 71.)

Ministry of Agriculture, Fisheries and Food, Welsh Office and Scottish Office Agriculture and Fisheries Department. 1994. *A guide to shellfish health controls.* Lowestoft, MAFF.

Ministry of Agriculture, Fisheries and Food, Welsh Office and Scottish Office Agriculture and Fisheries Department. 1994. *A guide to importing fish.* Lowestoft, MAFF.

Nature Conservancy Council. 1989. *Fish farming in the UK.* Memorandum to the House of Commons Agriculture Committee. Peterborough.

Pawson, M.G., & Rogers, S.I. 1989. *The coastal fisheries of England and Wales. Part ii: A review of their status in 1988.* Lowestoft, MAFF. (Directorate of Fisheries Research Internal Report No.19.) (Being updated.)

Ross, A. 1988. Fish farms and wildlife: are they really compatible? *Marine Conservation, summer 1988.*

Scottish Office Agriculture and Fisheries Department. 1993. *A report of the SOAFD annual survey of Shellfish farms for 1992.* Aberdeen, SOAFD.

Scottish Office Agriculture and Fisheries Department. 1993. *A report of the SOAFD annual survey of Salmon farms for 1992.* Aberdeen, SOAFD.

Spencer, B.E. 1990. *Cultivation of Pacific oysters.* Lowestoft, MAFF. (Directorate of Fisheries Research Laboratory Leaflet No. 63.)

Spencer, B.E., Edwards, D.B., & Millican, P.F. 1991. *Cultivation of Manila clams.* Lowestoft, MAFF. (Directorate of Fisheries Research Laboratory Leaflet No. 65.)

Scottish Salmon Growers Association. 1990. *Salmon farming and predatory wildlife.* Perth, Scottish Salmon Growers Association.

C. Contact names and addresses

Type of information	Contact address and telephone no.
Central contact for the local Sea Fisheries Committees and advice on general policy issues	Chief Executive, Association of Sea Fisheries Committees, Buckrose House, Commercial Street, Norton, Malton, North Yorkshire YO17 9HX, tel: 01653 698219
Shellfish reports and other publications, details of Fishery Orders and other advice and information on mariculture activities	Director, South Wales Sea Fisheries Committee (SWSFC), Queens Buildings, Cambrian Place, Swansea, West Glamorgan SA1 1TW, tel: 01792 654466
Shellfish reports and other publications, details of Fishery Orders and other advice and information on mariculture activities	Clerk and Chief Fisheries Officer, North Wales and North Western Sea Fisheries Committee (NW & NWSFC), Bailrigg, University of Lancaster, Lancaster, Lancashire LA1 4XY, tel: 01524 68745
Bivalve molluscs, water quality and environmental and shipping matters	Director of Port Health Services, Milford Port Health Authority, Gorsewood Drive, Hakin, Milford Haven, Pembrokeshire SA73 3EP, tel: 01646 692486
Bivalve molluscs, water quality and environmental and shipping matters	Director of Port Health Services, Swansea Bay Port Health Authority, Kings Dock Lock, Swansea SA1 8RU, tel: 01792 653523
Leases	The Crown Estate, Marine Estates, 16 Carlton House Terrace, London SW1Y 5AH, tel: 0171 210 4377
Scientific advice on marine fish and shellfish cultivation. Advice to assist with management and policy decisions for the coastal zone.	Head of Laboratory, MAFF Directorate of Fisheries Research, Fisheries Laboratory, Benarth Road, Conwy, Gwynedd LL32 8UB, tel: 01492 593883
Scientific advice relating to the mariculture industry	Director, MAFF Directorate of Fisheries Research, Fisheries Laboratory, Pakefield Road, Lowestoft, Suffolk NR33 OHT, tel: 01502 562244
Bivalve molusc production areas, the classification of shellfish waters and shellfish diseases	Director, MAFF Shellfish Division, Fish Diseases Laboratory, Barrack Road, The Nothe, Weymouth, Dorset DT4 8UB, tel: 01305 206600
Commercial advice and information on shellfish	Sea Fish Industry Authority, Sea Fish House, St Andrews Dock, Hull, North Humberside HU3 4QE, tel: 01482 27837
Reports and publications on mariculture	Director, Field Studies Council Research Centre, Oil Pollution Research Unit, Fort Popton, Angle, Pembroke, Dyfed SA71 5AD, tel: 01646 641404
Details of monitoring studies and reports produced for and compiled by the Steering Group	Trevor D. Lloyd, Milford Haven Waterway Environmental Monitoring Steering Group, Civil Protection Planning Unit, Dyfed County Council, Hill House, Picton Terrace, Carmarthen, Dyfed SA31 3BS, tel: 01267 236651
Funds projects and reports on various aspects of cultivating salmonids	Director, Scottish Salmon Growers Association, Drummond House, Scott Street, Perth PH1 5EJ, tel: 01738 635420
Commercial information and advice on shellfish	Director, Shellfish Association of the UK, Fishmongers Hall, London Bridge, London EC4R 9EL, tel: 0171 6263531
Administration of fisheries and mariculture in Wales including Several Orders	Welsh Office Agriculture Department, Fisheries Department, Division 2B, New Crown Buildings, Cathays Park, Cardiff CF1 3NQ, tel: 01222 823567
Fisheries Task Group paper and advice on interaction between mariculture activities and marine nature conservation issues	*Marine Advisory Officer, JNCC Peterborough, tel: 01733 62626
Information and advice on interaction between mariculture activities and marine nature conservation issues in the Skomer Marine Nature Reserve	*Marine Conservation Officer, CCW Skomer, Haverfordwest, tel: 01646 636736
Information and advice on interaction between mariculture activities and marine nature conservation issues in Wales	*Marine and Coastal Section, CCW HQ, Bangor, tel: 01248 370444
Information and advice on interaction between mariculture activities and marine nature conservation issues, especially in relation to birds	*Coastal Policy Officer, RSPB HQ, Sandy, Beds., tel: 01767 680551
Information and advice on interaction between mariculture activities and marine nature conservation issues	*Fisheries Officer, WWF-UK, Godalming, tel: 01483 426444
Information and advice on interaction between mariculture activities and marine nature conservation issues	*Conservation Officer, Marine Conservation Society, Ross-on-Wye, tel: 01989 566017

C. Contact names and addresses (continued)

Type of information	Contact address and telephone no.
Information and advice on interaction between mariculture activities and marine nature conservation issues in Cardigan Bay	*Projects Officer, Cardigan Bay Forum, Aberystwyth, tel: 01970 624471
Information and advice on interaction between mariculture activities and marine nature conservation issues in the Irish Sea Study Group area	*Chairman, Irish Sea Forum, University of Liverpool, tel: 0151 794 4089
Information and advice on interaction between mariculture activities and marine nature conservation issues	Administrator, The Marine Forum for Environmental Issues, Department of Zoology, The Natural History Museum, Cromwell Road, London SW7 5BD, tel: 0171 938 9114

* Starred contact addresses are given in full in the Appendix

9.2.5 Acknowledgements

Thanks to the following members of the Fisheries Working Group for their contributions and comments: Bill Cook (NW & NWSFC), Phil Coates (SWSFC), Brian Spencer (MAFF DFR Conwy), Dr McGovern (Crown Estate, Scotland), Paul Knapman (English Nature), Blaise Bullimore (Countryside Council for Wales), Indrani Lutchman (WWF UK), Clare Eno (JNCC), Mark Tasker (JNCC) and Nancy Harrison (RSPB). Additional information was contributed by David Rye (Milford Port Health Authority), Tony Green and Phil Stone (Cardigan Bay Forum), Alan Herbert and Andy Panayi (Crown Estate Commissioners). Thanks also go to the several others who have commented on drafts.

9.3 Wildfowling, grazing and collection of other plants and animals

Dr N.C. Davidson, D.A. Stroud, C.A. Crumpton and M.J. Goodwin

9.3.1 Wildfowling

A traditional coastal activity formerly commercially practised for food, wildfowling is now solely recreational. Quarry species and shooting seasons (the open season for coastal wildfowling is 1 September to 20 February) are regulated through the Wildlife and Countryside Act 1981: coastal quarry species are most ducks, some geese and three waders (only one of which (golden plover *Pluvialis apricaria*) is regularly coastal), and in this region it is chiefly ducks (especially wigeon *Anas penelope*, teal *A. crecca* and mallard *A. platyrhynchos*) that are targeted.

As well as statutory constraints on species shot, several sites are subject to further regulation self-imposed by wildfowlers. For example, since 1972 local shooting clubs on the Dyfi Estuary have voluntarily banned the shooting of Greenland white-fronted geese *Anser albifrons flavirostris*, although it is legal quarry in Wales (Fox & Stroud 1985). As elsewhere in Britain, much of the wildfowling in Region 12 is operated and managed through wildfowling clubs and syndicates. The representative body for sport shooting in the UK, the British Association for Shooting and Conservation (BASC), has 19,000 wildfowling members, most of whom belong to 200 affiliated wildfowling clubs: of these there are 31 clubs (15% of all affiliated clubs) with over 880 members operating in the counties of the region. Shooting at some coastal sites (such as the Dyfi) can involve clubs and individuals from inland areas also (in this case the West Midlands).

Much of the wildfowling in the region is coastal and focused on estuaries. Most of this activity is on the larger estuaries, notably Loughor, Carmarthen Bay, Milford Haven, Dyfi and Traeth Bach. It occurs occasionally, at low intensity or on small parts of at least ten of the smaller estuaries in the region but is usually absent from small urban and industrialised estuaries. Much of the wildfowling is well regulated through permit systems (e.g. on National Nature Reserves) and there is close liaison between the Countryside Council for Wales (CCW), the BASC and the wildfowling clubs. Since much of the land shot over is notified as SSSI, clubs that are owners and occupiers also operate under Notices of Consent from CCW, and there are refuge areas established on several estuaries, including the Loughor (see also section 5.12.3 and Owen (1992) for information on wildfowling regulation at several sites in the region).

Disturbance to waterfowl (including non-quarry species) from shooting during periods of severe winter weather risks the birds' survival: at these times national statutory wildfowling bans can be imposed after fourteen days of freezing conditions (voluntary restraint is called for after seven days). Such bans are important in this region since the weather is often relatively mild and the region is used as a refuge by birds moving from more severe weather further north and east (Ridgill & Fox 1990). Further information on the history and operation of cold-weather shooting bans is given by Stroud (1992).

9.3.2 Dune grazing

The dunes of Wales have been affected by agriculture for many centuries (see also section 3.2). During the National Sand Dune Survey grazing by domestic stock was recorded at 17 of the 49 sand dune sites, with undergrazing the norm (Dargie 1995). Most large sites are grazed, usually by sheep or cattle and occasionally by ponies and goats, although two of the larger sites, Laugharne and Pendine Burrows, are ungrazed (these sites do, however, have deer populations as alternative grazers). Information on grazing intensity is unavailable for most sites but it is known to vary by season. Over-grazing was recorded as occurring in this region only at Tywyn Gwyn. At Newborough Warren, a long-term experiment by the Institute of Terrestrial Ecology is underway on dune grazing. Small sites are rarely grazed (Penmaen and Pennard on the Gower Peninsula are notable exceptions). The absence of grazing from the majority of sites is due largely to displacement by other land uses, including leisure development and military use (see section 8.2.2).

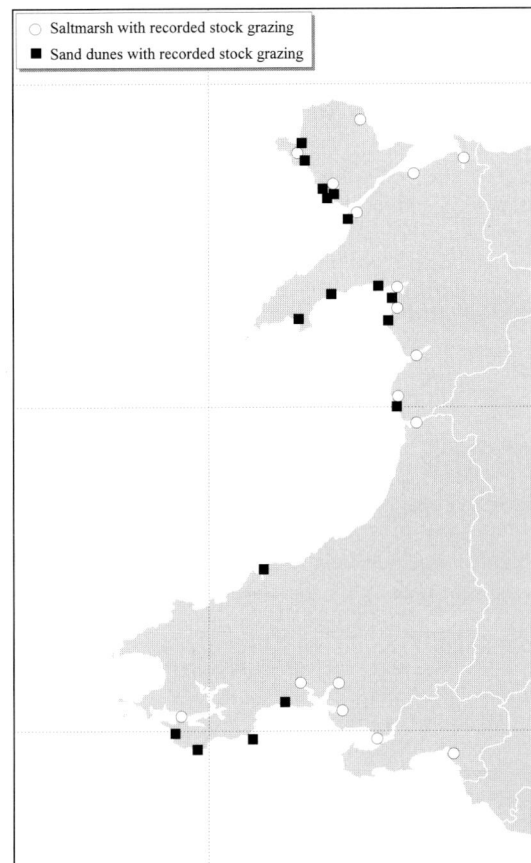

Map 9.3.1 Saltmarshes and sand dunes with recorded grazing. See Maps 3.6.1 and 3.2.1 for distribution of saltmarsh and sand dune sites. Source: JNCC Coastal Database.

9.3.3 Saltmarsh grazing

There are approximately 44,000 ha of saltmarsh in Great Britain, approximately 31,600 ha of which are grazed. Of the 5,461 ha of saltmarsh in the region, 4,995 ha (91%) is grazed to some extent - more than the national average (see also section 3.6). Significant saltmarsh grazing in this region occurs at the Dyfi Estuary, at Barmouth and at Traeth Bach (Map 9.3.1). It also takes place at the Burry Inlet, and to a lesser extent at the Neath Estuary and Milford Haven. Saltmarshes in south Wales are mostly ungrazed.

9.3.4 Collection of other plants and animals

Collection of seaweed and other plants and animals is controlled by the Coastal Protection Act (1949) and prohibited (with certain exceptions) by the Wildlife & Countryside Act (1981). No large-scale commercial collection of plants and animals (other than exploited fish and shellfish - see sections 5.5, 5.7 and 5.8) is known to occur in this region. The most significant collection, mainly in south Wales and around Milford Haven, is of the seaweed *Porphyra* from the shore for food (laver bread) (Eno 1991). Collection of laver weed is sometimes carried out using trailers, which can remove up to half a tonne at a time, but the total amounts involved are not known. Other collection, for small-scale or private consumption, is usually done by hand using simple tools and equipment. Curio collection in England and Wales mainly involves the species of sea fan *Eunicella verrucosa*, whose empty shells are collected in this region on south coast beaches (Eno 1991).

9.3.5 Information sources used

Some information about the distribution and management of wildfowling comes from the 1989 Estuaries Review data collection, now held as part of JNCC's integrated coastal database (see also Davidson *et al.* 1991), and some from the BASC. Information on sand dune and saltmarsh grazing was collected during national vegetation surveys of these habitats (Dargie 1995; Burd 1989).

9.3.6 Further sources of information

A. References cited

Dargie, T.C.D. 1995. *Sand dune vegetation of Great Britain. Part 3, Wales.* Peterborough, Joint Nature Conservation Committee.

Davidson, N.C., Laffoley, D.d'A., Doody, J.P., Way, L.S., Gordon, J., Key, R., Drake, M.C., Pienkowski, M.W., Mitchell, R., & Duff, K.L. 1991. *Nature conservation and estuaries in Great Britain.* Peterborough, Nature Conservancy Council.

Eno, N.C., *ed.* 1991. *Marine conservation handbook,* 2nd ed. Peterborough, English Nature.

Fox, A.D., & Stroud, D.A. 1985. Greenland white-fronted geese in Wales. *Nature in Wales, New Series,* 4(1-2): 20-27.

Owen, M. 1992. An analysis of permit systems and bag records on NNRs. *JNCC Report,* No. 68.

Ridgill, S.C., & Fox., A.D. 1990. *Cold weather movements of waterfowl in western Europe.* Slimbridge, International Waterfowl & Wetlands Research Bureau. (IWRB Special Publication No. 13.)

Stroud, J.M. 1992. Statutory suspension of wildfowling in severe weather: review of past winter weather and actions. *JNCC Report,* No. 75.

B. Further reading

Burd, F. 1989. *The saltmarsh survey of Great Britain.* Peterborough, Joint Nature Conservation Committee.

Beeftink, W.G. 1977. Saltmarshes. *In: The coastline,* ed. by R.S.K. Barnes. London, John Wiley and Sons.

Bell, D.V., & Fox, P.J.A. 1991. Shooting disturbance: an assessment of its impact and effects on overwintering waterfowl populations and their distribution in the UK. *Nature Conservancy Council, CSD Report,* No. 1242.

Doody, J.P. 1987. Botanical and entomological implications of saltmarsh management in inter tidal areas. *RSPB Symposium.* Sandy, Royal Society for the Protection of Birds.

Doody, J.P. 1988. The management of saltmarshes. *Coastal Habitat Network, No.2.* April.

Guiry, M.D., & Blunden, G., eds. 1991. *Seaweed resources in Europe: uses and potential.* Chichester, Wiley & Sons.

Mudge, G.P. 1989. Night shooting of wildfowl in Great Britain; an assessment of its prevalence, intensity and disturbance impact. *Nature Conservancy Council, CSD Report,* No.987.

Pain, D. 1990. Lead poisoning of wildfowl: the waste of a natural resource. *IWRB News, No.4, July.*

Rothwell, P. 1989. Saving our saltmarsh. *Shooting and countryside times, July/Aug. 1989.*

Scott, R., & Hodson, L.M. 1988. Preliminary review of management practices on the saltmarshes of north-west England. *Nature Conservancy Council, CSD Report,* No. 935.

Wells, S., & Wood, E., eds. 1991. *The marine curio trade. Conservation guidelines and legislation.* Ross-on-Wye, Marine Conservation Society.

C. Contact names and addresses

Type of information	Contact address and telephone no.
Wildfowl and wetlands (conservation)	*Publicity Officer, Wildfowl & Wetlands Trust HQ, tel. 01453 890333
Wildfowling (general, including information on affiliated clubs)	Information Officer, British Association for Shooting and Conservation, Marford Mill, Rossett, Wrexham, Clwyd LL12 0HL, tel. 01244 570881
Wildfowling (general information on wildfowl, habitats and conservation)	*RSPB HQ, Sandy, tel. 01767 680551
Wildfowling/saltmarsh grazing & dune grazing (policy and general information)	*CCW HQ, Bangor, tel. 01248 370444
Severe weather wildfowling bans	*Licensing Officer, CCW HQ Bangor, tel. 01248 370444
Dune grazing experiment, Newborough Warren	Unit Secretary, Institute of Terrestrial Ecology, Bangor Research Unit, University College of North Wales, Deiniol Road, Bangor, Gwynedd LL57 2UP, tel. 01248 370045
Saltmarsh and dune grazing and agriculture	Ministry of Agriculture Fisheries and Food, Whitehall Place, London SW1A 2HH, tel. 0171 270 8080
Shellfish (curios)	Secretary, Shellfish Association of Great Britain, Fishmongers' Hall, London Bridge, London EC4R 9EL, tel. 0171 283 8305

* Starred contact addresses are given in full in the Appendix

9.3.7 Acknowledgements

The authors wish to thank the BASC for help in compiling this section.

9.4 Quarrying and landfilling

C.A. Crumpton and M.J. Goodwin

9.4.1 Introduction

The main resources quarried in the region are limestone (seven quarries), sand and gravel (five), igneous rock (three), clay and shale (two) and coal (one quarry). End uses for these include construction, road building and domestic and industrial energy production (British Geological Survey 1994). Of the 2,505 quarries in the whole of GB, 18 (<1%) occur in the region, i.e. are less than 2 km inland (13% of the Welsh total of 144) (BGS 1994). Table 9.4.1 shows the output of the region's (coastal) quarries in a national context. The region is important in a national context for its output of igneous rock and common clay and shale.

Table 9.4.1 Quarry production in 1991 (thousand tonnes)

	Limestone and dolomite	Sand-stone	Igneous rock	Common clay and shale	Common sand and gravel
West Glamorgan	97	0	0	0	535
Dyfed	2,272	273	348	13	268
Gwynedd	82	0	1,253	423*	493
Region 12	2,451	273	1,601	436	1,296
Wales (whole country)	18,986	1,466	3,294	436	3,439
GB % in region	*2.3*	*2.1*	*3.5*	*3.3*	*1.3*
Great Britain (whole country)	*107,767*	*12,928*	*46,008*	*13,038*	*97,918*

Source: BGS (1994). * also includes Clwyd, Mid Glamorgan and Powys.

No figures are available for the percentage of coastal land devoted to landfilling in Wales, although for British estuaries in general it has been estimated that 34% of land claim is used for rubbish tips (the largest category of land use) (Davidson *et al.* 1991).

9.4.2 Important locations

The coastal quarries in the region are listed in Table 9.4.2 and shown on Map 9.4.1 (note that the two quarries at Kidwelly are represented on the map by a single symbol).

Map 9.4.2 shows the location of the region's currently used coastal landfill sites according to Aspinwall's Sitefile Digest (Aspinwall 1994); the status codes are defined in Table 9.4.3. Landfill sites were classed as coastal if they fell into a coastal 10 km National Grid square.

9.4.3 Management and issues

Further developments of existing quarries to 'superquarry' size appear unfeasible along the North Wales coast because of conflicts with centres of population and the shallowness of the water, which restricts access by deep-draught vessels (Whitbread & Marsay 1992).

Table 9.4.2 Coastal quarries

Location	Company	Resource
West Glamorgan		
Port Talbot	British Steel Plc.	Sand and gravel
Bishopston	Barland Quarry Ltd.	Limestone
Dyfed		
Kidwelly	Alfred McAlpine Quarry Products	Limestone
Kidwelly	R.M.C Wotton Roadstone	Limestone
Laugharne	F. Gilman	Limestone
Pembroke	J. Eynon and Sons	Sand and gravel
Pembroke	T. Scourfield	Limestone
Llanon	Venture Coal Ltd.	Coal
Borth	Evans and Owen	Common clay and shale
Gwynedd		
Penrhyndeudraeth	Wimpey Asphalt	Igneous
Chwilog	Wimpey Asphalt	Sand and gravel
Pwllheli	Nanhoron Quarry Ltd.	Igneous
Caernarfon	Butterley Brick Ltd.	Common clay and shale
Newborough	J. Vaughan	Sand and gravel
Moelfre	Anglesey Masonry Co.	Limestone
Benllech	Rhuddlan Stone (Brynteg) Ltd.	Limestone
Bangor	Tarmac North West	Sand and gravel
Penmaenmawr	A.R.C Northern	Igneous

Source: BGS (1994)

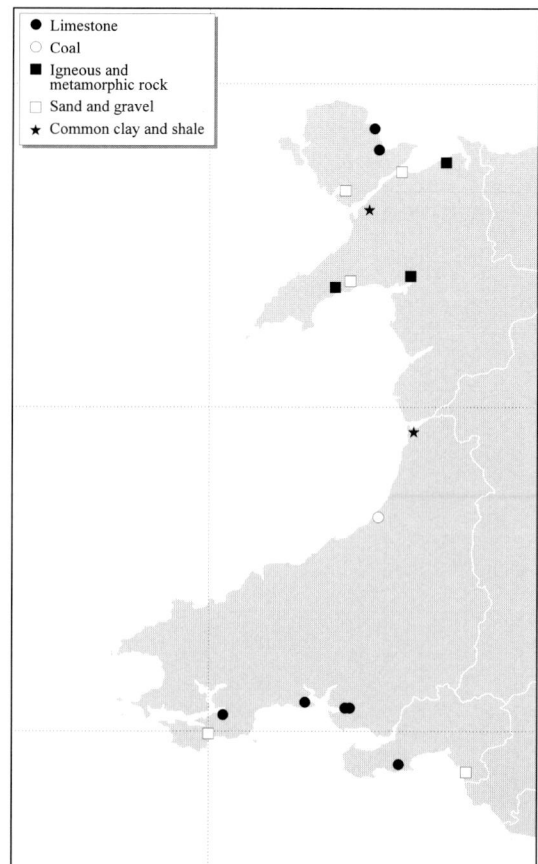

Map 9.4.1 Coastal quarries. Source: Welsh Office (1993). © Crown copyright.

Table 9.4.3 The status of the region's landfill sites (in support of Map 9.4.2)

Status code	Definition	Number in region
1	*Inert only*. Comprises uncontaminated excavated natural earth materials, and uncontaminated brick rubble and concrete with similar properties to natural earth materials.	29
2	*Non-hazardous*. Comprise mainly uncontaminated and industrial wastes such as packaging materials, wood and plastic. Some of these wastes are biodegradable but not rapidly so.	1
3	*Household/putrescible*. Comprise the typical contents of a household dustbin and similar wastes of industrial origin e.g. food processing wastes.	4
4	*Difficult wastes*. Any wastes which require particular handling techniques at the disposal site, e.g. vehicle tyres, dry feathers, animal carcasses. They are not the same as Special Wastes, which are toxic and require pre-notification of disposal to the Waste Regulation Authority.	9
Total		43

Source: Aspinwall & Co. (1994)

Landfill site licensing in Great Britain is the responsibility of the 152 Waste Regulation Authorities (WRAs). In Wales these are the District Councils, usually through the Environmental Health or Technical Services Departments. Each WRA is required to maintain a public register of waste management licences for private sites in its area and a register of resolutions referring to its own sites.

9.4.4 Information sources used

The figures for quarrying and mineral extraction are from the British Geological Survey's 1994 *Directory of Mines and Quarries*. Landfill data were provided by Aspinwall & Co. from their Sitefile Digest for waste treatment and disposal. This contains regularly updated information from the 152 WRAs and represents the most up to date collection of public information available on British waste management.

9.4.5 Further sources of information

A. References cited

Aspinwall & Co. 1994. *The sitefile digest: a digest of authorised waste treatment and disposal sites in GB*. Shrewsbury, Environment Press.

British Geological Survey (BGS). 1994. *Directory of mines and quarries 1994*. 4th ed. Nottingham, British Geological Survey.

Davidson, N.C., Laffoley, D.d'A., Doody, J.P., Way, L.S., Gordon, J., Key, R., Drake, M.C., Pienkowski, M.W., Mitchell, R., & Duff, K.L. 1991. *Nature conservation and estuaries in Great Britain*. Peterborough, Nature Conservancy Council.

Welsh Office. 1993. *Environmental digest for Wales. No.7, 1992*.

Whitbread, M., & Marsay, A. 1992. *Coastal superquarries to supply south-east England aggregate requirements*. Report to the Department of the Environment Geological and Minerals Planning Research Programme. London, HMSO.

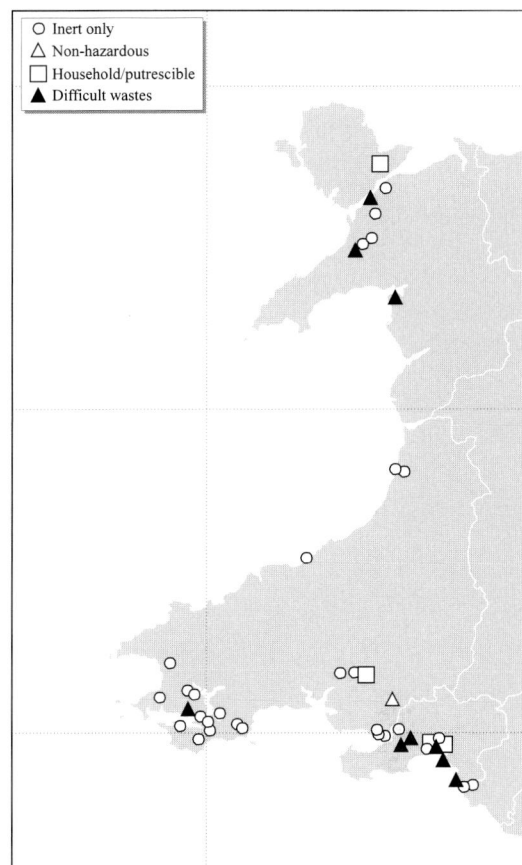

Map 9.4.2 Coastal landfill sites. Source: Site File Digest (Aspinwalls 1994).

B. Further reading

Eno, N.C. 1991. *Marine conservation handbook*. 2nd ed. Peterborough, English Nature.

C. Contact names and addresses

Type of information	Contact address and telephone no.
Quarries (Directory of Mines and Quarries)	Director, British Geological Survey, Keyworth, Nottingham NG12 5GG, tel. 0115 936 3393
Landfill sites (Sitefile Digest)	Senior Consultant, Aspinwall & Co., Walford Manor, Baschurch, Shrewsbury SY4 2HH, tel. 01939 261144
Waste regulation (Arfon)	Chief Environmental Health Officer, Arfon Waste Regulatory Authority, Swyddfa, Arfon, Penralt, Caernarfon LL55 1BN, tel. 01286 673113
Waste regulation (Carmarthen)	Director of Technical Services, Carmarthen Waste Regulatory Authority, (*District Council), tel. 01267 234567
Waste regulation (Ceredigion)	Director of Technical Services, Ceredigion Waste Regulatory Authority, (*District Council), tel. 01970 617911
Waste regulation (Llanelli)	Director of Technical Services, Llanelli Waste Regulatory Authority, (*Borough Council), tel. 01554 741100
Waste regulation (Neath)	Director of Engineering and Operations, Neath Waste Regulatory Authority, Tregelles Court, Neath Abbey, Neath SA10 7DF, tel. 01639 641121
Waste regulation (Port Talbot)	Borough Engineer, Port Talbot Waste Regulatory Authority, Civic Centre, Port Talbot SA13 1PJ, tel. 01639 883141
Waste regulation (South Pembrokeshire)	Director of Works and Services, South Pembrokeshire Waste Regulatory Authority, (*District Council), tel. 01646 683122
Waste regulation (Preseli Pembrokeshire)	Central Services Manager, Preseli Pembrokeshire Waste Regulatory Authority, (*District Council), tel. 01437 764551
Waste regulation (Swansea City)	City Engineer, Swansea City Waste Regulatory Authority, (*City Council), tel. 01792 301301
Waste regulation (Ynys Mon-Isle of Anglesey)	Director of Cont. Services, Ynys Mon-Isle of Anglesey Waste Regulatory Authority, (*Borough Council Office), tel. 01248 750057

* Starred contact addresses are given in full in the Appendix

9.4.6 Acknowledgements

Thanks to Dr Ron Moore and Susan Morley (Aspinwall & Co) for providing information on landfill sites from the Sitefile Digest.

9.5 Marine aggregate extraction, dredging, and disposal of dredge spoil

C.A. Crumpton and M.J. Goodwin

9.5.1 Introduction

Sand and gravel on the sea bed are important sources of industrial aggregate for concrete production, construction, beach replenishment and beach protection. They are extracted by commercial mineral companies under licence from the Crown Estate. Marine extraction in England and Wales reached a peak of 28 million tonnes in 1989 and fell steadily to 18 million tonnes in 1993, of which some six million tonnes was exported (Crown Estates 1994). In 1992 marine aggregates accounted for 15% of the national demand for aggregates. The quantity of marine dredged aggregate (692,513 tonnes) landed at the five ports in the region represents 3.7% of the total quantity of aggregate landed in 1993 (Crown Estate 1994).

Capital dredging refers to the one-off removal of sediment, chiefly when deepening shipping channels and during the construction of new dock facilities. Maintenance dredging is the regular dredging of existing ports and their approaches to maintain safe navigation. The majority of dredged material, which can range in composition from clay and silt to rock, is dumped at sea, but it may also be used for land claim and increasingly for beach recharge. Dredged material is the dominant input by man of inert solids to the Irish Sea and levels are considered to be unlikely to change significantly in the future. There may, however, be occasional peaks due to new harbour and marina developments (Irish Sea Study Group 1990a). During the Nature Conservancy Council's Estuaries Review surveys carried out in 1989, out of a total of 155 sites around Great Britain, capital dredging was taking place in 15 estuaries (10%) and maintenance dredging was taking place in 72 (47%) (Davidson et al. 1991), of which two and seven, respectively, were in the region.

The amount of dredged material dumped in the region in 1993 (1,401,365 tonnes) constitutes 4.7% of the total dredged material deposited around the UK as a whole (29,866,256 tonnes) in 1993. This contrasts with a figure of

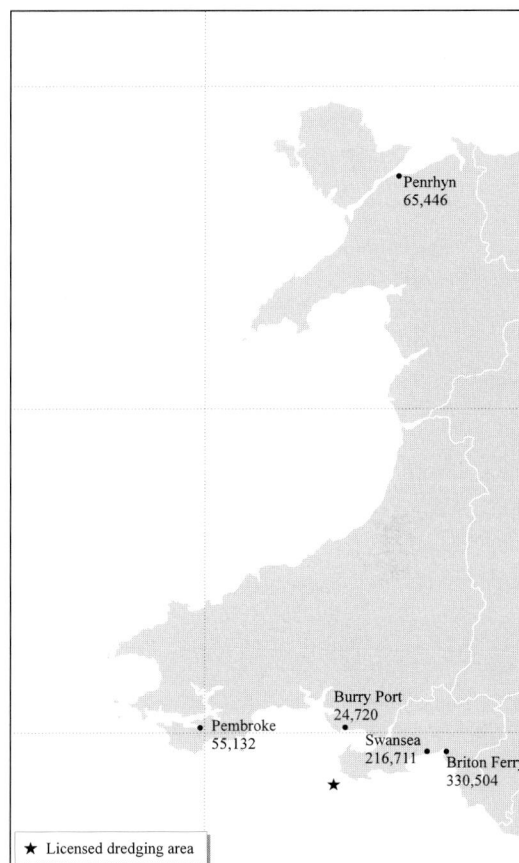

Map 9.5.1 Tonnages of marine dredged aggregates landed: 1993. Source: Crown Estate.

6.1% in 1992, when 1,792,192 tonnes were deposited in the region and 29,161,946 tonnes were deposited around the UK as a whole. During the Estuaries Review surveys carried out in 1989, dredged material was being dumped in 10 (6.5%) of the estuaries surveyed (Davidson et al. 1991), but none was in the region.

9.5.2 Important locations

Map 2.2.2 (in Chapter 2: Geology and Physical Environment) shows the seabed sediments in the region. Map 9.5.1 shows the landings of marine dredged aggregates in the regions's ports in 1993. The Helwick Bank, approximately 7 km south of Worms Head (see Map 1.2.1) is dredged by Llanelli Sand Dredging Limited. The greater part of the marine aggregate landed at Briton Ferry, Swansea and Pembroke Dock is dredged from Nash Bank and Holme Sand further east up the Severn Estuary: only that landed at Burry Port is likely to have come from Helwick Bank (Welsh Office, pers. comm.). A limited amount of material was landed at Briton Ferry and Swansea from the licensed area off Merseyside (Crown Estate pers. comm.). No aggregate prospecting or production takes

Table 9.5.2 The amounts of dredged material disposed of at each licensed site in the region in 1992 and 1993

Site name	MAFF code	Depth (m)	Dredging type	Dumped tonnage 1992	Dumped tonnage 1993
Swansea Bay (outer)	LU130	20	Capital	0	0
			Maintenance	1,632,692	1,401,365
Milford Haven	LU170	30	Capital	0	0
			Maintenance	156,000	0
Menai Strait	IS030	0-10	Maintenance	0	n/a
Holyhead Deep	IS040	50-80	Capital	0	0
			Maintenance	3,500	0
Holyhead East	IS042	64	Capital	0	n/a
Conwy Bay	IS055	20	Maintenance	0	0
Total				1,792,192	1,401,365

Source: MAFF

Map 9.5.2 Dredge spoil dumping sites. See Table 9.5.2. Source: MAFF (1994). © Crown copyright.

place in Cardigan Bay or Caernarfon Bay (Crown Estate 1994). Penrhyn in the north of the region is hampered by tidal conditions and a lack of space (Crown Estate 1994). Coarse gritty sand with a minor gravel component is worked on a small scale from two licences on a shared ground off the coast of north Wales. Few of the known gravel grounds in this area have been prospected (Nunney *et al.* 1986).

Map 9.5.2 shows the main marine disposal sites used for the dumping of dredged material in the region in 1992. The spoil dumping grounds in Swansea Bay take spoil from the maintenance dredging of Port Talbot Tidal Harbour (the greatest contributor) and the Neath River as well as from Swansea Docks (Welsh Office pers. comm.). Much less dredged material was disposed of in the Milford Haven dumping ground because the port of Milford Haven is relatively deep and so requires less dredging. In recent years, substantial quantities of material from the extensive capital dredging works involved in the Conwy estuary road tunnel project were dumped off-shore in Conwy Bay and north of Anglesey (Irish Sea Study Group 1990a).

9.5.3 Management and issues

Government policy for the provision of aggregate, formulated in 1982 and 1989, has encouraged marine extraction of sand and gravel: Minerals Planning Guidance Note 6 states that "it has a very important role to play in maintaining supplies of aggregate and, as far as possible, its use is to be encouraged" (Crown Estate 1992). Aggregates

from terrestrial sources are insufficient to meet demand (Doody *et al.* 1993). Dredging for marine aggregates tends to be a less controversial activity than terrestrial extraction, and 'high quality' aggregate exists in coastal areas adjacent to the main markets in south-east England (Kenny *et al.* 1994). The government promotes environmentally sustainable coastal defences, and as a result the use of sand and gravel for beach recharge is predicted to grow substantially (NERC undated). The national demand for aggregates increased steadily during the 1980s. In response, the aggregate industry invested in new ships, which allowed more efficient exploitation of licence areas and new, deeper waters to be dredged (Kenny *et al.* 1994).

Disposal of dredged material in the UK is controlled by the Water Resources Act (1991), the Food and Environmental Protection Act (1985) (dumping at sea and inter-tidal areas) and the Town and Country Planning and Environmental Protection Acts, both 1990 (dumping on land). The 1992 Paris Convention includes within its scope dumping of dredged material at sea. Licences to dump dredged material are granted in Wales by the Welsh Office. Each licence is subject to certain conditions, which have become more stringent in the last few years (Milford Haven Port Authority *pers. comm.*). Illegal dumping may occur; for instance, in 1986 and 1987 six and three cases respectively of alleged illegal dumping were investigated in England and Wales (MAFF 1989).

9.5.4 Information sources

The statistics on the tonnage of marine dredged aggregates from the Crown Estate relate to royalty returns for 1993. The regional landing port totals do not equal the amount dredged from each region because some is exported and some landed outside the region to meet home market demands.

9.5.5 Further sources of information

A. References cited

Crown Estate. 1994. *Marine aggregates - Crown Estate licences - summary of statistics 1993*. Crown Estate.

Crown Estate. 1992. *Marine aggregate extraction and the Government view procedure*. Crown Estate.

Davidson, N.C., Laffoley, D.d'A., Doody, J.P., Way, L.S., Gordon, J., Key, R., Drake, M.C., Pienkowski, M.W., Mitchell, R., & Duff, K.L. 1991. *Nature conservation and estuaries in Great Britain*. Peterborough, Nature Conservancy Council.

Doody, J.P., Johnston, C., & Smith, B. 1993. *Directory of the North Sea coastal margin*. Peterborough, Joint Nature Conservation Committee.

Irish Sea Study Group. 1990b. *The Irish Sea; an environmental review. Part 2; waste inputs and pollution*. Liverpool, Liverpool University Press.

Kenny, A.J., & Rees, H.L. 1994. The effects of marine gravel extraction on the macrobenthos: early post-dredging recolonisation. *Marine Pollution Bulletin*, 7: 442-447

Ministry of Agriculture, Fisheries and Food. 1989. *Coastal defence and the environment: a strategic guide for managers and decision makers in the National Rivers Authority, local authorities and other bodies with coastal responsibilities.* London, HMSO.

Ministry of Agriculture, Fisheries and Food. 1994. *Annual report: report on the disposal of waste at sea 1992.* London, HMSO.

Nunney, R.S., & Chillingworth, P.C.H. 1986. *Marine dredging for sand and gravel.* Department of the Environment. (Minerals Planning Research Project No. PECD 7/1/163 - 99/84.)

B. Further reading

Barne, J., Davidson, N.C., Hill, T.O., & Jones, M. 1994. *Coastal and Marine UKDMAP datasets: a user manual.* Peterborough, Joint Nature Conservation Committee.

BMAPA. 1993. *Aggregates from the sea : why dredge?* British Marine Aggregate Producers Association.

British Geological Survey. Undated. *Marine aggregate survey phase 4: Irish Sea, 53°N - 55°N and UK waters between 3°W and 5°30'W.* (BGS ref: WB/92/10.)

British Oceanographic Data Centre. 1992. UK Marine Digital Mapping Atlas Project (UKDMAP) (on diskette).

Campbell, J.A. 1993. *Guidelines for assessing marine aggregate extraction.* Lowestoft, MAFF (Directorate of Fisheries Research). (Laboratory leaflet No. 73.)

Collins, M.B., *et al.*, eds. 1979. *Industrialised embayments and their environmental problems: a case study of Swansea Bay.* University College, Swansea, Pergamon Press.

ICES. 1978. Input of pollutants to the Oslo Commission area. *Coop. Res. Rep., Int. Coun. Explor. Sea, 77*: 57.

Irish Sea Study Group. 1990. *The Irish Sea; an environmental review. Part 1; nature conservation.* Liverpool, Liverpool University Press.

Finney, N.H. 1987. Maintenance dredging and spoil disposal at UK ports. *Maintenance dredging.* London, TTL.

MAFF (Directorate of Fisheries Research). 1992. Monitoring of activities related to aggregate extraction. Monitoring and surveillance of non-radioactive contaminants in the aquatic environment and activities regulating the disposal of wastes at sea, 1990. *Aquatic Environment Monitoring Report, 30*: 46-49.

NERC. Undated. *Marine sand and gravel: resources and exploitation.* NERC.

Parker, M.M. 1987. The future for the disposal of dredged material in the UK. *Maintenance dredging.* London, TTL.

Posford Duvivier Environment. 1992. *Capital and maintenance dredging a pilot case study to review the potential benefits for nature conservation.* Unpublished report.

Pullen, S. Undated. *Dumping of dredged spoils from ports: contamination, pollution controls.*

Welsh Office, 1993. *Environment Digest for Wales; No. 7, 1992.*

C. Contact names and addresses

Type of information	Contact address and telephone no.
Marine sand and gravel extraction	Secretary, British Marine Aggregate Producers Association (BMAPA), 156 Buckingham Palace Road, London SW1 9TR, tel. 0171 730 8194
Marine aggregate extraction	Corporate Services Manager, Marine Estates (Offshore), The Crown Estate, 16 Carlton House Terrace, London SW1Y 5AH, tel. 0171 210 4377
Marine resource management	Technical Manager, Posford Duvivier (Managing Agents Offshore for The Crown Estate), Eastchester House, Harlands Road, Haywards Heath, West Sussex RH16 1PG, tel. 01444 458551
Offshore geoscience data including 1:250,000 maps of coastal geology	Director, British Geological Survey, Keyworth, Nottingham NG12 5GG, tel. 0115 936 3100
Sand and gravel	Director, Sand and Gravel Association (SAGA), 1 Bramber Court, 2 Bramber Road, London W14 9PB, tel. 0171 381 8778
Mineral Planning	Mineral Planning Officer, West Glamorgan County Council Minerals Planning Department, County Hall, Swansea SA1 3SN, tel. 01792 471111
Mineral Planning	Mineral Planning Officer, Dyfed County Council Minerals Section (Planning Dept), County Hall, Carmarthen, Dyfed SA31 1JP, tel. 01267 233333
Mineral Planning	Mineral Planning Officer, Gwynedd County Council. Minerals Section (Economic Development and Planning Dept), County Offices, Shire Hall Street, Caernarfon, Gwynedd LL55 1SH, tel. 01286 672255
Dumping of dredge spoil	The Oslo and Paris Commissions, New Court, 48 Carey Street, London WC2A 2JE, tel: 0171 242 9927
Database containing all dredge spoil dumping licensing information.	Marine Environmental Protection Division, Ministry of Agriculture, Fisheries and Food, Nobel House, 17 Smith Square, London SW1P 3JR, tel. 0171 238 6558
Dumping of dredge spoil at sea	Information Officer, International Maritime Organisation (IMO), 4 Albert Embankment, London SE1 7SR, tel. 0171 735 7611
Dumping of dredge spoil at sea	The Department of the Environment, 2 Marsham Street, London SW1P 3EB, tel. 0171 276 3000

C. Contact names and addresses (continued)

Type of information	Contact address and telephone no.
Dumping of dredge spoil at sea	Technical Secretary, Waste Management Forum (WMF), c/o Institute of Wastes Management, 9 Saxon Court, St Peter's Gardens, Northampton NN1 1SX, tel. 01604 20426
Dumping of dredge spoil in the region	Milford Haven Port Authority, P.O. Box 14, Milford Haven, Dyfed SA73 3ER, tel. 01646 693091
Dumping of dredge spoil at sea	International Council for the Exploration of the Seas, Palaegade 2-4, Dk 1261, Copenhagen K., Denmark, tel. 010 45 1154 225

* Starred contact addresses are given in full in the Appendix

9.6 Oil and gas development

C.A. Crumpton, M.J. Goodwin and J.H. Barne

9.6.1 Introduction

This section describes oil and gas exploration and related development in the region; information on oil and gas infrastructure and production is given in section 8.3.

There is increasing interest by the oil and gas industry in this region. Important sedimentary basins lie in the Irish Sea to the north and east of Anglesey (mainly covered in Region 13) and in Cardigan Bay stretching south-westwards into the Celtic Sea south of the Republic of Ireland. Exploration for oil and gas in the Irish Sea has been carried out since 1969, and significant discoveries have been made in the Irish Sea Basin to the north-east, and at Kinsale Head, near Cork, to the west. There has been less interest in the Bristol Channel. No oil or gas finds had been reported in the region as at 1 January 1994, and no oil or gas is currently produced in the region. Estimated 'undiscovered recoverable reserves' in the Southern Basin (Regions 5 and 6), the Irish Sea (mainly Region 13) and the Celtic Sea combined are 0-70 million tonnes for oil and 245-890 billion cubic metres for gas (Department of Trade and Industry 1994). Five exploration and four appraisal wells were commenced in the Irish Sea in 1993, out of a total of 110 such wells drilled in the UK continental shelf.

Much of the coastline of the region to the east of Llanelli (but excluding the Gower Peninsula) is held under an onshore petroleum licence. Areas such as the Menai Strait, the Burry Inlet and the Three Rivers are included in landward licensing rounds; elsewhere the offshore blocks are delineated right up to the coast. The 14th Offshore Licensing Round was announced in June 1993. Thirteen

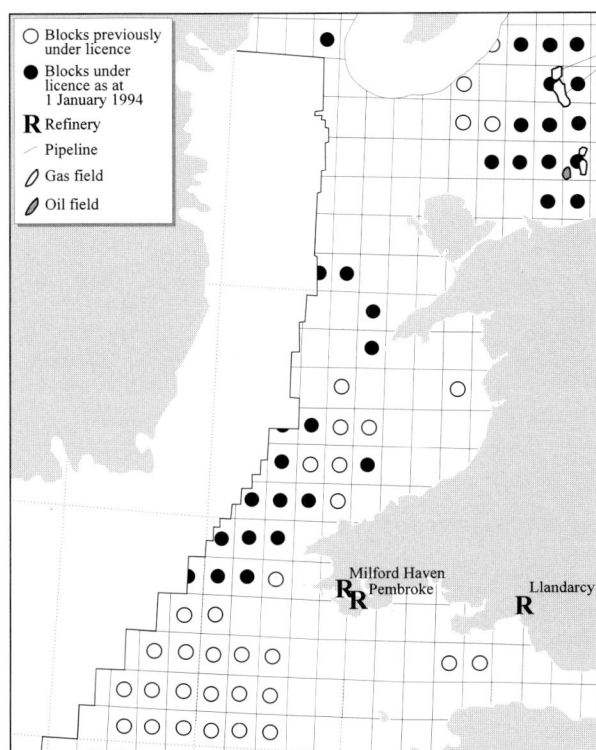

Map 9.6.2 UK Continental Shelf (UKCS) exploration. Source: DTI (1994). © Crown copyright.

blocks were awarded in Cardigan Bay and two in the Central Irish Sea, out of a total of 110 for the whole UK Continental Shelf (UKCS) (DTI 1994). No landward licensing round was held in 1993, and the 15th Round dealt only with areas in the North Sea. The 16th offshore oil and gas licensing round is currently under way, the results being due in June 1995.

9.6.2 Important locations

Map 9.6.1 shows blocks under licence in the region as at 1 January 1994, together with those previously held under licence. Locations of refineries are also shown (see also section 8.3.2). There are no subsea pipelines in the region. Map 9.6.2 shows sedimentary basins and structural 'highs' on the UK continental shelf. Both maps were adapted from DTI (1994).

9.6.3 Effects of human activities

Concern has been expressed about the possible environmental effects of oil and gas exploration and production in Cardigan Bay, should exploitable reserves be discovered, as important wildlife areas such as the Llyn

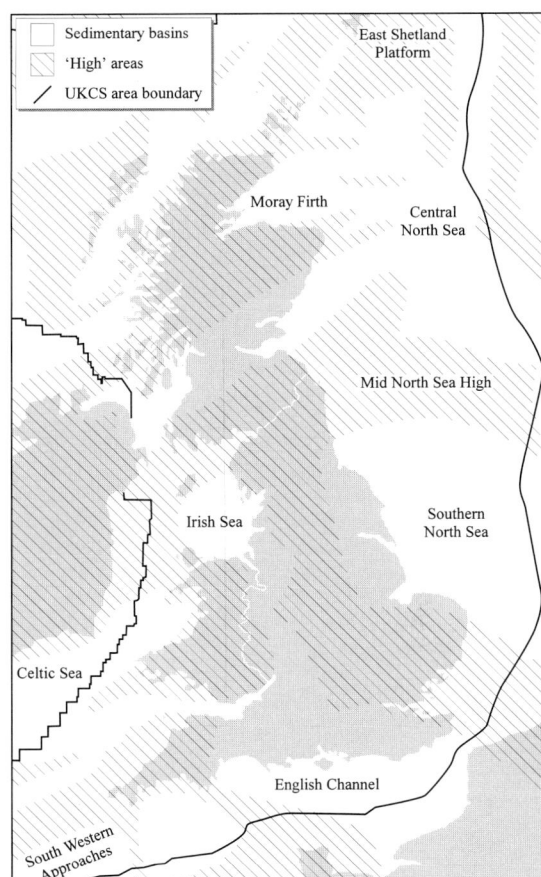

Map 9.6.1 Oil and gas. Source: DTI (1994). © Crown copyright.

211

Peninsula and the Pembrokeshire coast are nearby. Davies and Wilson (1995) describe a methodology for identifying areas unsuitable for licensing and for determining licensing conditions (see section 5.10 for seabird criteria).

9.6.4 Information sources used

Most of the data used here come from the DTI's 'Brown Book' *(The Energy Report, Volume 2: Oil and Gas Resources of the UK)*, which includes a number of caveats on the figures quoted and should be referred to for further explanation.

9.6.5 Further sources of information

A. References cited

Department of Trade and Industry. 1994. *The Energy Report: oil and gas resources of the UK.* London, HMSO.

Institute of Petroleum Information Service. 1993. *Know more about oil: the UK refining industry.* London Institute of Petroleum.

Davies, G.J. & Wilson, J.L.J. 1995. Wildlife sensitivity criteria for oil and gas developments in Great Britain. (Contractor: Environment & Resource Technology Ltd., Stromness). *Joint Nature Conservation Committee Report*, No. 206. (ERT Report No. 94/079.)

B. Further reading

ACOPS. 1990. *Survey of oil pollution around the coasts of the United Kingdom.* Advisory Committee on Pollution of the Sea. Annual Report.

British Gas. 1994. *Transportation & storage, March 1994.* British Gas.

Institute of Petroleum Information Service. 1993. *Know more about oil: the North Sea.* London, Institute of Petroleum.

Institute of Petroleum Information Service. 1993. *UK petroleum industry statistics: consumption and refinery production.* London, Institute of Petroleum.

Scottish Office. 1993. *The Scottish environment - statistics, No. 4 1993.* Edinburgh, The Government Statistical Service.

C. Contact names and addresses

Type of information	Contact address and telephone no.
Oil and gas developments	Public Relations Officer, Department of Trade and Industry, 1 Palace Street, London SW1E 5HE, tel: 0171 238 3214
Oil and gas industry issues	Public Relations Officer, UK Offshore Operators Association, 3 Hans Crescent, London SW1X 0LN, tel: 0171 589 5255
General information on the industry	Librarian, Institute of Petroleum Library and Information Service, 61 New Cavendish Street, London W1M 8AR, tel: 0171 828 7966
Oil refinery environmental problems and general marine environmental issues (Milford Haven)	The Chairman, Milford Haven Waterway Environmental Monitoring Steering Group, County Civil Protection Planning Unit, Hill House, Picton Terrace, Carmarthen, Dyfed SA31 3BS, tel: 01267 236651
Public health issues relating to oil refining (Milford Haven)	Director and Executive Officer, Milford Port Health Authority, Gorsewood Drive, Hakin, Milford Haven, Dyfed SA73 3EP, tel: 01646 692486
Oil spillages	Executive Secretary, British Oil Spill Control Association (BOSCA), 4th Floor, 30 Great Guildford Street, London SE1 0HS, tel: 0171 928 9199
Oil transportation and terminals	V, Oil Companies International Marine Forum (OCIMF), OCIMF, 15th Floor, 96 Victoria Street, London SW1E 5JW, tel: 0171 828 7966
The gas industry	Director and Secretary, Society of British Gas Industries, 36 Holly Walk, Leamington Spa, Warwickshire CV32 4LY, tel: 01926 334357
Oil developments and general issues	Projects Officer: Cardigan Bay Forum, Cardigan Bay Forum, Welsh Agricultural College, Llanbadarn Fawr, Aberystwyth SY23 3AL, te: 01970 624471
Research on local issues	The Director, Field Studies Centre, Fort Popton, Angle, Pembroke, Dyfed SA71 5AD, tel: 01646 641404

9.6.6 Acknowledgements

Thanks to Cardigan Bay Forum and the University of Greenwich for their kind assistance in obtaining information for this region.

9.7 Water quality and effluent discharges

C.A. Crumpton & M.J. Goodwin

9.7.1 Introduction

This section summarises information about water quality and effluent discharge from a number of sources. Full interpretation of the information base on pollutants and water quality is complex and beyond the scope of this book. Waste products and effluents containing contaminants reach the marine environment in this region in a number of ways; discharge ongoing outside the region may also have an effect. Sewage and trade effluents are discharged from outfalls into rivers or directly into the sea. Sewage sludge dumping at sea from ships has decreased in recent years and has now ceased (Welsh Office pers. comm.). Contaminants can reach the sea by airborne means, for example aerosols and rain. There are radioactive discharges within the region from the nuclear power station at Wylfa.

The region's waters suffer pollution particularly from the industrial and residential centres on the south and north coasts. Newport, Cardiff, Port Talbot and Swansea all contribute to the pollution of the region's south coast, with discharges of industrial and domestic waste. Milford Haven is another major industrial centre where pollution has been a problem. The north coast is affected by pollution from Merseyside and the Wirral. Estuarine water quality is summarised in section 4.1 (see especially Table 4.1.4). To date, cadmium is the only List 1 substance (i.e. on List 1 (highly toxic substances) of the EC Directive on the Discharge of Dangerous Substances to the Aquatic Environment (Directive 76/464/EEC)) discharged at significant levels in Wales, although levels are usually highest to the south of the region, in the Severn Estuary. Amongst the seven estuaries regularly monitored in Region 12, the Tawe estuary has the highest values (Welsh Office 1994).

Radioactivity levels increase progressively northwards in the region, probably in part because of the influence of discharges from Sellafield as well as those from Wylfa power station. Concentrations (for example of Caesium - 137) have decreased substantially over the last 15 years (Welsh Office 1994).

84% of EC-identified bathing waters in the region passed mandatory standards in 1993. The 1993 data for the UK as a whole, assessed by DoE, show a similar level of compliance with the mandatory coliform standards in the Bathing Water Directive (76/160/EEC) compared with 1992 (around 79%) (Table 9.7.1). Although the national percentage of bathing waters consistently complying with the mandatory

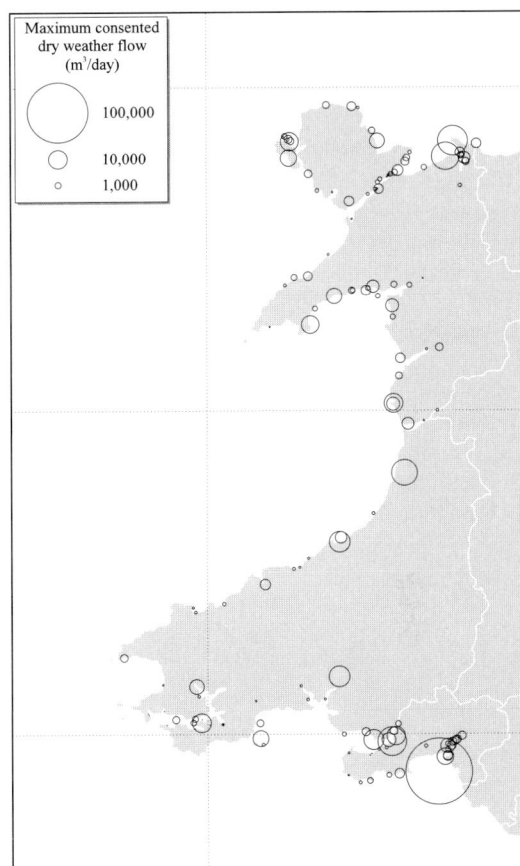

Map 9.7.1 Consented sewage outfalls. Area of circle is proportional to consented 'dry weather flow'. Map shows all outfalls with consented flow greater than 10 m³/day. Trade effluents not shown. Source: MAFF.

standards has remained at around 64%, the number consistently failing has been reduced. Analysis of faecal coliform values suggests that the improved water quality has been maintained over the last four years (Welsh Office 1994).

There were three European Blue Flag beach awards in the region in 1993, at Pembrey, Tenby North and Whitesands St. Davids, out of a total of twenty in the UK. There were 165 Tidy Britain Group Seaside Award beaches in the UK in 1994, including 47 in this region.

Coastwatch UK found that the main items of litter found along the coastline in this region are plastics (including sheeting, fishing gear, bottles and containers), textiles, paper and debris from ship wreckage (Coastwatch UK 1993). Sewage and sanitary materials are also present. Beachwatch '93, organised by Readers Digest and the Marine Conservation Society in parallel with surveys in 51 other countries, revealed that medical waste, including syringes and needles, is an increasing problem and the source is not known (McGilvray 1994).

Table 9.7.2 shows the quality of the region's beaches (for litter) in 1993 in a national context.

Table 9.7.1 Bathing waters survey - 1993 results for England, Wales and Scotland

	1993		1992	
	Pass	*Fail*	*Pass*	*Fail*
NRA Welsh Region	42	9	39	12
English NRA regions	290	77	289	76
Scotland	18	5	15	8
Northern Ireland	15	1	15	1

Source: DoE (1993)

Table 9.7.2 The quality of the region's beaches (for litter) in 1993

Area	% of beaches rated as excellent	% of beaches rated as moderate	% of beaches rated as polluted	Comments
West Glamorgan	9	44	47	All levels of littering better than national averages except for large metal objects, ship wreckage, dumped crops, oil and medical waste.
Dyfed	29	46	25	All litter types found to be consistent in quantity with national averages although general quality above average.
Gwynedd	8	44	48	Majority of litter types found at above national average.
Region 12	15	45	40	
Wales	7	39	54	
Great Britain	*8*	*42*	*50*	

(Source: Coastwatch UK 1993)

9.7.2 Important locations

Map 9.7.1 shows the locations in Region 12 of all the 166 consented (see section 9.7.3) sewage outfalls with a consented 'dry weather flows' (i.e. undiluted by rain) in excess of 10 m³ per day. Table 9.7.3 lists the nineteen sewage outfalls in the region whose consented 'dry weather flows' are in excess of 6,000 m³ per day, showing their locations and the type of discharge. These data do not include trade effluent discharges.

Table 9.7.4 and Map 9.7.2 show the 38 EU identified bathing waters in the region, 32 of which complied with mandatory coliform standards in the 1993 season (NRA 1994b). Bacterial quality of a selection of 130 non-EU identified bathing waters in the region in 1992 is listed in Welsh Office (1994). There are no statutory standards for these bathing waters: 12% were more polluted than the levels set for the EU bathing waters. Estuarine water quality is summarised in chapter 4.1 (see especially Table 4.1.4).

Table 9.7.3 Sewage outfalls in the region with consented 'dry weather flows' >6,000 m³ per day

Name of outfall	Location	Grid ref.	Type of discharge	Consented 'dry weather flow' in cu.m /day
The Baglan Sewage Outfall	Baglan	SS704883	Secondary Treated Sewage	119,000
Jersey Marine Outfall	Neath	SS723926	Untreated Sewage	6,520
Gowerton Sewage Treatment Works	Gowerton	SS562978	Secondary Treated Sewage	21,140
Llanant Sewage Treatment Works	Llanant	SS572995	Secondary Treated Sewage	9,544
Bynea And Halfway Sewage Treatment Works	Bynea	SS552981	Primary Treated Sewage	6,181
Llanelli Northumberland Ave Sewage Treatment Works	Llanelli	SS502984	Primary Treated Sewage	11,333
Parc Y Splotts Sewage Treatment Works	Carmarthen	SN401178	Secondary Treated Sewage	12,630
Tenby Marine Outfall	Tenby	SS155988	Macerated/Comminuted Sewage	7,953
Pembroke Supply Base Hancock Co	Pembroke	SM977040	Secondary Treated Sewage	9,308
Llanina Point Sewage Treatment Works	New Quay Llanina Point	SN403595	Primary Treated Sewage	11,100
Aberystwyth Sewage Treatment Works	Aberystwyth	SN600803	UV Treated Sewage	18,749
Tywyn Outfall	Tywyn	SH570018	Macerated/Comminuted Sewage	10,230
Pwllheli Outfall	Pwllheli	SH389348	Macerated/Comminuted Sewage	6,815
Abersoch Outfall	Abersoch	SH326262	Primary Treated Sewage	9,515
Porth Gwr Mawr Outfall	Trearddur	SH253774	Untreated Sewage	9,000
Turkey Shore Outfall	Holyhead	SH253827	Screened Sewage (>6mm)	9,400
Tynygongl Outfall	Benllech	SH525828	Untreated Sewage	6,140
Dwygyfylchi Outfall	Penmaenmawr	SH732779	Macerated/Comminuted Sewage	22,745
West Shore Outfall	Llandudno	SH756825	Macerated/Comminuted Sewage	26,740

Source: MAFF database of discharges to saline waters in England and Wales

Table 9.7.4 The state of the region's EU identified bathing
waters - 1993 season

Bathing water	Pass or fail
Swansea Bay	Fail
Bracelet Bay	Pass
Limeslade Bay	Pass
Langland Bay	Fail
Caswell Bay	Pass
Oxwich Bay	Pass
Port Eynon Bay	Pass
Rhossili Beach	Pass
Pembrey Beach	Pass
Pendine Beach	Pass
Amroth Beach	Pass
Saundersfoot Beach	Pass
Tenby N. Beach	Pass
Tenby S. Beach	Pass
Broadhaven	Pass
Newgale Beach	Pass
Whitesands	Pass
Newport Sands N.	Fail
Traeth Gwyn, New Quay	Pass
Aberystwyth S. Beach	Fail
Aberystwyth N. Beach	Pass
Aberdyfi	Fail
Borth	Pass
Tywyn	Pass
Fairbourne Beach	Pass
Barmouth	Pass
Llandanwg Beach	Pass
Harlech	Pass
Morfa Bychan	Pass
Criccieth Beach E.	Pass
Pwllheli Beach	Pass
Abersoch	Pass
Morfa Dinlle	Pass
Benllech	Pass
Treardurr Bay	Pass
Rhosneigr	Pass
Llandudno W.	Fail
Llandudno N.	Pass

Source: NRA (1993)

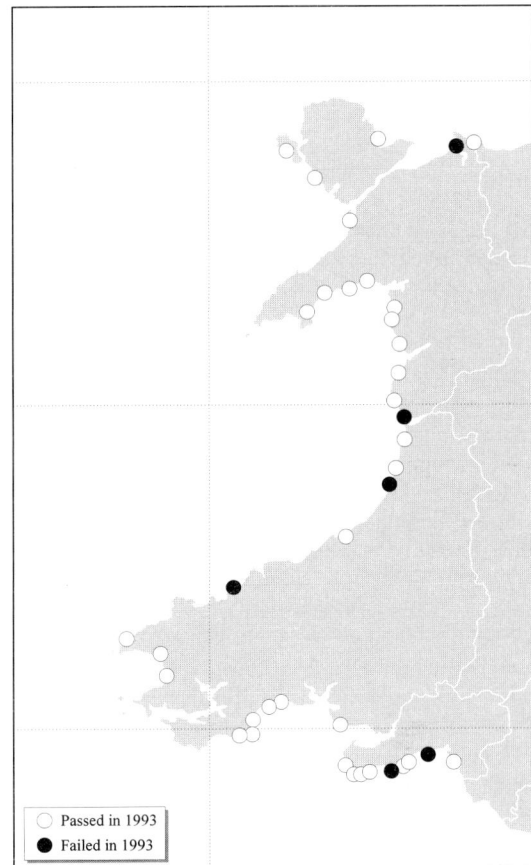

Map 9.7.2 Bathing water quality. Results of 1993 sampling of EC-
identified bathing waters. Source: NRA (1994b).
Adapted with permission.

9.7.3 Management and issues

The Water Resources Act (1991) is the main legislation that
controls discharges to the aquatic environment in Wales.
The National Rivers Authority (NRA) has overall
responsibility for the control of discharges and the
maintenance of water quality. It authorises sewage
discharges by issuing 'consents', with the Welsh Office
Agriculture Department (WOAD) as a statutory consultee to
take into account the fishery interests. Trade effluent
involving 'scheduled' (hazardous) processes must be
authorised by Her Majesty's Inspector of Pollution under
the Environmental Protection Act 1990, with the NRA as a
statutory consultee. WOAD issues licences for the dumping
of sewage at sea. From early 1992 all dumping of liquid
waste into the sea from ships ceased and all sewage sludge
dumping by marine vessels is set to be phased out by 1998,
under the Urban Waste Water Treatment Directive
(91/271/EEC). Under the same Directive all significant
sewage discharges, except those in 'High Natural
Dispersion Areas', will require minimum secondary
treatment, to be phased in by 2005. Sewage disposal on
land is controlled by the local Waste Regulation Authorities
(see section 9.4). The UK produces some 1.1 million tonnes
of dry solids (tds) of sewage sludge annually and disposes
of approximately 300,000 tds into the sea. UK sewage
sludge production is set to increase dramatically over the
next decade, with predicted increases totalling 2.2 million
tds by 2006. This will have to be disposed of on land, either
by dumping or by incineration.

215

9.7.4 Information sources

There are currently several schemes for assessing the quality of coastal waters and beaches. The NRA monitors identified bathing waters for levels of coliforms (bacteria that indicate sewage presence) under the EC Bathing Water Directive. There are schemes such as the European Blue Flags and Tidy Britain Group Seaside Awards for beaches which meet standards of beach and water quality. The Welsh Office publish an annual *Environmental Digest for Wales*, covering this region, which provides datasets on pollution indicators, including estuarine water quality, bathing waters and coastal water quality (heavy metals, sewage and radioactivity) (see Welsh Office 1994). The Ministry of Agriculture Fisheries and Food hold a database of consented sewage outfalls in England and Wales, and provide technical backup to WOAD.

Pollution levels in coastal waters north from Pembrokeshire are described further in Irish Sea Study Group (1990). The NRA's quarterly ship and air-borne National Coastal Baseline Survey monitors a large number of water quality parameters in coastal waters, including metals, nutrients and turbidity. Finally, there are the annual litter surveys of Coastwatch UK and Beachwatch, both of which use volunteers to survey lengths of coastline for litter and other signs of pollution. Coastwatch UK and Beachwatch do not sample the whole coastline in the region because of a shortage of volunteers. In consequence the results may be unrepresentative, especially as monitoring takes place over only one or two days per year.

9.7.5 Further sources of information

A. References

Coastwatch UK. 1993. *1993 survey report.* Farnborough College of Technology.

Department of the Environment. 1993. Minute No. 818. 1/12/93.

Irish Sea Study Group. 1990. *The Irish Sea. An environmental review. Part 2. Waste inputs and pollution.* Liverpool University Press. (Irish Sea Study Group Report.)

McGilvray, F. 1994. Marine debris on Britain's coast. *North Sea Monitor,* Vol. 12, Issue 1, March 1994.

National Rivers Authority. 1994. *Bathing water quality in England and Wales - 1993.* Bristol, National Rivers Authority.

National Rivers Authority. 1993. *Bathing waters report 1993, Welsh Region.* Bristol, National Rivers Authority.

Welsh Office. 1994. *Environmental digest for Wales. No. 8. 1993.* Cardiff.

B. Further reading

Anon. 1993. Lies, damned lies and statistics in the great water debate. *ENDS Report.* No. 227 (12/93): 16-19.

Anon. 1987. Shift on sewage sludge disposal methods. *Marine Pollution Bulletin,* Vol. 18, No. 12: 619.

Anon. 1989. Sewage sludge statistics. *Marine Pollution Bulletin, Vol. 20,* No. 2: 54.

Baker, B. 1993. The burning issue. *Surveyor.* 2/12/93, 18-19.

Clark, R.B. 1986. *Marine pollution.* Oxford, Blackwell Scientific Publications.

Department of Environment. 1990. *The digest of environmental protection and water statistics,* No. 13. London, HMSO.

Department of the Environment. 1992. *The UK environment.* London, HMSO.

Eno, N.C., ed. 1991. *Marine conservation handbook.* 2nd ed. Peterborough, English Nature.

European Community. 1991. *Directive on urban waste water treatment 1991.* (91/271/EEC.)

Hoare, R., & Hiscock, K. 1974. An ecological survey of the rocky coast adjacent to a bromine extraction works. *Estuarine and Coastal Marine Science,* 2: 329-348.

Horsman, P. 1982. The amount of garbage pollution from merchant ships. *Marine Pollution Bulletin, 13:* 167-169.

House of Commons Environment Committee. 1990. *Fourth report: pollution of beaches.* Vol.1. London, HMSO.

National Rivers Authority. 1994. *Discharge consents and compliance: the NRA's approach to control of discharges to water.* Bristol, National Rivers Authority.

Irish Sea Study Group. 1990. *The Irish Sea; an environmental review. Part 2; Waste inputs and pollution.* Liverpool, Liverpool University Press.

Irving, R. 1993. *Too much of a good thing: nutrient enrichment in the U.K.'s coastal waters.* A report to the World Wide Fund for Nature (WWF). London, WWF.

Kay, D., & Wyer, M. 1994. Making waves: recreational water quality. *Biologist, Vol. 41,* No. 1: 17-20.

Lees, D.N. Undated. Shellfish monitoring. *In: Viruses in the marine environment,* 43-57. Liverpool, Irish Sea Forum. (Irish Sea Forum Seminar Report.)

Marine Conservation Society. 1994. *The good beach guide.* Ross-on-Wye, Marine Conservation Society. (Details sewage outfalls close to beaches in the guide (not all coastal outfalls) and what treatment the sewage has had.)

Marine Pollution Monitoring Management Group (Monitoring Co-ordination Subgroup). 1994. *UK. national monitoring plan.* HMIP.

MAFF Directorate of Fisheries Research. 1991. *Utility of experimental measures of biological effects for monitoring marine sewage-sludge disposal sites.* MAFF, Lowestoft. (Aquatic Environment Monitoring Report No.24.)

MAFF Directorate of Fisheries Research. 1991. *Second report of the Marine Pollution Monitoring Management Group's Co-ordinating Group on monitoring of sewage sludge disposal sites.* MAFF, Lowestoft. (Aquatic Environment Monitoring Report No. 25.)

MAFF Directorate of Fisheries Research. 1991. *Monitoring and surveillance of non-radioactive contaminants in the aquatic environment and activities regulating the disposal of wastes at sea, 1988-89.* MAFF, Lowestoft. (Aquatic Environment Monitoring Report No.26.)

MAFF Directorate of Fisheries Research. 1991. *Third report of the Marine Pollution Monitoring Management Group's Co-ordinating Group on monitoring of sewage sludge disposal sites.* MAFF, Lowestoft. (Aquatic Environment Monitoring Report No.27.)

NRA. 1993. *Bathing water quality in England and Wales, 1992.* Bristol, National Rivers Authority. (Water Quality Series No. 11.)

Welsh Office. 1993. *Environment digest for Wales, No. 7, 1992.* Cardiff, Welsh Office.

Worldwide Fund for Nature UK. 1995. *Reassessing pollution: wildlife, humans and toxic chemicals in the environment.* Godalming, Worldwide Fund for Nature UK.

C. Contact names and addresses

Type of information	Contact address and telephone no.
Waste disposal. Statutory consultee for sewage discharges.	Welsh Office Agriculture Department, Fisheries Department, Division 2B, New Crown Buildings, Cathays Park, Cardiff CF1 3NQ, tel: 01222 823567
Aquatic environment research relating to waste disposal. Effects of dumping wastes at sea. Database of discharges to saline waters.	Senior Licensing Officer (Dumping), Ministry of Agriculture Fisheries and Food Fisheries Laboratory, Remembrance Ave., Burnham-upon-Crouch, Essex CM0 8HA, tel. 01621 782658
Bathing waters, as outlined in EC Directive (76/160/EEC)	Enquiries Officer, Department of the Environment (Public Enquiries Unit), tel. only: 0171 276 0900
Water quality, including bathing waters and National Coastal Baseline Survey. Discharge consents.	*Technical Manager, NRA Welsh Region, Cardiff, tel. 01222 770088
as above	Public Relations Manager, NRA, Highfield, Priestly Road, Caernarfon LL55 1HR, tel. 01286 672247
as above	Pollution Control Officer, NRA, Glan Teifi, Barley Mow, Lampeter, Dyfed SA48 7BY, tel. 01570 422455
Waste disposal, pollution, conservation issues	*Coastal ecologist, CCW HQ, Bangor, tel: 01248 370444
Sewage outfalls/effluent discharges	Chief Scientist (Environment), Dwr Cymru Cyfyngedig (Operating Company for Welsh Water Plc), Plas Y Ffyynnon, Cambrian Way, Brecon, Powys LD3 7HP, tel: 01874 623181
Industrial waste disposal	The Oslo and Paris Commissions, New Court, 48 Carey Street, London WC2A 2JE, tel. 0171 242 9927
Pollution from industrial sites. 'Scheduled' processes (hazardous discharges).	HM Inspector of Pollution (HMIP), Brunel House, 11th Floor, 2 Fitzalan Road, Cardiff CF2 1TT, tel. 01222 495558
Environmental pollution	Secretary, Royal Commission on Environmental Pollution, Church House, Great Smith Street, London SW1P 3BZ, tel. 0171 276 2080
Waste regulatory authorities (Local authority offices)	see table in section 9.4.5C.
Litter (Beachwatch '93) and "The Good Beach Guide"	*Campaigns Manager, Marine Conservation Society, Ross-on-Wye, tel. 01989 66017
Litter	Public Affairs Executive, Keep Wales Tidy Campaign, 8a Cambrian Estate, Pontyclun, Mid Glamorgan CF7 9EW, tel. 01443 228032
Seaside Awards	Information Officer, Tidy Britain Group, Trencherfield Mill, The Pier, Wigan, Lancs. WN3 4EX, tel: 01942 824620
Litter	Project Officer, Coastwatch UK, Farnborough College of Technology, Boundary Road, Farnborough, Hampshire GU14 6SB, tel. 01252 377503
Issues relating to Cardigan Bay	*Projects Officer, Cardigan Bay Forum, Aberystwyth, tel. 01970 624471
Issues relating to Carmarthen Bay	*Secretary, Carmarthen Bay Forum, Whitland, Dyfed, tel: 01994 419313
Issues relating to North Wales	*Chairman, North Wales Coastal Forum, Pwllheli, tel: 01758 83423
Marine processes and general research	Director, Centre for Marine and Coastal Studies, University of Liverpool, PO Box 147, Liverpool L69 3BX, tel: 0151 794 3653

* Starred contact addresses are given in full in the Appendix

9.8 Leisure and tourism

M.J. Dunbar, S.J. Everett and S.L. Fowler

9.8.1 Introduction

Tourism and the leisure industry are major contributors to the Welsh economy and provide many jobs in areas where there are otherwise few. Over 7 million residential holiday-makers visit Wales each year, as well as up to one million day visitors on fine summer weekends. More than 60% of the residential holiday-makers come to the coast. Most of the region's coast is of great leisure and tourist value because of its beautiful scenery, National Parks, historic towns, rocky coasts for angling and diving, fine beaches and clear, relatively warm sea water. It has been popular for leisure and tourism since the last century, especially for the population of the southern half of Britain, and is comparable in importance with the south-west peninsula of England. As well as attracting visitors from outside the region, coastal towns provide important leisure facilities for local people.

Virtually all kinds of leisure activities take place around the coast, including walking, camping, golf, bird-watching, climbing on sea cliffs, hang gliding and paragliding, land yachting on a few beaches, and general beach use by holiday-makers. Some of the most significant land-uses for tourism on the coast are golf courses, caravan/camping sites and rural car parks (which provide the access points necessary for many land- and water-based leisure activities). These are located on Map 9.8.1. A total of 133 caravan/camping sites have been identified along the coast. There were 23 golf courses and 86 car parks (excluding urban car parks not marked on the Ordnance Survey 1:50,000 maps from which these figures were obtained).

The main infrastructure developments for water-based leisure activities in the region include marinas, yacht moorings, dinghy parks and launching slips. Both long-established and modern yachting, power boating and other water sports centres are widely distributed along the coast. Many are concentrated in the sheltered waters of bays and inlets and near centres of population, where the newer centres are sometimes associated with the regeneration of waterfronts or areas where employment and/or tourism had been in decline. The northern half of Cardigan Bay, where the towns of Pwllheli and Abersoch were involved in the recent unsuccessful Manchester Olympic Games bid, has been described as the second most important sailing centre in Britain after the Solent (Heritage Coast Forum 1993). Limited facilities (primarily recreational craft moorings) are also found in most of the small fishing ports and harbours around the coastline, often where traditional harbour activities have declined. Other important water sports using the same basic recreational infrastructure or not requiring infrastructure, other than land access to the coast, include scuba diving, sea angling, jet-skiing, water skiing, canoeing, wind surfing, surfing and bathing. Boat trips are an important coastal activity in some areas during the main tourist season. Important areas for marine leisure are shown on Map 9.8.2.

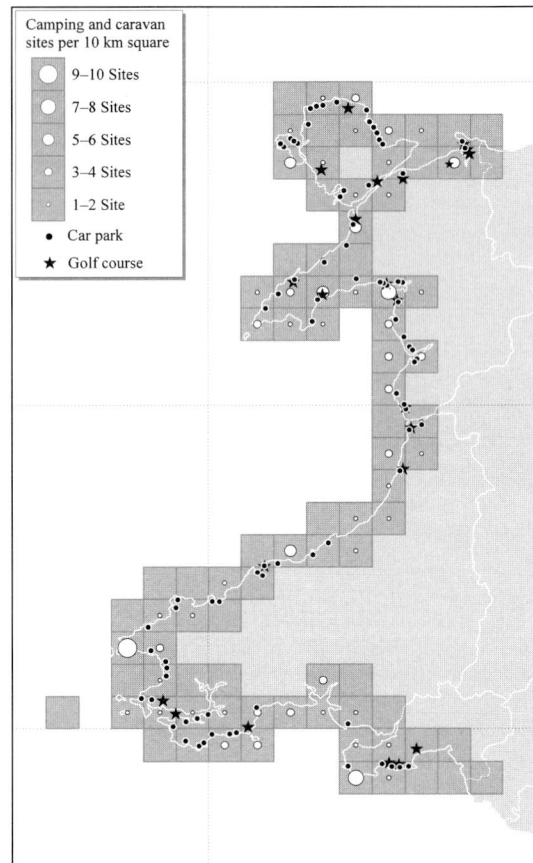

Map 9.8.1 Land-based leisure. Source: Ordnance Survey Landranger maps. © Crown copyright.

Table 9.8.1 Land- and water- based recreation sites within 10 km of the coast, by local authority district

District	No. of land-based sites	No. of water-based sites
Port Talbot	10	12
Neath	11	6
Swansea	36	42
Lliw Valley	6	12
Dinefwr	1	0
Llanelli	11	13
Carmarthen	12	22
South Pembrokeshire	19	36
Preseli	35	58
Ceredigion	25	45
Montgomery	2	1
Meirionnydd	53	57
Dwyfor	43	44
Arfon	43	21
Ynys Mon	23	57
Aberconwy	38	33
Total Region 12	*368*	*459*

Source: Natural Facilities Database (Sports Council for Wales/CCW). Figures for Preseli, Montgomery, Arfon, Lliw Valley and Neath include sites shared with adjoining districts (1 in each case). Figures for Swansea and Ynys Mon include sites shared with adjoining districts (2 in each case). Sites may be important for both land- and water-based leisure; the figures are not exclusive.

9.8.2 Important locations

In Wales as a whole there are currently 549 recorded sites of land- and air-based recreation identified as being within 10 km of the coast, the most numerous recorded activities being riding (at 138 sites), golf (78), hill-walking (65), rock climbing (58), orienteering (36) and cross-country races (30). 619 recorded sites of water-based recreation are identified as being within 10 km of the coast, the most numerous recorded activities being game angling (at 105 sites), sea bathing (86), sailing (74), boardsailing (53), sub-aqua (47) and canoeing (44). Table 9.8.1 shows the breakdown of land- and water-based sites within the region, by local authority district.

Table 9.8.2 shows the distribution of known accommodation in coastal districts in 1991: the original document (Wales Tourist Board 1991) should be referred to for an explanation of the assumptions and constraints in using the data. It is not known how much of this accommodation is on or near the coast, but in most areas it is probably a large proportion.

Table 9.8.2 Known bedspaces in tourist accommodation in coastal districts

District	Serviced	Self-catering	Caravan/camping
Port Talbot	215	96	0
Neath	269	4	240
Swansea	3,218	570	9,245
Lliw Valley	52	0	0
Llanelli	625	0	2,305
Carmarthen	1,675	1,285	2,281
South Pembrokeshire	6,488	1,476	15,260
Preseli	3,834	1,176	5,930
Ceredigion	4,095	2,038	12,680
Meirionnydd	4,731	1,531	13,248
Dwyfor	4,896	6,017	9,561
Arfon	3,269	1,262	4,466
Ynys Mon	2,887	1,212	6,683
Aberconwy	14,420	1,661	3,630
Total Region 12	*50,674*	*18,328*	*85,529*

Source: Wales Tourist Board (1991)

The Gower Peninsula is an important tourism centre in the south-east of the region, with a high concentration of caravan/camping sites and rural car parks, and many visitors as a result of its proximity to the conurbations of South Wales and the M4. Rhosilly Down on the peninsula is a popular area for hang gliding and paragliding.

Further west, a major concentration of leisure activities is located around the tourist centres of Tenby and Saundersfoot. This high density of leisure land-use decreases slightly around the Pembrokeshire National Park coastline and into the southern section of Cardigan Bay, but the National Park coastline is popular with visitors for walking and beach recreation. The Pembrokeshire Coast Path is the only National Trail in the region and extends from Amroth to Cardigan.

Much of the west Wales coast of Dyfed and Gwynedd is rugged and undeveloped, but there are significant tourist areas. These include (in Cardigan Bay): Aberporth, New Quay, Aberaeron, Aberystwyth, Borth, Tywyn, Barmouth, Harlech, Porthmadog, Criccieth, Pwllheli and Abersoch.

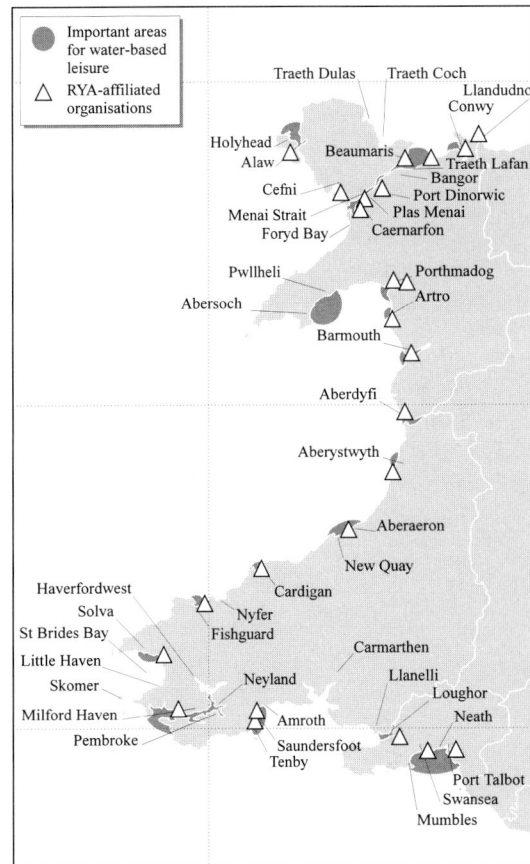

Map 9.8.2 Water-based leisure. Named locations are those listed in Table 9.8.4. (RYA: Royal Yachting Association). Sources: Tourist Offices.

Maps 9.8.1 and 9.8.2 show quite large numbers of facilities scattered along this coast, particularly bordering Snowdonia National Park. There is a large holiday camp (Starcoast World) between Pwllheli and Criccieth, major new tourism centres are planned for Harlech, Barmouth and Tywyn, and Barmouth has a new leisure centre. Walking and camping are popular activities on the Llyn peninsula, where remote lengths of coast remain free of leisure infrastructure.

The beaches of Caernarfon Bay and Anglesey have all attracted leisure developments. A major and regionally important tourist area is located at Llandudno on Conwy Bay, in the north-east corner of the region. This resort, along with Colwyn Bay to the east (in Region 13), serves many visitors from the industrial towns of north-west England, and is a significant traditional seaside recreational area. Great Orme is a popular Country Park and attracts many visitors, particularly for walking.

The sea cliffs of Gower, Pembrokeshire, Llyn, Holy Island and the Great Orme are popular climbing areas, but codes of conduct generally restrict this activity to outside the bird breeding season (see section 5.10 and 5.11).

Table 9.8.3 summarises the distribution of some land-based recreational activities in or near Heritage Coasts.

Many marinas are under construction or planned in this region: 39 potential Welsh marina sites were identified by the Council (now Campaign) for the Protection of Rural Wales in 1989 (Council for the Protection of Rural Wales 1989). Sixty-three affiliated sailing or yacht clubs are listed for the region by the RYA (1992), and there are numerous other water-sports clubs, particularly along the sheltered

Table 9.8.3 Sites of land-based recreational activities in (and within 1 km inland of) selected Heritage Coasts

Activity	Gower	S. Pemb.	Ceredigion	Llyn	Holyhead	Great Orme
Rock climbing	7	7	-	5	6	3
Pony trekking	1	-	1 (2)	(1)	(1)	(1)
Paragliding or hang gliding	1	-	-	1	-	1

Source: Sports Council for Wales (1992). Note: bracketed numbers of sites are inland within 1 km of the coast.

Table 9.8.4 Existing and proposed water-based leisure and tourism facilities

Site	Grid ref.	Marinas and leisure harbours	Additional moorings/ anchorages	Amenity barrages
Neath	SS7292	Monkstone Marina, Briton Ferry		
Swansea	SS6694	Swansea dock (recent redevelopment of 400-berth marina in old dock area)	yes	One present on the Tawe
Loughor	SS4897	New marinas proposed for Llanelli North Dock and Burry Port	yes	Proposed for Pembrey Dock and Burry Port (Doody unpub.)
Carmarthen	SN4020		yes	
Saundersfoot	SN1304		yes	
Tenby	SN1301	harbour	yes	
Milford Haven	SM9403	Pembroke, Milford Docks and Marina (151 berths), Neyland Yacht Haven (420 berths). New marinas proposed at Castle Pill, Pennar Park, Haverfordwest	Many. Major centre for sailing and water-sports	Proposed at Haverfordwest, Cosheston, Pembroke, Neyland
Skomer	SM7309		anchorage	
St Bride's Bay / Little Haven	SM8613		several anchorages	
Solva	SM8023		yes	
Fishguard	SM9638	proposed marina	yes	
Nyfer Estuary	SN0540		yes	
Cardigan	SN1648	proposed marina	yes	
New Quay	SN4060		yes	
Aberaeron	SN4663		yes	
Aberystwyth	SN5980	proposed marina	yes	
Aberdyfi	SN6495	yes	yes	
Barmouth / Mawddach	SH6416		yes	
Artro	SH5725		yes	
Portmadog / Traeth Bach (Glaslyn / Dwyryd)	SH5736	harbour, proposed marina	yes	
Pwllheli harbour	SH3835	yes (400 berths completed 1993 as part of unsuccessful Manchester Olympic bid)	yes, more proposed	
Abersoch	SH3128	Important sailing centre, part of Olympic bid.	yes	
Foryd Bay (Fort Belan)	SH4461	proposed marina		
Caernarfon	SH4863	proposed marina	yes	
Menai Strait	SH5471		yes, many	
Plas Menai	SH5066	(sailing centre)	yes	
Bangor / Penrhyn	SH5973	harbour, proposed marina	yes, many	
Beaumaris	SH6176	harbour	yes	
Port Dinorwic	SH5268	harbour, 230 berths	yes	
Cefni	SH4067		yes	
Alaw Estuary / Holyhead	SH3081	proposed marina at Holyhead	yes	
Traeth Dulas	SH4888		yes	
Traeth Coch	SH5380		yes	
Traeth Lafan	SH6375	proposed	yes	
Conwy	SH7976	marina, 243 berths	yes	

Sources: Buck (1993), D'Olivera & Featherstone (1993) and miscellaneous, e.g. tourist brochures

coastal areas such as Swansea Bay, Milford Haven, Carmarthen Bay, Tremadoc Bay, Abersoch to Pwllheli and the Menai Strait, where the Welsh National Water Sports Centre is based. Several other informal sailing groups use *ad hoc* beach hut facilities during the summer months. Casual surfing, canoeing and wind-surfing take place from many of the region's beaches and there has recently been a dramatic increase in jet-skiing, particularly in the Swansea Bay / Mumbles area and off the Pembrokeshire coast. Scuba diving is a widespread activity on the west coast, particularly off the Gower Peninsula (sixteen sites on the Heritage Coast listed in Sports Council (1992)), Pembrokeshire (50 sites on the Heritage Coasts) and the shores of the Llyn peninsula and Anglesey. Angling takes place from the shore and at sea.

Existing and major proposed water-based leisure developments are listed in Table 9.8.4. The activities undertaken at ports and harbours in the region are described in section 8.3.2 and listed in Table 8.3.2; their locations are shown on Map 8.3.3. Many of them have recreational moorings and launching slips.

9.8.3 Management and issues

The Wales Tourist Board is the independent statutory body financed primarily by the Welsh Office to encourage tourism in Wales. It liaises closely with private sector partners such as the three regional tourism companies (for North, Mid and South Wales), local authorities and statutory agencies such as the Welsh Development Agency, the Development Board for Rural Wales and Countryside Council for Wales. All the local authorities are concerned with tourism developments and consider them within their structure and local plans. Local authority coastal planning responsibilities and initiatives are described in section 10.4.

Since the 1950s there has been strong growth in many sectors of the tourist industry, including coastal camp sites and caravan parks. Many coastal campsites were initiated in the early days of planning controls and would not now be permitted by local authorities. More recently, efforts have been made to provide a greater choice of accommodation and interest away from the coastal zone, including the provision of 'gateway' facilities such as visitor centres in key locations. Coastal resorts have in the past acted somewhat as 'dormitories' for inland attractions such as Snowdonia National Park. The European Union's 'Leader' programme has been drawn upon to promote lesser known areas, often inland, in order to reduce tourist pressure on the 'honeypot' areas. As the structure of the tourist industry has changed, with more people travelling overseas for their holidays and expecting higher standards in domestic accommodation, hotels have been upgraded, whereas new campsites have become relatively less popular.

'Environmentally friendly' development is strongly favoured by the planning authorities. This includes crafts, bed-and-breakfast and farm-based tourism. There is increasing emphasis on the provision of quality accommodation rather than new caravan sites. Attention is also focused on expanding the tourist season outside the June-August season.

The popularity of Gower as a tourism centre has created problems for traffic management and, in some cases, the management of coastal habitats. Intensive tourist-related

developments are not now encouraged in this area. There are now restrictions on new coastal caravan and camping sites in Merionnydd. On the Llyn peninsula, cases of unsympathetic tourism development have been halted by the planning authority. Planning permission will no longer normally be granted for new camping and caravan sites on Anglesey.

A report by the Wales Tourist Board (1988) proposed a network of marinas all along the coast, but an up-to-date review is required for the current position to be assessed. Since the commercial viability of marina developments is closely related to that of property development in general, falling property prices over the last few years may be expected to have reduced enthusiasm for marina development, and some proposals may never come to fruition (Wales Tourist Board *pers. comm*).

The economic boom of the 1980s stimulated a substantial number of speculative developments associated with leisure and tourism. Amenity barrages became a particularly popular idea and some proposals are still under consideration in this region.

9.8.4 Information sources

Most of the above information is derived from materials received from Tourist Information Centres (up to date, but of varying detail within the region), from facilities shown on Ordnance Survey 1:50,000 Land Ranger maps and Admiralty Charts, from Huckbody *et al.* (1992) and from a nautical almanac (D'Olivera & Featherstone 1993). It is not possible to indicate the scale (size and capacity) of each campsite or car park from this information, and these will naturally vary considerably from the very small to the very large. The map and other information can only therefore be used to give an indication of the scale of this land use throughout the region's coastline. The Sports Council for Wales, in conjunction with the Countryside Council for Wales, is creating a Geographic Information System (GIS) database of Natural Facilities in Wales, logging more than 2,200 sites used for recreation, including information on location, activity type, club, access and site protection data.

9.8.5 Further sources of information

A. References cited

Buck, A.L. 1993. *An inventory of UK estuaries. Volume 2 South-west Britain*. Peterborough, Joint Nature Conservation Committee.

Council for the Protection of Rural Wales. 1989. *A green paper on marinas in Wales*. Welshpool, CPRW.

D'Olivera, B., & Featherstone, N.L. 1993. *The Macmillan and Silk Cut Nautical Almanac 1994*. Basingstoke, Macmillan Press Ltd.

Huckbody, A.J, Taylor, P.M., Hobbs, G. & Elliott, R. 1992. *Caernarfon and Cardigan Bays: an environmental appraisal*. London, Hamilton Oil Company.

Heritage Coast Forum. 1993. Llyn Heritage Coast. *In: Heritage Coasts in England and Wales: a gazetteer*. Manchester, Heritage Coast Forum.

Royal Yachting Association. 1992. *RYA affiliated organisations*. Eastleigh, RYA.

Sports Council for Wales. 1992. *Sport, recreation and protected areas in Wales*. Cardiff, Sports Council.

Wales Tourist Board. 1988. *Tourism in Wales. Developing the potential.* Cardiff.

Wales Tourist Board. 1991. *Compendium of statistical information on tourist accommodation.* Cardiff.

B. Further reading

British Tourist Authority. 1989. *Walking in Britain.* London, British Tourist Authority.

Doody, J.P. Undated. *Coastal habitat change - a historical review of man's impact on the coastline of Great Britain.* Peterborough, Joint Nature Conservation Committee (unpublished draft).

Evans, D.M., & Thomason, H. 1990. Tourism and recreational developments. *In: The Irish Sea, an environmental review. Part 4. Planning, development and management,* ed. by H.D. Smith & A.J. Geffen. Liverpool, Liverpool University Press. (Irish Sea Study Group.)

Robinson, A., & Millward, R. 1983. *The Shell book of the British coast,* 185 - 229. Newton Abbot, David and Charles.

Sports Council for Wales. 1991. *Sport and recreation in the natural environment: a digest for Wales.* Cardiff, Sports Council.

Sports Council. 1992. *Planning and managing watersports on the coast: lessons from Canada and the USA. Factfile 3: Countryside and water recreation.* London, Sports Council.

C. Contact names and addresses

Type of information	Contact address and telephone no.
Tourist facilities	Wales Tourist Board, Brunel House, 2 Fitzalan Road, Cardiff CG2 1UY, and 34 Piccadilly, London W1, tel. 0171 409 0969
Tourism information service	British Tourist Authority, Commercial Information Library, Thames Tower, Black's Road, Hammersmith, London W6 9EL, tel. 0181 846 9000 x 3011/3015
Tourist facilities	Tourist Information Centres Swansea, PO Box 59, Singleton Street SA1 3QG, tel. 01792 468321 Mumbles, Oystermouth Square SA3 4DQ, tel. 01792 361302 Llanelli, Public Library, Vaughan Street SA15 3AS, tel. 01554 772020 Tenby, The Croft SA70 8AP, tel. 01974 298144 Pembroke, Visitor Centre, Commons Road SA71 4EA, tel. 01646 622388 Milford Haven, 94 Charles Street SA73 2HL, tel. 01646 690866 Haverfordwest, Old Bridge SA61 2EZ, tel. 01437 763110 St. Davids, City Hall SA62 6SD, tel. 01437 720392 Fishguard, 4 Hamilton Street SA65 9HL, tel. 01348 873484 Cardigan, Theatr Mwldan, Bath House Road SA43 2JY, tel. 01239 613230 New Quay, Church Street SA45 9NZ, tel. 01545 560865 Aberaeron, The Quay SA46 0BT, tel. 01545 570602 Aberystwyth, Terrace Road SY23 2AG, tel. 01970 612125 Borth, High Street, The Promenade SY24 5HY, tel. 01970 871174 Aberdyfi, The Wharf Gardens LL35 0ED, tel. 01654 767321 Tywyn, High Street LL36 9AD, tel. 01654 710070 Barmouth, The Old Library, Station Road LL42 1LU, tel. 01341 280787 Harlech, Gwyddfir House, High Street LL46 2YA, tel. 01766 780658 Portmadog, High Street LL49 9LP, tel. 01766 512981 Pwllheli, Min y Don, Station Square LL53 5HG, tel. 01758 613000 Caernarfon, Oriel Pendeitsh, Castle Street LL55 2NA, tel. 01286 672232 Holyhead, Marine Square, Salt Island Approach LL65 1DR, tel. 01407 762622 Bangor, Theatr Gwynedd, Deiniol Road, Gwynedd LL57 2TL, tel. 01248 352786 Conwy, Conwy Castle Visitor Centre LL32 8LD, tel. 01492 592248 Llandudno, 1-2 Chapel Street LL30 2YU, tel. 01492 860490
Funding for tourism-related developments	Welsh Development Agency, Pearl House, Greyfriars Road, Cardiff CF1 3XX, tel. 01222 222666
Funding for tourism-related developments	The Development Board for Rural Wales, Lady Well House, Newtown, Powys SY16 1JB, tel. 01686 626965
Development in rural Wales	Campaign (formerly Council) for the Protection of Rural Wales, Ty Gwyn, 31 High Street, Welshpool, Powys SY21 7JP, tel: 01938 552525
Natural Facilities database	Rural Surveys Research Unit, Institute of Earth Studies, University College of Wales, Aberystwyth, Dyfed SY23 3DB, tel: 01970 622585

Sports Council. 1992. *Heritage Coasts: good practice in the planning, management and sustainable development of sport and active recreation.* London, Sports Council.

Sports Council. 1993. *Water skiing and the environment.* London, Sports Council.

Taylor, P.M., & Parker, J.G., *eds.* 1993. *The coast of north Wales and north-west England: an environmental appraisal.* London, Hamilton Oil Company Ltd.

Wales Tourist Board. 1994. *Tourism 2000 - a strategy for Wales.* Cardiff.

9.8.6 Acknowledgements

Thanks to Mr Elwyn Owen (Wales Tourist Board) and Professor Aitchison (Rural Surveys Research Unit) for providing information.

Chapter 10 Coastal management

10.1 Coastal management in the UK

S.L. Fowler, M.J. Dunbar and S.J. Everett

10.1.1 Introduction

In this chapter, unlike in most others in this book, the names and addresses of many contacts are given at the end of the relevant section, as well as the whole chapter concluding with a list of contacts with a wider involvement or interest in coastal management.

A great many, frequently competing, issues and activities affect the coastal environment and inshore waters. As a result, the task of coastal planning and management is a very complex one, not eased by the fact that numerous different authorities are individually responsible for particular statutory duties. Coastal management seeks to promote an inter-disciplinary approach to multiple use and the resolution of conflict between interest groups, "to ensure the long-term future of the resources of the coastal zone through environmentally sensitive programmes, based on the principle of balanced, sustainable use" (Gubbay 1990). Coastal management ensures that all land and sea use issues are co-ordinated, including development, conservation, waste disposal, fisheries, transport, and coastal protection and flood defence. The advantages of this have been recognised by coastal planners in many areas, with a number of local authorities and other bodies now promoting coastal management by various means. However, approaches differ from area to area, with overlap in some places and patchy coverage elsewhere (Earll 1994).

This chapter concentrates on those local and regional coastal management initiatives taking place wholly or partly within Region 12. GB and UK national initiatives, notably those led by non-governmental agencies and user groups, are outside its scope. Contact points for some of these organisations are, however, included in section 10.4C. The direction of national policy-making, within which many of the regional initiatives operate, is outlined below.

The House of Commons Environment Committee Second Report (House of Commons 1992), although limited in scope to England and the estuaries it shares with Wales (and Scotland), made recommendations for the planning and implementation of coastal management that have had policy and practical implications throughout the UK. Amongst these recommendations were:

- the endorsement of an integrated approach to coastal management, incorporating maritime land, sea and intertidal areas;
- a review of existing legislation; the need for international (EU-wide) policy initiatives; clearer responsibilities for planning and action in the coastal zone, based on a national strategic framework;
- appropriate funding for accountable bodies with responsibilities;

- research into the physical functioning of the coastal zone and associated protection and conservation measures;
- a review of planning mechanisms to allow effective safeguard of the coastal resource;
- monitoring and environmental assessment of coastal activities to assess their impacts;
- the involvement of local communities in coastal management planning;
- the integration of responsibility for coast protection and sea defence under one body;
- better statutory protection for sites of nature conservation importance;
- better provisions for control of marine pollution;
- the need for fisheries activities to take account of marine conservation issues.

Later in 1992, the Department of the Environment and the Welsh Office issued *Planning Policy Guidance: Coastal Planning (PPG 20)*, which made clearer the requirement for planning decisions to take account of environmental and conservation issues.

The Environment Select Committee's recommendations were followed up, in 1993, by the publication of *Development below low water mark: a review of regulation in England and Wales* (Department of the Environment/Welsh Office 1993a), in parallel with the discussion paper *Managing the coast: a review of coastal management plans in England and Wales and the powers supporting them* (Department of the Environment/Welsh Office 1993b). That same year, The Ministry of Agriculture, Fisheries and Food (MAFF) and the Welsh Office brought out their *Strategy for flood and coastal defence in England and Wales* (MAFF/WO 1993). In this their policy is spelled out: ". . . reducing the risks to people and the developed and natural environment from flooding and coastal erosion by encouraging the provision of technically, environmentally and economically sound and sustainable defence measures." Section 10.4B gives additional notes on the content of these publications.

By the end of 1994, Government had published its Regulations to implement the EU Habitats Directive (Department of the Environment/Welsh Office 1994). As they relate to the coast, these regulations provide for single management groups to be set up for whole sites, making the production of unified management plans a practical proposition. Where these sites are of European importance for their nature conservation interest, the conservation of that interest must be the primary consideration of the management plan. For this, the regulations require all relevant authorities to exercise a general duty of care for their long-term conservation. At the time of writing, discussions are continuing on how these requirements will work in practice.

10.1.2 National coastal management groups and initiatives

Partly as a result of these developments at a UK and international level, many national bodies are now becoming involved in the promotion of coastal management initiatives, despite most not having any direct management role through a statutory remit or ownership of coastal land. These include the National Coasts and Estuaries Advisory Group (NCEAG) and non-governmental organisations with a particular interest in the conservation of the coastal zone: the Marine Conservation Society, World Wide Fund for Nature (UK) and the Royal Society for the Protection of Birds (RSPB) (see section 10.3). Many other diverse interest groups and organisations now have national policies with regard to coastal management and estuaries management, for example the British Association for Shooting and Conservation, Royal Yachting Association, and their representatives are involved in most local or regional groups or fora.

Oxwich Bay, South Glamorgan (on the Gower Peninsula), where the variety of wildlife habitats coupled with many leisure activities presents a challenge for integrated management. Photo: J.P. Doody, JNCC.

10.2 Regional coastal management groups and initiatives

10.2.1 Introduction

There are currently numerous recent regional coastal management initiatives arising around the coastline under the leadership of local planning, harbours and ports authorities. For example, the Countryside Council for Wales is to launch its marine and coastal policy statement in mid 1995. Some local authorities are beginning to produce non-statutory coastal management plans to inform their statutory plans, and local authorities, harbour authorities, the National Rivers Authority, Sea Fisheries Committees and the Countryside Council for Wales will be amongst the wide range of statutory and non-statutory bodies that will have responsibilities in the management of marine Special Areas of Conservation under the EC Habitats Directive. Additionally, a number of local or regional coastal management projects are part of national initiatives being pursued by organisations such as the statutory nature conservation agencies or non-governmental bodies. Other initiatives, although not strictly integrated as defined in section 10.1, are also underway. These include Coastal Engineering Groups (section 10.2.5), which are primarily concerned with promoting co-ordination and liaison between organisations undertaking coastal works, and Shoreline Management Plans (sections 8.4.4, 8.4.5 and 10.2.6), National Rivers Authority River Catchment Management Plans (section 10.2.7), and Management Plans for protected areas of coast (section 10.2.8). Major regional coastal management initiatives are described in more detail below.

10.2.2 Local planning authority and ports/harbours initiatives

The maritime local planning authorities are involved in most, if not all, of the major coastal management initiatives described in this chapter. Their own planning documents (County Structure Plans and Local Plans) also usually pay particular attention to coastal matters, particularly when produced following PPG20 (DoE/WO 1992) (see sections 10.1 and 10.3). In Wales the Welsh Office invited the Assembly of Welsh Counties, in liaison with the District Councils, to draw up proposals for Strategic Planning Guidance, the equivalent of Regional Guidance in England. As part of this process a number of topic groups were formed, including a Coastal Strategy Working Party (chaired by David Bown, County Planning Officer of Dyfed). The report prepared by this group is, at the time of writing, with the Welsh Office awaiting their response.

Port and Harbour Authorities also have a statutory remit to control activities within their areas of authority, which may include coastal waters, and will have additional responsibilities in the management of marine Special Areas of Conservation under the EC Habitats Directive (section 10.2.1). The Milford Haven Port Authority Waterway Plan has control over a 'box' which extends approximately three

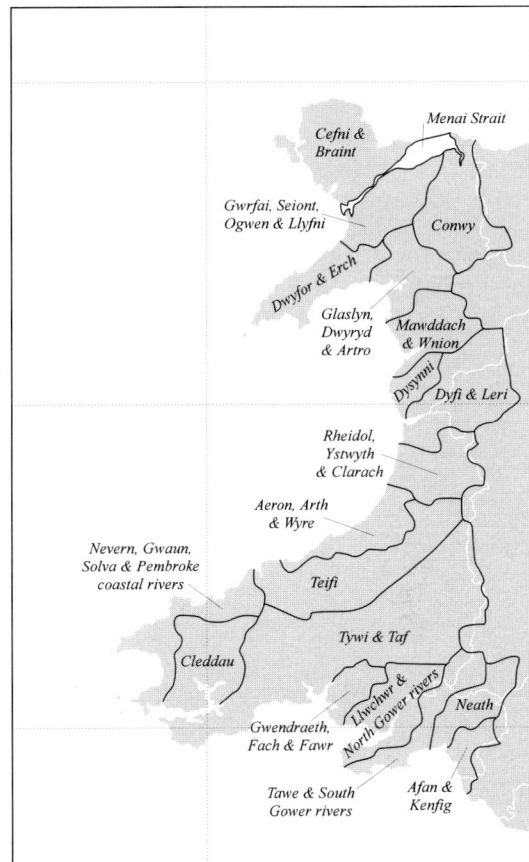

Map 10.2.1 River catchment areas. Reproduced by kind permission of the NRA.

miles out to sea outside the Haven. While its statutory concerns are primarily navigational, it also has a remit to investigate oil pollution incidents and prosecute, and has produced an oil pollution plan. Initiatives led by local authorities or port/harbour authorities are listed in Table 10.2.1.

10.2.3 Arfordir group

The Arfordir group is the local authority coastal officers' forum. It aims to promote integrated coastal management and best management practice for the whole of the Welsh coast, and to achieve Wales-wide representation after local government re-organisation. Membership is free and open to all maritime local authorities. Region 12 members include Ceredigion DC, Pembrokeshire Coast NP, Snowdonia NP, Dwyfor DC, Ynys Mon DC, Arfon DC, Aberconwy DC and Swansea City Council (plus local authorities from other Welsh regions).

Table 10.2.1 Local authority/port and harbour-based coastal management initiatives

Initiative name	Activities	Organisations involved	Contact name & address
Management Framework for the Crymlyn & Neath Estuary	Covers coast between Swansea and Neath including Swansea Bay and Neath Estuary. Provides a detailed planning framework, objectives and management prescriptions for the area.	West Glamorgan CC, Swansea CC, Neath BC and the Countryside Council for Wales (CCW).	Directorate of Development and Control, *Neath Borough Council, tel. 01639 641121
Gower Countryside Service	Covers AONB, Heritage Coast and the north-eastern part of the Burry Inlet and Loughor Estuary. 1990 Gower Management Plan currently in use, supplementing the draft Coast Zone Strategy (in prep.) for Black Pill to Loughor.	Managed by Swansea City Council's Gower Countryside Service. Assisted by the Gower Countryside Forum (see below)	Countryside Officer, Gower Countryside Service, Planning Department, Swansea City Council, Guildhall, Swansea SA1 4PH, tel: 01792 302741
Gower Countryside Forum	Provides liaison between numerous interest groups and assists the Countryside Service.	Cadw (Welsh Historic Monuments), Country Landowners Association, Glamorgan/Gwent Archaeological Trust, National Trust, Ramblers Association (Wales), Wales Tourist Board, Countryside Council for Wales, Gower Society, National Farmers Union, Gower Commoners Association, Farming and Wildlife Advisory Group (FWAG), West Glamorgan CC, Glamorgan Wildlife Trust, Welsh Office, West Glamorgan Association of Local Councils, Swansea City Council, British Horse Society, Gower Outdoor Education Centres, Campaign for the Protection of Rural Wales and 14 Community Councils.	Countryside Officer, Gower Countryside Service, Planning Department, Swansea City Council, Guildhall, Swansea SA1 4PH, tel. 01792 302741
Milford Haven Waterway Environmental Monitoring Steering Group	Covers Milford Haven Waterway below High Water Mean Tides. Co-ordinates and commissions a wide range of environmental monitoring within the waterway. The group hopes that its work will help to maintain and enhance a rich and diverse marine environment within the Haven.	Countryside Council for Wales, Dwr Cymru Welsh Water, Elf Oil Refinery, Gulf Oil Refinery, Dyfed CC, Field Studies Council Research Centre, Milford Haven Port Authority, National Power, National Rivers Authority, Pembrokeshire Coast National Park, Preseli Pembrokeshire and South Pembrokeshire District Councils, Texaco Refinery.	Trevor Lloyd, Dyfed County Council, Civil Protection Planning Unit, Hill House, Picton Terrace, Carmarthen, Dyfed SA31 3BS, tel. 01267 236651
Milford Haven Waterway Recreation Plan (published 1992)	Non-statutory document. Sets out guidance and a shared vision for the management of recreational activities and aims to strike a balance between these interests.	Milford Haven Port Authority, Pembrokeshire National Park Authority and National Rivers Authority (NRA)	Milford Haven Port Authority, PO Box 14, Milford Haven, Pembrokeshire, Dyfed SA73 3ER, tel. 01646 693091
Arfon (including Menai Strait)	Several management projects under way along the coast	Arfon Borough Council (in liaison with Countryside Council for Wales over Menai Strait proposed Marine Nature Reserve)	Countryside Officer, Arfon Borough Council, Penrallt, Caernarfon, Gwynedd LL55 1BN, tel: 01286 673113
Aberffraw Bay, Holyhead Mountain and North Anglesey Heritage Coasts	Managed under Coastal Management Plan for Isle of Anglesey (which covers the Area of Outstanding Natural Beauty (AONB)). Ynys Mon treats the whole island as an integrated management unit.	Managed by Anglesey Coastal Heritage, part of Ynys Mon Planning Department.	Coastal Officer, Treftadaeth Glannau Mon, Llys Llywelyn, Tyddyn Hwrdd, Aberffraw, Anglesey LL63 5AQ, tel. 01407 840845

*Starred contact addresses are given in full in the Appendix

10.2.4 The Welsh Coastal Groups Forum

The Welsh Coastal Groups Forum, established in 1991, co-ordinates the work of the Welsh Coastal Engineering Groups (section 10.2.5). Its remit includes the following: to promote the formation of coastal groups that include bodies with responsibilities for coastal defence and management in Wales and the strategic and local planning functions that would influence coastal defence; to further co-operation between those bodies; to act as a link between centrally-based organisations and coastal groups; to facilitate the development of a coastal zone appraisal and management approach, ensuring that the most environmentally consistent practice is adopted in relation to physical development in the coastal zone; to promote common standards of approach; and to identify policy, administrative and research requirements. Forum members include one representative from each coastal group in Wales (Cardigan Bay Coastal Group, Carmarthen Bay Coastal Engineering Group, Swansea Bay Coastal Group, Liverpool Bay Coastal Group, Tidal Dee Users Group (Region 13), Ynys Enlli to Llandudno Coastal Group, Severn Estuary Coastal Group (Region 13), Assembly of Welsh Counties, Council of Welsh Districts, Countryside Council for Wales and National Rivers Authority, Countryside Council for Wales, British Rail/Railtrack, Welsh Office Planning Division and the WO Environment Division). The Forum normally meets twice a year.

10.2.5 Coastal engineering groups

Five non-statutory coastal groups (sometimes known as coastal engineering groups) have been established within the region to improve co-ordination and liaison between agencies undertaking coastal works (see section 8.4 and Table 10.2.2). Map 8.4.1 shows the geographical coverage of these groups. (See Map 2.4.1 for further information on sediment cells in the region.) Their main aim is to seek a co-ordinated approach to all coastal engineering works by member authorities; reduce the risk of works adversely affecting the neighbouring coastline; and improve their understanding of coastal processes.

10.2.6 Shoreline management plans

Shoreline management plans are coastal defence plans compiled in accordance with government guidelines on assessing the environmental impacts of proposals (including soft defence and 'do nothing' options) (MAFF 1994). Their preparation is being considered by several of the coastal groups in the region (Carmarthen Bay Coastal Cell Group and Liverpool Bay Group); one is already in existence for Meirionnydd and others are proposed for other parts of the Cardigan Bay Coastal Group area.

10.2.7 Catchment management plans

River catchments, including estuaries and coastal waters, are the basic management unit around which the organisation, operations and statutory duties of the National

Rivers Authority (NRA) are based. Catchment management plans are prepared by the National Rivers Authority and express an agreed strategy to realise the environmental potential of the catchment, within prevailing economic and political constraints. River catchments are shown in Map 10.2.1, and the rivers themselves on Map 1.2.1. Table 10.2.3 gives the Welsh National Rivers Authority's five year programme for the completion of consultation reports for river catchment management plans in the region.

10.2.8 Designated sites

Discussed in detail in Chapter 7, statutory and non-statutory designations are also relevant here because they provide a degree of coastal management through their area/site management plans. These often tend to focus strongly on the conservation of landscapes, buildings and/or habitats and species, rather than wider and more integrated coastal issues, although in management planning for some sites a focus on visitor use and community involvement is important. Site-based initiatives in the region are listed in Table 10.2.4.

10.2.9 Coastal fora

In some places wider coastal fora have developed from a range of coastal designations and various management initiatives. There are three major coastal fora operating in the region, in Carmarthen Bay, Cardigan Bay and North Wales. A fourth, the Gower Countryside Forum, covers the whole of Gower, but is also involved in the work of the Gower Heritage Coast. The Burry Inlet and Loughor Estuary Liaison Group, whilst not constituted as a forum, acts in that capacity. The great value of these fora is that they bring all interest and user groups together and enable issues of concern to be examined from all points of view. The first of the coastal fora to be established, in 1991, was the Cardigan Bay Forum. This regional coastal liaison committee works to protect the environment of Cardigan Bay (coasts and marine areas) and promotes responsible use of its resources (see Table 10.2.5). The establishment of the Carmarthen Bay Forum and North Wales Coastal Forum were partly inspired by work of the Cardigan Bay Forum.

Table 10.2.2 Coastal engineering groups

Initiative name	Activities	Organisations involved	Contact address
Swansea Bay Coastal Group	Aims to improve co-ordination and liaison between agencies undertaking coastal works. Covers Lavernock Point (nr Penarth), to Worm's Head (SW Gower). Produced Swansea Bay Coastal Response Study (1993)	Ogwr Borough Council, Swansea City Council, Neath, Port Talbot and Vale of Glamorgan Borough Councils, National Rivers Authority, British Steel, Countryside Council for Wales, Welsh Office (observer)	Chairman: M E Thomas, Chief Technical Officer, Ogwr Borough Council, PO Box 4, Civic Offices, Angel Street, Bridgend, Mid Glamorgan CF31 1LX, tel. 01656 643643
Carmarthen Bay Coastal Engineering Group	Steering group, from Worm's Head to Milford Haven; aim as above. Database being compiled. Wave/tide computer model 1987-90. Carmarthen Bay Coastal Engineering Study Report (1989). Shoreline management plan under consideration.	Llanelli Borough Council, Swansea City Council, Carmarthen District Council, National Rivers Authority, Railtrack, Ministry of Defence, Countryside Council for Wales, National Power, Welsh Office (observer)	Chairman: R Paul Thomas, Director of Technical Services, Llanelli Borough Council, Ty Elwyn, Llanelli, Dyfed SA15 3AP, tel. 01554 741100
Cardigan Bay Coastal Group	Steering group, from Milford Haven to Ynys Enlli (Bardsey Island); aim as above. Database being compiled. Monitors beach cross sections and storm waves. Programme of beach profiling, study of coastal processes. Have produced Meirionnydd Coastal Management Study 1993, a Shoreline Management Plan for Meironnydd, and proposed Shoreline Management Plans for other parts of the coast.	Meirionnydd, Ceredigion, Dwyfor and Preseli District Councils, Dyfed County Council (Highways Dept), Gwynedd County Council (Snowdonia National Park Authority), Railtrack, National Rivers Authority (N and SW areas), Countryside Council for Wales, Welsh Office (observer). Associate membership: Aberdyfi Golf Club, Lord Harlech, Owners of various caravan sites	Chairman: Martin Wright, Meirionnydd District Council, Cae Penarlag, Dolgellau, Gwynedd LL40 2YB, tel. 01341 422341
Ynys Enlli to Llandudno Coastal Group	Aims to improve co-ordination and liaison between agencies undertaking coastal works. Photo monitoring dunes at Nefyn. Database being compiled. Analysis of coastal processes at Dinas Dinlle.	National Rivers Authority, Aberconwy, Arfon & Ynys Mon Borough Councils, Gwynedd County Council, Cyngor Dosbarth Dwyfor, Caernarfon Harbour Trust, Cadw (Welsh Historic Monuments), Railtrack, Countryside Council for Wales, Welsh Office (observer)	Chairman: M F Davies, National Rivers Authority, Bryn Menai, Holyhead Road, Bangor, Gwynedd LL57 2EF, tel. 01248 370970
Liverpool Bay Coastal Group	Aims to improve co-ordination and liaison between agencies undertaking coastal works. Databases of coastal structures and references, and flood risk areas map. Preparation of a shoreline management plan is under consideration.	Aberconwy, Colwyn, Delyn & Rhuddlan Borough Councils, West Lancs DC, Wirral & Sefton Metropolitan Borough Councils, National Rivers Authority (Welsh and NW regions), Railtrack, MAFF (observer), Welsh Office (observer). Other observers include Countryside Council for Wales	Chairman: A M Rhodes, Borough Engineer, Metropolitan Borough of Wirral, Town Hall, Bebington, Wirral L63 7PT, tel. 0151 645 2080

Table 10.2.3 Catchment management plans timetable

Action	Catchments
Consultation Plans published	Cleddau, Conwy, Menai Strait, Tawe, Taf, Tywi
Final Action Plans to be published by April 1995	Cleddau, Conwy, Menai Strait, Tawe, Taf
Final Action Plan to be published later in 1995	Twyi
Consultation Plans to be published in 1994/95	Afan/Kenfig, Dyfi/Leri, Glaslyn/Dwyryd/Artro
Consultation Plans to be published in 1995/96	Llwchwr/North Gower, Teifi, Rheidol/Ystwyth/Clarach, Cefni / Braint, Mawddach/Wnion
Consultation Plans to be published in 1996/97	Neath, Nevern/Gwaun/Solva, Gwyrfai/Seiont/Ogwen/Lyfni, Dwyfor/Erch
Consultation Plans to be published in 1997/98	Aeron/Arth/Wyre, Dysynni
Consultation Plans to be published in 1998/99	Gwaendraeth/Fach/Fawr

Source: NRA (1994). Note: Final Action Plans are normally published within six months of the Consultation Plan.

Table 10.2.4 Designated site-based coastal management initiatives

Initiative name	Activities	Organisations involved	Contact address
Pembrokeshire Coast National Park	Park boundary is the low water mark, includes most of the rocks and islets of the Pembrokeshire Coast. National Park Functional Strategy 1993-1996 in use.	Pembrokeshire Coast National Park Authority, Dyfed County Council, Countryside Council for Wales	Pembrokeshire Coast National Park, County Offices, St Thomas Green, Haverfordwest, Dyfed SA61 1QZ, tel. 01437 764591
South Pembrokeshire, Marloes & Dale, St Brides Bay, St David's Peninsula, Dinas Head, and St Dogmaels & Moylgrove Heritage Coasts	Work within coastal areas of the National Park, using the National Park Plan.	Managed by Pembrokeshire Coast National Park Authority (see above)	Pembrokeshire Coast National Park, County Offices, St Thomas Green, Haverfordwest, Dyfed SA61 1QZ, tel. 01437 764591
Ceredigion Coast Heritage Coast	Four separate areas within the HC (but most of Ceredigion's coast is managed to some degree). Now developing management proposals for the Marine Heritage Coast (1 nautical mile out to sea).	Managed by Ceredigion District Council Coastal Management Department, and 50% funded by Countryside Council for Wales.	Principal Planning Officer for the coast or Heritage Coast Project Officer, Dosbarth Cyngor Ceredigion, Planning Department, 1 North Road, Aberaeron, Dyfed SA46 6AT, tel. 01545 570881
Snowdonia National Park	Park boundary runs to the High Water Mark in places.	Snowdonia National Park Authority, Gwynedd County Council, CCW	Park Planning Officer, National Park Offices, Penrhydeudraeth, Gwynedd LL48 6LS, tel. 01286 673993
Llyn Heritage Coast	The draft Dwyfor Countryside Management Plan 1992 is in use for the whole area, not just the Heritage Coast	Managed by the Dwyfor Countryside Service, funded by Cyngor Dosbarth Dwyfor & Countryside Council for Wales	Planning Department, Cyngor Dosbarth Dwyfor, Swyddfeydd y Cyngor, Pwlheli LL53 5AA, tel. 01758 613131
Skomer Marine Nature Reserve	Management of intertidal and sublittoral areas for marine nature conservation	Countryside Council for Wales, South Wales Sea Fisheries Committee	Marine Warden, Fisherman's Cottage, Martin's Haven, Marloes, Haverfordwest, Dyfed SA62 3BJ, tel. 01646 636736
Menai Strait proposed Marine Nature Reserve	Management objectives and plan for the proposed MNR have been sent out for consultation	Countryside Council for Wales	North Wales Region, Plas Penrhos, Ffordd Penrhos, Bangor, Gwynedd, tel. 01248 370444
Great Orme's Head Heritage Coast	1990 Management Plan in use. Management Service also covers the whole of the Borough, with an increasing emphasis on managing the rest of the Aberconwy coast.	Managed by Aberconwy BC, reports to Great Orme Country Park Working Party, comprising Local Authority Planning Committee members, Mostyn Estates and Countryside Council for Wales.	Heritage Coast Officer or Countryside Officer, Tourism & Amenities Dept, Aberconwy Borough Council, 1/2 Chapel Street, Llandudno, Gwynedd LL32 8DU, tel. 01492 874151

Note: Management plans also exist for National Nature Reserves in the region (see section 7.3.1).

Table 10.2.5 Coastal fora

Initiative name	Activities	Organisations involved	Contact address
Burry Inlet and Loughor Estuary Liaison Group	Act as a forum; Conference in March 1995; considering other action for the future.	Countryside Council for Wales, Swansea City Council, Dyfed CC, Llanelli BC, Wildfowl and Wetlands Trust, West Glamorgan & Lliw Valley BCs, NRA, RSPB and South Wales Sea Fisheries Committee.	County Planning Department, Dyfed County Council, 40 Spilman Street, Carmarthen, Dyfed SA31 1LQ, or David Grace, Swansea City Council SA1 4PE, tel. 01792 302727
Carmarthen Bay Forum	Formed with SERA (Socialist Environmental Resources, Labour Party) and Friends of the Earth (Carmarthen) in 1993. Same general aims as Cardigan Bay Forum (see below)	About 12 members. Close links with Burry Inlet Group and Cardigan Bay Forum	Secretary: Jean Myers, Waungron, Cefnypant, Whitland, Dyfed SA34 0TS, tel. 01994 419313
Cardigan Bay Forum	A coastal liaison committee on a regional scale, established 1991. Aims to promote wider awareness & respect for the environmental importance, interest and natural beauty of Cardigan Bay and to encourage its harmonious use & enjoyment.	97 members, including user groups, interest groups, local authorities, statutory and voluntary national bodies, fisheries, tourism and recreational interests, scientific and conservation bodies, commercial organisations (including oil companies) etc.	*Projects Officer, Cardigan Bay Forum, Aberystwyth, tel. 01970 624471
North Wales Coastal Forum	Established 1992. Covers area extending south from lat. 53°40'N including coast and hinterland. Aims to help members exchange information and views on coastal issues, develop relationships with international and national government, agencies and bodies, and agree action on matters of mutual interest.	Clwyd County Council, District, Borough and Town Councils, Countryside Council for Wales, National Rivers Authority, Sea Fisheries Committee, non-governmental organisations including National Trust, RSPB, Wildlife Trust, commercial interests and scientific bodies.	Chairman, Stephen Pritchard, Ysgoldy, Bryncroes, Pwllheli, Gwynedd LL53 8EB, tel. 01758 83423

* Starred contact addresses are given in full in the Appendix

10.3 Further sources of information

A. References cited

DoE/Welsh Office. 1992. *Planning policy guidance - coastal planning.* PPG 20. London, HMSO.

Department of the Environment/Welsh Office. 1993a. *Development below low water mark: a review of regulation in England and Wales.* London, HMSO.

Department of the Environment/Welsh Office. 1993b. *Managing the coast: a review of coastal management plans in England and Wales and the powers supporting them.* London, HMSO.

Department of the Environment/Welsh Office. 1994. *The conservation (natural habitats etc.) Regulations.* London, HMSO (SI 2716).

Earll, R.C., ed. 1994. *Statutory and non-statutory plans in the estuarine and coastal environment. Overlapping plans - is this an issue?* Unpublished report of a meeting in July 1994.

Gubbay, S. 1990. *A future for the coast? Proposals for a UK coastal zone management plan.* A report to the World Wide Fund for Nature from the Marine Conservation Society (unpublished).

House of Commons. 1992. *Coastal zone protection and planning.* London, HMSO. (Environment Committee Second Report.)

National Rivers Authority. 1994. *Corporate Plan 1994/95.* Bristol, NRA.

Ministry of Agriculture, Fisheries and Food/Welsh Office. 1993. *Strategy for flood and coastal defence in England and Wales.* London, MAFF.

Ministry of Agriculture, Fisheries and Food. 1994. *Shoreline management plans.* London, MAFF. (4th draft, July 1994.)

B. Further reading

Countryside Council for Wales. 1994. *A policy framework for the coastal and marine zone of Wales: a discussion document.* Bangor.

Countryside Council for Wales. In press. *A review of coastal management of three test areas in Wales (Swansea Bay, Ceredigion coast and the Menai Strait).* University of Cardiff (unpublished report to CCW).

Gubbay, S. 1994. *Seas: the opportunity. Working together to protect our marine life.* Sandy, RSPB.

Jones, R. 1993. Coastal cell studies - a basis for coastal zone management. *Earth Science Conservation,* 32: 12-15.

King, G., & Bridge, L. 1994. *Directory of coastal planning and management initiatives in England.* Maidstone, National Coasts and Estuaries Advisory Group.

National Coasts and Estuaries Advisory Group. 1993. *Coastal planning and management: a good practice guide.* Maidstone.

Rendel Geotechnics. 1994. *Coastal planning and management: a review.* HMSO. (Report for the Department of the Environment.) (Supports recent coastal policy initiatives (including PPG20 Coastal Planning). Presents a broad synthesis of legislation, policy advice and research relevant to CZM. Measures effectiveness of coastal planning and management.)

Rothwell, P.I. Y, & Housden, S.D. 1990. *Turning the tide, a future for estuaries.* RSPB, Sandy.

RSPB. 1992. *A shore future. RSPB vision for the coast.* RSPB, Sandy.

Shaw, D. 1990. *Irish Sea Forum conference: an environmental review.* Liverpool University, Irish Sea Study Group.

Smith, H.D., & Geffen, A.J., eds. 1990. *The Irish Sea, an environmental review. Part 4. Planning, development and management.* Liverpool, Liverpool University Press.

Newsletters

Many national statutory, non-governmental and scientific bodies are now producing publications or newsletters on the subject of coastal management. These either provide information on particular local or national initiatives (such as the statutory or non-governmental organisations' estuaries and firths initiatives) or general information on a range of coastal news (for example the newsletters of Eurocoast UK and the European Union for Coastal Conservation). Some of these publications are listed below. Addresses of those publishing the newsletters are given in section 10.3C.

Coastal News. Newsletter of the Coastal Research and Management Group. Publication intended to stimulate co-operation and communication between the many disciplines working in the coastal zone. Contains information on coastal management, reviews of publications and notices of meetings. Published by JNCC.

Coastline. Quarterly magazine of the European Union for Coastal Conservation (EUCC). Intended to establish a pan-European forum on coastal issues, including coastal management. Published by EUCC.

CZM News. Occasional Newsletter of Eurocoast UK, reporting on projects and developments in the field of coastal zone management. Published by Eurocoast UK.

Coastline UK. Newsletter of the National Coasts and Estuaries Advisory group (NCEAG). Aimed at local authority planners. Published by NCEAG.

National and local planning/management publications

House of Commons Environment Committee. 1992. *Second report - coastal zone protection and planning.* London, HMSO. (Recommended that coastal zone management be adopted as the framework for all coastal zone planning and management practice in the United Kingdom. Called for a national coastal strategy, a review of the many organisations responsible for the coast, the extension of planning controls offshore, and the establishment of a Coastal Zone Unit in Department of the Environment.)

DoE/Welsh Office. 1992. *Planning policy guidance - coastal planning.* PPG 20. London, HMSO. (Recognises the need to define a coastal zone incorporating areas affected by natural near-shore processes. Advises local authorities to consider the impacts of off-shore and on-shore developments within the full coastal zone. Endorses the precautionary approach.)

DoE/Welsh Office. 1993. *Managing the coast: a review of coastal management plans in England and Wales and the powers supporting them.* London, HMSO. (Includes proposals for coastal management plans to be based on a voluntary, multi-agency approach, generally led by local authorities.)

DoE/Welsh Office. 1993. *Development below Low Water Mark - a review of regulation in England and Wales.* London, HMSO. (Rejects the 1992 Environment Committee's recommendations for the extension of development controls off-shore. Seeks to strengthen existing arrangements to overcome limitations and draw-backs in the present land-use planning system.)

MAFF. 1994. *Shoreline management plans.* (A procedural guide for operating authorities. 4th draft, July 1994.)

DoE/Welsh Office. In prep. *National coastal policy guidance statement.* (Government undertaking to produce this Statement made on 15 July 1994. Remit may go beyond PPG20 on coastal planning.)

Local planning authority plans and publications

Bown, D.P. Undated. *Strategic planning guidance for coastal Wales.* Carmarthen, Coastal Strategy Topic Group County Planning Department.

Ceredigion District Council. 1992. *Ceredigion Marine Heritage Coast: an introductory report.* Aberystwyth, Ceredigion District Council.

Dyfed County Council. 1980. *Dyfed county structure plan written statement.* Carmarthen, Dyfed County Council.

Dyfed County Council. 1987. *Dyfed county structure proposals for alteration.* Carmarthen, Dyfed County Council.

Gwynedd County Council. 1991. *Gwynedd county structure plan written statement.* Caernarfon, Gwynedd County Council.

Pembrokeshire Coast National Park. 1994. *Park functional strategies, 1995 - 1998.* Pembrokeshire Coast National Park.

Pembrokeshire Coast National Park. 1994. *National Park Plan. 2nd review: 1994 - 1995 (consultation draft).* Pembrokeshire Coast National Park.

Pembrokeshire District Council. 1994. *Draft local plan.* Pembrokeshire District Council.

West Glamorgan County Council. 1978. *West Glamorgan structure plan.* Swansea, West Glamorgan County Council.

C. Contact names and addresses

(See also Tables 10.2.1, 10.2.2, 10.2.4 and 10.2.5.)

Major regional and national bodies	Activities	Contact address and telephone no.
Welsh Coast Groups Forum	See section 10.2.4	Hugh Payne, Welsh Coastal Forum, Environment Division, Welsh Office, Parc Cathays, Caerdydd CF1 3NQ, tel. 01222 823176
GroupsArfordir Group	See section 10.2.3	*Arfordir Officer, CCW Aberystwyth, tel 01970 828314
Marine Conservation Society	Provides advice and supports local coastal management initiatives: runs grant-aided coastal management workshops and courses for coastal managers; promotes the establishment of voluntary coastal groups.	*Marine Conservation Society, Ross-on-Wye, tel: 01970 566017
Countryside Council for Wales Heritage Coast Forum	Coastal management of designated sites. Funded by the Countryside Commission. Provides up to date factual information on 45 Heritage Coasts in England and Wales. Provides contact between individuals and groups concerned with the management of Heritage Coasts in England and Wales.	*CCW HQ, Bangor. tel. 01248 370444 Heritage Coast Forum, Centre for Environmental Interpretation, The Manchester Metropolitan University, St Augustines, Lower Chatham Street, Manchester M15 6BY, tel. 0161 247 1067
Ministry of Agriculture, Fisheries and Food	Shoreline Management Plans (mainly aimed at formulating a coast protection strategy)	MAFF, Eastbury House, 30/34 Albert Embankment, London SE1 7TL, tel. 0171 238 3000
National Rivers Authority	Catchment management planning, 5-year programme	*Flood Defence Section, NRA HQ, Bristol, tel. 01454 624400, or NRA Welsh Region, Cardiff, tel. 01222 770088
Royal Society for the Protection of Birds Sandy,	Launched national campaign in 1990 to promote the importance of estuaries in the UK. Monitors the development of coastal zone initiatives around the UK. In 1994, launched Marine Life campaign, to increase awareness and to promote integrated coastal and marine management.	*Coastal Policy Officer, RSPB HQ, tel: 01767 680551
Coastal Research and Management Group	Established to aid the process of communication between research workers and managers in the field of coastal ecology. Concentrates on research and management issues relevant to landscape and wildlife conservation in the coastal zone (marine and terrestrial).	*Coastal Research and Management Group (CR&MG), Coastal Conservation Branch, JNCC Peterborough, tel. 01733 866825.
Coastal Technical Officers Group	The GB conservation agencies group (English Nature, Scottish Natural Heritage, Countryside Council for Wales, Department of the Environment for Northern Ireland, Joint Nature Conservation Committee and the Countryside Commission).	*Coastal Technical Officers Group, Secretariat: Coastal Conservation Branch, JNCC Peterborough, tel. 01733 866825
Esturiales Environmental Study Group	International programme for co-operation, the exchange of experience on estuarine management and personal contacts between local authority practitioners in Europe.	Professor Graham King, Esturiales Environmental Study Group, Swansea Institute of Higher Education, Faculty of Leisure and Tourism, Mount Pleasant Campus, Swansea SA1 6ED, tel. 01792 456326
Eurocoast UK	Aims to improve the basis for protection, development and management of the coastal zone. Projects and developments in the field of coastal management.	Eurocoast UK, Burderop Park, Swindon, Wiltshire SN4 0QD, tel. 01793 812479
European Union for Coastal Conversation	International grouping of organisations and individuals with an interest in coastal nature conservation matters, including coastal management.	Secretariat, European Union for Coastal Conservation (EUCC), P.O. Box 11059, NL-2301 EB Leiden tel. +31 71 122900/123952
Marine Forum	National network provides forum for discussion of marine issues relating to the seas around UK. Members include governmental and non-governmental organisations and individuals. Occasional seminars are held, covering a range of topics including coastal management.	Marine Forum, Natural History Museum, Cromwell Road, London SW7 5BD, tel. 0171 938 9114

Major regional and national bodies	Activities	Contact address and telephone no.
National Coasts and Estuaries Advisory Group	On behalf of local authorities, advises on the sustainable development of coastal and estuarine environments and promotes best practice in coastal management.	Secretary, National Coasts and Estuaries Advisory Group (NCEAG), Environment Programme, Kent County Council, Springfield, Maidstone ME14 2LX, tel: 01622 696180
World Wide Fund for Nature - UK	Provides funding for research, local voluntary policy development and local initiatives, and publications on integrated coastal management. Draws on considerable international experience with coastal management initiatives.	*World Wide Fund for Nature - UK, Godalming, tel. 01483 426444
National Trust	Has extensive coastal land holdings in the region (see section 7.5.1). Recently carried out a complete review of its Coastal Strategy Plans; has an ongoing review of coastal site management plans; produced an internal report *Coastal Strategy for Wales* (In prep.), which provides guidance for the acquisition of coastal sites under Enterprise Neptune and for responses to coastal issues.	*The National Trust: North Wales Office: Llandudno, tel. 01492 860123 *The National Trust: South Wales Office: Llandeilo, tel. 01558 822800

Addresses and telephone numbers of local planning authorities are given in full in the Appendix, as are * starred contact addresses.

10.4 Acknowledgements

The authors wish to thank S. Soffe, Countryside Council for Wales, for help in preparing this chapter.

Appendix

A.1 Frequently cited contact names and addresses

Name	Contact address and telephone no.	Name	Contact address and telephone no.
Statutory bodies		*Coastal fora*	
Countryside Council for Wales (CCW) HQ	Plas Penrhos, Fford Penrhos, Bangor, Gwynedd LL57 2LQ, tel: 01248 370444	Cardigan Bay Forum	Welsh Agricultural College, Llanbadarn Fawr, Aberystwyth, Dyfed SY23 3AL, tel: 01970 624471
CCW South Wales Region	43-44 The Parade, Roath, Cardiff CF2 3UH, tel: 01222 485111	Carmarthen Bay Forum	Secretary: Jean Myers, Waungron, Cefnypant, Whitland, Dyfed SA34 0TS, tel: 01994 419313
CCW Dyfed/Mid Wales Region	Plas Gogerddan, Aberystwyth, Dyfed SY23 3EE, tel: 01970 828551		
CCW North Wales Region	Hafod Elfyn, Penrhos Road, Bangor, Gwynedd LL57 2LQ, tel: 01248 372333	North Wales Coastal Forum	Chairman, Stephen Pritchard, Ysgoldy, Bryncroes, Pwllheli, Gwynedd LL53 8EB, tel: 01758 83423
CCW Fishguard	Sycamore Lodge, Hamilton Street, Fishguard, Dyfed, tel: 01348 874602	Irish Sea Forum	Irish Sea Forum Administrator, Oceanography Laboratories, Faculty of Science, University of Liverpool, PO Box 147, Liverpool L69 3BX, tel: 0151 794 4089
CCW Llandeilo	Yr Hen Bost, 56 Rhosmaen St, Llandeilo, Dyfed SA19 6HA, tel: 01558 822111		
CCW Skomer MNR	Fishermans Cottage, Martin's Haven, Marloes, Haverfordwest, Dyfed SA62 3BJ, tel: 01646 636736	*National voluntary bodies*	
		Marine Conservation Society	9 Gloucester Road, Ross-on-Wye, Herefordshire HR9 5BU, tel: 01989 566017
Institute of Terrestrial Ecology (ITE), Monks Wood	Abbots Ripton, Huntingdon, Cambridgeshire PE17 2LS, tel: 01487 773381	The National Trust HQ	33 Sheep Street, Cirencester, Gloucestershire GL7 1QW, tel: 01285 651818
ITE Merlewood	Windermere Road, Grange-over-Sands, Cumbria LA11 6JU, tel: 01539 532264	The National Trust North Wales Office	Trinity Square, Llandudno, Gwynedd LL30 2DE, tel: 01492 860123
Joint Nature Conservation Committee (JNCC), Peterborough	Monkstone House, City Road, Peterborough PE1 1JY, tel: 01733 62626	The National Trust South Wales Office	The Kings Head, Bridge Street, Llandeilo, Dyfed SA19 6BB, tel: 01558 822800
JNCC, Aberdeen	17 Rubislaw Terrace, Aberdeen AB1 1XE, tel: 01224 642863	Royal Society for the Protection of Birds (RSPB) HQ	The Lodge, Sandy, Bedfordshire SG19 2DL, tel: 01767 680551
National Rivers Authority	Rivers House, St Mellons Business (NRA), Welsh Region Park, St Mellons, Cardiff CF3 0LT, tel: 01222 770088	RSPB Wales Office	Bryn Adern, The Bank, Newtown, Powys SY16 2AB, tel: 01686 626678
NRA Head Office	Rivers House, Waterside Drive, Aztec West, Almondsbury, Bristol BS12 4UD, tel: 01454 624400	The Wildfowl & Wetlands Trust (WWT) HQ	Slimbridge, Gloucestershire GL2 7BX, tel: 01453 890333
Wildlife Trusts		WWT, Llanelli	Penclacwydd, Llwynhendy, Llanelli, Dyfed SA14 9SH, tel: 01554 741087
Dyfed Wildlife Trust	7 Market Street, Haverfordwest, Dyfed SA61 1NF, tel: 01437 765462		
Glamorgan Wildlife Trust	Nature Centre, Fountain Road, Tondu, Mid Glamorgan CF32 0E, tel: 01656 724100	Worldwide Fund for Nature - UK (WWF-UK)	Panda House, Weyside Park, Cattershall Lane, Godalming, Surrey GU7 1XR, tel: 01483 426444
North Wales Wildlife Trust	376 High Street, Bangor, Gwynedd LL57 1YE, tel: 01248 351541		

A.2 Local planning authorities

Name	Address and telephone no.
Aberconwy Borough Council	Bodlondeb, Conwy LL32 8DU, tel: 01492 592000
Arfon Borough Council	Town Hall, Bangor LL57 2RE, tel: 01248 370666
Carmarthen District Council	3 Spilman Street, Carmarthen SA31 1LE, tel: 01267 234567
Ceredigion District Council	Town Hall, Aberystwyth SY23 2EB, tel: 01970 617911
Dwyfor (Cyngor Dosbarth) District Council	Swyddfeydd y Cyngor, Pwllheli LL53 5AA, tel: 01758 613131
Dyfed County Council	County Hall, Carmarthen SA31 1JP, tel: 01267 233333
Gwynedd County Council	County Offices, Caernarfon LL55 1SH, tel: 01286 672255
Llanelli Borough Council	Town Hall, Llanelli SA15 3AH, tel: 01554 741100
Lliw Valley Borough Council	Civic Centre, Penllergaer, Swansea SA4 1GH, tel: 01792 893081
Merionnydd District Council	Cae Penarlag, Dolgellau, Gwynedd LL40 2YB, tel: 01341 422341
Neath Borough Council	Civic Centre, Neath, West Glamorgan SA11 3QZ, tel: 01639 641121
Pembrokeshire Coast National Park	County Offices, St Thomas Green, Haverfordwest, Dyfed SA61 1QZ, tel: 01437 764551
Port Talbot Borough Council	Civic Centre, Port Talbot SA13 1PJ, tel: 01639 875200
Preseli (Pembrokeshire) District Council	Cambria House, PO Box 27, Haverfordwest SA61 1TP, tel: 01437 764551
Snowdonia National Park	Park Planning Officer, National Park Offices, Penrhydeudraeth, Gwynedd LL48 6LS tel: 01766 770274
South Pembrokeshire District Council	Llanion Park, Pembroke Dock SA72 6DZ, tel: 01646 683122
Swansea City Council	Guildhall, Swansea SA1 4PE, tel: 01792 301301
West Glamorgan County Council	County Hall, Swansea SA1 3SN, tel: 01792 471111
Ynys Môn (Isle of Anglesey) Borough Council	Council Offices, Langefni LL77 7TW, tel: 01248 750057

A.3 Core reading list

There are a number of imporant publications that either provide information on a variety of topics covered in these regional reports (and so are frequently referred to) or give a good overview of regional and national information on coasts and seas. They are listed below.

Barne, J., Davidson, N.C., Hill, T.O., & Jones, M. 1994. *Coastal and Marine UKDMAP datasets: a user manual.* Peterborough, Joint Nature Conservation Committee.

British Oceanographic Data Centre. 1992. *United Kingdom Digital Marine Atlas. User Guide. Version 2.0.* Birkenhead, Natural Environment Research Council, British Oceanographic Data Centre.

Buck, A.L. 1993. *An inventory of UK estuaries. 2. South West Britain.* Peterborough, Joint Nature Conservation Committee.

Countryside Council for Wales. 1994. *A preliminary bibliography to the water and coast around Bardsey Island and the southwestern Lleyn Peninsula.* Unpublished draft.

Davidson, N.C., Laffoley, D.d'A., Doody, J.P., Way, L.S., Gordon, J., Key, R., Drake, M.C., Pienkowski, M.W., Mitchell, R., & Duff, K.L. 1991. *Nature conservation and estuaries in Great Britain.* Peterborough, Nature Conservancy Council.

Doody, J.P., Johnston, C., & Smith, B. 1993. *The directory of the North Sea coastal margin.* Peterborough, JNCC.

Eno, N.C., *ed.* 1991. *Marine conservation handbook.* 2nd ed. Peterborough, English Nature.

Gubbay, S. 1988. *A coastal directory for marine conservation.* Ross-on-Wye, Marine Conservation Society.

Hobbs, G., & Morgan, C.I., *eds.* 1992. *A review of the environmental knowledge of the Milford Haven Waterway.* Pembroke, Field Studies Council.

Huckbody, A.J, Taylor, P.M., Hobbs, G., & Elliott, R. 1992. *Caernarfon and Cardigan Bays: an environmental appraisal.* London, Hamilton Oil Company.

Irish Sea Study Group. 1990. *The Irish Sea; an environmental review. Part 1; Nature conservation. Part 2; Waste inputs and pollution. Part 3; Exploitable living resources. Part 4; Planning development and management.* Liverpool, Liverpool University Press.

Lee, A. J., & Ramster, J. W. 1981. *Atlas of the seas around the British Isles.* MAFF Atlas Office.

North Sea Task Force. 1993. *North Sea Quality Status Report 1993.* London; Oslo and Paris Commissions.

Robinson, A., & Millward, R. 1983. *The Shell book of the British coast,* 185 - 229. Newton Abbot, David and Charles.

Smith, J., Yonow, N., & Elliot, R. 1995. *The coast of Dyfed and south west Glamorgan: an environmental appraisal.* Aberdeen, Marathon Oil UK.

Steers, J.A. 1964. *The coastline of England and Wales.* 2nd ed., 112 - 183 (Geology and geomorphology). Cambridge, Cambridge University Press.

Taylor, P.M., & Parker, J.G., *eds.* 1993. *The coast of north Wales and north-west England: an environmental appraisal.* London, Hamilton Oil Company Ltd.

Young, G.A. 1992. *The Menai Strait: a review and bibliography of literature from the Wolfson Library.* (Contractor: University College of North Wales, Bangor.) Unpublished report to the Countryside Council for Wales.

Welsh Office. 1994. *Environmental digest for Wales. No. 8. 1993.* Cardiff.

A.4 Contributing authors

Author	Address	Author	Address
Dr M. Aprahamian	National Rivers Authority - North West Region, Fisheries Department, PO Box 12, Richard Fairclough House, Knutsford Road, Warrington WA4 1HG	Dr H.T. Gee	SGS Environment, Yorkshire House, Chapel St, Liverpool L3 9AG
Dr R.N. Bamber	Fawley Aquatic Research Labs Ltd, Marine and Freshwater Biology Unit, Fawley, Southampton, Hants. SO4 1TW	M.J. Goodwin	RSK Environment, 47 West Street, Dorking, Surrey RH4 1BU
J.H. Barne	Coastal Conservation Branch, JNCC, Monkstone House, City Road, Peterborough PE1 1JY	Dr M.I. Hill	SGS Environment, Yorkshire House, Chapel St, Liverpool L3 9AG
Dr R.S.K. Barnes	Department of Zoology, Downing Street, Cambridge CB2 3EJ	N.G. Hodgetts	Species Conservation Branch, JNCC, Monkstone House, City Road, Peterborough PE1 1JY
Dr J. M. Colebrook	Sir Alister Hardy Foundation for Ocean Science, c/o Plymouth Marine Laboratory, Citadel Hill, Plymouth, Devon PL1 2PB	R.A. Irving	14 Brookland Way, Coldwaltham, Pulborough, W. Sussex RH20 1LT
D.M. Craddock	Vertebrate Ecology and Conservation Branch, JNCC, Monkstone House, City Road, Peterborough PE1 1JY	A.W.G. John	Sir Alister Hardy Foundation for Ocean Science, c/o Plymouth Marine Laboratory, Citadel Hill, Plymouth, Devon PL1 2PB
C.A. Crumpton	RSK Environment, 47 West Street, Dorking, Surrey RH4 1BU	R.G. Keddie	Coastal Conservation Branch, JNCC, Monkstone House, City Road, Peterborough PE1 1JY
Dr T.C.D. Dargie	Loch Fleet View, Skelbo Street, Dornoch, Scotland IV25 3QQ	V.M. Morgan	2, Flaxen Walk, Warboys, Huntingdon PE17 2TR
Dr N.C. Davidson	Coastal Conservation Branch, JNCC, Monkstone House, City Road, Peterborough PE1 1JY	M.S. Parsons	3, Stanton Road, Raynes Park, London SW20 8RL
Dr J. P. Doody	Coastal Conservation Branch, JNCC, Monkstone House, City Road, Peterborough PE1 1JY	Dr M.G. Pawson	Ministry of Agriculture, Fisheries and Food, Directorate of Fisheries Research, Fisheries Laboratory, Pakefield Road, Lowestoft, Suffolk NR33 OHT
C.D. Duck	Sea Mammal Research Unit, Madingley Road, Cambridge CB3 OET	Dr G.W. Potts	The Marine Biological Association of the UK, The Laboratory, Citadel Hill, Plymouth PL1 2PB
M.J. Dunbar	Nature Conservation Bureau, 36, Kingfisher Court, Hambridge Road, Newbury, Berkshire RG14 5SI	Dr R.E. Randall	Girton College, Huntingdon Road, Cambridge CB3 0JG
Dr C.D.R. Evans	Coastal Ecology Group, British Geological Survey, Keyworth, Nottingham NG12 5GG	C.F. Robson	Coastal Conservation Branch, JNCC, Monkstone House, City Road, Peterborough PE1 1JY
Dr P.G.H. Evans	Seawatch Foundation, Dept of Zoology, University of Oxford, South Parks Road, Oxford OX1 3PS	Dr W.G. Sanderson	Marine Conservation Branch, JNCC, Monkstone House, City Road, Peterborough PE1 1JY
S.J. Everett	Nature Conservation Bureau, 36, Kingfisher Court, Hambridge Road, Newbury, Berkshire RG14 5SI	D.A. Stroud	Vertebrate Ecology and Conservation Branch, JNCC, Monkstone House, City Road, Peterborough PE1 1JY
A.P. Foster	61 Pittsfield, Cricklade, Swindon, Wiltshire SN6 7AW	S.E. Swaby	The Marine Biological Association of the UK, The Laboratory, Citadel Hill, Plymouth PL1 2PB
S.L. Fowler	Nature Conservation Bureau, 36, Kingfisher Court, Hambridge Road, Newbury, Berkshire RG14 5SI	Dr M.J.S. Swan	19 St Judith's Lane, Sawtry, Huntingdon, Cambs. PE17 5XE
A.B. Gale	Riverbank House, River Road, Taplow, Maidenhead SL6 0BG	M.L. Tasker	Seabirds and Cetaceans Branch, JNCC, 17 Rubislaw Terrace, Aberdeen AB1 1XE
		Dr C.E. Turtle	SGS Environment, Units 15 & 16, Pebble Close, Amington, Tamworth, Staffs B77 4RD